Lecture Notes in Computer Scie

T0253586

Commenced Publication in 1973
Founding and Former Series Editors:
Gerhard Goos, Juris Hartmanis, and Jan van Leeuwen

Editorial Board

Steve Renals   Samy Bengio (Eds.)

Machine Learning for Multimodal Interaction

Second International Workshop, MLMI 2005
Edinburgh, UK, July 11-13, 2005
Revised Selected Papers

 Springer

Volume Editors

Steve Renals
University of Edinburgh, Centre for Speech Technology Research
2 Buccleuch Place, Edinburgh EH8 9LW, UK
E-mail: s.renals@ed.ac.uk

Samy Bengio
IDIAP Research Institute
Rue du Simplon 4, Case Postale 592, 1920 Martigny, Switzerland
E-mail: bengio@idiap.ch

Library of Congress Control Number: 2006920577

CR Subject Classification (1998): H.5.2-3, H.5, I.2.6, I.2.10, I.2, I.7, K.4, I.4

LNCS Sublibrary: SL 3 – Information Systems and Application, incl. Internet/Web
and HCI

ISSN   0302-9743
ISBN-10   3-540-32549-2 Springer Berlin Heidelberg New York
ISBN-13   978-3-540-32549-9 Springer Berlin Heidelberg New York

Springer is a part of Springer Science+Business Media

springer.com

© Springer-Verlag Berlin Heidelberg 2006
Printed in Germany

Typesetting: Camera-ready by author, data conversion by Scientific Publishing Services, Chennai, India
Printed on acid-free paper   SPIN: 11677482   06/3142   5 4 3 2 1 0

Preface

This book contains a selection of refereed papers presented at the Second Workshop on Machine Learning for Multimodal Interaction (MLMI 2005), held in Edinburgh, Scotland, during 11–13 July 2005.

The workshop was organized and sponsored jointly by two European integrated projects, three European Networks of Excellence and a Swiss national research network:

- AMI, Augmented Multiparty Interaction, http://www.amiproject.org/
- CHIL, Computers in the Human Interaction Loop, http://chil.server.de/
- HUMAINE, Human–Machine Interaction Network on Emotion, http://emotion-research.net/
- PASCAL, Pattern Analysis, Statistical Modeling and Computational Learning, http://www.pascal-network.org/
- SIMILAR, human–machine interfaces similar to human–human communication, http://www.similar.cc/
- IM2, Interactive Multimodal Information Management, http://www.im2.ch/

In addition to the main workshop, MLMI 2005 hosted the NIST (US National Institute of Standards and Technology) Meeting Recognition Workshop. This workshop (the third such sponsored by NIST) was centerd on the Rich Transcription 2005 Spring Meeting Recognition (RT-05) evaluation of speech technologies within the meeting domain. Building on the success of the RT-04 spring evaluation, the RT-05 evaluation continued the speech-to-text and speaker diarization evaluation tasks and added two new evaluation tasks: speech activity detection and source localization.

MLMI 2005 was thus sponsored by the European Commission (Information Society Technologies priority of the Sixth Framework Programme), the Swiss National Science Foundation and the US National Institute of Standards and Technology.

Given the multiple links between the above projects and several related research areas, and the success of the first MLMI 2004 workshop, it was decided to organize once again a joint workshop bringing together researchers from the different communities working around the common theme of advanced machine learning algorithms for processing and structuring multimodal human interaction. The motivation for creating such a forum, which could be perceived as a number of papers from different research disciplines, evolved from an actual need that arose from these projects and the strong motivation of their partners for such a multidisciplinary workshop. This assessment was confirmed this year by a significant increase in the number of sponsoring research projects, and by the success of the workshop itself, which attracted about 170 participants.

The conference program featured invited talks, full papers (subject to careful peer review, by at least three reviewers), and posters (accepted on the basis of abstracts) covering a wide range of areas related to machine learning applied to multimodal interaction — and more specifically to multimodal meeting processing, as addressed by the various sponsoring projects. These areas included:

- Human–human communication modeling
- Speech and visual processing
- Multimodal processing, fusion and fission
- Multimodal dialog modeling
- Human–human interaction modeling
- Multimodal data structuring and presentation
- Multimedia indexing and retrieval
- Meeting structure analysis
- Meeting summarizing
- Multimodal meeting annotation
- Machine learning applied to the above

Out of the submitted full papers, about 50% were accepted for publication in the present volume, after having been invited to take review comments and conference feedback into account.

In the present book, and following the structure of the workshop, the papers are divided into the following sections:

1. Invited Papers
2. Multimodal Processing
3. HCI and Applications
4. Discourse and Dialog
5. Emotion
6. Visual Processing
7. Speech and Audio Processing
8. NIST Meeting Recognition Evaluation

Based on the successes of MLMI 2004 and MLMI 2005, it was decided to organize MLMI 2006 in the USA, in collaboration with NIST (US National Institute of Standards and Technology), again in conjunction with the NIST meeting recognition evaluation.

Finally, we take this opportunity to thank our Program Committee members, the sponsoring projects and funding agencies, and those responsible for the excellent management and organization of the workshop and the follow-up details resulting in the present book.

November 2005   Steve Renals
                                                                Samy Bengio

Organization

General Chairs

Steve Renals   University of Edinburgh
Samy Bengio   IDIAP Research Institute

Local Organization

Caroline Hastings   University of Edinburgh
Avril Heron   University of Edinburgh
Bartosz Dobrzelecki   University of Edinburgh
Jean Carletta   University of Edinburgh
Mike Lincoln   University of Edinburgh

Program Committee

Marc Al-Hames   Munich University of Technology
Tilman Becker   DFKI
Hervé Bourlard   IDIAP Research Institute
Jean Carletta   University of Edinburgh
Franciska de Jong   University of Twente
John Garofolo   NIST
Thomas Hain   University of Sheffield
Lori Lamel   LIMSI
Benoit Macq   UCL-TELE
Johanna Moore   University of Edinburgh
Laurence Nigay   CLIPS-IMAG
Barbara Peskin   ICSI
Thierry Pun   University of Geneva
Marc Schröder   DFKI
Rainer Stiefelhagen   Universitaet Karlsruhe

NIST Meeting Recognition Workshop Organization

Jon Fiscus   NIST
John Garofolo   NIST

Sponsoring Projects and Institutions

Projects:

- AMI, Augmented Multiparty Interaction, http://www.amiproject.org/
- CHIL, Computers in the Human Interaction Loop, http://chil.server.de/
- HUMAINE, Human–Machine Interaction Network on Emotion, http://emotion-research.net/
- SIMILAR, human–machine interfaces similar to human–human communication, http://www.similar.cc/
- PASCAL, Pattern Analysis, Statistical Modeling and Computational Learning, http://www.pascal-network.org/
- IM2, Interactive Multimodal Information Management, http://www.im2.ch/

Institutions :

- European Commission, through the Multimodal Interfaces objective of the Information Society Technologies (IST) priority of the Sixth Framework Programme.
- Swiss National Science Foundation, through the National Center of Competence in Research (NCCR) program.
- US National Institute of Standards and Technology (NIST), http://www.nist.gov/speech/

Table of Contents

III HCI and Applications

IV Discourse and Dialogue

V Emotion

VI   Visual Processing

VII   Speech and Audio Processing

VIII   NIST Meeting Recognition Evaluation

Gesture, Gaze, and Ground

David McNeill

University of Chicago

My emphasis in this paper is on floor control in multiparty discourse: the approach is psycholinguistic. This perspective includes turn management, turn exchange and coordination; how to recognize the dominant speaker even when he or she is not speaking, and a theory of all this. The data to be examined comprise a multimodal depiction of a 5-party meeting (a US Air Force war gaming session) and derive from a project carried out jointly with my engineering colleagues, Francis Quek and Mary Harper. See the Chen et al. paper in this volume for details of the recoding session.

Multiparty discourse can be studied in various ways, e.g., signals of turn taking intentions, marking the next 'projected' turn unit and its content, and still others. I adopt a perspective that emphasizes how speakers coordinate their *individual cognitive states* as they exchange turns while acknowledging and maintaining *the dominant speaker's status.* My goals are similar to Pickering & Garrod's interactive alignment account of dialogue (2004), but with the addition of gesture, gaze, posture, F-formations (Kendon 1990) and several levels of coreferential chains—all to be explained below. I adopt a theoretical position agreeing with their portrayal of dialogue as 'alignment' and of alignment as automatic, in the sense of not draining resources, but not their 'mechanistic' (priming) account of it (cf. Krauss et al. 2004 for qualms). The theory I am following is described in the next section. Alignment in this theory is non-mechanistic, does not single out priming, and regards conversational signaling (cf. papers in Ochs et al. 1996) as providing a synchrony of individual cognitive states, or 'growth points'.

1 Theoretical Background

The growth point. A growth point (GP) is a mental package that combines both linguistic categorial and imagistic components. Combining such semiotic opposites, the GP is inherently multimodal, and creates a condition of instability, the resolution of which propels thought and speech forward. The GP concept, while theoretical, is empirically grounded. GPs are inferred from the totality of communication events with special focus on speech-gesture synchrony and co-expressivity (cf. McNeill 2005 for extensive discussion). It is called a growth point because it is meant to be the initial pulse of thinking for and while speaking, out of which a dynamic process of organization emerges. Growth points are brief dynamic processes during which idea units take form. If two individuals share GPs, they can be said to 'inhabit' the same state of cognitive being and this, in the theoretical picture being considered, is what communication aims to achieve, at least in part. The concept of inhabitance was

S. Renals and S. Bengio (Eds.): MLMI 2005, LNCS 3869, pp. 1–14, 2006.

expressed by Merleau-Ponty (1962) in the following way: "Language certainly has inner content, but this is not self-subsistent and self-conscious thought. What then does language express, if it does not express thoughts? It presents or rather it *is* the subject's taking up of a position in the world of his meanings" (p. 193; emphasis in the original). The GP is a unit of this process of 'taking up a position in the world of meanings'. On this model, an analysis of conversation should bring out how alignments of inhabitance come about and how, as this is taking place, the overall conversational milieu is maintained by the participants.

The hyperphrase. A second theoretical idea—the 'hyperphrase'—is crucial for analyzing how these alignments and maintenances are attained in complex multi-party meetings. A hyperphrase is a nexus of converging, interweaving processes that cannot be totally untangled. We approach the hyperphrase through a multi-modal structure comprising verbal and non-verbal (gaze, gesture) data.

To illustrate the concept, I shall examine one such phrase from a study carried out jointly with Francis Quek and Mary Harper (the 'Wombats study'). This hyperphrase implies a communicative pulse structured on the verbal, gestural, and gaze levels simultaneously. The hyperphrase began part way into the verbal text (# is an audible breath pause, / is a silent pause, * is a self-interruption; F_0 groups are indicated with underlining, and gaze is in italics):

> we're gonna go over to # *thirty-five 'cause* / *they're ah** / *they're from the neigh borhood they know what's going on* #".

The critical aspect indicating a hyperphrase is that gaze turned to the listener in the middle of a linguistic clause and remained there over the rest of the selection. This stretch of speech was also accompanied by multiple occurrences of a single gesture type whereby the right hand with its fingers spread moved up and down over the deictic zero point of the spatialized content of speech. Considering the two non-verbal features, gaze and gesture, together with the lexical content of the speech, this stretch of speech is a *single production pulse* organized thematically around the idea unit, 'the people from the neighborhood in thirty-five.' This would plausibly be a growth point. Such a hyperphrase brings together several linguistic clauses. It spans a self-interruption and repair, and spans 9 F_0 groups. The F_0 groups subdivide the thematic cohesion of the hyperphrase, but the recurrence of similar gesture strokes compensates for the oversegmentation. For example, the F_0 break between "what's" and "going on" is spanned by a single gesture down stroke. It is unlikely that a topic shift occured within this gesture. Thus, the hyperphrase is a production domain in which linguistic clauses, prosody and speech repair all play out, each on its own time-scale, and are held together as the hyperphrase nexus.

Thus we have two major theoretical ideas with which to approach the topic of multiparty discourse—the growth point and the hyperphrase. The GP is the theoretical unit of the speaker's state of cognitive being. The hyperphrase is a package of multimodal information that presents a GP. Through hyperphrases GPs can be shared. Multiple speakers can contribute to the same hyperphrases and growth points. Speaker 2 synchronizes growth points with Speaker 1 by utilizing various turn-taking 'signals' to achieve synchrony. This hypothesis assumes that conversationalists align GPs—Speaker 2 emits signals in a hyperphrase until he/she senses alignment, then allows an exchange of the speaking turn. The signals can be seen as bringing one state of cognitive being into alignment with another, with the hyperphrase the package managing the coordination. We do not suppose that all turn exchanges are so organized, but we see evidence, in multiparty discourse, that much of it is.

2 The VACE Project[1]

The aim of our research project under the VACE program is to understand, across a wide multimodal front, interpersonal interactions during meetings of c. 5~6 individuals, US Air Force officers taking part in military gaming exercises at the Air Force Institute of Technology (AFIT), at the Wright Patterson Air Force Base, in Dayton, OH. The participants represent various military specialties. The commanding officer for the gaming session is always in position E. The task of this particular meeting was to figure out how a captured 'alien missile head' (which in fact looked rather like a coffee thermos with fins) functioned. The session lasted approximately 42 minutes. The examples to be studied are extracted from the latter half of this period. Figure 1 shows the meeting room and camera configuration.

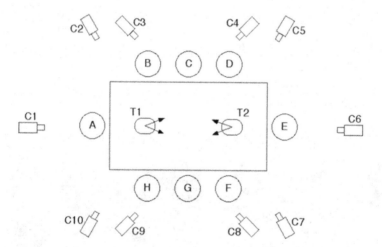

Fig. 1. Layout of the testing room. The participants were in positions C, D, E, F and G (positions A, B and H were vacant). Illustrations in later figures are from Camera 1's vantage point.

I shall give some general statistics for gesture (pointing) and gaze during the entire meeting, including notes on some coding difficulties in the case of gaze, and then analyze

[1] This research has been supported by the Advanced Research and Development Activity (ARDA), Video Analysis and Content Extraction VACE II grant #665661 (entitled *From Video to Information: Cross-Modal Analysis of Planning Meetings*).

two focus segments, concentrating on how the dominant participant (E) maintains his position, despite multiple shifts of speaker. I will also analyze the unique way the sole female participant seizes a speaking turn (participant C, who although of the same military rank as the others shows traits of marginalization in the group).

Pointing. The dominant participant, E, is the chief source of pointing but is the least frequent target of pointing by others. C and D are the least likely to point at anyone but are the most likely to be pointed at by others (D is notably passive in the group). So this pattern—rarely the source of pointing, often the target—may signal marginality, actual or felt, in a group setting. Table 1 summarizes the pointing patterns.[2]

Table 1. Pointing Patterns in the Meeting

	Source C	Source D	Source E	Source F	Source G	Total
Target C	3	2	17	8	10	40
Target D	1	4	21	11	3	40
Target E	4	0	5	2	0	11
Target F	3	2	13	0	2	20
Target G	4	4	8	7	0	23
Target others	*12*	*10*	*59*	*28*	*15*	
Target All	0	0	5	0	0	5
Target Some	1	2	10	2	0	15
Target Obj	3	6	20	12	24	65
Target Abstract	5	11	8	1	1	26
Total	24	31	107	43	40	245

(Note: 'target others' excludes self-pointing)

Fig. 2.1. E (head of table) points with right hand at C (left front). Participants are festooned with motion tracking (VICON) jewelry. (Ronald Tuttle is in the background.)

Fig. 2.2. F (right rear) points at G with origo shift toward E

---

[2] Coding of pointing and other features was carried by a dedicated research team—Irene Kimbara, Fey Parrill, Haleema Welji, Jim Goss, Amy Franklin, and (overseeing it all) Sue Duncan, all of the Gesture Lab at the University of Chicago (http://mcneilllab.uchicago.edu).

Figures 2.1 and 2.2 illustrate two pointing events, the first showing E with his right hand rising from rest on the table to point minimally at C (and thereby authorizing—weakly—her as speaker); the second is F pointing at G but in a curious way that shifts the origo or perspective base of the gesture to a locus in front of his own location, a maneuver that may unconsciously reflect the 'gravitational pull' of E on his right.

Gaze. Table 2 summarizes the distribution of gazes during the entire meeting. Again, as in pointing, E's dominant status is registered by an asymmetry, but now with reverse polarity: he is the most frequent gaze target but the least frequent gaze source. C, the sole female present, is unchivalrously the least frequent gaze target but the most frequent gaze source—a pattern also seen in a NIST interaction analyzed previously (unpublished data) again involving a female participant, although not the sole female in this case, but again seemingly the marginal participant in the group.

However, gaze *duration* by E is longer—duration and shift of gaze may perform distinct functions in this tradeoff. Table 3 compares the frequency and duration of gazes by E to G vs. those of G to E. Indeed, E looks with longer durations at G than G does at E, but this asymmetry does not hold for gazes at neutral space, the object, or papers—at these targets G gazes are actually longer. E's fewer, longer gazes at people but not at objects can be explained if he uses gaze to *manage* the situation—showing attentiveness (hence longer) but feeling no pressure to seek permission to speak (therefore fewer). Such fewer, longer gazes at people (but not at objects) are recognizably properties of a dominant speaker.

Table 2. Frequency of gaze during the meeting

	C Source	D Source	E Source	F Source	G Source	Total
C Target	X	38	45	59	67	209
D Target	70	X	83	112	94	359
E Target	212	136	X	144	149	641
F Target	150	107	98	X	116	471
G Target	75	52	63	68	X	258
Total	507	333	289	383	426	1938

Table 3. Comparison of E's gaze duration (fewest shifts) to G's (more shifts)

	E's gaze Number	(fewest shifts) Av. Duration secs	G's gaze Number	(more shifts) Av. Duration secs
At C	45	5.1	67	1.1
At D	82	4.0	93	2.6
At E	-	-	149	1.9
At F	98	3.9	116	1.6
At G	63	3.1	-	-
Neutral space	150	1.0	292	1.5
At object	58	1.7	42	2.8
At papers	33	3.2	18	8.2
Others	4	2.4	8	1.9
Average	67	3.0	98	2.7

To summarize dominance and marginality. Both pointing and gaze correlate with the social dimension of dominance, but in opposite directions:

> In *pointing*, the gesture has an active function—selecting a target; it is thus correlated positively with dominance and negatively with marginality. Marginal members may frequently be pointing targets as part of recruiting efforts.

> In *gaze*, the action has a passive or perceptual function—locating the source of information or influence; it is accordingly correlated negatively with dominance and positively with marginality, especially when brief.

> But in E's case, *gaze* is also active, not passive, and this is reflected in longer durations at people only, combined with fewer shifts of gaze overall; duration thus correlates with dominance positively.

Coding issues. Inferring gaze from video poses difficulties of coding, and it is well to say something about this. The following comments are based on notes by the coder (Haleema Welji): F and G wear glasses, making it difficult to see where their eyes are and even sometimes whether the eyes are open. Often it is necessary to look for a slight movement of the eye or eyelid, which can be hard to spot. Also, neutral space can coincide with the location of the object on the table and sometimes it is difficult to distinguish what is the target of gaze. A third difficulty is that at some orientations it is hard to get a good view of the eyes. Finally, when coding in slow motion a blink and a short glance away may be indistinguishable. Given the uncertainties, that no more than 8% of the gaze judgments for the be-glassed participants and less than 3% for the best participant were deemed tentative, is perhaps reassuring.

3 Focus Segments

Two segments were selected for detailed analysis. Both came from the second half of the 42 minute session.

Focus 1. The first focus segment highlights turn taking exchange in which hyperphrases carry multiple functions. The speech is as follows:

1. E: "okay. u-"
2. G: "So it's going to make it a little tough."
3. F: "It was my understanding that the- the whole head pivoted to provide the aerodynamic uh moment. But uh I could be wrong on. That uh ..."
4. G: "that would be a different design from-"
5. F: "From what-"
6. G: "from- from the way we do it."
7. F: "Okay."
8. E: "Okay so if we-"
9. G: "But we can look into that."
10. E: "If we're making that assumption ((unintel.)) as a high fidelity test"
11. F: "Yeah."

Turn taking at momentary overlap of GPs. An obvious case of a GP starting with one speaker and passing to the next appears at 5, where F says "from what" and G, at 6, takes over with "from- from the way we do it". The hyperphrase package of the joint inhabitance is seen in the deployment of gaze and gesture:

> F begins with a glance at E, then gestures interactively toward G, followed immediately by gaze at G and an iconic gesture depicting the alien coffee mug (see Figure 3).

The hyperphrase here is a multimodal unit within which dimensions of gesture and gaze exchange places in creating the GP concerning the 'way we do it', related to the imagery component depicting the object. We also see a hyperphrase being constructed by F that includes social information: E's standing as dominant speaker, in the quick glance at him at the start; G's status as current speaker, in the interactive gesture to him; and the ongoing role of the 'thermos' as the discourse theme.

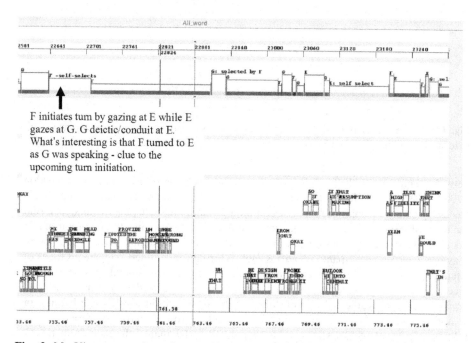

Fig. 3. MacVissta screenshot of turn taking in Focus 1. Notes added on how turn taking correlated with gaze and gesture (see the Chen et al paper for details on MacVissta).

Figure 4 displays how gesture was recruited at the onset of the new turn—a further component of the hyperphrase at this moment.

F-formation analysis. An F-formation is discovered by tracking gaze direction in a social group. The concept was introduced by Adam Kendon, who said, "An F-formation arises when two or more people cooperate together to maintain a space

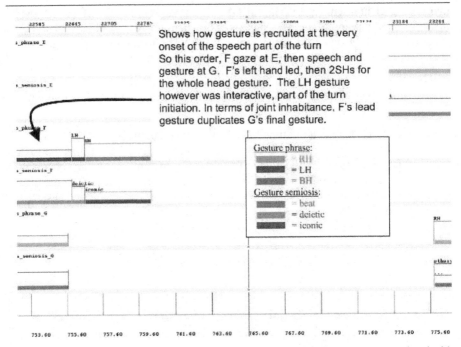

Shows how gesture is recruited at the very onset of the speech part of the turn
So this order, F gaze at E, then speech and gesture at G. F's left hand led, then 2SHs for the whole head gesture. The LH gesture however was interactive, part of the turn initiation. In terms of joint inhabitance, F's lead gesture duplicates G's final gesture.

Gesture phrase:
= RH
= LH
= BH
Gesture semiosis:
= beat
= deictic
= iconic

Fig. 4. MacVissta screenshot of gesture in Focus 1. Notes added on how gesture correlated with gaze and turn taking (see the Chen et al paper for details on MacVissta).

between them to which they all have direct and exclusive [equal] access." (Kendon 1990, p. 209). An F-formation, however, is not just about shared space. Crucially, it has an associated meaning, reveals a common ground, and helps us, the analysts, find the units of thematic content in the conversation. Figure 5 shows the F-formations in Focus 1. Tracking the appearance of the same color (see online version, shades of gray here) across participants identifies each F-formation, defined as a shared focus of attention. In the Focus segment, an F-formation defined by shared gaze at F (light green: lightest gray) is replaced by one defined by gaze at G (dark green: 4th darkest gray). Interestingly, there is a brief transition or disintegration with gaze either at E or at non-person objects (cf. online version: object=maroon, neutral space=yellow)—acknowledgement of E's status as dominant. But the main inference from the F-formation analysis is that speaker F was recognized as the next speaker *before* he began to speak, and this recognition was timed exactly with *his* brief gaze at E—a further signal of E's dominance. This gaze created a short F-formation with G, since both then looked at E. This in effect signaled the turn exchange, and is another component of the hyperphrase at this moment, ushering in a joint growth point.

Back to momentary sharing of GPs. So, what happened here at the turn exchange was a synchronizing of inhabitance by F (the next speaker) with G (the current speaker) via their joint F-formation with E the target. F's hyperphrase (a bundle of multimodal features) encompassed all these features. F's GP included the idea of his

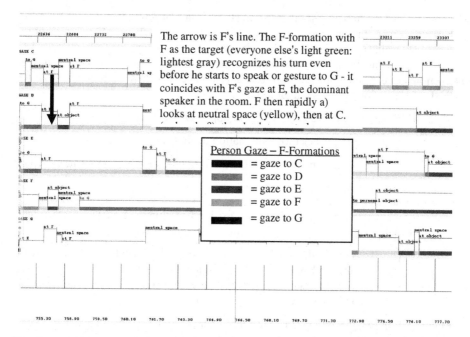

Fig. 5. MacVissta screenshot of F-formations in Focus 1. Notes added on how F-formations correlated with gesture, gaze and turn taking (see the Chen et al paper for details on MacVissta).

collaboration with G and with this he could lock-step their current cognitive states. F's first GP was in fact a continuation of G's. The details appear in how gaze and gesture deployed around the table:

> Dominant E continues to gaze at designated speaker G when G gestures at object and others apparently look at the object.

> G gazes at the dominant participant, and makes deictic/conduit gestures in his direction (cf. McNeill 1992 for these terms). G then shifts his gaze to the object, then quickly shifts back to E. Nonspeaker D doesn't shift to E when G shifts but keeps gaze at G—suggesting that what we see is the speaker affirming the dominant status of E, but the overhearers are free to respond to the speaker's new turn.

> Also, when F takes turn from G he waits until G finishes his ongoing sentence, but first turns to look at E in the middle of the sentence, and then starts his turn while still looking at E (only after this shifting to G).

The next example however displays a very different form of turn exchange, one based on *non*-joint inhabitance.

Focus 2. For reasons not entirely clear but possibly connected to the fact that, although of equal military rank, C was the sole female present, this speaker does not create a series of moves designed to synchronize idea units with any current speaker.

She appears instead to wait until there is no current state of joint inhabitance, and then embarks on a turn. In other words, C exploits the phenomena that we have seen but in reverse: she waits until a break in hyperphrasing; when it appears she plunges in. Focus 2 begins as F signaled the end of his turn and E's gaze briefly left the interaction space: C then quickly moved to speak. The speech is the following, but to understand the action requires a multimodal picture:

F: "to get it right the first time. So I appreciate that."

F relinquishes turn—intonation declines.

E gazes straight down table (no target?), setting stage for next step.

C intervenes, ferret-quick:

C: "I'm thinking graduation exercise kind of thing. You know we might actually blow something up. Obviously we don't want to".

E (not F, the previous turn-holder) acknowledges C's turn with gesture and gaze, but in a manner that suggests surprise—further confirming that C's strategy was to wait for a general lapse of inhabitance before starting to speak.

Figure 6.1 shows the moment C spots her chance to speak (the first line above). Figure 6.2 depicts 9 frames (0.3 s) later. Note how all the participants, in unison, are shifting their gaze to C and forming in this way a multiparty F-formation and hyperphrase with C the focal point.

Fig. 6.1. C leaps in. Gaze around the table is generally unfocused.

Fig. 6.2. 9 frames (0.3 s) later, gaze generally shifts to C and E points at C

One has to ponder the effects of a strategy like C's that avoids shared hyperphrasing and transitional GPs. C's experience of the interaction dynamics is seemingly quite different from the others and theirs equally from hers. Whether this is due to 'marginality' (as evident in pointing and gaze, Tables 1 and 2) or is a personal trait, is unclear. An all-female meeting would be of great interest, but we have not managed to assemble one to date.

4   Comparison of Focus 1 and Focus 2

In contrast to Focus 1, where we saw an intricate build up of a hyperphrase out of gaze and gesture, in Focus 2 C gazes at E (even though she is following G), and E provides authorizing back channels in the form of gaze and pointing, and this is the total exchange; there is no real hyperphrase or possibility of a shared transitional GP.

Taking the two focus segments together, it seems clear that speaker status can be allotted, negotiated, or seized in very short time sequences, but dominant speaker status is ascribed and changes slowly if at all.

5   Coreference, F-formations, and Gaze

The way in which discourse coheres—how segments beyond individual utterances take form—can be observed in various ways, but we have found tracking coreferential chains in speech to be highly useful. A 'reference' is an object or other meaning entity nominated in speech; a coreferential chain is a set (not necessarily consecutive) of linguistic nominations of the same referent. As a whole, the chain comprises a 'topic' in the conversation. A coreferential chain links extended text stretches and by its nature is interpretable on the level of meaning and can be the basis of hyperphrases. An important insight is that coreferential chains also can span different speakers, and so can tie together multiparty hyperphrases and shared growth points in dialogues.

Coreferential chains thread across different levels in the structure of discourse. A given chain might track over each of the following:

> **Object level:** cohesion through references to object world; e.g., "a confirming design".
> **Meta level:** cohesion through references to the discourse itself; e.g., "I propose assuming a US design".
> **Para level:** cohesion through references that include individual participants; e.g., "I agree with the assumption".

In Figure 7, a hyperphrase builds up between participants over each the above levels. In so doing it unites references to the alien object by tying them to the theme of how it is designed and what should initially be assumed about this design, each contribution from a different speaker and on a different level.

Coreferences also provide an overall profile of thematic content within a conversation. Figure 8 shows the cumulative distribution of coreferences over the total 42 minutes of the AFIT session. A small number of references account for the vast bulk of cohesion in this discourse. The curve can be read from left to right as listing the dominant topics and then less dominant topics—'FME people' (those who work on foreign material exploitation), operators of Air Force systems, and so forth, with the bulk of references on the long tail of single mentions.

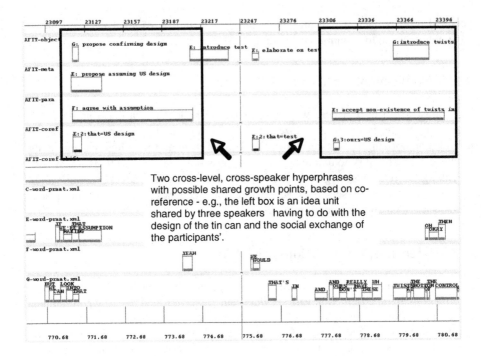

Fig. 7. MacVissta screenshot of coreference threads across multiple speakers creating F-formations

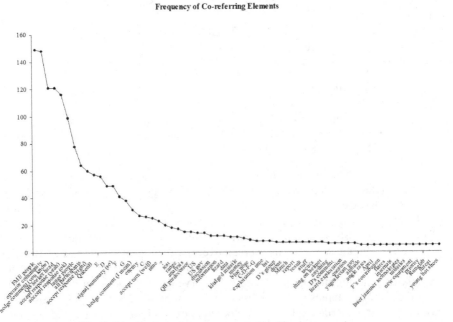

Fig. 8. Distribution of coreferences in the 42 minute session

Elaborations on the F-formation. In the discourse situations we observe, we see two types of F-formation:

1) *social,* in which the elements are other individals (Kendon's original version), and

2) *instrumental,* in which two or more people gaze at a common event or object in space.

The elaborations identify different kinds of social interactive configurations that can be seen in conversations that involve both participants and physical displays of objects (projection screens, the alien object of the AFIT session, etc.). Social F-formations are accompanied by significant shifts of the discourse levels of coreferential chains (object, meta, and para in various permutations); instrumental F-formations tend to stay on the same level (usually but not necessarily the object level). Table 4 shows the difference between social and instrumental F-formations in earlier data (a 4-party roundtable interaction recorded at NIST).

Table 4. Gaze and Level Shift

	Shift	Not Shift	N
Instrumental Gaze	44%	66%	32
Social Gaze	67%	33%	15

As hyperphrases, social F-formations thus open up a variety of trading relations with which to engender growth points during interactions. This richer variety is of course significant in itself. It makes sense in terms of the stimulus value of another person in a social context. The discovery is that social gaze has an immediate effect on the cohesive structure of discourse with coreference shifts strapped together into hyperphrases by gaze.

6   Conclusions and Application to Automatic Methods

For communication studies, the implications of this research seem clear: a multimodal approach uncòvers phenomena not otherwise observable. The concept of a hyperphrase, as a group of multimodal features in trading relationships, is particularly interesting from an instrumental viewpoint—you want to pick up these interacting features if you can. We focus currently on floor management: who is dominant, how are turns at speaking managed, what are the ways in which someone seizes a turn, and how does the alpha participant maintain control, etc.?, but the range can be broadened to include other aspects of meeting dynamics—the formation of coalitions, cleavages, and coups, etc.

The psycholinguistic interest in these meetings lies in the apparent synchronizing of states of joint inhabitance that the turn taking process engages. However, we see a different mode of turn taking in Officer C's case, in which her procedure was not the synchronization but rather exploitation of momentary lapses of joint inhabitance. While a single example cannot rule out individual style as the source of a pattern, it is the case that C's social isolation, as the sole female participant, is also a possible factor. Ever since Herbert Clark's pioneering studies of common ground (Clark 1996), it has been an assumption that for communication to take place at normal speeds and feasible resource allocations speaker and hearer need to establish a common ground, which then need not be further communicated. While common ground seems indisputable in a general sense (the officers all knew, for example, they were in the US Air Force, were at AFIT, were taking part in a training exercise, had before them an alien object—in fact, assumed all the high frequency topics seen in Fig. 8), C jumped in precisely when she sensed a lapse in the *local* common ground— F had given up his turn, E was drifting, no one else was starting to speak, etc. It is therefore worth considering that common ground has two orientations: a general one, which is, as Clark rightly emphasized, a precondition for all communication; and a local one, which is not a precondition but is a *product* of the interaction and is not a given in the conversation but is constantly unfolding. From this viewpoint, C, by interjecting, created a new common ground. With the general-local common ground distinction, we can track the dynamics of the interaction.

From a psycholinguistic and social psychology viewpoint, the management of turn taking, floor control, and speaker dominance (even if not speaking) are crucial variables, and the prospect of instrumentally recording clues to these kinds of things could be the basis for valuable interdisciplinary work. These descriptive features are the reality of the meeting to which instrumental recording methods need to make reference. The automatic or semi-automatic monitoring of meetings needs to be related to the actual events taking place in the meeting at the human, social level, and our coding is designed to provide an analytic description of these events. The coding emphasizes the multimodal character of the meeting, attending equally to speech, nonverbal behavior and the use of space, and the aim of the collaboration is to test which (if any) recoverable audio and video features provide clues to such events, thus warranting human inspection.

References

Chen, Lei, Rose, Travis, Parrill, Fey, Han, Xu, Tu, Jilin, Huang, Zhongqiang, Harper, Mary, Quek, Francis, McNeill, David, Tuttle, Ronald and Huang, Thomas. VACE Multimodal Meeting Corpus. This volume.

Clark, Herbert H. 1996.*Using Language*. Cambridge: Cambridge University Press.

Kendon, Adam 1990. *Conducting Interactions: Patterns of behavior in focused encounters.* Cambridge: Cambridge University Press.

Krauss, Robert M. and Pardo, Jennifer S. 2004. Is alignment always the result of automatic priming? *Behavioral and Brain Sciences* 27(02):203-204.

McNeill, David 1992. *Hand and Mind: What gestures reveal about thought.* Chicago: University of Chicago Press.

Merleau-Ponty, Maurice. 1962. *Phenomenology of Perception* (C. Smith, trans.). London: Routledge.

Ochs, Eleanor, Schegloff, Emanuel A, and Thompson, Sandra A. (Eds.) 1996. *Interaction and Grammar.* Cambridge: Cambridge University Press.

Pickering, Martin J. and Garrod, Simon 2004. Toward a mechanistic psychology of dialogue. *Behavioral and Brain Sciences* 27(02):169-226.

Toward Adaptive Information Fusion in Multimodal Systems

Xiao Huang and Sharon Oviatt

Center for Human-Computer Communication,
Computer Science Department,
Oregon Health and Science University,
Beaverton, OR 97006, USA
{huangx, oviatt}@csee.ogi.edu

Abstract. In recent years, a new generation of multimodal systems has emerged as a major direction within the HCI community. Multimodal interfaces and architectures are time-critical and data-intensive to develop, which poses new research challenges. The goal of the present work is to model and adapt to users' multimodal integration patterns, so that faster and more robust systems can be developed with on-line adaptation to individual's multimodal temporal thresholds. In this paper, we summarize past user-modeling results on speech and pen multimodal integration patterns, which indicate that there are two dominant types of multimodal integration pattern among users that can be detected very early and remain highly consistent. The empirical results also indicate that, when interacting with a multimodal system, users intermix unimodal with multimodal commands. Based on these results, we present new machine-learning results comparing three models of on-line system adaptation to users' integration patterns, which were based on Bayesian Belief Networks. This work utilized data from ten adults who provided approximately 1,000 commands while interacting with a map-based multimodal system. Initial experimental results with our learning models indicated that 85% of users' natural mixed input could be correctly classified as either unimodal or multimodal, and 82% of users' mulitmodal input could be correctly classified as either sequentially or simultaneously integrated. The long-term goal of this research is to develop new strategies for combining empirical user modeling with machine learning techniques to bootstrap accelerated, generalized, and improved reliability of information fusion in new types of multimodal system.

1   Introduction

In recent years, multimodal human-computer interaction systems have emerged as a dominant theme within HCI. Multimodal systems combine modalities into a whole system and provide a more usable, robust, and mobile-ready interface for users. Two mature types of multimodal system that integrate speech and lip movements and also speech and pen input are presented in [1] and [2], respectively. Temporal synchronization of users' input and multimodal signal fusion

S. Renals and S. Bengio (Eds.): MLMI 2005, LNCS 3869, pp. 15–27, 2006.

and integrated interpretation [3] [4] are major research topics of research for these time-critical systems.

At the heart of multimodal system design is adaptive information fusion. The goal is to model and adapt to users' multimodal integration patterns so that the system can develop an adaptive temporal threshold for robust fusion and interpretation. There are some studies on the topic of unimodal adaptation. For example, in [5], speech recognition systems are able to adapt to different speakers and environments. speech recognition systems are able to adapt to different speakers and environments. But research on adaptive multimodal interfaces still is in its infancy [6]. Fortunately, quite a few studies on machine learning can shed light on adaptive information fusion. Most of these studies use graphical models (i.e., Hidden Markov Model, Bayesian Belief Network and its extensions) to build the relation between different modalities and improve system task performance. For example, [7] [8] propose an asynchronous Hidden Markov Model for audio-visual speech recognition. Another approach is Dynamical Systems Trees [9] which has been applied to tracking football manuevers. In other recent work, Layered HMMs [10] [11] have been used to infer human activities in an office environment from audio-visual input.

In this paper, we adopt graphical models (i.e., Bayesian Belief Networks) to learn users' multimodal integration patterns and to adapt to each individual user. Results from a user-modeling study of multimodal integration patterns are summarized in section 2. Then three machine-learning models are presented and compared to demonstrate our new approach to developing user-adaptive multimodal systems.

1.1   State-of-the-Art Multimodal Systems

In [12] [13], two myths related to multimodal integration are discussed. One myth is that multimodal input always involves simultaneous signals. However, this assumption is contrary to actual objective data. More recent empirical evidence has clarified that multimodal input often is integrated sequentially [4]. The generation of multimodal systems should not only be able to process both unimodal and multimdal user input, but also both simultaneously and sequentially integrated multimodal constructions. Figure. 1 shows typical cases of simultaneous and sequential multimodal input.

Another myth is that all users' multimodal input is integrated in a uniform way. Recent studies has revealed an unusual bimodal distribution of user integration patterns. As illustrated in Figure. 2, previous data indicate that individual child, adult, and elderly users all adopt either a predominantly simultaneous or sequential integration pattern during speech and pen multimodal constructions [12] [14]. In these studies, users' dominant integration pattern was identifiable almost immediately, typically on the very first multimodal command, and remained highly consistent throughout a session. These findings imply that future multimodal systems that can detect and adapt to a user's dominant integration pattern potentially could yield substantial improvements in system robustness.

Simultaneous

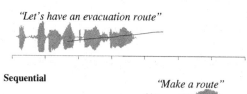

"Let's have an evacuation route"

Sequential

"Make a route"

0.0	0.5	1.0	1.5	2.0	2.5	3.0	3.5

Time (seconds)

Fig. 1. Simultaneous vs Sequential Integration Patterns: Typical Speech and Pen Constructions

Children			Adults			Seniors		
User	SIM	SEQ	User	SIM	SEQ	User	SIM	SEQ
SIM integrators:			SIM integrators:			SIM integrators:		
1	100	0	1	100	0	1	100	0
2	100	0	2	94	6	2	100	0
3	100	0	3	92	8	3	100	0
4	100	0	4	86	14	4	97	3
5	100	0	SEQ integrators:			5	96	4
6	100	0	5	31	69	6	95	5
7	98	2	6	25	75	7	95	5
8	96	4	7	17	83	8	92	8
9	82	18	8	11	89	9	91	9
10	65	35	9	0	100	10	90	10
SEQ integrators:			10	0	100	11	89	11
11	15	85	11	0	100	12	73	27
12	9	91				SEQ integrators:		
13	2	98				13	1	99
						Non -dominant		
						Integrators :		
						14	59	41
						15	48	52
Average Consistency 93.5%			Average Consistency 90%			Average Consistency 88.5%		

Fig. 2. Percentage of simultaneously-integrated multimodal constructions (SIM) versus sequentially-integrated constructions (SEQ) for children, adults, and seniors

Based on the above studies, it can be summarized that: 1) Previous lifespan data on speech and pen input shows users are classifiable as either simultaneous or sequential multimodal integrators (70% simultaneous, 30% sequential); 2) Users' dominant integration pattern is predictable early (i.e., 1st utterance); and 3) Their integration pattern remains highly consistent throughout an interaction (89-97% of consistency) and over time.

1.2   New Directions for Temporal Modeling and Multimodal Fusion

Due to large individual differences, estimates indicate that user-adaptive temporal thresholds could: 1) Reduce multimodal system processing delays by 50-60%;

2)Improve reliability of multimodal interpretation by 50% (including correct identification of multimodal vs. unimodal input); 3) Improve synchrony of user-system interaction [15]. As a new class of adaptive multimodal interfaces begins to be prototyped, our goal is to develop new techniques that can automatically learn and adapt to users' dominant multimodal integration patterns, and provide better assistances to users.

1.3 Why Combine Empirical User Modeling and Machine Learning Techniques?

One direction we are exploring involves combing empirical user modeling and machine learning techniques. The motivation for this work is that empirically-grounded user modeling can reveal: 1) What content is fertile territory for applying learning techniques (e.g., when major individual differences are present); 2) When different learning techniques should be applied to handle different subgroups of users adequately; 3) Which information sources should be learned; 4) What gains can be expected if learning techniques are applied; 5) How to apply learning techniques so they are transparent and avoid destabilizing users' performance; and 6) How to guide learning techniques more effectively by incorporating explicit, implicit, or combined forms of user feedback to the system. In addition, in some cases actually applying new machine learning techniques (e.g., asynchronous HMMs) to multimodal data can be computationally intractable unless prior knowledge can be incorporated based on user modeling to substantially constrain variability in the data (S. Bengio, personal communication, 10/05).

1.4 Goals of the Present Research

One goal of this research is to investigate users' speech and pen multimodal integration patterns, and to apply user modeling techniques for accurately learning to predict their future input patterns. If predictive information based on user modeling is sufficiently powerful, then it can be useful in bootstrapping machine learning techniques, substantially improving the speed and accuracy of the machine processing. Another goal of this research is to develop machine learning approaches for automatically learning users' multimodal integration patterns and adapting the system's temporal thresholds in real time during fusion.

2 User Modeling Study of User's Integration Patterns

Data was evaluated from a study that involved ten users spontaneously interacting with a multimodal system [13]. Their input and multimodal integration patterns then were analyzed empirically and also utilized for three different machine learning tests.

2.1 Methods Overview

Subjects. There were 10 adult subjects, aged 19-50, five male and five female, all were native speakers of English.

Application Scenario. Subjects were presented with a scenario in which they acted as non-specialists working to coordinate emergency resources during a major flood. To perform this task, they were given a multimodal map-based interface on which they received textual instructions from headquarters. They then used this interface to deliver input to the system by either speaking, inking on the map, or interacting multimodally. For details of the interface, tasks, and procedure, see [13].

Procedure. An experimenter was present and provided instructions, answered questions, and offered feedback or help during a training session. Following this orientation, the experimenter left the room and users began their session and completed 93 tasks. Users were told to complete tasks with this map-based system using their own words, and to use either pen input, speech input, or both modalities in any way they wished. The system was introduced to users as an open-microphone implementation, so they did not need to tap the pen on the screen before speaking. Upon completion, volunteers were interviewed about their interaction with the system, and were debriefed on the purpose of the study. The experiment lasted about one hour per participant.

Data Capture and Transcript Coding. All sessions were videotaped, and data were analyzed for type of input (i.e., unimodal speech or pen, versus multimodal) and multimodal integration patterns (i.e., simultaneous versus sequential). Analyses also provided fine-grained temporal synchronization information such as: 1) Absolute Intermodal Overlap/Lag, 2) Intermodal Overlap Ratio, 3) Intermodal Onset Differential, 4) Intermodal Offset Differential, 5) Speech Duration, 6) Pen Duration, and 7) Multimodal Command Duration. Details of these metrics have been described in [13].

2.2 Multimodal Integration Patterns for Individuals

For each subject, 93 commands total were recorded. The total available data for analysis was 930commands. Seven users predominantly provided multimodal input the system (i.e., over 60% of their commands), while three users predominantly provided unimodal input. In terms of individual differences in their multimodal integration pattern, Figure 3 taken from [14] illustrates the percentage of all multimodal commands that involved a sequential versus simultaneous integration pattern. There also were large individual differences among users in the percentage of unimodal versus multimodal input, and in their ratio of simultaneous to sequential multimodal integration. These large individual differences indicated that user-adaptive processing of multimodal input would be fertile territory for applying machine learning.

2.3 User Modeling Study Experimental Results

In this research, only 83 fully annotated commands for each user were used for modeling and machine learning purposes. Columns 2 and 3 in Table 1 show that the dominant pattern of subjects 1, 2, 3, 4, 5, 6, and 8 is multimodal

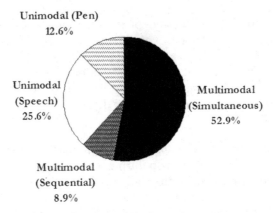

Fig. 3. Percentage of unimodal (pen only and speech only) and multimodal (sequentially integrated and simultaneously integrated) constructions for entire corpus

(60% of all commands), while the dominant pattern of subjects 7, 9 and 10 involves unimodal input to the system. The average consistency of users' dominant uni/multimodal pattern is 73.6%. Likewise, columns 4 and 5 show that the dominant multimodal integration pattern for subjects 7 and 10 is sequential (SEQ) when they do interact multimodally, whereas the dominant multimodal integration pattern of the other eight subjects is simultaneous (SIM). The overall average consistency for users' dominant SEQ/SIM pattern is a striking 93.5%. As this table illustrates, the dominant pattern of different subjects varies substantially, although each subject's own patterns are extremely consistent. This empirical result provides a basis for establishing reliable prior knowledge for machine learning, especially for users' multimodal integration pattern.

Since we planned to use the first 15 out of 83 commands from each subject as training samples, in Table 2 we have recalculated the percentages shown in Table 1 just for each subject's remaining 68 commands that our learning

Table 1. Percentage of unimodal versus multimodal commands delivered by each subject, and percentage of sequential versus simultaneous integration patterns for their multimodal com-mands (averaged over all data)

Subject	Multimodal	Unimodal	SIM	SEQ
1	69%	31%	87%	13%
2	92%	8%	100%	0%
3	62%	38%	90%	10%
4	62%	38%	97%	3%
5	84%	16%	99%	1%
6	89%	11%	98%	2%
7	22%	78%	5%	95%
8	69%	31%	72%	28%
9	41%	59%	97%	3%
10	28%	72%	0%	100%

Table 2. Percentage of unimodal versus multimodal commands delivered by each subject, and percentage of sequential versus simultaneous integration patterns for their multimodal commands (averaged over commands 16-83)

Subject	Multimodal	Unimodal	SIM	SEQ
1	70%	30%	94%	6%
2	90%	10%	100%	0%
3	62%	38%	91%	9%
4	65%	35%	98%	2%
5	88%	12%	98%	2%
6	96%	4%	97%	3%
7	14%	86%	10%	90%
8	69%	31%	69%	31%
9	39%	61%	100%	0%
10	33%	67%	0%	100%

models aimed to predict. Table 2 shows that the average consistency of users' patterns on their last 68 commands was even more stable than their grand means (i.e., 75.3% for uni/multimodal input, and 93.6% for integration pattern). In the present work, one major goal was to predict users' input using as few commands as possible. In this study, we tried to predict whether a subject's subsequent commands should be classified as unimodal or multimodal based on their first 5, 10, and then 15 commands. At each training step (i.e., 5, 10, 15), if the ratio of the subject's unimodal to total commands was larger than 60%, then they were classified as unimodal. If less then 40%, then they were classified as multimodal. For example, if subject 1 had 3 unimodal commands and 2 multimodal commands in their first 5 commands, the model would classify them as predominantly unimodal. This dominance classification also can be applied to other data variables (e.g., next signal, sequential/simultaneous, etc).

Table 3. Prediction result of user modeling study

# of training samples	Unimodal	Multimodal	SIM	SEQ
5	7,10	2,3,4,8	1,2,3,4,5,6,8, 9	7,10
10	7,10	2,3,4,6,8	1,2,3,4,5,6,8	7 ,9, 10
15	7,9,10	1,2,3,4,5,6, 8	1,2,3,4,5,6,8,9	7, 10

Table 3 shows the prediction accuracy of each subject's dominant pattern following just 5, 10, or 15 example commands. Based on 5 commands, we can correctly classify 6 subjects with respect to their dominant uni/multimodal pattern. With 15 commands, it is possible to classify users' dominant uni/multimodal input pattern with 100% accuracy. For classification of users' SIM/SEQ dominant integration pattern, the first 15 commands also are sufficient for 100% prediction accuracy.

It is worth noting that in principle we need a lot of training samples for machine learning models. If we can take advantage of user modeling results as prior knowledge to bootstrap machine learning, then substantial gains potentially could be achieved both in training time and model prediction accuracy. Furthermore, machine learning algorithms can be computationally intractable if there is no prior knowledge, especially for data as complex as multimodal input. Without good initialization, which can be specified by empirical results, machine learning algorithms can have substantial difficulty converging.

3   Machine Learning Model for Multimodal Integration Pattern Adaptation

In this section, we describe how to implement machine learning approaches to learn and adapt to each user's input pattern. We first introduce a general architecture of multimodal integration pattern adaptation. Then three machine learning models are presented with the goal of determining the best model for the present data and task. The experimental results of all three models are outlined in section 3.2.

3.1   Multi-layer Learning Architecture

The multi-layer learning architecture to predict users' multimodal integration patterns is shown in Fig. 4. At the first level, user modeling predicts the dominant pattern (Uni/Multmodal) of each user using a few training samples. Combing this prior knowledge, we can improve the BBN model to learn each user's pattern more accurately and rapidly (level 2). A more ambitious goal is to make the learned model adapt to new users through online learning (level 3).

In this section, we focus on adopting Bayesian Belief Network to learn users' input pattern (level 2 in Fig. 4). A Bayesian network [16] is a graphical model that encodes probabilistic relations among related variables. Bayesian Belief Network has the following advantages: 1) It can handle situations where some data are missing. 2) We can infer causal relations using BBN. Thus, it is possible to gain understanding about a problem domain and to predict the consequences of intervention. 3) It is an ideal representation for combining prior knowledge and new training samples.

The first machine learning model for multimodal integration pattern adaptation is shown in Fig. 5. We used the Matlab toolkit [17] to generate this model. The model represents the joint probability distribution of six variables (three inputs and three outputs). The model represents the joint probability distribution of six variables (three input, three output). These include: 1) Subject number: an input variable that denotes subject identification out of 10 total; 2) Task difficulty: an input variable that denotes the difficulty level of the current command out of four levels (easy, medium, difficult, very difficult); 3) Current signal: an input variable that represents the name of the modality generating the current signal (speech, pen, or neither/silence); 4) Uni/multimodal: an output variable that represents whether the command is unimodal or multimodal; 5)

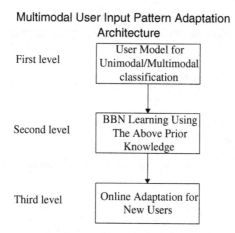

Fig. 4. Multimodal User Input Pattern Adaptation Architecture

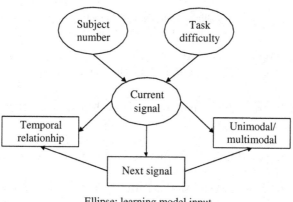

Fig. 5. Machine Learning Model 1 (Bayesian Belief Network) for multimodal integration pattern adaptation. [Ellipse denotes learning model input; Rectangle denotes learning model output].

Next signal: an output variable that represents what the next signal is (i.e., If the command is unimodal, then the next signal is silence. If multimodal, following a first signal input, the next signal could be speech or pen.); 6) Temporal relationship: an output variable that represents the predicted temporal relationship between the current signal and next signal. (There are three possible values: simultaneous, sequential and neither (i.e., for a unimodal command). The goal of this model is to incorporate a group of simple related variables in order to infer the pattern of subsequent user commands (i.e., Uni/Multi, SIM/SEQ). The

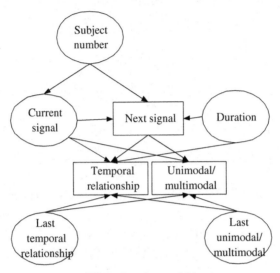

Bayesian Belief Network Model (2)
For Multimodal Integration Pattern Adaptation

Ellipse: learning model input
Rectangle: learning model output

Fig. 6. Machine Learning Model 2 (Bayesian Belief Network), with current signal duration and previous command features as additional input variables

goal of the model is to predict the pattern of each new input command, which then would be used by the system to more reliably cluster incoming signals and interpret their meaning.

In order to compare different machine learning models, we created an alternative one shown in Figure 6 based on different information sources. The major differences between Model 2 and Model 1 are: 1) Task difficulty level is omitted because during real-time processing the system does not have access to such information in advance; 2) Duration of current signal was added as an input variable. This variable has two values, 1 if the duration is long (longer than average duration), and 0 if not; and 3) The last command's input characteristics (i.e., uni/multimodal and SIM/SEQ) were added to determine whether further context regarding signal pattern could assist prediction.

The third model tested is a Naive Bayes model. The basic information sources are similar to Model 2, except the input variables are independent of each other. In other words, by removing the links between ellipses (i.e., input variables) we derive Machine Learning Model 3. The simple assumptions of this learning model are its advantage, especially when there are many variables. Even though studies in psychology show that multimodal input does not involve independence between modes, as a starting point for applying machine learning technology to multimodal adaptive interfaces, we have implemented this model to compare its performance with the others.

3.2   Machine Learning Study Experimental Results

To compare our alternative models, we used the first 15 commands from each subject's input to the system for training, and the remaining 68 commands from each subject for testing. The prediction accuracy of each model is shown in Table 4. Model 1 achieved 79% accuracy for predicting whether subsequent user commands were unimodal or multimodal, and 72% accuracy for predicting whether they were simultaneous or sequential in their multimodal integration pattern. This model is very simple, and the number of training sample it utilizes is very small compared with other machine learning apporaches. Moreover, information provided by including the last command did help prediction. Using model 2, the prediction rates improved to 85% and 82%, respectively, which is very promising. Although model 3 was the simplest, it nonetheless also provided good predictive information for adaptive information fusion. The Naive Bayes model is a good candidate for online-adaptation, and the simplicity of the independence assumption permits inclusion of more variables that can be useful in improving prediction accuracy.

Table 4. Comparison of prediction accuracy for 3 machine learning models

Model	Uni/Multi	SEQ/SIM
1	79%	73%
2	85%	82%
3	80%	81%

4   Conclusions and Future Work

In this paper, we investigated user-adaptive information fusion for multimodal systems. Our research reveals that there are large individual differences among users in multimodal input and integration patterns, although individual users show high internal consistency. Our user modeling results clarify that users' dominant multimodal integration patterns can be predicted based on very few samples. For our dataset, only 15 commands from each subject were needed to predict a given person's dominant input pattern (both uni/multimodal and sim/seq) with 100% accuracy. The present results also demonstrate the value of combining empirical user modeling with machine learning techniques in the development of a new generation of user-adaptive interfaces.

More specifically, in the present work we implemented three machine learning models (Bayesian Belief Networks) to predict each user's command input pattern. This is a much more difficult. This research constitutes an early attempt at applying machine learning techniques to prediction of complex multimodal data. With only a few training samples and relatively simple learning models, we were able to achieve good prediction accuracy. In fact, our second model correctly classified 85% of users' natural mixed input as unimodal or multimodal, and 82% of users' multimodal input as sequentially or simultaneously integrated.

The study of adaptive information fusion for multimodal systems is still in its infancy. Future research will investigate the performance of different learning techniques, such as that achievable with asynchronous HMM models [8] which previously have been applied to audio-visual speech and lip movement data. Future work also will examine the extent to which these machine learning models generalize to predicting users' input in different tasks and with different input modes. The long-term goal of this research is to develop new strategies for combining empirical user modeling with machine learning techniques to bootstrap accelerated, generalized, and improved reliability of information fusion in new types of multimodal systems.

Acknowledgments

Thanks to Benfang Xiao and Josh Flanders for assistance with data collection, and Rebecca Lunsford for her insightful comments and suggestions. This research was supported by DARPA Contract No. NBCHD030010 and NSF Grant No. IIS-0117868. Any opinions, findings or conclusions expressed in this material are those of the author(s) and do not necessarily reflect the views of the Defense Advanced Research Project Agency, or the Department of the Interior.

References

1. C. Benoit, J.-C. Martin, C. Pelachaud, L. Schomaker, and B. Suhm. Audio-visual and multimodal speech-based systems. In *the Handbook of Multimodal and Spoken Dialogue Systems: Resources, Terminology and Product Evaluation*, pages 102– 203, Boston, MA, 2000.
2. S. Oviatt. Multimodal interfaces. In *the Handbook of Human-Computer Interaction*, pages 286–304. Law. Erlb., 2003.
3. D. Massaro and D. Stork. Sensory ntegration and speech reading by humans and machines. *American Sciences*, 86:236–244, 1998.
4. S. Oviatt. Integration and sychronization of input modes during multimodal human computer interaction. In *Proc. of CHI'97*, pages 415–422.
5. I. Illina. Tree-structured maximum a posteriori adaptation for a segment-based speech recognition system. In *Proc. of ICSLP'02*, pages 1405–1408, 2002.
6. B. Xiao, R. Lunsford, R. Coulston, M. Wesson, and S.L. Oviatt. Modeling multimodal integration patterns and performance in seniors: Toward adaptive processing of individual differences. In *Proc. of ICMI'03*, pages 265–272, Vancouver, B.C.
7. S. Bengio. An asynchronous hidden markov model for audio-visual speech recognition. In *Advances in Neural Information Processing Systems*, volume 15, pages 1213–1220, 2003.
8. S. Bengio. Multimodal authentication using asynchronous hmms. In *AVBPA*, pages 770–777, 2003.
9. A. Howard and T. Jebara. Dynamical systems trees. In *Uncertainty in Artificial Intelligence*, 2004.
10. X. Huang, J. Weng, and Z. Zhang. Office presence detection using multimodal context information. In *Proc. of ICASSP'04*, Montreal, Quebec, Canada, USA.

11. N. Oliver, A. Garg, and E. Horvitz. Layered representations for learning and inferring office activity from multiple sensory channels. *Int. Journal on Computer Vision and Image Understanding*, 96(2):227–248, 2004.

12. S. Oviatt. Ten myths of multimodal interaction. *Communications of the ACM*, 42(11):74–81, 1999.

13. S. Oviatt, R. Coulston, and R. Lunsford. When do we interact multimodally? Cognitive load and multimodal communication patterns. In *Proc. of ICMI'04*, pages 129–136, Pennsylvania, USA. ACM Press.

14. S. Oviatt, R. Coulston, S. Tomko, B. Xiao, R. Lunsford, M. Wesson, and L. Carmichael. Toward a theory of organized multmodal integration patterns during human-computer interaction. In *Proc. of ICMI'03*, pages 44–51, Vancouver, B.C. ACM Press.

15. S. Oviatt, R. Lunsford, and R. Coulston. Individual differences in multimodal integration patterns: What are they and why do they exist? In *Prof. of CHI'05*, pages 241–249. ACM Press.

16. D. Heckerman. A tutorial on learning with Bayesian networks. In *Learning in Graphical Modals*. MIT Press, 1999.

17. K. Murphy. The Bayes net toolbox for matlab. *Computing Science and Statistics*, 33, 2001.

The AMI Meeting Corpus: A Pre-announcement*

Jean Carletta, Simone Ashby, Sebastien Bourban, Mike Flynn,
Mael Guillemot, Thomas Hain, Jaroslav Kadlec, Vasilis Karaiskos,
Wessel Kraaij, Melissa Kronenthal, Guillaume Lathoud, Mike Lincoln,
Agnes Lisowska, Iain McCowan, Wilfried Post,
Dennis Reidsma, and Pierre Wellner

AMI Project Consortium
J.Carletta@edinburgh.ac.uk

Abstract. The AMI Meeting Corpus is a multi-modal data set consisting of 100 hours of meeting recordings. It is being created in the context of a project that is developing meeting browsing technology and will eventually be released publicly. Some of the meetings it contains are naturally occurring, and some are elicited, particularly using a scenario in which the participants play different roles in a design team, taking a design project from kick-off to completion over the course of a day. The corpus is being recorded using a wide range of devices including close-talking and far-field microphones, individual and room-view video cameras, projection, a whiteboard, and individual pens, all of which produce output signals that are synchronized with each other. It is also being hand-annotated for many different phenomena, including orthographic transcription, discourse properties such as named entities and dialogue acts, summaries, emotions, and some head and hand gestures. We describe the data set, including the rationale behind using elicited material, and explain how the material is being recorded, transcribed and annotated.

1 Introduction

AMI is a large, multi-site and multi-disciplinary project with the aim of developing meeting browsing technologies that improve work group effectiveness. As part of the development process, the project is collecting a corpus of 100 hours of meetings using instrumentation that yields high quality, synchronized multimodal recording, with, for technical reasons, a focus on groups of four people. All meetings are in English, but a large proportion of the speakers are non-native English speakers, providing a higher degree of variability in speech patterns than in many corpora. We expect the corpus to become an invaluable resource to a range of research communities, since it should be of interest to those working on

---

* This work was supported by the European Union 6th FWP IST Integrated Project AMI (Augmented Multi-party Interaction, FP6-506811).

speech, language, gesture, information retrieval, and tracking, as well as being useful for organizational psychologists interested in how groups of individuals work together as a team. We describe the data set and explain how the material is being recorded, transcribed and annotated.

2   The Shape of the Corpus

Any study of naturally-occurring behaviour such as meetings immediately encounters a well-known methodological problem: if one simply observes behaviour "in the wild", one's results will be difficult to generalize, since not enough will be known about what is causing the individual (or individuals) to produce the behaviour. [1] identifies seven kinds of factors that affect how work groups behave, ranging from the means they have at their disposal, such as whether they have a way of communicating outside meetings, to aspects of organizational culture and what pressures the external environment places on the group. The type of task the group is trying to perform, and the particular roles and skills the group members bring to it, play a large part in determining what the group does; for instance, if the group members have different roles or skills that bear on the task in different ways, that can naturally increase the importance for some contributions, and it can also be a deciding factor in whether the group actually needs to communicate at all or can leave one person to do all of the work. Vary any of these factors and the data will change in character, but using observational techniques, it is difficult to get enough of a group history to tease out these effects. One response to this dilemma is not to make completely natural observations, but to standardize the data as much as possible by eliciting it in a controlled manner for which as many as possible of the factors are known. Experimental control allows the researcher to find effects with much greater clarity and confidence than in observational work. This approach, well-established in psychology and familiar from some existing corpora (e.g., [2]), comes with its own danger: results obtained in the laboratory will not necessarily occur outside it, since people may simply behave differently when performing an artificial task than they do in their daily lives.

Our response to this methodological difficulty is to collect our data set in parts. The first consists of elicited material using a design task in which the factors that [1] describe are all fixed as far as they can be. Since it constitutes the bulk of the data, the details of how it was elicited are important, and so we describe it below. The second consists of other, less controlled elicitations for different tasks. For instance, in one set of five meetings, forming one coherent set, which draws personnel from an existing work group to plan where to place people, equipment, and furniture in a fictionalized move to a new site that simplifies a real situation the group faces. These again provide more control than in natural data, but give us a first step towards thinking about how one combines data from disparate sources. The third contains naturally occurring meetings in a variety of types, the purpose of which is to help us validate our findings from the elicitation and determine how well they generalize by seeing how badly variation in the factors affects our models. The goal in this part of the collection was not to constrain the type of meeting in any way apart from keeping the recording manageable, but to allow the factors to vary freely. Taking histories that would allow us to classify the groups by factor would be a formidable task, and so the recorded data is included "as is", without supplementary materials.

3   The Meeting Elicitation Scenario

In our meeting elicitation scenario [3], the participants play the roles of employees in an electronics company that decides to develop a new type of television remote control because the ones found in the market are not user friendly, as well as being unattractive and old-fashioned. The participants are told they are joining a design team whose task, over a day of individual work and group meetings, is to develop a prototype of the new remote control. We chose design teams for this study for several reasons. First, they have functional meetings with clear goals, so making it easier to measure effectiveness and efficiency. Second, design is highly relevant for society, since it is a common task in many industrial companies and has clear economic value. Finally, for all teams, meetings are not isolated events but just one part of the overall work cycle, but in design teams, the participants rely more heavily on information from previous meetings than in other types of teams, and so they produce richer possibilities for the browsing technology we are developing.

3.1   Participants and Roles

Within this context, each participant in the elicitation is given a different role to play. The *project manager* (PM) coordinates the project and is responsible overall. His job is to guarantee that the project is carried out within time and budget limits. He runs the meetings, produces and distributes minutes, and produces a report at the end of the trial. The *marketing expert* (ME) is responsible for determining user requirements, watching market trends, and evaluating the prototype. The *user interface designer* (UI) is responsible for the technical functions the remote control provides and the user interface. Finally, the *industrial designer* (ID) is responsible for designing how the remote control works including the componentry. The user interface designer and industrial designer jointly have responsibility for the look-and-feel of the design.

For this elicitation, we use participants who are neither professionally trained for design work nor experienced in their role. It is well-known that expert designers behave differently from novices. However, using professional designers for our collection would present both economic and logistical difficulties. Moreover, since participants will be affected by their past experience, all those playing the same role should have the same starting point if we are to produce replicable behaviour. To enable the participants to carry out their work while lacking knowledge and experience, they are given training for their roles at the beginning of the task, and are each assigned a (simulated) personal coach who gives

sufficient hints by e-mail on how to do their job. Our past experience with elicitations for similar non-trivial team tasks, such as for crisis management teams,
suggests that this approach will yield results that generalize well to real groups.
We intend to validate the approach for this data collection both by the comparisons to other data already described and by having parts of the data assessed
by design professionals.

3.2 The Structure of the Elicited Data

[4] distinguishes the following four phases in the design process:

- *Project kick-off*, consisting of building a project team and getting acquainted
  with both each other and the task.
- *Functional design*, in which the team sets the user requirements, the technical
  functionality, and the working design.
- *Conceptual design*, in which the team determines the conceptual specification
  for the components, properties, and materials to be used in the apparatus,
  as well as the user interface.
- *Detailed design*, which finalizes the look-and-feel and user interface, and during which the result is evaluated.

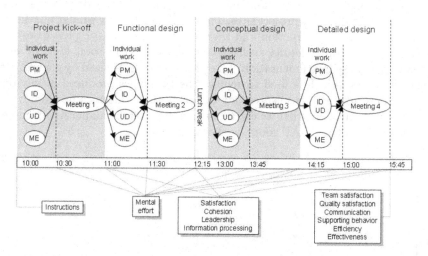

Fig. 1. The meeting paradigm: time schedule with activities of participants on top and
the variables measured below. PM: Project Manager; ID: industrial designer; UI: user
interface designer; ME: marketing expert.

We use these phases to structure our elicitation, with one meeting per design
phase. In real groups, meetings occur in a cycle where each meeting is typically
followed by production and distribution of minutes, the execution of actions that
have been agreed on, and the preparation of the next meeting. Our groups are
the same, except that for practical reasons, each design project was carried out

in one day rather than over the usual more extended period, and we included questionnaires that will allow us to measure process and outcomes throughout the day. In future data collections we intend to collect further data in which the groups have access to meeting browsing technology, and these measures will allow us to evaluate how the technology affects what they do and their overall effectiveness and efficiency. An overview of the group activities and the measurements used is presented in fig. 1.

3.3   The Working Environment

Our collection simulates an office environment in which the participants share a meeting room and have their own private offices and laptops that allow them to send e-mail to each other, which we collect; a web browser with access to a simulated web containing pages useful for the task; and PowerPoint for information presentation. During the trials, individual participants receive simulated e-mail from other individuals in the wider organization, such as the account manager or their head of department, that are intended to affect the course of the task. These emails are the same for every group.

4   Data Capture: Instrumented Meeting Rooms

The data is being captured in three different instrumented meeting rooms that have been built at different project sites. The rooms are broadly similar but differ in overall shape and construction and therefore in their acoustic properties, as well as in some recording details, such as microphone and camera placement and the presence of extra instrumentation. All signals are synchronized by generating a central timecode which is used to replace the timecodes produced locally on each recording device; this ensures, for instance, that videos same frames at exactly the same time and that we can find those times on the audio. An example layout, taken from the IDIAP room, is shown in figure 2.

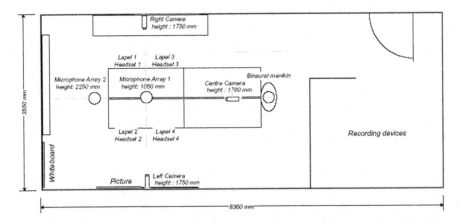

Fig. 2. Overhead Schematic View of the IDIAP Instrumented Meeting Room

4.1   Audio

The rooms are set up to record both close-talking and far-field audio. All microphone channels go through separate pre-amplification and analogue to digital conversion before being captured on a PC using Cakewalk Sonar recording software. For close-talking audio, we use omni-directional lapel microphones and headset condenser microphones. Both of these are radio-based so that the participants can move freely. For far-field audio, we use arrays of four or eight miniature omni-directional electret microphones. The individual microphones in the arrays are equivalent to the lapel microphones, but wired. All of the rooms have a circular array mounted on the table in the middle of the participants, plus one other array that is mounted on either the table or the ceiling and is circular in two of the rooms and linear in the other. One room also contains a binaural manikin providing two further audio channels.

4.2   Video

The rooms include capture of both videos that show individuals in detail and ones that show what happens in the room more generally. There is one close-up camera for each of four participants, plus for each room, either two or three room view cameras. The room view cameras can be either mounted to capture

| Closeup | Corner | Overhead |

Fig. 3. Camera views in the Edinburgh room

the entire room, with locations in corners or on the ceiling, or to capture one side of the meeting table. All cameras are static, with the close-up cameras trained on the participants' usual seating positions. In two of the rooms, output was recorded on Mini-DV tape and then transferred to computer, but in the other, output was recorded directly. Figure 3 shows sample output from cameras in the Edinburgh room.

4.3   Auxiliary Data Sources

In addition to audio and video capture, the rooms are instrumented to allow capture of what is presented during meetings, both any slides projected using a beamer and what is written on an electronic whiteboard. Beamer output is recorded as a timestamped series of static images, and whiteboard activity as timestamped x-y co-ordinates of the pen during pen strokes. In addition, individual note-taking uses Logitech I/O digital pens, where the output is similar to what the whiteboard produces. The latter is the one exception for our general approach to synchronization; the recording uses timecodes produced locally on the pen, requiring us to synchronize with the central timecode after the fact as best we can. We intend to subject all of these data sources to further processing in order to extract a more meaningful, character-based data representation automatically [5,6].

5   Orthographic Transcription

Our first and most crucial annotation is orthographic transcription of the recorded speech.

5.1   The Transcription Process

Transcribers work to a written manual, the features of which are described in the next section. We use several steps in the transcription process in order to ensure the quality of the results.

First pass. First pass transcribers are expected to achieve a balance between speed and accuracy. They start not with the raw audio signals but with a blank transcription that uses a simple energy-based technique to segment silence from speech for each person in the meeting, a technique originally developed and tested in [7]. Transcribers only listen to and transcribe the areas identified as speech by the auto-segmentation, using special marks for transcription of which they are unsure or that is unintelligible. They adjust segment boundaries where the given ones clearly begin too late or end too early, but without care to be accurate at this stage.

Second pass. In this step the checker reviews all segments, both speech and silence. The first-pass transcription is verified, any missed speech is transcribed, segment boundaries are carefully reviewed and adjusted to better fit the speech, and any uncertainties (items in parentheses) are resolved. If a sequence remains unintelligible, it is marked permanently as such.

Some meetings also receive a third pass from a transcription manager as a quality control step. Each transcription is then validated using a script that checks for spelling errors against the evolving AMI dictionary, uninterpretable symbols, and problems with the data format before being marked as 'finished'.

It is important to manage any large transcription effort carefully in order to avoid inconsistencies in the set of transcriptions, as well as to keep the work flowing smoothly. We have found Wikis invaluable in this regard. We use them to allocate work to individual transcribers, record their progress, discuss and resolve difficulties with interpreting the manual or with the audio files, and create official spellings for words that are not already in the dictionary used for spell checking. The transcriptions themselves are held in a CVS repository with symbolic tags representing their status, to which the transcribers have access via a simple web form.

5.2   Features of AMI Transcriptions

Speech is transcribed verbatim using British spellings, without correcting grammatical errors, e.g. 'I seen him', 'me and him have done this'. Additionally, certain common 'nonstandard' forms signifying linguistic reduction are employed, such as 'gonna' and 'kinda'. Normal capitalization on proper nouns and at the beginning and end of sentences is used, along with simplified standard English punctuation, including commas, hyphens, full stops and question marks. Other types of punctuation are used for specific purposes. Neologisms are flagged with an asterisk, e.g. 'bumblebeeish*'. Where mispronunciations are simply due to interference from the speaker's mother tongue, and therefore could be considered how one would expect a speaker of that language to pronounce the English word involved, they are ignored. Other mispronunciations are flagged with an asterisk as for neologisms, with the word transcribed using its correct spelling, not a spelling representing how it was pronounced. Discontinuity and disfluency, at the word or the utterance level, are indicated with a hyphen, e.g. 'I think basi- '; 'I just meant—I mean ...'. Particular care is also taken with punctuation at the end of a speech segment, where it indicates either that the turn continues (comma or no punctuation) or does not (full stop, question mark or hyphen). Qualitative and non-speech markers are kept to a minimum. Simple symbols are used to denote laughing '$', coughing '%' and other vocal noises '#', while other types of nonverbal noises are not indicated in the transcription. Whispered or emphasized speech, for example, are not tagged in any special way. A special category of noises, including onomatopoetic and other highly meaningful sounds, are indicated with a meta-noise tag within square brackets, e.g. '[sound imitating beep]'.

Sample transcription given in a human-readable format is shown in figure 4. The transcribers used Channel Trans (http://www.icsi.berkeley.edu/Speech/mr/ channeltrans.html), which adapts Transcriber (http://www.etca.fr/CTA/gip/ Projets/Transcriber/) for multiple speakers. Transcribers worked from headset audio except in a few instances where the lapel audio was of higher quality.

6   Forced Alignment

Automatically generated word and phoneme level timings of the transcripts are provided. Firstly this allowed more effective annotation of higher level information, secondly the time-segmentation is provided with the corpus for further processing. As the process for obtaining the time-segmentation has several implications on future processing we include a brief description of the steps involved. The timings were generated using acoustic models of an automatic speech recognition system [8]. The system was specifically developed for the transcription of

```
(ID) That's our number one prototype.
(PM)                            /@ like a little lightning in it.
(ID) Um do you wanna present the potato,
(ID) or shall I present the Martian?
(UI)    /Okay, um -
(PM)        /The little lightning bolt in it, very cute.
(UI)                        /What -
(UI) We call that one the rhombus, uh the rhombus.
(ME)        /I could -
(PM)                        /The v- the rhombus rhombus?
(ID)                                   /That's
(ID) the rhombus, yep.
(UI) Um this one is known as the potato, uh it's
(UI) it's a $ how can I present it? It's an ergonomic shape,
(ID)    /$
(ME)    /$
(UI) so it it fits in your hand nicely. Um,
{UI) it's designed to be used either in your left hand or or
(UI) in your right hand.
```

Fig. 4. Transcription Sample

the AMI meetings using all input channels and is based on the Hidden Markov Model Toolkit (HTK, http://htk.eng.cam.ac.uk). The time level information itself was obtained in a multi-step process:

Preprocessing of transcripts. Normalisation of transcripts to retain only events that are describable by phonemes. Text normalisation to fit the following dictionary creation.

Generation of a pronunciation dictionary. For the alignment a pronunciation for each word is required. This is either a fully automatic or a semi-automatic process. Dictionaries are based on the UNISYN dictionary [9], pronunciations for words not in that dictionary were created using pronunciation prediction (for more details on this process see [8]). In the case of semi-automatic processing, the suggested pronunciation is manually checked.

Viterbi Alignment. The acoustic recordings from the independent headset microphones are encoded and processed using the Viterbi algorithm, and the text and dictionaries created in the previous steps. Utterance time boundaries are used from the previous segmentation. Two passes of alignment are necessary to ensure a fixed silence collar for each utterance.

The acoustic models used in this process are trained on data from conversational telephone speech recordings (CTS) and more than 100 hours of close-talking microphone recordings from meetings, including the AMI corpus.

Post-processing. The output of the alignment stage includes silence within words. This is corrected.

The output of the above process is an exact time and duration for each pronounceable word in the corpus according to close talking microphones.

Furthermore phoneme level output is provided, again with exact timing. In each case times and durations are multiples of 10 milliseconds. Due to the automatic processing errors in the times are inevitable. Word level times should be broadly correct, however problems arise in the vicinity of overlapped speech (i.e. multiple speakers talking at the same time) and non-speech sounds (like door-closing etc). Furthermore problems can be expected where it was impossible to derive pronunciation for human generated sounds.

Phoneme level transcripts and timings should be used with caution. Meeting speech is conversational and spontaneous, hence similar in nature to CTS data. Greenberg et al. [10] have shown that there are considerable differences between human and automatic phone labelling techniques. Since the cost of manual labelling is prohibitive for corpora of this size one has to be aware of the properties of automatic methods as used here: Firstly, canonical pronunciations from dictionaries are used to represent arbitrary acoustic realisations of words. Secondly acoustic models for alignments make use of phoneme context. This and general model building strategies imply that phone boundaries can be inaccurate for frequently occurring phone sequences.

7   Annotation

In addition to orthographic transcription, the data set is being annotated for a wide range of properties:

- Named entities, focusing on references to people, artefacts, times, and numbers;
- Dialogue acts, using an act typology tailored for group decision-making and including some limited types of relations between acts;
- Topic segmentation that allows a shallow hierarchical decomposition into subtopics and includes labels describing the topic of the segment;
- A segmentation of the meetings by the current group activity in terms of what they are doing to meet the task in which they are engaged;
- Extractive summaries that show which dialogue acts support material in either the project manager's report summarizing the remote control scenario meetings or in third party textual summaries;
- Emotion in the style of FeelTrace [11] rated against different dimensions to reflect the range that occurs in the meeting;
- Head and hand gestures, in the case of hands focusing on those used for deixis;
- Location of the individual in the room and posture whilst seated;
- for some data, where on the video frames to find participant faces and hands; and
- for some data, at which other people or artefacts the participants are looking.

These annotations are being managed by a process similar to that used by the transcribers. For each one, reliability, or how well different annotators agree on how to apply the schemes, is being assessed.

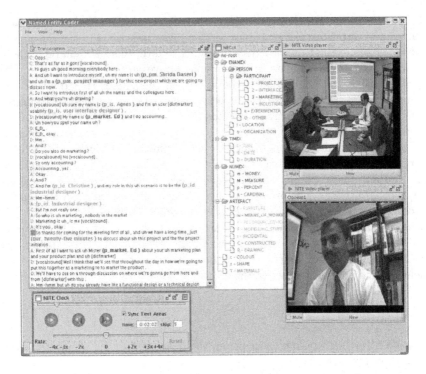

Fig. 5. Screenshot of the named entity annotation tool

Creating annotations that can be used together for such a wide range of phenomena requires careful thought about data formats, especially since the annotations combine temporal properties with quite complex structural ones, such as trees and referential links, and since they may contain alternate readings for the same phenomenon created by different coders. We use the NITE XML Toolkit for this purpose [12]. Many of the annotations are being created natively in NXT's data storage format using GUIs based on NXT libraries — figure 5 shows one such tool — and others require up-translation, which in most cases is simple to perform. One advantage for our choice of storage format is that it makes the data amenable to integrated analysis using an existing query language.

8   Release

Although at the time of submission, the data set has not yet been released, we intend to allow public access to it via http://mmm.idiap.ch, with a mirror site to be established at Brno University of Technology. The existing Media File Server found there allows users to browse available recorded sessions, download and upload data by HTTP or FTP in a variety of formats, and play media (through RTSP streaming servers and players), as well as providing web hosting and streaming servers for the Ferret meeting browser [13].

References

1. McGrath, J.E., Hollingshead, A.: Interacting with Technology: Ideas, Evidence, Issues and an Agenda. Sage Publications, Thousand Oaks (1994)
2. Anderson, A.H., Bader, M., Bard, E.G., Boyle, E., Doherty, G., Garrod, S., Isard, S., Kowtko, J., McAllister, J., Miller, J., Sotillo, C., Thompson, H., Weinert, R.: The HCRC Map Task Corpus. Language and Speech **34** (1991) 351–366
3. Post, W.M., Cremers, A.H., Henkemans, O.B.: A research environment for meeting behavior. In Nijholt, A., Nishida, T., Fruchter, R., Rosenberg, D., eds.: Social Intelligence Design, University of Twente, Enschede, the Netherlands (2004)
4. Pahl, G., Beitz, W.: Engineering design: a systematic approach. Springer, London (1996)
5. Chen, D., Odobez, J.M., Bourlard, H.: Text detection and recognition in images and video frames. Pattern Recognition **37** (2004) 595–608
6. Liwicki, M., Bunke, H.: Handwriting recognition of whiteboard notes. In Marcelli, A., ed.: 12th Conference of the International Graphonomics Society, Salerno (2005)
7. Lathoud, G., McCowan, I.A., Odobez, J.M.: Unsupervised location-based segmentation of multi-party speech. In: ICASSP-NIST Meeting Recognition Workshop, Montreal (2004) http://www.idiap.ch/publications/lathoud04a.bib.
8. Hain, T., Dines, J., Garau, G., Moore, D., Karafiat, M., Wan, V., Oerdelman, R., Renals, S.: Transcription of conference room meetings: an investigation. In: InterSpeech 2005, Lisbon (submitted)
9. Fitt, S.: Documentation and user guide to UNISYN lexicon and post-lexical rules. Technical report, Centre for Speech Technology Research, University of Edinburgh (2000)
10. Greenberg, S.: Speaking in shorthand - a syllable-centric perspective for understanding pronunciation variation. In: ESCA Workshop on modelling pronunciation variation for automatic speech recognition, Kerkrade, Netherlands (1998) 47–56
11. Cowie, R., Douglas-Cowie, E., Savvidou, S., McMahon, E., Sawey, M., Schröder, M.: 'FEELTRACE': An instrument for recording perceived emotion in real time. In Douglas-Cowie, E., Cowie, R., Schrder, M., eds.: ISCA Workshop on Speech and Emotion: A Conceptual Framework for Research, Belfast (2000) 19–24
12. Carletta, J., Evert, S., Heid, U., Kilgour, J., Reidsma, D., Robertson, J.: The NITE XML Toolkit. (submitted)
13. Wellner, P., Flynn, M., Guillemot, M.: Browsing recorded meetings with Ferret. In Bengio, S., Bourlard, H., eds.: Machine Learning for Multimodal Interaction: First International Workshop, MLMI 2004, Martigny, Switzerland, June 21-23, 2004, Revised Selected Papers. Lecture Notes in Computer Science 3361. Springer-Verlag, Berlin (2005) 12–21

VACE Multimodal Meeting Corpus

Lei Chen[1], R. Travis Rose[2], Ying Qiao[2], Irene Kimbara[3], Fey Parrill[3],
Haleema Welji[3], Tony Xu Han[4], Jilin Tu[4], Zhongqiang Huang[1], Mary Harper[1],
Francis Quek[2], Yingen Xiong[2], David McNeill[3],
Ronald Tuttle[5], and Thomas Huang[4]

[1] School of Electrical Engineering, Purdue University, West Lafayette, IN
[2] CHCI, Department of Computer Science, Virginia Tech, Blacksburg, VA
[3] Department of Psychology, University of Chicago, Chicago, IL
[4] Beckman Institute, University of Illinois Urbana Champaign, Urbana, IL
[5] Air Force Institute of Technology, Dayton, OH
quek@vt.edu

Abstract. In this paper, we report on the infrastructure we have developed to support our research on multimodal cues for understanding meetings. With our focus on multimodality, we investigate the interaction among speech, gesture, posture, and gaze in meetings. For this purpose, a high quality multimodal corpus is being produced.

1 Introduction

Meetings are gatherings of humans for the purpose of communication. Such communication may have various purposes: planning, conflict resolution, negotiation, collaboration, confrontation, etc. Understanding human multimodal communicative behavior, and how witting or unwitting visual displays (e.g., shoulder orientations, gesture, head orientation, gaze) relate to spoken content (the words spoken, and the prosody of the utterances) and communicative acts is critical to the analysis of such meetings. These multimodal behaviors may reveal static and dynamic social structuring of the meeting participants, the flow of topics being discussed, the high level discourse units of individual speakers, the control of the flow of the meeting, among other phenomena. The collection of rich synchronized multimedia corpora that encompasses multiple calibrated video streams, audio channels, motion tracking of the participants, and various rich annotations is necessary to support research into these phenomena that occur at varying levels of temporal resolution and conceptual abstraction.

From the perspective of the technology, meetings challenge current audio and video processing approaches. For example, there is a higher percentage of crosstalk among audio channels in a six party meeting than in a two party dialog, and this could reduce the accuracy of current speech recognizers. In a meeting setting, there may not be the ideal video image size or angle when attempting to recognize a face. Recorded meetings can push forward multimodal signal processing technologies.

S. Renals and S. Bengio (Eds.): MLMI 2005, LNCS 3869, pp. 40–51, 2006.

To enable this research, we are assembling a planning meeting corpus that is coded at multiple levels. Our research focuses not only on low level multimodal signal processing, but also on high level meeting event interpretation. In particular, we use low-level multimodal cues to interpret the high-level events related to meeting structure. To carry out this work, we require high quality multimodal data to jointly support multimodal data processing, meeting analysis and coding, as well as automatic event detection algorithms. Our corpus is designed to support research both in the understanding of the human communication and the engineering efforts to meet the challenges of dealing with meeting audio and video content. This collection, which is supported by the ARDA VACE-II program, is called the VACE meeting corpus in this paper.

We describe our efforts in collecting the VACE meeting corpus, the infrastructure we have constructed to collect the data, and the tools we have developed to facilitate the collection, annotation, and analysis of the data. In particular, Section 2 describes the ongoing multimodal meeting corpus collection, Section 3 describes audio and video data processing algorithms needed for corpus production, and Section 4 briefly summarizes some of the research that this corpus enables.

2   Meeting Data Collection

To investigate meetings, several corpora have already been collected, including the **ISL** audio corpus [1] from Interactive Systems Laboratory (ISL) of CMU, the **ICSI** audio corpus [2], the **NIST** audio-visual corpus [3], and the **MM4** audio-visual corpus [4] from Multimodal Meeting (MM4) project in Europe. Using these existing meeting data resources, a large body of research has already been conducted, including automatic transcription of meetings [5], emotion detection [6], attention state [7], action tracking [8, 4], speaker identification [9], speech segmentation [10, 11], and disfluency detection [12]. Most of this research has focused on low level processing (e.g., voice activity detection, speech recognition) or on elementary events and states. Research on the structure of a meeting or the dynamic interplay among participants in a meeting is only beginning to emerge. McCowan et al. [4] have used low level audio and video information to segment a meeting into meeting actions using an HMM approach.

Our multimodal meeting data collection effort is depicted schematically in Figure 1. We next discuss three important aspects of this meeting data collection effort: (1) meeting room setup, (2) elicitation experiment design, and (3) data processing.

2.1   Multimodal Meeting Room Setup

Under this research effort, Air Force Institute of Technology (AFIT) modified a lecture room to collect multimodal, time-synchronized audio, video, and motion data. In the middle of the room, up to 8 participants can sit around a rectangular conference table. An overhead rail system permits the data acquisition

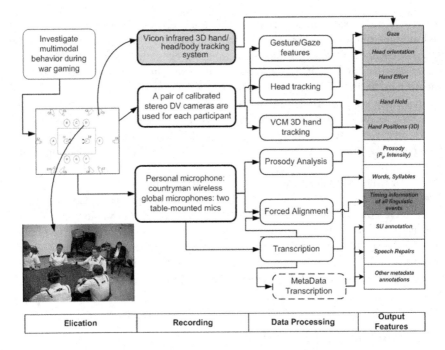

Fig. 1. VACE meeting corpus production

technician to position the 10 Canon GL2 camcorders in any configuration required to capture all participants by at least two of the 10 camcorders. Using S-video transfer, 10 Panasonic AG-DV2500 recorders capture video data from the camcorders. The rail system also supports the 9 Vicon MCam2 near-IR cameras and are driven by the Vicon V8i Data Station. The Vicon system records temporal position data. For audio recording, we utilize a setup similar to the ICSI and NIST meeting rooms. In particular, participants wear Countryman ISOMAX Earset wireless microphones to record their individual sound tracks. Table-mounted wired microphones are used to record the audio of all participants (two to six XLR-3M connector microphones configured for the number of participants and scenario, including two cardioid Shure MX412 D/C microphones and several types of low-profile boundary microphones (two hemispherical polar pattern Crown PZM-6D, one omni-directional Audio Technica AT841a, and one four-channel cardioid Audio Technica AT854R). All audio signals are routed to a Yamaha MG32/14FX mixing console for gain and quality control. A TASCAM MX-2424 records the sound tracks from both the wireless and wired microphones.

There are some significant differences between our video recording setup and those used by previous efforts. For example, in the NIST and MM4 collections, because stereo camera views are not used to record each participant, only $2D$ tracking results can be obtained. For the VACE meeting corpus, each participant is recorded with a stereo calibrated camera pair. Ten video cameras are placed facing different participants seated around the table as shown in Figure 1.

To obtain the $3D$ tracking of 6 participants, 12 stereo camera pairs are setup to ensure that each participant is recorded by at least 2 cameras. This is important because we wish to accurately track head, torso and hand positions in 3D. We also utilize the Vicon system to obtain more accurate tracking results to inform subsequent coding efforts, while also providing ground truth for our video-tracking algorithms.

2.2   Elicitation Experiment

The VACE meeting corpus involves meetings based on wargame scenarios and military exercises. We have selected this domain because the planning activity spans multiple military functional disciplines, the mission objectives are defined, the hierarchical relationships are known, and there is an underpinning doctrine associated with the planning activity. Doctrine-based planning meetings draw upon tremendous expertise in scenario construction and implementation. Wargames and military exercises provide real-world scenarios requiring input from all functionals for plan construction and decision making. This elicits rich multimodal behavior from participants, while permitting us to produce a high confidence coding of the meeting behavior. Examples of scenarios include planning a Delta II rocket launch, humanitarian assistance, foreign material exploitation, and scholarship award selection.

2.3   Multimodal Data Processing

After obtaining the audio and video recordings, we must process the data to obtain features to assist researchers with their coding efforts or to the train and evaluate automatic event detection algorithms. The computer vision researchers on our team from University of Illinois and Virginia Tech focus on video-based tracking, in particular, body torso, head, and hand tracking. The VCM tracking

Table 1. Composition of the VACE meeting corpus

Video	MPEG4 Video from 10 cameras
Audio	AIFF Audio from all microphones
Vicon	3D positions of Head, Torso, Shoulders and Hands
Visual Tracking	Head pose, Torso configuration, Hand positions
Audio Processing	Speech segments, Transcripts, Alignments
Prosody	Pitch, Word & Phone duration, Energy, etc.
Gaze	Gaze target estimation
Gesture	Gesture phase/phrase, Semiotic gesture coding, e.g., deictics, iconics
Metadata	Language metadata, e.g., sentence boundaries, speech repairs, floor control change

approach is to obtain $3D$ positions of the hands, which is important for obtaining a wide variety of gesture features, such as gesture hold and velocity. The change in position of the head, torso, and hands provide important cues for the analysis of the meetings. Researchers on our team from Purdue handle the audio processing of the meetings. More detail on video and audio processing appear in the next section.

Our meeting room corpus contains time synchronized audio and video recordings, features derived by the visual trackers and Vicon tracker, audio features such as pitch tracking and duration of words, and coding markups. Details on the data types appear in an organized fashion in Table 1.

3   Multimodal Data Processing

3.1   Visual Tracking

Torso Tracking. Vision-based human body tracking is a very difficult problem. Given that joint-angle is a natural and complete way to describe human body motion and human joint-angles are not independent, we have been investigating an approach to learn these latent constraints and then use them for articulated body tracking [13] After learning the constraints as potential functions, belief propagation is used to find the MAP of the body configuration on the Markov Random Field (MRF) to achieve globally optimal tracking. When tested on the VACE meeting corpus data, we have obtained tracking results that will be used in future experiments. See Figure 2 for an example of torso tracking.

Fig. 2. Torso tracking

Head Pose Tracking. For the video analysis of human interactions, the head pose of the person being analyzed is very important for determining gaze direction and the person being spoken to. In our meeting scenario, the resolution of a face is usually low. We therefore have developed a hybrid 2D/3D head pose tracking framework. In this framework, a 2D head position tracking algorithm [14] tracks the head location and determines a coarse head orientation (such as the frontal view of the face, the side view and the rear view of the head) based on the appearance at that time. Once the frontal view of a face is detected, a 3D head pose tracking algorithm [15] is activated to track the 3D head orientation. For 2D head tracking, we have developed a meanshift tracking algorithm with an online updating appearance generative mixture model. When doing meanshift tracking, our algorithm updates the appearance histogram online based on some key features acquired before the tracking, allowing it to be more accurate and robust. The coarse head pose (such as frontal face) can be inferred by simply checking the generative appearance model parameters. The 3D head pose tracking algorithm acquires the facial texture from the video based on the 3D face model. The appearance likelihood is modelled by an incremental PCA subspace, and the 3D head pose is inferred using an annealed particle filtering technique. An example of a tracking result can be found in Figure 3.

Fig. 3. Head pose tracking

Hand Tracking. In order to interpret gestures used by participants, exact 3D hand positions are obtained using hand tracking algorithms developed by researchers in the Vislab [16, 17]. See [18] for details on the Vector Coherence Mapping (VCM) approach that is being used. The algorithm is currently being ported to the Apple G5 platform with parallel processors in order to address the challenge of tracking multiple participants in meetings. An example of a tracking result can be found in Figure 4.

3.2 Audio Processing

A meeting involves multiple time synchronized audio channels, which increases the workload for transcribers [19]. Our goal is to produce high quality transcrip-

Fig. 4. VCM hand position tracking

tions that are time aligned as accurately as possible with the audio. Words, and
their components, need to be synchronized with video features to support coding
efforts and to extract prosodic and visual features used by our automatic meeting event detection algorithms. To achieve this goal, we need an effective way
to transcribe all audio channels and a highly accurate forced alignment system.
As for the transcription convention, we are utilizing the Quick Transcription
(QTR) methodology developed by LDC for the 2004 NIST Meeting Recognition
Evaluations to achieve a balanced tradeoff between the accuracy and speed of
transcription. Meeting audio includes multi-channel recordings with substantial
cross-talk among the audio channels. These two aspects make the transcription
process more challenging than for monologs and dialogs. We use several tools to
improve the effectiveness and efficiency of audio processing: a tool to pre-segment
audio channels into transcribable and non-transcribable regions, tools to support
the transcription of multiple channels, and tools to enable more accurate forced
alignments. These are described in more detail below.

Automatic Pre-segmentation. Since in meetings typically one speaker is
speaking at any given time, the resulting audio files contain significant portions
of audio that do not require transcription. Hence, if each channel of audio is
automatically segmented into transcribable and non-transcribable regions, the
transcribers only need to focus on the smaller pre-identified regions of speech,
lowering the cognitive burden significantly compared with handling a large undif-
ferentiated stream of audio. We perform audio segmentation based on the close-
talking audio recordings using a novel automatic multi-step segmentation [20].
The first step involves silence detection utilizing pitch and energy, followed by

BIC-based Viterbi segmentation and energy based clustering. Information from each channel is employed to provide a rough preliminary segmentation. The second step makes use of the segment information obtained in the first step to train a Gaussian mixture model for each speech activity category, followed by decoding to refine the segmentation. A final post-processing step is applied to remove short segments and pad silence to speech segments.

Meeting Transcription Tools. For meetings, transcribers must utilize many audio channels and often jump back and forth among the channels to support transcription and coding efforts [19]. There are many transcription and annotation tools currently available [21]; however, most were designed for monologs and dialogs. To support multi-channel audio, researchers have either tailored currently available tools for dialogs (e.g., the modification of Transcriber [22] for meeting transcription by ICSI (http://www.icsi.berkeley.edu/Speech/mr/channeltrans.html) or designed new tools specific for the meeting transcription and annotation process, (e.g., iTranscriber by ICSI).

We have evaluated ICSI's modified Transcriber and the beta version of ICSI's iTranscriber currently under development. Although these tools can not be used in their current form for our transcription and annotation process, they highlight important needs for transcribing meetings: transcibers need the ability to easily load the multiple channels of a meeting and efficiently switch back and forth among channels during transcription. Hence, we have developed two Praat [23] extensions to support multi-channel audio transcription and annotation. We have chosen to use Praat for the following reasons: 1) it is a widely used and supported speech analysis and annotation tool available for almost any platform, 2) it is easy to use, 3) *long sound* supports the quick loading of multiple audio files, and 4) it has a built-in script language for implementation of future extensions. We have added two menu options to the Praat interface: the first supports batch loading of all the audio files associated with a meeting, and the second enables transcribers to switch easily among audio files based on the transcription tiers.

Improved Forced Alignment. Forced alignment is used to obtain the starting and ending time of the words and phones in the audio. Since such timing information is widely used for multimodal fusion, we have investigated factors for achieving accurate alignments. In the first step, the forced alignment system converts the words in the transcript to a phoneme sequence according to the pronunciations in the dictionary. For out of vocabulary (OOV) words, the typically used method is to use a special token, such as UNK, to replace the OOV words. However, this approach can significantly degrade forced alignment accuracy. Hence, we have created a script to identify all of the OOV words in the finished transcription and have designed a Praat script to prompt the transcriber to provide an exact pronunciation for each OOV word given its audio and then to subsequently update the dictionary with that word and pronunciation. Although this approach is more time consuming, it provides a more accurate alignment result important to our corpus production task. Based on a systematic study [24], we have also found more accurate forced alignments are obtained by having transcribers directly transcribe pre-identified segments of speech (supported by the presegmentation tool described previously) and by using a sufficiently trained, genre matched speech recognizers to produce the alignments. For meeting room alignments, we have been using ISIP's ASR system with a triphone acoustic model trained from more than 60 hours long spontaneous speech data [25] to force align transcriptions provided for segments of speech identified in the pre-segmentation step. Alignments produced given this setup requires little hand fixing. We are currently evaluating *SONIC* [26] for future use in our system.

4   Meeting Interaction Analysis Research

The VACE meeting corpus enables the analysis of meeting interactions at a number of different levels. Using the visualization and annotation tool *Macvissta*, developed by researchers at Virginia Tech, the features extracted from the recorded video and audio can be displayed to support psycholinguistic coding efforts of researchers on our team at University of Chicago. Some annotations of interest to our team include: F-formation [27], dominant speaker, structural events (sentence boundary, interruption point), and floor control challenges and change. Given the data and annotations in this corpus, we are carrying out measurement studies to investigate how visual and verbal cues combine to predict events such as sentence or topic boundaries, interruption points in a speech repair, or floor control changes. With the rich set of features and annotations, we are also developing data-driven models for meeting room event detection along the lines of our research on multimodal models for detecting sentence boundaries [28].

Visualization of visual and verbal activities is an important first step for developing a better understanding of how these modalities interact in human communication. The ability to add annotations of important verbal and visual events further enriches this data. For example, annotation of gaze and gesture activities is important for developing a better understanding of those activities in floor control. Hence, the availability of a high quality, flexible multimodal visualization/annotation tool is quite important. To give a complete display of a meeting, we need to display any of the multimodal signals and annotations of all participants. The Vissta tool developed for multimodal dialog data has been recently ported to the Mac OS X while being adapted for meeting room data [29]. Currently the tool supports the display of multiple angle view videos, as shown in Figure 5. This tool can display transcriptions and visual features, together with the spoken transcripts and a wide variety annotations. It has been widely used by our team and is continually being refined based on feedback.

Using MacVissta, researchers at the University of Chicago are currently focusing on annotating gesture and gaze patterns in meetings. Gesture onset and offset are coded, as well as the semiotic properties of the gesture as a whole, in relation to the accompanying speech. Because gesture is believed to be as relevant to a person's communicative behavior as speech, by coding gesture, we are attempting to capture this behavior in its totality. In addition, gaze is coded for each speaker

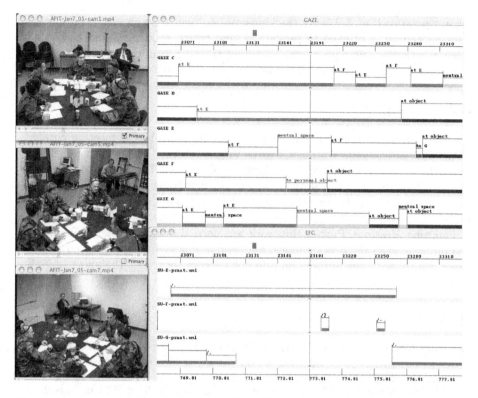

Fig. 5. A snapshot of the MacVissta multimodal analysis tool with multiple videos shown on the left, gaze annotations and speech mark-ups shown on the right

in terms of the object of that gaze (who or what gaze is directed at) for each moment. Instances of shared gaze (or "F-formations") are then extractable from the transcript, which can inform a turn-taking analysis. More fine-grained analyses include the coding of mimicry (in both gesture and speech), and the tracking of lexical co-reference and discourse cohesion, which permits us to capture moments where speakers are negotiating how to refer to an object or event. These moments appear to be correlated with shared gaze. To date, we have finished annotation of one complete meeting, AFIT_Jan_07, involving five participants lasting forty minutes. Video and annotations can be viewed in the MacVissta tool after download from the VACE site at Virginia Tech.

5   Conclusions

In this paper, we have reported on the infrastructure we have developed to support our research on multimodal cues for understanding meetings. With our focus on multimodality, we investigate the interaction among speech, gesture, posture, and gaze in meetings. For this purpose, a high quality multimodal corpus is being produced. Each participant is recorded with a pair of stereo calibrated camera pairs so that $3D$ body tracking can be done. Also an advanced motion tracking system is utilized to provide ground truth. From recorded audio and video, research on audio processing and video tracking focus on improving quality of low features that support higher level annotation and modeling efforts.

Acknowledgments

We thank all team members for efforts to produce the VACE meeting corpus: Bing Fang, and Dulan Wathugala from Virginia Tech, Dr. Sue Duncan, Matt Heinrich, Whitney Goodrich, and Alexia Galati from University of Chicago, Dr. David Bunker, Jim Walker, Kevin Pope, Jeff Sitler from AFIT. This research has been supported by the Advanced Research and Development Activity ARDA VACEII grant 665661: *From Video to Information: Cross-Model Analysis of Planning Meetings*. Part of this work was carried out while the tenth author was on leave at NSF. Any opinions, findings, and conclusions expressed in this paper are those of the authors and do not necessarily reflect the views of NSF or ARDA.

References

[1] Burger, S., MacLaren, V., Yu, H.: The ISL meeting corpus: The impact of meeting type on speech type. In: Proc. of Int. Conf. on Spoken Language Processing (ICSLP). (2002)

[2] Morgan, N., et al.: Meetings about meetings: Research at ICSI on speech in multiparty conversations. In: Proc. of ICASSP. Volume 4., Hong Kong, Hong Kong (2003) 740–743

[3] Garofolo, J., Laprum, C., Michel, M., Stanford, V., Tabassi, E.: The NIST Meeting Room Pilot Corpus. In: Proc. of Language Resource and Evaluation Conference. (2004)

[4] McCowan, I., Gatica-Perez, D., Bengio, S., Lathoud, G., Barnard, M., Zhang, D.: Automatic analysis of multimodal group actions in meetings. IEEE Trans. on Pattern Analysis and Machine Intelligence **27** (2005) 305–317

[5] Schultz, T., Waibel, A., et al.: The ISL meeting room system. In: Proceedings of the Workshop on Hands-Free Speech Communication, Kyoto Japan (2001)

[6] Polzin, T.S., Waibel, A.: Detecting emotions in speech. In: Proc.of the CMC. (1998)

[7] Stiefelhagen, R.: Tracking focus of attention in meetings. In: Proc. of Int. Conf. on Multimodal Interface (ICMI), Pittsburg, PA (2002)

[8] Alfred, D., Renals, S.: Dynamic bayesian networks for meeting structuring. In: Proc. of ICASSP. Volume 5., Montreal, Que, Canada (2004) 629–632

[9] Gatica-Perez, D., Lathoud, G., McCowan, I., Odobez, J., Moore, D.: Audio-visual speaker tracking with importance particle filters. In: Proc. of Int. Conf. on Image Processing (ICIP). Volume 3., Barcelona, Spain (2003) 25–28

[10] Renals, S., Ellis, D.: Audio information access from meeting rooms. In: Proc. of ICASSP. Volume 4., Hong Kong, Hong Kong (2003) 744–747

[11] Ajmera, J., Lathoud, G., McCowan, I.: Clustering and segmenting speakers and their locations in meetings. In: Proc. of ICASSP. Volume 1., Montreal, Que, Canada (2004) 605–608

[12] Moore, D., McCowan, I.: Microphone array speech recognition: Experiments on overlapping speech in meetings. In: Proc. of ICASSP. Volume 5., Hong Kong, Hong Kong (2003) 497–500

[13] Han, T.X., Huang, T.S.: Articulated body tracking using dynamic belief propagation. In: Proc. IEEE International Workshop on Human-Computer Interaction. (2005)

[14] Tu, J., Huang, T.S.: Online updating appearance generative mixture model for meanshift tracking. In: Proc. of Int. Conf. on Computer Vision (ICCV). (2005)

[15] Tu, J., Tao, H., Forsyth, D., Huang, T.S.: Accurate head pose tracking in low resolution video. In: Proc. of Int. Conf. on Computer Vision (ICCV). (2005)

[16] Quek, F., Bryll, R., Ma, X.F.: A parallel algorighm for dynamic gesture tracking. In: ICCV Workshop on RATFG-RTS, Gorfu,Greece (1999)

[17] Bryll, R.: A Robust Agent-Based Gesture Tracking System. PhD thesis, Wright State University (2004)

[18] Quek, F., Bryll, R., Qiao, Y., Rose, T.: Vector coherence mapping: Motion field extraction by exploiting multiple coherences. CVIU special issue on Spatial Coherence in Visual Motion Analysis (submitted) (2005)

[19] Strassel, S., Glenn, M.: Shared linguistic resources for human language technology in the meeting domain. In: Proceedings of ICASSP 2004 Meeting Workshop. (2004)

[20] Huang, Z., Harper, M.: Speech and non-speech detection in meeting audio for transcription. In: MLMI-05 NIST RT-05S Workshop. (2005)

[21] Bird, S., Liberman, M.: (Linguistic Annotation: Survey by LDC http://www.ldc.upenn.edu/annotation/)

[22] Barras, C., Geoffrois, D., Wu, Z., Liberman, W.: Transcriber : Development and use of a tool for assisting speech corpora production. Speech Communication (2001)

[23] Boersma, P., Weeninck, D.: Praat, a system for doing phonetics by computer. Technical Report 132, University of Amsterdam, Inst. of Phonetic Sc. (1996)

[24] Chen, L., Liu, Y., Harper, M., Maia, E., McRoy, S.: Evaluating factors impacting the accuracy of forced alignments in a multimodal corpus. In: Proc. of Language Resource and Evaluation Conference, Lisbon, Portugal (2004)

[25] Sundaram, R., Ganapathiraju, A., Hamaker, J., Picone, J.: ISIP 2000 conversational speech evaluation system. In: Speech Transcription Workshop 2001, College Park, Maryland (2000)

[26] Pellom, B.: SONIC: The University of Colorado continuous speech recognizer. Technical Report TR-CSLR-2001-01, University of Colorado (2001)

[27] Quek, F., McNeill, D., Rose, T., Shi, Y.: A coding tool for multimodal analysis of meeting video. In: NIST Meeting Room Workshop. (2003)

[28] Chen, L., Liu, Y., Harper, M., Shriberg, E.: Multimodal model integration for sentence unit detection. In: Proc. of Int. Conf. on Multimodal Interface (ICMI), University Park, PA (2004)

[29] Rose, T., Quek, F., Shi, Y.: Macvissta: A system for multimodal analysis. In: Proc. of Int. Conf. on Multimodal Interface (ICMI). (2004)

Multimodal Integration for Meeting Group Action Segmentation and Recognition

Marc Al-Hames[1], Alfred Dielmann[2], Daniel Gatica-Perez[3], Stephan Reiter[1], Steve Renals[2], Gerhard Rigoll[1], and Dong Zhang[3,*]

[1] Institute for Human-Machine-Communication, Technische Universität München, Arcisstr. 21, 80290 Munich, Germany
[2] Centre for Speech Technology Research, University of Edinburgh, 2 Buccleuch Place, Edinburgh EH8 9LW, UK
[3] IDIAP Research Institute and Ecole Polytechnique Federale de Lausanne (EPFL), P.O. Box 592, Martigny, CH-1920, Switzerland

Abstract. We address the problem of segmentation and recognition of sequences of multimodal human interactions in meetings. These interactions can be seen as a rough structure of a meeting, and can be used either as input for a meeting browser or as a first step towards a higher semantic analysis of the meeting. A common lexicon of multimodal group meeting actions, a shared meeting data set, and a common evaluation procedure enable us to compare the different approaches. We compare three different multimodal feature sets and our modelling infrastructures: a higher semantic feature approach, multi-layer HMMs, a multi-stream DBN, as well as a multi-stream mixed-state DBN for disturbed data.

1 Introduction

Recordings of multi-party meetings are useful to recall important pieces of information (decisions, key-points, etc.), and eventually share it with people who were not able to attend those meetings. Unfortunately, watching raw audio-video recordings is tedious. An automatic approach to extract high-level information could facilitate this task.

In this paper we address the problem of recognising sequences of human interaction patterns in meetings, with the goal of structuring them in semantic terms. Our aim is to discover repetitive patterns into natural group interactions and associate them with a lexicon of meeting actions or phases (such as discussions or monologues). The detected sequence of meeting actions will provide a relevant summary of the meeting structure. The investigated patterns are inherently group-based (involving multiple simultaneous participants), and multimodal (as captured by cameras and microphones).

Automatic modelling of human interactions from low-level multimodal signals is an interesting topic for both theoretical and practical reasons. First, from the theoretical point of view, modelling multichannel multimodal sequences provides a particular challenging task for machine learning techniques. Secondly, from the application point of view, automatic meeting analysis could add value to the raw data for browsing and retrieval purposes.

---

* Authors listed in alphabetical order.

S. Renals and S. Bengio (Eds.): MLMI 2005, LNCS 3869, pp. 52–63, 2006.

Starting from a common lexicon of meeting actions (section 2) and sharing the same meeting data-set (section 3), each site (TUM, IDIAP and UEDIN) has selected a specific feature set (section 4) and proposed relevant models (section 5). Then a common evaluation metric (section 6) has been adopted in order to compare several experimental setups (section 7).

2   Action Lexicon

Two sets of meeting actions have been defined. The first set (lexicon 1, defined in [8]) includes eight meeting actions, like discussion, monologue, or presentation. The monologue action is further distinguished by the person actually holding the monologue (e.g. monologue 1 is meeting participant one speaking). The second set (lexicon 2, defined in [15]) comprehends the full first set, but also has combinations of two parallel actions (like a presentation and note-taking). The second set includes fourteen group actions. Both sets and a brief description are shown in table 1.

Table 1. Group action lexicon 1 and 2

Action	Lexicon	Description
Discussion	lexicon 1 and 2	most participants engaged in conversations
Monologue	lexicon 1 and 2	one participant speaking continuously without interruption
Monologue+ Note-taking	contained only in lexicon 2	one participant speaking continuously others taking notes
Note-taking	lexicon 1 and 2	most participants taking notes
Presentation	lexicon 1 and 2	one participant presenting using the projector screen
Presentation+ Note-taking	contained only in lexicon 2	one participant presenting using projector screen, others taking notes
White-board	lexicon 1 and 2	one participant speaking using the white-board
White-board+ Note-taking	contained only in lexicon 2	one participant speaking using white-board, others taking notes

3   Meeting Data Set

We used a public corpus of 59 five-minute, four-participant scripted meetings [8]. The recordings took place at IDIAP in an instrumented meeting room equipped with cameras and microphones[1]. Video has been recorded using 3 fixed cameras. Two cameras capture a frontal view of the meeting participants, and the third camera captures the white-board and the projector screen. Audio was recorded using lapel microphones attached to participants, and an eight-microphone array placed in the centre of the table.

---

[1] This corpus is publicly available from http://mmm.idiap.ch/

4   Features

The investigated individual actions are multimodal, we therefore use different audio-visual features. They are distinguished between *person-specific* AV features and *group-level* AV features. The former are extracted from individual participants. The latter are extracted from the white-board and projector screen regions. Furthermore we use a small set of lexical features. The features are described in the next sections, for details please refer to the indicated literature.

From the large number of available features each site has chosen a set, used to train and evaluate their models. The complete list of features, and the three different sets IDIAP, TUM, UEDIN are listed in table 2.

Table 2. Audio, visual and semantic features, and the resulting three feature sets

		Description	IDIAP	TUM	UEDIN
Person-Specific Features	Visual	head vertical centroid	X		
		head eccentricity	X		
		right hand horizontal centroid	X		
		right hand angle	X		
		right hand eccentricity	X		
		head and hand motion	X		
		global motion features from each seat		X	
	Audio	SRP-PHAT from each seat	X		
		speech relative pitch	X		X
		speech energy	X	X	X
		speech rate	X		X
		4 MFCC coefficients		X	
		binary speech and silence segmentation		X	
	Semantic	individual gestures		X	
		talking activity		X	
Group Features	Visual	mean difference from white-board	X		
		mean difference from projector screen	X		
		global motion features from whiteboard		X	
		global motion features from projector screen		X	
	Audio	SRP-PHAT from white-board	X		
		SRP-PHAT from projector screen	X		
		speaker activity features			X
		binary speech from white-board		X	
		binary speech from projector screen		X	

4.1   Audio Features

MFCC: For each of the speakers four MFC coefficients and the energy were extracted from the lapel-microphones. This results in a 20-dimensional vector $x_S(t)$ containing speaker-dependent information.

A binary speech and silence segmentation (BSP) for each of the six locations in the meeting room was extracted with the SRP-PHAT measure [8] from the microphone array. This results in a six-dimensional discrete vector $x_{BSP}(t)$ containing position dependent information.

Prosodic features are based on a denoised and stylised version of the intonation contour, an estimate of the syllabic rate of speech and the energy [5]. These acoustic features comprise a 12 dimensional feature vector (3 features for each of the 4 speakers).

Speaker activity features rely on the active speaker locations evaluated using a sound source localisation process based on a microphone array [8]. A 216 element feature vector resulted from all the 6^3 possible products of the 6 most probable speaker locations (four seats and two presentation positions) during the most recent three frames [5]. A speaker activity feature vector at time t thus gives a local sample of the speaker interaction pattern in the meeting at around time t.

Further audio features: From the microphone array signals, we first compute a speech activity measure (SRP-PHAT). Three acoustic features, namely energy, pitch and speaking rate, were estimated on speech segments, zeroing silence segments. We used the SIFT algorithm to extract pitch, and a combination of estimators to extract speaking rate [8].

4.2   Global Motion Visual Features

In the meeting room the four persons are expected to be at one of six different locations: one of four chairs, the whiteboard, or at a presentation position. For each location L in the meeting room a difference image sequence $I_d^L(x, y)$ is calculated by subtracting the pixel values of two subsequent frames from the video stream. Then seven global motion features [16] are derived from the image sequence: The centre of motion is calculated for the x- and y-direction, the changes in motion are used to express the dynamics of movements. Furthermore the mean absolute deviation of the pixels relative to the centre of motion is computed. Finally the intensity of motion is calculated from the average absolute value of the motion distribution. These seven features are concatenated for each time step in the location dependent motion vector. Concatenating the motion vectors from each of the six positions leads to the final visual feature vector that describes the overall motion in the meeting room with 42 features.

4.3   Skin-Colour Blob Visual Features

Visual features derived from head and hands skin-colour blobs were extracted from the three cameras. For the two cameras looking at people, visual features extracted consist of head vertical centroid position and eccentricity, hand horizontal centroid position, eccentricity, and angle. The motion magnitude for head and hand blobs were also extracted. The average intensity of difference images computed by background subtraction was extracted from the third camera. All features were extracted at 5 frames per second, and the complete set of features is listed in table 2. For details refer to [15].

4.4 Semantic Features

Originating from the low level features also features on a higher level have been extracted. For each of the six locations in the meeting room the talking activity has been detected using results from [7]. Further individual gestures of each participant have been detected using the gesture recogniser from [16]. The possible features were all normalised to the length of the meeting event to provide the relative duration of this particular feature. From all available events only those that are highly discriminative were chosen which resulted in a nine dimensional feature vector.

5   Models for Group Action Segmentation and Recognition

5.1 Meeting Segmentation Using Semantic Features

This approach combines the detection of the boundaries and classification of the segments in one step. The strategy is similar to that one used in the BIC-Algorithm [14]. Two connected windows with variable length are shifted over the time scale. Thereby the inner border is shifted from the left to the right in steps of one second and in each window the feature vector is classified by a low-level classifier. If there is a different result in the two windows, the inner border is considered a boundary of a meeting event. If no boundary is detected in the actual window, the whole window is enlarged and the inner border is again shifted from left to the right. Details can be found in [13].

5.2 Multi-stream Mixed-State DBN for Disturbed Data

In real meetings the data can be disturbed in various ways: events like slamming of a door may mask the audio channel or background babble may appear; the visual channel can be (partly) masked by persons standing or walking in front of a camera. We therefore developed a novel approach for meeting event recognition, based on mixed-state DBNs, that can handle noise and occlusions in all channels [1, 2]. Mixed-state DBNs are an HMM coupled with a LDS, they have been applied to recognising human gestures in [10]. Here, this approach has been extended to a novel multi-stream DBN for meeting event recognition.

Each of the three observed features: microphone array (BSP), lapel microphone (MFCC) and the visual global motion stream (GM) is modelled in a separate stream. The streams correspond to a multi-stream HMM, where each stream has a separate representation for the features. However, the visual stream is connected to a LDS, resulting in a mixed-state DBN. Here the LDS is a Kalman filter, using information from all streams as driving input, to smooth the visual stream. With this filtering, movements are predicted based on the previous time-slice and on the state of the multi-stream HMM at the current time. Thus occlusions can be compensated with the information from all channels. Given an observation O and the model parameters E_j for the mixed-state DBN, the joint probability of the model is the product of the stream probabilities: $P(O, E_j) = P_B \cdot P_M \cdot P_G$. The model parameters are learned for each of the eight event classes j with a variational learning EM-algorithm during the training phase. During the classification an unknown observation O is presented to all models E_j. Then $P(O|E_j)$

is calculated for each model and O is assigned to the class with the highest likelihood: $\text{argmax}_{E_j \in E} P(O|E_j)$. Applying the Viterbi-algorithm to the model, leads to a meeting event segmentation framework. The mixed-state DBN can therefore easily be combined with other models presented in this work.

5.3 Multi-layer Hidden Markov Model

In this section we summarise the multi-layer HMM applied to group action recognition. For a detailed discussion, please refer to [15].

In the multi-layer HMM framework, we distinguish group actions (which belong to the whole set of participants, such as *discussion and presentation*) from individual actions (belonging to specific persons, such as *writing and speaking*). To recognise group actions, individual actions act as the bridge between group actions and low-level features, thus decomposing the problem in stages, and simplifying the complexity of the task.

Let I-HMM denote the lower recognition layer (individual action), and G-HMM denote the upper layer (group action). I-HMM receives as input audio-visual (AV) features extracted from each participant, and outputs posterior probabilities of the individual actions given the current observations. In turn, G-HMM receives as input the output from I-HMM, and a set of group features, directly extracted from the raw streams, which are not associated to any particular individual. In the multi-layer HMM framework, each layer is trained independently, and can be substituted by any of the HMM variants that might capture better the characteristics of the data, more specifically asynchrony [3], or different noise conditions between the audio and visual streams [6]. The multi-layer HMM framework is summarised in figure 1.

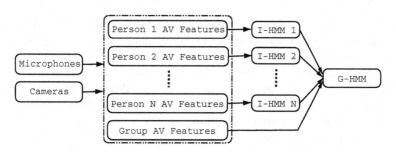

Fig. 1. Multi-layer HMM on group action recognition

Compared with a single-layer HMM, the layered approach has the following advantages, some of which were previously pointed out by [9]: (1) a single-layer HMM is defined on a possibly large observation space, which might face the problem of overfitting with limited training data. It is important to notice that the amount of training data becomes an issue in meetings where data labelling is not a cheap task. In contrast, the layers in our approach are defined over small-dimensional observation spaces, resulting in more stable performance in cases of limited amount of training data. (2) The I-HMMs are person-independent, and in practice can be trained with much more data

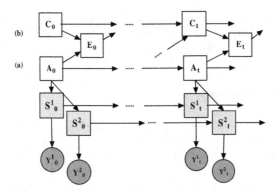

Fig. 2. Multistream DBN model (a) enhanced with a "counter structure" (b); square nodes represent discrete hidden variables and circles must be intend as continuous observations

from different persons, as each meeting provides multiple individual streams of training data. Better generalisation performance can then be expected. (3) The G-HMMs are less sensitive to slight changes in the low-level features because their observations are the outputs of the individual action recognisers, which are expected to be well trained. (4) The two layers are trained independently. Thus, we can explore different HMM combination systems. In particular, we can replace the baseline I-HMMs with models that are more suitable for multi-modal asynchronous data sequences. The framework thus becomes simpler to understand, and amenable to improvements at each separate level.

5.4 Multistream DBN Model

The DBN formalism allows the construction and development of a variety of models, starting from a simple HMM and extending to more sophisticated models (hierarchical HMMs, coupled HMMs, etc). With a small effort, DBNs are able to factorise the internal state space, organising it in a set of interconnected and specialised hidden variables.

Our multi-stream model (bottom of figure 2) exploits this principle in two ways: decomposing meeting actions into smaller logical units, and modelling parallel feature streams independently. We assume that a meeting action can be decomposed into a sequence of small units: meeting subactions. In accordance with this assumption the state space is decomposed into two levels of resolution: meeting actions (nodes A) and meeting subactions (nodes S^F). Note that the decomposition of meeting actions into meeting subactions is done automatically through the training process.

Feature sets derived from different modalities are usually governed by different laws, have different characteristic time-scales and highlight different aspects of the communicative process. Starting from this hypothesis we further subdivided the model state space according to the nature of features that are processed, modelling each feature stream independently (multistream approach). The resulting model has an independent substate node S^F for each feature class F, and integrates the information carried by each feature stream at a 'higher level' of the model structure (arcs between A and S^F, $F = [1, n]$). Since the adopted *lexicon 1* (section 2) is composed by 8 meeting actions, the action node A has a cardinality of 8. The cardinalities of the sub-action nodes S are part of parameter set, and in our experiments we have chosen a value of 6 or 7.

The probability to remain in an HMM state corresponds to an inverse exponential [11]: a similar behaviour is displayed by the proposed model. This distribution is not well-matched to the behaviour of meeting action durations. Rather than adopting ad hoc solutions, such as action transition penalties, we preferred to improve the flexibility of state duration modelling, by enhancing the existing model with a counter structure (top of figure 2). The counter variable C, which is ideally incremented during each action transition, attempts to model the expected number of recognised actions. Action variables A now also generate the hidden sequence of counter nodes C, together with the sequence of sub-action nodes S. Binary enabler variables E have an interface role between action variables A and counter nodes C.

This model presents several advantages over a simpler HMM in which features are "early integrated" into a single feature vector: feature classes are processed independently according to their nature; more freedom is allowed in the state space partitioning and in the optimisation of the sub-state space assigned to each feature class; knowledge from different streams is integrated together at an higher level of the model structure; etc. Unfortunately all these advantages, and the improved accuracy that can be achieved, are balanced by an increased model size, and therefore by an increased computational complexity.

6 Performance Measures

Since group meeting actions are high level symbols and their boundaries are extremely vague. In order to evaluate results of the segmentation and recognition task we used the Action Error Rate, a metric that privileges the recognition of the correct action sequence, rather than the precise temporal boundaries. AER is defined as the sum of *insertion* (Ins), *deletion* (Del), and *substitution* (Subs) errors, divided by the total number of actions in the ground-truth:

$$\text{AER} = \frac{\text{Subs} + \text{Del} + \text{Ins}}{\text{Total Actions}} \times 100\% \tag{1}$$

Measures based on *deletion* (Del) and *insertion* (Ins) and *substitution* (Subs) are also used to evaluate action recognition results.

7 Experiments and Discussions

7.1 Higher Semantic Feature Approach

The results of the segmentation are shown in table 3 (BN: Bayesian Network, GMM: Gaussian Mixture Models, MLP: Multilayer Perceptron Network, RBF: Radial Basis Network, SVM: Support Vector Machines). Each row denotes the classifier that was used. The columns show the insertion rate (number of insertions in respect to all meeting events), the deletion rate (number of deletions in respect to all meeting events), the

Table 3. Segmentation results using the higher semantic feature approach (BN: Bayesian Network, GMM: Gaussian Mixture Models, MLP: Multilayer Perceptron Network, RBF: Radial Basis Network, SVM: Support Vector Machines). The columns denote the insertion rate, the deletion rate, the accuracy in seconds and the classification error rate (using lexicon 1 in Table 1).

Classifier	Insertion (%)	Deletion (%)	Accuracy	Error (%)
BN	14.7	6.22	7.93	39.0
GMM	24.7	2.33	10.8	41.4
MLP	8.61	1.67	6.33	32.4
RBF	6.89	3.00	5.66	31.6
SVM	17.7	0.83	9.08	35.7

accuracy (mean absolute error) of the found segment boundaries in seconds and the recognition error rate. In all columns lower numbers denote better results. As can be seen from the tables, the results are quite variable and heavily depend on the used classifier. These results are comparable to the ones presented in [12]. With the integrated approach the best outcome is achieved by the radial basis network. Here the insertion rate is the lowest. The detected segment boundaries match pretty well with a deviation of only about five seconds to the original defined boundaries.

7.2   Multi-stream Mixed-State DBN for Disturbed Data

To investigate the influence of disturbance to the recognition performance, the evaluation data was cluttered: the video data was occluded with a black bar covering one third of the image at different positions. The audio data from the lapel microphones and the microphone array was disturbed with a background-babble with 10dB SNR. 30 undisturbed videos were used for the training of the models. The remaining 30 unknown videos have been cluttered for the evaluation.

The novel DBN was compared to single-modal (audio and visual) HMMs, an early fusion HMM, and a multi-stream HMM. The DBN showed a significant improvement of the recognition rate for disturbed data. Compared to the baseline HMMs, the DBN reduced the recognition error by more than 1.5% (9% relative error reduction) for disturbed data. It may therefore be useful to combine this approach with the other models presented in this work, to improve the noise robustness. Please refer to [1, 2] for detailed recognition results, as well as a comprehensive description of the model.

7.3   Multi-layer Hidden Markov Model

Table 4 reports the performance in terms of action error rate (AER) for both multi-layer HMM and the single-layer HMM methods. Several configurations were compared, including audio-only, visual-only, early integration, multi-stream [6] and asynchronous HMMs [3]. We can see that (1) the multi-layer HMM approach always outperforms the single-layer one, (2) the use of AV features always outperforms the use of single modalities for both single-layer and multi-layer HMM, supporting the hypothesis that the group actions we defined are inherently multimodel, (3) the best I-HMM model is the asynchronous HMM, which suggests that some asynchrony exists for our task of group action recognition, and is actually well captured by the asynchronous HMM.

Table 4. AER (%) for single-layer and multi-layer HMM (using lexicon 2 in Table 1)

Method		AER (%)
	Visual only	48.2
	Audio only	36.7
Single-layer HMM	Early Integration	23.7
	Mutli-stream	23.1
	Asynchronous	22.2
	Visual only	42.4
	Audio only	32.3
Multi-layer HMM	Early Integration	16.5
	Multi-stream	15.8
	Asynchronous	15.1

7.4   Multistream DBN Model

All the experiments depicted in this section were conducted on 53 meetings (subset of the meeting corpus depicted in section 3) using the lexicon 1 of eight group actions. We implemented the proposed DBN models using the Graphical Models Toolkit (GMTK) [4], and the evaluation is performed using a leave-one-out cross-validation procedure.

Table 5 shows experimental results achieved using: an ergodic 11-states HMM, a multi-stream approach (section 5.4) with two feature streams, and the full counter enhanced multi-stream model. The base 2-stream approach has been tested in two different sub-action configurations: imposing $|S^1| = |S^2| = \{6\,or\,7\}$. Therefore four experimental setups were investigated; and each setup has been tested with 3 different feature sets, leading to 12 independent experiments. The first feature configuration ("UEDIN") associates prosodic features and speaker activity features (section 4.1) respectively to the stream S^1 and to S^2. The feature configuration labelled as "IDIAP" makes use of the multimodal features extracted at IDIAP, representing audio related features (prosodic data and speaker localisation) through the observable node Y^1 and video related measures through Y^2. The last setup ("TUM") relies on two feature families extracted at the Technische Universität München: binary speech profiles derived from IDIAP speaker locations and video related global motion features; each of those has been assigned to an independent sub-action node. Note that in the HMM based experiment the only observable feature stream Y has been obtained by merging together both the feature vectors Y^1 and Y^2. Considering only the results (of table 5) obtained within the UEDIN feature setup, it is clear that the simple HMM shows much higher error than any other multi-stream configuration. The adoption of a multistream based approach reduces the AER to less than 20%, providing the lowest AER (11%) when sub-action cardinalities are fixed to 7. UEDIN features seem to provide a higher accuracy if compared with IDIAP and TUM setups, but it is essential to remember that our DBN models have been optimised for the UEDIN features. In particular sub-action cardinalities have been intensively studied with our features, but it will be interesting to discover optimal values for IDIAP and TUM features too. Moreover overall performances achieved with the multistream approach are very similar (AER are always in the range from 26.7% to 11.0%), and all my be considered promising. The TUM setup seems to be the configu-

Table 5. AER (%) for an HMM, and for a multi-stream (2 streams) approach with and without the "counter structure"; the models have been tested with the 3 different feature sets (using lexicon 1)

Model	Feature Set	Corr.	Sub.	Del.	Ins.	AER
	UEDIN	63.3	13.2	23.5	11.7	48.4
HMM	IDIAP	62.6	19.9	17.4	24.2	61.6
	TUM	60.9	25.6	13.5	53.7	92.9
	UEDIN	86.1	5.7	8.2	3.2	17.1
2 streams $(|S^F| = 6)$	IDIAP	77.9	8.9	13.2	4.6	26.7
	TUM	85.4	9.3	5.3	6.8	21.4
	UEDIN	85.8	7.5	6.8	4.6	18.9
2 streams $(|S^F| = 6)$ + counter	IDIAP	79.4	10.0	10.7	4.3	24.9
	TUM	85.1	5.7	9.3	6.4	21.4
	UEDIN	90.7	2.8	6.4	1.8	11.0
2 streams $(|S^F| = 7)$	IDIAP	86.5	7.8	5.7	3.2	16.7
	TUM	82.9	7.1	10.0	4.3	21.4

ration for which switching from a HMM to a multistream DBN approach provides the greatest improvement in performance: the error rate decreases from 92.9% to 21.4%. If with the UEDIN feature set the adoption of a counter structure is not particularly effective, with IDIAP features the counter provides a significant AER reduction (from 26.7% to 24.9%). We are confident that further improvements with IDIAP features could be obtained by using more than 2 streams (such as the 3 multistream model adopted in [5]). Independently of the feature configuration, the best overall results are achieved with the multistream approach and a state space of 7 by 7 substates.

8 Conclusions

In this work, we have presented the joint efforts of the three institutes (TUM, IDIAP and UEDIN) towards structuring meetings into sequences of multimodal human interactions. A large number of different audio-visual features have been extracted from a common meeting data corpus. From this features, three multimodal sets have been chosen. Four different approaches towards automatic segmentation and classification of meetings into action units haven been proposed. We then deeply investigated the three feature sets, as well as the four different group action modelling frameworks:

The first approach from TUM exploits higher semantic features for structuring a meeting into group actions. It thereby uses an algorithm that is based on the idea of the Bayesian-Information-Criterion. The mixed-state DBN approach developed by TUM compensates for disturbances in both the visual and the audio channel. It is not a segmentation framework but can be integrated into the other approaches presented in this work to improve their robustness. The multi-layer Hidden Markov Model developed by IDIAP decomposes group actions as a two-layer process, one that models basic individual activities from low-level audio-visual features, and another one that models the group action (belonging to the whole set of participants). The multi-stream DBN model proposed by UEDIN operates an unsupervised subdivision of meeting actions into sequences of group sub-actions, processing multiple asynchronous feature streams independently, introducing also a model extension to improve state duration modelling.

All presented approaches have provided comparable good performances. The AER are already promising, but there is still space for further improvements both in the feature domain (i.e.: exploit more modalities) and in the model infrastructure. Therefore in the near future we are going to investigate combinations of the proposed systems to improve the AER and to exploit the complementary strengths of the different approaches.

Acknowledgement. This work was partly supported by the European project M4 (MultiModal Meeting Manager) and European Union 6th FWP IST Integrated Project AMI (Augmented Multi-party Interaction, FP6-506811, publication AMI-87).

References

1. M. Al-Hames and G. Rigoll. A multi-modal graphical model for robust recognition of group actions in meetings from disturbed videos. In *Proc. IEEE ICIP*, Italy, 2005.
2. M. Al-Hames and G. Rigoll. A multi-modal mixed-state dynamic Bayesian network for robust meeting event recognition from disturbed data. In *Proc. IEEE ICME*, 2005.
3. S. Bengio. An asynchronous hidden markov model for audio-visual speech recognition. In S. Becker, S. Thrun, and K. Obermayer, editors, *Advances in NIPS 15*. MIT Press, 2003.
4. J. Bilmes. Graphical models and automatic speech recognition. *Mathematical Foundations of Speech and Language Processing*, 2003.
5. A. Dielmann and S. Renals. Multistream dynamic Bayesian network for meeting segmentation. *Lecture Notes in Computer Science*, 3361:76–86, 2005.
6. S. Dupont and J. Luettin. Audio-visual speech modeling for continuous speech recognition. *IEEE Transactions on Multimedia*, 2(3):141–151, September 2000.
7. G. Lathoud, I. A. McCowan, and J.-M. Odobez. Unsupervised Location-Based Segmentation of Multi-Party Speech. In *Proc. 2004 ICASSP-NIST Meeting Recognition Workshop*, 2004.
8. I. McCowan, D. Gatica-Perez, S. Bengio, G. Lathoud, M. Barnard, and D. Zhang. Automatic analysis of multimodal group actions in meetings. *IEEE Transactions on Pattern Analysis and Machine Intelligence (PAMI)*, 27(3):305–317, 2005.
9. N. Oliver, E. Horvitz, and A. Garg. Layered representations for learning and inferring office activity from multiple sensory channels. In *Proc. ICMI*, Pittsburgh, Oct. 2002.
10. V. Pavlovic, B. Frey, and T.S. Huang. Time series classification using mixed-state dynamic Bayesian networks. In *Proc. IEEE CVPR*, 1999.
11. L. R. Rabiner. A tutorial on hidden markov models and selected applications in speech recognition. *Proc. of the IEEE*, 2(77):257–286, 1989.
12. S. Reiter and G. Rigoll. Segmentation and classification of meeting events using multiple classifier fusion and dynamic programming. In *Proc. IEEE ICPR*, pages 434–437, 2004.
13. S. Reiter and G. Rigoll. Multimodal meeting analysis by segmentation and classification of meeting events based on a higher level semantic approach. In *Proc. IEEE ICASSP*, 2005.
14. A. Tritschler and R.A. Gopinath. Improved speaker segmentation and segments clustering using the bayesian information criterion. In *Proc. EUROSPEECH '99*, 1999.
15. D. Zhang, D. Gatica-Perez, S. Bengio, I. McCowan, and G. Lathoud. Modeling individual and group actions in meetings: a two-layer hmm framework. In *IEEE Workshop on Event Mining at the Conference on Computer Vision and Pattern Recognition (CVPR)*, 2004.
16. M. Zobl, F. Wallhoff, and G. Rigoll. Action recognition in meeting scenarios using global motion features. In J. Ferryman, editor, *Proc. PETS-ICVS*, pages 32–36, 2003.

Detection and Resolution of References to Meeting Documents

Andrei Popescu-Belis[1] and Denis Lalanne[2]

[1] University of Geneva,
School of Translation and Interpretation (ETI), TIM/ISSCO,
40, bd. du Pont d'Arve,
CH-1211 Geneva 4, Switzerland
andrei.popescu-belis@issco.unige.ch
[2] University of Fribourg,
Faculty of Science,
DIUF/DIVA,
3, ch. du Musée,
CH-1700 Fribourg, Switzerland
denis.lalanne@unifr.ch

Abstract. This article describes a method for document/speech alignment based on explicit verbal references to documents and parts of documents, in the context of multimodal meetings. The article focuses on the two main stages of dialogue processing for alignment: the detection of the expressions referring to documents in transcribed speech, and the recognition of the documents and document elements that they refer to. The detailed evaluation of the implemented modules, first separately and then in a pipeline, shows that results are well above baseline values. The integration of this method with other techniques for document/speech alignment is finally discussed.

1 Introduction

Documents are often the main support for communication in group meetings. For instance, slides are used for talks, and are generally displayed in sequence, being thus naturally aligned with the presenter's utterances. This is not the case, however, when the supporting documents are not so obviously set into focus, for instance when reports or articles are discussed during a meeting.

When meetings are recorded and stored in a database that can be accessed by a meeting browser, it is necessary to detect the temporal alignment between speech and documents or sub-document elements. This kind of alignment has to be derived from the linguistic content of speech and documents, and from clues in other modalities.

We study in this paper the alignment of transcribed speech and electronic documents, based on the references that are made explicitly in speech, such as "the title of our latest report" or "the article about ...". A number of processing modules required to carry out this task are described in Section 2, and techniques

S. Renals and S. Bengio (Eds.): MLMI 2005, LNCS 3869, pp. 64–75, 2006.

for document structuring are briefly outlined (2.2). Section 3 defines reference-based document/speech alignment, then describes the proposed methods for the detection of expressions referring to documents and the recognition of the document elements they refer to. The press-review meetings used in this experiment and the evaluation methods that we designed are described in Section 4. Results appear in Section 5. Finally, the place of reference-based alignment among other document/speech alignment techniques is discussed in Section 6.

2   Document/Speech Alignment for Meeting Browsing

Meeting processing and retrieval applications target several types of users. For instance, a professional who missed a meeting could use such an application to browse through the meeting's content directly to the most relevant points, without viewing or listening to the entire recording. Likewise, someone who attended a meeting but who would like to review some points, such as the decisions that were made, could benefit from a meeting browser, as well as someone who would like to track the progress of issues over several meetings. Once an episode of interest has been spotted in a meeting, a meeting browser should allow the user to explore the transcript, or to watch/listen to the episode, or to check the documents that were discussed.

2.1   Importance of References to Documents for Meeting Browsing

When meetings deal with one or several documents, it becomes important to align in a precise manner each episode of the meeting to the sections of the documents that are discussed in it, and vice-versa. This allows a meeting browser to retrieve the episodes of a meeting in which a particular section of a document was discussed, so that the user can find out what was said about it. Conversely, the application can also display the documents relevant to a given episode of a meeting, while the user browses through that episode. A study of user requirements has shown that queries frequently involve information related to meeting documents [1].

The references made in speech to the meeting documents are a fined-grained type of information that allows document/speech alignment. Using these references, the multimodal rendering of the meeting can be enhanced as shown in Fig. 1. The expressions that refer to documents are coded, in this implementation, as hyperlinks towards the right part of the window: clicking on such a link highlights the article referred to by that expression. This approach can of course be integrated to larger, more complex browsers.

The resolution of references to documents is a cross-channel task that enhances dialogue and document browsing. The task requires significant pre-processing of data (Fig. 2). The most significant tasks are: the generation of a transcript of the utterances produced by each speaker; the generation of an abstract representation of each document structure; the detection of the expressions from the transcripts that refer to meeting documents; and the identification of the document element each of these expressions refers to. The latter two tasks are the main object of this chapter.

Fig. 1. Aligned browsing of meeting transcript and documents. Clicking on a referring expression (underlined) highlights the corresponding document element.

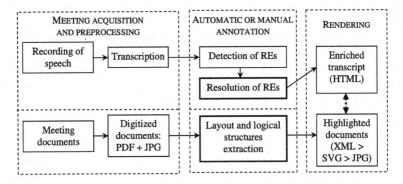

Fig. 2. Components of an application for the resolution of references to documents

2.2 Construction of the Logical Structure of Documents

The PDF format has become very common for disseminating nearly any kind of printable documents, since it can be easily generated from almost every other document format. However, because its use is limited to displaying and printing, its value for retrieval and extraction is considerably reduced. Our experience has shown that the reading order of a text is often not preserved, especially in documents having a complex multi-column layout, such as newspapers. Even recent tools that extract the textual content of PDF documents do not reveal the physical and logical structures of documents. To overcome these limitations, we designed and implemented Xed, a tool that reverse engineers electronic documents and extracts their layout structure [2]. This approach merges low-level text extraction methods with layout analysis performed on synthetically generated TIFF images. Xed has been tested with success on various document classes with complex layouts, including newspapers.

In the present study, we consider that newspaper front pages have a hierarchical structure. The following elements (in Typewriter font) are used. A Newspaper front page bears the newspaper's Name, the Date, one Master Article, zero, one or more Highlights, one or more Articles, etc. Each content element has an ID attribute bearing a unique index. An `Article` is composed of a `Title`, a `Subtitle`, a `Source`, the `Content` (mandatory), and one or more `Authors` and `References`.

To obtain data with 100% correct document structure for the application to document/speech alignment, the XML document segmentations have been validated manually according to the structure mentioned above, encoded in a DTD. Information about the layout structure, i.e. the bounding boxes of each logical block, topological positions, fonts, etc., was stored in separate annotation files, using pointers to the ID attributes of the logical blocks.

3   Reference-Based Document/Speech Alignment

3.1   What Are References to Documents?

From a cognitive point of view, speakers use *referring expressions (REs)* to specify the entities about which they talk, or more accurately the representations of entities in the speaker's mind. When speakers discuss one or more documents, as in press-review meetings, they often refer explicitly to documents or various parts of documents (e.g. 'the title', 'the next article', etc.).

Reference resolution amounts to the construction of links between each RE and the corresponding document element. For example, if a speaker says: "I do not agree with the title of our latest report", then 'our latest report' refers to a paper or electronic document, and 'the title of our latest report' refers precisely to its title, an element that can be retrieved from the document structure.

Two important notions are *coreference* and *anaphora*. RE_1 and RE_2 are co-referent if they refer to the same entity, here a document element. RE_2 is an anaphor with respect to RE_1 if the element it refers to cannot be identified without making use of RE_1, then called the antecedent of RE_2. In the following example, 'the first article' is the antecedent and the pronoun 'it' is the anaphor: "The first article is particularly relevant to our company. It discusses ...". Note that anaphora may occur without coreference, as is the case with 'the first chapter' and 'the title' in this example: "The first chapter is nicely written. The title suggests that ...". The resolution of references to documents offers the advantage of a restricted set of candidate entities, when compared to anaphora or coreference resolution [3–6].

3.2   The Detection of REs

The reference resolution process has in our view two main stages: (1) the detection of the REs that refer to documents; (2) the identification of the document and document element that each RE refers to. In a preliminary study [7], only the second stage could be automated: no results were available for the entire process. We present here an automated solution for the first stage as well, and evaluate the accuracy of the two combined stages.

We designed a grammar-based component that spots the REs referring to documents in the transcript of meeting dialogues (in French). We chose to consider a manual speech transcript because an automatic one would contain too many recognition errors, which would make the evaluation of our alignment impossible. Each channel is segmented into utterances following the SDA.XML format used in our project [8]. We used the CLaRK XML environment [9][1] to write a tokenizer and a grammar.

In order to detect REs that refer to documents, we created a set of pattern matching rules applying to the words of the utterances, with sometimes a left or a right context. The challenge in writing the detection grammar was to combine a priori linguistic knowledge about the form of REs with the empirical observations on our corpus[2], summarized elsewhere [7]. The resulting grammar has about 25 pattern matching rules, but since most of them contain one or more logical disjunctions and optional tokens, they are equivalent to several hundred possible REs. Another challenge was to tune the coverage of the grammar to avoid too many false positives or true negatives, corresponding respectively to precision and recall errors for the RE detection task (see 4.2).

The main improvement that should be made to this method – apart from increasing the coverage and accuracy of the grammar – is the intrinsic ambiguity of certain REs, which may or may not refer to documents, depending on their context. A typical example are pronouns such as 'it' and indexicals such as 'this' or 'this one', which seem to require some knowledge of their antecedent in order to be tagged as referring to documents or not. A possible solution would be to develop a classifier for this task, based on surface features present in the left and right contexts and surrounding REs, or to extend the above grammar to filter out pronouns that cannot refer to documents. In the meanwhile, we tested several pattern matching rules, and kept the ones that increased recall without reducing precision too much. The failure to detect the pronouns is, however, quite penalizing for the document/speech alignment task, shown in Section 5.3.

3.3   The Recognition of References to Documents

Once the REs are detected, the second task is to recognize to which document and document element each RE refers, among the set of potential referents that is derived from the document structure. A first idea is to consider co-occurrences of words between the RE and the documents. For each RE, its words and the words surrounding it are matched using the cosine metric with the bag of words of each document element: Title, Author, Content, etc. The most similar document element could be considered as the referent of the RE, provided the similarity value exceeds a fixed threshold.

The theories of reference resolution emphasize, however, the importance of keeping track of the referents that were mentioned, in particular of the "current" referent [10]. We integrated therefore this important feature and the word-based

---

[1] Available at: http://www.bultreebank.org/clark/.

[2] For instance, most of the references are made to entire articles, using REs such as 'the article', 'the [first/last] article', 'a short article about …', or 'the front page of Le Monde'. These examples are translated from French; 'Le Monde' is the name of a French newspaper.

comparison into a more complex algorithm which processes anaphoric and non-anaphoric REs differently.

The resulting algorithm processes the REs in sequence. First, it determines the document referred to by each RE, among the list of documents associated to the meeting. The criterion is that REs that make use of a newspaper's name are considered to refer to the respective newspaper, while all the other ones are supposed to refer to the current newspaper[3].

The algorithm then attempts to determine the document *element* that the current RE refers to. It first decides whether the RE is anaphoric or not by matching it against a list of typical anaphors for document elements (e.g. 'the article' or 'it'). If the RE is anaphoric (and not the first RE of the meeting), then its referent is the current document element. If the RE is not anaphoric, then co-occurrences of words are used as above to find the document element it refers to: the words of the RE and the surrounding ones are matched with document elements; the one that scores the most matches is considered to be the referent of the RE. Then, the 'current document' and the 'current document element' (a single-level focus stack [10]) are updated, before processing the next RE.

Several parameters govern the algorithm, in particular the relative importance of the various matches between words of the RE and of its left/right context, with the words from document elements. Another parameter is the span of the left and right contexts, that is, the number of preceding and following words and utterances considered for matching. These parameters are tuned empirically in Section 5.2.

4   Data and Evaluation

The data was recorded in the document-centric meeting room set up at the University of Fribourg. Several modalities related to documents were recorded, thanks to a dozen cameras and eight microphones. These devices are controlled and synchronized by a meeting capture and archiving application, which also helps the users to organize the numerous data files [11].

In this study, we use 22 press-review meetings of ca. 15 minutes each, recorded between March and November 2003, in which participants discuss the front pages of one or more newspapers of the day, in French[4]. Each participant introduces one or more articles. For each article, a short monologue is followed by a brief discussion. The meetings were manually transcribed using the Transcriber tool[5] and exported as XML files. The structure of the 30 documents (front pages, cf. Section 2.2) was also encoded into XML files.

4.1   Annotation of Ground Truth REs and References

The annotation model for the references to documents was described in an earlier paper [7]. The main idea is to separate the annotation of REs from the annotation of the references to documents. REs are tagged on the XML transcript

---

[3] This method does not handle complex references such as 'the other newspaper'.

[4] Available at: http://diuf.unifr.ch/im2/data.html.

[5] Available at: http://www.etca.fr/CTA/gip/Projets/Transcriber.

using an opening `<re ID="...">` and a closing `</re>` tag. The documents and elements they refer to are encoded in a separate block at the end of the XML transcript, as links between the index of the RE (ID attribute), a document filename, and an XPath designation of the document element referred to, in the XML representation of the document structure.

In a first pass, the annotators marked the REs using their own understanding of references to documents. The most litigious cases were the impersonal references to the creator of an article, such as (in English) *"they say that ..."*. We assumed this was a reference to the author of the article, or at least to the entire article (the actual scoring procedure allows this flexibility). REs that correspond only to quotations of an article's sentences were not annotated, since they refer to entities mentioned by the documents, rather than to the document elements.

A total of 437 REs were annotated in the 22 meetings of the corpus. This number is not due to the subjects being instructed to refer more often to documents, but is due to the document-centric meeting genre.

In a second pass, the annotators were instructed to code, for each RE, the name of the document and the XPath to the respective document element, using the templates that were generated automatically after the first pass. Examples of XPath expressions were provided. When in doubt, annotators were instructed to link the RE to the most general element, that is, the article or front page.

Inter-annotator agreement for the second pass [7], with three annotators on 25% of the data, is 96% for document assignment and 90% for document element assignment (see evaluation metric below). After discussion among annotators, we reached 100% agreement on documents, and 97% agreement on elements.

4.2   Evaluation of RE Detection

The evaluation of the first processing stage, RE detection, is done by comparing the correct REs with those found automatically, using precision and recall. To apply these metrics, two problems must be solved. First, to what extent is some variability on the RE boundaries tolerated? And second, how are embedded REs processed?

We consider here that the detection of only a fragment of an RE counts the same as the detection of the entire RE, i.e. a correct hit is counted if the `<re>` and `</re>` tags found by the RE detector are identical to, or comprised within the correct ones. This is somewhat similar to the MUC-7 guidelines [4], with the difference that here, no minimal fragment is required for an RE. This indulgent scoring procedure is due to the nature of our application: detecting only a fragment of an RE is indeed sufficient for document/speech alignment, if the fragment is correctly linked to a document.

Embedded REs correspond in general to embedded NPs, such as "[the title of [the next article]]" (non-embedded but intersecting REs seem to be ruled out by the recursive nature of syntax). The difficulty in scoring embedded REs is related to the above decision to score RE fragments. If only exact matches counted as correct, there would be no risk of confusion between embedded REs. But because RE fragments count as well, one should avoid counting them more than once. For in-

stance, if the RE detector generates the following markup: "the title of the first
</re>chapter</re>", then "chapter" should count either as a match for "the
first chapter" or for "the title of the first chapter", but not for both REs.

We propose therefore the following error counting algorithm, which loops
through all the correct REs in sequence (for embedded REs, it starts with the
deepest one). For each correct RE, if the system has tagged it, or has tagged an
RE included it, then no error is counted, and this RE is removed from the set
of system REs; if it hasn't, count one recall error. When all correct REs have
been thus tested, *recall error* is the number of recall errors that were counted,
divided by the total number of correct REs. *Precision error* is the number of
system REs remaining in the list (that is, not matching correct ones), divided
by the total number of REs tagged by the system.

4.3   Evaluation of RE Resolution

If the resolution of REs is attempted on the correct set of REs, then its evaluation
is done simply in terms of correctness or accuracy [7]. For each RE the referent
found by the system is compared with the correct one using three criteria, and
then three global scores are computed. The first one is the number of times
the document is correctly identified. The second one is the number of times the
document element at the `Article` level (characterized by its `ID` attribute) is
correctly identified. The third one is the number of times the exact document
element (characterized by its full XPath) is correctly identified. These values are
normalized by the total number of REs to obtain scores between 0 and 1. The
third metric is the most demanding one. However, we will use only the first two,
since our resolution algorithms do not target sub-article elements yet.

When the resolution of REs is combined with their recognition, the evaluation method must be altered so that it does not count wrongly-detected REs,
which are necessarily linked to erroneous document elements, since these are
evaluated by the precision score at the level of RE detection. The method must
however count the REs that were not detected (to count the missing links) and
examine the detected RE fragments, which may or may not be correctly linked
to documents.

We used the algorithm that scores RE detection (Section 4.2) to synchronize
the indexes of the detected REs with the correct ones. This allows us to compute
the three accuracy scores as defined above. These adapted metrics of the accuracy
of RE resolution thus take partially into account the imperfect RE detection, but
they are not influenced by detection "noise". Therefore, to evaluate the combined
process of detection and resolution, the scores for RE detection are still required.

5   Results

5.1   Scores for the Detection of REs

The grammar for the detection of REs is evaluated in terms of recall (R), precision (P) and f-measure (f). The initial grammar based on prior knowledge and
on corpus observation reaches $R = 0.65$, $P = 0.85$ and $f = 0.74$.

Experimental analysis can help to assess the value of certain rules. For instance, when adding a rule that marks *all* third person pronouns as referring to documents, precision decreases dramatically, with insufficient increase in recall: $R = 0.71$, $P = 0.52$ and $f = 0.60$. Similarly, adding a rule that marks *all* indexicals as referring to documents produces an even lower performance: $R = 0.70$, $P = 0.46$ and $f = 0.56$. It appears however that in for the present meeting genre, the indexicals 'celui-ci' and 'celui-là' ('this one' and 'that one', masculine forms) are almost always used to refer to articles. Therefore, the best scores are obtained after tuning and adding the previous rule: $R = 0.68$, $P = 0.88$ and $f = 0.76$. However, even without this particular rule, f-measure after tuning the grammar is only 1% lower.

5.2   Scores for the Resolution of REs

Several baseline scores can be proposed for comparison purposes, depending on the choice of a "minimal" algorithm. For the RE/document association metric, always choosing the most frequent newspaper leads to ca. 80% baseline accuracy. However, when considering meetings with at least two newspapers, the score of this random procedure is 50%, a much more realistic, and lower, baseline. Regarding the RE/element association metric, if the referent is always the front page as a whole, then accuracy is 16%. If the referent is always the main article, then accuracy is 18% – in both cases quite a low baseline.

The RE resolution algorithm applied on the set of *correct* REs reaches 97% accuracy for the identification of documents referred to by REs, i.e., 428 REs out of 437 are correctly resolved. The accuracy is 93% if only meetings with several documents are considered. This is a very high score which proves the relevance of the word co-occurrence and anaphora tracking techniques.

The accuracy for document element identification is 67%, that is, 303 REs out of 437 are correctly resolved at the level of document elements. If we consider only REs for which the correct document was previously identified, the accuracy is 68% (301 REs out of 428). This figure is basically the same since most of the RE/document associations are correctly resolved.

The best scores are obtained when only the right context of the RE is considered for matching, i.e. only the words *after* the RE, and not the ones *before* it. Empirically, the optimal number of words to look for in the right context is about ten. Regarding the other optimal parameters, a match between the RE and the title of an article appears to be more important than one involving the right context of the RE and the title, and much more important than matches with the content of the article: optimal weights are about 15 vs. 10 vs. 1. If anaphor tracking is disabled, the accuracy of document element identification drops to ca. 60%. The observation of systematic error patterns could help us improve the algorithm.

5.3   Combination of RE Detection and Resolution

When the two modules are combined in a pipeline, their errors cumulate in a way that is *a priori* unpredictable, but which can be assessed empirically as follows. The best configurations were selected for the two modules and, on a perfect transcript, the obtained results were: 60% document accuracy (265 REs out of 437) and 32% document element accuracy (141 REs out of 437). If we compute document element accuracy only on the REs which have the correct document attached, the score increases to 46% (123 REs out of 265). It appears thus that the error rates do not combine linearly: if they did, the scores would have been, respectively, ca. 73% and ca. 50%.

The reason for the lower than expected scores lies probably in the context-based algorithm used for RE resolution, in which each RE depends on the correct resolution of the previous one, through the monitoring of the "current document element". This is a pertinent feature when REs are correctly detected, but when too many REs are missing (here recall is only 67%), and especially when most of the pronouns are missing, the algorithm loses track of the current document element. Therefore, an improvement of the RE detector should considerably increase the overall detection-plus-resolution accuracy.

6   Other Document/Speech Alignment Techniques

The resolution of references to documents is not the only method for the cross-channel alignment of meeting dialogues with meeting documents. We have implemented and evaluated two other methods: *citation-based alignment*, a pure lexical match between terms in documents and in speech transcription, and *thematic alignment*, a semantic match between sections of documents (sentences, paragraphs, logical blocks, etc.) and units of dialogue structure (utterances, turns, and thematic episodes).

The robust thematic alignment method uses various state-of-the-art metrics (cosine, Jaccard, Dice), considering document and speech units as bags of weighted words [11]. After suppression of stop-words, proper stemming, and after calculation of terms frequency in their section relative to their frequency in the whole document (TF.IDF), the content of various types of document elements is compared with the content of various speech transcript units.

When matching spoken *utterances* with document *logical blocks*, using cosine metric, recall is 84%, and precision is 77%, which are encouraging results. And when matching speech *turns* with logical blocks, recall stays at 84% and precision rises to 85%. On the other hand, alignment of spoken *utterances* to document *sentences* is less precise but is more promising since it relies on less processing. Using Jaccard metric, recall is 83%, and precision is 76% [11]. Furthermore, thematic alignment of spoken *utterances* to document *sentences* has been used for joint thematic segmentation of documents and speech transcripts. The evaluation of this method shows that this bi-modal thematic segmentation outperforms standard mono-modal segmentation methods, which tends to prove that the combination of modalities considerably improves segmentation scores [12].

In another recent, integrative evaluation, we measured the effect of combining the various document/speech alignments (reference-based, citation-based, and thematic) on the general document/speech alignment performance [13]. Eight meetings were tested, with a total of 927 utterances, and 116 document logical blocks. After combination of the three methods, the values of recall, precision, and f-measure were respectively 67%, 72% and 68%, whereas their independent use reaches at best, respectively, 55%, 75% and 63%. These results tend to prove the benefit of combining the various methods of document/speech alignment.

7   Conclusion

Printed documents and spoken interaction are two important modalities in communication. This article presented an attempt to align these modalities based on their semantic content, in the context of a meeting browser that makes use of the mentions of documents in the dialogue.

The results presented here demonstrate the feasibility of a reference-based alignment technique using a grammar-based module for RE detection, followed by a module implementing word co-occurrence and anaphora tracking for RE resolution. The two modules were evaluated separately, then in sequence: the scores for the overall task remain still above the baseline when the two modules are combined. Future feasibility studies could also evaluate the degradation induced in a pipelined alignment process by other automated modules, such as speech recognition or document structuring. Together with other alignment techniques, we believe that our approach will contribute to the design of a robust multi-modal meeting browser.

Acknowledgements

This work is part of (IM)2, a project supported by the Swiss National Science Foundation (see http://www.im2.ch). The authors would like to thank Dalila Mekhaldi, Emmanuel Palacio and Didier von Rotz for help with data preparation, as well as the three anonymous MLMI'05 reviewers for their valuable suggestions.

References

1. Lisowska, A., Popescu-Belis, A., Armstrong, S.: User query analysis for the specification and evaluation of a dialogue processing and retrieval system. In: LREC'04, Lisbon (2004) 993–996
2. Hadjar, K., Rigamonti, M., Lalanne, D., Ingold, R.: Xed: a new tool for extracting hidden structures from electronic documents. In: Workshop on Document Image Analysis for Libraries, Palo Alto, CA (2004)
3. Mitkov, R.: Anaphora Resolution. Longman, London, UK (2002)
4. Hirschman, L.: MUC-7 Coreference task 3.0. Technical report, MITRE (1997)
5. van Deemter, K., Kibble, R.: On coreferring: Coreference in MUC and related annotation schemes. Computational Linguistics 26(4) (2000) 629–637
6. Popescu-Belis, A.: Evaluation-driven design of a robust reference resolution system. Natural Language Engineering 9(3) (2003) 281–306

7. Popescu-Belis, A., Lalanne, D.: Reference resolution over a restricted domain: References to documents. In: ACL'04 Workshop on Reference Resolution and its Applications, Barcelona (2004) 71–78

8. Popescu-Belis, A., Georgescul, M., Clark, A., Armstrong, S.: Building and using a corpus of shallow dialogue annotated meetings. In: LREC'04, Lisbon (2004) 1451–1454

9. Simov, K., Simov, A., Ganev, H., Ivanova, K., Grigorov, I.: The CLaRK system: Xml-based corpora development system for rapid prototyping. In: LREC'04, Lisbon (2004) 235–238

10. Grosz, B.J., Joshi, A.K., Weinstein, S.: Centering: A framework for modeling the local coherence of discourse. Computational Linguistics **21**(2) (1995) 203–225

11. Lalanne, D., Mekhaldi, D., Ingold, R.: Talking about documents: revealing a missing link to multimedia meeting archives. In: Document Recognition and Retrieval XI, San Jose, CA (2004)

12. Mekhaldi, D., Lalanne, D., Ingold, R.: Using bi-modal alignment and clustering techniques for documents and speech thematic segmentations. In: CIKM'04, Washington D.C. (2004)

13. Mekhaldi, D., Lalanne, D., Ingold, R.: From searching to browsing through multimodal documents linking. In: ICDAR'05, Seoul (2005)

Dominance Detection in Meetings Using Easily Obtainable Features

Rutger Rienks and Dirk Heylen

Human Media Interaction (HMI),
University of Twente, Enschede, The Netherlands
{rienks, heylen}@ewi.utwente.nl
http://hmi.ewi.utwente.nl/

Abstract. We show that, using a Support Vector Machine classifier, it is possible to determine with a 75% success rate who dominated a particular meeting on the basis of a few basic features. We discuss the corpus we have used, the way we had people judge dominance and the features that were used.

1 Introduction

In many cases it is beneficial for the effectiveness of a meeting if people assume a cooperative stance. Grice [1975] formulated four maxims that hold for cooperative conversations. The maxims of quantity, quality, relevance and manner state that one should say nothing more or less than is required, speak the truth or say only things for which one has enough evidence, only say things that are relevant for the discussion at hand and formulate the contribution such that it can be easily heart and understood by the interlocutors. These maxims are all formulated from the perspective of producing utterances in a conversation. One could define similar maxims for cooperative behavior, more generally. One can also think of several tasks of chairpersons in meetings as being guided by such maxims. The chair should facilitate the participants to have their say, to cut off people who make their contribution too long or to intervene when contributions are not relevant to the discussion at hand. Discussions should be properly organized to have arguments develop, so that all positions are put to the fore, and all relevant pros and cons are raised. People that are too dominant in meetings may violate one or more of the cooperative maxims and thereby frustrate the process of collective decision making for which many meetings are intended. The chair of the meeting should avoid this from happening or intervene when it does.

Nowadays, in order to maximize the efficiency, meetings can be assisted with a variety of tools and supporting technologies [Rienks et al., 2005]. These tools can be passive objects such as microphones facilitating better understanding or semi-intelligent software systems that automatically adjust the lighting conditions. In the near future, meetings will be assisted with various similar sorts of active, and perhaps even autonomous, software agents that can make sense of what is happening in the meeting and make certain interventions [Ellis and Barthelmess,

S. Renals and S. Bengio (Eds.): MLMI 2005, LNCS 3869, pp. 76–86, 2006.

2003]. An example of such meeting assisting agents could be an agent that signals possible violations of cooperative maxims in the decision making process to the chairperson. One of the major issues to be addressed in this case is how the agent can detect that there is such a disturbance. In the research described in the following sections we looked at a way to automatically detect the relative level of dominance of meeting participants on the basis of a set of simple features. We start with introducing the concept of dominance (Section 2). To establish a corpus, we asked several people to rank a collection of meetings. We investigated whether the rankings by different people were similar (Section 3). Next, we describe the features we used for our classifier (Section 4), how we obtained the feature values from our corpus (Section 5) and what the performance of our classifier was when using the best features (Section 6).

The only work that we are aware of which is in some sense comparable is described in Zhang et al. [2005] who created a two-level influence model. A dynamic Bayesian network (DBN) was proposed to learn the influence of each participant in meetings using both acoustic and language features. As 'ground truth' input for their model, a set of thirty meetings of about five minutes each was used together with the averaged results of three annotators.

2   Dominance

According to Hoffmann [1979], there are three types of behavioral roles that can be identified in groups or teams. These roles can be classified as task-oriented, relation-oriented and self-oriented. Each group member has the potential of performing all of these roles over time. *Initiators, Coordinators* and *Information Givers* are task-oriented roles that facilitate and coordinate the decision making tasks. The Relations-Oriented role of members deals with team-centered tasks, sentiments and viewpoints. Typical examples are : *Harmonizers, Gatekeepers* and *Followers*. The Self-Oriented role of members focusses on the members' individual needs, possibly at expense of the team or group. Examples here are *Blockers, Recognition Seekers* and *Dominators*. The Dominator is a group member trying to assert authority by manipulating the group or certain individuals in the group. Dominators may use flattery or proclaim their superior status to gain attention and interrupt contributions of others. According to Hellriegel et al. [1995], a group dominated by individuals who are performing self-oriented subroles is likely to be ineffective.

In psychology, dominance refers to a social control aspect of interaction. It involves the ability to influence others. One can refer to it as a personality characteristic - the predisposition to attempt to influence others - or one can use the term to describe relationships within a group. Dominance is a hypothetical construct that is not directly observable. However, there appear to be certain behavioral features displayed by people that behave dominantly that make it possible for observers of these behaviors to agree on judgments of dominance. In Ellyson and Dovidio [1985] the nonverbal behaviors that are typically associated with dominance and power are investigated. In several of the papers in that volume, human perceptions of dominance are discussed as well. Behaviors such as proxemic relations, facial expressions and gaze were investigated.

In 'A System for Multiple Level Observation of Groups' (SYMLOG), [Bales and Cohen, 1979], Bales distinguishes three structural dimensions in group interactions: status, attraction and goal orientation. Goal orientation refers to the question whether people are involved with the task or rather with socio-emotional behaviours. This dimension was already present in Bales' earlier work on Interaction Process Analysis [Bales, 1951]. The attraction dimension refers to friendly versus unfriendly behaviours. The status dimension has to do with dominant versus submissive behaviours. Bales developed a checklist that observers can use to structure their observations of groups. He has also developed a number of self-report scales that group members can use to rate themselves (and other group members) on these three dimensions. SYMLOG presents a questionnaire containing 26 questions from which 18 relate to the concept of dominance. The factors involved in these questions provide a way to explicate the concept. An overview of these factors in their most general form are shown in Table 1.

Table 1. Aspects of dominance according to SYMLOG

Positive contributions	Negative contributions
active, dominant, talks a lot	passive, introverted, said little
extraverted, outgoing, positive	gentle, willing to accept responsibility
purposeful, democratic task-leader	obedient, worked submissively
assertive, business-like, manager	self-punishing, worked too hard
authority, controlling, critical	depressed, sad, resentful, rejecting
domineering, tough-minded, powerful	alienated, quit, withdrawn
provocative, egocentric, showed-off	afraid to try, doubts own ability
joked around, expressive, dramatic	quietly happy just to be in group
entertaining, sociable, smiled, warm	looked up to others, appreciative

When we look at these factors we see that most of them are very hard to operationalize. For example to automatically determine when someone is 'purposeful' or 'alienated' is quite complex and highly dependent on human interpretative skills. For the automatic classification task, we need easy to extract and automatically detectable features that can be quantified and transformed as a series of digits into our system.

To train a classifier that can determine who is the person that dominated a meeting, we need a corpus of meeting recordings with the relevant features that the classifier is using either extracted or annotated and also we need to know how the participants of the various meetings scored on the dimension of dominance. We will provide more details on the corpus and the features used by the classifier in Section 4. Now, we will first describe how we established the dominance ranking for the meetings we used.

3 Dominance Judgements

For our study, We used a corpus of eight four-person meetings[1]. The meetings varied in length between 5 and 35 minutes. We collected 95 minutes in total. We used different kinds of meetings, including group discussions where topics had to be debated, discussions about the design of a remote control, book club meetings and PhD. evaluation sessions.

We asked ten people to rank the participants of the meetings with respect to their perceived dominance. Each person ranked four, i.e. half of, the meetings. We thus had a total of five rankings for every meeting. We simply told people to rate the four people involved in the meeting on a dominance scale. We did not tell the judges anything more about what we meant by that term. The results are shown in Table 2. The first cell shows that in the first meeting (M1), judge A1 thought that the most dominant person was the one corresponding to the fourth position in this list, second was the first person in this list, third the second person in the list and least dominant was the third person in the list: 2,3,4,1. If one looks at the judgements by the other judges for this meeting (A2 to A5), by comparing the different columns for this first row, one can see that A3's judgments are identical to A1's. All but A4 agree that the fourth person on the list was most dominant. All but A5 agree that the third person was least dominant. All but A2 agree that the first person was the second dominant person. This seems to suggest that on the whole judgements were largely consistent across judges at first sight.

Table 2. Rating of meeting participants for all the annotators per meeting

	A1	A2	A3	A4	A5	'Average'	'Variance'
M1	2,3,4,1	3,2,4,1	2,3,4,1	2,1,4,3	2,4,3,1	2,3,4,1	8
M2	2,3,4,1	2,3,4,1	2,3,4,1	2,3,1,4	3,2,4,1	2,3,4,1	8
M3	2,1,3,4	3,1,2,4	2,1,4,3	3,1,2,4	1,2,3,4	2,1,3,4	8
M4	2,4,3,1	2,4,3,1	1,4,2,3	2,3,4,1	1,4,3,2	1,4,3,1	4
	A6	**A7**	**A8**	**A9**	**A10**	**'Average'**	**'Variance'**
M5	4,3,2,1	4,3,1,2	3,4,1,2	4,3,1,2	3,4,1,2	4,3,1,2	6
M6	1,3,2,4	1,4,3,2	3,1,4,2	3,1,4,2	1,3,4,2	1,3,4,2	12
M7	1,4,3,2	2,4,3,1	3,2,1,4	2,4,1,3	1,4,3,2	1,4,2,3	14
M8	1,2,4,3	1,4,2,3	2,1,3,4	2,1,3,4	1,2,4,3	1,2,3,4	12

To establish the degree of agreement, we compared the variance of the judgements with the variance of random rankings. If the variance of the annotators is smaller than the variance of the random rankings, we have a strong indication that people agree on how to create a dominance ranking.

---

[1] The first three meetings are meetings from for the AMI project (cf. http://www.amiproject.org), M1 and M2 are the AMI pilot meetings AMI-Pilot-2 and AMI-Pilot-4, M3 is a meeting from the AMI spokes corpus (AMI-FOB 6). The last five are meetings recorded for the M4 project (cf. http://www.m4project.org: M4TRN1, M4TRN2, M4TRN6, M4TRN7 and M4TRN12).

If we add up the dominance scores for each person in the meeting, this results for the first meeting in scores 11, 13, 19 and 7, with results in an overall ranking of 2, 3, 4, 1. We call this the 'average' ranking. In case of similar scores, we scored them an equal rank by giving them both the highest value. The next one highest in the ranking was ranked with a gap of two. Example: if the sum of the total scores ended up 8, 10, 12, 10 the resulting ranking became 1,2,4,2. For each of the judges we compare how they differ for each person from this average.

As a measure for the variance we calculated the sum of all the (absolute) differences of each of the annotators judgments (A^i) with their corresponding average. The difference with the average was calculated as the sum of the pairwise absolute differences for all the annotators values of the meeting participants A_p with their corresponding average value $Average_p$. See Table 2 for the results.

$$'Variance' = \sum_{i=1}^{5} \sum_{p=1}^{4} |A_p^i - Average_p|$$

In this case A1 and A3 judgments are identical to the average. A2 made different judgments for the first person (scoring him as 3 instead of 2) and the second person (scoring him as 2 instead of 3). So this results in a variance of 2 adding up the variance 4 and 2 of judges A4 and A5 respectively this ends up in an overall variance of 8 for judgements on the first meeting.

When comparing the variance of the judges with the variance resulting from randomly generated rankings, the distribution of the variance of the annotators ($\mu = 9$, $\sigma = 3.38$, $n = 8$) lies far more left of the distribution coming from randomly generated rankings. ($\mu = 17.8$, $\sigma = 3.49$, $n = 1.0 * 10^6$). The two distributions appeared to be statistically significant ($p < 0.001$) according to the 2-sided Kolmogorov Smirnov test. It thus appears that judges agree very well on dominance rankings. We may have to be conservative to generalize this though as we have only a small (n=8) amount of real samples.

These results support our initial thoughts, where we expected humans to agree (to a reasonable extent) on the ranking of meeting participants according to their conveyed dominance level.

4   Features Used by the Classifier

Dominance can be regarded as a higher level concept that might be deduced automatically from a subset of lower level observations [Reidsma et al., 2004], similar to the assignment of the value for dominance by humans on the basis of the perception and interpretation of certain behaviours.

For our classifier we considered some easily obtainable common sense features that possibly could tell us something about the dominance of a person in relation to other persons in meetings. We deliberately did not use semantically oriented features. For each person in the meeting we calculated scores for the following features.

- The person's influence diffusion (IDM)
- The speaking time in seconds (STS)

- The number of turns in a meeting (NOT)
- The number of times addressed (NTA)
- The number of successful interruptions (NSI)
- The number of times the person grabbed the floor (NOF)
- The number of questions asked (NQA)
- The number of times interrupted (NTI)
- The ratio of NSI/NTI (TIR)
- Normalised IDM by the amount of words spoken. (NIDF)
- The number of words spoken in the whole meeting (NOW)
- The number of times privately addressed (NPA)

The *Influence diffusion model* [Ohsawa et al., 2002] generates a ranking of the participants by counting the number of terms, reused by the next speaker from the current speaker. The person who's terms are re-used the most is called the most influential.

Most of the features appear as simple metrics with variations that measure the amount to which someone is involved in the conversation and how others allow him/her to be involved. These are all measures that are easy to calculate given a corpus with appropriate transcriptions and annotations provided. Metrics used in the literature, as in SYMLOG, depend on the interpretation of an observer.

We defined a *successful interruption* in line with Leffler et al. [1982]. We counted as a successful interruption any occurrence where a speaker A starts talking while another speaker B is talking and speaker B finishes his turn before speaker A. So we did not make a distinction between overlap and interruption. A *floorgrab* was defined each time a participant started speaking after a silence larger than 1.5 seconds.

After the judges that rated our corpus had finished their ratings, we asked them to write down a list of at least five aspects which they thought they had based their rankings on. The following features were mentioned.

> Dominant is the person: who speaks for the longest time, who speaks the most, who is addressed the most, who interrupts the others the most, who grabs the floor the most, who asks the most questions, who speaks the loudest, whose posture is dominant, who has the biggest impact on the discussion, who appears to be most certain of himself, who shows charisma, who seems most confident.

From the features identified by the annotators we can see that e.g. *charisma* and *confidence* are again typical examples of features that are very hard to measure and to operationalize. Most of this is again due to the fact that a proper scale does not exist, and as a result the valuation becomes too subjective and values from one annotator might not correlate with the values from another annotator. Several of the other features are similar to the ones we are exploring for their predictive power in our classifier.

5   Acquiring and Preprocessing the Data

For each of the eight meetings ranked by our annotators, we calculated the values for the measures identified in the previous section. This was done on the basis of simple calculations on manual annotations and on the results of some scripts processing the transcriptions[2]. With respect to addressee annotation 25% of the data was not annotated due to the cost involved[3].

In order to make the values for the same feature comparable, we first made the feature values relative with respect to the meeting length. This was done in two steps. First the fraction, or share, of a feature value was calculated given all the values for that feature in a meeting.

$$\text{The share of a feature value } (F'_{Pn}) = \frac{F_{Pn}}{\sum F_{P1}..F_{P4}}$$

Then, according to the value of the fraction, the results were binned in three different bins. As we are dealing with four person meetings the average value after step 1 is 0.25 (=25% share). The features were grouped using the labels 'High' ($F'_{Pn} > 35\%$), 'Normal' ($15\% < F'_{Pn} < 35\%$), and 'Low' ($F'_{Pn} < 15\%$).

As a consequence, apart from the fact that features were now comparable between meetings, the feature values that originally had 'approximately' the same value now also ended up in the same bin. This seemed intuitively the right thing to do. Table 3 shows the value of the NOW feature ('The number of words used' per participant per meeting) before and after applying the process. If we look at the number of words used for person 2 (P2) and person 4 (P4) we see that they both end up labelled as 'High'. Although they did not speak the same amount of words, they both used more than 90000 words, which is a lot in comparison with P1 (38914) and P3 (26310), both ending up classified as 'Low'.

Now, as the feature values were made comparable, we were almost ready to train our model. The only step left was to define the class labels determining the dominance level. For this we decided to use the same technique as for the features, labelling them also as 'High', 'Normal' and 'Low'. We calculated the shares of each of the participants by dividing the sum of the valuations of all judges for this participant by the total amount of points the judges could spend $(5 * (1 + 2 + 3 + 4) = 50)$.

The results were then again binned using the same borders of 15 and 35 percent. When a share was smaller than 15% the dominance level was labelled as 'High'; if the share lay between 15% and 35% the dominance level was labelled 'Normal' and when it was higher than 35 % the label 'Low' was used. This way, also the persons who received more or less similar scores ended up in the same bin.

---

[2] All transcriptions used were created using the official AMI and M4 transcription guidelines of those meetings [Moore et al., 2005, Edwards, 2001].

[3] Addressee information takes over 15 times real time to annotate [Jovanovic et al., 2005].

Table 3. The feature 'Number of Words' before and after preprocessing for person 1,2,3 and 4 respectively for each meeting

	NOW before preprocessing				NOW after preprocessing			
	P1	P2	P3	P4	P1	P2	P3	P4
M1	38914	93716	26310	98612	low	high	low	high
M2	33458	11602	14556	37986	high	low	low	high
M3	3496	7202	8732	2774	low	high	high	low
M4	2240	1956	4286	7642	low	low	normal	high
M5	4470	1126	9148	1974	normal	low	high	low
M6	2046	17476	1828	4058	low	high	low	high
M7	4296	6812	8258	1318	normal	high	high	low
M8	1586	13750	1786	1540	low	high	low	low

This resulted in a data-set of 32 samples with twelve samples receiving the class label 'High', ten 'Normal' and ten 'Low'. We define our baseline performance as the share of the most frequent class label ('High') having a share of 37.5% of all labels.

6   Detecting Dominance

We wanted to predict the dominance level of the meeting participants with the least possible features, in accordance with Occam's razor [Blumer et al., 1987], trying to explain as much as possible with as little as possible. The fewer features we required, the easier it would be to eventually provide all information to the system. This way we reduced the risk of over fitting our model to the data as well. To decrease the amount of features we evaluated the features on their discriminative force using WEKA's Support Vector Machine (SVM) attribute evaluator.

The top five of most discriminative features appeared to be (in order of importance) NOF, NOT, NSI, NOW, and NOQ. We obtained the best performance by training a SVM using the two most discriminative features: NOF and NOT. Ten-fold cross validation resulted in a performance of 75%, much higher than our 37.5% baseline. This means, that given the number of times the meeting participants grab the floor after a silence together with the number of turns a participant has, our classifier is in 75 % of the cases able to correctly classify the behavior of the participants as being 'Low', 'Normal' or 'High'on dominance. The confusion matrix is shown in Table 4.

From the confusion matrix it can be seen that our classifier performs better on the classes 'Low' and 'High' than on the class 'Normal'. This seems in line with our intuition that people showing more extreme behavior are easier to classify. To test the significance it appeared that the 90% confidence interval for our classifier lies between a performance of 62% and 88%, having a lower bound much higher than the 37.5% baseline. This confidence interval is important due

Table 4. Confusion matrix using the features NOF and NOT. The rows are showing the actual labels and the columns the labels resulting from the classifier.

	Low	Normal	High
Low	8	1	1
Normal	2	7	1
High	0	3	9

to the relatively small number of data samples. The fact that we would over fit our classifier when using all the features appeared when we trained on all the features. Ten fold cross validation resulted in that case in a performance of 50%.

It is interesting to see that the number of successful interruptions as a feature on its own results in a performance of 59% which, although not significant, implies a correlation with the concept of dominance. This is in line with the claim of West and Zimmerman [1983] calling interruption 'a device for exercising power and control in conversation'. Tannen [1993] on the other hand claims that interruptions not necessarily need to be a display of dominance as people can interrupt each other to show enthusiastic listenership and participation as well.

7   Applying the Model

Aware of the fact that our sample size is relatively small and that not all meetings follow the same format, we do think that our results suggest that it is possible to have a system analyzing the level of dominance of the meeting participants. If we look at the features used by our model, and the fact that their values should be just as informative during the meeting as after the meeting, we expect these systems not to function just after the meeting, but just as well in real time.

We crafted a very simplistic model based on the top three features: NOF, NOT and NSI. The model grants one point for each turn a participant takes in a meeting and if the turn is acquired, either after a silence greater than 1.5 seconds, or by an interruption, another extra point is given. This model enabled

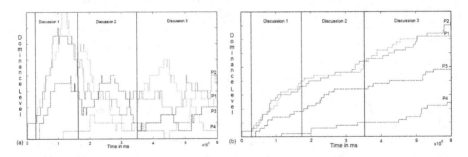

Fig. 1. Graphical outputs of the simplistic dominance model applied to M3 for a 100 seconds window (a) and for a window spanning the whole meeting (b)

us to produce figures similar to Figure 1, where we counted the points for all the participants of the AMI-FOB6 meeting in a time window of 100 seconds for each participant (a) and cumulatively counted the points for each participant over a whole meeting (b). It should be noted that the resulting heights of the participants levels correspond to the averaged annotator value of meeting M3 in Table 2.

8   Conclusions and Future Work

We have shown that in the future systems might be extended with modules able to determine the relative dominance level of individual meeting participants. We were able to reach an accuracy of 75% using just two easily obtainable features. The concept *dominance* appears in the meeting domain to be mainly reflected by the number of floorgrabs and the number of turns someone takes. As all the features are made relative to the total value of all participants, one is able to apply the model both during as well as after the meeting.

Possible directions for opportunities to improve our model could be to extend the feature set with more semantically oriented features, such as 'Who is using the strongest language?', or 'Who gets most suggestions accepted?'. Although these features seem very intuitive and might increase the performance, one does have to realize that being able to measure these, costly and complex inferencing systems have to be developed.

Another possible thing to look at is to use more samples, this will be more expensive on one side, but also decreases the confidence interval and thus further increase the reliability of the performance on the other side.

Typical applications of systems that track the dominance levels of participants are other systems using the dominance information in order to inform the meeting participants or a meeting chairman about this. With this information a chairman could alter his style of leadership in order to increase the meeting productivity. Combined with other information, recommender systems could be created that directly suggest how to change the leadership style. The next thing one could think of is a virtual chairman as mentioned in Rienks et al. [2005] which is able to lead a meeting all by itself, giving turns, keeping track of a time-line and most important: keeping the meeting as effective and efficient as possible.

Acknowledgements

This work was partly supported by the European Union 6th FWP IST Integrated Project AMI (Augmented Multi-party Interaction, FP6-506811, publication AMI-96). We would like to thank our volunteers as well as Natasa Jovanovic for providing us the addressee data of most of our used meetings and finally Lynn Packwood for helping improving the text.

References

R.F. Bales. *Interaction Process Analysis.* Addison-Wesley, 1951.

R.F. Bales and S.P. Cohen. *SYMLOG: A System for the Multiple Level Observation of Groups.* The Free Press, 1979.

A. Blumer, A. Ehrenfeucht, D. Haussler, and M. K. Marmuthh. Occam's razor. In *Information Processing Letters*, pages 377–380. 24 edition, 1987.

J. A. Edwards. *Transcription in Discourse*, chapter in Handbook of Discourse, pages 321–348. Mass: Blackwell Publishers, 2001.

C.(S.) Ellis and P. Barthelmess. The Neem dream. In *Proceedings of the 2003 conference on Diversity in computing*, pages 23–29. ACM Press, 2003. ISBN 1-58113-790-7.

Ellyson and Dovidio. *Power, Dominance, an Nonverbal Behavior.* Springer Verlag, 1985.

H.P. Grice. *Logic and conversation*, chapter Syntax and Semantics: Speech Acts, pages 41–58. Academic Press, 1975.

D. Hellriegel, J.W. Slocum Jr., and R.W. Woodman. *Organizational Behavior, seventh edition.* West publising company, 1995.

L.R. Hoffmann. Applying experimental research on group problem solving to organizations. *Journal of applied behavioral science*, 15:375–391, 1979.

N. Jovanovic, R. Op den Akker, and A. Nijholt. A corpus for studying addressing behavior in multi-party dialogues. In *Proc. of The sixth SigDial conference on Discourse and Dialogue*, 2005.

A. Leffler, D.L. Gillespie, and C. Conaty. The effects of status differentiation on non-verbal behaviour. *Social Psychology Quarterly*, 45(3):151–161., 1982.

J. Moore, M. Kronenthal, and S. Ashby. Guidelines for AMI speech transcriptions. Technical report, IDIAP, Univ. of Edinburgh, February 2005.

Y. Ohsawa, N. Matsumura, and M. Ishizuka. Influence diffusion model in text-based communication. In *Proc. of The eleventh world wide web conference*, 2002. ISBN 1-880672-20-0.

D. Reidsma, R. Rienks, and N. Jovanovic. Meeting modelling in the context of multimodal research. In *Proc. of the Workshop on Machine Learning and Multimodal Interaction*, 2004.

R. Rienks, A. Nijholt, and D. Reidsma. *Meetings and Meeting support in ambient intelligence*, chapter in Ambient Intelligence, Wireless Networking, Ubiquitous Computing. Artech House, Norwood, MA, USA, 2005. In Press.

D. Tannen. *Interpreting Interruption in Conversation*, chapter in Gender and Discourse, pages 53–83. Oxford University Press, 1993.

C. West and D.H. Zimmerman. *Small Insults: A study of interruptions in cross-sex conversations between unaquainted persons*, chapter in Language, Gender and Society, pages 103–117. Newbury House, 1983.

D. Zhang, D. Gatica-Perez, S. Bengio, and D. Roy. Learning influence among interacting markov chains. *Advances in Neural Information Processing Systems (NIPS)*, 18, 2005.

Can Chimeric Persons Be Used in Multimodal Biometric Authentication Experiments?

Norman Poh and Samy Bengio

IDIAP Research Institute, Rue du Simplon 4, CH-1920 Martigny, Switzerland
{norman, bengio}@idiap.ch

Abstract. Combining multiple information sources, typically from several data streams is a very promising approach, both in experiments and to some extent in various real-life applications. A system that uses *more than one* behavioral and physiological characteristics to verify whether a person is who he/she claims to be is called a *multimodal* biometric authentication system. Due to lack of large true multimodal biometric datasets, the biometric trait of a user from a database is often combined with another different biometric trait of yet another user, thus creating a so-called *chimeric user*. In the literature, this practice is justified based on the fact that the underlying biometric traits to be combined are assumed to be independent of each other given the user. To the best of our knowledge, there is no literature that approves or disapproves such practice. We study this topic from two aspects: 1) by clarifying the mentioned independence assumption and 2) by constructing a pool of chimeric users from a pool of *true* modality matched users (or simply "true users") taken from a bimodal database, such that the performance variability due to chimeric user can be compared with that due to true users. The experimental results suggest that for a large proportion of the experiments, such practice is indeed questionable.

1 Introduction

Biometric authentication (BA) is a problem of verifying an identity claim using a person's behavioral and physiological characteristics. BA is becoming an important alternative to traditional authentication methods such as keys ("something one has", i.e., by possession) or PIN numbers ("something one knows", i.e., by knowledge) because it essentially verifies "who one is", i.e., by biometric information. Therefore, it is not susceptible to misplacement or forgetfulness. Examples of biometric modalities are fingerprints, faces, voice, hand-geometry and retina scans [1].

Due to inherent properties in each biometric and external manufacturing constraints in the sensing technologies, no single biometric trait can achieve 100% authentication performance. This problem can be alleviated by combining two or more biometric traits, also known as the field of multimodal biometric authentication. In the literature, there are several approaches towards studying fusion of modalities. One practice is to construct a large database containing several biometric traits for each user. This, however, can be very time-consuming and expensive. Another practice is to combine biometric modalities of a database with biometric modalities of another biometric database. Since both databases do not necessarily contain the *same* users, such combination results in

S. Renals and S. Bengio (Eds.): MLMI 2005, LNCS 3869, pp. 87–100, 2006.

chimeric users. From the experiment point of view, these biometric modalities belong to the same person. While this practice is commonly used in the multimodal litera-ture, e.g., [2,3] among others, it was questioned whether this was a right thing to do or not during the 2003 Workshop on Multimodal User Authentication [4]. To the best of our knowledge, there is no work in the literature that approves or disapproves such assumption.

There are at least two arguments that justify the use of chimeric users, i.e., i) *modal-ity independence assumption* – that two or more biometric traits of a single person are independent of each other; and ii) *privacy issue* – participants in the multimodal biomet-ric experiments are not ready to let institutes keep record of too much of their personal information (raw biometric data) at the same place. If such information is misused, it could be dangerous, e.g., identity theft. It is for this same reason that processed bio-metric features are preferred for storage rather than raw biometric data. Note that the first argument is *technical* while the second one is *ethical*. Although both arguments are equally important, the second one is beyond an experimenter's control and is related to the policy related to a database. For instance the policy should address who can use the database and how it should be used. When a database is carefully designed to protect the participants' privacy right, this issue should be resolved. For this reason, this paper focuses on the first argument.

We set out to investigate the validity of the modality independence assumption by using two approaches, namely : 1) by pinning down the concept of *independence* and 2) by simulating the effect of chimeric users experimentally and measuring the discrep-ancy in terms of performance between the use of chimeric users and the use of true users. Note that these two approaches represent *two different ways* of thinking about the problem: one theoretical and the other experimental. To verify this hypothesis, we limit our scope to studying such effect to bimodal as generalization to more than two modalities is direct. It should be emphasized that the use of chimeric users is not lim-ited to biometric authentication, but may be in general applicable to problems involving multimodal streams. Hence, this study is of interest to researchers studying multimodal fusion.

This paper is organized as follows: Section 2 underpins the concept of independence between biometric traits (the first approach of studying the validity of chimeric users); Section 3 describes the database to be used; Section 4 details the experimental pro-cedure and presents the results (the second approach); and finally this is followed by conclusions in Section 5.

2   On the Independence Assumption

2.1   Preliminary

Suppose that each authorized person is identified by a unique identity claim $j \in \mathcal{J} \equiv \{1, \ldots, J\}$ and there are J identities. We sometimes call these users as clients to oppose a set of other unauthorized persons known as impostors. Hence, a biometric authentica-tion system is aimed at distinguishing clients from impostors, which is an *aggregated* two-class problem, i.e., a two-class problem with J distinctive users. In this problem, it is common to represent a user by his/her feature template or *model*, i.e, a set of parameters derived from the features. Suppose that the output due to comparing a user model C_j to a feature X is $y(j)$. For each client or user model C_j, there is a corresponding impostor model I_j. Lacking a proper definition[1], the impostor model is often *naively* defined as the model of other finite users $\forall_{j'} | j' \in \mathcal{J} - j$. We the purpose of clarity, we will drop the client index j such that writing C is equivalent to writing C_j and writing y is equivalent to writing $y(j)$. To decide whether to accept or reject the access request represented by feature X claiming identity j, previous theoretical studies such as [5,6] often use the following decision function:

$$\text{decision}(P(C|X)) = \begin{cases} \text{accept} & \text{if } P(C|X) > 0.5 \\ \text{reject} & \text{otherwise,} \end{cases} \quad (1)$$

where by the probability law, $P(C|X) + P(I|X) = 1$. Although this decision rule is correct, such formulation does not allow the interpretation of a threshold-based decision function such as:

$$\text{decision}(y) = \begin{cases} \text{accept} & \text{if } y > \Delta \\ \text{reject} & \text{otherwise,} \end{cases} \quad (2)$$

where Δ is the user-independent decision threshold. It can be easily seen that $y = P(C|X)$ and $\Delta = 0.5$ when comparing both decision functions. The decision function in Eqn. (2) is found in most biometric authentication systems. For instance, if the matching score y is based on a distance between a user template X_{tmplt} and the submitted feature X, i.e., $y \equiv dist(X_{tmplt}, X)$, where $dist$ is a distance measure, the decision function in Eqn. (1) cannot reflect such measure since it applies to probability outcome only. To allow the interpretation of threshold in the case of a distance measure, we propose that the classification be carried out such that:

$$\text{decision}(\text{LPR}) = \begin{cases} \text{accept} & \text{if LPR} > 0 \\ \text{reject} & \text{otherwise,} \end{cases} \quad (3)$$

where LPR is *logarithmic posterior ratio*. It is defined as:

$$\text{LPR} \equiv \log\left(\frac{P(C|X)}{P(I|X)}\right) = \log\left(\frac{P(X|C)P(C)}{P(y|I)P(I)}\right)$$
$$= \underbrace{\log\frac{P(X|C)}{P(X|I)}} + \underbrace{\log\frac{P(C)}{P(I)}} \equiv \text{LLR} - \Delta, \quad (4)$$

where we introduced the two terms: $y \equiv \text{LLR}$ or Log-Likelihood Ratio and a threshold Δ. The first term corresponds to the *interpretation of* score y as an LLR. The second term is a constant. It handles the case of different priors (hence fixed *a priori*), i.e., it reflects the different *costs* of false acceptance and false rejection. Note that y is a direct function of X and the model variable associated to it (say θ), i.e., $y = f_\theta(X)$. We

---

[1] Ideally, this impostor model should be the world population minus the user j. In terms of computation and data collection effort, this is not feasible and in practice not necessary.

use the function f with parameter θ to explicitly represent the *functional relationship* between the variables y and X.

Although y is interpreted as an LLR here, many different machine-learning algorithms (e.g., Gaussian Mixture Models, Multi-Layer Perceptrons, Support Vector Machines) can be viewed as an approximation to this relationship, without necessarily giving it a probabilistic interpretation, i.e., y being a probability. Suppose that y is an instance of the variable Y and is drawn from the distribution $\mathcal{Y}$. The decision function in Eqn. (2) then implies that $E_{\mathcal{Y}|C}[Y] > E_{\mathcal{Y}|I}[Y]$, where $E_{\mathcal{Z}}[Z]$ is the expectation of Z under the law $\mathcal{Z}$. In words, this means that the expected client score has to be greater than that of impostor. To allow interpretation of a distance measure, one can simply interchange between C and I, such that $E_{\mathcal{Y}|C}[Y] < E_{\mathcal{Y}|I}[Y]$.

Depending on the outcome of the decision (as a function of the threshold Δ), a biometric authentication system can commit two types of errors, namely, False Acceptance (FA) and False Rejection (FR). The error rates of FA and FR are defined as:

$$\text{FAR}(\Delta) = 1 - P(Y|I \le \Delta)$$
$$\text{FRR}(\Delta) = P(Y|C \le \Delta),$$

where $P(Y|k \le \Delta)$ is the cumulative density function of conditional variable Y within the range $[-\infty, \Delta]$ for each class k. Note that a unique point with Δ^* where $\text{FAR}(\Delta^*) = \text{FRR}(\Delta^*)$ is called Equal Error Rate (EER). EER is often used to characterize a system's performance. Another useful performance evaluation point for *any given threshold* Δ (not necessarily Δ^*) is called Half Total Error Rate (HTER) and is defined as the average of FAR and FRR, i.e.,:

$$\text{HTER}(\Delta) = \frac{1}{2}(\text{FAR}(\Delta) + \text{FRR}(\Delta)).$$

The discussion until here concerns only a particular client. In reality, one has extremely few examples of genuine accesses $y|C$ and relatively large impostor accesses $y|I$, as mentioned earlier. As a result, the estimation of user-specific threshold is extremely unreliable. For this reason, the user-independent versions of FAR, FRR and EER, as well as the threshold are often used. Although there exists abundant literature to estimate user-specific threshold (see for instance a survey in [7,8]), common threshold is by far a standard practice.

2.2   Different Levels of Dependency Assumption

There are a number of different assumptions that can be made about the levels of dependency when one considers combining multimodal information sources. These dependencies have implications for the mathematical modeling and classifier used. Two notions of dependencies can be distinguished here, i.e, *feature-oriented* dependency and *score-oriented* dependency. The former assumes dependency at the feature-level while *not considering* the dependency at the score level. The latter, on the other hand, assumes *independence at the feature level* but handles dependency uniquely at the score level. These two dichotomies thus give rise to four types of dependencies in *decreasing order*:

- **Strict Feature Dependence.** It is characterized uniquely by the feature-oriented dependence assumption.
- **Loose Feature Dependence.** It is characterized by feature-oriented independence but score-oriented dependence
- **Loose Feature Independence.** It is characterized by both feature-oriented and score-oriented independence.
- **Strict Feature Independence.** It is characterized uniquely by the feature-oriented independence assumption.

Suppose that X_1 and X_2 are features of two different biometric modalities. Using the same Bayesian formulation (with focus on LLR) as in the previous Section, the four categories can be formally stated as follows:

- **Strict Feature Dependence:**

$$y_{SD}(j) = \log \frac{p(X_1, X_2|C_j)}{p(X_1, X_2|I_j)} \tag{5}$$

$$\equiv f_{\theta_j}(X_1, X_2), \tag{6}$$

where the function f explicitly represents any classifier with the associated parameter θ_j. By so doing, we actually provide a Bayesian interpretation of the classifier f. One possible weakness of this approach is known as the "curse of dimensionality", whereby modeling the joint features in higher dimension can cause a degraded performance compared to methods resulting from the other assumptions (to be discussed below).

- **Strict Feature Independence:**

$$y_{SI}(j) = \log \frac{p(X_1|C_j)p(X_2|C_j)}{p(X_1|I_j)p(X_2|I_j)} \tag{7}$$

$$= \log \frac{p(X_1|C_j)}{p(X_1|I_j)} + \log \frac{p(X_2|C_j)}{p(X_2|I_j)} \tag{8}$$

$$= y_1(j) + y_2(j) \tag{9}$$

$$\equiv f_{\theta_j^1}(X_1) + f_{\theta_j^2}(X_2) \tag{10}$$

where $y_i(j) \equiv \log \frac{p(X_i|C_j)}{p(X_i|I_j)}$ and θ_j^i is the model parameter associated to modality i and user j. Note that in theory the two classifiers involved, $f_{\theta_j^i}|i = \{1, 2\}$, do not have to be homogeneous (the same type). In practice, however, some form of normalization may be needed if they are not homogeneous, e.g., from different vendors or based on different algorithms. It can be seen that using this Bayesian framework, the independence assumption leads to the well-known sum rule. On the other hand, using the probabilistic framework $y(j) \equiv p(C_j|X)$, this dependency would have led to the well-known product rule (proof not shown here).

- **Loose Feature Dependence:**

$$y_{LD}(j) = \log \frac{p(y_1(j), y_2(j)|C_j)}{p(y_1(j), y_2(j)|I_j)} \tag{11}$$

$$\equiv f_{\theta_j^{COM}}(y_1(j), y_2(j)) \tag{12}$$

$$= f_{\theta_j^{COM}} \left(f_{\theta_j^1}(X_1), f_{\theta_j^2}(X_2) \right), \tag{13}$$

where $f_{\theta_j^{COM}}$ can be considered as a second-level classifier, also called a fusion classifier. The loose feature dependence is a result of committing to the feature independence assumption – which means that the scores $y_1(j)$ and $y_2(j)$ can be derived separately – and score-oriented dependence assumption – implying that the dependency at the score level should be modeled. This formulation actually motivates the use of trainable classifiers in fusion. Suppose that $\boldsymbol{y}(j) = [y_1(j), y_2(j)]^T$ is a vector and an instance of the variable $\boldsymbol{Y}(j)$. If $\boldsymbol{Y}(j)$ is drawn from a class-conditional Gaussian distributions and that both the client and impostor distributions share a common covariance matrix $\boldsymbol{\Sigma}$, it is possible to show that:

$$f_{\theta_j^{COM}} = w_1(j)y_1(j) + w_2(j)y_2(j), \tag{14}$$

where $\boldsymbol{w}(j) = [w_1(j), w_2(j)]^T$ has the following solution:

$$\boldsymbol{w}(j) \propto \boldsymbol{\Sigma}^{-1} \left(E[\boldsymbol{Y}(j)|C_j] - E[\boldsymbol{Y}(j)|I_j] \right) . \tag{15}$$

The linear opinion pool (or weighted sum) shown here is a typical solution given by Fisher's linear discriminant [9, Sec. 3.6]. Other solutions using the same linear discriminant function (but possibly *more powerful* since they do not make the class-conditional Gaussian assumption) includes Support Vector Machines with a linear kernel [10] and the perceptron algorithm [9, Chap. 6], the latter of which generalizes to the least square and the logistic discrimination/regression solutions (depending on the error criterion). It can thus be seen that the loose feature dependence assumption motivates the use of a fusion classifier. It should be noted that the Bayesian framework using Eqn. (11) as a departure point does not dictate that a linear classifier has to be used. In practice, however, to the best of our knowledge, non-linear classifiers have not been reported to provide *significantly* better results over their linear counterparts in this application. Often, due to small training sample size on a *per user basis*, the classifier at this level is trained across all users. Although user-specific fusion classifiers have been proposed, e.g., [3], global fusion classifier is by far the most commonly used approach. We will study this case here. Hence, as long as fusion is concerned, the index j in the term $f_{\theta_j^{COM}}$ of Eqn. (12) can be dropped, so as the weights in Eqn. (14).

– **Loose Feature Independence:**

$$y_{LI}(j) = \log \frac{p(y_1(j)|C_j)p(y_2(j)|C_j)}{p(y_1(j)|I_j)p(y_2(j)|I_j)} \tag{16}$$

$$= \log \frac{p(y_1(j)|C_j)}{p(y_1(j)|I_j)} + \log \frac{p(y_2(j)|C_j)}{p(y_2(j)|I_j)} \tag{17}$$

$$\equiv f_{\theta_j^1}(y_1(j)) + f_{\theta_j^2}(y_2(j)) \tag{18}$$

$$= f_{\theta_j^1} \left(f_{\theta_j^1}'(X_1) \right) + f_{\theta_j^2} \left(f_{\theta_j^2}'(X_2) \right), \tag{19}$$

where $f_{\theta_j^i}'$ is a classifier taking features X_i and $f_{\theta_j^i}$ is another classifier taking the score $y_i(j)$, for all $i \in \{1, 2\}$. Since $f_{\theta_j^i}$ is a one-input one-output function, this procedure is also called *score normalization* [11]. Among the score normalization techniques, user-specific Z-score normalization is perhaps the most representative one. Z-norm and other techniques are surveyed in [7]. It turns out that the fusion classifier is a sum rule. Again, due to lack of user-specific data, the score normalization is treated the same across users. Hence, we can replace $f_{\theta_j^i}$ by f_{θ^i} (without the subscript j) in Eqns. (18) and (19), for all $i = \{1, 2\}$.

The above four types of architecture as a result of different levels of dependence assumption are certainly not exhaustive. It is possible to combine say strict feature dependence and strict feature independence assumption such that the resultant architecture compensates for both assumption (see for instance [12]).

As can be seen, depending on the level of dependency between X_1 and X_2 that one is willing to commit to, one arrives at any of the four choices of architectures. In multimodal biometrics, where two (or more) biometric modalities are captured using different sensors, it is well accepted that the strict feature dependence assumption (the first one) is *in general* not true [2]. Hence, as long as the use of chimeric users is concerned, only the last three levels of dependency are relevant. In the experimental setting with chimeric users, one simply uses the concatenated score with modalities of *other users* , i.e.,

$$\boldsymbol{y}_{chimeric} = [y_1(j), y_2(j')]^T \text{ where } j \neq j'.$$

and combines the concatenated score by using classifiers such as Eqns. (9), (12) and (18), respectively for the last three levels of dependency.

Thus we arrive at the crucial question: "*Do the different levels of dependency allow one to switch the identities?*". If one follows strictly (and agrees with) the Bayesian framework presented so far, none of these assumptions provide any hint about the use of chimeric users in practice. They merely guide how one should model the final score y just before making the accept/reject decision. Lacking any plausible justification and theoretical explanation, we resolve to an experiment-driven approach to study the effects of switching identities. Before presenting the experimental approach, we first present the database used in the next section.

3   The XM2VTS Database

There exists several bimodal biometric authentication databases for this purpose, e.g., M2VTS, XM2VTS and BANCA databases. We will use the XM2VTS for two reasons: it has among the largest number of users, i.e., 200 clients and 95 casual impostors; and the results of many single modal experiments (in scores) are available for fusion. These scores are also publicly available[2] and are reported in [13].

The XM2VTS database [14] contains synchronised video and speech data from 295 subjects, recorded during four sessions taken at one month intervals. On each session, two recordings were made, each consisting of a speech shot and a head shot. The speech shot consisted of frontal face and speech recordings of each subject during the recital of a sentence. The database is divided into three sets: a training set, an evaluation set

---

[2] http://www.idiap.ch/~norman/fusion

Table 1. The Lausanne Protocols as well as the fusion protocol of XM2VTS database

Data sets	Lausanne Protocols		Fusion
	LP1	LP2	Protocols
LP Train client accesses	3	4	NIL
LP Eval client accesses	600 (3 × 200)	400 (2 × 200)	Fusion dev
LP Eval impostor accesses	40,000 (25 × 8 × 200)		Fusion dev
LP Test client accesses	400 (2 × 200)		Fusion eva
LP Test impostor accesses	112,000† (70 × 8 × 200)		Fusion eva

†: Due to one corrupted speech file of one of the 70 impostors in this set, this file was deleted, resulting in 200 less of impostor scores, or a total of 111,800 impostor scores.

and a test set. The training set (LP Train) was used to build client models, while the evaluation set (LP Eval) was used to compute the decision thresholds (as well as other hyper-parameters) used by classifiers. Finally, the test set (LP Test) was used to estimate the performance.

The 295 subjects were divided into a set of 200 clients, 25 evaluation impostors and 70 test impostors. There exists two configurations or two different partitioning approaches of the training and evaluation sets. They are called Lausanne Protocol I and II, denoted as **LP1** and **LP2** in this paper. In both configurations, the test set remains the same. Their difference is that there are three training shots per client for LP1 and four training shots per client for LP2. Table 1 is the summary of the data. More details can be found in [15]. The first column shows the data set, divided into training, evaluation and test sets. Columns two and three show the the partition of the data according to LP1 and LP2 whereas column four shows the partition of data for the fusion protocols that are *consistent* with the Lausanne Protocols. As far as fusion is concerned, there are only two data sets, labeled as "Fusion dev" (for development) and "Fusion eva" (for evaluation), since the data used in LP training sets are reserved to construct the base systems[3]. Note that the fusion development set is used to calculate the parameters of fusion classifier as well as the optimal global threshold. They are then applied to the fusion evaluation set. Since the threshold is *calculated from the development set*, the reported HTER obtained from the evaluation set is thus called an *a priori* HTER.

4   An Experimentally Driven Approach

This Section aims at answering the following question: "Is an experiment carried out using chimeric users *equivalent* to the one carried out using true users in terms of a given performance measure?". Suppose that the performance measure of interest is *a priori* HTER. The above question can then be rephrased as: "Is the *a priori* HTER obtained using chimeric users *similar to* (or *not significantly* different from) the one obtained using the true users?". We can formally specify the null hypothesis and its corresponding alternative hypothesis as follows:

---

[3] Given the naming conventions of the XM2VTS corpus which are admitably rather confusing, we *consistently* use the term "developemnt set" to mean training set and "evaluation set" to mean test set.

- H_0: The *a priori* HTER obtained from chimeric users is *equivalent* to the one obtained from true users.
- H_1: The *a priori* HTER obtained from chimeric users is *different from* the one obtained from true users.

Suppose that the HTER value due to chimeric users, v, is an instance of a random variable V which follows an unknown distribution. We are interested in:

$$p(v \in {}^c[a, b]|H_0) = \alpha, \tag{20}$$

where ${}^c[a, b]$ is the complementary of $[a, b]$ – or the *critical region*, i.e., the set of values for which we will reject H_0 – and α is the level of the test – or the Type I error, i.e., the probability of selecting H_1 when H_0 is true. By convention, α is usually set to 1% or 5%. Note that the critical region is computed such that the Type I error is only meaningful for a given α level.

Since the distribution of HTER due to chimeric users is unknown, we need to estimate it using a random permutation procedure such that in each permutation, a biometric modality of one user is paired with another biometric modality of yet another user. This procedure is somewhat similar to the bootstrap-based non-parametric statistical test [16,17] but different in two aspects: a bootstrap manipulates samples whereas the permutation process here manipulates user identities; and a bootstrap draws samples with replacement whereas the permutation process, as its name implies, permutes identities, which means it draws identity *without replacement*. Since each permutation creates a "new" set of fusion scores, a fusion classifier has to be constructed before the HTER value can be computed. By repeatedly applying the random permutation procedure, we can then obtain a set of HTER values, which represents our non-parametric estimate of the distribution V. Evaluating Eqn. (20) is simply a matter of determining if the HTER due to true users is in $[a, b]$ (hence in favor of H_0) or in its complement ${}^c[a, b]$ (hence in favor of H_1). The values a and b are chosen such that $p(v \in [a, b]) = 1 - \alpha$ for a given α and $p(v < a) = p(v > b)$. Under such constraints, it is obvious to see that $p(v < a) = p(v > b) = \alpha/2$. To illustrate this idea, we took an experiment from the XM2VTS score-level fusion benchmark database, and applied the hypothesis test procedure mentioned. The results are plotted in Figure 1.

Two fusion classifiers are used in the experiments, namely the mean operator and the Gaussian Mixture Model (GMM). Both of these fusion classifiers are representative approaches of the *loose feature independence* assumption and the *loose feature dependence* assumption, respectively. For the mean operator, prior to fusion, scores are normalized to zero mean and unit variance such that none of the two expert scores dominate just because of a larger variance. The normalization parameters are calculated from the development set. For the GMM, the number of Gaussian components is tuned by simple validation.

According to the fusion protocol, there are 21 multimodal data sets available. The HTER distribution due to random identity match is sampled 1000 times and there are 200 users. This means that the 1000 samples are a sheer portion of $1000 \left(\dfrac{200^2}{200} \right)^{-1} \approx 10^{-542}$ (since we can have as many as 200×199 chimeric users in addition to the

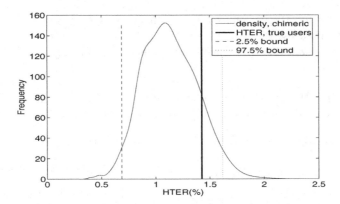

Fig. 1. The distribution of *a priori* HTER (thin curve) estimated from 1000 random samplings of chimeric users versus the HTER of true users (bold vertical line). All thresholds were calculated to minimize HTER on the development set. The HTER of the true users is in the 87.7 percentile (or 1.42% HTER) and is within the 2.5 (dashed vertical line) percentile (or 0.69% HTER) and 97.5 percentile (dotted vertical line) (or 1.62% HTER). Hence, this experiment supports the null hypothesis.

original 200 users and from these users we sample 200 users each time), i.e., one cannot possibly evaluate all the possible permutations. Table 2 lists the HTER range at 95% of confidence due to 1000 samples of random identity match (chimeric-user effect) and the corresponding HTER of true identity match. The first 15 are fusion datasets taken from LP1 while the rest are from LP2. For the values of HTER of true identity match falling outside the confidence range, a * sign is marked. There are two *'s for the mean operator and three for the GMM.

Since Table 2 is limited to the criterion of EER only, we also plot the whole spectrum of the so-called Expected Performance Curve (EPC) [18], which selects different thresholds for different criteria, on a separate validation set, as follows:

$$\Delta_* = \arg\min_{\Delta} \omega \text{FAR}(\Delta) + (1 - \omega)\text{FRR}(\Delta) \tag{21}$$

where ω ranges from 0 to 1. Using this threshold, the EPC then plots the corresponding HTER on the test set, with respect to ω, i.e., $\text{HTER}(\Delta_*, \omega)$. This enables us to obtain unbiased estimates of the HTER since all hyper-parameters, including the threshold, are selected on some separate validation set.

Figures 2 and 3 show EPC curves of the distribution due to random identity match (with a 95% confidence interval) and the EPC curve of true identity match, for the mean operator and the GMM, respectively. As can be observed, there are much more points where the HTER of true identity match falls out of the 95% confidence range. Precisely, exactly 8/21 of experiments for the mean operator and 7/21 of experiments for the GMM. Hence, based on the available fusion datasets, about one third of them shows that the experiments with chimeric users are *inconsistent* with those carried out with the true identity match setting. Considering the fact that the mean operator has no parameters to be estimated and that the GMM has some, the free parameters in the

Table 2. The *a priori* HTER range (whose confidence falls between 2.5% and 97.5% quantiles, corresponding to the usual middle 95% confidence bound) of 1000 samples of random identity match (chimeric-user effect) versus the *a priori* HTER of true identity match for both the mean operator and the GMM fusion classifiers, for each of the 21 fusion datasets. For each experiment, the threshold is calculated to fulfill the EER criterion on the training set. For the values of *a priori* HTER of true identity match falling outside the confidence range, a "∗" sign is marked.

No.	LP	Data set	HTER (%)			
			Mean		GMM	
		(Face) (Speech) experts	chimeric	true	chimeric	true
1	1	(FH,MLP)(LFCC,GMM)	[0.36, 1.02]	0.79	[0.10, 0.60]	0.35
2	1	(FH,MLP)(PAC,GMM)	[0.70, 1.36]	1.13	[0.38, 1.13]	1.08
3	1	(FH,MLP)(SSC,GMM)	[0.54, 1.24]	0.87	[0.32, 1.03]	0.72
4	1	(DCTs,GMM)(LFCC,GMM)	[0.16, 0.68]	0.53	[0.11, 0.58]	0.44
5	1	(DCTs,GMM)(PAC,GMM)	[0.71, 1.59]	1.44	[0.69, 1.62]	1.42
6	1	(DCTs,GMM)(SSC,GMM)	[0.60, 1.38]	1.14	[0.55, 1.39]	1.21
7	1	(DCTb,GMM)(LFCC,GMM)	[0.13, 0.47]	∗ 0.55	[0.04, 0.51]	0.47
8	1	(DCTb,GMM)(PAC,GMM)	[0.30, 0.93]	∗ 1.13	[0.29, 0.97]	∗ 1.06
9	1	(DCTb,GMM)(SSC,GMM)	[0.27, 0.82]	0.75	[0.22, 0.82]	∗ 0.86
10	1	(DCTs,MLP)(LFCC,GMM)	[0.52, 1.16]	0.84	[0.09, 0.58]	0.50
11	1	(DCTs,MLP)(PAC,GMM)	[0.95, 1.77]	1.12	[0.54, 1.40]	0.86
12	1	(DCTs,MLP)(SSC,GMM)	[0.84, 1.64]	1.37	[0.45, 1.19]	1.02
13	1	(DCTb,MLP)(LFCC,GMM)	[1.31, 2.62]	1.62	[0.23, 1.08]	0.58
14	1	(DCTb,MLP)(PAC,GMM)	[2.42, 3.84]	3.65	[1.41, 2.91]	2.60
15	1	(DCTb,MLP)(SSC,GMM)	[2.07, 3.43]	2.88	[1.00, 2.22]	1.55
16	2	(FH,MLP)(LFCC,GMM)	[0.34, 0.91]	0.69	[0.01, 0.64]	0.13
17	2	(FH,MLP)(PAC,GMM)	[0.53, 1.21]	1.14	[0.27, 0.98]	0.73
18	2	(FH,MLP)(SSC,GMM)	[0.50, 1.10]	0.98	[0.17, 0.83]	∗ 0.89
19	2	(DCTb,GMM)(LFCC,GMM)	[0.00, 0.33]	0.13	[0.00, 0.38]	0.38
20	2	(DCTb,GMM)(PAC,GMM)	[0.04, 0.46]	0.18	[0.03, 0.51]	0.16
21	2	(DCTb,GMM)(SSC,GMM)	[0.01, 0.38]	0.18	[0.01, 0.51]	0.17

fusion classifier *does*, to some extents, contribute to the variability observed by HTER due to the chimeric-user effect. Note that in both experiments, the 1000 random identity permutations were constrained to be the *same*. This is essential to keep the possible experiment-induced variation to be minimal.

5   Conclusions

In this paper, the following issue was addressed: "Can chimeric persons be used in multimodal biometric authentication experiments?". This topic was tackled by 1) identifying the different levels of dependency assumptions as a result of two dichotomies: feature-oriented dependence and score-oriented dependence; and 2) by experimentally comparing the effects due to using chimeric users with those using the original true modalities of same users (or simply "true users"). One major conclusion from the first approach is that the independence assumption does not imply that one can use the chimeric users in experiments. Instead, such assumption only guides how one should

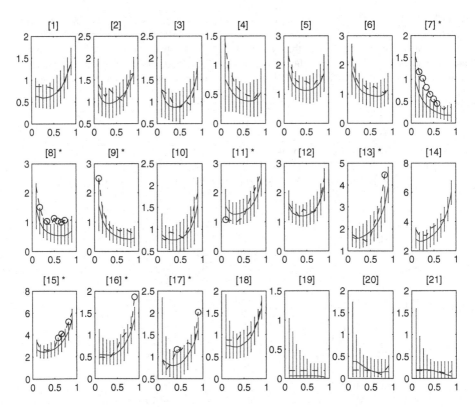

Fig. 2. The EPC curve range, whose X-axis is the cost ω and whose Y-axis is HTER in %, due to 1000 samples of random identity match, at 95% of confidence versus the EPC curve (dashed line) of true identity match, for each of the 21 experiments, using the *mean operator* as the fusion classifier. They are labeled accordingly from 1 to 21 corresponding to the experiment numbers in Table 2. A ∗ sign is marked for the experiments whose one or more HTERs of true identity match fall outside the confidence range. For these points, circles are plotted on the corresponding EPC curve.

construct a classifier to combine information from different modalities. Neither does the second more empirical approach support the use of chimeric users. Indeed based on 21 fusion datasets and two fusion classifiers, only about two thirds of the data indicate that chimeric users can be used, or in other words, the use of true users does not vary significantly, at 95% of confidence, compared to the case when chimeric users are used in experiments. The rest of the rather large one-third of datasets suggest that the use of chimeric users cannot appropriately replace the dataset of the true modality matched dataset. Considering the high variability of HTER due to the effect of chimeric users, several runs of fusion experiments with different identity match are *strongly recommended*. Although such remedial procedure does not necessarily reflect the case when true modality matched identity is used, it *at least* gives a more accurate figure about the possible range of HTER values when the true identities are used. If the 21 fusion datasets are representative of this scenario, then, one might have a 2/3 chance of better

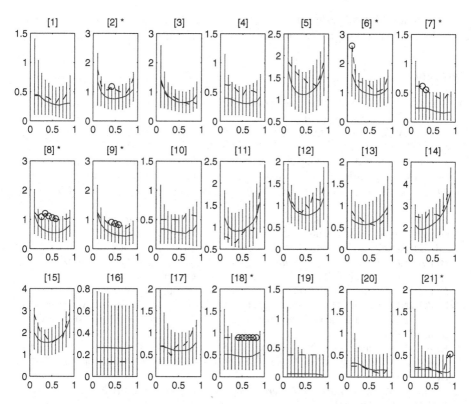

Fig. 3. As per Figure 2, except that a Gaussian Mixture Model fusion classifier is used in place of the mean operator. There are 7 data sets reporting that the EER due to true identity match is *significantly* different from the EER distribution due to random identity match at 95% of confidence, contrary to 8 in Figure 2.

reflecting the real HTER, after performing a large number of fusion experiments (1000 in our case!). However, one should *probably not* use the obtained HTER as a claim that the performance reflects the actual case where the real multimodal datasets are used. The current experimental approach adopted here is somewhat preliminary and in some ways limited in scope. It does not answer for instance, "how far the score distribution estimated with the independence assumption is from the one estimated with the dependence assumption?". Secondly, it does not yet answer the question: "Are the relative HTER values, in contrast to absolute values as done here (e.g., in comparing two fusion methods) *consistent* between experiments with chimeric users and those with true users?". These issues will be dealt with in the near future.

Acknowledgment

This work was supported in part by the IST Program of the European Community, under the PASCAL Network of Excellence, IST-2002-506778, funded in part by the

Swiss Federal Office for Education and Science (OFES) and the Swiss NSF through the NCCR on IM2. This publication only reflects the authors' view.

References

1. A.K. Jain, R. Bolle, and S. Pankanti, *Biometrics: Person Identification in a Networked Society*, Kluwer Publications, 1999.
2. A. Ross, A. Jain, and J-Z. Qian, "Information Fusion in Biometrics," *Pattern Recognition Letter*, vol. 24, no. 13, pp. 2115–2125, September 2003.
3. J. Fierrez-Aguilar, J. Ortega-Garcia, J. Gonzalez-Rodriguez, and J. Bigun, "Kernel-Based Multimodal Biometric Verification Using Quality Signals," in *Defense and Security Symposium, Workshop on Biometric Technology for Human Identification, Proc. of SPIE*, 2004, vol. 5404, pp. 544–554.
4. J-L. Dugelay, J-C. Junqua, K. Rose, and M. Turk, *Workshop on Multimodal User Authentication (MMUA 2003)*, no publisher, Santa Barbara, CA, 11–12 December, 2003.
5. L.I. Kuncheva, "A Theoretical Study on Six Classifier Fusion Strategies," *IEEE Trans. Pattern Analysis and Machine Intelligence*, vol. 24(2), pp. 281–286, February 2002.
6. J. Kittler, M. Hatef, R. P.W. Duin, and J. Matas, "On Combining Classifiers," *IEEE Trans. Pattern Analysis and Machine Intelligence*, vol. 20, no. 3, pp. 226–239, 1998.
7. N. Poh and S. Bengio, "Improving Single Modal and Multimodal Biometric Authentication Using F-ratio Client Dependent Normalisation," Research Report 04-52, IDIAP, Martigny, Switzerland, 2004.
8. K.-A. Toh, X. Jiang, and W.-Y. Yau, "Exploiting Global and Local Decision for Multimodal Biometrics Verification," *IEEE Trans. on Signal Processing*, vol. 52, no. 10, pp. 3059–3072, October 2004.
9. C. Bishop, *Neural Networks for Pattern Recognition*, Oxford University Press, 1999.
10. V. N. Vapnik, *Statistical Learning Theory*, Springer, 1998.
11. A. Jain, K. Nandakumar, and A. Ross, "Score Normalisation in Multimodal Biometric Systems," *Pattern Recognition (to appear)*, 2005.
12. A. Ross and R. Govindarajan, "Feature Level Fusion Using Hand and Face Biometrics," in *Proc. SPIE Conf. on Biometric Technology for Human Identification II*, Orlando, 2005, vol. 5779, pp. 196–204.
13. N. Poh and S. Bengio, "Database, Protocol and Tools for Evaluating Score-Level Fusion Algorithms in Biometric Authentication," Research Report 04-44, IDIAP, Martigny, Switzerland, 2004, Accepted for publication in *AVBPA 2005*.
14. J. Matas, M. Hamouz, K. Jonsson, J. Kittler, Y. Li, C. Kotropoulos, A. Tefas, I. Pitas, T. Tan, H. Yan, F. Smeraldi, J. Begun, N. Capdevielle, W. Gerstner, S. Ben-Yacoub, Y. Abdeljaoued, and E. Mayoraz, "Comparison of Face Verification Results on the XM2VTS Database," in *Proc. 15th Int'l Conf. Pattern Recognition*, Barcelona, 2000, vol. 4, pp. 858–863.
15. J. Lüttin, "Evaluation Protocol for the XM2FDB Database (Lausanne Protocol)," Communication 98-05, IDIAP, Martigny, Switzerland, 1998.
16. Ruud M. Bolle, Nalini K. Ratha, and Sharath Pankanti, "Error analysis of pattern recognition systems: the subsets bootstrap," *Computer Visioin and Image Understanding*, vol. 93, no. 1, pp. 1–33, 2004.
17. M. Keller, J. Mariéthoz, and S. Bengio, "Significance Tests for *bizarre* Measures in 2-Class Classification Tasks," IDIAP-RR 34, IDIAP, 2004.
18. S. Bengio and J. Mariéthoz, "The Expected Performance Curve: a New Assessment Measure for Person Authentication," in *The Speaker and Language Recognition Workshop (Odyssey)*, Toledo, 2004, pp. 279–284.

Analysing Meeting Records: An Ethnographic Study and Technological Implications

Steve Whittaker, Rachel Laban, and Simon Tucker

Department of Information Studies, University of Sheffield, Regent Court,
211 Portobello Street, Sheffield, S1 4DP, UK
{s.whittaker, lip03ral, s.tucker}@shef.ac.uk

Abstract. Whilst there has been substantial research into the support of meetings, there has been relatively little study of how meeting participants currently make records and how these records are used to direct collective and individual actions outside the meeting. This paper empirically investigates current meeting recording practices in order to both understand fundamental collaboration processes and to determine how these might be better supported by technology. Our main findings were that participants create two types of meeting record. Public records are a collectively negotiated contract of decisions and commitments. Personal records, in contrast, are a highly personalised reminding tool, recording both actions and the context surrounding these actions. These observations are then used to informally evaluate current meeting support technology and to suggest new directions for research.

1 Introduction

Despite their importance and prevalence there is a general perception that meetings are not as efficient as they might be. Self-estimates of meeting productivity for many different types of managers range from 33-47% [1]. Early psychological studies of meeting processes identified problems such as process loss and free riding - documenting how individual efforts are dissipated by collective group processes. However, another inefficiency is information loss, i.e. the failure to record important information, decisions and actions and how this affects future actions. Here, we are interested in information capture and use: how people record different types of meeting information and how this affects future individual and collaborative work. Further to this we are interested in how well current technology addresses these needs and what is required to enhance the technological support available to meetings.

Studies of meeting practices examined information capture, documenting the importance of recording semi-structured information such as dates, announcements, phone numbers and names. They have observed a conflict for participants between taking adequate notes and contributing to meetings [2,3,14]. However with some exceptions [2] these studies did not investigate how the captured information was used to direct future individual and collective activities. The same work also explored technologies for capturing discussions. Many of these techniques were invented over

S. Renals and S. Bengio (Eds.): MLMI 2005, LNCS 3869, pp. 101–113, 2006.

10 years ago, but despite their promise, there is still little sign of their being used in meetings. And despite the interest in yet more powerful capture tools [5,6], the predominant 'technologies' used today are pen, paper and whiteboards, and nontraditional technologies such as laptops tend to be used only for private note-taking.

Our study therefore addresses this paradox. We revisit the issue of capture, looking at current recording practices and exploring how they support collective action. We carried out an ethnographic study of two organisations investigating both individual and group practices for recording and representing meeting information. We investigate both the types of records groups and individuals make and what the benefits and problems associated with these records are. We then use these observations to critique current meeting access technology.

2 Participants and Study Context

The setting for our fieldwork was two UK service firms, one responsible for national and international mail deliveries and the other for supplying software services. In each firm we studied a core team through a sequence of multiple meetings. We chose to follow two teams in repeated interactions, rather than a large set of individual meetings, as an important issue concerned how information in earlier meetings was invoked and followed up on in later meetings.

The core teams had 5 and 7 members, and the target meetings had between 3 and 16 participants. This discrepancy arose because not all team members were able to attend all team meetings, and in the software company some meetings included customers from outside the organisation. In the delivery company the meetings were held on a weekly basis and their main objective was reporting and team co-ordination, as the team worked through issues arising during the previous week. In the software services company, meetings were between customers and suppliers. The main objective was to iron out difficulties associated with supply and delivery of services. Both sets of meetings were task-oriented rather than being about idea generation and they tended to be structured around written agendas. In both cases participants were familiar with each other, having worked together for over 6 months.

We collected many different types of data, including observations of participants' behaviour during meetings - when they took notes, when they talked and what they noted down. We carried out interviews with participants before and after meetings, and we analysed private notes and public minutes of the meetings. Overall we observed 7 separate one-hour meetings, generating 12 hours of observation, along with 25 hours of interviews over the course of a three-month period. We also made audio recordings of a subset of 3 meetings and then transcribed these recordings. Our principal observer had previously worked at the delivery company and had also dealt with the software company and was therefore familiar with both companies, allowing her to gain access to employees.

One issue that required careful negotiation was confidentiality. At the outset, we asked all participants whether they were comfortable being observed and recorded. All transcripts were anonymized by removing all identifying information such as participant, supplier and dealer names. All participants were informed that they could stop recordings being made at any point. They were also given copies of the meeting transcripts and asked whether they wanted information to be excised from the transcript and the original record.

We begin by describing the nature and functions of public records of meetings such as minutes. We identify the limitations of minutes, and how participants respond to these problems by taking their own notes in meetings. Next we describe the nature and functions of personal notes, as well as the problems users experience with these.

3   Results

3.1   The Nature and Function of Public Meeting Records

Our participant observations, analysis of minutes and interviews revealed that public records such as minutes had four main functions:

- To track group progress.
- To serve as a public record of past actions and decisions.
- To remind people about their commitments.
- To resolve disputes about commitments.

Minutes are an abstract record of attendees, group decisions, past actions and future commitments. They also document whether previous commitments and actions by group members have been carried out. On some occasions, they might include background information relating to a decision or action, but this tends to be the exception rather than the rule. Minutes are also general: they document all major decisions and actions, rather than focusing on specific aspects of the meeting.

Minutes were used in a variety of ways. People firstly used them as a public record against which to track group progress in order to determine whether recent actions or commitments had been carried out. Meetings often began with a run through the previous meeting's minutes. Participants would quickly review the main items minuted from prior meetings, check whether actions had been carried out, and explore whether there were follow up items resulting from those actions. In this sense minutes help individuals co-ordinate their own actions with each other and with what was publicly agreed. One manager commented:

It is like a checkpoint for me, just to make sure what we are doing is what we agreed we'd do at the last meeting. Are we still on track with what we said we'd do?

Minutes also serve as a long-term archive of the group's commitments and actions. Very occasionally teams would be asked about past events or commitments, and here the minutes were used as the document of record, stating what had been decided or what had been done about a particular issue.

A slightly different function of minutes was to remind people about their commitments. Here minutes serve as a 'todo' list for the various group members detailing their individual commitments. If those commitments have not been met, then other team members or the manager will invoke the minutes as way of enforcing that the action is carried out.

*Minutes are an important record of what we said we'd do and when we said we'd do it.
I go back to them when people aren't happy that a particular situation has occurred
because someone hasn't done something they said they'd do.*

This highlights a critical aspect of minutes - their use as an implicit contract
between the different group members about the actions they each agreed to carry out.
Managers or other team members will refer to the minutes as a way of questioning
individuals about the status of one of their commitments.

*It is generally where something has not happened or something has not gone to plan.
Probably the key thing from my point of view is say two or three weeks after a meeting
has taken place if somebody had agreed to take an action or do something and the
situation has not improved or someone has escalated a problem I'll refer back to the
meeting minutes to find out what was agreed and therefore what somebody should have
done.*

The contractual nature of the minutes is further underlined by the practice we
observed of having people 'sign off' on the minutes. Participants were encouraged to
review the minutes of the prior meeting to correct discrepancies between what was
written in the minutes and what participants recalled being discussed. These
discrepancies need to be resolved before the minutes can become the official
document of record. One manager semi-jokingly used quasi-legal language when
giving team members the opportunity to approve or challenge the minutes: 'are these
minutes a true and fair record of what happened on 24/11?'

In a similar contractual way, minutes are used as the document of record to resolve
group disputes. There were occasional disagreements between team members about
what had been decided. Usually the disputes focused on who had agreed to undertake
an action item. When this happened, rather than relying on memory, the minutes were
used to determine what was agreed:

*I think you find over time that some people are generally more honourable about what
they have said than other people, so some people you can trust what they have said and
that they'll do things, other people will change there mind over time about what they
said they would do and I think perhaps where I have felt in the past that someone has
said something in a meeting and then backed away from it or not done what they have
said then I'll generally capture what they have said or done and I'll make sure it is
minuted.*

3.2 The Limitations of Public Records

Although minutes had clear benefits in serving as a group contract and memory aid,
they nevertheless had several critical failings, including:

- Not all meetings had minutes taken.
- The minutes are occasionally inaccurate.
- The minutes lack sufficient detail to allow participants to carry out personal
  actions or to allow non-attendees to determine what went on in the meeting.
- They are selective sometimes omitting politically sensitive information.
- They are not timely.
- They are laborious to produce.

- They don't capture the experience of being in the meeting.
- They don't capture more peripheral aspects of the meeting such as 'awareness' information that is relevant to the group's functioning but not directly related to a decision or action.

Only 56% of the meetings that we observed had minutes taken. This seemed to depend on factors such as importance, meeting context and meeting type. Minutes were taken more often in the software than the delivery company. A possible reason for this was that the software meetings were contractual in nature involving discussions between customers and suppliers, where various promises were being made about what services would be delivered. Both parties felt that it was advantageous for decisions and commitments to be a matter of record. When there were no minutes participants relied on the manager's notes if these were available, or a combination of different team members' personal notes.

However, even when minutes were taken, participants complained that they had significant limitations. They pointed out that minutes were sometimes inaccurate. All participants routinely checked meeting minutes against what they had personally noted or remembered. They stated this was because important information was occasionally misstated or misrepresented in the minutes. These inaccuracies could arise because a discussion was complex, or poorly structured, or when the official minute-taker was not an expert in the topic under discussion. Inaccuracy is clearly a serious problem if minutes are being used both as a group archive and a contract between members about what they have agreed to do.

if someone else had taken a key action in a meeting I would make a note of that possibly, mainly to compare with the minutes of the meeting when they come out to check whether the meeting minutes were accurate particularly when I think something important or significant has been agreed.

Another major problem was that public minutes often did not provide enough information to allow participants to carry out their individual commitments. Bare statements of action items and who was responsible for each, often did not provide enough background contextual information, making it hard for participants to carry out their action items.

I take notes because the minutes sometimes don't tell me everything I need to know about my own actions.

Lack of detail also meant that it wasn't always clear even to attendees exactly what had happened in the meeting:

if you don't have a more detailed record of the meeting that sometimes you lose the meaning, you lose a lot of the richness about what happened so if you just see actions it doesn't always give you a clear view of what was discussed.

This lack of detail made it even harder for non-attendees to use the minutes to discover what went on at a meeting.

Well normally minutes aren't enough, you need someone to giveyou a briefing afterwards, because the minutes don't tell you everything that has gone on and the discussions that took place.

The minimal nature of minutes also made it hard to revisit prior decisions or reuse prior work. We asked participants whether they ever referred to past minutes when a related issue had occurred in a prior meeting. Again the minutes were felt to be too cursory - providing insufficient context about what had been discussed to make them useful.

Another limitation is that minutes can be selective, containing deliberate omissions such as when there is a politically sensitive discussion. We noted several such 'off record' discussions which were sometimes prefaced by instructing the minute-taker not to minute subsequent comments. Though these off-record comments often contained significant information (on one occasion, unofficial confirmation of a £3.6 million contract was discussed), this was not recorded and was therefore unavailable to non-attendees.

Another factor that undermined the utility of minutes as a group 'todo' list was that they were not timely, often taking several days to produce. If individuals relied on the minutes as a reminder about their outstanding actions, then several days might elapse before they can begin those actions. This not only left them with less time to execute actions before the next meeting, and but also increased the likelihood that they might forget important details associated with those items, especially as minutes tended to record minimal information about each action.

A further problem with minutes is that they are laborious to produce. A meeting participant has to be delegated to take highly detailed notes, reducing their ability to contribute. In addition, transposing these detailed notes, possibly checking their accuracy with various stake-holders, all means additional work.

A less frequently mentioned limit of minutes was they didn't recreate the feeling of being in the meeting. Two participants mentioned wanting records that were richer than descriptions of decisions and actions, saying they wanted to be able to reconstruct the meeting context and what it felt like to be at it:

> it's just not remembering a list of some key points from a meeting but being able to transport yourself back in some instances if you are discussing what happened, so it is more of a transporting your memory back into the actual situation to remember the actual discussion to remember what actually happened.

Another limitation of minutes related to their focus on decisions, actions and commitments. Participants pointed out that a key part of meetings is to provide awareness information, unrelated to specific actions or decisions but which provides a backdrop to the group's activities. Examples here included personnel changes in other groups or high level management. A related point was that an important function of meetings was to establish a culture or modus operandi for the group and that this type of information never appeared in the minutes.

3.3 The Nature and Function of Personal Meeting Records

Participants addressed some of the limitations of public records by taking their own personal notes. 63% of our informants reported that they 'always' took personal notes. The remaining 37% said that they 'sometimes' did so, and pointed to various factors such as chairing meetings - which prevented them from taking their own notes.

It was clear that personal records were highly valued. Most participants routinely took personal notes, which were always accessed, often multiple times. All informants reported referring back to meeting records at least once -with 75% of doing this 'frequently'. Another sign of their importance was that informants took great care to ensure that they were accurate. Half of them 'occasionally' rewrote their notes. Others stated a desire to rewrite their own notes but lacked the time to do this. They also took care to preserve their notes; 75% filed meeting records, keeping these records for a year on average.

Personal notes generally had a less predictable structure than minutes. Like minutes, personal notes mentioned important decisions, names, dates and actions. However one major difference was that personal notes reflected the note-taker's personal perspective, unlike the minutes - which were a general and often formulaic record of what transpired in the meeting.

> *I think my notes are a reflection of the things that interest me, the things that are of a particular interest to me in the meeting. When people are talking but I'm not interested that I don't note anything. My notes are subjective.*

These comments were also supported by our observations, where it was clear that different participants took personal notes at different times and about different agenda items.

In their personal notes, participants often supplemented information about group decisions and actions with detailed factual information they thought they might forget, or which was relevant to the execution of their own personal actions. For example, participants might note personal actions on the right of the page with supporting information on the left. People might also note down actions associated with others if these had relevance for their own activities.

We analysed the content of people's notes. We classified each note depending on whether it concerned decisions, actions, or contextual information. Consistent with minutes, we found that a significant proportion of personal notes concerned decisions (19%) and actions (48%). However in contrast to minutes, we found that 30% of personal notes concerned comments supplying context for actions.

Another characteristic of personal notes is that they could be cryptic, often consisting of a few words about a topic. There are two main reasons for this. Firstly participants are aware that taking detailed notes detracts from their ability to contribute to the discussion, so they write as little as possible. Secondly personal notes are intended to be associative triggers or reminders for the note-taker, rather than verbatim transcripts of exactly what was said. If a participant is highly familiar with a given topic, or if a discussion outcome is exactly what they anticipated, then there is no need to record detailed information, if one or two carefully chosen words will suffice.

> *I don't usually write in sentences sometimes I just write one word that will be enough for me to remember what it was about.*

People's roles also had an important effect on their note-taking. Managers tended to be involved in discussions around most agenda points which meant that they had fewer opportunities to take detailed notes. Note taking strategies were also influenced by whether or not the meeting was being minuted. Specifically, if participants knew that public notes were being taken they tended to take fewer notes.

> *these days I probably tend to take very few notes from meetings generally just things that are of importance to me or actions that I have taken out of a meeting, generally most important meetings would tend to be minuted anyway so I tend to rely on the minutes of the meeting.*

We identified four main reasons why personal records were important to meeting participants:

- As personal reminders.
- To provide enough contextual information to carry out personal actions.
- To check the accuracy of the minutes.
- To brief others about what went on.

We have already seen that a major function of meetings is to agree on various actions that participants will carry out. People therefore take notes to remind themselves about what actions they have committed to. We have seen too, however, that the official minutes may contain insufficient contextual information to allow participants to carry out their actions. The need for context about personal actions explains why personal notes tend to be esoteric and personalised; notes are intended to help participants carry out their own jobs rather than serving as a general public record. In other words, personal notes serve to record personal 'todo' items and their context, which participants fear they may otherwise forget:

> *if I failed to [carry out the action] immediately as time goes on it would start to slip out, there could be key points that I forget, or key actions that I forget to take. With a recorded note I can always check and make sure I've done them, or check what I have to do.*

When no official minutes were taken of the meeting, then personal notes were sometimes shared among attendees to ensure that commitments were not forgotten:

> *I have so many meetings I would forget what happened if I didn't write them down. It is a memory aid for me and quite often it is a memory aid for other people at meetings so quite often other people will come to me and ask me what happened and I'll check my notes and see what I have written down.*

Another important function of personal notes is to check the accuracy of the meeting minutes. All our participants reported using personal notes for this purpose. As the minutes are used both as the document of record and also as a group 'todo' list, participants were keen to ensure that they were accurate, particularly about issues relating to themselves. For 25% of participants checking the minutes was the main function of their notes; after checking the minutes they discarded their own notes.

Finally, personal notes were sometimes used to report what went on in a meeting to non-attendees. However, when personal notes were taken to brief non-attendees, they tended to be less cryptic or personalised. Here note-takers felt they had to provide greater details of all aspects of the meeting that were thought to be relevant to the group being briefed.

3.4 The Limitations of Personal Records

Despite the value of personal notes, participants also complained about their limitations:

- Taking notes reduces one's ability to contribute to discussion
- Personal notes sometimes lack both accuracy and comprehensibility
- Their esoteric nature made them difficult for non-attendees to understand

One major problem was that taking accurate personal notes reduced participants' ability to participate in discussion. Participants' estimates of the time they took note-taking in meetings ranged from 5-40%, and all felt that this compromised their contributions:

> *if you are writing things down you are not listening to what is being said and it is probably more important to listen to what is being said rather than writing your own notes about things that have been discussed previously.*

Indeed one of our informants pointed out that when he was chairing a meeting, he was so focused on the conversation and management of the meeting that he found it impossible to take notes.

This view is supported by our observations of informants. We noted down the frequency of note-taking and contributions to the meeting, and confirmed the expected negative impact of note-taking on people's contributions, with those taking detailed notes contributing least to the conversation

A second limitation of personal notes was that they were sometimes inaccurate or hard to interpret - even for those who had created them. One reason for this was the difficulty of simultaneously taking notes while listening to what is currently being said. Participants found themselves unable to process new information while writing detailed notes about an important prior point. The result was that personal notes could be cursory, disjointed and incomplete.

> *I can't understand my notes all the time probably because I have started to write down what I think I need to capture but then I have heard something else that has stopped me in my tracks, so what I have already written isn't joined up enough to understand what I was supposed to be capturing in the first place.*

Others focused on trying to take fairly minimal notes, allowing them to contribute to and track the conversation, relying on their memories to reconstruct what went on. Again however there are limits to this strategy as such notes often weren't detailed or accurate enough to determine what went on in the meeting or what actions to undertake as follow up.

4 Technological Implications

The observations detailed above have shown that there are clear problems associated with current techniques for the production and use of public and personal meeting records. In a previous paper [7], the state of the art of technology designed to review automatically produced meeting records was examined. Briefly, such systems primarily make audio and video recordings of meetings (although participant notes taken, projected slides, and whiteboard annotations are also often recorded) and then construct indices using raw data which allow users of meeting browsers to access and navigate the meeting record.

As a result of the analysis of current meeting records we are now in a position to critique current meeting browsers with regard to their support for public and personal recordings. It is clear that, in order to be beneficial, browsers should support current record taking practices while addressing their main problems. Below, current meeting browsers are assessed with regard to public and personal meeting records in turn.

4.1 Public Meeting Records

Current meeting browsers are highly focused on *single meetings* and are, therefore, poorly placed to support the collection of data from a long-term series of meetings. In cases where browsers make use of multiple meetings as a raw data set (e.g. [9]) the user is required to search the meeting set in order to identify a point of interest. There is little opportunity to perform a high level analysis on the meeting series; for example, tracking the progress of a task assigned in one meeting over a series of meetings.

Equally, the use of public meeting records as a record of past actions and decisions is not well supported by current meeting browsers. The core of the problem in this area is that there is no associated abstraction over each meeting, similar to the abstract representation of actions and decisions seen in the meeting minutes. There is a further question regarding the *formality* of the meeting record. Recall that one of the uses of public records was as a contractual record of the events of a meeting. It is unlikely, due to the errorful nature of automatically recognised speech, whether such a formal summary of the meeting could be produced. It is unclear, too, whether the verbatim record is too fine grained to perform the same function. It is also unclear whether hybrid access to the meeting record (e.g. [8]) would prove effective. If a more concrete abstract record is required, however, it is likely that browsers could be employed as a tool to clarify and identify key points.

Although current meeting browsers have difficulty in matching the benefits of current public meeting records they are able to overcome some of the problems associated with such records. Most notably since the meeting record is automatically produced public records are no longer laborious to produce, selective, or untimely (although there is some delay in constructing the indices; for example, the transcript is generally produced off line). Furthermore, although there may be errors in the automatically generated annotations, the underlying recording is accurate; any inaccuracies in the annotations can be resolved by reverting to the original recording. It is also possible to determine contextual information, if it is assumed that the indices provided are suitable for locating the relevant points in the meeting.

It is also easier to generate automatic records for all meetings, since a chosen minute taker is no longer required; this also means that the minuter can increase their contribution to the meeting. Most meeting recording systems are, however, designed for a specific room where the setup and calibration of the recording equipment is relatively straightforward to maintain. There is, therefore, a requirement that, to be recorded, meetings take place in this specific room. This precludes spontaneous meetings which research has shown are prevalent [4]. A novel approach to addressing this problem is outlined in [10], with the use of a portable recording device which allows for audio and video recording; whiteboard annotations, notes etc. are not included in this recording.

Finally, it is difficult to say whether browsing a meeting will account for the more peripheral experiences in which the public records were described to be lacking. It is clear that the inclusion of audio-visual recordings should increase the experience of attending the meeting compared with a textual record and, since a verbatim record is produced, no information is lost in the meeting record. Novel browsers which aim to construct virtual meeting spaces (e.g. [11]) may be required to fully present an immersive meeting review environment.

4.2 Personal Meeting Records

Personal meeting records are less concerned with providing information for long-term analysis and so the supplementation of these records is less problematic for current meeting browsers. The personalised nature of such records are not often reflected in meeting browsers, however mappings between personal notes and meeting records are well described in the literature (e.g. [2]). Filochat [14], for example, allows the user to take notes as they normally would, these notes then acting as an index into a recording of the meeting. Whilst such systems are typically successful, current media rich meeting browsers (e.g. [13,6,13]) do not yet leverage the use of this functionality - although it is likely that personal notes could form an index which could be used by such browsers.

Most of the benefits of personal notes such as providing contextual information, to check the accuracy of public records and to brief others about the meeting are addressed by current meeting browsers. However, current meeting browsers are built around low level annotations (e.g. speaker turns, presented slides etc.) and do not support the extraction of personal actions. Browsers which index personal notes taken during the meeting can support this process but the support is inherently indirect. In Filochat, for example, there is no explicit way of qualifying the purpose of the each note -the user must generate their own notation to achieve this. It is possible that, in the future, text processing techniques can be used to determine the purpose of each note and can supplement these indices

Personal records are no longer required to brief others about the meeting since non-attendees can now just have access the meeting record. Again, however, the problem of abstraction is raised since a non-attendee has no means of quickly determining the salient points of a meeting; for example, there is no means of identifying the actions that were assigned to them. The problem of personal notes being too esoteric for sharing no longer applies and, furthermore, there is arguably considerable information to be gathered from a group analysis of note taking practices of the meeting participants [14] that would not be possible without the automatic processing.

A significant problem with personal notes, as noted in our observations, was that taking notes reduces the ability to participate in the meeting. Whilst meeting browsers do not necessarily negate the need to take notes, it can be seen that the time required to note something is significantly reduced if personal notes are being used to construct an index into the meeting since the note need not include all the contextual information required [2,4].

4.3 Summary

Due to the reciprocal nature of public and personal meeting records, the current generation of meeting browsers are largely able to both address the limitations of public records and replicate the benefits of personal records. The main failings of meeting browsers seem to be that they are largely only able to offer a view of a single meeting, that there is not layer of abstraction between the user and the underlying data and annotations and finally that data collected from personal notes are not exploited in media rich meeting browsers. Furthermore, an unanswered question is whether a formal set of minutes are required now that users have access to the verbatim record.

5   Conclusion

Our study shows how two types of public and personal record are used together to co-ordinate different aspects of collaborative activity. Minutes are a minimal description of collectively agreed actions and decisions serving as a contract and group archive. However individuals supplement these with personal notes that are customised, providing themselves with information that allows them to carry out their personal objectives, as well as to check the veracity of the official minutes. Our analysis of new technical opportunities indicates that current browsers lack abstractions but there is much leverage to be gained by exploiting more data sources.

Acknowledgements

This work was partly supported by the European Union 6th FWP IST Integrated Project AMI (Augmented Multi-party Interaction, FP6-506811, publication AMI-97).

References

1. Green, W.A., and Lazarus, H.: Are today's executives meeting with success, Journal of Management Development (10) 1, (1991), 14-25.
2. Moran, T.P., Palen, L., Harrison, S., Chiu, P., Kimber, D., Minneman, S., Melle, W. and Zellweger, P.:"I'll get that off the audio": A Case study of salvaging multimedia meeting records. In: Proceedings of the CHI '97, Atlanta, Georgia (1997).
3. Wilcox, L., Schilit, B.N., and Sawhney, N.: Dynomite: A Dynamically Organized Ink And Audio Notebook. In: Proceedings of CHI 97, Atlanta, Georgia (1997).
4. Whittaker, S., P. Hyland, and M. Wiley: Filochat: Handwritten Notes Provide Access To Recorded Conversations. In: Proceedings of CHI '94, Boston, Massachusetts, USA (1994).
5. Chiu, P., Boreczky, J., Girgensohn, A., Kimber, D.: LiteMinutes: An Internet-Based System For Multimedia Meeting Minutes. In: Proceedings of 10th WWW Conference, Hong Kong (2001) 140-149.

6. Cutler, R., Rui, Y., Gupta, A., Cadiz, J.J., Tashev, I., He, L., Colburn, A., Zhang, Z., Liu, Z. and Silverberg, S.: Distributed Meetings: A Meeting Capture And Broadcasting System. In: Proc. of the 10th ACM International Conference on Multimedia (2002), 503-512.

7. Tucker, S., Whittaker, S.: Accessing Multimodal Meeting Data: Systems, Problems and Possibilities, In: Bengio, S., Bourlard, H. (Eds.) LectureNotes In Computer Science, 3361, (2005) 1-11.

8. Whittaker, S., Hitschberg, J., Amento, B., Stark, L., Bacchiani, M., Isenhour, P., Stead, L., Zamchick, G., Rosenberg, A.: SCANMail: A Voicemail Interface That Makes Speech Browsable, Readable and Searchable. In: Proceedings of CHI 2002, Minneapolis, Minnesota, USA (2002)

9. Colbath, S. and Kubala, F.: Rough 'n' Ready: A Meeting Recorder and Browser. In: Proceedings of the Perceptual User Interface Conference, November 1998, San Francisco, CA. (1998), 220-223

10. Lee, D., Erol, B., Graham, J., Hull, J.J., and Murata, N.:, Portable Meeting Recorder. In: Proceedings of the ACM Multimedia (2002), 493-502.

11. Reidsma, D., Akker, R., Rienks, R., Poppe, R., Poppe, R., Nijholt, A., Heylen, D. and Zwiers, J.: Virtual Meeting Rooms: From Observation to Simulation. In: Proceedings of Social Intelligence Design, (2005).

12. Wellner, P., Flynn, M. and Guillemot, M.: Browsing Recordings of Multi-party Interactions in Ambient Intelligent Environments, In: CHI 2004 Workshop #9: Lost in Ambient Intelligence, (2004).

13. Lalanne, D., Sire, S., Ingold, R., Behera, A., Mekhaldi, D. and Rotz, D: A Research Agenda For Assessing The Utility Of Document Annotations In Multimedia Databases Of Meeting Recordings. In: Proceedings of the 3rd International Workshop on Multimedia Data And Document Engineering, Berlin, Germany (2003).

14. Davis, R.C., Landay, J.A., Chen, V., Huang, J., Lee, R.B., Li, F.C., Lin, J., Morrey, C.B., Schleimer, B., Price, M.N., Schilit, B.N.:NotePals: Lightweight Sharing by the Group, for the Group, In: Proceedings of CHI 99, (1999) 338-345.

Browsing Multimedia Archives Through Intra- and Multimodal Cross-Documents Links

Maurizio Rigamonti, Denis Lalanne, Florian Evéquoz, and Rolf Ingold

DIVA Group, Department of Informatics, University of Fribourg, Bd. de Pérolles 90,
CH-1700 Fribourg, Switzerland
{firstname.lastname}@unifr.ch
http://diuf.unifr.ch/diva

Abstract. This article proposes to consider all the links existing between documents, as a new artifact for browsing through multimedia archives. In particular, links between static documents and other media are presented in this article
through Inquisitor, FriDoc and FaericWorld, i.e. three distinct document-centric
systems, which allow (a) browsing (b) validation of annotations, and (c) edition
of annotations or documents. *Inquisitor* illustrates the intra-document links between a raw document and its abstract representations. It is the base level, i.e.
the closest to the raw media. *FriDoc* illustrates the cross-documents links, in
particular temporal ones, between documents at the event level, which strictly
connect documents captured at the same occasion (e.g. a meeting, a conference,
etc.). Finally, *FaericWorld* proposes cross-documents linking as a novel artifact
for browsing and searching through a cross-event multimedia library. This article describes those three systemvs and the various types of links that can be
built between documents. Finally, the paper presents the result of a user evaluation of *FriDoc* and briefly discusses the usefulness of cross-documents linking,
and in particular document alignments, for browsing through multimedia
archives.

1 Introduction

Graphical user interfaces to textual-document libraries are good and getting better, but
search and browsing interfaces in multimedia-document libraries are still in their early
stages of development [13]. Most existing systems are mono-modal and allow searching for images, videos, sound, etc. For this reason, current researches in image and
video analysis target to automatically create indexes and pictorial video summaries to
help users browse through multimedia corpuses. However, those methods are often
based on low-level visual features and lack of semantic information. High-level index
carrying semantic information are hard to extract through a complete automatic recognition and human manual annotation is too costly to be considered. Even though
high-level index are missing, few mono-modal systems succeed to provide browsing
artifacts for filtering information and displaying the relevant one. For image search
and browsing, Janecek [3] proposed an interface based on semantic fisheye views,
which uses alternatively similarity- or semantic-guided browsing for exploring a

S. Renals and S. Bengio (Eds.): MLMI 2005, LNCS 3869, pp. 114–125, 2006.

manually and professionally labeled collection. Another remarkable system dealing with images is *Flamenco* [16] that uses hierarchical faceted metadata to navigate. Videos management and retrieval is the aim of *ViCoDe* project [10], which uses similarity between various features to sort the collection. Finally, Hu and Dannenberg [2] proposed a system for retrieving music information using sung queries. However, a good example of successful multimedia browsing system is harder to find.

There is a recent significant research trend on recording and analyzing meetings [7], mostly in order to advance the research on multimodal content analysis and on multimedia information retrieval, which are key features for designing future communication systems, dealing with multi-modal archives. Many research projects aim at archiving meeting recordings in suitable forms for later browsing and retrieval. *Ferret* [17] is a framework for prototyping and testing meeting browsers into an event-based context, where instances of different media coexist within a specific meeting. *Archivus* [9] extends the concept of intra-event navigation, and uses constraint-based searching mechanisms to browse a collection of meetings through a library metaphor where books represent meetings. Various taxonomies of meeting browsers have been already proposed; Tucker and Whittaker organized meeting browsers according to the type of control stream they use: video, audio and artifact browsers [15]. Lalanne and Sire [5] proposed earlier a complete taxonomy based on the type of streams handled, control streams, derived streams and finally higher-level annotations available. However, most of these projects do not take into account the printed documents that are often parts of the information available during a meeting and in our daily lives. We believe printable documents could provide a natural and thematic mean for browsing and searching through large multimedia repository.

2   Using Links as a Browsing Artifact

Even though search engines like Google are nowadays very powerful, defining the proper query is not a one-step process and requires several trials. Browsing thus remains very useful when users do not have enough knowledge of the domain in order to know how and what to look for. Furthermore, searching through multimedia archives is often limited due to the difficulty to produce automatically high-level semantic annotations from audio, image and video streams.

Document linking has been recently used as a way to structure information and to bypass searching lacks [5, 6]. For instance, *citeseer* [1] uses various mechanisms in order to connect scientific publications through citation links mainly, i.e. bibliographical references, but also through similarity calculations, or simply by linking documents having the same author or belonging to the same website. In this case, links become the main browsing artifact and users can access similar documents, related documents, or even use the most linked publications as entry points to a novel domain. *Kartoo* and *Alice in Wonderland* also use similarity and hyper links as an artifact for browsing [4, 14]. Finally, *LinkedIn* uses the social links between persons as a way to create thematic communities [8].

This article proposes to design and implement link-based systems for navigating, editing and validating a multimedia world composed of documents. Those documents can be raw media, combination of media and annotations, or even clusters of documents. Our main hypothesis is that cross-documents linking mechanisms is a way to connect independent multimedia documents and de facto a powerful artifact for browsing through multimedia archives. Inquisitor and FriDoc are two document-centric systems we implemented, which operate at different levels of granularity in a multimedia archive and offer complementary functionalities. FaericWorld build upon these experiences to create a linked multimedia world. First, this paper presents Inquisitor, a system specialized for validating static documents analysis and recognition tools. This system will illustrate the creation of a new annotation and its linking with the media stream, i.e. the raw document. In the rest of this paper, a link between raw data and its annotations is called an **intra-document link**. The next system presented is FriDoc, a system implemented and evaluated for replaying and browsing through meeting recordings. A user evaluation of FriDoc is presented that shows that document-centric alignment allows using static documents as structured and thematic vectors towards multimedia meeting archives. The multimodal relationships in FriDoc illustrate **cross-documents links**. Finally, FaericWorld will present a multimedia document world composed of heterogeneous media and multimodal cross-documents links. All the links and media used in these three complementary systems are summarized respectively in table 1 and 2.

Table 1. Links supported by the systems. The top of the table represents links hierarchie.

			link			
				cross-document		
				thematic	strict (un-weighted)		
type		intra-document	(weighted)	temporal	reference	hyperlink
system	Inquisitor	√				
	FriDoc	√	√	√	√	
	FaericWorld	√	√	√	√	√

Table 1 classifies cross-documents links according to two main sub-categories: thematic and strict relationships. Thematic links are weighted ($0 < w < 1$), in order to characterize the similarities between two documents content. At opposite, strict links are un-weighted links, i.e. with distance $w = 1$, and can represent different relationships such as:

1. A temporal coexistence of media (e.g. within a meeting, a video recorded at time t coexists with a static document discussed at the same time t);
2. Bibliographic references, citations, authors' name, etc. are implicit reference to other related documents;
3. Hyperlinks are explicit references.

Table 2. Relationship between systems and documents

		Document			
		Media	Multimedia	People	Events
system	Inquisitor	√			
	FriDoc	√	√		√
	FaericWorld	√	√	√	√

Table 2 presents the document types supported by Inquisitor, FriDoc and Faeric-World. Media are either instances of static documents (i.e. newspapers, articles, etc.), images, videos, or audio recordings. Multimedia documents are composed of various types of media (e.g. slideshows or websites containing textual part, images and videos). People consist in the information related to single person or groups (i.e. person name, its publications, etc.). Finally, events are clusters of independent media, multimedia documents and people, which coexist within a particular time interval, context and geographical area. Conferences and meetings are good example of events.

Table 3. Functionalities offered by the systems

		Document		
		Navigation	Edition	Validation
system	Inquisitor	√	√	√
	FriDoc	√		
	FaericWorld	√	√	√

Table 3 shows the different tasks supported by the systems: the **navigation** consists in browsing through archives, in order to retrieve or look for specific information; the **edition** allows end-users to modify, delete or create documents, annotations and links in the world; finally, the **validation** is an edition sub-task provided to interact with incremental systems that exploits users feedbacks for learning. For instance, the validation of logical structures could consist in accepting or refusing a logical label.

To wrap it up, Inquisitor is handling relationships within static documents; FriDoc is cross-documents and uses document alignment for browsing through meeting recordings; finally, FaericWorld is also a cross-documents system, using static documents as a way to connect all types of media.

3 Inquisitor: Editing and Validating Documents' Annotations for Further Multimodal Cross-Documents Linking

Inquisitor focuses on printable electronic documents, e.g. books, articles, newspapers, which are defined as **static documents**. Inquisitor is therefore a system, which is used to (a) visualize a single static document, its annotations and the existing intra-document links, (b) validate annotations and links and finally (c) edit them. Since static documents are considered being a meaningful entry point for cross-media navigation in FriDoc and FaericWorld, the main conceptual task of Inquisitor is to prepare these static documents and ensure the consistency of annotations.

In the context of static documents, the physical structure is the base annotation, which is directly derived from the raw media, i.e. a PDF document, and can be extracted automatically using classical methods of document analysis. Other annotations include the reading order, the logical structure, the table of content, the thumbnail view, etc. Those derived annotations can be computed either automatically using recognizers or manually by the user. Physical structures are composed of clusters grouping homogenous document primitives (text, graphics and images), which respect topologic, stylistic and typographic proximity. Fig. 1 shows an example of (a) a newspaper page and (b) its physical structure. The logical structure regroups the physical blocks, logically labeled, in a logical hierarchy. For instance, physical blocks of a newspaper belong to articles, which are composed of titles, authors, body, etc. Fig.1 (c) represents the newspaper segmented into articles. In general, physical structures can be represented in a universal form for all types of documents whereas logical structures depend on a specific class of document. Finally, other document annotations will be derived from already existing ones. For instance, a table of content will be represented as a list of links on the title of all the articles delimited by the logical structure.

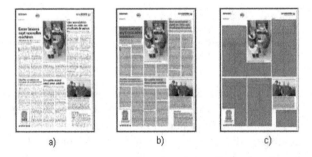

Fig. 1. An example of document (a) enriched with physical (b) and logical structures (c)

There are two levels of links in Inquisitor. The first level of links connects the base annotation to the raw data; in our case, it is the document physical structure. The second level of links is cross-annotations and connects various document annotations. For instance, the previous table of content is linked with the document logical structure, which is itself linked with the document physical structure.

Fig. 2 illustrates the visualization paradigm of Inquisitor: the document itself is represented as an image; physical structures are drawn as rectangles superposed on the image, reinforcing the strict relationship between this base annotation and the raw data; successive annotations, such as the logical structure, are represented with rhombs, in order to clearly separate first level annotations, i.e. based directly on raw-data, from the derived ones.

Fig. 2. The logical structure is linked with the physical structure, and the physical structure is itself linked with the document image using rectangles superposed to document image

Inquisitor supports users through three different tasks, i.e. 1) mono-modal naviga-tion, 2) validation of annotations and links and finally 3) their edition.

The validation task is inherited from systems for supervised analysis of documents [13]. In fact, the content of the documents handled by Inquisitor is first extracted from PDF files and structured in a canonical XML format [12]. Further, the physical struc-ture can be automatically labeled and structured in a logical hierarchy. Concerning the validation of the physical structure, Inquisitor major functionalities are merging, split-ting, resizing and moving of blocks, in order to correct over- and under-segmentation errors of extraction. On the other hand, validation of others annotations consist either in correcting wrong logical labels, either in modifying, destroying and creating intra- or cross-annotations links. Fig. 3 shows (a) a menu for labeling text blocks and (b) the fusion of an over-segmented text block. Actually, validation guarantees annotations consistency and consequently allows a valid mono-modal navigation.

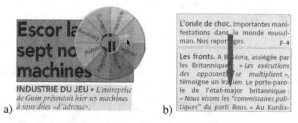

Fig. 3. Inquisitor supports (a) the labeling of physical text blocks and (b) the fusion of blocks. The arrow is a graphical artifact for defining the source and destination implied in the merging operation.

The creation of new annotations fully uses the link metaphor. Users firstly create a novel abstraction (i.e. a cluster of rhombs and links such as in fig. 2) and, secondly, connect the latter and the already existing ones through intra-document links. For instance, creating a table of content consist in 1) building a new annotation that contains a hierarchical structure composed of *table* entities and 2) link the latter with document logical blocks (titles, figures, etc.).

Finally, Inquisitor's last task is the navigation, which fully takes benefit from the validated annotations and links. The physical structure highlights the different regions of the original document whereas the logical structure and other similar annotations are interfaces to access the structured document content. For instance, users clicking on the title of the document table-of-content will access the related document zone.

4 FriDoc: Document-Centric Multimedia Meeting Browsing

FriDoc [6] is a multimedia meeting browser that plays synchronously meeting documents using cross-documents links. Users can first search at a cross-meeting level (Fig. 4.a), by typing a combination of keywords, in order to retrieve all the relevant static documents. In fact, the navigation paradigm is first of all document-centric; Clicking on a chosen static document open all the linked multimedia data in the intra-meeting navigator (Fig. 4.b), in which all the components (static documents, audio/video, transcription, and annotations) are fully synchronized through the meeting time, thanks to the document alignments; clicking on one of them causes all the components to visualize their content at the same time. For instance, clicking on a journal article positions audio/video clips at the time when it was discussed, scrolls the speech transcription at the same time, and displays the document that was projected.

Fig. 4. In FriDoc, both cross (a) and intra-meeting navigation are available (b)

The TileBar visualization at the bottom of the interface represents the complete meeting's duration. It is a visual overview of the overall meeting and can serve as a control bar. Each layer stands for a different temporal annotation: speaker turns, utterances, document logical blocks and slides projected. Those temporal annotations hold timestamps for each state change (i.e. new speaker, new topic, slide change, etc.) and spatial information for documents. For example, the speech transcript contains speaker turns, divided in speech utterances, with their corresponding start and end times. The TileBar reveals the temporal links and semantic relationships between meeting annotations and can potentially bring to light synergies or conflicts, and new methods in order to improve the automatic generation of annotations.

About 30 meetings, i.e. roughly eight hours of multimedia meeting recordings, have been integrated in FriDoc. Based on those data, a user evaluation has been performed on 8 users. The goal was to measure the usefulness of document alignments for browsing and searching through a multimedia meeting archive. Users' performance in answering questions, both mono-modal and multimodal has been measured on both qualitative and quantitative basis (e.g. task duration, number of clicks, satisfaction, etc.). Mono-modal questions involve looking through one modality to answer ("What did Florian say about Iraq?"), whereas multi-modal questions require inspecting at least two modalities. For instance, "Which articles of the Herald Tribune's front page have not been discussed during the press review meeting?" requires both looking at the speech transcript to know which articles have been discussed and consulting the newspaper's content to have the complete list of articles. The 8 users, mostly students in computer science among which several women, had to answer in total to 8 questions (4 mono-modals and 4 multi), with a limited time for answering of 5 minutes per question, using two exact similar prototypes in order to avoid measuring their usability instead of the document alignments usefulness. One prototype had the document alignments enabled, and the other one not. Questions have been prepared so that their complexities were balanced over the 2 meetings used for the evaluation and over the 2 prototypes tested.

76% of the questions have been solved when users disposed of the document alignments, whereas 66% without. The performance difference becomes particularly significant for multi-modal questions, i.e. requiring information from at least two modalities, where around 70% of the questions were solved when users were benefiting from the alignments and 50% of the questions were solved without. This user evaluation shows that static documents are good vectors to access other media and that document multimodal alignments improve user performances in browsing and searching through multimedia meeting recordings.

5 FaericWorld: Multimedia Archives Management

Currently, FaericWorld is at its early development and intends to visualize at a glance a large collection of heterogeneous multimedia documents, which belong to all the categories presented in section 2 (media, multimedia, people and events). The collection is considered as being a **world**, where documents are connected through cross-documents links and in which clusters are developed around static documents: media exist in the world only if linked with static documents.

Figure 5 shows an image of a low fidelity prototype of FaericWorld, which is composed of the following parts:

1. On the background, static documents in the world are connected by cross-documents links, i.e. thematic similarities, implicit references and hyperlinks;
2. On the foreground, the currently selected static document is used as an hyper-mark to access a cluster of linked media;
3. On the left, the navigation artifacts, dynamic queries and filtering criteria can be defined such as media types, links layers, and annotations to take into account.

The major tasks targeted by FaericWorld are: 1) the cross-media navigation, 2) the validation of annotations and links and 3) the annotation and creation of new documents, hyper-linking regions of the world.

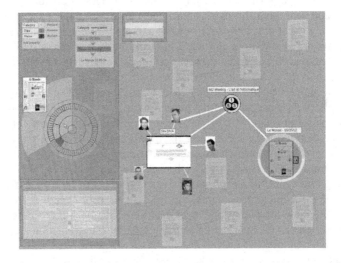

Fig. 5. An overview of FaericWorld built around static documents and events

The navigation allows users to consult and retrieve documents. Static documents and links are the main artifact for browsing into FaericWorld. In fact, queries and filter criteria create a focused view of the world, where only linked clusters of static documents are visualized. Selecting a static document allows accessing to all the other media, connected through cross-documents links. Moreover, each category of document and each link discovered during the navigation can be used as filters for refining the users query.

The documents world can be organized for navigation using quantity of links per document, category of connected media and other basic criteria. An alternative organization consists in creating a different world representation through layers, which filter the media to display in function of link types selected by the user. These filtering features not only take into account the existing cross-documents links such as citation or thematic distance, but also create dynamic links between documents thanks to annotations such as the logical structure or the thematic relationships between documents. Fig. 6 illustrates the various phases necessary for organizing the world, using an inverse sunburst-menu as a hierarchical representation of the world, where each level of the tree corresponds to a filtering feature, e.g. the date, type of document, theme, etc.

Another mechanism envisioned for pre-structuring the world for browsing is based on textual queries. A research is launched on static documents content, fulfilling the query when the searched words belong to content linked with at least an annotation. For instance, a collection of results is restituted because logical or physical structures contain the word sequence in a unique textual block.

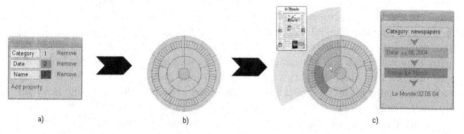

Fig. 6. A possible entry point to our FaericWorld based on (a) criteria definition, (b) the corresponding hierarchical view of the world, where first criterion belongs to external circle and last one to second from center and finally (c) the selection of a portion of the world

The validation task ensures the consistency of the world and allows refining automatic indexing systems. In fact, this task consists in validating annotations, i.e. creating or destroying links established between documents. For instance, we currently compute annotations and links automatically using our tools specialized for static documents. Currently, mono-modal extraction of PDF document physical structure is almost perfect and document alignment is robust. Future works will provide automatically annotations such as logical structures and category of static documents. FaericWorld is a validation platform and will help evaluating and correcting multimodal indexing systems.

Finally, the edition task consists in creating completely new documents and annotations linking on existing information. For instance, this edition task will allow the creation of meeting minutes, table of content, etc. and in general views of the world.

To wrap it up, the following use-case illustrates how to browse a collection of documents with FaericWorld in order to find the image of a painting discussed during a meeting. The user remembers an article of newspapers discussed during the same meeting, or a meeting participant name, or any piece of information. Browsing works by association. For example the user types the name of the newspaper, then selects the time interval corresponding to the meeting and asks the system to retrieve all the related images and filters them according to the color feature that he remembers well being yellow. The user finally finds the painting and depending on the filter or linker selected can find by association all the related information, e.g. the biography of the painter, all the audio/video recording in which a speaker talked about it, other painting by the same artist, etc.

6 Conclusion

Nowadays, browsing is well supported when dealing with large databases of textual documents. Various research projects have investigated novel retrieval strategies to search and browse through multimedia libraries containing either images, videos or audio data, with successful and interesting results, but highlighting the difficulty of indexing automatically those media. Other recent projects have explored novel interaction paradigms for browsing through multi-modal event recordings, such as meetings, lectures or conferences. However, most of those browsers ignore static documents, from which it is possible to extract robustly high-level indexes. Because of their intrinsic structures and textual content, static documents constitute good thematic and structured vectors to multimedia archives, when linked with other media. We have shown in this paper that using static documents structures together with multimodal document linking methods can greatly improve search and browsing in multimedia meeting archives. In particular, this paper presents two main categories of links: intra- and cross-documents links. On one hand, intra-document links connect annotations to raw-data and allow creating incrementally other annotations on the document; on the other hand, cross-documents links cluster multimedia data together and enrich mutually connected documents. Links between documents can be easily created using basic techniques and as such can be good vectors for transmitting information from automatically richly-annotated documents to weakly-annotated ones such as videos, images or sound.

In this paper we presented three complementary document-centric systems, fully implementing this idea of intra-document links and multimodal cross-documents links for browsing in large multimedia collections. Inquisitor is the first system, the base system, which allows validating and editing static documents' annotations such as physical and logical structures, which are interconnected by the way of intra-documents links. The validation in Inquisitor ensures the consistency of the derived data and further can be used for indexing other media. FriDoc is a document-centric multimedia meeting browser. It uses static documents structures to access to linked multimedia data and annotations. All the meeting multimedia data are synchronized on the meeting time through document alignment techniques. A preliminary evaluation of FriDoc demonstrated that document alignments, i.e. cross-documents links, improve user performances in browsing multimedia archives. Finally, FaericWorld allows browsing in a large cross-media library. The main motivation of FaericWorld is to fully use multimodal cross-documents links, at first between static documents and other media, for creating thematic and strictly related clusters.

Future works include 1) assessing Inquisitor usability with a user evaluation, 2) implementing the first FaericWorld prototype along with a preliminary evaluation, 3) developing of rapid means for extracting other annotations that can be useful for browsing and finally 4) integrating in a common framework the three systems presented in this paper.

References

1. Bollacker, K. D., Lawrence, S., Lee Giles, C.: CiteSeer: an autonomous web agent for automatic retrieval and identification of interesting publications. 2nd International Conference on Autonomous Agents, ACM Press, New York, USA (1998) 116-123

2. Hu, N., Dannenberg, R. B.: A comparison of Melodic Database Retrieval Techniques Using Sung Queries. International Conference on Digital Libraries, Proceedings of the 2nd ACM/IEEE-CS joint conference on Digital libraries, Portland, USA (2002) 301-307

3. Janecek, P., Pu, P.: An Evaluation of Semantic Fisheye Views for Opportunistic Search in an Annotated Image Collection, Journal of Digital Libraries, 5 (1). Special Issue on Information Visualization Interfaces for Retrieval and Analysis, (2005) 42-56

4. Kartoo, http://www.kartoo.com

5. Lalanne, D., Sire, Ingold, R., Behera, A., Mekhaldi, D., von Rotz, D.: A research agenda for assessing the utility of document annotations in multimedia databases of meeting recordings. 3rd International Workshop on Multimedia Data and Document Engineering, in conjunction with VLDB-2003, Berlin, Germany (2003) 47-55

6. Lalanne, D., Ingold, R., von Rotz, D., Behera, A., Mekhaldi, D., Popescu-Belis, A.:Using static documents as structured and thematic interfaces to multimedia meeting archives. In Bourlard, H., Bengio S. (eds.), LNCS:, Multimodal Interaction and Related Machine Learning Algorithms, Springer-Verlag, Berlin Germany (2004) 87-100.

7. Lalanne, D., Lisowska, A., Bruno, E., Flynn, M., Georgescul, M., Guillemot, M., Janvier, B., Marchand-Maillet, S., Melichar, M., Moenne-Loccoz, N. Popescu-Belis, A., Rajman, M., Rigamonti, M., von Rotz, D., Wellner, P.: The IM2 Multimodal Meeting Browser Family, IM2 technical report, (2005)

8. LinkedIn, https://www.linkedin.com

9. Lisowska, A., Rajman, M., Bui, T.H.: ARCHIVUS: A System for Accessing the Content of Recorded Multimodal Meetings. Proceedings of the Joint AMI/PASCAL/IM2/M4 Workshop on Multimodal Interaction and Related Machine Learning Algorithms, Martigny, Switzerland, (2004) 291-304

10. Marchand-Maillet, S., Bruno, E.: Collection Guiding: A new framework for handling large multimedia collections. First Workshop on Audio-visual Content and Information Visualization In Digital Libraries, AVIVDiLib05, Cortona, Italy, (2005)

11. Rigamonti, M., Bloechle, J.-L., Hadjar, K., Lalanne, D., Ingold, R.: Towards a Canonical and Structured Representation of PDF Documents through Reverse Engineering, ICDAR 2005, Seoul, Korea (2005) 1050-1054

12. Rigamonti, M., Hitz, O., Ingold, R.: A Framework for Cooperative and Interactive Analysis of Technical Documents. Fifth IAPR International Workshop on Graphics Recognition, Barcelona, Spain (2003) 407-414

13. Shneiderman, B., Plaisant, C.: Designing the User Interface: Strategies for Effective Human-Computer Interaction (4th Edition), Addison-Wesley, Hardcover, 4th edition, Published March 2004, 652 pages

14. Alice in Wonderland, TextArc, http://www.textarc.org/

15. Tucker, S., Whittaker, S.: Accessing Multimodal Meeting Data: Systems, Problems and Possibilities. LNCS 3361, Machine Learning for Multimodal Interaction, Springer, New York, USA (2004) 1-11

16. Yee, K.-P., Swearingen, K., Li, K., Hearst, M.: Faceted Metadata for Image Search and Browsing. Proceedings of the SIGCHI conference on Human factors in computing systems, Ft. Lauderdale, USA (2003) 401-408

17. Wellner, P., Flynn, M., Tucker, S., Whittaker, S.: A Meeting Browser Evaluation Test, Presented at the Conference on Human Factors in Computing Systems), Portland, Oregon, USA (2005) 2021-2024

The "FAME" Interactive Space

F. Metze[1], P. Gieselmann[1], H. Holzapfel[1], T. Kluge[1], I. Rogina[1], A. Waibel[1],
M. Wölfel[1], J. Crowley[2], P. Reignier[2], D. Vaufreydaz[2], F. Bérard[3], B. Cohen[3],
J. Coutaz[3], S. Rouillard[3], V. Arranz[4], M. Bertrán[4], and H. Rodriguez[4]

[1] Universität Karlsruhe (TH)
[2] Institut National Polytechnique de Grenoble (INPG)
[3] Université Joseph Fourier (UJF), Grenoble
[4] Universitat Politecnica de Catalunya (UPC), Barcelona
metze@ira.uka.de
http://www.fame-project.org/

Abstract. This paper describes the "FAME" multi-modal demonstrator, which integrates multiple communication modes – vision, speech and object manipulation – by combining the physical and virtual worlds to provide support for multi-cultural or multi-lingual communication and problem solving.

The major challenges are automatic perception of human actions and understanding of dialogs between people from different cultural or linguistic backgrounds. The system acts as an information butler, which demonstrates context awareness using computer vision, speech and dialog modeling. The integrated computer-enhanced human-to-human communication has been publicly demonstrated at the FORUM2004 in Barcelona and at IST2004 in The Hague.

Specifically, the "Interactive Space" described features an "Augmented Table" for multi-cultural interaction, which allows several users at the same time to perform multi-modal, cross-lingual document retrieval of audio-visual documents previously recorded by an "Intelligent Cameraman" during a week-long seminar.

1 Introduction

Current advances in language and vision technology as well as user interface design are making possible new tools for human-human communication. Integration of speech, vision, dialog, and object manipulation offers the possibility of a new class of tools to aid communication between people from different cultures using different languages.

The "FAME" project (EU FP5 IST-2000-28323) develops a new vision for computer interfaces, which replaces and extends conventional human-computer interaction by computer-enhanced human-to-human (CEHH) interaction. The crucial difference lies in the role that the computer plays and the demands it makes on the human user's attention in a living and working environment.

Like an invisible information butler, such systems observe and learn their users' ways and preferences, and "understand" enough about the context and purpose of their activity, to be able to provide helpful and supportive services that are informed by, and appropriate for that context. A broad range of applications can profit from CEHH interfaces, including office work, communication, entertainment and many more. What

S. Renals and S. Bengio (Eds.): MLMI 2005, LNCS 3869, pp. 126–137, 2006.

is common in most of these settings is that the goal and preoccupation of visitors is to interact with other humans and not with machines.

The work presented here demonstrates an interactive space using intelligent agents to facilitate communication among researchers from different linguistic backgrounds, who discuss several scientific topics, which have been presented at a seminar series. The agents provide three services:

1. Provide information relevant to context, i.e. make users aware of existing information in an audio-visual database, then retrieve and present it appropriately
2. Facilitate human to human communication through multi-modal interaction as well as presentation of speech and text in multiple languages
3. Make possible the production and manipulation of information, blending both electronic and physical representations

The agents therefore do not explicitly intervene, but remain in the background to provide appropriate support (this mode is known as *implicit interaction*), unless explicitly called for to provide a particular service, such as playing a video.

The remainder of Section 1 will formulate the concepts behind "FAME" and introduce the functions our "intelligent room" [1] can perform. Section 2 will present the individual components and evaluate their performance individually, while Section 3 will present an overall evaluation of the integrated system from the user's point of view.

1.1   The Functions of the "FAME" Demonstrator

The functions of the "FAME – Facilitating Agents for Multi-Cultural Exchange" multi-modal demonstrator are split into an off-line and on-line part, as shown in Fig. 1:

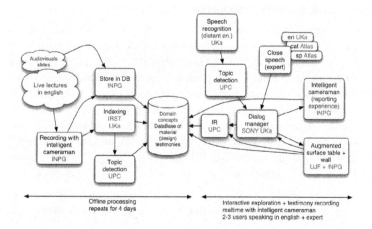

Fig. 1. Components of the "FAME" demonstrator: the database connects the off-line "Intelligent Cameraman" and indexing to the left, the and on-line multi-modal document retrieval using the "Augmented Table" on the right

Off-line Part. To provide audio-visual documents, an "Intelligent Cameraman" [2] recorded a four day seminar on Language Technology and Language, Cognition, and Evolution [3], which were held on the premises of the FORUM2004 [4] in Barcelona. The cameraman runs fully automatically and does not interfere with the lecture or its visitors.

The resulting videos, which contain audio from the presenter, the translator, and the audience, are then segmented, automatically transcribed and processed by a topic detection system, which assigns one topic to every segment. The videos can then be retrieved during the on-line use of the system in different ways.

On-line Part. The goal of the "Augmented Table" is to aid and support multi-cultural interaction and multi-modal document retrieval [5]. Students and researchers can come to the table and discuss with each other, retrieve information about the seminar as well as see recordings or automatically generated transcriptions of the lectures themselves, or see or give "testimonies".

The Database. The database is the interface between the off-line and on-line parts. In addition to the videos, their transcription and topic segmentation, it contains speakers' CVs, a picture, and contact information. For every lecture, we also added information on time and place as well as course material (slides) and other meta information.

1.2   The "Interactive Space"

At a conference, attendees usually use the physical conference program organized as a time-schedule and they ask other attendees what's interesting to attend. Therefore, the design of our showcase must maintain these two forms of interaction (browsing a time-schedule and chatting with colleagues for reporting their experience and asking for advice) in a seamless and complementary way.

Preliminary Analysis. In a user-centered approach, domain concepts that users manipulate are classified to provide guidelines for the design of the user interface. In particular, *1st-class* concepts should be observable at all time, and *2nd-class* concepts should be browsable at all time, i.e. they are not necessarily observable but accessible through additional user's actions such as scrolling, selecting a navigation button such as "next-previous-top", "show details". After analysis of 15 CHI (Computer Human Interaction) conference programs, our demonstrator ranks 1st-class domain concepts as follows: *Lecture* (in terms of: Title, Place, Date, BeginHour, EndHour), *Speakers* and *Topics*; while we use the 2nd-class domain concepts *Documents* (papers, slides, video, audio) and *Testimonies* (recorded audio-visual "opinions" about lectures).

Design Solution. Given the current state-of-the-art in automatic speech recognition without close-talking microphones [6], our design is based on the hypothesis that there should be two types of users: one *manager* and up to five *users*:

Users are researchers knowledgeable in the task domain, i.e. they are skilled at manipulating the notions of session, lecture, topics; they are familiar with the lectures' topic, but not with augmented reality. To ensure a reliable functioning of the system, the users do not issue spoken commands to the system, but the topic spotter component of the system recognizes their speech and acts upon it. Visitors to the demonstration can be "users".

A manager is skilled both in the task domain and in the interaction techniques. His spoken requests are recognized by the system, so there is no need for extra explicit interaction with the system. He can conduct a rich dialog with the system using speech and direct manipulation, he acts as a "moderator".

The manager and several users can interact with the system at the same time, i.e. they can speak between themselves, move tokens or select items etc. As shown in Fig. 2, the overall setting includes:

- A shared horizontal surface (the "Augmented Table") for exploring information about the conference and recording testimonies
- A microphone in the middle for acquiring user's utterances and detecting information of interests (i.e. topics and/ or speakers' names) as well as a loud-speaker, so that the system can talk back to users
- A shared vertical surface (the "Wall") for peripheral activities, such as a presentation of the detected topics, lecture slides, or other text information from the database
- A second vertical surface for video projections from the database
- A camera to record testimonies

Compared to the "un-augmented" setting (i.e. browsing a paper brochure or asking colleagues in the hallway), the added value of FAME comes from (see Fig. 2):

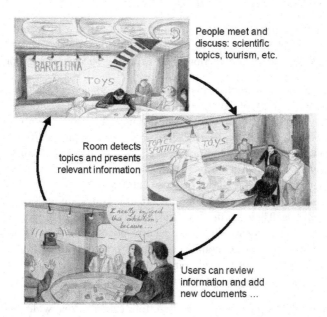

Fig. 2. The overall setting of the "interactive space": table for focused search activity and walls for peripheral activities and information. The Feedback loop made possible by the FAME room improves engagement within communities.

- The interaction itself (manipulating tokens and chatting at the same time),
- The nature of the information that can be retrieved (lecture videos, presentation slides, testimonies, biographical or contact information, etc.),
- The capacity to produce feedback (e.g. reporting a testimony, which is added to the database), which improves the feeling of engagement in the event.

2   Components of the FAME Demonstrator

The components of the FAME demonstrator were developed in parallel by the FAME partners, each using their own software and tools. Integration of the individual components into one system was achieved during two integration workshops held at different sites using different hardware to provide backup and to ensure that the demonstrator would not depend on specifics of either location, so as to avoid problems during several days of public exhibits at the FORUM2004 in Barcelona and IST2004 in The Hague.

Communication between components is assured through Open Agent Architecture (OAA) [7], which allows agents running on several machines with different operating systems to communicate and also access the database. In total, the on-line part of the FAME demonstrator requires six PCs in a mixed configuration of Linux and Windows, which supported three speech recognizers, speech synthesis, video processing for the "Augmented Table", projection of the table itself and the walls, video player and recorder, room control, and database/ communication server.

2.1   Cameraman and Speech Activity Detection

The automatic cameraman is a context aware system designed to record lectures or meetings. It creates movies by dynamically selecting camera views based on context analysis using a speech activity detection system running on several microphones.

The Context Aware Framework. This is based on the concept of entities, roles, relations, situations and a graph of situations [8]. An *entity* is a group of observable properties detected by perceptual components. For instance, a person (an entity with (x, y) properties) can be detected by a video tracker. A *role* is an acceptance test which selects entities based on their properties. For instance, a long and thin object can play the role of a pointer. A *relation* is a predicate over entities: person 1 is near person 2. A situation is defined as a set of roles and relations between entities.

Context is described as a graph. Nodes are situations, arcs are temporal constraints between the situations. They are decorated using Allen's temporal operators [9]. For each Allen temporal operator we composed a corresponding Petri Net pattern. By applying those patterns, the context graph can be transformed in an equivalent synchronized Petri Net. The Petri Net is then compiled in a set of forward production rules (Jess) that will check the situation activation sequence.

The Cameraman. The room is equipped with four cameras: one wide-angle view of the scene, one for the audience, one for the lecturer, and one filming the slides. The lecturer has a lapel microphone, there are ambient microphones for the audience. The perceptual components, a video tracker [10] for the lecturer, a "new slide" detector based on image difference, and a speech activity detector, model four situations, each with an associated camera: *lecturer speaks*, *audience asks a question*, *new slide*, and *unspecified*.

Speech Activity Detection (SAD). The SAD system is composed of an *energy detector*, a *basic classifier* and a *neural net* trained to recognize voiced segments. The energy detector uses pseudo energy (sum of absolute sample values) to determine if a signal is speech or not. The basic classifier works in frequency bands and tags specific sound classes: fricatives, low frequency sounds like fans, and other sounds. The neural net is a multi-layer perceptron with 2 hidden layers. Input consists of band crossing, energy and 16 LPC coefficients. This module is the only sub-system that needs to be trained. Training was done on 1h of speech extracted from the BREF [11] corpus. A rule based automaton determines the final result using the three sub-system's decision as input.

The results from the evaluation conditions, one dealing with close-talking data from the lecturer's lapel microphone, the other dealing with far-field microphone audio, and from field experiments suggest that the SAD system accuracy is satisfying for the purpose of the context analysis. Results in terms of Mismatch Rate (MR), Speech Detection Error Rate (SDER), and Non-speech Detection Error Rate (NDER) are as follows [12]:

	MR	SDER	NDER
Close-Talking	10.8%	5.8%	27.9%
Far-Field	13.4%	12.9%	15.4%

2.2 Information Retrieval and Topic Detection

Information Retrieval (IR). Conventional IR allows a user to type a query, the system performs a search on a previously indexed single collection of information sources and then provides the results. FAME needs to go beyond this scheme, because it deals with on-line access to documents from a *set of different collections* triggered by explicit or implicit interaction [13].

Indexing is done using textual features (words, stems, lemmas, multiword terms, phrases, etc.). These can also include morphological, syntactic or semantic information. Textual features can be automatically extracted from multimedia documents or manually attached to them.

Querying can be done using text or speech. The system allows cross-lingual and conceptual-based query expansion using EuroWordNet [14] as lexical resource (both queries and indexed documents ara allowed to be in Catalan, English and Spanish, conceptual-based query expansion is performed using the synonymy relations present in EuroWordNet, no attempt to word sense disambiguation has been done because several experiments regarding this issue have not resulted on improving the global accuracy of the system) . Cross-lingual IR is useful, as a speaker's ability to understand a document in a foreign language is usually higher than his active command of that language.

Topic Detection (TD). Detection of topics consists of assigning topics to lecture segments, or detecting that no in-domain topic is currently being discussed.

In order to perform (on-line) TD, topics first need to be described during a preparation phase. We refer to this off-line and highly time-consuming task as Topic Characterization (TC). The most widely used form of performing TC consists in attaching a collection of units to each topic. The problems which need to be addressed here are *selecting* the appropriate type of unit, *choosing the criteria* for selecting the appropriate units to describe each topic, and *choosing a representation schema* for the collection of units describing the set of topics.

Topic Signatures (TS) are used to represent topics. TS are lists of weighted units or terms. Building a TS for a collection of topics was done semi-automatically. Different TS for a topic collection depend on each other.

With the set of "topics" pre-defined and each topic being described by its TS, the input stream is examined sequentially and its features are extracted and compared with the features (TS) of the different topics. If there is enough evidence, the presence of a new topic (a change of topic) is detected and communicated [15].

2.3 The Augmented Table and Token Tracker

The token tracker component of the "Augmented Table" analyzes in real time the video stream coming from the camera located above the table. The positions of all tokens (red disks) are extracted from the video stream and converted into a stream of APPEAR, MOTION and DISAPPEAR events with associated positions (x, y). The FAME token tracker will be evaluated in terms of its *resolution* and *latency*.

Resolution. The smallest motion that will be detected and reported by the tracker depends on the video stream, which is processed at 388 x 284 pixels in order to maintain full video frame rate and low latency. Setting a 2 pixel motion threshold for static stability before reporting a motion event because of the instability of the video signal, the actual resolution on the surface depends on the geometry of the setup. Typically, an accuracy of 0.5 cm or 5 pixels for the projection, is reached, which is sufficient for the task.

Latency. The time lag between the moment a user moves a token and the moment the associated feedback is moved accordingly has a strong effect on human performance with interactive systems. [16] recommends that devices should not have more than 50 ms latency. As shown in [17], it is not necessary for latency to be very stable: no effect on human performance is detected with standard deviation of latency at or below 82 ms.

Following the approach reported in [18], we designed a latency measuring device for the token tracker: on a 1.4 Ghz PowerPC G4 machine, the resulting latency value is distributed between 61 ms and 141 ms, with an average at 81 ms, which is tolerable given a standard variation on latency of 16 ms in our system, which means FAME is well within the 82 ms requirement expressed in [17]. We mainly attribute the latency variation to the difference in camera delay (25 Hz frame rate) and projector refresh rate (60 Hz).

2.4 Dialog Manager

The dialog manager is the central on-line component that mediates and executes messages of the various components, maintaining a shared multi-modal context with the

"Augmented Table". In this function, the dialog manager interprets speech input from the manager (*explicit interaction*), input from the topic spotter using distant speech recognition (*implicit interaction*) and events stemming from users' actions on the table (*explicit interaction*). The dialog manager will call requested services as dictated by the context, for example IR queries, highlighting information on the table, playing video segments, showing slides or pieces of information on the information wall, controlling testimony recording, controlling room devices (lamps) and generating spoken output.

If the dialog manager detects clarification needs, or information is missing to execute a command, it requests further information from the speaker or calls on other services, such as IR, to obtain the information required to execute the command.

For dialog management and multi-modal integration we use the TAPAS dialog management framework, which is based on ARIADNE dialog algorithms [19] with extensions to support multilingual input and output [20]. The dialog manager can restrict the search space of the close-talking speech recognizers to the given context. Performance numbers for these recognizers and the dialog manager are summarized here:

Performance on	Spanish	English
Overall Number of Turns	597	1029
Word Error Rate	18.6%	17.2%
Sentence Error Rate	21.3%	20.7%
Turn Error Rate	20.7%	17.5%
Finalized Goal Rate	75.2%	71.5%

2.5 Speech Recognition

Apart from the close-talking recognizers for the managers, the augmented table uses two other speech recognition systems:

Lecture Transcription. To automatically segment and transcribe the lectures given at the seminar and make them accessible to indexing, transcriptions were generated by ITC-irst [21]; here we describe a smaller backup system developed by UKA, which was run during pauses between demonstrations. Development of lecture transcription components used the TED [22] corpus, because of its similarity to the Barcelona seminar presentations. The acoustic model has been trained on 180 h Broadcast News (BN) and close-talking "Meeting" data [6], summing up to a total of 300 h of training material. Models were first trained on Meeting and BN, then adapted to TED by MAP and MLLR.

To generate language models (LMs), we used corpora consisting of BN (160 M words), proceedings (17 M words) of conferences such as ICSLP, Eurospeech, ICASSP or ASRU and talks (60 k words) by the TED adaptation speakers. The baseline LM is based on BN. Our final LM was generated by interpolating a 3-gram LM based on BN and proceedings, a class based 5-gram LM based on BN and proceedings and a 3-gram LM based on the talks. The overall out-of-vocabulary rate is 0.3% on a 25 k vocabulary including multi-words and pronunciation variants.

The TED decoding and perplexity results using the acoustic and language models described above are shown below. The first run did not use TED model adaptation, while the last run used MLLR model adaptation on the hypothesis of the "TED-Adapted" run.

Performance on TED database	Native		Non-native	
	WER	PP	WER	PP
First run	42.8%	300	53.9%	160
TED Adapted, Baseline LM	36.7%	300	35.2%	160
Adapted to Speaker, Final LM	28.5%	171	31.0%	142

Comparing the first runs between the native vs. the non-native test data sets we see a big gap in performance which is due to the fact that the acoustic model was trained on mostly native speech. The gain of acoustic adaptation was higher for the non-native test set as for the native test set, which may be explained by the fact that the amount of adaptation material was four times smaller for the native speakers than for the non-native speakers. Word error rates of transcriptions of the Barcelona lectures are about the same as those of the TED development set.

Topic Spotting using Room Microphones. A real-time speech recognition system derived from the ISL "Meeting" system [6], running on a single microphone placed in the middle of the "Augmented Table" is used to detect topics from the conversation between visitors to FAME.

The initial system using a BN LM interpolated with data collected from the Internet had a topic error rate of 41% at a speech recognition accuracy of 17%. Re-weighting the keywords for topic spotting and taking confidence scores into account reduced the topic spotting error rate to 38%.

2.6   Component Integration

We have conducted an evaluation to measure response time over a distributed OAA system including different components. OAA offers two kinds of method calls: *asynchronous* calls (messages without response) and *synchronous* calls (response is returned to the caller). We have evaluated both message types with sequential calls and parallel calls for maximum throughput.

We found that the first call to OAA of an agent plus registration time was quite large with an average of 667 ms. All following calls are much faster. The average delay in our distributed system for a single synchronous method call (including request and reply) ranges between 20 ms and 25 ms. The numbers have been evaluated for an agent calling himself (routed over the OAA facilitator), chained calls (a call stack of depth 10), and a single agent calling another agent. The same setting has been used to create parallel tests, where 10 agents send a message concurrently. The average response time was 157 ms. The delay from sending the first request and receiving the last response was 207 ms. Divided by 10, this corresponds to an average processing time of 21 ms per message. We thus assume the total message throughput to be 47 messages (including responses) per second. The results of the sequential tests and sequential chained calls correspond to the final setting of the demonstrator and provide realistic numbers of the expected delay of messages. In the demonstration setup, the delays of the messages are small enough. However, the tested setup can not be applied to a larger system or one that needs a significantly higher message throughput.

3   The FAME Demonstrator and User Study

Over 150 persons used FAME during the Barcelona demonstration. We randomly selected 5 groups of 3 users among them for a user study [23]. After a brief introduction to the system, users were asked to perform predefined tasks, such as "Can you retrieve Mr. Harold Somer's lecture?" or "What topics are being addressed in the lecture about Machine Translation?", etc. We observed their behavior while interacting within the FAME interactive space and finally, the users answered some questions about their impression of the system.

We observed two general kinds of behavior: *actors* who wanted to experiment with the system, and *spectators* who enjoyed observing the scene. People felt confident with the system in less then one minute. They were more interested in playing with it than learning from the content: unfortunately, the social context did not favor a "learning" experience, although most visitors had a "science" background. We summarize the results in two categories:

General Impression. The function and the manipulation of tokens are easy to learn and to understand. The existence of multiple tokens brings a playful note to the system. We observed users dropping multiple tokens randomly on the table to see what happens. The multiplicity of tokens supports simultaneous actions but does not necessarily favor collaboration. In turn, this lack of collaboration between users may lead to confusion, because, as a result of the quasi-simultaneity of different output modalities, users did not know whether the replies of the system corresponded to their own or someone else's request.

Most users would have preferred to be able to ask IR requests directly, instead of asking the manager to do it for them. Most users did not pay attention to the fountain of words (on the wall) that correspond to the topics recognized by the topic spotter as users were talking freely around the table. From the social perspective, the testimony function was a big success. At first, some users were shy at recording themselves. Others enjoyed it for the possibility to watch themselves through the replay function.

General Impression	Yes	Sometimes	No	No Answer
Is it useful to have multiple places to look for information?	5	8	1	1
Is it fun to have multiple places to look for information?	7	6	0	2
Is it useful to be able to play with the system with other people?	9	5	0	1
Is it fun to be able to play with the system with other people?	11	3	0	1
Would you prefer to issue speech commands yourself?	7	4	2	2
Is the system reliable?	12	0	2	1
Would you be interested in using it?	12	1	0	2

User Ratings For Different Parts of the System. In general, users' opinions are quite enthusiastic, but overall, the system is viewed as a prototype. Some users judged the quantity of information insufficient to really test the system. Some videos were perceived as too short but the content was supposed to be relevant. The icons and numbers denoting video clips in the flower menus should be replaced by a representative image of the video content and a textual title. Multi-surface and multi-user interaction were

Rating on	Very Easy	Easy	Difficult	Very Hard	No Answer
Working with the tokens	1	13	0	0	1
Understanding organization of the seminar, topics and speakers	0	13	1	0	1
Choosing lectures to visit, discovering topics and speakers	2	11	1	0	1
Retrieving audio-visual content from lectures	1	13	0	0	1
Retrieving course materials	2	11	1	0	1
Giving a testimony	3	10	0	1	1

considered useful and fun but sometimes confusing. In addition, users would like to navigate within a video clip. Some users complained about the speed of the system reactions.

In summary, the overall design and technical integration of the FAME interactive space were very well perceived, fun to use, and provided a special experience. However, at the detail level, there is room for both design and technical improvements, such as speeding up the response time, allowing easier navigation within videos and slides, and better spatial arrangements for projection walls and augmented table, etc.

4   Conclusions

From the interaction perspective, the system is easy to learn and provides people with an enjoyable experience based on the tangibility of the tokens, the table, the walls and spoken interaction. The novelty of the interaction style and the fact that it is fun, draw users' attention away from the content itself. The "testimony" feedback service provides a new social experience, although, in our experiment, users exploited this facility more to look at themselves and not to produce information for others.

We have not been able to demonstrate the benefit of implicit interaction supported by the topic spotter. We believe that implicit interaction cannot be tested in sessions of short duration, but can only be appreciated over a long period of use, which was not possible in our setting.

The experiment also showed the necessity for systems to automatically adapt to the physical environment: spatial relationships between surfaces, distance from the actuators, background color of surfaces, etc. For example, one third of the users were wearing the same color as that of the tokens, which could be a problem in bad lightning conditions. Our continuing work on context modeling and adaptation is an attempt to solve this problem.

References

1. Gieselmann, P., Denecke, M.: Towards multimodal interaction within an intelligent room. In: Proc. Eurospeech 2003, Geneva; Switzerland, ISCA (2003)
2. Crowley, J.L., Reignier, P.: Dynamic composition of process federations for context aware perception of human activity. In: Proc. International Conference on Integration of Knowledge Intensive Multi-Agent Systems, KIMAS'03, 10, IEEE (2003)

3. Consorci Universitat Internacional Menéndez Pelayo de Barcelona: "Tecnologies de la llengua: darrers avenços" and "Llenguatge, cognició i evolució". http://www.cuimpb.es/ (2004)
4. FORUM2004: Universal Forum of Cultures. http://www.barcelona2004.org/ (2004)
5. Lachenal, C., Coutaz, J.: A reference framework for multi-surface interaction. In: Proc. HCI International 2003, Crete; Greece, Crete University Press (2003)
6. Metze, F., Fügen, C., Pan, Y., Waibel, A.: Automatically Transcribing Meetings Using Distant Microphones. In: Proc. Int. Conf. on Acoustics, Speech, and Signal Processing, Philadelphia, PA; USA, IEEE (2005)
7. SRI AI Center: Open Agent Architecture 2.3.0. http://www.ai.sri.com/~oaa/ (2003)
8. Rey, G., Crowley, J.L., Coutaz, J., Reignier, P.: Perceptual components for context aware computing. In: Proc. UBICOMP 2002 – International Conference on Ubiquitous Computing, Springer (2002)
9. Allen, J.: Towards a general theory of action and time. Artificial Intelligence 13 (1984)
10. Caporossi, A., Hall, D., Reignier, P., Crowley, J.: Robust visual tracking from dynamic control of processing. In: PETS04, Workshop on Performance Evaluation for tracking and Surveillance, ECCV04, Prague; Czech Republic (2004)
11. Lamel, L., Gauvain, J., Eskenazi, M.: BREF, a large vocabulary spoken corpus for French. In: Proc. Eurospeech 1991, Geneva, Switzerland (1991)
12. Surcin, S., Stiefelhagen, R., McDonough, J.: Evaluation packages for the first chil evaluation campaign. CHIL Deliverable D4.2 (2005) http://chil.server.de/.
13. Bertran, M., Gatius, M., Rodriguez, H.: FameIr, multimedia information retrieval shell. In: Proceedings of JOTRI 2003, Madrid; Spain, Universidad Carlos III (2003)
14. The Global WordNet Association: EuroWordNet. http://www.globalwordnet.org/ (1999)
15. Arranz, V., Bertran, M., Rodriguez, H.: Which is the current topic? what is relevant to it? a topic detection retrieval and presentation system. FAME Deliverable D7.2 (2003)
16. Ware, C., Balakrishnan, R.: Reaching for objects in vr displays: Lag and frame rate. ACM Transactions on Computer-Human Interaction (TOCHI) 1 (1994) 331–356
17. Watson, B., Walker, N., Ribarsky, W., Spaulding, V.: The effects of variation of system responsiveness on user performance in virtual environments. Human Factors, Special Section on Virtual Environments 3 (1998) 403–414
18. Liang, J., Shaw, C., Green, M.: On temporal-spatial realism in the virtual reality environment. In: ACM symposium on User interface software and technology, Hilton Head, South Carolina (1991) 19–25
19. Denecke, M.: Rapid prototyping for spoken dialogue systems. In: Proceedings of the 19th International Conference on Computational Linguistics, Taiwan (2002)
20. Holzapfel, H.: Towards development of multilingual spoken dialogue systems. In: Proceedings of the 2nd Language and Technology Conference. (2005)
21. Cettolo, M., Brugnara, F., Federico, M.: Advances in the automatic transcription of lectures. In: International Conference on Acoustics, Speech, and Signal Processing (ICASSP 2004), Montreal; Canada, IEEE (2004)
22. Lamel, L., Schiel, F., Fourcin, A., Mariani, J., Tillmann, H.: The translanguage english database (ted). In: Proc. ICSLP1994, Yokohama; Japan, ISCA (1994) 1795 – 1798
23. Coutaz, J., et al.: Evaluation of the fame interaction techniques and lessons learned. FAME Deliverable D8.2 (2005)

Development of Peripheral Feedback to Support Lectures

Janienke Sturm, Rahat Iqbal, and Jacques Terken

Department of Industrial Design, Eindhoven University of Technology,
P.O.Box 513, 5600 MB Eindhoven, The Netherlands
{J.Sturm, R.Iqbal, J.M.B.Terken}@tue.nl

Abstract. In this paper we describe a service that provides peripheral feedback on participation level of the audience in lectures and seminars to presenters. The peripheral display makes the lecturer aware of the attention level as well as the interest level of their students. We hypothesise that providing this kind of feedback can help lecturers or presenters to adjust their behaviour to the cognitive demands of the audience. In this paper we report on the results obtained from a focus group and two surveys that were carried out. Following that we describe the development of peripheral displays focusing on the design considerations and process of the teacher support service. We describe the service by addressing its technological components and visualisations. Finally we briefly discuss the issues to be considered for the evaluation of such an unobtrusive service.

1 Introduction

We are moving away from traditional desktop computing towards *ubiquitous computing*, where people and environments are augmented with computational resources that provide information and services unobtrusively, wherever and whenever required. One of the prime features of *ubiquitous computing* and *calm technology* is to provide information in the periphery of attention [1]. The term 'periphery' describes what we are attuned to without attending to consciously. In this way, peripheral displays portray non-critical information without distracting or burdening the user. The information in the periphery can be provided in a multimodal way, for example by video and audio or a dedicated device acting as a truly peripheral display. Within the framework of the EU-funded CHIL project (http://chil.server.de), we are developing a peripheral display to support the lecturer in a classroom where students are allowed to use laptops during the lecture. This service will make the lecturer aware of the students' attention level as well as their interest level, which may help the teacher to decide when and how to continue the lecture.

Technological progress is increasingly changing the traditional classrooms into a ubiquitous environment. Such an environment is equipped with a variety of applications including note taking tools that can facilitate students as well as lecturers [2, 3, 4, 5, 6, 7]. Many teachers already make use of notebooks to deliver their lectures and or to post their slides to students in real time. Similarly, students also bring their laptops to the classroom. The usage of laptops with internet or intranet facilities in classrooms has many advantages, but it also bears the risk of students doing other things than attending to the lecture and taking notes, such as playing games, browsing the

S. Renals and S. Bengio (Eds.): MLMI 2005, LNCS 3869, pp. 138–149, 2006.
© Springer-Verlag Berlin Heidelberg 2006

internet, chatting, e-mailing. Now imagine the following scenario. A teacher is presenting complex content using slides, and cognitive load for the students is high, since they need to simultaneously take notes of what was said and listen to new input (in fact, this situation easily results in both incomplete notes and lack of understanding for the new input). Therefore, the teacher might want to reduce cognitive load by waiting until most students finished writing their notes before moving on to the next slide. However, now that students may use their laptops for other things than taking notes, it is unclear to the teacher how to interpret the observable activities of the students: if the teacher would know that most students who are typing are in fact chatting rather than taking notes, it makes no sense to wait until they finished before moving on to the next slide. Moreover, the teacher might want to know whether the attending students are still paying attention or whether they are losing their interest. This suggests that it would be useful for teachers to get feedback of the students' attention and interest levels. In this paper, we present a service that was developed within CHIL. Using this service, teachers receive real-time feedback about the activities and attention level of the audience in the lecture. We hypothesize that providing this kind of feedback in an unobtrusive manner may help lecturers to adjust their behaviour to the demands of the lecture without disrupting them unduly from their primary activities.

The remainder of the paper is organized as follows. Section 2 describes two user studies that were carried out to get a view of user behaviour and needs in relation to taking notes and using electronic equipment in lecture rooms. Section 3 provides a description of the development of a peripheral display providing feedback on student activity and interest to the lecturer. In Section 4 we draw conclusions and outline some points for future research.

2   User Studies

2.1   Focus Group

As a first step towards the development of an unobtrusive service providing feedback about the participation level of students in a classroom we conducted a focus group study aiming at collecting teachers' opinions concerning the use of electronic devices during their lectures. The main questions were whether they make use of electronic devices during their lectures, either for students or for themselves, and what types of services they would consider to be useful. The focus group consisted of five experienced teachers and professors at Eindhoven University of Technology. It took place in a friendly environment and was led by a facilitator. One person was appointed to take notes of the most important remarks and the whole discussion was recorded on tape for back-up purposes. The duration of the focus group was about 90 minutes.

The main conclusions of the focus group substantiate the general merits and demerits of services. Teachers appreciated the use of electronic devices for asking questions to intermittently test the understanding of the students, to make the lectures more appealing, etc. Some teachers preferred to use blackboard and chalk, rather than static slide presentations, because they actually create their story on the spot. Teachers did see the advantages for students to use laptops during class, for example to get access to electronic summaries, to get relevant documents, to follow along with the online lecture notes provided by the teacher, or to take electronic notes. Most teachers agreed that electronic note-taking should be done with a pen rather than using a keyboard for input, because typed input would reduce flexibility and increase cognitive load for the students. However, it worried the teachers a lot that they will lose eye contact with the students when the students are sitting behind their laptops and that they will not be able to see what students are doing: whether they are attending the lecture and taking notes, or misusing the notebook for gaming, e-mailing, web browsing, etc. They believe that students need to be taught how to use the laptop during class, but teaching them rules of laptop etiquette, such as those mentioned by Campbell and Pargas, may well be infeasible [8].

2.2 Teacher and Student Survey

In addition to the focus group, we conducted a survey through the Internet among teachers and students, addressing the way they deliver and participate in lectures. The survey is an adapted version of a similar survey that was carried out within the CHIL project by AIT, but which was tuned to presentations in small-group meetings rather than lectures [9]. The survey covers important aspects of both delivering and attending lectures, such as how, and how often do students take notes, what students do if they find a lecture boring, how teachers gauge the understanding and interest of their audience, etc. The survey has given us a better understanding of the possible impact of the service we propose. The most signification results are presented below.

2.2.1 Student Survey

In addition to several general questions, such as age and sex, the student questionnaire contained 13 questions that are related to the way students behave during lectures. In total 319 students (233 male, 86 female) filled out the questionnaire. Most respondents are between 19 and 25 years of age. The lion's share of students is related to the TU/e, a small part to other universities or colleges.

General: The following aspects were considered important to finish a course successfully: the lecture itself, related literature, homework assignments, notes, and discussions both with students and the teacher. Especially the lecture itself, literature and homework were considered to be important or very important by most students.

Activities during lecture: As described in Table 1, listening to the lecture and taking notes are the main activities of students during the lecture. Interestingly, 4% of the students indicate that they never or almost never listen to a lecture. From Table 1 it can also be seen that 92% of the students take notes during the lecture. Only 8% never take notes. Activities that are less related to the lecture, such as talking to fellow students and thinking about irrelevant things, also happen quite often (around 95% do this at least sometimes). Sleeping and doing other things (either with or without using a laptop) are done only rarely.

Table 1. What do you do during a lecture? (in %[1])

	Never	Sometimes	Often	Always
Listen	1	5	61	34
Take notes	8	27	47	17
Come up with questions	26	55	17	2
Talk to other students	4	59	29	8
Think about irrelevant things	6	63	27	4
Sleep	74	23	3	0
Do other things	46	50	3	1
Do other things on laptop	84	15	0	0

Note-taking: Despite the fact that all students at our university possess a laptop, half of the students never bring their laptop to lectures. Only 14% of the students often or always bring their laptops to class. 65% of the students often or always take notes during a lecture. As mentioned previously, a minority of 8% of the students never takes notes.

As can be seen in Table 2 most students usually take notes on paper. 26% of the students say that they usually or always take notes on hand-outs, whereas 18% of the students indicate that they never use hand-outs for taking notes. The explanation for the fact that only a few students use handouts for taking notes may be twofold. Either the students prefer to use normal paper, or the students never receive any hand-outs. The majority of the students never use the laptop for taking notes. Only 9% of the students use the laptop sometimes or often.

Table 2. What do you use to take notes? (in %)

	Never	Sometimes	Often	Always
Paper	0	6	34	60
Hand-outs	18	55	23	3
Laptop	92	8	1	0

When taking notes, catch words, summaries, explanations, figures, and formulas all are used sometimes or often by the majority of the students (see Table 3). However, almost none of the students use short-hand to take notes.

Notes are most often used to prepare for an exam and for later reference to interesting topics. Only a few students use their notes to prepare for the next lecture. 24% of the students indicate that they usually do not use their notes after the lecture.

If handouts are distributed before the lecture, they are most often used for later reference. 80% of the students indicate that they (sometimes or often) use the handouts to read along with the lecture and to take notes on (76%). This suggests that the second explanation for the observation that only a few students use handouts for taking notes must be true: students do not receive handouts very often.

---

[1] Due to truncation some rows in the tables throughout this paper may not add up to 100%.

Table 3. What do you write down? (in %)

	Never	Sometimes	Often	Always
Bullet points	7	40	44	9
Summary	21	41	35	3
Explanation	4	25	60	11
Short hand	76	17	7	0
Figures	8	36	47	9
Formulas	1	17	59	23

Questions: 33% of the students never ask questions during or after a lecture, whereas 60% sometimes ask questions.

Table 4. At which moment do you ask a question? (in %)

	Never	Sometimes	Often	Always
Interrupt teacher	66	26	3	0
When teacher pauses	24	37	30	7
Lift hand	4	27	40	28
At designated points	30	49	17	2
End of the lecture	34	49	15	2

If students do want to ask a question, most of them do not interrupt the teacher; they usually raise their hand or else they wait until the teacher pauses (see Table 4).

Understanding and interest: In case students do not *understand* what is being told, most of them (71%) will usually try to keep paying attention. Students never or rarely walk out of the classroom or fall asleep. 76% sometimes or often "switch off". Only 54% of the students sometimes or often ask for additional explanation, 46% never does so (see Table 5 below).

Table 5. What do you do when you do not understand the teacher? (in %)

	Never	Sometimes	Often	Always
Stay alert	2	26	57	14
Ask for explanation	46	44	9	1
Switch off	34	54	12	0
Sleep	76	20	4	0
Walk out	78	20	1	0

If students lose their *interest* in the lecture, most of them (64%) will usually try to keep paying attention anyway (see table 5). Many students say they sometimes "switch off" and start thinking about irrelevant things. 38 % of the students occasionally start to do other things (e.g. SMS or talk to fellow students) and 32% sometimes leave the lecture.

Finally, aspects of speaker volume, knowledge, explanations and environmental factors are all considered to be important for keeping a high level of attention by the majority of the students. Only accent is considered to be less important by many students.

Table 6. What do you do when you lose interest? (in %)

	Never	Sometimes	Often	Always
Stay alert	3	32	57	7
Switch off	22	59	18	2
Do other things	49	38	13	0
Do other things on laptop	85	10	5	0
Sleep	74	23	4	0
Walk out	62	32	6	0

2.2.2 Teacher Survey

In addition to several general questions addressing e.g. age and sex of the participant, the teacher survey consists of 13 questions concerning the way teachers prepare and deliver their lectures. 13 teachers (12 male, 1 female) filled out the questionnaire. They are between 21 and 65 years of age and have different amounts of teaching experience. All teachers are currently related to TU/e.

Preparation of lecture: Almost 80% of the teachers often or always prepare transparencies or electronic slides and use those as a guide through the lecture.

Delivering a lecture: Most teachers use either chalk and blackboard or transparencies or electronic slides as tools during their lecture. A flip-over is used only rarely. If they use transparencies or electronic slides, only 25% of the teachers never use hand outs. 42% of the teachers always use hand outs in this case.

The majority of the teachers (62%) always use their laptop during lectures, whereas only 2 teachers (15%) never use one. The teachers mainly use their laptops for presenting electronic slides, but about half of the teachers sometimes use the laptop for looking up information from previous lectures and as a memory aid.

About half of the teachers never allow their students to use a laptop during the lecture. Those who do allow the use of laptops (see Table 7) most often allow students to take notes on their laptops or make exercises.

Table 7. What are students allowed to use their laptop for? (in %)

	Never	Sometimes	Often	Always
Reading along	38	38	0	25
Taking notes	29	29	0	43
Lookup information	43	57	0	0
Exercises	0	38	25	38

Understanding and interest: To find out whether students understand the contents of the lecture (See Table 8), cues like eye-contact, facial expression, body posture and active participation are used by all teachers. For gauging interest level (Table 9), eye-contact, facial expression and body posture are used often by most teachers as an indication of students' interest. Body posture is used less often.

Table 8. How do you gauge whether students understand the lecture? (in%)

	Never	Sometimes	Often	Always
Eye contact	0	8	62	31
Body posture	0	15	69	15
Facial expression	0	8	69	23
Active participation	0	23	62	15

Table 9. How do you gauge whether students are interested? (in %)

	Never	Sometimes	Often	Always
Eye contact	0	23	54	23
Body posture	8	62	23	8
Facial expression	0	15	77	8
Active participation	0	23	54	23

Teachers never walk out of their own lecture neither when students don't understand the lecture nor when they are just not interested (see Table 10 and Table 11). Speeding up the lecture is also only rarely used in these situations. If students appear not to understand the lecture, most teachers explain more and ask more questions. The most common solution when students are not interested in the lecture is to ask more questions and to use humour. Many teachers also (sometimes or often) continue as planned.

Table 10. What do you do when students are not interested in the lecture? (in %)

	Never	Sometimes	Often	Always
Continue as planned	23	38	38	0
Ask more questions	0	54	38	8
More humour	0	54	23	23
Next topic	50	50	0	0
Go faster	85	15	0	0
Short break	31	69	0	0
Leave lecture	100	0	0	0

Table 11. What do you do when students do not understand? (in %)

	Never	Sometimes	Often	Always
Continue as planned	33	58	8	0
Ask more questions	0	38	54	8
More humour	31	54	15	0
Go faster	100	0	0	0
Explanation	0	15	54	31
Leave lecture	100	0	0	0

Summarising, the user studies provided the following insights:

- The use of electronic tools in the lecture room is still uncommon. Students mostly use conventional means for taking notes, also because many lecturers prohibit use of electronic means.
- Lecturers see advantages for the use of laptops by students, but are concerned about unintended use and about losing eye contact.
- Lecturers use nonverbal cues to estimate students' understanding and interest.

So, we conclude that there are opportunities for the use of electronic equipment by students, provided that we provide lecturers with feedback about what the students are actually doing and about their interest level.

3 Development of Peripheral Display

3.1 Teacher Support Service

Following the main findings from the user studies, we propose a service that supports the teacher by providing information about students' attention and interest levels during the lecture. As an indication of the *level of attention*, the service shows how many students are actively taking notes, as opposed to playing games, chatting, or browsing the web. *Interest level* represents the interest of the students who attend to the lecture (either taking notes or not). We assume that students who are doing other things have low interest in the lecture and therefore we do not include these students in the calculation of interest level.

Although it is generally assumed that a teacher should intuitively know whether students can still keep pace with the lecture or not, the information may be ambiguous and with larger groups of students it may be difficult. Our intention is to substantiate the teacher's subjective feeling with quantitative data about the attention and interest level of the students. The benefit of such a service is that the teacher can concentrate on tailoring the lecture to the students, rather than being occupied with guessing the attention and interest levels of the audience.

Students' laptops will be equipped with a digital note-taking application (Agilix GoBinder[TM]) as shown in Figure 1. The application allows students to take electronic notes that are handwritten or drawn by means of a pen mouse or typed using the keyboard. Different styluses and colors are available and notes can easily be selected and moved or deleted. Figure 1 shows a screen shot of this application.

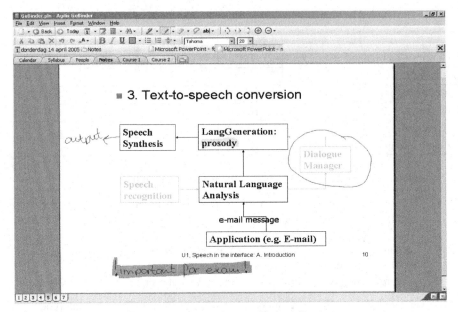

Fig. 1. Screenshot of note-taking application

In contrast with traditional pen and paper notes, students can draw digital notes on a local copy of the teacher's slides without requiring the teacher to hand out printed copies. Moreover, digital notes can be saved electronically and they can be selected, moved and resized or highlighted easily. If used on a Tablet PC, handwritten digital notes can be converted into text through handwriting recognition, allowing for easy indexing and searching. At a later stage, we intend to make audio and video recordings of the lecture and link those recordings to the time-stamped electronic notes, to facilitate access to the lecture content (cf. [2]).

3.2 Peripheral Displays

In order to shield the teacher from information overload, it is important that the student monitoring service be as little interruptive for the teacher as possible. Therefore, the information should be presented in the periphery of the teacher's attention, so that it can be viewed whenever required, and ignored when the teacher is not interested. Moreover, in order to minimize the additional cognitive load for the teacher, the visualizations should be easy to interpret. There are numerous ways in which this information can be presented to the teacher, using for example video or audio or a truly peripheral display such as a set of lamps on the desk. For the moment we choose to show the relevant information in graphical form in a separate window in the margin of the teacher's notebook screen. For attention level and interest level we propose the visualizations as depicted in Figure 2.

Attention level is depicted in the form of a pie chart, showing the percentage of students that are actively using the note-taking application in red ("BUSY") and the

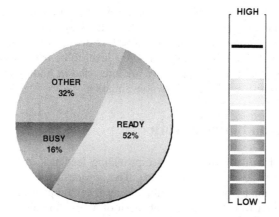

Fig. 2. Visualization of attention level (left) and interest level (right)

percentage of students that have the application as the active window, but are not actually using it in green ("READY"). Green in this case means that the teacher may move on, whereas red denotes students who are not yet ready to move on. The idea is that, if the BUSY area is small relative to the READY area, the teacher may move on, but if the BUSY area is large relative to the READY area, s/he might wait a moment before moving on until more students finished their notes. The grey area (or "OTHER") indicates students who are doing other things on their notebooks, such as chatting or browsing the web. This category is assumed to be irrelevant to the teacher's decision to move on or wait. The current Interest level is represented as a scale, with red indicating a low interest level and green indicating a high interest level and is calculated across BUSY and READY students (as said before, students doing other things are considered by definition not to be interested in the lecture). The horizontal line indicates the average interest level since the start of the lecture. Both visualizations are updated dynamically in real-time. The update rate of the information will be optimized by experimentation, so as to make sure that the information accurately and meaningfully reflects the current situation, but is not too distracting for the teacher.

3.3 Technology

As mentioned before, for measuring attention level we distinguish three groups of students: students who are actively taking notes using the Agilix GoBinder™ application, students who have the note-taking application as the active window, but are not actively using it and students who are using other applications on their laptop. To collect this information, monitoring software will be installed on the students' notebooks, which provides information about the application which is currently active or has been used most recently. The individual information is sent to a central server in real-time; the server collects the information and changes it into a graphical representation that is sent to the teacher's laptop.

Interest level can be measured in many different ways. Initially, we will ask the students to actively provide information about their own level of interest by means of a slider bar that they can adjust using their laptops (such as in [10]). In the future, we hope to be able to detect level of interest automatically on the basis of the students' nonverbal behaviour (eye gaze, posture, etc.). In this way, the information provided will be more objective and reliable and it will be less disruptive for the students. Mota et al. have shown automatic detection of interest level to be feasible for a single student / single application situation [11]. We are interested in finding out whether such a set-up would also be feasible in a classroom situation.

4 Conclusions and Future Work

We have presented an unobtrusive service providing feedback to lecturers about the attention and interest level of the audience. The service intends to support human-human communication by providing peripheral feedback on participation level. In the near future we plan a formative user evaluation of a first implementation of the service. With this evaluation we want to find out whether the visualizations are clear, what teacher and students' attitudes are towards the service and in what way using the service influences the lecture. In this user test, the service will be made available during a series of lectures. After the first evaluation and depending on its outcomes, we will optimise the visualizations and further develop the service. One aspect that we may need to address in the future is the possibility to provide the teacher with support on how to improve the lecture in case attention and interest are decreasing, e.g. by telling him/her when to slow down, rather than only signalling what is going on. Furthermore, we may extend the note-taking facilities for the students with the possibility to link keywords that were taken down during the class to recorded audio or video streams, for easy access to the lecture content afterwards.

We believe that services like the one described here may overcome some of the concerns associated with the use of electronic equipment in classrooms and that the feedback provided to lecturers will help the lecturers to reduce the cognitive load for the students. Obviously, these beliefs need to be substantiated by further research.

Acknowledgments

The work reported in this paper was supported by the Integrated Project CHIL (IP 506909), funded in the thematic area Information Society Technologies under the Sixth Research Framework Programme of the European Union.

References

1. Weiser M. and Seely Brown, J.: The Coming Age of Calm Technology. In P. J. Denning and R. M. Metcalfe (eds.): Beyond Calculation - The Next Fifty Years of Computing, Copernicus/An Imprint of Springer-Verlag, 1996.
2. Brotherton, J. and Abowd, G.: Lessons learned from eClass: Assessing automated capture and access in the classroom. ACM Transactions on Computer-Human Interaction (TOCHI), Vol. 11(2), 2004, 121-155.
3. Beecher, J.: Note-taking: What do we know about the benefits? ERIC Clearinghouse on Reading, English and Communication Digest #37 (EDO-CS-88-12), 1988

4. Chiu, P., Kapuskar, A., Reitmeier, S., and Wilcox, L.: NoteLook: Taking notes in meetings with digital video and ink. In Proceedings of ACM Multimedia, 1999, 149-158.
5. Stifelman, L., Arons, B., and Schmandt, C.: The Audio Notebook: paper and pen interaction with structured speech. In Proceedings of the SIGCHI conference on Human factors in Computing Systems: CHI2001, 2001, 182-189.
6. Whittaker, S., Hyland, P., and Wiley, M.: Filochat: Handwritten notes provide access to recorded conversations. In Proceedings of Human Factors in Computing Systems: CHI94, 1994, 271-277.
7. Wilcox, L., Schilit, B., and Sawhney, N.: Dynomite: A dynamically organized ink and audio notebook. In Proceedings of Human Factors in Computing Systems: CHI97, 1997, 186-193.
8. Campbell, A. and Pargas, R.: Laptops in the classroom. In Proceedings of the 34th SIGCSE Technical Symposium on Computer Science Education, Reno, NV, 2003, 98-102.
9. Terken, J. (ed.): Report on observation studies with requirements for CHIL services. Deliverable 7.1 of the CHIL project, Technische Universiteit Eindhoven, 2004.
10. Sung, M., Gips, J., Eagle, N., Madan, A., Caneel, R., DeVaul, R., Bonsen, J., and Pentland, S.: MIT.EDU: M-learning applications for classroom settings. Journal of Computer Assisted Learning (JCAL), 2004.
11. Mota, S. and Picard, R.: Automated posture analysis for detecting learner's interest level. In Proceedings of the IEEE Workshop on Computer Vision and Pattern Recognition for Human Computer Interaction (CVPRHCI), 2003.

Real-Time Feedback on Nonverbal Behaviour to Enhance Social Dynamics in Small Group Meetings

Olga Kulyk, Jimmy Wang, and Jacques Terken

Department of Industrial Design, Eindhoven University of Technology,
P.O.Box 513, 5600 MB Eindhoven, The Netherlands
{O.Kulyk, C.Wang, J.M.B.Terken}@tue.nl

Abstract. We present a service providing real-time feedback to participants of small group meetings on the social dynamics of the meeting. The service visualizes non-verbal properties of people's behaviour that are relevant to the social dynamics: speaking time and gaze behaviour. The service was evaluated in two studies, in order to test whether the feedback influences the participants' visual attention and speaking time and enhances the satisfaction with the group interaction process. In a qualitative evaluation it was found that groups in general perceive the social feedback during the meeting as a useful and positive experience, which makes them aware of their group dynamics. In a second study, aiming at a more quantitative analysis, we obtained preliminary evidence that the feedback service affected participants' behaviour and resulted in more balanced participation and gaze behaviour. We conclude that services providing automatic feedback about relatively low-level behavioural characteristics can enable groups to adjust the social dynamics in group meetings.

1 Introduction

Current technology supports mainly content and information exchange during meetings, whereas social aspects have been addressed only recently. The use of technology to support group meetings has appeared as early as 1971 [8]. Tools like electronic whiteboard, projector, video and audio recorders, and electronic minutes have been used for brainstorming, idea organizing and voting, and the associated methods for working with these tools have been refined over the last two decades. The methods focused on the content and information exchange and productivity in meetings.

Technologies to support group cohesion and satisfaction of meeting members have received much less attention [9]. Cohesiveness is the descriptive term that psychologists use to refer to an important property of groups. It is captured in common usage by a wider range of terms like solidarity, cohesion, team spirit, group atmosphere, unity, 'groupness' [5]. It is known from psychological studies that cohesive groups can achieve goals more efficiently and with higher satisfaction [16].

In this paper we focus on social dynamics. In this context, we define social dynamics as the way verbal and nonverbal communicative signals of the participants in a meeting regulate the flow of the conversation [1], [14]. Analyses of conversations

S. Renals and S. Bengio (Eds.): MLMI 2005, LNCS 3869, pp. 150–161, 2006.

in meetings have shown that there are two mechanisms governing the flow of conversation [14]. Either the current speaker selects the next speaker, by a combination of verbal and nonverbal signals, e.g., by addressing a participant explicitly and/or by gaze behaviour and additional cues. Or the next speaker selects him/herself: if the current speaker has finished, one of the other participants may take the turn (possibly after a brief transition phase where several participants try to get the floor simultaneously). The first mechanism has prevalence over the second one. From these observations it follows that the nonverbal behaviour of the participants influences the flow of the conversation. Here, we summarize the most important mechanisms.

- Plain speaking time is a first determinant of social dynamics. Since interrupting the speaker is bound to social conventions, within certain limits the current speaker determines how long s/he remains speaking. Speaking means having the opportunity to control the flow of conversation and influence the other participants. Depending on personality, speakers may try to monopolize the discussion, with the risk that not all arguments relevant to the topic of discussion come to the surface, which may ultimately lead to a "groupthink" situation, when a member of the group attempts to conform his or her opinion to what s/he believes to be the consensus of the group [6].

- Speaker eye gaze is a second determinant of the social dynamics, in two ways. The current speaker controls the flow of conversation by having the privilege of selecting the next speaker. Often, this is indicated by non-verbal means such as eye gaze [2], [7], [19]. In addition, when addressing all participants, the speaker should take care to look at all participants in due time to avoid giving the impression that s/he is neglecting particular participants. However, due to the nature of conversation, it is highly likely that the next speaker reacts to what the current speaker said. As a result, the respondent will look at the previous speaker, and interactive sequences involving two speakers may arise [11], leaving little opportunity for the other members of the group to participate in the discussion.

- Listener eye gaze is a third determinant of the social dynamics. The participant who is speaking is being looked at by the other participants, indicating that s/he is in the focus of attention [20], [17]. However, when the speaker is speaking for a long time, other participants may lose interest, which is signalled by gazing elsewhere.

Recently, researchers have taken inspiration from the observation that socially inappropriate behavior such as imposing one's own views instead of giving the others the opportunity to contribute may rezsult in suboptimal group performance, and they have developed systems that monitor and give feedback on social dynamics [3], [4]. Research has mostly focused on group decision-making tasks where balanced participation is essential to solving the task at hand. The systems capture observable properties like speaking time, posture and gestures of the meeting participants, analyze the interaction of people and give feedback through offering visualizations of the social data. For instance, DiMicco offered feedback about the speaking time of different participants visualized through a histogram presented on a public display. Evaluations showed that real-time feedback on speaking activity can result in more equal participation of all meeting members [4].

These findings and observations lead us to believe that audio-visual cues of human behaviour, namely eye-gaze and speaking time, directly relate to the dynamics of the meeting at the social level. In the framework of the EU-funded CHIL project, we designed a service that generates an unobtrusive feedback to participants about the social dynamics during the meeting, on the basis of captured audio-visual cues. Our goal is to make the members aware of their own and others behaviour, and in this way influence the group's social dynamics. It is assumed that such feedback may influence the participants' behaviour to create more appropriate social dynamics in a group, and therewith increase the satisfaction of the group members with the discussion process.

In the remainder of the paper, we first describe a focus group study, aiming at getting feedback on our ideas. We proceed with the design concept, which presents information on current and cumulated speaking activity in combination with the visual focus of attention of speakers and listeners. We then present the outcomes of two evaluations, one qualitative study to inform the design, and one quantitative evaluation, to assess the effects of the service on participants' behaviour in meetings. We conclude with a discussion of our findings and future prospects.

2 Focus Group

A focus group meeting was arranged to get insight into social dynamics problems that group members encounter during meetings. Our interest was whether information on the social dynamics of a meeting to be useful for them. The focus group addressed the following five main questions:

1. Do you remember any problematic situations during meetings?
2. To what extent do you feel social dynamics was the cause of the problem?
3. Do you think feedback about social dynamics can be useful? If so, at what moment, how and where?
4. Do you think this type of visualized feedback (examples as demonstrated on slides) would be useful during the meeting?
5. Do you have any ideas about other solutions for solving problems related to social dynamics in meetings?

The focus group consisted of 8 participants (two project teams of a post-graduate curriculum at the Technische Universiteit Eindhoven) and lasted about 90 minutes. Before the focus session we recorded 2 real meetings on video to obtain illustrative materials for the focus group session. The focus discussion was led by a facilitator and one participant was appointed to take notes. After each question the participants were asked to note down their answers for our later reference.

The most important outcome was that participants considered the social dynamics feedback during the meeting potentially useful, as it might improve the efficiency of the meetings. It was also considered useful for people who want to participate more in a meeting but do not manage to do so: participants indicated that it is important to make the group aware of the degree to which individual group members participate in the discussion. They all had experience with problems during the meetings related to the social dynamics, such as: two people discussing for a long time in a subgroup; one person talking for a long time and behaving like a chair of the meeting without being appointed as such, etc. The fact that one person speaks for a long time, neglecting the others, can cause a bad mood and annoyance.

Participants agreed that feedback, such as a notification to the speaker that the audience is bored, should be provided during the meeting rather than afterwards. Furthermore, feedback should be objective, positive, general, and public. In addition to public feedback, private feedback providing more details might be useful as well.

3   Design

We applied an iterative design process: we worked out a first concept, set up a series of group meetings in which the initial concept was applied and then adjusted the concept on the basis of the remarks by the meeting participants and ran a further evaluation.

Design concept. Concept development was guided by the literature, the results from the focus group, the group meetings, a CHIL deliverable on user requirements for the various CHIL services [13], unpublished ethnographical studies of meetings conducted at TUE and general usability considerations. The concept emerged from discussions within the design team and with an expert in information visualization and interaction design. The resulting concept consisted of a visualization of the ongoing social dynamics on a shared display, showing the following aspects of social dynamics:

- Cumulative speaking time of each participant.
- Duration of the current turn.
- Cumulative and current visual attention for speakers.
- Cumulative and current visual attention for listeners.

The visualization is projected in the centre of a table, as shown in Figure 1 for a four meeting participants setting.

Fig. 1. Left: Visualization of current and cumulative speaking activity and visual attention for each participant P#, with P2 as the current speaker. Right: Snapshot from experimental session. Further explanation in text.

The four "wind directions" (corresponding to four sides of the meeting table) represent participants P1, P2, P3 and P4, respectively. The visualization contains the following components: (1) The right-hand circle (coded **Sa**) represents how much attention a participant received while speaking from the other participants since the beginning of the meeting. (2) For the current speaker, this circle is surrounded by an outer, lighter-coloured ring representing how much visual attention s/he receives from the other participants. (3) The middle circle (coded **S**) represents the participant's cumulative speaking time since the beginning of the meeting. (4) Again, for the current speaker, this circle is surrounded by an outer, lighter-coloured ring, the size of which represents the duration of the ongoing turn. (5) The left-most circle (coded **A**) indicates how much visual attention the participant – as a listener - has received from the other participants while they were speaking (added up across all other participants). The different circles are distinguished by different colours (the codes are not included in the visualization). The information is updated dynamically in real-time. Visual attention is derived from eye gaze. In order to facilitate users' memory of the meaning of the different circles, we designed icons serving as mnemonics which are displayed underneath the circles (see Figure 2).

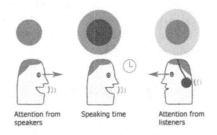

Fig. 2. Icons explaining the meaning of each circle

The visualization is generated on the basis of combined audio (speech) and visual (focus of attention) cues, captured in real-time during the meeting. In order to implement the concept, different technologies might be applied (some of which are being developed in the CHIL project). In order to determine speaking time for individual participants, it suffices to equip individual participants with close-talking microphones and to detect onset and offset of voice activity from the separate microphone signals. In order to determine visual focus of attention, eye gaze might be determined from a panoramic camera in combination with a context model. Or, depending on the spatial arrangement of participants, eye gaze might be inferred from head orientation, determined from a panoramic camera, as in [17], or from special devices mounted to the heads of the participants that can be tracked with an Infrared camera.

4   Qualitative Evaluation

In order to get a first impression of whether the concepts under development make sense and to identify problems, we conducted a formative evaluation. Several groups consisting of 4 people engaged in discussion sessions during which feedback was provided on the social dynamics by means of the visualization concept. We invited both pre-existing teams and ad-hoc groups. Pre-existing teams may be expected to behave differently from ad-hoc teams as they have already an established social structure. The discussion was followed by a semi-structured interview with a focus on identifying usability problems and soliciting suggestions for improvement, alternative solutions, and preferences for design options.

Since the purpose of the current experiments was to evaluate the visualization concept, rather than implementing the technologies we applied a Wizard of Oz approach. A simple web interface was developed to enable 4 wizards to simulate the perceptual components of visual attention tracking and speech activity detection for meetings of four participants, where each wizard monitored the speaking activity and the eye gaze of one participant. The four wizards monitored the meeting through one-sided mirrors and/or tv-screens. During the meeting, wizards indicated the state of the eye-gaze and speaking activity whenever there was a change in the behaviour of the participant. All the wizards' codings were recorded by the central server. Obviously, such a set-up requires that we calculate the inter-wizard reliability and the reliability of the wizard codings vis-a-vis the actual events. These checks are still in progress and will be reported in later publications.

The results of the experiment were encouraging: groups in general perceived the social feedback during their meeting as a useful and positive experience which made them aware of their group dynamics. Importantly, most of the group members expressed their satisfaction with the visualisation feedback and indicated that the changes in the feedback were noticeable, even though the feedback was provided in the periphery of the visual field. A few participants indicated that they were distracted at the beginning and this was mainly because they wanted to see explicitly how the patterns of verbal and non-verbal communication were reflected in the display. Some of the participants said that the visualised feedback influenced their behaviour and as a result the participants were enthusiastic and motivated to establish balanced participation in the meeting. Ultimately, they tried to provide others with the opportunity to speak.

5   Quantitative Evaluation

Hypotheses and setup. Small adjustments were made to the visualization on the basis of the formative evaluation, mainly concerning the increment reflecting changes over time for the different visualization components. Next, a comparative evaluation was conducted to assess the influence of the feedback on the social dynamics during the meeting both qualitatively and quantitatively, comparing meetings without and with feedback. With the second evaluation we aimed to validate the following hypothesis:

1. Speaking time will be balanced more equally in sessions with feedback than in sessions without feedback. Concretely, participants who under-participate in NoFeedback conditions will participate more in Feedback conditions and participants who over-participate in NoFeedback conditions will participate less in Feedback conditions.

2. Attention from the speaker will be divided more equally between listeners in Feedback conditions than in NoFeedback conditions. Concretely, listeners who receive less attention from the speaker in NoFeedback conditions will receive more attention in Feedback conditions and listeners who receive more attention from the speaker in NoFeedback conditions will receive less attention in Feedback conditions

3. Shared attention (attention from listeners for the speaker) will be higher in Feedback conditions.

4. Participants' satisfaction about group communication and performance will be higher in the presence of feedback visualization.

In order to evaluate hypothesis 4, subjective judgments about participant's satisfaction with the visualization feedback were collected by means of a questionnaire. Group satisfaction was assessed by a satisfaction questionnaire combining questionnaires about group process and decision making [10], [12]. An additional set of questions was included to address participants' subjective judgements about usefulness and usability of the service (including aspects such as participation, distraction, awareness and privacy).

The experiment applied a within-subjects (or rather "within-group") design. Every group participated in two discussion sessions in which the members discussed the best solution for a particular topic. In one condition feedback was provided, in the other no feedback was provided. At the beginning participants were told that participation was voluntary and they were asked to sign the consent form. All groups were asked for a written permission for audio and video recording. Next they filled in a standard personality questionnaire. In each condition (with and without feedback), the groups first had a 5 minutes discussion about a topic that they could select from a list provided by the experimenter. The 5 minutes discussion served for the group members to get used to each other and to the environment, and to familiarize with the feedback. The five minutes discussion in the Nofeedback condition was included to ensure that both target conditions would be preceded by an initial discussion. To avoid order effects, order of feedback and Nofeedback conditions was balanced across groups. It was left up to the participants to reflect or not on the displayed information.

Experimental task. First we planned to use a hidden profile decision task [18], making groups discussing the selection of a student from a set of students for admission in a programme in one session and the choice of a location for a shop from a number of possible locations in the other session [4]. However, a pilot test showed that people started reading their hidden facts from the paper during the discussion in order to find the best decision. As our intention was to observe the visual attention, it was decided to redesign the hidden profile tasks. All members received the same facts, but each participant had to defend a different position, representing a particular set of beliefs and values (a profile). E.g., for the student selection task one participant would emphasize financial incentives associated with admission of particular students whereas another member would emphasize intellectual ability. The goal of each task for the group was to reach consensus about the optimal choice during a 20 minutes group discussion. Users were told in advance that no task description would be available during the discussion. First the experimenter instructed the participants to study their profile and the alternatives independently and make a preliminary choice. They had 15 minutes to write down and memorize the important arguments. In order to simplify the memorizing task, the amount of choice parameters was reduced and the number of options to choose from was limited to three for each task. The discussion began only when every member is ready; additional time was given on request. A pilot test showed that people discussed actively and defended their beliefs and values according to the profile very enthusiastically. The main tasks were counterbalanced with feedback conditions. The total duration of an experiment was about 2 hours. As in the first test, for the visualization condition a Wizard of Oz approach was applied.

Participants. In total 44 (18 female and 26 male) participants took part in the experiment in groups of 4 persons. Members of at least two groups knew each other in advance. Participants were Dutch and foreign students and researchers of the different departments of the University (Technische Universiteit Eindhoven). The average age of participants was 29,5. All groups had members of both genders and were composed of the people of the same or close social status in order to prevent higher-status dominance [15]. In particular, students were in different group than senior researchers. One of the groups was eliminated from the data analysis due to missing speaking activity data for one participant, leaving 10 groups, comprising 40 subjects.

Measures. Measures for speaking time, attention from speaker and shared focus of attention were obtained from the log files of the Wizard codings, indicating speaking time and gazing behaviour for individual participants once a second. All parameters were expressed as percentages. For Speaking time, each participant's speaking time was expressed as the percentage of time that participant had been speaking of the overall speaking time for that session. For Attention from the speaker, the attention for each individual participant when listening was expressed as the percentage of time that the participant had been looked at by the speaker, summing over the different speakers throughout the session. Shared attention for the speaker was expressed as the number of participants that had been looking at the speaker simultaneously, converted to percentages, for each individual participant when speaking. For instance, if during a particular turn all other three members had been looking at the speaker all the time, it would amount to 100% shared attention for that turn. If two speakers had been looking all of the time and the third listener not at all, it would amount to 67% shared attention. Percentages were summed across all turns of each individual participant.

Quantitative results

Speaking time. Figure 3 shows a scatter plot containing the speaking time (%) for each individual participant in the NoFeedback and the difference score in the Feedback and NoFeedback condition. As can be seen, there is a clear negative trend, meaning that participants who speak relatively much in the NoFeedback condition show a decrease in Speaking Time (a negative difference score) and participants who underparticipate in the NoFeedback condition speak relatively more in the Feedback condition (show a positive difference score). The Pearson correlation is -.53, with an associated t of –3.88 (df = 38), p<.05. The same results are obtained if we compute the correlation on deviation scores for individual participants against the group mean. However, this analysis assumes that scores of individual participants are independent, which is clearly not the case. Therefore, we also computed deviation scores for each participant from the group mean ($|i_{i=1,4}$-group mean|) and calculated the mean deviation per group in the no-feedback and feedback condition. In this analysis, the difference between no-feedback and feedback conditions was in the predicted direction (group mean deviation no-feedback: 9.07, feedback: 7.74) but not significant (t(9)=1.26, p=.24). Thus, although we find some evidence supporting hypothesis 1, stating that speaking time will be balanced more equally in sessions with feedback than in sessions without feedback, the difference between the two conditions is not significant.

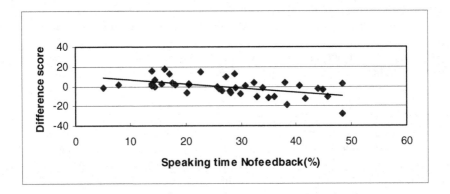

Fig. 3. Scatter plot of speaking time in NoFeedback condition and Difference score Speaking time Feedback-NoFeedback, for individual participants

Attention from speaker. Fig. 4 shows a scatter plot containing the attention from the speaker (%) for each individual participant in the NoFeedback and the difference score in the Feedback minus the NoFeedback condition. As can be seen, there is a clear negative trend, meaning that participants who get relatively little attention from the speaker in the NoFeedback condition receive more attention from the speaker in the Feedback condition, while the reverse holds for participants who receive relatively much attention from the speaker in the NoFeedback condition. The Pearson correlation is -.36, with an associated t of –2.36 (df = 38), p<.05. Again, computing deviations from the group mean and comparing the mean deviation per group in the no-feedback and feedback condition showed that the difference between the no-feedback and feedback condition was in the predicted direction but not significant: no-feedback: 9.45, feedback: 8.38 (t(9)=0.94, p=.37). Thus, although we find some evidence supporting hypothesis 2, holding that the attention from the speaker will be divided more equally between listeners in Feedback conditions than in NoFeedback conditions, the difference between conditions is not significant.

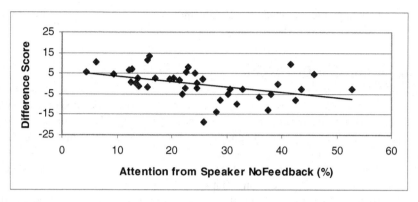

Fig. 4. Scatter plot of Attention from speaker in NoFeedback condition and Difference score Attention from Speaker Feedback-NoFeedback, for individual participants

Shared attention. For shared attention, our hypothesis stated that there would be an overall increase in shared attention from the NoFeedback condition to the Feedback condition. This was not supported by the data, neither for individual scores ($t(39)$=-1.81, p=.08) nor for group means ($t(9)$=-1.78, p=.11), although the difference between the NoFeedback and Feedback conditions was in the predicted direction: 68.17% shared attention for NoFeedback and 70.64 %shared attention for Feedback. So, hypothesis 3 is not confirmed.

Questionnaire results. The results of the group process satisfaction show that the feedback had a positive influence on the group process satisfaction. All questionnaires used 7-point Likert-scales. Analysis of questions on satisfaction with the group process showed a significant difference between answers for Feedback and NoFeedback in favour of Feedback in 7 out of 15 questions.

Table 1. Paired T-test for the Difference D between Feedback and NoFeedback condition

Feedback-NoFeedback	Mean D	SD	t	Sig.
Group participation worked very well	0.53	1.57	2.12	.04
There was no disruptive conflict	0.63	1.74	2.28	.03
Comments reflected respect for one another	0.40	1.24	2.05	.05
Participants reached agreement	0.78	2.07	2.37	.02
People were friendly	0.48	1.06	2.83	.01
General quality of participants' contributions was very good	0.43	1.22	2.21	.03

Table 1 shows the results for the statements where the largest scores were observed. Analysis of the satisfaction with the decision making process showed no significant result. Results for questions about satisfaction with the service were quite positive and all above the middle value. Results for additional questions demonstrated that it was not embarrassing for the users to have the feedback in front of the group (mean=4.97), and they didn't find the information distracting (mean=4.25). Interestingly, even though participants often looked at the information, they also could easily forget about it. In our vision this is the advantage of peripheral information.

6 Conclusion and Discussion

We have presented a visualization service that generates feedback on speech activity and visual attention for participants in small group meetings. Evaluations provided preliminary evidence that the feedback service affected the amount of time participants spoke during the meeting; also, we obtained preliminary evidence that feedback influenced the way speakers distributed their visual attention across listeners during the meeting. Finally, we found that the feedback had a positive influence on the group process satisfaction. No effect was found for Shared attention. Possibly, the presence of the visualization itself may have drawn visual attention of the participants away from the speakers, interfering with our predicted effects. Further analyses are needed to get a better understanding of the data.

Several explanations may be conceived to explain the preliminary effects that we observed. At a basic level, the visualization may create a global awareness for social dynamics, as a result of which participants adjust their speaking behaviour and gazing behaviour. Alternatively, or in addition, the concrete moment to moment feedback may make participants aware that their current turn is getting rather long and that they are systematically neglecting particular listeners. Again, further analyses are needed to shed light on possible explanations.

Finally, it needs to be pointed out that our current experiments and results concern situations where equal participation is valuable, since participants need to reach agreement and each participant's viewpoint should receive due attention. Obviously, equal participation is not always useful. In a meeting where there is a chairman whose main purpose is to inform the audience, or when a team has invited an expert, one would not want the chairman or expert to pursue equal participation as an aim in itself, and a completely different rhythm of the conversation will be appropriate. However, even in those cases the speaker's eye gaze may serve to make feel people connected and committed to contribute when appropriate. Thus, even though the precise patterns will differ across different types of meetings, we believe that feedback on social dynamics will help to improve meeting behaviour.

Acknowledgements

The work reported in this paper was supported by the Integrated Project CHIL IP 506909, funded in the thematic area Information Society Technologies under the Sixth Research Framework Programme of the European Union. We thank Janienke Sturm and Rahat Iqbal for assistance in various stages of the research and Joan DiMicco from MIT for making available the hidden profile tasks. We also thank an anonymous reviewer for suggestions for improving the paper.

References

1. Argyle, M. *Social Interaction*. London: Methuen (1969)
2. Bakx, I., Turnhout, K. van, Terken, J.: Facial orientation during multi party interaction with information kiosks. In *Proceedings of Interact* 2003
3. Basu, S.: Towards measuring human interactions in conversational settings. In *Proceedings of the IEEE International workshop on Cues in Communication CUES*. 2001.
4. DiMicco, J., Pandolfo, A., Bender, W.: Influencing group participation with a shared display. In *Proceedings of the 2004 ACM conference on Computer Supported Cooperative Work. CSCW*. (2004) p. 614-623
5. Hogg, M.A.: *The Social Psychology of Group Cohesiveness. From Attraction to Social Identity*, Harvester Wheatsheaf (1992)
6. Janis, I.: Victims of Groupthink: *A Psychological Study of Foreign-Policy Decisions and Fiascoes*, Boston: Houghton Mifflin (1972)
7. Kendon, A.: Some functions of gaze direction in social interaction. *Acta Psychologica* 26 (1967), p. 22-63
8. Kraemer, K. and King, J.: Computer-based systems for cooperative work and group decision making. *ACM Computing Surveys* 20, 1988 p. 115-146
9. McGrath, J.: Time, interaction and performance (TIP): A theory of groups. *Small Group Research* 22, 1991, p. 147-174
10. Olaniran B.A.: A Model of Group Satisfaction in Computer-Mediated Communication and Face-to-Face Meetings. In *Behaviour and Information Technology*, 15, 1996, p. 24-36
11. Parker, K.: Speaking turns in small group interaction: A context sensitive event sequencing model. *Journal of Personality and Social Psychology*, 54, 1988, p. 956-971
12. Paul, S., Seetharaman P., Ramamurthy K.: User Satisfaction with System, Decision Process, and Outcome in GDSS Based Meeting: An Experimental Investigation. *Hawaii International Conference on System Sciences*. 2004
13. Pianesi, F. (Ed.): *User Requirements and Scenarios Evaluation for the Various Services*. Deliverable 3.1 of the CHIL project. ITC-IRST 2005
14. Sacks, H., Schegloff, E., J.efferson, G.: A simplest systematics for the organisation of turn-taking for conversation. *Language. Journal of the linguistic society of America* 50, 1974, p. 696-735
15. Silver, S. D., Cohen, B. P., & Crutchfield, J. H.: Status differentiation and information exchange in face-to-face and computer-mediated idea generation. *Social Psychology Quarterly* 57, 1994, p. 108-123
16. Shaw, M.: *Group Dynamics: The Psychology of Small Group Behavior*. McGraw Hill, New York 1981
17. Stiefelhagen, R., & Zhu, J.: Head orientation and gaze direction in meetings. In *Proceedings of Human Factors in Computing Systems*. CHI2002, 2002, p. 858-859
18. Stasser, G., D. Stewart: Discovery of Hidden Profiles by Decision Making Groups: Solving a Problem versus Making a Judgment. *Journal of Personality and Social Psychology* 63, 1992, p. 426-434
19. Takemae, Y., Otsuka, K., and Mukawa, N.: Video cut editing rule based on participants' gaze in multiparty conversation. In *Proceedings of the 11th ACM International Conference on Multimedia*, 2003, p. 303-306
20. Vertegaal, R., Slagter, R., Veer, G. van der, and Nijholt, A.: Eye gaze patterns in conversations: There is more to conversational agents than meets the eye. In *Proceedings of Human Factors in Computing Systems. CHI2001*, 2001, p. 301-308

A Multimodal Discourse Ontology
for Meeting Understanding

John Niekrasz and Matthew Purver

Center for the Study of Language and Information, Stanford University,
Cordura Hall, 210 Panama St., Stanford, CA 94305-4115, USA
{niekrasz, mpurver}@csli.stanford.edu

Abstract. In this paper, we present a multimodal discourse ontology
that serves as a knowledge representation and annotation framework for
the discourse understanding component of an artificial personal office
assistant. The ontology models components of natural language, multimodal communication, multi-party dialogue structure, meeting structure, and the physical and temporal aspects of human communication.
We compare our models to those from the research literature and from
similar applications. We also highlight some annotations which have been
made in conformance with the ontology as well as some algorithms which
have been trained on these data and suggest elements of the ontology
that may be of immediate interest for further annotation by human or
automated means.

1   Introduction

People can communicate with great efficiency and expressiveness during natural interaction with others. This is perhaps the greatest reason that face-to-face
conversations remain such a significant part of our working lives despite the numerous technologies available that allow communication by other means. Nevertheless, businesses spend millions of dollars each year conducting meetings that
are often seen as highly inefficient [1], and there is great interest in researching these interactions to better understand them, create technology to facilitate
them, and assist in the recording and dissemination of their content.

To do this in a manner that is truly useful to organizations and desirable to
individuals, automated "meeting understanding" should encompass not only the
annotation of video and audio for playback, but the extraction of relevant information at the level of semantics and pragmatics: what subjects were discussed,
what decisions were made, and what tasks were assigned [2]. Because natural
multi-party interactions are vastly complex, and because this information we
wish to extract is equally complex, of many different types, and expressed in
many different modalities, a meeting understanding system must have an *integrated* and *expressive* model of meetings, discourse, and language supporting it
to effectively manage its knowledge.

For our meeting understanding system, a component of the Cognitive Assistant that Learns and Organizes (CALO), knowledge integration and expression

S. Renals and S. Bengio (Eds.): MLMI 2005, LNCS 3869, pp. 162–173, 2006.

is performed through the use of a formal ontology. Our work in the design of this ontology parallels that which has has been termed "meeting modelling" [3], "meeting ontology" [4], or "meeting data model" [5] elsewhere in the literature. While other efforts of this kind are similar in purpose, to our knowledge, our ontology is the only implementation that (1) integrates such a wide variety of components, (2) is directly linked to a domain of understanding, and (3) uses an expressive semantics for representation and inference.

In the following sections, we present our multimodal discourse ontology (henceforth, MMDO) and describe its purpose in the CALO system. Section 2 provides a clearer problem definition in relation to similar research. In Sect. 3, we describe the ontology itself in detail. Finally, in Sect. 4, we present some of the current and potential functional uses of the ontology in performing automatic understanding and annotation.

2   Background

There are currently multiple efforts being undertaken to create systems that observe, organize, facilitate, or otherwise understand meetings automatically. Each effort has brought forth distinct proposals for models of meetings and their associated data. Many commonalities may be found between these models, while in some cases, differing motivations and requirements have caused new approaches to be taken.

One nearly universal motivation is for the support of human end-user applications. [5] proposes a model for meetings and meeting data intended for a meeting browsing web tool; [3] describes a generic model for corpus-based multimodal interaction research supporting remote conferencing and virtual simulation; [4] describes an ontology of collaborative spaces and activities for meeting argumentation structuring, navigation, and replay. Our ontology is designed similarly to support human end-user applications like these, including a meeting browser with search, summary, and playback capabilities and a proactive assistant for relevant document retrieval during the meeting. Additionally, the system is designed to answer user queries similar to those obtained in user studies such as [6] and [2], each of which is formally encoded as a knowledge base query which uses the ontology's terminology.

In addition to considering the human end-user, the MMDO is also designed to facilitate inter-process communication within an adaptive automatic discourse and natural-language understanding architecture, which requires the modelling of concepts that may *not* play a role for the user. Any information generated by individual components, e.g. the speech recognizer or natural language parser, must be specified in the model in order to be communicated system-wide, increasing the ontology's complexity and requiring that it take into account constraints imposed by the functioning of system components.

The MMDO, as one of many subontologies in the CALO system ontology, is a model and representation which is directly compatible with the ontologies supporting CALO's other functions, such as event calendaring, email and contact management, and task monitoring. Since these concepts and knowledge about them are the very subject matter of the meetings we wish to automatically understand, this compatibility allows our ontology to elegantly connect to representations of discourse subject matter.

Another driving factor in our design is the system's upper ontology. All ontologies in the CALO system are designed using the Component Library (CLib) ontology [7], a library of generic atomic and complex concepts, each representing a type of entity, event, role, or property. While we will not describe implementation specifics in this paper, the reader should be aware that CLib and CALO's component ontologies, including the MMDO, are implemented by the CLib maintainers in the Knowledge Machine language [8], an expressive frame-based knowledge representation language with first-order logic semantics.

Our design of the MMDO, following the motivations presented above (see [9] for a comparable set of motivations in the design of a dialogue act taxonomy), is meant to remain flexible and generic. In many cases models are purposefully underspecified to support further theory development. In others, system requirements have prompted full specification of models that may change to accommodate a more generic architecture. We will now turn to describing the core ontology that is a foundation for the MMDO.

2.1   Upper Ontology

The CLib [7] serves as the CALO system's upper ontology. Its components are designed to be reusable and composable by non-experts and therefore take inspiration from natural language, causing its concepts to be relatively intuitive to users. The principal division in the library is between *Entities* (things that are) and *Events* (things that happen). Events are divided into *States* and *Actions*, where states are relatively static and brought about or changed by actions. In addition, a *Role* is something an entity *is* in the context of an event. Composition is then achieved through the use of *relations* between components and *properties*. Every concept in the MMDO described below is designed through composition and relation to these and other previously defined components.

2.2   The CLib Communication Model

The CLib ontology includes a Communication Model (CM), a model of communication and knowledge exchange between agents. It includes three layers, representing the physical, symbolic, and informational components of individual communicative acts (the *Communicate* event); the events in these three layers typically occur simultaneously, transforming the communicated domain-level *Information* into an encoded symbolic *Message*, from this message into a concrete physical *Signal*, and back again (see Fig. 1, where dashed lines divide the layers). *Events* are depicted as ovals and *Entities* are depicted as darker rectangles. The arrows signify *relations*. The three layers may be interpreted as aligning with the layers of joint action described in [10] at which communicative

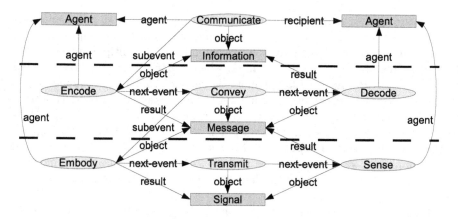

Fig. 1. The CLib Communication Model

grounding takes place. To complete the first layer, there must be *attention*; for the second, *identification*; and for the third, *understanding*.

As a foundation for further development of the MMDO, we posit a functional interpretation of the *Communicate* event that is appropriate for structuring multi-party human dialogue. Namely, the *Communicate* event is taken to serve the role of an atomic *communicative act*: a temporally contiguous communicative action with a possible interpretation and contextual significance, along the lines of what may be called a *speech act*, *dialogue move*, *dialogue act*, or *conversational act/move* in the literature. Its role in the ontology as described below will serve as its formal definition.

3   The Multimodal Discourse Ontology

We now turn to describing the details of the MMDO. We present the ontology in three parts proceeding conceptually from local to global elements. First, Sect. 3.1 describes extensions to the CM required to apply its internal model of communicative acts to natural multimodal communication; Sect. 3.2 then goes beyond these internals to describe the discourse model that connects communicative acts together and that defines their relationship to individual participants in a multiparty discourse; finally, Sect. 3.3 describes our model of the meeting activity and its relationship to the participants, the discourse, and the meeting environment.

3.1   Extending the Communication Model

At the level of individual communicative acts, our model uses the CM as a starting point, but requires several extensions to take into account both the constituent structure of natural language and the multimodal, multi-party nature of meeting dialogue.

Multimodal Communication. The basic CM assumes a one-to-one mapping across its three layers, neglecting the multimodal co-expression of speech and gesture that is found in natural conversation [11] (e.g. simultaneous verbal and gestural reference, as in "Can you pass me that [point] cup please?"). To model multimodal communication, we extend this to multiple media via the CLib concepts of *Medium* and *Language*, where a *Signal* must be transmitted over some *Medium* and a *Message* must be encoded in some *Language*. For a single *Communicate* event, we now allow the *Encode* action to produce a multiplicity of *Messages*, each in their own *Language*, which each generate their own physical signal in some *Medium*. Speech is characterized as employing any *SpokenLanguage* such as *SpokenEnglish* and the medium of *Sound*; writing of text employs a *WrittenLanguage* such as *WrittenEnglish* and the medium of *Ink*; natural human gesture employs the language of *HumanGesture* and the medium of *Light*.

Additionally, the basic association of physical-layer events with various media are encoded as definitional axioms for subclasses of the *Embody* event such as *Speak*, *Draw*, and *Gesticulate* (*Hear*, *Read*, and *See* are encoded as subclasses of *Sense* for the sensory half of the model). By asserting these latter physical-layer events independent from the symbolic or informational layers, they may optionally serve to represent events like coughing or accidental ink-marks that are produced in the appropriate mode but determined to be without linguistic or communicative function.

Constituent Structure. Despite our addition of a dimension supporting multi-modality to the CM, there remains a single symbolic entity (a *Message*) between the physical signal and the domain interpretation for each mode. In extending our model to natural language, and in particular when providing a basis for automatic NL processing, we of course require a more complex representation which includes not only the multiple layers of utterance representation in the CM but also their internal constituent structure (representations of individual words and phrases within utterances). While keeping to the CM model, we therefore take *Messages* as our equivalent of *signs*, with lexical, syntactic, semantic, phonological, or semaphoric (gestural) representations expressed as properties thereof.

Our framework follows that of the General Ontology for Linguistic Description [12], positing a recursively-defined *LinguisticUnit*, which is the building-block of *Messages* and is a *Message* itself. Units are then built into constructions through composition, generating a *LinguisticConstruction* (a collection of units forming its own unit), a *LinguisticConstituent* (one of two or more units that form a construction), and a *LinguisticAtom* (a unit that is not a construction). These generic classes are realized through medium- and language-specific subclasses, allowing information in all modalities to be expressed in the same framework. For written and spoken language, these specific subclasses include *Word* and *Sentence*, together with sub-lexical units such as spoken *Phonemes* and written *OrthographicUnits*. For graphical representations such as whiteboard diagrams, they include atomic and compound *DiagramObjects*. For gestural communication, they include units such as *DeicticGesture* and *IconicGesture*, modelling the set of gestures termed "semaphoric" in [11].

Physical Embodiment and Signal Segmentation. If we are to be able to replay particular constituents for analysis, or to train processing components (e.g. speech recognizers) based on their observed realizations, this linguistic constituent structure must be linked to a parallel structure in the layer of physical signals, and we therefore elaborate the CM one step further. We take the *Embody* event to be composed of *subevents* that realize the individual constituents of the *Message*, resulting in temporal sub-constituents of the overall *Signal*. This provides us with an event-based (temporal) representation for the physical realization of linguistic constituents, allowing a representation for language-based signal segmentation of audio, ink, and video, a common task and important requirement for linguistic and multimedia annotation (see [13] for a discussion).

Semantics. In the case of gestural acts such as *DeicticPoint*, knowledge of its referent is enough to fully characterize the *Information* component in the communication model. Units of natural language, however, are semantically more complex and need to be annotated for meaning at their multiple constituent levels. In the MMDO, this is handled by each linguistic constituent (including the *Message* as a whole) potentially having a *logical-form* component, allowing us to express not only the propositional content of the constituent, but also the referential content of individual words and phrases where suitable. This component is expressed using the CLib ontology and its component domain ontologies, realizing a direct link to the system's knowledge base. Additionally, given the high levels of uncertainty due to speech recognizer errors and ungrammatical speech, full propositional semantic annotation will often not be possible for the highest-level *Message*. However, in application we take a robust fragment-parsing approach within a Davidsonian semantics, allowing us to posit event, entity, and role representations wherever possible, while leaving other entities or roles underspecified.

Communicative Roles. The basic CM contains a simple representation for the relations that individuals have to a communicative act. They are either the *recipient* or *agent* of the events in the model. For natural multi-party conversation, this is overly simplistic. People may be overhearers of acts even though they are not the direct addressees; and the intended addressee of an utterance or gesture may be the entire group (e.g. lecturing), a subset (e.g. third-party talk), or an individual. The basic model will therefore not support algorithms for addressee detection (and subsequently turn-taking and initiative management in an interactive system). We therefore add *Addressee* and *Overhearer* to the set of *Roles* that a *Person* may play in a *Communicate* event.

3.2 Modeling Discourse Structure

The extensions described so far are restricted to individual communicative acts. This section describes further extensions that allow us to express relations between these acts, providing an integrated model of a *Discourse* event and its structure.

Dialogue Structure. Our notion of discourse structure is expressed by considering a set of *Communicate* events as *dialogue moves*, expressed via membership of particular subclasses and with their interrelation expressed via the properties associated with these subclasses. Following e.g. [14], we class moves at more than one nominally independent layer. At the most fundamental level, we consider only a move's effect on the immediate short-term context, and use the *generic* act level of MALTUS [14] (compatible with the MRDA scheme [15]). This includes the basic acts *Statement*, *Question*, *Backchannel* and *Floorholder*, but not more intentional acts such as e.g. *propose*, *challenge* (see below).

However, rather than simply label moves, we use their *antecedent* property to express discourse structure directly, relating each move to its antecedent. At this level we restrict moves to having a single antecedent, but allow multiple moves to share the same antecedent; this results in a tree structure (following [16]) able to express not only simple adjacency pairs but multiple possibly simultaneous threads represented by the branches of the tree. We take each tree to be a *Discourse*, a structurally related set of individual *Communicate* acts, required to be semantically or pragmatically coherent via constraints on their structural relations.

These constraints on the classes of move that can serve as each others' antecedents can of course be expressed directly by constraints on the *antecedent* property associated with those classes (e.g. answers must have queries as antecedents, backchannels must have antecedent moves with different speakers). However, our intention is to model not only the move structure of the discourse, but its effect on the emerging context, and so we combine this approach with a notion of *information state* and constraints on its update. This allows us to express the information-state update approach familiar in dialogue processing ([17] among others) directly within the MMDO, rather than requiring a separate dialogue management module or rule set. As set out below, we believe this is advantageous for automated processing and learning, allowing multiple constraint types to be considered simultaneously. The exact constraints will depend on the model of information state used: in an obligation-based model an *Ask* move can be associated directly with the introduction of an addressee's obligation to address the question; in a question-based model it can be associated with the direct introduction of a new question under discussion [17]. Importantly, including these fine-grained semantic constraints does not commit us to a bottom-up approach, building semantic interpretations and using them to derive move type; on the contrary, standard dialogue move classifiers can be used to hypothesize move types, and the information state constraints used to influence or disambiguate semantic interpretation.

Argumentation and Decision-making. At a higher level of abstraction, we also allow for a coarser-grained level of structure intended to model the argumentative and decision-making processes of meeting discourse (embodying a notion similar to that of "rhetorical relations" or "discourse structure" in the analysis of text) such as the raising of issues and the proposal, defense, rejection and acceptance of alternative solutions to the issue [18]. We do not regard it as either practicable or desirable to assign this structure at the level of individual utterances (the level of individual *Communicate* acts assumed in the dialogue structure of the previous section). Instead, raising issues or proposing alternatives is a function often performed by segments of multiple utterances. A single coherent proposal sequence might consist of multiple atomic statements and questions, and it will be most useful to users to report it in this way. We therefore posit *Communicate* events that have multiple *Encode* subevents, spanning those events which characterize dialogue moves. These higher-level acts of communication characterize steps in a negotiative process such as *Propose*, *Reject*, and *Accept*, each acting on an *Issue* which is represented using the domain ontology in the same manner as the logical form content of dialogue-level communicative acts.

3.3   Modeling the Meeting Activity

The previous sections describe a bottom-up discourse model, assembling a pragmatically unified *Discourse* structure out of interrelated *Communicate* events. However, meetings are not just discourse; they may include non-communicative activities (e.g. note-taking, waiting for all to arrive) and multiple discourses (e.g. simultaneous side conversations, dialogues separated by breaks for equipment setup). The MMDO therefore models a *Meeting* as an independent class of collaborative *Activity*, an event that has a collection of component *subevents*, the majority of which are *Discourses*. Our only restriction on the subevents is that they occur in one location over a contiguous period of time. As well as the bottom-up characterization, we can therefore also segment *Meeting* and *Discourse* activities in a top-down, coarser-grained way.

Coarse Segmentation. User studies such as [6] demonstrate that a temporally-coarse characterization of a meeting can help users to extract information from annotated meeting records. Automatic coarse segmentation of meetings has correspondingly been the subject of much research, but approaches differ widely in the concepts of *segment* used. One approach is to segment according to "group actions", recognizing physical group activities using speech and/or multimodal features of the discourse [19–21]. The taxonomies used combine a high-level analysis of discourse type (e.g. monologue and discussion) with physical actions of the participants (e.g. presence at the whiteboard and note-taking). In earlier work [22, 19], the taxonomy included activities based on an argumentative dimension of the discourse (e.g. consensus and disagreement), though these do not appear in later analysis. [5] suggest a similar set of "meeting activities" but include a wide variety of other concepts like voting, multiple simultaneous discussions, and silence. A contrasting approach [23] suggests a simple taxonomy contrasting multi-party, multi-directional exchange of information with uni-directional exchange, to attain high coverage and low ambiguity. In addition, segmentation can also be driven by content – e.g. [24] incorporate lexical features to segment discourse by topic.

It is clear from this variety of segmentation methods that no single segmentation nor taxonomy of segments is objectively optimal. Nevertheless, each type of segmentation is likely to provide a useful means for meeting browsing, summary and information retrieval. Therefore, rather than identifying a single taxonomy of segment classes in the MMDO, we have adopted the aims of high coverage, low ambiguity, and high inter-annotator agreement highlighted in [23] and [9], and have identified a number of nominally independent dimensions over which either a *Meeting* or *Discourse* can be usefully segmented and classified.

At a coarse-grained level, a *Meeting* may be segmented along the dimensions of *physical state* and *agenda state*. *Physical state* depends only on the physical activities of the participants (for example, all participants being seated around a table, vs. one being at the whiteboard while the rest are in their seats). *Agenda state* refers to the position within a previously defined meeting structure, whether specified explicitly as an agenda document (providing a list of classes) or as directed by a meeting leader.

At a similar level of granularity, *Discourses* may be segmented along the dimensions of *information flow* and *topic*. *Information flow* describes the general discourse type (e.g. is the subject matter open for discussion with participation by several parties, or is there a one-directional flow as in a presentation or briefing) [23]. *Topic* then describes the coherence of the theme or semantic content of the discussion (we expect this to align significantly with the agenda state for some meeting types). We anticipate that both of these dimensions will be useful for browsing and summarization of meetings, and have produced annotations and initial algorithms to support doing this [25]. We also anticipate that finer-grained segmentations of *Discourses* may be useful, for example according to *floor-holding* activity, and include this ability in the MMDO.

Participant Roles and Segment Classes. In each of the above dimensions, segments may then be classified and participants assigned roles in those events. While we have yet to define a comprehensive set, we provide some potential examples to clarify.

In the dimension of physical state, a frequent suggestion in the literature is for a segment class of "presentation" or "whiteboard" [19–21]. In our model, the *physical state* of being at the whiteboard is represented independently of an *information flow* dimension. Thus, for the segment in the latter dimension, the roles of *InformationProvider* and *InformationConsumer* are specified (see [23]); while the segment in the former dimension will require a single role of one person at the whiteboard.

As a further example, in the turn-taking dimension, a single person may be said to be the *FloorHolder* for some segment of a *Discourse*, and the ontology may assert the constraint that only one person may play this role. Of course, this state will be affected by the floor-handling nature of communicative acts and constraints may be imposed on this relationship in the ontology as well.

4   Automatic Processing and Annotation

The depth and breadth of the ontology mean that it provides not only a complete basis for knowledge storage and annotation, but also a framework for automated communication between software agents. A multi-agent system has been built in collaboration with other project partners that populates a knowledge base with the fundamental physical signal information (video, audio, and sketch) recorded during a meeting. Given that information, separate interpretive agents populate the knowledge base with instances of the classes described above, building up a representation of the discourse, using each others' assertions as a foundation (see [26] for a more application-relevant discussion of the ontology along these lines).

Our first step in applying this software framework as part of CALO has been to create algorithms for adaptive topic segmentation and classification. A number of different approaches have been investigated, both discriminative (including decision trees based on lexical and discourse information such as speaker activity changes and the proportion of silence, following [24], and maximum entropy models based on simple lexical features) and generative (adapting [27] to model discourse topic shifts as changes between states in a topic-word Markov model). Results so far are encouraging, with P_k error levels against a set of human annotations approaching 30% (a level not far from typical human annotator agreement, see [25]) for individual classifiers.

5   Future Work

Both human and automated annotation of meetings is currently being performed using this framework for a set of meetings being collected at multiple institutions. However, some elements of the MMDO framework have not yet been applied to these data, and in the future we expect to address these elements, which include principally the argumentative and decision-making aspects, semantic alignment with domain ontologies, and detection of floor-holding mechanisms and addressee detection. Additionally, we are planning to use the availability of simultaneous multimodal information to learn classifiers for multimodal speech act detection (using not only prosodic and lexical information, but the semantic parser output). We are also working on a software framework called *NOMOS* to support flexible human annotation and visualization using this and other ontology-based models [25].

Acknowledgments

The authors would like to thank Satanjeev Banerjee, Ken Barker, Vinay Chaudhri, Jerry Hobbs, and Sanjeev Kumar for their help and suggestions toward the design of this ontology, as well as Bill Jarrold for his implementation of the design in KM. We also wish to express our appreciation to David Demirdjian, Lynn Voss, Yitao Sun, and the other CALO developers who have worked with us to align their components with the ontology to create CALO 2.0. This work was supported by DARPA grant NBCH-D-03-0010.

References

1. Romano, Jr., N.C., Nunamaker, Jr., J.F.: Meeting analysis: Findings from research and practice. In: Proceedings of the 34th Hawaii International Conference on System Sciences. (2001)
2. Lisowska, A., Popescu-Belis, A., Armstrong, S.: User query analysis for the specification and evaluation of a dialogue processing and retrieval system. In: Proceedings of the 4th International Conference on Language Resources and Evaluation. (2004)
3. Reidsma, D., Rienks, R., Jovanović, N.: Meeting modelling in the context of multimodal research. In: Lecture Notes in Computer Science. Volume 3361. Springer-Verlag (2005) 22–35
4. Bachler, M.S., Shum, S.J.B., Roure, D.C.D., Michaelides, D.T., Page, K.R.: Ontological mediation of meeting structure: Argumentation, annotation, and navigation. In: Proceedings of the 1st International Workshop on Hypermedia and the Semantic Web. (2003)
5. Marchand-Maillet, S.: Meeting record modelling for enhanced browsing. Technical Report 03.01, Computer Vision and Multimedia Laboratory, Computing Centre, University of Geneva, Switzerland (2003)
6. Banerjee, S., Rose, C., Rudnicky, A.: The necessity of a meeting recording and playback system, and the benefit of topic-level annotations to meeting browsing. In: Proceedings of the 10th International Conference on Human-Computer Interaction. (2005)
7. Barker, K., Porter, B., Clark, P.: A library of generic concepts for composing knowledge bases. In: Proceedings of the 1st International Conference on Knowledge Capture. (2001)
8. Clark, P., Porter, B.: KM - The Knowledge Machine 2.0: Users manual (2004) http://www.cs.utexas.edu/users/mfkb/RKF/km.html.
9. Popescu-Belis, A.: Dialogue acts: One or more dimensions? ISSCO Working Paper 62 (2005) University of Geneva.
10. Clark, H.H., Krych, M.A.: Speaking while monitoring addressees for understanding. Journal of Memory and Language **50** (2004) 62–81
11. Quek, F., McNeill, D., Bryll, R., Duncan, S., Ma, X.F., Kirbas, C., McCullough, K.E., Ansari, R.: Multimodal human discourse: Gesture and speech. ACM Transactions on Computer-Human Interaction **9**(3) (2002) 171–193
12. Farrar, S., Langendoen, T.: A linguistic ontology for the semantic web. Glot International **7**(3) (2003) 97–100
13. Ide, N., Romary, L., de la Clergerie, E.: International standard for a linguistic annotation framework. In: Proceedings of the HLT-NAACL Workshop on the Software Engineering and Architecture of Language Technology. (2003)
14. Clark, A., Popescu-Belis, A.: Multi-level dialogue act tags. In: Proceedings of the 5th SIGdial Workshop on Discourse and Dialogue. (2004)
15. Shriberg, E., Dhillon, R., Bhagat, S., Ang, J., Carvey, H.: The ICSI Meeting Recorder Dialog Act Corpus. In: Proceedings of the 5th SIGdial Workshop on Discourse and Dialogue. (2004)
16. Lemon, O., Gruenstein, A.: Multithreaded context for robust conversational interfaces: Context-sensitive speech recognition and interpretation of corrective fragments. ACM Transactions on Computer-Human Interaction **11**(3) (2004)
17. Traum, D., Bos, J., Cooper, R., Larsson, S., Lewin, I., Matheson, C., Poesio, M.: A model of dialogue moves and information state revision. In: Task Oriented Instructional Dialogue (TRINDI): Deliverable 2.1. University of Gothenburg (1999)

18. Pallotta, V., Niekrasz, J., Purver, M.: Collaborative and argumentative models of natural discussions. In: Proceedings of the 5th Workshop on Computational Models of Natural Argument. (2005)
19. Dielmann, A., Renals, S.: Dynamic bayesian networks for meeting structuring. In: Proceedings of the IEEE International Conference on Acoustics, Speech, and Signal Processing. (2004)
20. Reiter, S., Rigoll, G.: Segmentation and classification of meeting events using multiple classifier fusion and dynamic programming. In: Proceedings of the International Conference on Pattern Recognition. (2004)
21. McCowan, I., Gatica-Perez, D., Bengio, S., Lathoud, G., Barnard, M., Zhang, S.: Automatic analysis of multimodal group actions in meetings. IEEE Transactions on Pattern Analysis and Machine Intelligence 27(3) (2005) 305–317
22. McCowan, I., Bengio, S., Gatica-Perez, D., Lathoud, G., Monay, F., Moore, D., Wellner, P., Bourlard, H.: Modeling human interaction in meetings. In: Proceedings of the IEEE International Conference on Acoustics, Speech, and Signal Processing. (2003)
23. Banerjee, S., Rudnicky, A.: Using simple speech-based features to detect the state of a meeting and the roles of the meeting participants. In: Proceedings of the 8th International Conference on Spoken Language Processing. (2004)
24. Galley, M., McKeown, K., Fosler-Lussier, E., Jing, H.: Discourse segmentation of multi-party conversation. In: Proceedings of the 41st Annual Meeting of the Association for Computational Linguistics. (2003)
25. Gruenstein, A., Niekrasz, J., Purver, M.: Meeting structure annotation: Data and tools. In: Proceedings of the 6th SIGdial Workshop on Discourse and Dialogue, Lisbon, Portugal. (2005)
26. Niekrasz, J., Purver, M., Dowding, J., Peters, S.: Ontology-based discourse understanding for a persistent meeting assistant. In: Proceedings of the AAAI Spring Symposium Workshop on Persistent Assistants: Living and Working with AI. (2005)
27. Blei, D., Moreno, P.: Topic segmentation with an aspect hidden Markov model. In: Proceedings of the 24th Annual International Conference on Research and Development in Information Retrieval. (2001) 343–348

Generic Dialogue Modeling
for Multi-application Dialogue Systems

Trung H. Bui, Job Zwiers, Anton Nijholt, and Mannes Poel

Human Media Interaction, Department of Computer Science, University of Twente,
Postbox 217, 7500 AE Enschede, The Netherlands
{buith, zwiers, anijholt, mpoel}@cs.utwente.nl

Abstract. We present a novel approach to developing interfaces for multi-application dialogue systems. The targeted interfaces allow transparent switching between a large number of applications within one system. The approach, based on the Rapid Dialogue Prototyping Methodology (RDPM) and the Vector Space Model techniques, is composed of three main steps: (1) producing finalized dialogue models for applications using the RDPM, (2) designing an application interaction hierarchy, and (3) navigating between the applications based on the user's application of interest.

1 Introduction

A multi-application dialogue system is defined as a dialogue system allowing the user to navigate between a set of applications. Applications considered range from simple tasks such as operating a home device or booking a flight to more complex tasks such as controlling a smart-room or managing the (road) traffic.

To date, due to the complexity of the management of language interfaces and their strong dependence on the interaction context, a really generic approach for multi-application dialogue design does not yet exist; each application or a set of applications requires the development of a specific model. Multi-application dialogue model prototyping therefore represents a significant part in the development process of multi-application interactive systems. However, most current prototyping methods are limited to the development of dialogue systems working on a single application or a small set of applications [3], [8], [10], [12].

In this perspective, we aim at developing a generic dialogue modeling methodology for the efficient production of interfaces for multi-application dialogue systems. The targeted interface allows transparent switching between a large number of applications within one system. The approach, based on the Rapid Dialogue Prototyping Methodology (RDPM[1]) [1] and the Vector Space Model (VSM) techniques, is composed of three main steps: (1) producing finalized dialogue models for applications using the RDPM, (2) designing an application interaction hierarchy based on VSM techniques, and (3) navigating between the applications based on the user's application of interest.

---

[1] A methodology allowing a quick production of frame-based dialogue models.

S. Renals and S. Bengio (Eds.): MLMI 2005, LNCS 3869, pp. 174–186, 2006.

These steps are described in sections 2, 3, and 4 respectively. A scenario example for producing a dialogue system accessing 10 applications in the ICIS domain [2] is presented in section 5. Finally, in sections 6 and 7 we summarize the main points of the paper and possible further extensions of the methodology respectively.

2 Producing Finalized Dialogue Models for Applications Using the RDPM

The finalized dialogue model for each application can be quickly produced using the RDPM.

The general idea underlying the RDPM is that the dialogue model is a frame-based model that can be quite easily and systematically derived from a relational representation of the application itself, hereafter called the task model. More precisely, the RDPM consists of five main consecutive steps, namely: (1) *producing a task model* for the targeted application; (2) automatically *deriving an initial dialogue model* from the produced task model; (3) using the generated interface to *carry out Wizard-of-Oz experiments* (i.e. dialogue simulations) to improve the initial dialogue model; (4) *carrying out an internal field test* to further refine the dialogue model (reformulation of system messages, improved feedback, etc.), and to validate the evaluation procedure (coherence, understandability); and (5) *carrying out an external field test* to evaluate the final dialogue model according to the evaluation procedure defined during the internal field test. Steps 1 and 2 are briefly described in the next sections in the context of producing finalized dialogue models for applications, the remaining steps are described in detail in [1].

2.1 Task Model

In the RDPM, an application is seen as a set of functions the user can invoke through a multimodal interface to perform the various functionalities provided by the application. In this perspective, an application is modeled as a *solution table* [1], where the rows correspond to the possible functions (also called "solutions" or "targets") and the columns are the attributes needed to uniquely identify each of the functions, and to invoke it. In other words, the values of the attributes in a row of the solution table (also referred to as canonical values) correspond to the values of the arguments of the function, the call of which results in the fulfillment of the corresponding application functionality. For example, in the ICIS domain, the task model for the patient search can reduce to a single generic function select_patient(name, age, address,...), the attributes of which identify the selection features available for the patient search. Therefore, the task model of the patient search is a solution table with as many columns as there are attributes, the rows of which are the various value combinations corresponding to

---

[2] ICIS stands for Interactive Collaborative Information Systems, a Dutch research project which aims at developing intelligent collaborative information systems technology in order to reduce risks and damages in chaotic complex environments.

patients. At the computational level, the calls to the select_patient() function are implemented in the form of SQL queries to the solution table containing the required information.

2.2 Finalized Dialogue Model for a Single Application

In our approach, a finalized dialogue model is defined as a set of interconnected multimodal Generic Dialogue Nodes (referred to as mGDNs [9]), where each of the dialogue nodes is associated with one of the attributes (also called "slots" or "fields") in the solution table. In complex applications, these mGDNs are divided into groups, where each group is considered as an object and the mGDNs in the group are attributes of the object. For instance, the *First Name, Last Name,* and *Function* mGDNs belong to the *Person* group. For any given slot, the role of the associated mGDN is to perform the simple interaction with the user that is required to obtain a valid value for the associated attribute. In the architecture that we have selected for the implementation of our multimodal dialogue-driven interfaces, the processing of the mGDNs (i.e. the actual interaction with the user according to the specification of the mGDNs) is performed by a specific module called the *local dialogue manager.* However, this is, of course, not sufficient to carry out any real dialogue: some form of global dialogue management also has to be integrated. For example, in addition to the definition of the mGDNs and the specification of the local dialogue manager, some branching logic responsible for the management of the global dialogue flow needs to be specified. In our approach, this branching logic is hard-coded in a specific dialogue management module, called the *global dialogue manager.* The underlying assumption is that the encoded local and global dialogue flow management strategies are indeed application-independent, i.e. that, in most situations, they lead to an acceptable, though not always optimal behavior for the system. Consequently, in our approach, dialogue model design essentially reduces to the application-dependent, declarative specification of the mGDNs, the encoded dialogue management strategies being used without modification for all applications. In short, a finalized dialogue model consists of two main parts: (1) the application-dependent, declarative specification of the mGDNs; and (2) the application-independent (local and global) dialogue flow management strategies encoded in the corresponding (local and global) dialogue manager. Both of these components are described in more detail in [1].

2.3 System Architecture

The general architecture of the dialogue system corresponding to each single application produced by the RDPM is represented in Fig. 1.

Three input modalities: voice, text and pointing can be used independently or simultaneously depending on the configuration of the current active mGDN [9]. These inputs are pre-processed by the Natural Language Understanding (NLU) modules and the Pointer Understanding (PU) module. The outputs from NLU and PU modules are semantic triples (attribute, value, time-stamp). The fusion

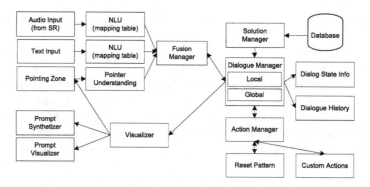

Fig. 1. Architecture of dialogue systems produced by RDPM

manager integrates the semantic triples receiving from the NLU and PU modules and sends a set of integrated semantic triples to the dialogue manager. In the current implemented version, the fusion manager simply collects the semantic triples based on their time-stamp relation and forwards them to the dialogue manager.

The dialogue manager encodes the local dialogue flow management strategy and global dialogue management strategy. Therefore, the input to the dialogue manager is first processed by the local dialogue management strategy in which we define five types of generic situations: *OK, Request for Repetition, Request for Help, NoInput,* and *NoMatch* [1].

In the case of the *OK* situation, control is handed back to the global dialogue manager which applies the global dialogue management strategy for the activation of the next mGDN. The dialogue state information (e.g. the current dialogue state, the active mGDN, etc.) and the recognized semantic triples are updated to the dialogue state info module and the dialogue history module respectively. When the dialogue manager gathers enough constraints [3], it sends the request to the action manager, the application connected with this module performs the task and sends the feedbacks to the action manager, the action manager then forwards these feedbacks to the dialogue manager. In addition, functions related with user modeling and system customization have been integrated such as *Reset Patterns* and *Custom Actions*. Reset Patterns allows the system to adapt to the behavior of a specific user or population of users by anticipating their next decisions. The idea is to develop an intelligent reset algorithm that estimates the most probable values for some mGDNs slots in a new dialogue session according to the previous interactions with the user. Custom Actions allows the users to dynamically associate sequences of solutions with a single new solution. The main goal of these two functions is to reduce the time to perform a task with the interface. The hypothesis is that these functions will indeed increase the quality

---

[3] This happens when the number of solutions (extracted from the solution manger) satisfying the current constraints is smaller than or equal to a pre-defined solution threshold.

of the interaction as perceived by the user. These two functions are described in detail in [2].

The outputs from the dialogue manager to the visualizer are multimedia prompts containing messages and a pointing zone update content. The messages are visualized in the user interface (Prompt Visualizer) and/or uttered by the mGDN during the interaction (Prompt Synthesizer). The messages are combined with the pointing zone update content (the content is a map, a calendar or a table depending on the nature of the mGDN) to allow the user to provide the desired values using keyboard, microphone or mouse click/touchscreen.

3   Designing an Application Interaction Hierarchy

In section 2, we showed that it is possible to produce n finalized dialogue models $M_0, M_1, ..., M_{n-1}$ from n applications $A_0, A_1, ..., A_{n-1}$ using the RDPM [4], the question is how to integrate these applications in one unique system (i.e. multi-application dialogue system).

Vrugt and Portele [12] introduced a dialogue system accessing multiple applications with a dynamic setup that can be changed at run-time. Their goal is achieved by application-independent knowledge processing inside the dialogue system based on modular ontological descriptions. They also define a clear interface between a dialogue system and applications by realizing a generic dialogue functionality on top of the application independent knowledge processing. This approach assumes that the user knows exactly which application he is going to interact with and therefore it is not scalable to the development of dialogue systems with a large number of applications.

Carroll and Carpenter [3] developed a call-routing dialogue system using the VSM techniques. The system allows routing the user's telephone call to the right department. Two main modules in the system are the routing module and the disambiguation module. When the routing module returns more than one candidate applications, the disambiguation module is invoked. The disambiguation module determines the number of terms relevant to the user's request (say n) and uses a YN-question ($n = 1$) or a WH-question ($n > 1$) to identify the desired application (i.e. the department) or transfers the call to the operator ($n = 0$). The authors do not view each application as a finalized dialogue model, therefore no further interaction happens when an application is identified.

We organize applications in a hierarchy since it allows flexible dealing with a large number of applications [4]. The hierarchy can be created manually or automatically. When the number of application is large (hundreds, thousands, or more [5]), it is difficult to create the hierarchy manually, therefore an automatic process is suitable for this case. In our approach, the hierarchy is produced automatically using VSM techniques and an hierarchical clustering algorithm.

---

[4] Each application can have its own set of input modalities as described in section 2.3.

[5] We assume that each application is described by an associated textual document and the main goal is to find out the user's application of interest.

3.1   Application Interaction Hierarchy

An application interaction hierarchy is an m levels hierarchy of n finalized dialogue models consisting of three types of nodes:

1. Root (level: m-1): unique node on the top of the hierarchy.
2. Internal nodes (level: from m-2 to 1): each internal node consists of at least two child nodes, a child node can be an internal node or a leaf. The hierarchy accepts lattice nodes (i.e. internal nodes, each of them has more than one father node).
3. Leaves(level: 0): correspond to n applications.

An application interaction hierarchy ($n = 10$) is represented in Fig. 4.

3.2   Vector Space Model for the Finalized Dialogue Models

We assume each finalized dialogue model which the production is described in section 2 is characterized by a textual description of the associated application. The textual description can be extracted from the mapping tables (cf. Fig. 1). We represent these descriptions by k-dimension vectors $d_0, d_1, ..., d_{n-1}$ using the VSM techniques.

The following paragraph presents the process of producing vectors and computing the similarity between the textual descriptions of the applications using the standard VSM technique (in the implementation phase, a suitable VSM and the number of index terms are selected based on the content of textual descriptions. For example, in case the textual description is a set of sentences, a semantic VSM taking into account the dependence between terms such as [11] is appropriate):

1. Produce index terms from the textual descriptions
   We analyze the textual descriptions using Natural Language Processing (NLP) techniques (syntactic analysis, morphological & stop words filtering, term extraction) to produce k index terms: $t_1, t_2, ..., t_k$.
2. Construct occurrence matrix F
   A description is represented by a lexical profile: $d_i = (w_{i0}, w_{i1}, ..., w_{ik-1})$. w_{ij} is the weight (or importance) of the jth indexing term t_j in the textual description d_i. w_{ij} is often simply the number of occurrences of t_j in d_i or the inverted occurrence frequency.
   The $n \times k$ occurrence matrix F:

$$
F = \begin{pmatrix} d_0 \\ d_1 \\ ... \\ d_{n-1} \end{pmatrix} = \begin{pmatrix} w_{00} & w_{01} & ... & w_{0k-1} \\ w_{10} & w_{11} & ... & w_{1k-1} \\ ... & ... & ... & ... \\ w_{n-10} & w_{n-11} & ... & w_{n-1k-1} \end{pmatrix}
$$

3. Compute the score (or measure the similarity)
   The most common similarity measure for the standard VSM is the cosine of
   the angle between the vectors:

$$sim(d_i, d_j) = \cos(\overrightarrow{d_i}, \overrightarrow{d_j}) = \frac{\sum_{p=0}^{k-1}(w_{i_p} \times w_{j_p})}{\sqrt{\sum_{p=0}^{k-1} w_{i_p}^2 \times \sum_{p=0}^{k-1} w_{j_p}^2}}.$$

We use this measure to determine the similarity between two applications,
i.e. the score between A_i and A_j : $s(A_i, A_j) = sim(d_i, d_j)$.

3.3   Hierarchical Clustering Algorithm

From the vectors $d_0, d_1, ..., d_{n-1}$ and their similarity computation produced in
3.2, we use the hierarchical clustering algorithm [7] to produce the application
interaction hierarchy:

1. Consider each d_i is a single cluster, we have n clusters, the distances between
   a pair of clusters i and j (in this step): $D(i, j) = 1 - sim(d_i, d_j)$.
2. Find the most similar pair of clusters (i.e. $\min(D(i, j))$) and merge them into
   a single cluster, so that we have one cluster less.
3. Compute distances between the new cluster and each of the old clusters.
4. Repeat steps 2 and 3 until all items are clustered into a single cluster of
   size n.

Step 3 can be done in several ways such as single-linkage, complete-linkage,
or average-linkage clustering [6]. Applying the single-linkage, the formula to calculate the distance between two clusters C_1, C_2:

$$D(C_1, C_2) = \min_{i \in C_1, j \in C_2}[D(i, j)]$$

The output of the presented clustering algorithm is a binary tree (Fig. 3), this
tree is transformed to an application interaction hierarchy based on the degree
of similarity between the applications [6] (Fig. 4).

4   Navigating Between Applications Based on the User's Application of Interest

The system aims to find out the target application with a minimal number
of dialogue turns. Based on the application interaction hierarchy produced in
section 3, the preliminary experimented work presented in [5], and the textual
content provided by the user, the user-system interaction process is described in
detail in the following algorithm:

---

[6] For example, if a node N_1 has two child nodes (N_2, N_3) and N_2 has two child nodes
N_4, N_5 and $[D(N_2, N_3) - D(N_4, N_5)] \leq \alpha$, α is a predefined threshold, then N_2 is
removed; N_4, N_5 become the child nodes of N_1.

1. **Start**

   The system starts with a generic prompt: "What can I do for you?" (similar to the internal GDN "Start" described in [1]).

2. **Active node determination**

   When receiving a user's request, the system first represents the request in the form of a vector $q = (q_1, q_2, ..., q_k)$ using the set of k index terms described in section 3.2, and then determines the active node on the hierarchy by the following steps:

   (a) Score computation

   Compute the similarity between q and $d_0, d_1, ..., d_{n-1}$, we obtain a set of scores $s_0, s_1, ..., s_{n-1}$: $s_i = sim(d_i, q)$.

   For example, in Fig. 2 we have $s_0 = 0.85$, $s_1 = 0.9$, ..., $s_9 = 0.15$.

   (b) Upward propagation

   Select the best scores at each level and propagates them upward until the root is reached.

   For example, in Fig. 2 we have $s_{0-2} = max(s_0, s_1, s_2) = 0.9$.

   (c) Downward traversal to determine the active node

   Start from the root, compute the difference between two highest score child nodes, if this difference is below a certain threshold (we call this threshold the internal node stop threshold $t_s : (0 < t_s \leq 1)$), then stop. If not, go down to the highest score child node and continue to determine the active node.

   For example, in Fig. 2, starting from M_{0-9}, we calculate the difference between M_{0-4} and M_{5-9}: $dif(M_{0-4}, M_{5-9}) = 0.4$, it is greater than $t_s = 0.15$, then we go down to M_{0-4}, we still have $dif(M_{0-2}, M_{3-4}) = 0.2$ is greater than t_s then we go down to M_{0-2}, we have $dif(M_0, M_1) = 0.05 < t_s$ then M_{0-2} is the active node.

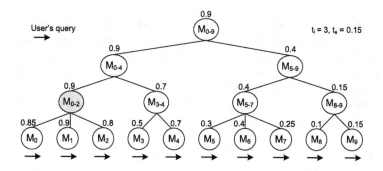

Fig. 2. Determine the active node based on the user's query

3. **Response generation**

   The active node identified in the previous steps can be a root, an internal node or a leaf. Two types of response depending on the position of the active node are:

(a) The active node is the root or an internal node

In this case, the functionality of the active node is similar to the list processing GDN described in [1]. The system shows a list of application candidates belonging to the active node and their score is not below the highest score leaf outside the active node (e.g. in fig. 2, M_4 is the highest score leaf outside the active node M_{0-2}). To avoid showing a bulky list to the user (particularly in case of vocal dialogue), the maximum number of application candidates is limited by a threshold called the list processing threshold t_l, with t_l is a positive interger. The user can determine to go **next** (i.e. show the t_l following application candidates), **previous** (i.e. show the t_l previous application candidates), **stop** (i.e. restart the dialogue), **up** (i.e. move to the upper level on the hierarchy), **down** (i.e. move to the highest score child node), or **select** the desired application. If the user does not change the active node (i.e he does not use the command up or down) and after browsing all the applications (belonging to the active node) he could not find his desired applications, the system temporarily assigns the scores of the browsed leaves to zero and goes back to step 2b.

(b) The active node is a leaf

The application takes control and interacts with the user as an application-specific dialogue system. If the user's request is out of the application's domain, go back to step 2.

An example of the algorithm with $n = 10$ and $t_l = 3$ is presented in Fig. 5 and explained in detail in section 5.3.

5   Scenario Example

This section illustrates, on the global level, the process of developing a dialogue system accessing 10 applications in the ICIS domain using three steps presented in sections 2, 3, 4. The applications are: car route navigation (A_0), air route navigation (A_1), traffic lanes (A_2), map and fire management (A_3), tunnel sensors management (A_4), weather forecast (A_5), virtual control room (A_6), road surface temperature monitoring (A_7), patient information search (A_8), and medical worker verification (A_9).

5.1   Step 1

Applying the RDPM, we produce the finalized dialogue models: $M_0, M_1, ..., M_9$.

5.2   Step 2

From the finalized dialogue models, we create the application interaction hierarchy (cf. Fig. 4). Finalized dialogue models for the root and internal nodes are the list processing mGDNs produced by the RDPM.The role of each node is to

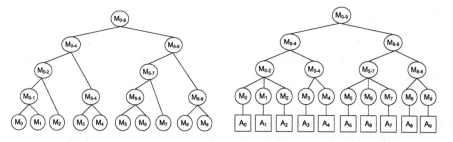

Fig. 3. Binary tree   **Fig. 4.** Application Interaction Hierarchy

select a subset of the applications belonging to it, for example the role of M_{0-2} is to select a subset of $\{A_0, A_1, A_2\}$.

5.3   Step 3

An example of the system-user interaction is presented in Fig. 5. The "Start" mGDN sends the system's prompt S_1 to the user. According to the content of the user's prompt U_2, the active node M_{0-2} is determined. M_{0-2} asks the user to select an application from the list $\{A_0, A_1, A_2\}$ (all three applications are shown because $t_l = 3$). Based on the user's answer in U_4, M_0 is activated. In steps from 5 to $k-1$, M_0 interacts with the user as an application-specific dialogue system. In step k, the user's request U_k is out of M_0's application domain, M_0 then forwards U_k to the system. The system analyzes U_k and activates M_8. M_8 continues the interaction with the user and processes the out of the application domain case in a similar manner M_0 has done.

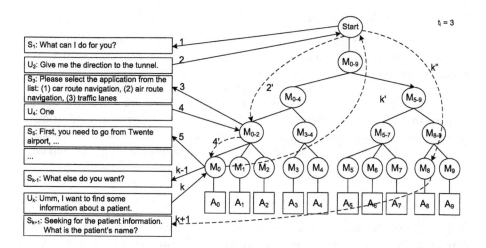

Fig. 5. Navigating between the applications

6   Conclusion

We have presented a framework for the development of interfaces for multi-application dialogue systems. Three important steps in the framework are described and illustrated by a scenario example.

Currently, the RDPM software toolkit is available for the development of finalized dialogue models for single applications. It has been used in three research projects: InfoVox [7], INSPIRE [8], IM2.MDM [9] to validate the principle idea of the methodology, and is being extended for the development of a large number of applications in the ICIS domain. The practical result shows that from a simple application, we can develop an initial dialogue model in several hours. The dialogue manager, the most important part of dialogue prototyping, covers most of the application independent dialogue functionalities (i.e. branching logic, dialogue dead-end management strategy, confirmation strategy, dialogue termination strategy, incoherencies, strategy defining level of initiative, etc.) Therefore, we can re-use the dialogue manager and the other modules described in section 2.3 for the development of multi-application dialogue systems.

Some initial work toward developing the application interaction hierarchy and navigating between the applications (sections 3 and 4) has been analyzed and implemented (e.g. NLP Pre-Processing Tool, VSM). The multi-application dialogue system for ICIS domain presented in section 5 is currently under development.

7   Future Work

Two main possible extensions of the generic dialogue modeling methodology we plan to study in the future are *crossing-application* and *task selection*.

7.1   Crossing-Application

The application interaction hierarchy created in section 3 can be used to manage several concurrent applications (i.e. crossing-application). This extension is significant when the user wants to simultaneously execute several applications in order to achieve his goal in an optimal way. For example, in the scenario presented in section 5, the user's goal is to find out an optimal route for sending a rescue team to the disaster site. Suppose that the system contains two applications, the car root navigation application and the traffic lanes application. Obviously, if the user can interact with both these applications simultaneously, his goal can be more quickly satisfied than he does with each application sequentially.

7.2   Task Selection

In the definition of the application interaction hierarchy in the section 3.1, we mentioned that each leaf corresponds to an application. In task-oriented dia-

---

[7] http://liawww.epfl.ch/Research/infovox.html

[8] http://www.knowledge-speech.gr/inspire-project/index.html

[9] http://www.issco.unige.ch/projects/im2/mdm/

logues, each application usually consists of several tasks. We can extend the hierarchy for identifying a task or a set of tasks in an application. To achieve this goal, the hierarchy will be constructed from the set of tasks in the same way we have done for the set of applications. Further work on task sharing (i.e. one task appears in several applications) will be studied.

Acknowledgements

We would like to thank Martin Rajman for his useful suggestions and comments about the generic dialogue modeling idea presented in this paper, Lynn Packwood for her advices in English writing, and the two anonymous reviewers for their useful comments on the first version of this paper. This work is part of the ICIS program (http://www.decis.nl/html/icis.html). ICIS is sponsored by the Dutch government under contract BSIK 03024.

References

1. T.H. Bui, M. Rajman, and M. Melichar. Rapid dialogue prototyping methodology. In *Proceedings of the 7th International Conference on Text, Speech & Dialogue (TSD 2004), P. Sojka, I. Kopecek & K. Pala (Eds.), Lecture Notes in Computer Science, Springer-Verlag, Berlin Heidelberg New York*, pages 579–586, Brno, Czech Republic, September 2004.
2. T.H. Bui, M. Rajman, and S. Quarteroni. Extending the Rapid Dialogue Prototyping Methodology: User Modeling. Technical Report WP4 Deliverable 4.3, Ecole Polytechnique Federale de Lausanne, Lausanne, Switzerland, August 2004.
3. J. Chu-Carroll and B. Carpenter. Vector-based natural language call routing. *Computational Linguistics*, 25(3):361–388, 1999.
4. D.R. Cutting, D.R. Karger, J.O. Pedersen, and J.W. Tukey. Scatter/gather: a cluster-based approach to browsing large document collections. In *SIGIR '92: Proceedings of the 15th annual international ACM SIGIR conference on Research and development in information retrieval*, pages 318–329, New York, NY, USA, 1992. ACM Press.
5. E. Forler. *Intelligent user interface for specialized web sites*. Ecole Polytechnique Federale de Lausanne (EPFL), Lausanne, Switzerland, diploma thesis edition, 2000.
6. A.K. Jain, M.N. Murty, and P.J. Flynn. Data clustering: a review. *ACM Computing Surveys*, 31(3):264–323, 1999.
7. S.C. Johnson. Hierarchical Clustering Schemes. *Psychometrika*, (2):241–254, 1967.
8. B. Lin, H. Wang, and L. Lee. Consistent dialogue across concurrent topics based on an expert system model. In *Sixth European Conference on Speech Communication and Technology (EUROSPEECH'99)*, Budapest, Hungary, 1999.
9. A. Lisowska, M. Rajman, and T.H. Bui. Archivus: A system for accessing the content of recorded multimodal meetings. In Samy Bengio and Hervé Bourlard, editors, *Machine Learning for Multimodal Interaction, First International Workshop,MLMI 2004, Martigny, Switzerland, June 21-23, 2004, Revised Selected Papers*, volume 3361, pages 291 – 304. Springer.

10. H.I. Ng and K.T. Lua. Dialog Input Ranking in a Multi-Domain Environment Using Transferable Belief Model. In *Proceedings of the 4th SIGdial Workshop on Discourse and Dialogue*, Sapporo, Japan, July 2003.
11. M. Rajman, R. Besanon, and J.-C. Chappelier. Le modèle DSIR : une approche à base de sémantique distributionnelle pour la recherche documentaire. *revue Traitement Automatique des Langues (TAL), 41(2), Paris*, 2001.
12. J. Vrugt and T. Portele. Application-Independent Knowledge-Processing in a Task-Oriented Speech-Dialog-System. *it – Information Technology*, 46(6):306–314, December 2004. `http://www.it-inftech.de`.

Toward Joint Segmentation and Classification of Dialog Acts in Multiparty Meetings

Matthias Zimmermann[1], Yang Liu[1],
Elizabeth Shriberg[1,2], and Andreas Stolcke[1,2]

[1] International Computer Science Institute
[2] SRI International, USA
{zimmerma, yangl, ees, stolcke}@icsi.berkeley.edu

Abstract. We present baseline results for the joint segmentation and classification of dialog acts (DAs) of the ICSI Meeting Corpus. Two simple approaches based on word information are investigated and compared with previous work on the same task. We also describe several metrics to assess the quality of the segmentation alone as well as the joint performance of segmentation and classification of DAs.

1 Introduction

As spoken language technology research moves toward more complex domains, further processing of the stream of words provided by a recognizer is often necessary. To support higher-level tasks such as information retrieval and summarization [1, 2], the input speech signal must be segmented into meaningful units, for example dialog acts (DAs). The five DA types used in this work are statements, questions, backchannels, floorgrabbers, and disruptions. The task we investigate here is how to split a stream of words into non-overlapping segments of text and assigning mutually exclusive DA types mentioned above to these segments. While this task description suggests a sequential solution, an approach based on joint segmentation and classification most likely performs best because knowledge of the classification might also improve the segmentation. We use the term *joint segmentation and classification* for systems that do not implement this task in the form of two independent modules running in sequence but produce their final result by taking into account information from both the segmentation and the classification.

Previous work mainly concentrated on either the segmentation of speech into sentences [3, 4] or the classification of already segmented text into various sets of DA types [5–8]. For automatic segmentation of speech it remains unclear how well a subsequent component can handle segmentation errors. For the latter case, the classification of DAs, it is typically assumed that the true segmentation boundaries are provided. As a consequence, a degradation of the performance due to imperfect segmentation boundaries must be expected. To provide more realistic results for the task of automatic segmentation and classification of DAs, a sequential approach is described in [9]. Results for the related task of

S. Renals and S. Bengio (Eds.): MLMI 2005, LNCS 3869, pp. 187–193, 2006.

subtype detection for sentence-like units (statements, backchannels, questions, or incomplete) for broadcast news and spontaneous telephone conversations were reported in [10]. In this paper we make a first attempt toward joint segmentation and classification of DAs on the ICSI (MRDA) Corpus [11].

2   Methodology and Performance Metrics

For the joint segmentation and classification of DAs, two simple techniques are investigated in this paper. The first technique is based on a hidden-event language model (HE-LM) described in [12], and the second relies on a hidden Markov model (HMM) based tagger. The HE-LM is frequently used for detection of sentence boundaries [9, 4], where after each word the model predicts a nonboundary or a sentence boundary event. In contrast, we use the HE-LM to predict not only a DA boundary or a nonboundary event, but the type of the DA boundary at the same time. This extension to [12] was also used in [3] to detect sentence boundaries and 5 different types of disfluencies. In our case the DA-specific boundary posterior probabilities are computed using forward-backward dynamic programming. The model can be seen as an nth order HMM in which the word/event pairs correspond to states and the words to observations, with the transition probabilities given by the n-gram LM.

The second technique relies on the concept of disambiguation of words, which is widely used in the form of HMM-based part of speech (POS) taggers. In our case a conventional n-gram LM is used to model the priors of sequences $((w_1, d_1), (w_2, d_2), \dots (w_n, d_n))$. The w_i are the words from the lexicon provided by the speech to text (STT) system and the d_i represent specific DAs, such as statements, questions, etc. To model segmentation boundaries between words of the same DA type, the lexicon of the DA types also includes special symbols indicating the first word of a new DA (e.g. the symbol $S+$ tags the first word of a statement, while the other words of a statement are tagged with an S). Mapping probabilities $p(w|(w, d))$ are then estimated from the LM training corpus. Note that compared to the conventional way of POS tagging based on HMMs, our model states do not correspond to the tags only, but to joint events of words and tags. Simple add-1 smoothing is applied to account for unseen word-DA combinations. Finally, the sequence $((w_1, d_1), (w_2, d_2), \dots)$ with the highest posterior probability is computed for a provided input sequence $(w_1, w_2, \dots)$.

To assess the performance of joint segmentation and classification of DAs, a number of measures have been proposed. We first describe two metrics for the measurement of the segmentation performance before metrics for the joint segmentation and classification of DAs are explained. The NIST-SU metric was used to report the segmentation performance in previous work [9] and has been defined by NIST for the EARS MDE evaluations [13]. As this measure takes into account only the local correspondence of reference boundaries and boundaries computed by the system, a direct interpretation of the resulting error rates is not always easy. To provide a more intuitive metric we propose the DA segmentation error rate (DSER), which measures the percentage of wrongly segmented DA

Reference	S|Q.Q.Q|S.S.S|B|S.S|
System	S|Q|S|Q.Q|D.D.D|S.S|S|
NIST-SU	C E E C C E E C
DSER	C| E | C |E| E |

Metric	Errors	Reference Units	Error Rate
NIST-SU	3 FA, 1 miss	5 boundaries	80%
DSER	3 match errors	5 DAs	60%

Fig. 1. Two metrics for the assessment of segmentation performance. S, Q, B, and D represent words of statements, questions, backchannels, and disruptions. DA boundaries are indicated using the symbol '\|', while '.' is used for nonboundaries. Errors and correct cases are indicated using letters E and C.

Reference	S|Q.Q.Q|S.S.S|B|S.S|
System	S|Q|S|Q.Q|D.D.D|S.S|S|
NIST-SU	C E E C E E E C
Lenient	C C E C C E E E E C C
Strict	C E E E E E E E E E E
DER	C| E | E |E| E |

Metric	Errors	Reference	Error Rate
NIST-SU	1 sub., 3 FAs, 1 miss	5 boundaries	100%
Lenient	5 match errors	11 words	45%
Strict	10 match errors	11 words	91%
DER	4 match errors	5 DAs	80%

Fig. 2. Comparison of metrics to measure joint performance of segmentation and classification of DAs

segments. A DA is considered to be mis-segmented if and only if its left and/or right boundary does not correspond to the reference segmentation exactly. This implies that the DSER metric penalizes missed cases more than false alarm (FA) cases, compared to the NIST-SU metric. See Fig. 1 for an illustration.

For the assessment of the joint performance of the segmentation and classification of DAs, four different metrics are used in the experiments described in Sec. 3. These metrics are illustrated in Fig. 2. First, the NIST-SU error metric is adapted to also include substitutions, not only missed boundaries or false alarms. Substitutions occur when the system outputs a DA boundary at the correct position, but the reference and the system disagree on the DA type on the left side of the boundary. The word-based "lenient" and "strict" metrics have been introduced in [9]. The lenient metric does not take into account the segmentation boundaries and only compares the DA types assigned to corresponding words. For the strict metric, a word is considered to be correctly classified if and only if it has been assigned the correct DA type and it lies in exactly the same DA segment as the corresponding word of the reference.

As a metric for the joint segmentation and classification of DAs that is easy to interpret, we propose the DA error rate (DER). This metric is derived from the

DSER and not only requires a DA to have exactly matching boundaries but also to be tagged with the correct DA type. The DER thus measures the percentage of the misrecognized DA and can be seen as a length-normalized version of the strict metric.

For completeness we also mention the recognition accuracy as described in [14], which corresponds to the classical word error rate. As in the case of the word error rate, the accuracy metric of [14] only relies on the sequence of symbols (DA types in our case) and does not consider the actual segmentation boundaries. Scoring is then based on the string edit distance. This metric is not used in the experiments below.

3   Experiments and Discussion

For all experiments reported here the experimental setup used is as described in [9]. Of the 75 available meetings in the ICSI MRDA corpus, two meetings of a different nature are excluded (Btr001 and Btr002). From the remaining meetings we use 51 for training, 11 for development, and 11 for evaluation. For the segmentation and classification of the DA types, the available speech is first sorted according to the speaker, and then by time. The available DA types are mapped to the following five distinct types: backchannels (B), disruptions (D), floor grabbers (F), questions (Q), and statements (S). Each system is then optimized and evaluated under both reference and STT conditions. Under the reference condition it is assumed that we have access to the true sequence of spoken words, while under the STT condition the recognizer's top-choice sequence of words is provided. The sequential approach to segmentation and classification of DAs described in [9] differs in a number of aspects from the systems investigated in this paper. Major differences lie in its sequential nature and the usage of prosodic and word-based information for both segmentation and classification of DAs. Prosody has been shown to help both the segmentation [4] and the classification of DAs [7]. While this system has the potential drawback of working in a sequential fashion, it is taking advantage of prosody in the segmentation step and requires access to the complete DA segment for classification. The potential advantage of the systems described in this paper lies in their ability to produce segmentation boundaries that are based on the estimation of the previous DA type for the last n words. However, both the HE-LM and the HMM tagger approach decide to segment and classify DAs based on local information only. Since the classification of the DA is implicitly done by predicting a corresponding DA boundary, valuable information is lost when the beginning of the current DA has fallen out of the current n-gram context.

Segmentation performance results of the different systems are provided in Table 1. To better compare the integrated approaches with the previous results, we report the segmentation error rate for [9] using the HE-LM alone without taking into account the prosodic pause feature. Note that, due to a minor difference in the counting of errors under STT conditions, the error rates given in Table 1 are slightly lower than those previously reported in [9]. Comparing the HE-LM

Table 1. Comparison of the segmentation error rates of the different systems under both reference and STT conditions

Condition	System	NIST-SU	DSER
Ref	[9]	34.5	40.8
	[9] np[1]	46.0	53.0
	HE-LM	46.3	55.3
	Tagger	51.1	61.7
STT	[9]	45.5	49.4
	[9] np[1]	59.5	62.0
	HE-LM	59.6	62.4
	Tagger	62.8	66.9

[1] reduced system, no prosody features

Table 2. Comparison of the segmentation and classification performance of the different systems under both reference and STT conditions

Condition	System	NIST-SU	Lenient	Strict	DER
Ref	[9]	52.6	20.0	64.4	54.4
	[9] np[1]	62.3	21.0	72.4	64.1
	HE-LM	62.2	23.3	74.3	66.5
	Tagger	69.5	22.6	78.6	72.6
STT	[9]	68.3	25.1	75.4	64.3
	[9] np[1]	78.3	25.0	82.9	73.2
	HE-LM	78.0	26.2	83.8	73.9
	Tagger	81.3	22.4	85.4	77.3

[1] reduced system, no prosody features

and the tagger approach of this paper, we notice that the HE-LM consistently outperforms the tagger on both segmentation metrics.

Performance results for the joint segmentation and classification of DAs are provided in Table 2 for the different systems. Again, performance results for the reduced version of [9] (not including prosody) is used for better comparison with the HE-LM and the tagger based methods. Compared with these results, the HE-LM approach shows a comparable performance, which is promising, given the simplicity of the approach. As we would expect, the system described in [9] in its original form outperforms the approaches investigated here. A notable result from these experiments is the observation that the tagger based approach shows the lowest lenient error rates and, at the same time, the highest error rates for the NIST-SU, the strict, and the DER metrics. This observation suggests that the lenient metric is most useful when used in combination with other metrics that take into account the quality of the segmentation as well.

4   Conclusion and Outlook

We have investigated two simple approaches based on word information for joint segmentation and classification of DAs in multiparty meetings. Furthermore, with the DSER and the DER we propose additional performance metrics for segmentation and joint segmentation and classification of DAs with a simple semantic interpretation. The DSER measures the percentage of the correctly segmented DAs, while the DER quantifies the percentage of correctly segmented and tagged DAs. Based on the experiments, we suggest that the lenient metric proposed in [9] should not be used alone but in combination with other metrics that also take into account the quality of the segmentation.

The results provided in this paper serve as a baseline against which we will measure the results of future work on joint segmentation and classification. As a next step we will investigate approaches that do not rely only on local evidence, but rather are able to take into account complete DA hypotheses along the lines of [14]. In such a framework it is also possible to integrate prosodic information and to consider word lattices.

Acknowledgments

We thank Barbara Peskin for her valuable comments. This work was supported by the EU Framework 6 project on Augmented Multiparty Interaction, DARPA Contract NBCHD030010, NSF Awards IIS-0121396 and IRI-9619921, and the Swiss National Science Foundation through the research network IM2.

References

1. Armstrong, S., et al.: Natural language queries on natural language data. In: Proc. NLDB, Burg, Germany (2003) 14–27
2. Waibel, A., et al.: Advances in automatic meeting record creation and access. In: Proc. ICASSP. Volume 1., Rhodes, Greece (2001) 207–210
3. Stolcke, A., et al.: Automatic detection of sentence boundaries and disfluencies based on recognized words. In: Proc. ICSLP. Volume 5., Sydney, Australia (1998) 2247–2250
4. Shriberg, E., et al.: Prosody-based automatic segmentation of speech into sentences and topics. Speech Communication **32** (2000) 127–154
5. Ji, G., Bilmes, J.: Dialog act tagging using graphical models. In: Proc. ICASSP. Volume 1., Philadelphia, USA (2005) 33–36
6. Ries, K.: HMM and neural network based speech act detection. In: Proc. ICASSP. Volume 1., Rhodes, Greece (2001) 207–210
7. Stolcke, A., et al.: Dialogue act modeling for automatic tagging and recognition of conversational speech. Computational Linguistics **26** (2000) 339–371
8. Webb, N., Hepple, M., Wilks, Y.: Dialog act classification based on intra-utterance features. Cs-05-01, Dept. of Comp. Science, University of Sheffield, UK (2005)
9. Ang, J., et al.: Automatic dialog act segmentation and classification in multiparty meetings. In: Proc. ICASSP. Volume 1., Philadelphia, USA (2005) 1061–1064
10. Liu, Y., et al: Structural metadata research in the EARS program. In: Proc. ICASSP. Volume 5., Philadelphia, USA (2005) 957–980
11. Shriberg, E., et al.: The ICSI meeting recorder dialog act (MRDA) corpus. In: Proc. SIGDIAL, Cambridge, USA (2004) 97–100

12. Stolcke, A., Shriberg, E.: Automatic linguistic segmentation of conversational speech. In: Proc. ICSLP. Volume 2., Philadelphia, USA (1996) 1005–1008
13. NIST website: Rt-03 fall rich transcription.
   http://www.nist.gov/speech/tests/rt/rt2003/fall/ (2003)
14. Warnke, V., et al.: Integrated dialog act segmentation and classification using prosodic features and language models. In: Proc. 5th Europ. Conf. on Speech, Communication, and Technology. Volume 1., Rhodes, Greece (1997) 207–210

Developing a Consistent View on Emotion-Oriented Computing

Marc Schröder[1] and Roddy Cowie[2]

[1] DFKI GmbH, Saarbrücken, Germany
[2] Queen's University, Belfast, Northern Ireland
http://emotion-research.net

Abstract. The network of excellence HUMAINE is currently making a co-ordinated, interdisciplinary effort to develop a consistent view on emotion-oriented computing. This overview paper proposes a "map" of the research area, distinguishing core technologies from application-oriented and psychologically oriented work. First results from the ongoing research in the thematic workpackages are reported.

1 Introduction

It is increasingly recognised that emotional factors in a broad sense are central to improving the naturalness of interaction between machines and their users. As humans, users react emotionally to aspects of their environment that matter to them [1], and these emotions will influence their way of acting [2], their way of thinking [3], and their decisions [4]. Furthermore, as social animals, humans expect their interaction partners to pick up signs of emotion and to react to them in some appropriate way [5]. Currently machines that interact with human users do not take account of the emotional dimension that humans expect to find in interaction, and that is a recurrent source of frustration. A simple example for emotionally inadequate system behaviour is a message window suggesting a software update which is triggered while the user is under time pressure or giving a presentation: it is likely to induce panic or anger rather than appreciation. A more sophisticated example is a multi-modal dialogue system that cannot anticipate the emotional impact of a piece of information on the user: if the system informs the user that, e.g., there are no more seats left on the flight the user wants to book, a standard happy-sounding voice will not improve customer relations.

Creating competent emotion-oriented systems is a large scale challenge. The European Network of Excellence HUMAINE (HUman-MAchine Interaction Network on Emotions) was established to prepare the scientific and technological ground for this task, with funding from the EU IST programme from 2004 to 2007.

HUMAINE follows a principled approach to addressing the large number of issues involved. As the network brings together researchers with a very wide range of backgrounds, a first phase of 18 months was scheduled in the work plan, whose

S. Renals and S. Bengio (Eds.): MLMI 2005, LNCS 3869, pp. 194–205, 2006.

aim was to identify an appropriate set of sub areas into which research can be structured, and to come to a common understanding of the core issues in each of these thematic areas. In several iterations, this first phase led to the establishment of plans for "exemplars", i.e. achievable pieces of work illustrating how things should be done in a principled way in a given area. In each thematic area, a workshop was held (or will soon be held), in which the subject matter is highlighted from a broad range of perspectives. The proceedings of these workshops are available on the HUMAINE portal (http://emotion-research.net/ws). The discussions of phase one are now basically complete, and the second phase is starting, in which these exemplars are actually built.

This paper reports on some of the key outcomes of the first phase, mainly by outlining the "exemplars" envisaged in order to advance the state of the art in the different thematic areas.

2   Mapping the Research Area

A key part of the first project phase is reaching an understanding of the various tasks and disciplines relevant to emotion-oriented computing, and the ways in which they may interact. The ideas incorporated in the initial HUMAINE proposal have fared reasonably well, but they have developed with experience. Figure 1 summarises what seem to be the key divisions and connections at this stage.

The central column represents the areas where purely technological challenges loom largest. It is not self-evident that detection and synthesis should function as separate sub-disciplines, and HUMAINE initially proposed a different division: but it has become clear that they draw on different background technologies. 'Planning action' involves modelling the kind of action pattern that might be expected in a particular emotional state, either so that an artificial agent can generate appropriate action patterns or so that it can anticipate the kinds of action pattern that a human might produce in a given state - which in turn may be used to recognise emotion or to select among various responses that might be considered.

The left hand column deals with issues where application is most obviously of concern. The special character of usability issues in this area has gradually become clearer. Finding out how users respond to an emotion-oriented system is both more difficult than it is for technologies with more objective aims, and more important. It is more difficult because emotional responses are subtle, and easily disrupted by interventions that are meant to measure them. It is more important because designing an emotion-oriented system is centrally concerned with accommodating to non-rational preferences and dispositions in the user. In that situation, iterative user-centred design methods seem likely to be indispensable. Work on emotion-related language could in principle be divided up among the sub-disciplines in the central column, but in practise it draws on different conceptual roots and has particular links to applications in the relatively near future. It has become clear that HUMAINE's workpackage on persuasion and communication in effect represents that area.

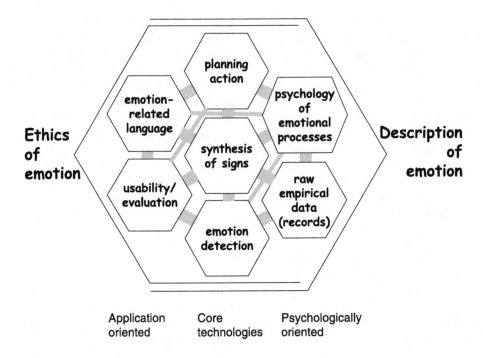

Fig. 1. Graphical representation of the sub-areas involved in achieving emotion-oriented computing

The right hand column contains the sub-areas with the strongest roots in psychology. These are divided between one concerned with theory and one concerned with empirical data, which was described in the original proposal as 'databases'. Of course existing theory is informed by data, but for a variety of reasons, it has not generally been the kind of data that it is natural to collect with a view to developing emotion-oriented systems. As a result, there are creative tensions between that kind of data collection and existing psychological theory. Similarly, psychological theory does not simply inform technological work. Technological work is a test of its accuracy and completeness in a general sense. It also promises to provide unparallelled tools to test theories, in the form of artificial agents whose actions can be controlled with a precision that is impossible with humans, and which therefore provide unparallelled opportunities to test theoretical ideas.

It is not an accident that synthesising signs of emotion is at the centre of the diagram. There are rich connections among all the areas, but the task of synthesising agents that can interact emotionally seems at the present time to be the one that best summarises the state of the art - in the sense that it cannot be done well without satisfactory progress in all the others. Conversely, failures in this area may expose problems in any of the other areas.

At either edge of the diagram are issues with a strong philosophical element which affect the whole enterprise, though they do not impact all of the areas equally. One, whose strongest effect is on the areas related to psychology, is finding appropriate ways to describe emotions and emotion-related states. The other, whose strongest effect is on the areas close to application, is the ethics of emotion-oriented systems.

This summary is deliberately at a broad level. The sections that follow look at individual thematic areas in more detail.

3   Describing Emotions

It is difficult to work with phenomena unless one has good ways of describing them. In the broad area of emotion, it is widely accepted that words in common use are an unsatisfactory medium. It is not simply that potentially interesting states elude description: even core terms like "emotion" or "affect" are defined differently by different experts, and they point non-experts in various directions according to context [6,7]. HUMAINE has chosen to confront the issue by making the description of emotion an explicit focus of research. It is being addressed on several levels.

At the first level, there has been vigorous discussion within HUMAINE about the domain that needs to be addressed [8]. The surface argument involves questions about how widely or narrowly to use words like 'emotion' and 'affect', but it reflects a deeper issue, which is to mark out a practically important set of problems that yield to conceptually related solutions. As a first step, HU-MAINE aims to map out states which are or might be considered to be related to emotion, and which are both reasonably common and potentially relevant in human-computer interaction. HUMAINE aims to carry out that kind of 'actuarial' exercise, and initial steps have been taken [9]. Words then need to be found (or invented) that allow the domains that matter practically to be described in a way that is convenient and intuitive.

At a second level, the Theory workpackage in HUMAINE has started to build up a glossary of emotion-related terms, drawing on the existing literature [10]. This conceptual and terminological clarification task will differentiate the different types of affective phenomena that should be distinguished from a theoretical perspective, while at the same time staying close to application concerns. Comments from the potential users of this vocabulary (e.g., the "system-builders" in the network) will be sought in several iterations, leading to successive clarification and re-formulation, culminating in definitions that can be used by researchers from any theoretical background. Establishing a common terminology will significantly reduce the barrier to cross-disciplinary cooperation in this area.

The third level involves the practical methods of describing individual emotional states. Newcomers to the field tend to use short lists of basic emotions, often not realising that these were proposed in the specific context of evolutionary, "Darwinian" emotion theories [6]. A key aim of the Theory workpackage is to promote awareness of the available choices of emotion descriptions, and the circumstances in which they may be useful. For example, lists of emotion words are being established that are particularly useful in the context of emotion-oriented technological systems [8]; descriptions of individual cognitive appraisal components can be related to aspects of facial expression; and broad dimensional labelling can be used to track the general emotional tone over time. As these options become better known in the technological community, system-builders can select the most suitable formalisms for their application.

The Databases workpackage in HUMAINE approaches the issue of emotion descriptions from a different angle [11]. Rather than formulating and specifying descriptions out of theory, this workpackage will explore the phenomena that can be found in "real" data, i.e. in naturalistic recordings of persons experiencing emotions [12]. Often, the phenomena observed in such contexts differ substantially from the clear-cut ideas that come to the fore in emotion theories. For example, emotion-related states of low intensity, as they often occur in natural dialogue, cannot easily be described by emotion theories which focus on intense, fullblown emotions. In addition, word-based emotion representations ("anger", "sadness" etc.) cannot easily capture the composites and shades of emotion that are frequently observed in naturalistic data, e.g. when two emotions are simultaneously present, or when one emotion is expressed in order to mask another one that is experienced [13]. One of the aims of the Databases workpackage is to provide "provocative" data which exposes these issues. On that basis, it aims to identify labelling schemes that are genuinely suited to describe that kind of material. These are expected to combine elements of several existing approaches – description using everyday verbal categories, broad dimensional descriptions, and descriptions based on appraisal theory.

4   Detecting and Generating Signs of Emotion

One fundamental of natural human-machine interaction is the ability to detect the signs of emotion emitted by the user, intentionally or unintentionally. This task is, on the one hand, heavily dependent on the emotion models used, e.g. whether the emotion is described as a category or as a region in a multidimensional space. The task is also highly dependent on the material from which to recognise emotion: for example, classifiers that work very well with acted emotional material may fail on naturalistic material [14]. The challenge involves events with an emotional component as well as "pure" emotions, such as dialogue success [15], and classification may well depend on contextual knowledge as well as local features [16].

HUMAINE has prioritised three modalities for study – facial expression in video; speech in audio; and physiological parameters. In each of these, its first priority is to establish the reliability of alternate signal analysis algorithms for extracting basic features. Building on that, it aims to clarify the principles of effective cross-modal integration. One challenge that is immediately apparent is to deal with the different temporal structures that characterise the modalities. Most algorithms in biosignal processing operate on a continuous, and relatively slow time scale. Speech tends to be analysed in discrete units, ranging from phonemes to phrases and even sequences of phrases; whereas the best known approaches to facial expression analysis deal with essentially instantaneous 'stills'. Beyond that, several theoretical models of multimodal integration will be compared. The simplest types of integration model to be considered include the "direct identification" model, where all input signals are directly transmitted to one multimodal classifier, and the "separate identification" model, where emotion is recognised from each modality separately. More complex integration models include the "dominant modality recoding" model, where a dominant modality drives the perception of other modalities, and the "common space recoding" model, where all the modalities are projected upon a common space prior to categorisation (as audiovisual speech recognition is thought to involve mapping information from both modalities into a common motor space).

Cutting across these issues is the question of which type of emotion descriptor to predict. Key options include discrete, dimensional and appraisal models of emotions. There is evidence that some types of descriptor relate particularly directly to the information available in some modalities [17]. HUMAINE will study the extent to which there are privileged relationships between descriptors and particular sources of evidence.

There is no unambiguous measure of success for such emotion recognition components: Should it perform as closely as possible like a human, i.e., make the same errors as humans, or should it be as accurate as possible, i.e. possibly more accurate than a human? The answer to this question is likely to depend on the application area. In a stress detection module for drivers, high accuracy is important; in a conversational interface, acting as human-like as possible will be more important. As a baseline for comparison, work is being performed within the Theory workpackage to assess the recognition capabilities of humans. Presenting the same audiovisual material to both human raters and classification algorithms will provide interesting insights in the similarity of their judgements.

Synthesising emotional signs is as important as their recognition for natural human-machine interaction. From a human point of view, it could be seen as just "the other side of the medal". However, the technologies involved in the two endeavours differ completely. HUMAINE investigates how emotions can be expressed by Embodied Conversational Agent (ECA) systems [18]. This work has started by compiling a list of capabilities that go beyond the current state of the art, but which would be required for an emotionally competent ECA. They can be grouped into three areas: perception, interaction, and generation. In the perception domain, an important pre-requisite for believable emotional interaction is an ECA's capability to perceive the user, events, or other agents. A key means for modelling this capability is an affect-related attention mechanism. On the level of interaction, rather than modelling the ECA merely as a speaker, it is important to attempt the generation of *listener* behaviour. Among other things, this includes backchannel utterances, which can signal to the user that the ECA is listening; what it does or does not understand; and how it evaluates what is being said [19]. On the generation side, the existing capabilities such as gestural and vocal expressivity need to be refined both in richness and in control, in order to model more closely what humans do in expressive situations.

This last point is obviously linked to the analysis of naturalistic databases of emotional behaviour. Conceptually, the insights gained from such analyses can be used for improving the rendered ECA behaviour. But the link can be made even more direct: given a suitable description format, a database annotation can be used to "drive" an ECA, so that the ECA can serve as an analysis-by-synthesis framework for validating the annotation scheme. First promising steps in this direction have been undertaken [20].

5   Emotions in Computational Cognitive Architectures

Going beyond shallow descriptions of emotions requires an understanding of the emotional aspects of the cognitive architecture that processes them. Existing systems that predict emotional reactions from situation descriptions are often based on the cognitive emotion model proposed by Ortony, Clore and Collins [21], which provides a useful but limited account.

HUMAINE attempts to understand and describe the emotional aspects of cognitive architectures more fully by a combination of two approaches.

Conceptually, a "blueprint" description for an affectively competent agent will be compiled in the Theory workpackage [10], with the aim to describe the mechanisms involved in emotional processing. It will gather the different points of view taken by current theorists from different disciplines, including psychology, cognitive neuroscience, philosophy, and ethology, and should be the starting point for a fruitful dialogue with engineer-oriented groups regarding the issues encountered during the implementation process. It should be seen as an evolving source "book", where state-of-the-art questions could be asked and where attempts to address them will be described.

Practically, HUMAINE also works with existing cognitive system architectures, and investigates the various ways in which emotions can be incorporated in such architectures [22]. The workpackage on emotion in Cognition and Action explores emotional phenomena in a range of very different approaches to cognitive architectures.

The "low-level" or sub-symbolic approach is concerned with the investigation of the influence of emotions in cognition and action from the perspective of their embodiment. Following this view, cognition and action are inseparable, tightly coupled perception-action loops rather than separable input-output elements. In this line of research, HUMAINE investigates robots endowed with a relatively simple cognitive architecture inspired by biological perception-action loops. First results indicate that minor modifications to the architecture, modelled after biological neuromodulation, can give rise to emergent "emotional" behaviour. Ethological methods, which are usually applied to studying animal behaviour, can be used to interpret the behaviour of such a robot. For example, in one scenario, two motivated robots competed for a resource ("food"). Usually, their bumpers would signal an obstacle that must be avoided. However, when the architecture was altered so that the bumper sensitivity dropped when the "hunger" became too big, the robots could be observed to show "aggressive" behaviour when trying to attain the resource, pushing each other away [23]. Another example is a visual homeostasis mechanism leading to "bonding" behaviour as displayed by Lorentz' geese [24].

The "high-level" or symbolic approach works on extensions of existing belief-desire-intention (BDI) models with emotion. This approach is studied in HUMAINE in the scope of dialogue simulation, and is based on Bayesian networks as a method to represent uncertain knowledge and reasoning. Existing cognitive models of emotion activation are being revised in the light of a document [25] produced by the Theories workpackage concerning emotion theories and classification of emotion models. Furthermore, it is envisaged to design an affective user modelling component to be combined with a linguistic parser of the user moves, in order to integrate 'recognition' and 'interpretation' functions. How to integrate these in a single cognitive model is another research question that will be addressed.

The "hybrid" approach attempts to bridge the gap between sub-symbolic and symbolic aspects of cognition and emotion. It will do so using agents that combine both levels, being at the same time embodied/reactive and deliberative. Studying the way in which these two levels are interrelated with respect to emotions first requires clear definitions of key properties, such as representational features, degree of autonomy, or independence from the outside world. On that basis, one can then start to deal with issues such as management of timing and prioritisation between both levels, or how to achieve mappings between the contents of these levels. For example, it would be interesting to know that an avoidance tendency on the reactive level is somehow linked to an emotion named "fear" on the symbolic level. Making this link explicit is not trivial. Similarly, where the reactive component generates a behaviour that appears contradictory to the symbolic emotional assessment of the situation, it will be most relevant to model the negotiation and decision-making process required between the two levels to generate behaviour.

All these approaches focus on modelling the cognitive mechanisms and resulting behaviour of an individual. Complementarily, HUMAINE also addresses the social and interpersonal mechanisms of regulating the emotions of individuals. Here, the unit of analysis is the *relation* in groups of two or more agents rather than the behaviour or mental state of an individual. This work includes a broad range of aspects, from the study of human politeness [26] to modelling the links between personality, emotion, and mood [27].

6 Affecting the User

The ultimate goal of HUMAINE is to enable the community to build emotion-oriented technological systems. Even if this is still an ambitious, long-term goal, work is underway in HUMAINE to prepare the ground.

The workpackage Emotion in Communication and Persuasion explores ways to purposefully induce emotions in the human user [28,29]. Models of persuasion are developed and tested in both monological and dialogical situations. Natural language is one important means for inducing emotions in human users. A first application in this area is the creative humour testbed, where the system generates potentially funny slogans based on semantic properties of natural language [30]. This example shows the direction in which first applications of emotion-oriented technology are emerging: Rather than fully competent stand-alone systems, the language-based creative humour testbed can produce a number of *potentially* funny slogans out of which the really funny ones need to be selected by a human user.

Several types of communicative strategy are investigated in the context of persuasion. One such strategy is politeness, currently being explored in a conversational context [26]. Another is deception: the recognition and generation of lying expressions. As a scenario for investigating lying behaviour in human-machine interaction, an interactive dice game was developed, played by two humans and an ECA. The game can only be won by lying occasionally [31]. In this controlled scenario, various aspects of lying can be studied, related to system behaviour (simulated lying), user reactions to simulated lying, and user lying.

Affective issues in user interfaces present a new set of challenges to usability research. Work in the Usability workpackage focuses on finding methods that can help guide future design and evaluation of affective systems [32,33]. Existing usability criteria such as control, predictability or transparency are not the most suitable for describing emotional systems. For that reason, the exemplar in this workpackage will first of all develop a set of criteria by which to measure successful, usable affective interaction systems. These criteria will not be objective, independently measurable entities, but will make sense relative to the specific application domain, aim to capture subjective experiences of the user, and foremost, be related to the designer's intention for the application. These criteria will then need to be translated into evaluation metrics, accompanied by suggested evaluation methods. Existing user-centred methods for design and evaluation will be investigated with respect to their use for emotion-oriented systems. At the same time, new methods will be proposed that are targeted specifically at capturing the unique aspects of affective interaction. Examples for such methods are: a sensual method for non-verbal mediation of affective state, a Wizard-of-Oz environment for multimodal emotional interaction, and an extended think-aloud protocol designed to capture emotional interactions.

7   HUMAINE Conscience

When dealing with machines that might one day be able to influence human emotions, there is a real need to think about the ethical dimension of such systems. It is only too easy to imagine, e.g., persuading machines used for "enhancing" product sales, or surveillance systems measuring continually the degree of friendliness exhibited by call-centre staff.

HUMAINE takes a proactive approach to these issues in its Ethics workpackage – few projects in the IST domain investigate ethical implications so thoroughly. An ethical audit [34] marked the starting point of this endeavour:

it consisted of a questionnaire assessing participants' previous experience with ethical issues in emotion-oriented systems and in emotion research including human participants. It was completed by all HUMAINE partner institutions. Its results showed a serious lack of preparation among the organisations carrying out research in the area. More importantly, the parties involved were not necessarily aware of this shortcoming.

The challenge faced by HUMAINE's Ethics team is thus to set up a whole new body of procedures and criteria by which to make sure that research and its results are not used to put humans to unethical risks. The theoretical framework in which these issues are now being addressed [35] is called Principlism [36]. It is based on the four universally shared moral principles of nonmaleficence, autonomy, beneficence, and justice. It is acknowledged that applying these principles to a concrete situation involves delicate judgments. Any set of general recommendations will therefore need to be complemented by a panel of humans, e.g. by an ethics committee that can address specific situations.

8   Conclusion: Steps Ahead

This paper has given a short overview of the broad range of activities under way in the Network of Excellence HUMAINE. Despite the multitude of angles from which network members address the complex set of thematic areas, people have come to a common understanding of key research issues. Joint specification of plans for exemplars has been a crucial mechanism to bring perspectives closer.

In the second phase of HUMAINE, which is starting now, these exemplars will actually be built. Due to its nature as a network, HUMAINE will not produce full-scale demonstrator or prototype systems. This allows us to avoid the need to make the usual short-term shortcuts required to make a system look coherent. Instead, we will produce illustrations at various levels of technological sophistication. The core intention behind building this type of exemplars is to do things "right", in the interest of a well-founded, iterative build-up of competences. With this approach, we believe we can make a real, lasting contribution.

Acknowledgements

The preparation of this paper was supported by the EU project HUMAINE (IST-507422).

References

1. Scherer, K.R.: Introduction: Cognitive components of emotion. In Davidson, R.J., Goldsmith, H., Scherer, K.R., eds.: Handbook of the Affective Sciences. Oxford University Press, New York, Oxford (2003) 563–571
2. Frijda, N.H.: The Emotions. Cambridge University Press, Cambridge, UK (1986)
3. Sokolowski, K.: Emotion und Volition. Hogrefe, Göttingen (1993)

4. Damasio, A.R.: Descartes' Error: Emotion, Reason, and the Human Brain. Grosset/Putnam, New York (1994)
5. Frijda, N.H., Mesquita, B.: The social roles and functions of emotions. In Kitayama, S., Markus, H.R., eds.: Emotion and Culture. United Book Press, Baltimore, MD, USA (1994) 51–87
6. Cornelius, R.R.: The Science of Emotion. Research and Tradition in the Psychology of Emotion. Prentice-Hall, Upper Saddle River, NJ (1996)
7. Russell, J., Barrett-Feldman, L.: Core affect, prototypical emotional episodes and other things called emotion: dissecting the elephant. Journal of Personality and Social Psychology **76** (1999) 37–63
8. Cowie, R., Douglas-Cowie, E., Cox, C.: Beyond emotion archetypes: databases for emotion modelling using neural networks. Neural Networks (Special Issue Emotion and Brain: Understanding Emotions and Modelling their Recognition) (2005) to appear.
9. Douglas-Cowie, E., Cowie, R.: Report on the first HUMAINE summer school. http://emotion-research.net/ws/summerschool1 (2004)
10. Scherer, K.R., Roesch, E., et al.: HUMAINE deliverable D3d: Description of potential exemplars: "WP3: Theories and Models of Emotion". http://emotion-research.net/deliverables (2004)
11. Douglas-Cowie, E., et al.: HUMAINE deliverable D5d: Multimodal data in action and interaction: a library of recordings and labelling schemes. http://emotion-research.net/deliverables (2004)
12. Douglas-Cowie, E., Campbell, N., Cowie, R., Roach, P.: Emotional speech: Towards a new generation of databases. Speech Communication Special Issue Speech and Emotion **40** (2003) 33–60
13. Abrilian, S., Devillers, L., Buisine, S., Martin, J.C.: EmoTV1: Annotation of real-life emotions for the specifications of multimodal affective interfaces. In: Proceedings of HCI International 2005, Las Vegas, USA (2005) to appear.
14. Batliner, A., Fischer, K., Huber, R., Spilker, J., Nöth, E.: Desperately seeking emotions or: Actors, wizards, and human beings. In: Proceedings of the ISCA Workshop on Speech and Emotion, Northern Ireland (2000) 195–200
15. Steidl, S., Hacker, C., Ruff, C., Batliner, A., Nöth, E., Haas, J.: Looking at the last two turns, I'd say this dialogue is doomed - measuring dialogue success. In P. Sojka, I.K., Pala, K., eds.: Proceedings of Text, Speech and Dialogue, 5th International Conference, September 9-12, 2002, Brno, Czech Republic. Lecture Notes in Artificial Intelligence, Berlin, Springer (2004) 629–636
16. Wallace, M., Raouzaiou, A., Tsapatsoulis, N., Kollias, S.: Facial expression classification based on MPEG-4 FAPs: The use of evidence and prior knowledge for uncertainty removal. In: Proceedings of the IEEE International Conference on Fuzzy Systems (FUZZ-IEEE), Budapest, Hungary (2004)
17. Laukka, P.: Vocal expression of emotion: discrete-emotions and dimensional accounts. PhD thesis, Uppsala University (2004)
18. Pélachaud, C., et al.: HUMAINE deliverable D6c: Description of potential exemplars: Interaction. http://emotion-research.net/deliverables (2004)
19. Pfleger, N., Alexandersson, J.: Modeling non-verbal behavior in multimodal conversational systems. Information Technology **46** (2004) 341–345
20. Pélachaud, C.: Non-verbal communication. Presentation at the workshop of the HUMAINE workpackage 6, Emotion in Interaction, Paris, France (2005) http://emotion-research.net/ws/wp6.
21. Ortony, A., Clore, G.L., Collins, A.: The Cognitive Structure of Emotion. Cambridge University Press, Cambridge, UK (1988)

22. Cañamero, L., et al.: HUMAINE deliverable D7c: Description of potential exemplars: Emotion in Cognition and Action. http://emotion-research.net/deliverables (2004)

23. Avila-Garcia, O., Cañamero, L.: Using hormonal feedback to modulate action selection in a competitive scenario. In: From Animals to Animats: Proceedings of the 8th International Conference of Adaptive Behavior (SAB'04), Cambridge, MA, MIT Press (2004) 243–252

24. Blanchard, A.J., Cañamero, L.: Using visual velocity detection to achieve synchronization in imitation. In: Proceedings of the 3rd International Symposium on Imitation in Animals and Artifacts, Symposium of the AISB'05 Convention, Hertfordshire, UK (2005)

25. Scherer, K.R., et al.: HUMAINE deliverable D3c: Preliminary plans for exemplars: Theory. http://emotion-research.net/deliverables (2004)

26. Rehm, M., André, E.: Informing the design of embodied conversational agents by analysing multimodal politeness behaviors in human-human communication. In: Proc. AISB 2005 Symposium on Conversational Informatics for Supporting Social Intelligence & Interaction. (2005)

27. Gebhard, P.: ALMA – a layered model of affect. In: Proceedings of the Fourth International Joint Conference on Autonomous Agents and Multiagent Systems (AAMAS-05), Utrecht (2005) To appear.

28. Stock, O., et al.: HUMAINE deliverable D8a: Report on basic cues and open research topics in Communication and Emotions. http://emotion-research.net/deliverables (2004)

29. Stock, O., et al.: HUMAINE deliverable D8c: Description of potential exemplars: Communication & Persuasion. http://emotion-research.net/deliverables (2004)

30. Stock, O., Strapparava, C.: The act of creating humorous acronyms. Applied Artificial Intelligence 19 (2005) 137–151

31. Rehm, M.: Keeping users engaged – analysing gaze behaviours in a multiparty interaction with an eca. Presentation at the workshop of the HUMAINE workpackage 6, Emotion in Interaction, Paris, France (2005) http://emotion-research.net/ws/wp6.

32. Höök, K., et al.: HUMAINE deliverable D9c: Description of potential exemplars: Usability. http://emotion-research.net/deliverables (2004)

33. Höök, K., et al.: HUMAINE deliverable D9a: Usability of emotion oriented systems recommendations green paper. http://emotion-research.net/deliverables (2005)

34. Goldie, P., Döring, S.A.: HUMAINE deliverable D0f: Report on Ethical Audit. http://emotion-research.net/deliverables (2004)

35. Goldie, P., Döring, S.A., et al.: HUMAINE deliverable D10b: Interim report to plenary meeting on ethical frameworks for emotion-oriented systems 2005. http://emotion-research.net/deliverables (2005)

36. Beauchamp, T.L., Childress, J.F.: Principles of Biomedical Ethics. 5th edn. Oxford University Press, Oxford (2001)

Multimodal Authoring Tool for Populating a Database of Emotional Reactive Animations

Alejandra García-Rojas, Mario Gutiérrez, Daniel Thalmann, and Frédéric Vexo

Virtual Reality Laboratory (VRlab),
École Polytechnique Fédérale de Lausanne (EPFL),
CH-1015 Lausanne, Switzerland
{alejandra.garciarojas, mario.gutierrez, daniel.thalmann,
frederic.vexo}@epfl.ch

Abstract. We aim to create a model of emotional reactive virtual humans. This model will help to define realistic behavior for virtual characters based on emotions and events in the Virtual Environment to which they react. A large set of pre-recorded animations will be used to obtain such model. We have defined a knowledge-based system to store animations of reflex movements taking into account personality and emotional state. Populating such a database is a complex task. In this paper we describe a multimodal authoring tool that provides a solution to this problem. Our multimodal tool makes use of motion capture equipment, a handheld device and a large projection screen.

1   Introduction

Our goal is to create a model to drive the behavior of autonomous Virtual Humans (VH) taking into account their personality and emotional state. This model does not aim to work by itself, it should be supported by a more generic model of behavior, but our model will complement the realistic behavior by enabling VHs to perform reflex movements triggered by events in the Virtual Environment (VE). Reflex movements can be modulated by inner personality and emotions of the VH e.g. there is a ball thrown towards the VH, the virtual character should avoid it, they way it performs the avoidance reflex will depend on its inner state: an energetic motion or a more lethargic one depending on the level of excitement and personality.

We intend to build our animation model on the basis of a large set of animation sequences described in terms of personality and emotions. In order to store, organize and exploit animation data, we need to create a knowledge-based system, an animations database.

This paper focuses on the authoring tool that we designed for populating such animation database. We observe that the process of animating is inherently multimodal because it involves several inputs such as motion capture (mocap) sensors and user control on an animation software. For simplifying the process of animating we propose to integrate the required inputs into a multimodal interface composed of a handheld device (providing a mobile GUI), motion capture

S. Renals and S. Bengio (Eds.): MLMI 2005, LNCS 3869, pp. 206–217, 2006.

equipment and a large projection screen (to ease the interaction with virtual characters). One of the added values of our system is that it provides an immersive multimodal environment for animating characters. Our tool allows for interacting within the Virtual Environment as if the user were inside. Animation data produced with this tool is organized considering personality traits and emotional states.

The rest of the paper is organized as follows: next chapter presents related work on multimodal interfaces and knowledge-based proposals for VH animation. This will be followed by our system proposal, its architecture and implementation. Finally we present our results and plans for future work.

2   Related Work

Our authoring tool is intended to facilitate the process of producing character animation in an innovative way. Our approach is to animate a character from "inside", having the actor (animator) immersed in a Virtual Environment and looking at the world through the eyes of the character. For this we need to address multiple interaction modalities: body motion, 3D visualization, etc. Moreover, animation data created by the user should be stored and organized in an efficient way. The following section presents a brief overview on multimodal interfaces research. The second subsection deals with models and strategies for organizing animation data in a knowledge-based system.

2.1   Multimodal Interfaces

A multimodal system has two or more input/output communication channels. The benefit of using multimodal systems is to get more transparent, flexible, efficient and expressive means of human-computer interaction. A descriptive conception of multimodal interfaces can be found in Oviatt's work [25].

Multimodal interfaces are implemented in Virtual Environments (VE) because they help to produce the effect of immersion. This immersion is provided through a natural interaction between the user and the environment. One pioneer multimodal application is the "Media Room" by Bolt [6]. This application combines images projected on a screen and user gestures. The fact of positioning one or more users in front of a large rear-projection screen displaying the virtual world is an approach in semi-immersive VE that has given encouraging results.

Examples of systems implementing the semi-immersive approach are: "The Enigma of the sphinx" [1] and the "Magic Wand" [7]. In the same line of research, "Conducting a virtual orchestra" [26] proposes a semi-immersive VE based on a large projection screen, a handheld device and 3D sound rendering. A PDA-based GUI was implemented to conduct the orchestra. User's gestures while conducting were captured with a magnetic tracker attached to the PDA. Handheld devices are innovate interfaces for VE. Another example of integration of handheld devices in VE can be found in [14]. These works explore the potential of using handheld devices to interact with Virtual Environments and VH.

Multimodal interfaces allows us to create more immersive Virtual Environments and they have the advantage of facilitating user interaction. It is interesting to incorporate handheld devices as an interaction device because they reinforce human-human contact in a Virtual Environment, avoiding the need to sit in front of a screen with a mouse and keyboard. We will use these ideas to build our multimodal interface. Next subsection deals with models for organizing animation, data management is essential for exploiting and reusing information.

2.2 Knowledge-Based Systems for Virtual Human Animation

The animation model we are developing will require a large amount of animation sequences. We need a database for storing and organizing animation data. The following is a brief review of research targeted at organizing animation data for Virtual Humans.

The Amoba system [12] uses a database structure to organize motion. This is a very spread and ambiguous organization structure. We require something more specialized and with richer annotations -metadata- describing the content -animation.

The work presented in [17] proposes the use of a database to retrieve the desired animation and manipulate it from a GUI. This work is interesting from the point of view of the process needed to reuse animations and models. Another implementation for reusing animation data is presented in [21] this research considers the importance of a database to animate avatars in real time. These couple of works do not deal with the process of populating the database.

A new approach towards incorporating semantics into Virtual Humans and their animation is presented in [13]. This work intends to define in a formal way, the components of a VH, including its animation, by means of an ontology.

We observe that in order to maximize the reuse and exploitation of animation data, we need to incorporate a semantic layer that enables both computer systems and human users to acquire, organize, and understand the information. For realistic animations, we need to have as much data as possible in the database. The tool we propose intends to facilitate both the data acquisition and organization.

3   Multimodal Tool for Populating an Animation Database

This section presents the conceptual description of our authoring tool based on the multimodal interaction concepts presented in previous section and the requirements for associating the desired data to the animation.

3.1 Knowledge-Base Structure

In order to define a model for emotional reactive VH we need to associate traits of personality and emotions to the animations. By considering such inner variables we expect to increase believability of the characters.

Improving believability in computer generated characters is one of the main challenges in computer animation. A believable behavior has many aspects to consider: realism, emotions, personality and intent [9]. There are many models that approach a realistic behavior following the principle of action selection, goal-oriented animation, etc. They frequently use synthesized animations, created by means of specialized algorithms. The most realistic results are obtained with prerecorded animations performed by human actors using mocap. Several models consider that personality and emotional states are the more general traits that influence behavior [22]. This is why we consider interesting to have animations influenced by these traits.

We organize animations in terms of emotions and personality because they are key components of a believable behavior. There are models of personality and emotion for VH that allow to design an emotionally personified virtual human. Among the most complete personality models for virtual humans are: [20] [19] and other less complex such as [10].

We took some of the common factors proposed by the models mentioned before to describe the metadata (attributes describing animation sequence) of our knowledge-based system. To represent personality we use the Five Factor Model (FFM) [23] that describes personality in five dimensions. The parameters that compose this model are described in table 1.

We have found two popular models of emotion used in character animation: The Cognitive Structure of Emotions Model (OCC - Ortony, Clore and Collins) [24] categorizes several types of emotions based on the positive or negative reactions to events, actions, and objects, it defines 22 emotions; and Ekman's 6 basic emotions for facial expression [11] (joy, sadness, anger, surprise, fear, and disgust) that can be combined to obtain other expressions. As the multilayered model says [19] only 4 expressions of Ekman (joy, sadness, fear and anger) are defined in the OCC model. Surprise and disgust do not find place in the OCC model, mainly because they do not involve much cognitive processing. They group OCC and Ekman's emotions within 6 expressions to represent the emotional states and to reduce the computational complexity. This emotions are explained and categorized in the table 1.

Table 1. Models of personality (FFM) and emotion (OCC)

Five Factor Model of Personality		OCC Model of Emotion	
Factor	Description	Emotion	Description
Extraversion	Preference for and behavior in social situations.	Joy	Happy-for, Gloating, Joy, Pride, Admiration, Love, Hope, Satisfaction, Relief, Gratification, Gratitude
Agreeableness	Interactions with others.	Sadness	Resentment, Pity, Distress, Shame, Remorse
Conscientiousness	Organized, persistent in achieving goals	Anger	Anger, Reproach, Hate
Neuroticism	Tendency to experience negative thoughts	Surprise	Surprise
		Fear	Fear, Fear-confirmed
Openness	Open minded-ness, interest in culture	Disgust	Disgust

The FFM and OCC models are ideally suited to the task of creating concrete representations of personality and emotions with which to enhance the illusion of believability in virtual characters [3].

The models we have defined describe an individualization of VH humans. Each VH is defined by a specific combination of attribute values corresponding to the FFM. Each VH can have many configurations of the attributes of emotional states (OCC model), and each attribute can be defined in different levels.

To describe animations we consider also events in the environment, these events are represented by objects in the VE. For example we can have a sphere that represents a ball. The ball can then produce the event "thrown ball".

One event is associated to one animation because this event will make the VH move in reaction. One animation is performed as reaction to one event, under one configuration of emotional state for one specific personality of a VH. This conception is translated into a database diagram presented in figure 1.

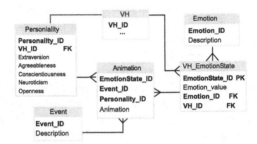

Fig. 1. Diagram of the knowledge-base system

Under this structure, when an event occurs in the environment, the animation engine will look into the knowledge base for an animation suitable to perform a reaction, taking into account the specific conditions of emotional state and personality. Next subsection gives more details on the components of the multimodal interface and how they are interconnected.

3.2   Multimodal Structure

The multimodal authoring tool we propose makes use of motion capture, a large projection screen and a handheld device.

The motion capture system, as main input device, allows the animator to acquire high quality animations and give the appropriate intention and expressiveness to each movement. The second input modality is the handheld device that will work as a remote control. In combination with the PDA, a large screen will provide visual feedback to the user. With the PDA device we reduce the amount of people required in the production process, and make a more interactive interface, the same person using the mocap can drive the authoring. Moreover, this mobile interface allows for previewing the animation and accessing the database without the need to be in front of a PC.

The interaction of the elements above mentioned with the knowledge-based system is illustrated in figure Figure 2. These elements are described as follows:

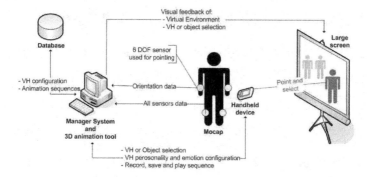

Fig. 2. Multimodal interaction between elements

- Main control of the authoring resides in the Manager system. This Manager receives commands from the PDA device and executes an action in response; it can also send information to the PDA, such as metadata (attributes) or animation data (the actual animation).
- Sensors continuously send information about the actor's position and the Manager system reads them depending of the command in process; it could be reading only the right hand orientation or all the sensors information (recording an animation).
- The Manager makes transactions in the knowledge-base system, can store or retrieve information of the metadata or animation sequences.
- The manager system communicates with the 3D viewer in which the VE is represented. A VE contains VHs and objects that trigger events, the scene is projected on the large screen.

The authoring process is driven through the PDA device. First, the user selects a VH or object by pointing at the large screen and pressing a button in the PDA. Objects can be associated to an event. Events can be triggered from the PDA. Depending of the event some of its parameters can be modified, for example a ball can be thrown in different directions.

From the PDA, personality traits and emotion parameters of a VH can be configured for each sequence to be recorded. Many combinations of parameters of emotional states can be recorded for one event. This configurations are saved in the knowledge base system. The GUI in the PDA with this functionality implemented is illustrated in the figure 3.

Animating a VH can be done in two modalities: watching the VH mimic the user movements, or viewing the VE through the VH eyes (see figure 7). The character moves in real time according to the data acquired by the mocap system.

For recording, there is a mechanism similar to a VCR with a big button to start and stop recording. To start recording we give 5 seconds for the user to get an initial posture before recording the animation. After those 5 seconds the sequence starts to be recorded until the user presses stop. When storing the recorded animation, the last three seconds are removed to avoid storing undesired motions due to the movement for pressing the stop button on the

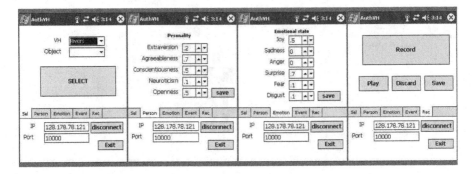

Fig. 3. Screen shots of the GUI in the PDA

Fig. 4. Previewing animation on the handheld device

PDA. User can Save or discard a sequence. The animation is stored with the current configuration of emotional states, event, personality and VH. Finally, "Stop animating" option stops animating from the mocap and "Stop authoring", the VH is deselected.

To reproduce animations the user can Play a sequence. It consists on reproducing the last sequence recorded in the large screen, or any of the other saved sequences. This last option will only work when the VH is neither being animated nor in pause. User can also preview recorded sequences in the PDA (figure 4). We have explained the main components of the multimodal tool and its work-flow. Next section provides technical details concerning the implementation.

4   Implementation

Motion capture is performed using the motion capture system from Ascension Technology [4], composed of 13 6-DOF magnetic sensors. As interface with the Mocap we used an utility developed at VRlab: Shared Input Devices (SID) [16]. The SID program gets the sensor information and puts it in a shared memory zone in the host machine. The manager program access to this shared memory to obtain the sensors data. This information is translated and sent to the 3D animation tool.

The animation tool used was Maya 5.0 [8]. Maya provides a rich set of tools for rendering, modeling and animating. It is one of the leader solutions in the market and can be considered as a defacto standard in the animation industry.

In Maya we modelled VH with H-Anim [15] skeleton. H-Anim is a W3C standard for animating humanoid models. We used a Plug-in presented in [2] to export the animation in MPEG-4 BAP [18]. This encoding animation is a low bit-rate representation suitable for networked applications.

Data from mocap sensors are sent to Maya using Maya's motion capture API. We created a component that uses this API and also applies the right transformation to the raw sensors data. Each 6-DOF sensor needs to be calibrated to provide its data in the same coordinate space used by Maya. Calibration was implemented following the method described in [5], it computes the correspondence between the initial orientation of each sensor and the default initial orientation of each H-Anim body part. We implemented in maya several MEL (Maya Embedded Language) scripts for: linking the sensors data with the skeleton used to animate the VH; start and stop recording movements and exporting animations. This commands are executed by the Manager system.

Virtual Humans modeled in Maya are animated through their H-Anim skeleton. We used inverse kinematics to compute proper joint rotation values for the VH limbs, and applied orientation constraints to some joints (root, column and skull) with the suitable weights. We created in Maya one locator for each sensor and constrained them to the proper effector or joint. The association of the sensors in the actor with the mocap and the locators in Maya and the skeleton are shown in figure 5.

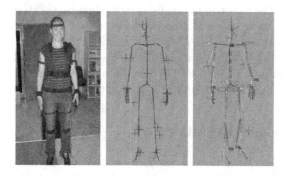

Fig. 5. Association of the mocap's sensors with the skeleton effectors/joints

As handheld device we used a PDA iPAQ HP 4700. We built the GUI for the PDA in C# with controls to drive the animation process. To preview the recorded animations on the PDA we switch application and use a mobile 3D viewer based on the "Mobile Animator" [14].

The knowledge-based system was set up in MySQL. This database is free, easy to implement and provides enough performance for our needs. Data transmission to and from the database is done using ODBC for MySQL.

The Manager system was implemented in C++. The communication with the PDA is done through sockets. Interaction with maya is done through the "Command Port" interface (MEL command: commandPort).

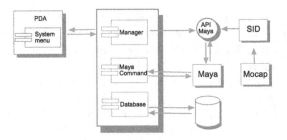

Fig. 6. Component diagram implementation

The components diagram in figure 6 shows the interaction between the described components.

The GUI in the PDA (see fig 3) has a "Tab menu" for selecting VH or objects, configuring personality, emotions or events and recording animation. Events can be selected from the PDA and modified and activated. The data configured in the PDA is sent as a character stream.

For selecting VHs or objects we read the position and orientation of the 6-DOF sensor on the right hand, within this we exploit the fact of having the sensors already set on the user. We calibrate the initial position as the center of the screen and transform sensor orientation into 2D coordinates corresponding to the computer screen. 2D screen coordinates are used to drive the mouse pointer position. This way the user can naturally interact just by pointing at the screen.

To save animations we use a MEL script to execute a plug-in that exports the skeleton animation to MPEG-4 BAP format. The BAP file created is placed into a shared directory in the host machine and the path saved in the database. If the user wants to play the animation on the PDA the Manager sends the path and name of the animation and the Mobile animator is able to preview the animation.

5   Discussion and Results

To start populating the database, we have tested our multimodal tool with different examples. We used the example mentioned in the introduction, a ball being thrown towards the VH. We defined the event "Ball thrown". Figure 7 shows the animation process: the user configures a VH, performs an animation, and previews the saved animation on the PDA.

The combination of Mocap with a large projection screen proved to be an efficient and intuitive way to produce multiple sequences of realistic animation and had good feed-back to the user. The lightweight interface (PDA) was more comfortable than using a PC, but disturbed the user because he had to decide between keeping the PDA in the hand while recording or leave it. We believe that the handheld device could be enhanced with speech recognition, in particular for the start/stop recording functionality. The multimodal interface provided a useful mechanism for populating the animation database that we have defined, but we still need to populate it with different reflex movements that a human

Fig. 7. Using the multimodal authoring tool

being could perform under specific emotional and personality conditions. For this we may need to record in video several people and evaluate their inner state and then use the video with an actor to reproduce the movement.

Describing animation sequences by means of metadata introduces a semantic layer that promote the reuse and increases the productivity of animation.

6   Conclusions and Future Work

We have presented a multimodal tool to populate a knowledge based system for VH animation. The tool involves the use of motion capture, a handheld interface, a semi immersive VE (large projection screen) and the incorporation of semantics (metadata) to the animation. Animation data is organized in a knowledge base taking into account personality traits and emotional state of the VH. The multimodal interface provides a fast and intuitive tool for populating the animation database. However there may still be need for fine-tunning animation due to the inherent noise of the Mocap data.

Future work consists on populating the animations repository in order to provide a rich repertoire for the animation model. The model for reactive VH will be described in future publications. The current paper focused on describing the tools for acquiring and organizing the information.

Acknowledgments. This research has been partially funded by the Swiss Federal Office for Education and Science in the framework of the European Networks of Excellence IST - HUMAINE (http://emotion-research.net) and IST - AIM@SHAPE (http://www.aim-at-shape.net).

References

1. T. Abaci, R. de Bondeli, J. Ciger, M. Clavien, F. Erol, M. Gutierrez, S. Noverraz, O. Renault, F. Vexo, and D. Thalmann. Magic wand and enigma of the sphinx. *Computers & Graphics*, 28(4):477–484, August 2004.
2. Y. Amara, M. Gutierrez, F. Vexo, and D. Thalmann. A maya exporting plug-in for mpeg-4 fba human characters. In *Proceedings of the First International Workshop on Interactive Rich Media Content Production: Architectures, Technologies, Applications and Tools. (RICHMEDIA 2003)*, pages 121–130, 2003.

3. E. André;, M. Klesen, P. Gebhard, S. Allen, and T. Rist. Integrating models of personality and emotions into lifelike characters. pages 150–165, 2000.

4. Ascension Technology Corporation. http://www.ascension-tech.com/.

5. C. Babski and D. Thalmann. Real-time animation and motion capture in web human director (whd). In *VRML '00: Proceedings of the fifth symposium on Virtual reality modeling language (Web3D-VRML)*, pages 139–145, 2000.

6. R. A. Bolt. Put-that-there: Voice and gesture at the graphics interface. In *SIG-GRAPH '80: Proceedings of the 7th annual conference on Computer graphics and interactive techniques*, pages 262–270, New York, NY, USA, 1980. ACM Press.

7. J. Ciger, M. Gutierrez, F. Vexo, and D. Thalmann. The magic wand. In *SCCG '03: Proceedings of the 19th spring conference on Computer graphics*, pages 119–124, New York, NY, USA, 2003. ACM Press.

8. A. S. Corp. Maya, 3d animation and effects software. http://www.alias.com.

9. P. Doyle. Believability through context using "knowledge in the world" to create intelligent characters. In *AAMAS '02: Proceedings of the first international joint conference on Autonomous agents and multiagent systems*, pages 342–349, New York, NY, USA, 2002. ACM Press.

10. A. Egges, S. Kshirsagar, and N. M. Thalmann. A model for personality and emotion simulation. In *Knowledge-Based Intelligent Information and Engineering Systems (KES2003)*, 2003.

11. P. Ekman. *Emotion in the Human Face*. Cambridge University Press, New York,, 1982.

12. S. Grunvogel, J. Piesk, S. Schwichtenberg, and G. Buchel. Amoba: A database system for annotating captured human movements. In *CA '02: Proceedings of the Computer Animation*, pages 98–102. IEEE Computer Society, 2002.

13. M. Gutierrez, D. Thalmann, F. Vexo, L. Moccozet, N. Magnenat-Thalmann, M. Mortara, and M. Spagnuolo. An ontology of virtual humans: incorporating semantics into human shapes. In *Proceedings of Workshop towards Semantic Virtual Environments (SVE05), March 2005*, pages 57–67, 2005.

14. M. Gutierrez, F. Vexo, and D. Thalmann. The mobile animator: Interactive character animation in collaborative virtual environments. In *VR '04: Proceedings of the IEEE Virtual Reality 2004 (VR'04)*, page 125, Washington, DC, USA, 2004. IEEE Computer Society.

15. H-anim. The humanoid animation working group. http://www.h-anim.org.

16. B. Herbelin. Shared Input Device Controller, http://vrlab.epfl.ch/ bhbn/birdnet/ index.html.

17. A. Huang, Z. Huang, B. Prabhakaran, and J. C. R. Ruiz. Interactive visual method for motion and model reuse. In *GRAPHITE '03: Proceedings of the 1st international conference on Computer graphics and interactive techniques in Australasia and South East Asia*, pages 29–36. ACM Press, 2003.

18. ISO/IEC 14496-2:1999. Information Technology – Coding of Audio-Visual Objects, Part 1: Systems (MPEG-4 v.2), December 1999. ISO/IEC JTC 1/SC 29/WG 11 Document No. W2739.

19. S. Kshirsagar. A multilayer personality model. In *SMARTGRAPH '02: Proceedings of the 2nd international symposium on Smart graphics*, pages 107–115, New York, NY, USA, 2002. ACM Press.

20. S. Kshirsagar and N. Magnenat-Thalmann. Virtual humans personified. In *AA-MAS '02: Proceedings of the first international joint conference on Autonomous agents and multiagent systems*, pages 356–357, New York, NY, USA, 2002.

21. J. Lee, J. Chai, P. S. A. Reitsma, J. K. Hodgins, and N. S. Pollard. Interactive control of avatars animated with human motion data. In *SIGGRAPH '02: Proceedings of the 29th annual conference on Computer graphics and interactive techniques*, pages 491–500, New York, NY, USA, 2002. ACM Press.

22. S. Marsella and J. Gratch. A step toward irrationality: using emotion to change belief. In *AAMAS '02: Proceedings of the first international joint conference on Autonomous agents and multiagent systems*, pages 334–341, New York, NY, USA, 2002. ACM Press.

23. R. R. McCrae and O. P. John. An introduction to the five-factor model and its applications. *Journal of Personality*, (60):175–215, 1992.

24. A. Ortony, G. L. Clore, and A. Collins. *The Cognitive Structure of Emotions.* Cambridge University Press, 1998.

25. S. Oviatt. Multimodal interfaces. pages 286–304, 2003.

26. S. Schertenleib, M. Gutierrez, F. Vexo, and D. Thalmann. Conducting a virtual orchestra. *IEEE MultiMedia*, 11(3):40–49, 2004.

A Testing Methodology for Face Recognition Algorithms

Aristodemos Pnevmatikakis and Lazaros Polymenakos

Athens Information Technology, Autonomic and Grid Computing, Markopoulou Ave.,
19002 Peania, Greece
{apne, lcp}@ait.edu.gr
http://www.ait.edu.gr/research/RG1/overview.asp

Abstract. Many face recognition methods have been reported in the literature. Also many face databases and face recognition methodologies are available to test them. Unfortunately most authors test their methods using restricted databases, or random subsets of them. This does not facilitate the comparison of the methods. In this paper we propose an evaluation methodology that utilizes three publicly available databases and an evaluation protocol that offers numerous splits of the images between training and testing images. We also evaluate many different face recognition methods using our methodology, offering a comparison between them.

1 Introduction

Face recognition from still images or video sequences has an ever growing number of applications; recent examples include security and smart room deployments [1]. If performance could be boosted to the level achieved by other biometric features, face recognition would rank among the most desirable methods, because of the non-intrusiveness and the simplicity of the infrastructure required.

Many algorithms have been proposed, both feature-based (EBGM [2]) and appearance-based (PCA [3,4], LDA [4,5], ICA [6], correlation filters [7], HMM [8] and kernel methods [9]) to mention a few. Those methods have been introduced in the literature, but in most cases their testing has followed a proof-of-concept approach: the methods are shown to work, but they are tested on different face databases, sometimes databases created for the task, without following a particular testing methodology. Hence their performance is often difficult to properly estimate and compare.

There exist many databases that can be used for the evaluation of face recognition algorithms. Some of them offer many images per subject, but have limited number of subjects (Aberdeen [10], ORL [8], HumanScan [11], Yale [12] and CMU Expression [13]). ORL and CMU Expression have close-cropped faces with expression variations that are extreme for some subjects. Unfortunately the expressions are not captured systematically, thus there are different expressions for different subjects. The Yale database extensively and systematically covers different lighting conditions and slight pose variations, but neither expressions nor occlusions. HumanScan has moderate but non-systematic lighting and pose variations and some occlusions by glasses and even hands. The presence of many images per person in these databases allows the testing of methods using either few or many training images per class.

S. Renals and S. Bengio (Eds.): MLMI 2005, LNCS 3869, pp. 218–229, 2006.

The FERET database [14] has hundreds of subjects but offers only four neutral images for the majority of subjects. Nevertheless, the most established testing methodology utilizes this database, allowing a comparison of performance but only for applications that are limited in number of training images per class. The AR database [15] consists of faces of 126 persons. The images have systematic expression, illumination and occlusion impairments, but unfortunately there are too few neutral faces. Hence this database is mostly suited for the assessment of the effect of specific situations to face recognition and not for a general performance assessment.

This lack of uniform testing approach across methods and databases often leads to confusing or even contradicting results in the literature. For example, regarding PCA and LDA methods, the results in [5,15-21] fail to clarify the effect of factors like the distance metrics, the number of training images per class, the pre-processing scheme used and the removal of the eigenvectors with the largest associated eigenvalues. Also, regarding HMM, excellent performance is reported on the ORL database [8]. This is indeed the case, but only for that database. We have found that the performance of the method using the HumanScan database is much worse.

In order to facilitate the complete assessment of the performance of face recognition methods, covering different number of training images per class, expressions, illumination conditions, pose variations and occlusions, a new testing methodology is proposed, covering the databases and the evaluation protocol for the partition of the images into training and testing. Numerous such partitions are defined, allowing the statistical evaluation of the methods.

With the proposed testing methodology, we proceed to compare the performance of several methods (PCA variants, LDA, EBGM variants and HMM variants) and several pre-processing schemes (intensity normalization, histogram equalization and edginess [22]). This offers a fair comparison of all the methods under the common testing methodology.

This paper is organized as follows: In section 2 the evaluation methodology is detailed. Then, in section 3 the results obtained from many different algorithms are presented. Finally in section 4 the conclusions are drawn.

2 Evaluation Methodology

In the following subsections, the proposed evaluation methodology is detailed. First the databases are presented and their choice is justified. Then, the evaluation protocol is detailed.

2.1 Databases

The goal of the proposed methodology is to provide the means for comparison of face recognition methods, not the combination of face detection and recognition. Hence the databases that are to be used should allow for the extraction of the faces from the images. Also, most of the methods deal with faces that are geometrically normalized to some standard size. Furthermore, they require the eyes to be located in predefined pixels in some template. To complicate matters, feature-based methods need more feature than just the eyes to be marked on the images. Hence it is desirable to use databases with some feature points marked on them. These points must include the eyes, as the geometric normalization is based on their position. Alternatively, a face database can provide close-cropped faces, approximately normalized in size and in eye position. Such databases can be useful for the assessment of the methods under non-ideal detection.

Taking into account the available databases, we propose a methodology that utilizes three databases: the HumanScan, the CMU Expression and two subsets of the Yale B database.

The HumanScan database, although originally developed for face detection, is very well suited for face recognition evaluations because it depicts faces in normal but not ideal conditions. Such conditions characterize images with faces that are approximately frontal and with mostly neutral expressions. The occlusions are normal glasses (not dark sunglasses), blinking eyes and fingers. Lighting conditions vary, but not to the extreme. HumanScan offers high resolution non-cropped faces of 21 people and many images per person. Unfortunately the pose, illumination and expression changes are not performed systematically, nor can the same conditions be found across all people in the database. A set of 20 facial features are marked on the images, allowing the evaluation of feature-based methods. The images are not cropped, allowing geometric normalization based on the given eye positions, or imperfect geometric normalization and cropping to evaluate the effect of non-ideal detection. Finally, the images are not normalized in terms of intensity, allowing the evaluation of intensity normalization pre-processing schemes.

The CMU Expression database depicts 13 people, offering 75 close-cropped images per person. The people in it pose with different and sometimes extreme facial expressions, albeit in a non-systematic way.

The Yale B database comprises of 10 people, under 65 different illumination conditions and 9 different poses, so in total 585 images per person. Both the illumination conditions and the poses are carefully controlled. The illumination conditions can be very extreme, while the poses are frontal with small rotations. The faces are not cropped and hand-annotated coordinates are given for the geometric normalization. For the frontal faces, the coordinates of the eyes and the mouth are given. For the non-frontal, only the center of the head is marked, but the head size is inferred from the equivalent frontal images. Hence normalization of the faces is possible in this database, but not its use for feature-based methods. In the proposed evaluation methodology, two databases are generated out of the Yale B database. The YaleIllum database comprises of all the frontal images under any illumination. The YalePose comprises of all the poses under approximately frontal lighting conditions. Nine out of the 64 lighting conditions are considered as approximately frontal. These are those with azimuth between -10 and +10 degrees and elevation between -20 and +20 degrees. As a result, the YalePose subset comprises of 81 images per person.

The four databases used for the proposed evaluation methodology are summarized in Table 1.

Table 1. The four databases used for the proposed evaluation methodology

Name	Persons	Images per person	Total images	Annotated features or cropped	Pose	Illumina-tion	Expres-sion	Occlu-sion
HumanScan	21	25-145	1373	20 features	Minimal, non-systematic	Moderate, non-systematic	Minimal, non-systematic	Glasses, hands
CMUExpr	13	75	975	Cropped	None	None	Extreme, non systematic	None
YaleIllum	10	65	650	Eyes, mouth	None	Extreme, systematic	None	None
YalePose	10	81	810	Head center	Moderate, systematic	Minimal, systematic	None	None

2.2 Evaluation Protocol

The evaluation protocol defines many different partitions of training and testing images, with various numbers of training images per person for each database. The face recognition methods are trained and tested on those partitions. Hence, adhering to the protocol allows the evaluation of the face recognition methods in terms of number of training images per person, pose, illumination and expression. The large number of partitions allows for many runs and hence a comparison across the different methods of results, either of individual runs, or of statistics of groups of runs.

For those databases that the impairments (variations on pose, illumination and expression) are introduced non-systematically, the selection of the different training and testing partitions can be random. The number of partitions can be any that the number of images per class and training images allows. The R_N runs for N training images per class are selected as follows: If the minimum number of images per person is K_{min}, then a set of L indices $i_k^{(N)} \in \{1, 2, \ldots K_{min}\}$, $k = 1, 2, \ldots L$ is selected. The set $\{i_k^{(N)}\}$ is the pool from which the R_N different N-tuples of training image indices for each person are formed. The first R_N from the possible $R_L^{(N)}$ N-tuples are selected, starting from the smallest of the $i_k^{(N)}$ indices. Note that since

$$R_L^{(N)} = \frac{L!}{N!(L-N)!} \tag{1}$$

care should be taken not to select $L \gg N$ and end up with R_N being very small relative to $R_L^{(N)}$, as in this case some of the larger $i_k^{(N)}$ are not included in the N-tuples. The parameters for the N-tuples generation of the protocol for HumanScan and CMU Expression are shown in Table 2. In these two databases the primary measure of performance is the average Probability of Misclassification (PMC), given by the ratio of the falsely recognized faces over the total number of faces tried per run.

Table 2. The parameters for the N-tuples generation of the protocol for the non-systematic databases

Database	N	L	R_N	$R_N/R_L^{(N)}$ (%)	$\{i_k^{(N)}\}$
	1	25	25	100	1:1:25
	2	25	300	100	1:1:25
HumanScan	3	15	400	87.9	1:1:10, 12:2:20
$K_{min} = 25$	5	12	400	50.5	1:1:4, 6:2:20
	7	12	400	50.5	1:1:4, 6:2:20
	10	14	400	40.0	1:1:7, 8:2:20
	2	29	400	98.5	1:29
CMU Expr	3	38	400	87.9	1:2:29
$K_{min} = 75$	4	38	400	80.8	1:2:10, 11:3:29
	5	38	400	86.6	1, 3, 5:3:29

For the databases derived from Yale B, where the pose and illumination changes are systematic, the selection of the different training and testing partitions needs also be systematic. For the Yale Illumination database, extensive experiments have shown that optimum results are obtained when the central and extreme azimuth and elevation lighting are represented in the training set. Hence the $L = 15$ indices of the possible training images are $\{1,4,6,27,28,29,32,33,34,56,57,58,61,62,63\}$. For Yale Pose, extensive testing has indicated that the optimum choices for training images are those that capture the different poses and not the minor differences in illumination. Hence the $L = 9$ indices of the possible training images are $\{1,10,19,28,37,46,55,64,73\}$.

Table 3. The numbers of runs for the various numbers of training images per person of the protocol for the systematic databases

Database	N	L	$R_N = R_L^{(N)}$
	2		105
	3		455
Yale	4		1365
Illumination	5	15	3003
	7		6435
	10		3003
	2		36
	3		84
	4		126
Yale Pose	5		126
	6	9	84
	7		36
	8		9
	9		1

For these two databases, where the impairments are introduced systematically, all the $R_L^{(N)}$ runs have to be tried. The numbers of runs for the various numbers of training images per person are shown in Table 3.

3 Evaluation Results

Some face recognition methods are evaluated using the proposed methodology. These include:

- three variants of the linear subspace projection methods, namely PCA and PCA without the three eigenvectors corresponding to the largest eigenvalues (PCAw/o3), representing unsupervised projection matrix estimation [3,4] and LDA, representing unsupervised projection matrix estimation [4,5],
- Elastic Bunch Graph Matching (EBGM) [2], a feature-based method, and
- Pseudo 2D Hidden Markov Models (HMM) [8].

EBGM, as a feature-based method is restricted to the HumanScan database that offers 20 hand-annotated features.

These methods are evaluated using the different databases and intensity normalization schemes. The latter include zero-mean unity-variance normalization, histogram equalization and edginess [22]. The median values of the PMC results are used for visualization of the variation of performance, but the results are also analyzed statistically using boxplots [23]. In these plots, the medians are represented by horizontal lines, the boxes around the median values represent the inter-quartile ranges and the whiskers represent the extend of the data. Outliers are marked by crosses. The notches on the boxes represent the uncertainty of the median value estimation: difference in the median values is statistically significant at the 5% significance level only if the notches of the boxes do not overlap.

The evaluation results on HumanScan are shown in Fig. 1. In Fig. 1a the median values of the probability of misclassification are given as a function of the number of training faces per person. The performance of all methods improves as more training faces are used. This is expected since the excess training captures more variation of the appearance of the person. The best preprocessing scheme is histogram equalization. LDA outperforms all methods for three or more training faces per person. For fewer, PCAw/o3 with histogram equalization is the clear winner. In Fig. 1.b the statistical analysis of the best methods for 10 training faces per person using boxplots is performed. The analysis shows that the best median of PMC of LDA compared to PCAw/o3 with histogram equalization, no matter the preprocessing scheme has statistical significance. It also shows that LDA without any preprocessing is not very robust; its inter-quartile range and the extend of the data exceeds that of PCAw/o3 with histogram equalization. The usage of with histogram equalization makes LDA robust, with performance significantly better than the other two.

The evaluation results on Yale Illumination are shown in Fig. 2. In Fig. 1a the 10th percentile values of the probability of misclassification are given as a function of the number of training faces per person. In this case we do not report the median, since the particular choice of training images is very important; the different lighting conditions have to be represented in training as uniformly as possible. The best preprocessing scheme is edginess, but it is not very effective for PCAw/o3. LDA outperforms all methods for five or more training faces per person. For fewer, PCA with edginess preprocessing is the clear winner. To demonstrate the robustness added to the classifiers when edginess preprocessing is used, the statistical analysis using boxplots is shown in Fig. 1.b. Both the median and the inter-quartile range drop. Also, since the notches of the PCA and LDA methods with edginess preprocessing do not overlap, the fact that LDA performs better has statistical significance at the 5% significance level.

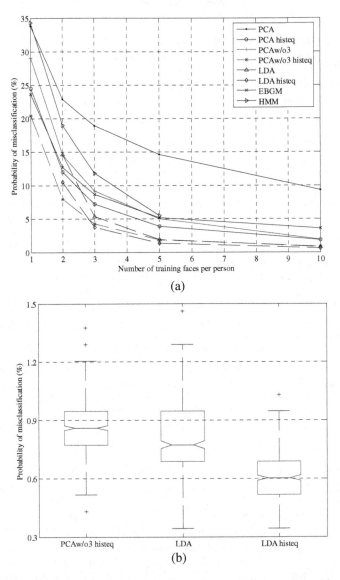

(a)

(b)

Fig. 1. Results on HumanScan. (a) Median of the PMC as a function of the number of training faces per person. (b) Boxplot of the three best methods for 10 training faces per person.

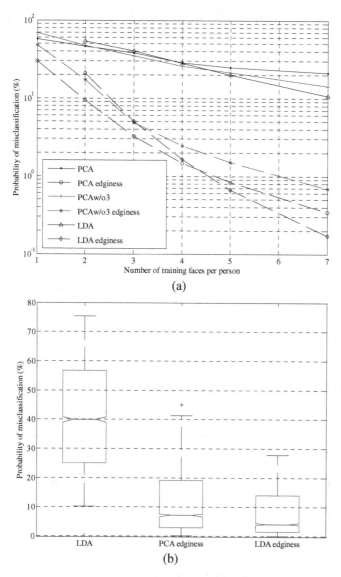

Fig. 2. Results on Yale Illumination. (a) 10th percentiles of the PMC as a function of the number of training faces per person. (b) Boxplots of three methods for 5 training faces per person that indicate how preprocessing enhances robustness.

The evaluation results on Yale Pose are shown in Fig. 3. As in Yale Illumination, the 10th percentile values of the probability of misclassification are given as a function of the number of training faces per person. The effect of preprocessing is not as straightforward here. Depending on the method and the number of training faces per person no preprocessing or histogram equalization are the best choices. Histogram equalization is beneficial to the two PCA variants for many training faces per person, but should not be used with LDA. LDA outperforms all methods for three or more training faces per person. For fewer, PCA should be used. Finally, note the catastrophic effect of ignoring the three eigenvectors with the largest associated eigenvalues.

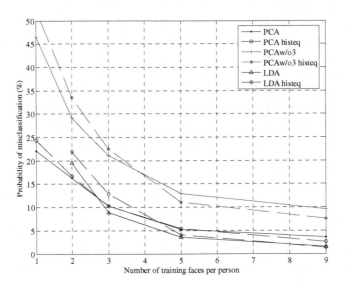

Fig. 3. 10th percentile values of the PMC as a function of the number of training faces per person for Yale Pose

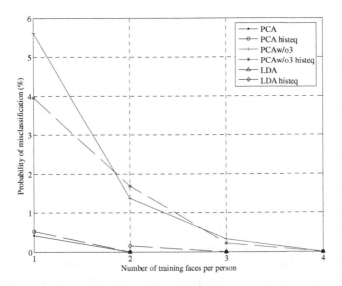

Fig. 4. Median values of the PMC as a function of the number of training faces per person for CMU Expression

The evaluation results on CMU Expression are shown in Fig. 4. As the variations in this database are not systematic, the median values of the probability of misclassification are given as a function of the number of training faces per person. This database does not provide a challenge to face recognition, as both PCA and LDA result to zero median PMC values for two or more training faces per person. As in the case of pose variation, the effect of preprocessing is not straightforward. Depending on the method and the number of training faces per person no preprocessing or histogram equalization are the best choices. Nevertheless, the effect of preprocessing is not as pronounced as in other cases. Finally, as in the case of pose variation, also here in the case of expression variation, it is catastrophic to ignore the three eigenvectors with the largest associated eigenvalues.

4 Conclusions

An evaluation methodology is proposed in this paper, comprising of four face databases and an evaluation protocol. The protocol is different in the various databases, taking into account whether the impairments each introduces to the images are performed systematically or not. The protocol allows for a large number of different partitions between the training and testing data.

The proposed evaluation methodology allows for a thorough study of the face recognition methods in terms of number of training images per person, pose, illumination and expression variations, and geometric and intensity normalization. Some face recognition methods (linear subspace projection variants, EBGM, HMM, correlation filters) and different intensity normalization schemes (zero mean/unity variance, histogram equalization and edginess) are thus evaluated, leading to the following conclusions: The methods perform differently when applied on different databases. This is because the databases depict different impairments, in which some methods are better suited than others. Under ideal geometric normalization, linear subspace projection performs best, with LDA being more robust than PCA for more than 3 training images per person. EBGM is impressive for one training image per class. Intensity normalization is very important for illumination changes, with edginess performing best, but leads to performance degradation for pose and expression changes. Histogram equalization has a more mild effect in the case of pose and expression changes, whereas it is quite good for illumination changes. Finally, ignoring the three eigenvectors with the largest associated eigenvalues enhances performance only if there are no pose or expression changes. For the latter case, the performance degradation is severe.

Thus, a face recognition system that is applied on unconstraint images, without any a-priori knowledge of the illumination, pose and expression the person under test will assume should not discard the three eigenvectors with the largest associated eigenvalues and should use histogram equalization to preprocess the images. The designer of the system should try to include examples of the extreme illuminations and poses that are expected in the training faces.

Additional work is underway both in terms of methods and databases. Both other linear subspace projection methods (direct LDA [24], OFLD [25]), as well as non-linear extensions (kernel methods [9], LaplacianFaces [26]) are being investigated.

Regarding databases, the ORL [8] and AR [15] databases are under integration in the proposed methodology. The PIE [27] database is also under consideration.

Acknowledgements

This work is sponsored by the European Union under the integrated project CHIL, contract number 506909.

References

[1] Waibel, A., Steusloff, H., Stiefelhagen, R. et. al, CHIL: Computers in the Human Interaction Loop, 5th International Workshop on Image Analysis for Multimedia Interactive Services (WIAMIS), (April 21-23, 2004), Lisbon, Portugal.

[2] Wiskott, L., Fellous, J.-M., Krueger, N. and Malsburg, C., Face Recognition by Elastic Bunch Graph Matching, in *Intelligent Biometric Techniques in Fingerprint and Face Recognition*, eds. Jain, L.C. et al., CRC Press, Chapter 11, (1999), 355-396.

[3] Turk, M. and Pentland, A., Eigenfaces for Recognition, *J. Cognitive Neuroscience, 3* (March 1991), 71-86.

[4] Pnevmatikakis , A. and Polymenakos, L., Comparison of Eigenface-Based Feature Vectors under Different Impairments, *Int. Conf. Pattern Recognition 2004,* (Aug. 2004), 296-300.

[5] Belhumeur, P., Hespanha, J. and Kriegman, D., Eigenfaces vs. Fisherfaces: Recognition Using Class Specific Linear Projection, *IEEE Trans. Pattern Analysis and Machine Intelligence, 19, 7* (July 1997), 711-720.

[6] M. Bartlett, J. Movellan and T. Sejnowski, 'Face Recognition by Independent Component Analysis', *IEEE Trans. Neural Networks*, vol. 13, no. 6, pp. 1450-1464, Nov. 2002.

[7] C. Xie, B. V. K. Vijaya Kumar, S. Palanivel and B. Yegnanarayana, 'A Still-to-Video Face Verification System Using Advanced Correlation Filters', *International Conference on Biometric Authentication*, pp. 102-108, 2004.

[8] F. Samaria and A. Harter, 'Parametrisation of a Stochastic Model for Human Face Identification', *Proc. 2ⁿᵈ IEEE Workshop on Applications of Computer Vision,* pp. 138-142, Dec. 1994.

[9] J. Yang, A. Frangi, J.-Y. Yang, D. Zhang, and Z. Jin, 'KPCA Plus LDA: A Complete Kernel Fisher Discriminant Framework for Feature Extraction and Recognition', *IEEE Transactions On Pattern Analysis And Machine Intelligence*, Vol. 27, No. 2, Feb. 2005.

[10] http://pics.psych.stir.ac.uk

[11] O. Jesorsky, K. Kirchberg, R. Frischholz, 'Robust Face Detection Using the Hausdorff Distance', in J. Bigun and F. Smeraldi, eds., Audio and Video based Person Authentication - AVBPA 2001, pp. 90-95, Springer, 2001.

[12] A. Georghiades P. Belhumeur and D. Kriegman, 'From Few to Many: Illumination Cone Models for Face Recognition under Variable Lighting and Pose', *IEEE Trans. Pattern Anal. Mach. Intelligence*, vol. 23, no. 6, pp. 643-660, 2001.

[13] Xiaoming Liu, Tsuhan Chen and B.V.K. Vijaya Kumar, 'On Modeling Variations For Face Authentication', *International Conference on Automatic Face and Gesture Recognition*, pp. 369-374, May 2002.

[14] P. Philips, H. Moon, S. Rizvi and P. Rauss, 'The FERET Evaluation Methodology for Face-Recognition Algorithms', *IEEE Trans. Pattern Analysis and Machine Intelligence*, vol. 22, no. 10, pp. 1090-1104, Oct. 2000.

[15] A. Martínez , A. Kak, 'PCA versus LDA', *IEEE Transactions on Pattern Analysis and Machine Intelligence*, vol. 23 no. 2, pp. 228-233, Feb. 2001.

[16] W. Yambor, B. Draper and J. Beveridge, 'Analyzing PCA-based face recognition algorithms: Eigenvector selection and distance measures', *Workshop on Empirical Evaluation in Computer Vision*, Dublin, Ireland, July 2000.

[17] J. Beveridge, K. She, B. Draper, and G. Givens, 'A nonparametric statistical comparison of principal component and linear discriminant subspaces for face recognition', *IEEE Conference on Pattern Recognition and Machine Intelligence*, pp. 535 – 542, Dec. 2001.

[18] J. Beveridge, K. She, B. Draper, and G. Givens, 'Parametric and nonparametric methods for the statistical evaluation of human id algorithms', *Workshop on the Empirical Evaluation of Computer Vision Systems*, Dec. 2001.

[19] J. Beveridge and K. She, 'Fall 2001 Update to CSU PCA Versus PCA+LDA Comparison', http://www.cs.colostate.edu/evalfacerec/papers.html, Tech. Rep., Colorado State University, Fort Collins, CO, Dec. 2001.

[20] W. Zhao, R. Chellappa, and A. Krishnaswamy, 'Discriminant analysis of principal components for face recognition', in Wechsler, Philips, Bruce, Fogelman-Soulie, and Huang, editors, Face Recognition: From Theory to Applications, pp. 73–85, 1998.

[21] W. Zhao, R. Chellappa, and P. Phillips, 'Subspace linear discriminant analysis for face recognition', *UMD*, 1999.

[22] B. S. Venkatesh, S. Palanivel and B. Yegnanarayana, Face Detection and Recognition in an Image Sequence using Eigenedginess, *3rd Indian Conference on Vision Graphics and Image Processing,* Ahmedabad, December 16-18, 2002.

[23] R. McGill, J. W. Tukey and W. A. Larsen, Variations of Boxplots. *The American Statistician*, pp. 12-16, 1978.

[24] H. Yu and J. Yang, A direct LDA algorithm for high-dimensional data with application to face recognition, *Pattern Recognition.*, Vol. 34, pp. 2067–2070, 2001.

[25] J. Yang and J.Y. Yang, Why can LDA be performed in the PCA transformed space, *Pattern Recognition*, Vol. 36, pp. 563–566, 2003.

[26] X. He, S. Yan, Y. Hu, P. Niyogi and H.-J. Zhang, Face Recognition Using Laplacianfaces, *IEEE Trans. Pattern Analysis and Machine Intelligence*, pp. 328-340, March 2005.

[27] T. Sim, S. Baker, and M. Bsat, The CMU Pose, Illumination, and Expression Database, *IEEE Trans. Pattern Analysis and Machine Intelligence*, Vol. 25, No. 12, , pp. 1615 – 1618, Dec. 2003.

Estimating the Lecturer's Head Pose in Seminar Scenarios - A Multi-view Approach

Michael Voit, Kai Nickel, and Rainer Stiefelhagen

Interactive Systems Lab, Universität Karlsruhe (TH), Germany
{voit, nickel, stiefel}@ira.uka.de

Abstract. In this paper, we present a system to track the horizontal head orientation of a lecturer in a smart seminar room, which is equipped with several cameras. We automatically detect and track the face of the lecturer and use neural networks to classify his or her face orientation in each camera view. By combining the single estimates of the speaker's head orientation from multiple cameras into one joint hypothesis, we improve overall head pose estimation accuracy. We conducted experiments on annotated recordings from real seminars. Using the proposed fully automatic system we are able to correctly determine the lecturer's head pose in 59% of the time and for 8 orientation classes. In 92% of the time, the correct pose class or a neighbouring pose class (i.e. a 45 degree error) were estimated.

1 Introduction

In recent years there has been much research effort spent on building smart perceptive environments. The challenge is to build environments which support humans during their activities without obliging them to concentrate on operating complicated technical devices.

In the framework of the European Union Research project CHIL, we are therefore developing services that aim at proactively assisting people during their daily activities and in particular during their interaction with others. Here, we focus on office and lecture scenarios, as they provide a wide range of useful applications for computerized support.

To provide intelligent services in a smart lecture environment it is necessary to acquire basic information about the room, the people in it and their interactions. This includes for example the number of people, their identities, location, posture, body and head orientation, speech etc.

A person's head orientation can be a valuable cue to determine his or her focus of attention and interaction partners. This could be useful to index seminar recordings, to detect context switches such as interruptions, discussions, etc. and in particular to tell the "smart room" about the lecturer's target of attention, for instance the audience, a whiteboard, his or her laptop etc.

In this work, we present a fully automated system for tracking a lecturer's head pose. By using multiple cameras we cover the entire room and are able to combine head pose estimates coming from various camera views into one single, more robust hypothesis. To estimate head pose in each view, we use an

S. Renals and S. Bengio (Eds.): MLMI 2005, LNCS 3869, pp. 230–240, 2006.

appearance-based approach as proposed in [8], as it has proven to provide useful results even from low-resolution facial images such as the ones captured with the smart room cameras.

The remainder of this paper is organized as follows: In Section 1.1 we discuss related work. Section 2 introduces the Sensor setup used in our smart room. Section 3 gives a system overview and describes the technical components – head detection and extraction, frontal-face classification, head pose estimation and fusion – in detail. Section 4 presents experimental results on recorded seminars. In Section 5 we conclude this paper.

1.1 Related Work

In recent years, various approaches for visually estimating head pose were presented. Yet, the interacting person whose pose was to be recognized often had to limit its movement and rotation to a fixed area around the camera. This prohibits natural behaviour and only allows to embed those systems in environments where the user's freedom of movement is restricted anyway (like in a car or in front of a screen).

Especially model-based approaches as presented in [3], [2], [7] are affected by this constraint. Since in these approaches, a number of facial features need to be detected to compute head pose, they require facial images of quite high resolution and also suffer of tracking problems due to fast head movements.

In contrast, appearance-based approaches tend to achieve satisfactory results even with lower resolutions of extracted head images. In [8] a neural-network-based approach was demonstrated for head pose estimation from very low resolution facial images which were captured by a panoramic camera. Here, however, the output only covered ranges from the left to the right profile. Also only one camera view was used, thereby limiting the application of the system to an area around a meeting table.

Another interesting work is described by Ba and Obodez in [1]. They classify facial images by modelling the responses of Gabor and Gaussian filters for a number of pose classes. An interesting contribution of their work is the combination of head detection and pose estimation in one particle filter framework. However, their work was limited to a monocular system.

Tian et al. [9] described the use of wide baseline overhead stereo-cameras in a room to classify an observed head pose into one of a fixed set of discrete pose classes. Neural networks were implemented for estimating the head pose seen by each camera. A maximum-likelihood search results in the final pose hypothesis. Though the architecture of the presented system seems to be usable for more than two cameras, the work lacks an example with more than one camera pair. To our knowledge, this is the only work combining multiple views for head pose estimation.

2 Sensor Setup

Figure 1 depicts our sensor setup: four calibrated colour cameras (Sony DFW-500) are mounted in the upper corners of the smart-room at a height of about

$2.7m$. The size of the room is $5.9m \times 7.1m$. Because of this layout, the entire room is covered by the cameras' field of view, such that at least one facial view of the user's head can always be obtained. The missing ability to zoom optically results in very low-resolution images of the extracted head, depending on where the person is standing. Using the native camera resolution of 640×480 pixels, the typical size of a head is about 20×30 to 50×65 pixels in our data. Figure 4 shows the four views of the room as seen by the cameras.

In addition to the low resolution facial views, our recordings also suffer from non-optimal lighting conditions due to the non-uniform illumination coming from different light sources in the room (halogene lamps as well as sunlight coming through the windows). In our recordings, therefore, mostly two camera views are always confronted with strong back light.

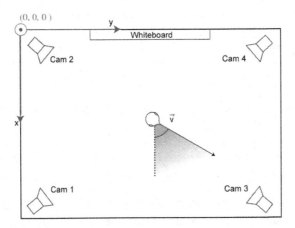

Fig. 1. Four cameras are placed in the upper corners of the smart-room, such that at least one facial view of the head can be obtained. We estimate the horizontal rotation angle (pan) of a person's head by combining the estimates from multiple cameras. The overal pose estimation is relative to the room coordinate system, situated in the north-western corner of the room.

3   System Overview

Our system for tracking a lecturer's head pose consists of the following main components:

1. Tracking of the lecturer
2. Head detection and alignment
3. Classifying frontal views vs. views at the head's back
4. Pose estimation for each camera view
5. Building a joint pose hypothesis

The following sections describe these components in detail.

3.1   Tracking the Lecturer's Head

In order to track the location of the lecturer's head, we follow the approach presented in [5]: A particle filter framework integrates multiple cues from all of the camera views and hypothesizes the lecturer's 3D position. It does so by performing sampled projections of 3D hypotheses and scoring them, thus avoiding the need for explicit triangulation.

Intuitively, the lecturer is the person that is standing and moving most, while people from the audience are generally sitting and not moving much. In order to exploit this behavior, we decided to use dynamic foreground segmentation based on adaptive background modeling [6] as primary feature. To support the track, we use detectors for face and upper body [10] [4].

In order to evaluate a hypothesis, we project a person-sized cuboid centered around the head position to the image plane, and count the number of foreground pixels inside the projected polygon. The fraction of foreground pixels within the polygon is then used as the particle's score. This calculation is sped-up by first computing an integral image of the foreground map, so that a particle can be scored in constant time independently from image resolution.

Furthermore, for each particle, the head cuboid projection on the image plane is classified by a single run of the face-detector. The overlap between the projected head box and all detected faces is used to refine the particle's score. In the same manner, upper body detection is incorporated to support the track.

Using this tracking scheme, computationally expensive features are evaluated locally at the particles' projected positions in the respective images. Thus, the complexity of the tracking algorithm is related linearly to the image size, the number of cameras, and the number of particles. The average tracking error was evaluated to be about $23cm$ throughout all video sequences.

3.2   Head Alignment

Since the estimated position of the lecturer given by the tracking module does not provide consistently aligned bounding boxes of the lecturer's face, a further face alignment step becomes necessary, before faces can be extracted for later processing.

In order to align and extract the lecturer's face in each camera view, we use a frontal and profile face detector which are based on Haar-feature cascades as proposed in [10]. The search space for these face detectors is limited to a search window around the initially estimated position of the lecturer, projected into the respective camera view (see Figure 4 for an example - the big boxes around the lecturer's head depict the search windows for the face detectors).

Since the face detectors sometimes fail to detect a face, we predict the face bounding boxes in those camera views, in which the lecturer's face could not be detected in order to get a facial view for later pose estimation. This can be done if the face was detected in at least two other camera views. From the detected faces, we then compute the lecturer's 3D position by triangulation and project a 3D cuboid around the 3D head location into those camera views where no face was detected (see also Figure 2).

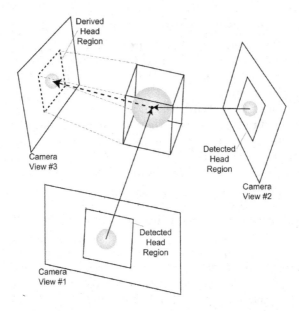

Fig. 2. We detect heads using both frontal and profile face cascades in each camera view. The 3D position of the head is computed by triangulating the centroid of each detected head region in associate camera pairs and searching for the 3D position with the smallest residual. In camera views where no head was found at all, the head's region is derived by placing a fixed-size cuboid around the computed head's centroid in 3D and re-projecting the cube onto the corresponding camera's image plane. The edges of the projection describe the derived head region then.

If - due to false face detections - more than one face is detected in a camera view, those face bounding boxes that lead to the minimal triangulation residual are chosen as the correct ones.

3.3   Classifying Frontal Views vs. Views at the Head's Back

In our experiments, we observed that neural networks for head pose estimation performed worse if views of the back of a head (showing hair only) were included in the training data set. Therefore, we try to automatically detect back-views of heads in our data. To do this, we trained a neural network classifier which outputs the a-posteriori probability, that a given image depicts a frontal view in the range from left to right profile ([$-90°, +90°$]). Following the work we presented in [11], we use a three-layered, feed-forward network, trained with frontal views and views of the head's back only. For the latter the target output was defined to be 0, else 1. Finally, we use a likelihood threshold of 0.5 above which all captures are classified as (near-) frontal views of the head. As input to the neural net, a histogram-normalized grayscale image of the head as well as horizontal and vertical edge images were used. All these were downsampled to 16×16 pixels each, and concatenated into one single feature vector.

The network was trained using standard error backpropagation, minimizing the output error on a cross evaluation set within 100 training cycles.

3.4   Single-View Head Pose Estimation

We first try to estimate the lecturer's head orientation relative to each camera position in the range of $[-90°, +90°]$. Doing the estimation relative to each camera (position) first - instead of estimating head orientations relative to the world coordinate system - allows us to train and use only one single neural network to estimate head pose for all cameras (see Figure 3). This has the advantage that all available facial images from all cameras can be used for training the network. Also, this makes our system independent of the positioning of the cameras in the room and allows us to add further cameras without the necessity of retraining the network.

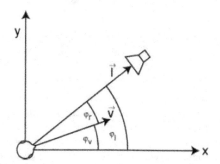

Fig. 3. Each camera's line of sight points straight to the corresponding head's 3D centroid. By using relative head pose angles, the very same head pose estimating neural network may be used for each additional camera view, thus preventing the necessity to train one single network for each camera view respectively.

To estimate head pose, we follow our previous work [11] using a three-layered, feed-forward network with one single output unit. Head pose is estimated continously in the range of $[-90°, +90°]$. As input images, again downsampled histogram normalized grayscale images as well as horizontal and vertical edge images of heads are used.

The network is trained with standard error backpropagation, using a dataset that consists of frontal views of the head only, ranging from left to right profile. As noted above, we experience a more robust performance of the system by limiting its output and therefore the training data to the $[-90°, +90°]$ range.

3.5   Building the Joint Hypothesis

We define $\Theta = \{\theta_i\}$, with $\theta_i \in \{0°, 45°, \ldots, 315°\}$ as the set of all possible head pose classes. These are defined to be relative to the world coordinate system in the room.

Fig. 4. Example output of our discrete head pose estimation system. The arrows indicate the final head pose estimation (long red arrow) and the groundtruth head pose (short green arrow). Further, the position of the arrows indicate the position of the user in the smart-room. The rectangles in each camera view indicate both our search window (large rectangle) in which the system tries to detect a head, and the actual detected head region (small rectangle).

Further, at each timestamp we have $H = \{h_1, h_2, \ldots, h_n\}$, the set of all single orientation estimations made. n represents the number of cameras used, depicting frontal views at the lecturer's head only.

In making a final decision about the true head pose, we score a pose hypothesis θ_i by summing up the a-posteriori probabilities of all available estimations as follows:

$$\pi(\theta_i) = \sum_{j=1}^{n} P(\theta_i | h_j) \tag{1}$$

Finding the best hypothesis then consists in maximizing the score by searching for the best fitting hypothesis $\hat{\theta}$:

$$\hat{\theta} = \arg\max_{\theta_i \in \Theta} \pi(\theta_i) \tag{2}$$

The described procedure guarantees increasing hypothesis scores, the more camera views are being used and easily allows to extend an existing setup by adding more cameras in order to stabilise the estimation. Hereby, the algorithm's complexity increases linearly with the number of cameras C and the number of possible head orientation classes according to $O(C \cdot |\Theta|)$.

The a-posteriori probabilities in equation (1) are derived from confusion matrices that were built for each camera whilst evaluating the classification performance of the trained neural network on the cross evaluation set. Since confusion matrices transcribe the amount of estimated facial views when the true head pose is known, they allow to compute the a-posteriori probabilities of pose classes when a specific single estimation is given. That way, the posterior probability of a class θ_i given the observation h_j can be computed as

$$P(\theta_i|h_j) = \frac{k_{ij}}{\sum_m k_{mj}} \tag{3}$$

where k_{ij} denotes the matrix element in row i and column j. While the matrix columns define the different estimation classes and the rows describe the groundtruth head pose classes.

4   Experiments and Results

Considering the educational smart-room scenario we already described earlier, we evaluated our implementation on real videos that were recorded during a seminar lecture in 2003. Overall we recorded 7 persons, further splitting each recording into 4 segments of 5 minutes each, on which training and evaluation was realised separately. However, in order to reduce redundancy, we annotated and evaluated every 10th frame only. In the multiuser scenario, we trained the underlying neural networks on segments 1 and 2, using segment 3 as cross evaluation set. Segment 4 was used for evaluation purposes, thus evaluating the networks with video data that has not been seen before in the training stage, though resulting from the same persons. In the unknown user scenario, we implemented a round robin evaluation, thus excluding a person's recording from training and cross evaluation when evaluation is being done on this person's video data.

For providing groundtruth information regarding the true head pose, we manually annotated the videos with the observed head pose of the lecturer, classifying the head's pose manually into one of eight equidistant classes such as $0°, 45°, 90°, ...315°$.

4.1   Multiuser System

In case of the multiuser system, the networks have been evaluated with the same persons they have been trained with, although not the very same segments have been used. In this case, with the use of our earlier described head position tracking module, classifying frontal views of the head performed with an accuracy of 83.5%.

As Table 1 shows, head orientation estimation performed correctly with approximately 59% in our fully automatic scenario. This means, the networks were evaluated using unsupervised head extractions, thus including outliers and variance resulting from imperfect alignment of the corresponding bounding box.

In case of manually annotated 3D positions of the head's centroid and manual removal of extreme outliers, the performance increased to approximately 74% correct detection of the pose class thus showing the impact of imperfect face detections and outliers in the complete system.

One major problem regarding outliers in alignment comes from views where the head region has been derived from other views: Using a fixed-size cuboid surely is ineffective in assigning a hard edged region of interest. Estimating the head's approximate size in 3D and using a secondary triangulation step regarding the bounding box' vertices might therefore provide an alternative for future work.

Table 1. System's performance on head pose estimation in percent. We evaluate both the results for automatic recognizing of facial views as well as choosing near frontal views manually. Using a fully automatic system, the correct pose class is detected 58.9% of the time. In 91.7% of the time, the correct class or a neighbouring pose class is detected (*error* < 45°). When choosing frontal views manually, the correct head pose is recognized in 74.6% of the time.

	correct class	correct or neighbour class
multiuser manual view selection	74.6	96.4
multiuser automatic view selection	58.9	91.7
unknown user automatic view selection	48.4	82.9

The second limitation is clearly resulting from the error produced by the facial view classifier, especially considering the fact how such a false positive classification shifts the range of possible head poses that are to be considered. If, for example, camera 1 and 2 depict frontal captures of the user's head and camera 3 estimates a false positive, the range of possible head poses clearly shifts up to the third camera's view range. Since the orientation estimation network only gets trained up to profile faces captures, the output of the third camera is taken into account as if the head is truly rotated into that direction. This leads to the best matching head pose for a wrongfully extended range, which clearly produces false hypotheses in the end. Regarding these outcasts, temporal filtering could help in reducing this negative effect.

4.2   Unknown Users

The unknown user scenario was realised by implementing the leave-one-out method, where one person was removed from the training data set and exclusively used for evaluation purposes only. The results are shown in Table 1. In this unknown user scenario, the initial facial view recognition step achieved a correct recognition rate of 79.6%.

Overall, correct pose class detection was achieved in 48.4% of the time. In 82.9% of the time the estimated pose class fell in either the correct class or a neighbouring class (*error* < 45°). Although the obtained performance is worse than in the multiuser case, we can see that - as in the multiuser case - the performance increases as more facial views are available for pose classification (see Table 2). The results furthermore indicate that it might be advantageous to train the system with much more data in order to increase the networks' capability of generalisation on unseen people.

Table 2. Correct classification in percent in case of both a multiuser and an unknown user scenario. In both cases, using more frontal views at the head enhances the system's performance.

	1 frontal view	2 frontal views	3 frontal views	avg.
multiuser	37.5%	58.3%	72.5%	58.9%
unknown users	27.3%	55.2%	55.3%	48.4%

5   Conclusions

In this work, we have presented an approach for estimating the horizontal head orientation of a lecturer in a multi-camera smart-room environment. We estimate head orientation in each camera view using a neural network. Multiple head pose estimates coming from various camera views are then fused in order to obtain a more accurate estimate of the lecturer's head orientation.

Since head pose is initially estimated with respect to each camera, our approach is flexible and allows for easy change of camera positions and use of additional cameras without the necessity of retraining the system.

We conducted experiments on a set of real seminar recordings. Our experiments show that the overall error significantly decreases as more facial views are included in the estimation. In a multiuser evaluation, the correct pose class could be detected in 58.9% of the frames. In 91.7% of the time, the correct class or a neighbouring pose class (i.e. a 45 degree error) were estimated. In case of unseen users, in 48.4% of the frames the pose class was correctly determined (82.9% when including the neighbouring pose classes).

Our setup provides an unobtrusive estimation of a lecturer's rough head orientation. We believe that this will be useful for many applications in smart seminar rooms, e.g. in order to detect people's focus of attention and interaction among each other.

As our experiments show, pose estimation results were quite heavily affected by false detections of near frontal facial views. In future work we will try to circumvent these problems by soft classification of near frontal views (instead of hard decisions as it is the case right now). We furthermore hope to improve results by using temporal filtering to stabilize the system output.

Acknowledgements

This work has been funded by the European Commission under contract nr. 506909 within the project CHIL (http://chil.server.de).

References

1. S. O. Ba and J.-M. Obodez. A probabilistic framework for joint head tracking and pose estimation. In *Proceedings of the 17th International Conference on Pattern Recognition*, 2004.
2. A. H. Gee and R. Cipolla. Non-intrusive gaze tracking for human-computer interaction. In *Proceedings of Mechatronics and Machine Vision in Practise*, pages 112–117, 1994.
3. T. Horprasert, Y. Yacoob, and L. S. Davis. Computing 3-d head orientation from a monocular image sequence. In *Proceedings of the 2nd International Conference on Automatic Face and Gesture Recognition*, 1996.
4. R. Lienhart and J. Maydt. An extended set of haar-like features for rapid object detection. In *Proceedings of the IEEE International Conference on Image Processing*, 2002.
5. K. Nickel, T. Gehrig, R. Stiefelhagen, and J. McDonough. A joint particle filter for audio-visual speaker tracking. In *International Conference on Multimodal Interfaces ICMI 05, Trento, Italy*, 2005.
6. C. Stauffer and W. Grimson. Adaptive background mixture models for real-time tracking. In *Proceedings of the IEEE Conference on Computer Vision and Pattern Recognition*, pages 246–252, 1999.
7. R. Stiefelhagen, J. Yang, and A. Waibel. A modelbased gaze tracking system. In *Proceedings of the IEEE International Joint Symposia on Intelligence and Systems*, pages 304–310, 1996.
8. R. Stiefelhagen, J. Yang, and A. Waibel. Simultaneous tracking of head poses in a panoramic view. In *International Conference on Pattern Recognition*, 2000.
9. Y.-L. Tian, L. Brown, J. Connell, S. Pankanti, A. Hampapur, A. Senior, and R. Bolle. Absolute head pose estimation from overhead wide-angle cameras. In *IEEE International Workshop on Analysis and Modeling of Faces and Gestures*, 2003.
10. P. Viola and M. Jones. Rapid object detection using a boosted cascade of simple features. In *Proceedings of the IEEE Conference on Computer Vision and Pattern Recognition*, 2001.
11. M. Voit, K. Nickel, and R. Stiefelhagen. Multi-view head pose estimation using neural networks. In *Second Workshop on Face Processing in Video (FPiV'05), in Proceedings of Second Canadian Conference on Computer and Robot Vision. (CRV'05), 9-11 May 2005, Victoria, BC, Canada*, 2005.

Foreground Regions Extraction and Characterization Towards Real-Time Object Tracking

José Luis Landabaso and Montse Pardàs

Technical University of Catalunya, Barcelona, Spain
{jl, montse}@gps.tsc.upc.edu

Abstract. Object localization and tracking are key issues in the analysis of scenes for video surveillance or scene understanding applications. This paper presents a contribution to the object tracking task in indoor environments surveyed by multiple fixed cameras. The method proposed uses a foreground separation process at each camera view. Then, a 3D-foreground scene is modeled and discretized into voxels making use of all the segmented views, preventing the difficulties of inter-object occlusions in 2D trackers, and increasing the robustness for not having to rely only in one view. The voxels are grouped into meaningful blobs, whose colors are modeled for tracking purposes, using a novel voxel-coloring technique that considers possible inter/intra-object occlusions. Finally, color information together with other characteristic features of 3D object appearances are temporally tracked using a template-based technique which takes into account all the features simultaneously in accordance with their respective variances. Extensive experiments dealing with several hours of video sequences in real-world scenarios have been conducted, showing a very promising performance.

1 Introduction

One of the important objectives of image and video analysis is the development of accurate and robust tracking techniques for multiple moving objects in dynamic and cluttered visual scenes. It is particularly desirable in the video surveillance field where an automated system allows fast and efficient access to unforeseen events that need to be attended by security guards or law enforcement officers. It also enables tagging and indexing interesting scene activities / statistics in a video database for future retrieval on demand. In addition, such systems are the building blocks of higher-level intelligent vision-based or assisted information analysis and management systems with a view to understanding the complex actions, interactions, and abnormal behaviors of objects in the scene.

Vision-based surveillance systems can be classified in several different ways, considering the environment in which they are designed to operate. In this paper our focus is on processing videos captured by multiple fixed camera overlooking indoor areas in visual monitoring scenarios.

S. Renals and S. Bengio (Eds.): MLMI 2005, LNCS 3869, pp. 241–249, 2006.
© Springer-Verlag Berlin Heidelberg 2006

Multiple camera surveillance has two key advantages over single camera systems. First, the occlusion problem automatically vanishes when using enough cameras. And second, the process gains robustness for not having to rely only in one camera.

There have been several attempts to fuse video information from different cameras. Some approaches start with the assumption that the scene develops in flat areas with large distances between objects and cameras. The tracking becomes then only a problem of 2D localization in a plane. In such situations it is commonplace to project tracking regions from one camera view to another [1]. The process, known as homography between images, can be employed to select which projection is used based on the localization of the object, in order to avoid occlusions present in a camera but not in others.

Although homographic transformations between images have proved to solve some problems, they fail when the assumptions of large distances and flat areas do not hold, such as indoor scenarios. To overcome this limitation, there have been some works which try to do a 2D-based tracking and then fuse the results into a 3D space; and others which try to fuse 3D features first, to use them later in a single tracker.

1.1   Our Approach

We focus on the second approach. In particular, we propose using the camera views to extract foreground voxels, i.e., the smallest distinguishable box-shaped part of a three-dimensional image. Indeed, foreground voxels provide enough information for precise object detection and tracking. Furthermore, there are several alternatives for the voxel extraction process, such as laser range scanners that although providing very precise volumetric information, suffer from very low scanning rates, making them unsuitable for our application. Other non-invasive reconstruction methods use intensity-based techniques [2] that compute correspondences across images and then recover the 3D structure by triangulation and surface fitting. Unfortunately, for effective operation of these techniques the camera views must be close so that the correspondence is effective. Besides, a huge number of points have to be usually matched and fused into a consistent model, making it a slow and difficult task.

Instead, we propose using shape from silhouette, which is another non-invasive and faster technique. A calibrated [3] set of cameras must be placed around the scene of interest, and the camera pixels must be provided as either part of the shape (foreground) or background. Each of the foreground camera point defines a ray in the scene space that intersects the object at some unknown depth along this ray; the union of these visual rays for all points in the silhouette defines a generalized cone within which the 3D object must lie. Finally, the object is guaranteed to lie in the volume defined by the intersection of all the cones. The main drawback of the method is that it doesn't always capture the true shape of the object, as concave shape regions are not expressed in the silhouettes. However, this is not a severe problem in a tracking application as the aim is not to reconstruct photorealistic scenes.

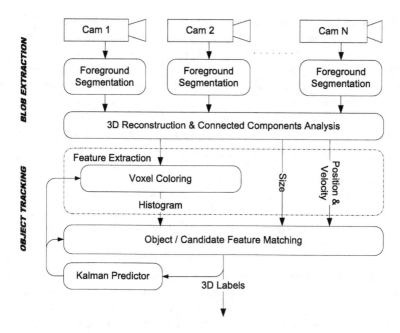

Fig. 1. The system block diagram showing the chain of functional modules

After the voxelization process (see figure 1), a connected component analysis *CCA* is followed to cluster and label the voxels into meaningful 3D-blobs, from which some representative features are extracted. Finally, there is a template-based matching process aiming to find persistent blob correspondences between consecutive frames.

The paper is structured as follows. In the next section the techniques for pixel-domain analysis leading to the segmented foreground views are described. Section 3 is devoted to discussion on issues concerning 3D-blob extraction, including the voxelization process and the voxel coloring. Section 4 describes the object tracking approach adopted. Section 5 illustrates the experimental evaluations of the system. And, finally the paper concludes in Section 6 .

2 2D Foreground Segmentation

The 2D foreground extraction technique that we have used [4, 6] is based on the adaptive background subtraction method proposed by Stauffer and Grimson [7]. A mixture of K Gaussian distributions is used to model RGB color changes, at each pixel location, in the imaging scene over the time. With each incoming frame the Gaussian distributions are updated, and then used to determine which pixels are most likely to result from a background process. This model allows a proper representation of the background scene undergoing slow lighting and scene changes as well as momentary variations.

The foreground pixels thus obtained, however, are not exempt from false detections due to noise in the background and camera jitters. A false-foreground pixels suppression procedure is introduced to alleviate this problem. Basically, when a pixel is initially classified as a foreground pixel, its 8-connected neighboring pixels' models are examined. If the majority of these models, when applied to this pixel, agree that it's a background pixel, then it's considered as a false detection and removed from foreground.

Once the foreground objects pixels have been identified, an additional scheme [5] is applied to find out if some of these foreground pixels correspond to areas likely to be cast shadows or specular reflections. The working mechanism of this novel scheme is the following:

As the first step, we evaluate the variability in both brightness and color distortion [8] between the foreground pixels and the adaptive background, and possible shadows and highlights are detected. It was observed though that this procedure is less effective in cases that the objects of interest have similar colors to those of presumed shadows. To correct this, an assertion process comparing the gradient / textures similarities of the foreground pixels and corresponding background is incorporated. These processing steps, effectively removing cast shadows, also invariably delete some object pixels and distort object shapes. Therefore, a morphology-based conditional region growing algorithm is employed to reconstruct the object's shapes. This novel approach gives favorable results compared to the current state-of-the-art to suppress shadows / highlights.

3   3D Blob Extraction

Once the foreground region has been extracted in each camera view, the blobs in the 3D space are constructed. In our implementation, the bounding volume (the room) is discretized into voxels. Each of the foreground camera points defines a ray in the scene. Then, the voxels are marked as *occupied* when there are intersecting rays from enough cameras $MINC$ over the total N.

The relaxation in the number of intersecting rays at a voxel prevents typical missing-foreground errors at the pixel level in a certain view, consisting in foreground pixels incorrectly classified as background. Besides, camera redundancy also prevents analog false-foreground errors, since a wrongly defined ray in a view will unlikely intersect with at least $MINC$ -1 rays from the rest of the cameras at any voxel.

3.1   Voxel Connectivity Analysis

After marking all the *occupied* voxels, with the process described above, a connectivity analysis is performed to detect clouds of connected voxels, i.e. 3D-blobs, corresponding to tracking targets. We choose to group the voxels with 26-connectivity which means that any possible contact between voxels (vertices, edges, and surfaces) makes them form a group. Then, from all the possible blobs, we consider only the ones with a number of connected voxels greater than a certain threshold B_SIZE, to avoid spurious detections.

3.2   Voxel Coloring

After voxel grouping, the blobs are characterized with their color (dominant color, histogram, histogram at different heights, etc.), among other features. This characterization is employed later for tracking purposes. However, a trustworthy and fast voxel coloring technique has to be employed before any color extraction method is applied to the blob.

We need to note that during the voxelization and labeling process, inter/intra-object occlusions are not considered, as it is irrelevant whether the ray came from the occluded or the occluding object. However, in order to guarantee correct pixel-color mapping to visible voxels in a certain view, occlusions have to be previously determined.

We discard slow exhaustive search techniques, which project back all the *occupied* voxels to all the camera views to check intersecting voxels along the projection ray. Instead, for the sake of computational efficiency, we propose a faster technique, making use of target localization, which can be obtained from the tracking system.

As photorealistic coloring is not required in our application, intra-object occlusions are simply determined by examining if the voxel is more distant to the camera than the centroid of the blob the voxel belongs to. On the other hand, inter-object occlusions in a voxel are simply determined by finding objects (represented by their centroid) in between the camera and the voxel. This is achieved by computing the closest distance between the segment voxel-to-camera and the objects' centroids $(dist(\underline{\mathbf{vc}}, \mathbf{o_c}))$. The process is schematized in the Voxel-Blob level in figure 2.

To reduce even further the computational complexity, the voxels can be approximated by the position of the centroid of the blob they belong to, as it's shown in the Blob level in figure 2, and intra-object occlusions are not examined.

Finally, the color of the voxels is calculated as an average of the projected colors from all the non-occluding views.

4   Object Tracking

After labeling and voxel coloring, the blobs are temporally tracked throughout their movements within the scene by means of temporal templates.

Each object of interest in the scene is modeled by a temporal template of persistent features. In the current studies, a set of three significant features are used for describing them: the velocity at its centroid, the volume, and the histogram. Therefore at time t, we have, for each object l centered at (p_{lx}, p_{ly}, p_{lz}), a template of features $M_l(t)$. Prior to matching the template l with a candidate blob k in frame $t + 1$, centered at $(p'_{kx}, p'_{ky}, p'_{kz})$ with a feature vector $B_k(t+1)$, Kalman filters are used to update the template by predicting its new velocity and size in $\hat{M}_l(t+1)$. The mean $\overline{M}_l(t)$ and variance $V_l(t)$ vector of the templates are updated when a candidate blob k in frame $t + 1$ is found to match with it. The updates are computed using the latest corresponding L blobs that the object has matched.

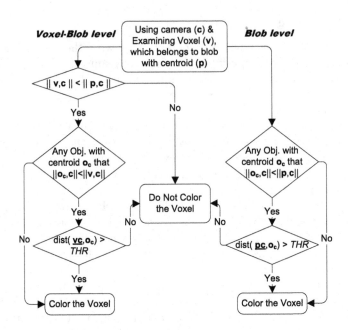

Fig. 2. Voxel Coloring block diagram, showing the two proposed methods. On the left, the Voxel-Blob level, which addresses voxel coloring individually. On the right, a faster approach using only the centroids of the blobs.

For the matching procedure we choose to use a parallel matching strategy. The main issue is the use of a proper distance metric that best suits the problem under study. The template for each object being tracked has a set of associated Kalman filters that predict the expected value for each feature (except for the histogram) in the next frame. Obviously, some features are more persistent for an object while others may be more susceptible to noise. Also, different features normally assume values in different ranges with different variances. Euclidean distance does not account for these factors as it will allow dimensions with larger scales and variances to dominate the distance measure.

One way to tackle this problem is to use the Mahalanobis distance metric, which takes into account not only the scaling and variance of a feature, but also the variation of other features based on the covariance matrix. Thus, if there are correlated features, their contribution is weighted appropriately.

However, with high-dimensional data, the covariance matrix can become non-invertible. Furthermore, matrix inversion is a computationally expensive process, not suitable for real-time operation. So, in the current work a weighted Euclidean distance between the template l and a candidate blob k is adopted, assuming a diagonal co-variance matrix. For a heterogeneous data set, this is a reasonable distance definition. Further details of the technique have been presented in the past [4].

5   Results

The voxelization and tracking methods have been evaluated extensively using, among others, our own recordings at the *UPC* smart-room and the benchmarking video sequences provided by the *CHIL* project [9]. The *CHIL* sequences are provided with manually labeled tags of the tracking target corresponding to thousands of frames of seminar presentations in a smart room.

The room discretization was done using $5 \times 5 \times 5$ cm^3 cubes. During the voxelization process we used 4 cameras, accepting voxel reconstruction with at least $MINC = 3$ intersecting rays. Blobs with B_SIZE lower to 700 were filtered out and voxel coloring was performed with the Blob-level faster approach, setting $THR = 40$ cms.

Under the above mentioned conditions, the voxelization and tracking process performs at 5 fps; with an average tracking error under 20 cms (see the complete results in Table 1).

The algorithm performs extremely well except in object grouping situations, not being able to segment them. In spite of that, the tracker is able to recover the correct tags after the objects ungroup. Some videos are available in our web at: http://gps-tsc.upc.es/imatge/_jl/Tracking.html

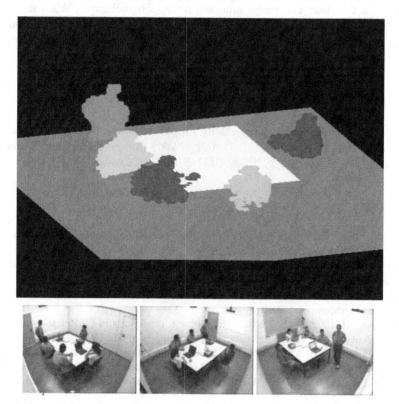

Fig. 3. Voxel reconstruction and labeling of a video sequence recorded at the *UPC* smart-room

Table 1. First column shows the mean of Euclidian distance between the estimated position of the centroid, and the ground truth of the head center. Note that for this evaluation, not 3D distances are used, but rather the 2D distance between the projection on the ground of the estimated head centre and that of the ground truth labels. The second column expresses the percentage of frames where the distance between the estimated distance and the ground truth was worse than 30 cms.

30 minutes of video	Error	Results with Error > 30 cms
Results	148.2 mms	3.8%

6   Conclusions and Future Work

In this paper, we have presented a system able to create a 3D-foreground scene, characterize objects with 3D-blobs and track them, preventing the difficulties of inter-object occlusions in 2D trackers, and increasing the robustness for not having to rely only in one view. The system uses a novel voxel coloring scheme which allows fast object histogram retrieval used later with other features in a parallel matching technique during the tracking.

Some of the directions to take to improve results include projecting back the 3D-blobs to assist the foreground segmentation technique. Also, dynamic adjustment of the required number of intersecting rays at a voxel $MINC$ will be investigated. The parameter may be set depending on the position of the tracking target, allowing tracking in areas where only fewer cameras have visibility.

Acknowledgments

This material is based upon work partially supported by the European Union under the Integrated Project *CHIL IST-2004-506909* and by the Spanish Ministry of Education under actions *TIN2004-0171-E* and *TEC2004-01914*

References

1. Black, J., Ellis, T., Rosin, P.: Multi view image surveillance and tracking. Proceedings of the Workshop on Motion and Video Computing 2002
2. Hartley, R., Zisserman, A.: Multiple view geometry in computer vision. Cambridge University Press 2000
3. Zhang, Z.: A flexible new technique for camera calibration. Technical report, Microsoft Research, August 2002
4. Landabaso, J.L., Xu, L-Q., Pardàs, M.: Robust Tracking and Object Classification Towards Automated Video Surveillance. Proceedings of ICIAR **2** 2004 463–470
5. Xu, L-Q., Landabaso, J.L. Pardàs, M.: Shadow removal with blob-based morphological reconstruction for error correction. Acoustics, Speech, and Signal Processing, 2005. Proceedings. (ICASSP '05). IEEE International Conference on, **Vol.2**, Iss., March 18-23, 2005 729–732

6. Landabaso, J.L., Pardàs, M., Xu, L-Q.: Hierarchical representation of scenes using activity information. Acoustics, Speech, and Signal Processing, 2005. Proceedings. (ICASSP '05). IEEE International Conference on, **Vol.2**, Iss., March 18-23, 2005 677–680
7. Stauffer, C., Grimson, W.E.L.: Learning patterns of activity using real-time tracking. IEEE trans. on Pattern Analysis and Machine Intelligence, **22(8)**, August 2000
8. Horpraset, T., Harwood, D., Davis, L.: A statistical approach for real-time robust background subtraction and shadow detection. Proceedings of International Conference on Computer Vision, 1999
9. *CHIL* project home page: http://chil.server.de

Projective Kalman Filter: Multiocular Tracking of 3D Locations Towards Scene Understanding

C. Canton-Ferrer[1], J.R. Casas[1], A.M. Tekalp[2], and M. Pardàs[1],[*]

[1] Technical University of Catalonia, Barcelona, Spain
{ccanton, josep, montse}@gps.tsc.upc.es
[2] Koc University, Istanbul, Turkey
mtekalp@ku.edu.tr

Abstract. This paper presents a novel approach to the problem of estimating and tracking 3D locations of multiple targets in a scene using measurements gathered from multiple calibrated cameras. Estimation and tracking is jointly achieved by a newly conceived computational process, the Projective Kalman filter (PKF), allowing the problem to be treated in a single, unified framework. The projective nature of observed data and information redundancy among views is exploited by PKF in order to overcome occlusions and spatial ambiguity. To demonstrate the effectiveness of the proposed algorithm, the authors present tracking results of people in a SmartRoom scenario and compare these results with existing methods as well.

1 Introduction

Estimating the 3D position and velocity of objects in a scene is of interest in a number of applications such as visual surveillance, SmartRoom monitoring, human-computer interfaces and scene understanding. Multiple view geometry has been addressed in [12] from a mathematical viewpoint, but there is still work to be done for the efficient fusion of redundant camera views and its combination with image analysis techniques for object detection and tracking. In this framework, the current paper proposes a novel technique to address the problem of tracking multiple 3D locations based on the data obtained from a set of calibrated cameras.

Many vision based tracking techniques have been developed to deal with sequences from a single perspective [11, 6] but considerably less work has been published on tracking of 3D locations with multiple cameras. One of the main problems within this topic is establishing correspondences among features from different perspectives [4]. On the other hand, multiple viewpoints allow exploiting

[*] This material is based upon work partially supported by the European Union under the Integrated Project CHIL IST-2004-506909 and by the Spanish Ministry of Education under actions TIN2004-0171-E and TEC2004-01914.

spatial redundancy and overcome ambiguities caused by occlusion or segmentation errors and provide 3D position information as well.

The common methodology to this problem in existing approaches is composed by two disjoint successive steps: estimation of the 3D location and Kalman tracking over this estimation. Bayesian networks [5, 7], algebraic methods [17, 9] or homographies [3] have been employed to establish correspondences among the projections of the 3D tracked points on all views and then perform a Kalman tracking directly on this estimated 3D location. The main drawbacks of these methods are sensitivity to occlusions and spatial ambiguity when resolving the multiple view correspondence problem [4].

In this paper, we present a novel technique that performs a joint estimation and tracking of multiple 3D locations allowing the problem to be posed in a single, unified framework. Projective geometry underlying the image formation process is exploited allowing the definition of our Projective Kalman Filter. Information redundancy among views is taken into account to define a data association process to deal with occlusions and keep a coherent track. This filter has found applicability in a SmartRoom scenario in the fields of body and gesture analysis (see Fig.1) or person tracking.

The outline of this work is as follows. Background topics on projective geometry and Kalman filtering required in forecoming sections are reviewed in Sec.2. Projective Kalman Filter theory is presented on Sec.3. Experimental results are presented in Sec.4. Finally, conclusion and further improvements are given in Sec.5.

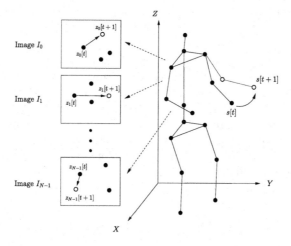

Fig. 1. Example of an application of tracking of 3D locations from its projections within the framework of body analysis (based on [8]). Tracking of the hidden state $s[t]$ among time from its projections $z_k[t]$, $0 \leq k < N$, would allow obtaining the position of body joints.

2   Projective Geometry and Kalman Tracking Basics

In order to define a joint estimation-tracking scheme that exploits the underlying projective geometry of a multiple view scenario, some basic concepts are presented. Formation of images formulation and Kalman filtering theory are briefly reviewed but the reader is addressed to [12] and [15] for more references.

2.1   Multiple View Systems and Projective Geometry

Obtaining two-dimensional coordinates (pixel positions) of an image from a three-dimensional magnitude (a 3D location) is a process where a dimension is lost. Formally, projection can be seen as a many-to-one morphism $\psi : \mathbb{R}^3 \to \mathbb{N}^2$ that transforms 3D Euclidean coordinates in the world reference frame into 2D coordinates in the camera reference frame. The usual mathematical way to model this process passes through projective geometry as an efficient description of the image formation process. Essentially, a camera is regarded as a projective device where an image is the result of the central projection of 3D world points onto the image plane. Specifically, the pinhole camera model is employed in this paper. Projective effects due to vanishing points can be easily modeled and understood if we take into consideration projective coordinate systems. Many authors take advantage from projective geometry and homogeneous coordinates when addressing computer vision problems [12].

Projection operation can be fully described in homogeneous coordinates by the linear application $\mathbf{P} : \mathbb{P}^3 \to \mathbb{P}^2$ denoted as the *projection matrix*[1]. So,

$$\mathbf{x} = \mathbf{PX}, \qquad \mathbf{P} = \mathbf{K}[\mathbf{R}|\mathbf{t}], \qquad \mathbf{x} \in \mathbb{P}^2, \qquad \mathbf{X} \in \mathbb{P}^3, \qquad (1)$$

where the *calibration matrix* $\mathbf{K}$ models the intrinsic parameters of the camera (focal length, scaling and projection center) and $\mathbf{R}$ and $\mathbf{t}$ its extrinsic parameters (rotation and translation of the camera).

It must be noted that projection is essentially a non-linear operation when defined by the application $\psi : \mathbb{R}^3 \to \mathbb{N}^2$. In fact, when adopting the pinhole camera model and the associated projective geometry model, the relation between the image coordinates $\tilde{\mathbf{x}} = [\tilde{x} \ \tilde{y}]^\top \in \mathbb{N}^2$ and the projected coordinates $\mathbf{x} = [x \ y \ z]^\top \in \mathbb{P}^2$ is stated as:

$$\tilde{x} = \left\lfloor \frac{x}{z} \right\rfloor, \qquad \tilde{y} = \left\lfloor \frac{y}{z} \right\rfloor. \qquad (2)$$

For the sake of simplicity in the notation, let us re-define $\psi_{\mathbf{P}} : \mathbb{R}^3 \to \mathbb{N}^2$ as the projection operator from 3D coordinates to image coordinates embedding Eq.1 and Eq.2.

---

[1] The notation employed in this paper follows the one described by [12,10].

2.2 Standard Kalman Filter Data Model

The Kalman filter addresses the general problem of estimating the state $\mathbf{s} \in \mathbb{R}^n$ of a discrete-time controlled process that is governed by the linear stochastic difference equation:

$$\mathbf{s}[t+1] = \mathbf{F}\,\mathbf{s}[t] + \mathbf{w}[t], \tag{3}$$

with a measurement $\mathbf{z} \in \mathbb{R}^m$ that is

$$\mathbf{z}[t+1] = \mathbf{H}\,\mathbf{s}[t+1] + \mathbf{v}[t+1]. \tag{4}$$

The random variables $\mathbf{w}[t]$ and $\mathbf{v}[t]$ represent the state and measurement noise respectively. The matrix $\mathbf{F}$ in the difference Eq.3 relates the state at the future step $t+1$ to the state at the current step t and the matrix $\mathbf{H}$ in the measurement Eq.4 relates the state to the measurement $\mathbf{z}[t+1]$. Matrices $\mathbf{F}$ and $\mathbf{H}$ might change with each time step despite most of the approximations in Kalman filtering assume they are constant. In order to define a convergent Kalman filter, the random variables $\mathbf{w}[t]$ and $\mathbf{v}[t]$ are assumed to be independent of each other, white and with normal probability distributions

$$p(\mathbf{w}) \sim \mathcal{N}(0, \mathbf{Q}), \tag{5}$$
$$p(\mathbf{v}) \sim \mathcal{N}(0, \mathbf{R}). \tag{6}$$

2.3 Standard Kalman Filter Evolution

In summary, we have the following situation: starting from an initial estimate $\hat{\mathbf{s}}[0|-1]$, with an initial state covariance matrix denoted as $\mathbf{\Sigma}[-1|-1]$, for each observation $\mathbf{z}[t+1]$, the estimate of the state is updated using the following steps:

1. **State estimate extrapolation:**

$$\hat{\mathbf{s}}[t+1|t] = \mathbf{F}\hat{\mathbf{s}}[t|t] \tag{7}$$

2. **Error covariance extrapolation:**

$$\mathbf{\Sigma}[t+1|t] = \mathbf{F}\mathbf{\Sigma}[t|t]\mathbf{F}^\top + \mathbf{Q} \tag{8}$$

3. **Kalman gain:**

$$\mathbf{K}[t+1] = \mathbf{\Sigma}[t+1|t]\mathbf{H}^\top[t+1]\left(\mathbf{H}[t+1]\mathbf{\Sigma}[t+1|t]\mathbf{H}^\top[t+1] + \mathbf{R}\right)^{-1} \tag{9}$$

4. **State estimate update:**

$$\hat{\mathbf{s}}[t+1|t+1] = \hat{\mathbf{s}}[t+1|t] + \mathbf{K}[t+1]\left(\mathbf{z}[t+1] - \mathbf{H}[t+1]\hat{\mathbf{s}}[t+1|t]\right) \tag{10}$$

5. **Error covariance update:**

$$\mathbf{\Sigma}[t+1|t+1] = \left(\mathbf{I} - \mathbf{K}[t+1]\mathbf{H}[t+1]\right)\mathbf{\Sigma}[t+1|t] \tag{11}$$

3   Projective Kalman Filter (PFK)

Kalman filtering is the optimal strategy when dealing with estimation problems that involve linear relationships between the observed and real state variables and the distorting noise has a normal probability density. In the current analysis scenario, Kalman theory has still applicability and allows defining a joint estimation-tracking scheme exploiting the projective nature of the data gathered from the cameras.

3.1   Multi-camera 3D Tracking Scenario

Let us define $\tilde{\mathbf{X}}^i[t] = [\tilde{X}^i[t]\ \tilde{Y}^i[t]\ \tilde{Z}^i[t]]^\top$, $0 \le i < M$, as the M 3D locations, targets, to be tracked along time. The available data of each of the N cameras is noted as $\tilde{\mathbf{x}}_k^i[t] = [\tilde{x}_k^i[t]\ \tilde{y}_k^i[t]]^\top$, $0 \le i < M$, $0 \le k < N$ and its formation process can be described as:

$$\tilde{\mathbf{x}}_k^i[t] = \psi_{\mathbf{P}_k}\left(\tilde{\mathbf{X}}^i[t]\right) + \boldsymbol{\xi}_k^i[t], \tag{12}$$

where $\boldsymbol{\xi}_k^i[t]$ is a noise factor present at time t in the projection of the i-th tracked object on the k-th camera and $\psi_{\mathbf{P}_k}$ is the projection operator associated to this camera. The noise factor $\boldsymbol{\xi}_k^i[t]$ is mainly formed by two contributions

$$\boldsymbol{\xi}_k^i[t] = \mathbf{g}_k^i[t] + \mathbf{d}_k^i[t], \tag{13}$$

where $\mathbf{g}_k^i[t]$ is the noise introduced by the inaccuracies of the calibration process, camera resolution, lens distortion,... considered to have a normal probability distribution in virtue of the Central Limit Theorem. On the other hand, $\mathbf{d}_k^i[t]$ is modeled as an impulsive noise result of a bad foreground region detection, occlusions or heavy lens distortion (borders of the image).

3.2   Kalman Filtering on Multiple Projective Planes

Defining a scheme embedding estimation and tracking based on a direct application of Kalman equations Eq.3 and Eq.4 is not straightforward. Let us define our state variable $\mathbf{s}[t]$ as the position and velocity that describe the dynamics of the tracked 3D location in homogeneous coordinates:

$$\mathbf{s}[t] = [\mathbf{X}^i[t]\ \dot{\mathbf{X}}^i[t]]^\top = [\tilde{X}^i[t]\ \tilde{Y}^i[t]\ \tilde{Z}^i[t]\ 1\ \dot{\tilde{X}}^i[t]\ \dot{\tilde{Y}}^i[t]\ \dot{\tilde{Z}}^i[t]\ 0]^\top. \tag{14}$$

The measure process described by Eq.4 must be modelled according to the projective nature of the observations. The data captured by the N cameras, that is the projections of the 3D tracked location given by Eq.12 (pixel positions), forms the observation vector $\mathbf{z}[t]$:

$$\begin{aligned}\mathbf{z}[t] &= [\mathbf{x}_0^i[t]\ \mathbf{x}_1^i[t]\ \cdots\ \mathbf{x}_{N-1}^i[t]]^\top \\ &= [\tilde{x}_0^i[t]\ \tilde{y}_0^i[t]\ 1\ \tilde{x}_1^i[t]\ \tilde{y}_1^i[t]\ 1\ \cdots\ \tilde{x}_{N-1}^i[t]\ \tilde{y}_{N-1}^i[t]\ 1]^\top,\end{aligned} \tag{15}$$

that is the detected projections of $\tilde{\mathbf{X}}^i[t]$ on every view.

It can be seen that the problem of tracking a 3D location (hidden state) from its projections on calibrated cameras (observation) does not fit with the standard Kalman filter formulation. Relations between the real state, $\tilde{\mathbf{X}}^i[t]$, and the observations, $\tilde{\mathbf{x}}_k^i[t]$, are non-linear. Thus, statistical distributions when processed by a projective device, $\psi_{\mathbf{P}_k}$, do not usually keep the same statistical properties. Hence Kalman filtering theory can not be applied directly. Solutions to this problem have arisen as the Extended Kalman Filter (EKF) [16], the Unscented Kalman Filter (UKF) [13] or Particle Filtering [1]. Moreover, normal distribution of the involved random variables is not fulfilled. The random variables modelling the movement of the 3D location to be tracked (position and velocity) are modelled as a normal distribution but the observed variables, that are affected by the noise factor $\boldsymbol{\xi}_k^i[t]$ described by Eq.13, are not. This problem can be coarsely solved by approximating $\boldsymbol{\xi}_k^i[t]$ by a normal distribution however, this solution leads to poor results in presence of occlusions (large values of $\boldsymbol{\xi}_k^i[t]$).

Projective Kalman filter is able to perform a joint estimation and tracking by adding some modifications on the parameters introduced by Eq.3 and Eq.4 in order to deal with the data model defined by Eq.14 and Eq.15. Filter evolution follow the standard Kalman equations defined in Sec.2.3. Regarding the state equation Eq.3:

- **State Transition Matrix:** Matrix $\mathbf{F}$ is set to be constant over time and defined as:

$$\mathbf{F} = \begin{bmatrix} 1 & 0 & 0 & 0 & \frac{1}{T} & 0 & 0 & 0 \\ 0 & 1 & 0 & 0 & 0 & \frac{1}{T} & 0 & 0 \\ 0 & 0 & 1 & 0 & 0 & 0 & \frac{1}{T} & 0 \\ 0 & 0 & 0 & 1 & 0 & 0 & 0 & 0 \\ 0 & 0 & 0 & 0 & 1 & 0 & 0 & 0 \\ 0 & 0 & 0 & 0 & 0 & 1 & 0 & 0 \\ 0 & 0 & 0 & 0 & 0 & 0 & 1 & 0 \\ 0 & 0 & 0 & 0 & 0 & 0 & 0 & 1 \end{bmatrix}. \tag{16}$$

- **Process noise:** The statistics of process noise $\mathbf{w}[t]$ are set to be normal. The covariance matrix $\mathbf{Q}$ defining this random variable is learnt from groundtruth data and set invariant through time.

In order to define a Kalman scheme to track 3D positions from multiple camera data, the measure process described by Eq.4 must be modelled accordingly to the projective nature of the observations.

- **Observation Matrix:** The key point of our Kalman filter scheme relies in the definition of the observed data. A first proposal for this matrix would be:

$$\mathbf{H} = \begin{bmatrix} \mathbf{P}_0 & \mathbf{0}_{3\times4} \\ \vdots & \vdots \\ \mathbf{P}_{N-1} & \mathbf{0}_{3\times4} \end{bmatrix}. \tag{17}$$

However, this matrix, when applied to the state vector $s[t]$ would generate coordinates that might not be on the image plane ($z \neq 1$). Hence, the projection non-linearity must be compensated to obtain coordinates fulfilling $z = 1$ in order to have a coherent data model. Our proposal for the adaptive design of the matrix $\mathbf{H}[t+1]$ is as follows:

$$\mathbf{H}[t+1] = \begin{bmatrix} \alpha_0 & \cdots & 0 \\ \vdots & \ddots & \vdots \\ 0 & \cdots & \alpha_{N-1} \end{bmatrix} \cdot \begin{bmatrix} \mathbf{P}_0 & \mathbf{0}_{3\times 4} \\ \vdots & \vdots \\ \mathbf{P}_{N-1} & \mathbf{0}_{3\times 4} \end{bmatrix},$$

$$\alpha_k = \frac{1}{\mathbf{P}_k^3 \cdot \hat{\mathbf{s}}[t+1|t]} \mathbf{I}_{4\times 4}, \tag{18}$$

where $\mathbf{P}_k^3$ is the 3th row of $\mathbf{P}_k$ and $\hat{\mathbf{s}}[t+1|t]$ is the predicted state given by Eq.7. In this way, when computing Eq.10 the observed, $\mathbf{z}[t+1]$, and predicted term, $\mathbf{H}[t+1]\hat{\mathbf{s}}[t+1|t]$, can be compared (both have $z = 1$) leading to a meaningful result. The non-linearity introduced by the projection operator, $\psi_{\mathbf{P}_k}$, is therefore overcome and successfully modelled.

- **Observation noise:** The statistics of the observation noise $\boldsymbol{\xi}_k^i[t]$ can not be modelled as a random variable with normal distribution. Nevertheless, despite Kalman theory would seem not to be applicable, we propose an scheme to design an adaptive covariance matrix $\mathbf{R}[t]$ that will be able to handle occlusions and make Kalman theory fit in our scheme. Covariance matrix $\mathbf{R}[t]$ can be seen as a matrix that controls how reliable is the observed data in order to use it for the estimation of the hidden state $\hat{\mathbf{s}}[t+1|t+1]$. In the observation process, there could be two situations: if there is no occlusion in the projection of $\mathbf{X}^i[t]$ onto the k-th view, then the distorting noise $\boldsymbol{\xi}_k^i[t]$ reduces to be the AWGN $\mathbf{g}_k^i[t]$ part or if there is occlusion and the predominant noise term turns out to be the impulsive $\mathbf{d}_k^i[t]$ factor. Under this model, $\mathbf{R}$ matrix can be defined for every time step as:

$$\mathbf{R}[t] = \begin{bmatrix} \beta_0 & \cdots & 0 \\ \vdots & \ddots & \vdots \\ 0 & \cdots & \beta_{N-1} \end{bmatrix}, \tag{19}$$

where

$$\beta_k = \begin{cases} \sigma_k & \text{if there is no occlusion } (\boldsymbol{\xi}_k[t] \approx \mathbf{g}_k[t]) \\ \infty & \text{if there is occlusion } (\boldsymbol{\xi}_k[t] \approx \mathbf{d}_k[t]) \end{cases}. \tag{20}$$

where σ_k is the observation covariance noise at k-th view. With this scheme, non-informative data coming from occluded views is disregarded when computing the estimation of the hidden state and projections corrupted with AWGN are correctly handled. The algorithm to decide whether a view is occluded or not is described in Sec.3.3.

3.3   Data Association Problem

In presence of multiple objects, occlusion and noisy measurements, it is important to assign the correct measurement to each tracked object. This is called the data association problem [2]. The following algorithm describes how to associate data to every tracked object in the scene (inspirated by [17]) and decide whether an occlusion has occurred in some views.

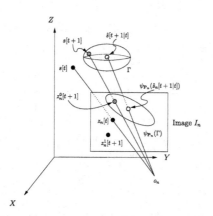

Fig. 2. Data association scenario. State estimation $\hat{s}[t+1|t]$ and the uncertainty region defined by Γ when projected into image I_n allow associating the correct observation, $\mathbf{z}_n^0[t+1]$, to the interest track dismissing false detections, $\mathbf{z}_n^1[t+1]$.

Data association must determine the spatial correspondence of two projections generated by the same 3D feature at two consecutive time instants in the same image. In this way, when tracking multiple targets, the algorithm will be able to perform properly. Moreover, in the case when a correspondence can not be established probably due to an occlusion, the data association algorithm should modify the $\mathbf{R}[t+1]$ matrix accordingly. The proposed data association procedure is described by the following steps:

1. **State estimate extrapolation:** In order to perform a search for the most likely correspondence on time $t+1$, the algorithm estimates the state at this time through Eq.7 thus obtaining $\hat{s}[t+1|t]$.
2. **Data bounding:** From the state evolution equation Eq.3, it can be assumed that the uncertainties of the 3D tracked location, the state, are modelled by the process noise described by the covariance matrix $\mathbf{Q}$. Assuming that this matrix has been correctly estimated, it can be inferred that the 3D position, $s[t+1]$, fulfills the condition:

$$s[t+1] \in \Gamma, \tag{21}$$

$$\Gamma : \left\{ \mathbf{X} / \left(\mathbf{X} - \hat{s}[t+1|t]\right) \mathbf{W}^{-1} \left(\mathbf{X} - \hat{s}[t+1|t]\right)^\top \leq 0 \right\}. \tag{22}$$

That is, $\mathbf{s}[t+1]$ is inside the ellipsoid Γ in homogeneous coordinates defining an uncertainty region proportional to the state noise covariance. The conic matrix $\mathbf{W}$ [12] contents information about the topology of the ellipsoid and we define it from $\mathbf{Q}$ as:

$$
\mathbf{W} = \begin{bmatrix} & & 0 \\ & \gamma\mathbf{Q} & 0 \\ & & 0 \\ 0 & 0 & 0 & -1 \end{bmatrix} = \begin{bmatrix} \gamma\sigma_x & 0 & 0 & 0 \\ 0 & \gamma\sigma_y & 0 & 0 \\ 0 & 0 & \gamma\sigma_z & 0 \\ 0 & 0 & 0 & -1 \end{bmatrix}. \tag{23}
$$

In our experiments, a value $\gamma = 6$ has provided effective results.

3. **Data Association:** The geometric property defined in Eq.21 and Eq.22 must be also fulfilled when dealing with a projection of this 3D scenario as depicted in Fig.2. A process to associate the most likely projection at time $t+1$ with respect to t can be defined straightforward. Since our input data are pixels detected on the projected images we could associate the pixel that minimizes a given criteria related to the projection of Γ, $\psi_{\mathbf{P}_k}(\Gamma)$, to the i-th track. Generally, the perspective projection of an ellipsoid is an ellipse defined by the matrix $\mathbf{V}$ fulfilling the following condition [12]:

$$
\mathbf{V} \propto \left(\mathbf{P}_k \mathbf{W}^{-1} \mathbf{P}_k^\top \right)^{-1}. \tag{24}
$$

Then, a proposal to establish the best association between the i-th track at the time $t+1$ with the input data $\mathbf{z}_n^l[t+1]$, $0 \le l < L$ (there could be uncountable input data coming from the real tracks, false detections,...) can be done through the Mahalanobis distance:

$$
\mathbf{z}_n^i[t+1] = \tag{25}
$$
$$
\min_{\mathbf{z}_n^l[t+1]} \sqrt{(\mathbf{z}_n^l[t+1] - \psi_{\mathbf{P}_k}(\hat{\mathbf{s}}[t+1|t]))\, \mathbf{V}\, (\mathbf{z}_n^l[t+1] - \psi_{\mathbf{P}_k}(\hat{\mathbf{s}}[t+1|t]))^\top}.
$$

4. **Occlusion detection:** In the case when the condition related to the i-th track association

$$
\sqrt{(\mathbf{z}_n^i[t+1] - \psi_{\mathbf{P}_k}(\hat{\mathbf{s}}[t+1|t]))\, \mathbf{V}\, (\mathbf{z}_n^i[t+1] - \psi_{\mathbf{P}_k}(\hat{\mathbf{s}}[t+1|t]))^\top} > \delta, \tag{26}
$$

is fulfilled, being δ a threshold, we can say that there is an occlusion or the data is too corrupted to be taken into account in next steps of the Kalman filter. Hence, a criterium to set the parameter β_k from Eq.20 is defined. For our experiments, we took $\delta = 0.2$.

4   Results

In order to evaluate the performance of the proposed tracking method, two experiments were carried out. We applied the described algorithm to both synthetic and real data to demonstrate the efficiency of our solution and compare it to the performance of the existing approaches to this problem within a SmartRoom framework [9, 17]. The scenario where this algorithm was applied (in both synthetic and real data) was the SmartRoom at UPC provided with 5 fully calibrated wide angle lense cameras with a resolution of 768x576 pixels at 25 fps.

Experiment 1: Synthetic Data

A synthetic path was created simulating the movement of a single person walking inside a SmartRoom. For this scenario two possibilities of the noise factor ξ_k were studied: only Gaussian noise or Gaussian noise and occlusions added in the projected views. For the first case, different Gaussian noise levels were added in the projected views according to the measurement equation Eq.4. For the second case, occlusions were simulated by adding high amplitude noise bursts of a duration of 10 frames with $P_{\text{occlusion}} = 0.3$. For these input data, PKF and the standard KF [17, 9] algorithms were applied to test and compare the performance of our joint estimation-tracking scheme. Fig.3(a) and 3(b) depict the error curves for different levels of noise in the two situations. Fig.3(c) shows the zenital view of the grountruth and PKF and KF estimated paths. Finally, Table 1 shows some quantitative results comparing PKF and KF performances.

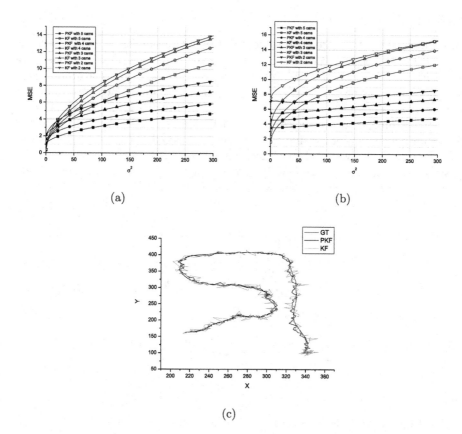

Fig. 3. Results on synthetic data. In (a), the error curves for the PKF and KF for diverse levels of Gaussian noise. In (b), the error curves for the PKF and KF operating in the same noise conditions with a $P_{\text{occlusion}} = 0.3$ and an occlusion length of 10 samples. In (c), the groundtruth trajectory of the location of interest and the results of PKF and KF (zenital view).

Table 1. Mean and standard deviation of the error for tracks with different levels of Gaussian noise for PKF and KF with 5 cameras and no occlusions (Values in mm)

Gaussian Noise σ^2	PKF μ	σ	KF μ	σ
50	7.93	3.90	9.48	4.38
100	10.31	5.09	13.13	6.17
150	11.90	5.90	15.87	7.54
200	13.11	6.55	18.15	8.68
250	14.01	7.10	20.12	9.66
300	14.90	7.58	21.83	10.54

Experiment 2: Real Data

In order to test our system, a sequence of 400 frames with two people spontaneously interacting with each other was recorded. Foreground regions were segmented and the top of each region in every view was taken as the input data in order to track the 3D head of each person. By applying PKF, we obtained the tracking results depicted in Fig.4 but, when applying KF, occlusions made the tracker unable to keep a coherent track along time. In the case were the foreground regions representing the two people merged in one view, the redundancy in the other views allowed keeping coherent tracks but accuracy of the position estimation decreased. Video results for this sequence can be obtained at http://gps-tsc.upc.es/imatge/_Ccanton/pkf.zip.

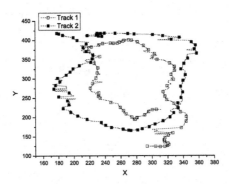

Fig. 4. Results on real data. Zenital plot showing simultaneous tracking of two people.

5   Conclusions and Future Work

A new approach towards tracking 3D locations from its projections on multiple calibrated cameras has been presented. The proposed scheme performs a joint estimation and tracking by taking advantage of the projective nature of the observations, defining the Projective Kalman Filter. Results on synthetic and real data proved this scheme to produce more reliable results in comparison with the standard Kalman approaches to this problem. The accuracy of PKF was good, even though the error in the experiments with real data were conditioned by calibration, foreground segmentation and camera positions.

Future research perspectives involve the development of schemes more robust to occlusions, input data inconsistencies and position of the cameras. Applications of this technique to body analysis and person tracking are under research as well.

References

1. Arulampalam, M.S., Maskell, S., Gordon, N., Clapp, T.: A tutorial on particle filters for online nonlinear/non-Gaussian Bayesian tracking. IEEE Trans. on Signal Proc. **50-2** (2002), 174–188.
2. Bar-Shalom, J., Fortmann, T.E.: Tracking and Data Association. Academic Press. 1988.
3. Black, J., Ellis, T.: Multi Camera Image Tracking. Proc. Work. on Motion and Video Computing (2001).
4. Canton-Ferrer, C., Casas, J.R., Pardàs, M.: Towards a Bayesian Approach to Robust Finding Correspondences in Multiple View Geometry Environments. LNCS, **3515:2** (2005), 281–289.
5. Chang, T.H., Gong, S.: Tracking Multiple People with a Multi-Camera System. Proc. IEEE Work. on Multi-Object Tracking (2001).
6. Darrell, T., Gordon, G., Harville, M.: Integrated person tracking using stereo, color and pattern detection. Int. J. of Computer Vision, **37-2** (2000), 175–185.
7. Dockstader, S.L., Tekalp, A.M.: Multiple camera tracking of interacting and occluded human motion. Proc. of IEEE **89-10** (2001), 1441–1455.
8. Dockstader, S.L., Berg, M.J., Tekalp, A.M.: Stochastic Kinematic Modeling and Feature Extraction for Gait Analysis. IEEE Trans. on Imag. Proc. **12-8** (2003), 962–976.
9. Focken, D., Stiefelhagen, R.: Towards vision-based 3D people tracking in a smart room. Proc. IEEE Int. Conf. on Multimodal Interfaces (2002), 400–405.
10. Garcia, O.: Mapping 2D images and 3D world objects in a multicamera system. Ms. Thesis. Technical University of Catalonia. 2004.
11. Haritaoglu, I., Harwood, D., David, L.: W^4: Who?When?Where?What?A real time system for detecting and tracking people. LNCS, **1406** (1998), 877–892.
12. Hartley, R.I., Zisserman, A.: Multiple View Geometry in Computer Vision. 2nd Edition. Cambridge University Press. 2004.
13. Julier, S.J., Uhlmann, J.K.: A New Extension of the Kalman Filter to Nonliner Systems. Proc. of AeroSense: The 11th Int.Symp. on Aerospace/Defence Sensing, Simulation and Controls (1997).
14. Jung, S.K., Wohn, K.Y.: 3D Tracking and Motion Estimation using Hierarchical Kalman Filter. Proc. IEE Visual Image Signal Process. **144-5** (1997)
15. Kalman, R.E.: A New Approach to Linear Filtering and Prediction Problems. Trans. of the ASME–J. of Basic Engineering, **82-D** (1960), 35–45.
16. Lewis, F.L.: Optimal Estimation. John Wiley and Sons, New York. 1986.
17. Mikic, I., Santini, S., Jain, R.: Tracking Objects in 3D using Multiple Camera Views. Proc. Asian Conf. on Computer Vision (2000), 234–239.

Least Squares Filtering of Speech Signals for Robust ASR

Vivek Tyagi[1,2] and Christian Wellekens[1,2]

[1] Institute Eurecom, Sophia-Antipolis, France
[2] Swiss Federal Institute of Technology (EPFL), Lausanne, Switzerland
`vivek.tyagi@eurecom.fr, christian.welleken@eurecom.fr`

Abstract. The behavior of the least squares filter (LeSF) is analyzed for a class of non-stationary signals that are composed of multiple sinusoids whose frequencies, phases and the amplitudes may vary from block to block and which are embedded in white noise. Analytic expressions for the weights and the output of the LeSF are derived as a function of the block length and the signal SNR computed over the corresponding block. Recognizing that such a sinusoidal model is a valid approximation to the speech signals, we have used LeSF filter estimated on each block to enhance the speech signals embedded in white noise. Automatic speech recognition (ASR) experiments on a connected numbers task, OGI Numbers95[20] show that the proposed LeSF based features yield an increase in speech recognition performance in various non-stationary noise conditions when compared directly to the un-enhanced speech and noise robust JRASTA-PLP features.

1 Introduction

Speech enhancement, amongst other signal de-noising techniques, has been a topic of great interest for past several decades. The importance of such techniques in speech coding and automatic speech recognition systems can only be understated. Towards this end, adaptive filtering techniques have been shown to be quite effective in various signal de-noising applications. Some representative examples are echo cancellation[9], data equalization [10-12], narrow-band signal enhancement[8,13], beamforming[14,15], spectral estimation[3], radar clutter rejection, system identification[16] and speech processing[8].

Most of the above mentioned representative examples require an explicit external noise reference to remove additive noise from the desired signal as discussed in [8]. In situations where an external noise reference for the additive noise is not available, the interfering noise may be suppressed using a Wiener linear prediction filter (for stationary input signal and stationary noise) if there is a significant difference in the bandwidth of the signal and the additive noise [8,3,2]. One of the earliest use of the least mean square filtering for speech enhancement is due to Sambur[5]. In his work, the step size of the LMS filter was chosen to be one percent of the reciprocal of the largest eigenvalue of the correlation matrix of the first voiced frame. However, speech being a non-stationary

S. Renals and S. Bengio (Eds.): MLMI 2005, LNCS 3869, pp. 262–273, 2006.

signal, the estimation of the step size based on the correlation matrix of just single frame of the speech signal, may lead to divergence of the LMS filter output. Nevertheless, the exposition in [5] helped to illustrate the efficacy of the LMS algorithm for enhancing naturally occurring signals such as speech. In [3], Zeidler et. al. have analyzed the steady state behavior of the adaptive line enhancer (ALE), an implementation of least mean square algorithm that has applications in detecting and tracking stationary sinusoidal signals in white noise.

In [2], Anderson et al extended the above mentioned analysis for a stationary input consisting of finite band-width signals in white noise. These signals consist of white Gaussian noise (WGN) passed through a filter whose band-width α is quite small relative to the Nyquist frequency, but generally comparable to the bin width $1/L$. They have derived analytic expressions for the weights and the output of the LMS adaptive filter as function of input signal band-width and SNR, as well as the LMS filter length and bulk delay 'z^{-P}' (please refer to Fig. 1).

In this paper, we extend the previous work in [2,3] for enhancing a class of non-stationary signals that are composed of multiple sinusoids whose frequencies and the amplitudes may vary from block to block and which are embedded in white noise. The key difference in the approach proposed in this paper is that we relax the assumption of the input signal being stationary. Therefore the input signal is blocked into frames and we analyze a L-weight least squares filter (LeSF), estimated on each frame which consists of N samples of the input signal.

We have derived the analytical expressions for the impulse response of the L-weight least squares filter (LesF) as a function of the input SNR (computed over the current frame), effective band-width of the signal (due to finite frame length), filter length 'L' and frame length 'N'. Recognizing that such a time-varying sinusoidal model[7] is a reasonable approximation to the speech waveforms, we have applied the block estimated LeSF filter for de-noising speech signals embedded in broad-band noise. Sinusoidal model is particularly suitable for voiced speech which consists of sinusoids with frequencies at the multiple of the fundamental frequency (pitch). The ASR experiments were performed on the OGI Numbers95[19] database which consists of free-format connected numbers. The clean utterances were corrupted by realistic additive noise from the Noisex[20] database. The usual Mel-frequency cepstral coefficient (MFCC) [17] features are derived from the LeSF enhanced speech signal for automatic speech recognition (ASR) application. The experimental results indicate a significant improvement in the ASR performance.

2   Least Squares Filter (LeSF) for Signal Enhancement

The basic operation of the LeSF is illustrated in figure (1) and it can be understood intuitively as follows. The autocorrelation sequence of the additive noise $u(n)$ that is broad-band decays much faster for higher lags than that of the speech signal. Therefore the use of a large filter length ('L') and the bulk delay P causes de-correlation between the noise components of the input signal, namely $(u(n-L-P+1), u(n-L-P+2), ..., u(n-P))$ and the noise component

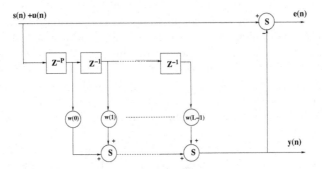

Fig. 1. The basic operation of the LeSF. The input to the filter is noisy speech, $(x(n) = s(n) + u(n))$, delayed by bulk delay $=P$. The filter weights w_k are estimated using the least squares algorithm based on the samples in the current frame. The output of the filter $y(n)$ is the enhanced signal.

of the reference signal, namely $(u(n))$. The LeSF filter responds by adaptively forming a frequency response which has pass-bands centered at the frequencies of the formants of the speech signal while rejecting as much of broad-band noise (whose spectrum lies away from the formant positions). Denoting the clean and the additive noise signals by $s(n)$ and $u(n)$ respectively, we obtain the noisy signal $x(n)$.

$$x(n) = s(n) + u(n) \tag{1}$$

The LeSF filter consists of L weights and the filter coefficients w_k for k $\in$ $[0, 1, 2..L-1]$ are estimated by minimizing the energy of the error signal $e(n)$ over the current frame, $n \in [0, N-1]$.

$$e(n) = x(n) - y(n) \tag{2}$$

$$\text{where } y(n) = \sum_{i=0}^{L-1} w(i)x(n-P-i) \tag{3}$$

Let $\mathbf{A}$ denote the $(N+L) \times L$ data matrix[6] of the input frame $\mathbf{x} = [x(0), x(1), ...x(N-1)]$ and $\mathbf{d}$ denote the $(N+L) \times 1$ desired signal vector which in this case is just a delayed version of signal $\mathbf{x}$. The LeSF weight vector $\mathbf{w}$ is then given by

$$\mathbf{w} = \left(\mathbf{A}^H \mathbf{A}\right)^{-1} \mathbf{A}^H \mathbf{d} \tag{4}$$

As is well known, $\mathbf{A}^H \mathbf{A}$ is a symmetric $L \times L$ Toeplitz matrix whose (i,j) element is the temporal autocorrelation of the signal vector $\mathbf{x}$ estimated over the frame length [6].

$$\left[\mathbf{A}^H \mathbf{A}\right]_{i,j} = r(|i-j|) \tag{5}$$

$$= \sum_{n=0}^{N-|i-j|} x(n)x(n+|i-j|) \tag{6}$$

In practice, $\mathbf{A}^H \mathbf{A}$ can always be assumed to be non-singular due to presence of additive noise[6] for filter length $L < N$. The weight vector $\mathbf{w}$ in (4) can be obtained using Levinson Durbin algorithm[6] without incurring a significant computational cost.

3   LeSF Applied to Sinusoidal Model of Speech

As proposed in [7], speech signals can be modeled as a sum of multiple sinusoids whose amplitudes, phases and frequencies can vary from frame to frame. Let us assume that a given frame of speech signal $\mathbf{s(n)}$ can be approximated as a sum of M sinusoids. Then the noisy signal $x(n)$ can be expressed as

$$x(n) = \sum_{i=1}^{M} A_i \cos(\omega_i n + \phi_i) + u(n) \tag{7}$$

where $n \in [0, N-1]$ and $u(n)$ is a realization of white noise. Then the kth lag autocorrelation can be shown to be,

$$\begin{aligned} r(k) &= \sum_{n=0}^{N-k-1} x(n)x(n+k) \\ &\simeq \sum_{i=1}^{M}(N-k)A_i^2 \cos(2\pi f_i k) + N\sigma^2 \delta(k) \end{aligned} \tag{8}$$

where it is assumed that $N \gg 1/(f_i - f_j)$ for all frequency pairs (i,j) and the noise $u(n)$ is white, ergodic and uncorrelated with the signal s(n). The LeSF weight vector $w(k)$ is then obtained as the solution of the Normal equations,

$$\begin{aligned} \sum_{k=0}^{L-1} r(l-k)w(k) &= r(l+P) \\ l &\in [0,1,2..L-1] \end{aligned} \tag{9}$$

The set of L linear equations described in (9) can be solved by elementary methods if the z-transform $(S_{xx}(z))$ of the symmetric autocorrelation sequence $(r(k))$ is a rational function of 'z' [1].

$$S_{xx}(z) = \sum_{k=-\infty}^{\infty} r(k)z^{-k} \tag{10}$$

Consider then, a real symmetric rational z transform with M pairs of zeros and M pairs of poles.

$$S_{xx}(z) = G \frac{\prod_{m=1}^{M}(z - e^{-\beta_m + j\Psi_m})(z^{-1} - e^{-\beta_m - j\Psi_m})}{\prod_{m=1}^{M}(z - e^{-\alpha_m + j\omega_m})(z^{-1} - e^{-\alpha_m - j\omega_m})} \tag{11}$$

If the signal $\mathbf{x}$ is real, then so is its autocorrelation sequence, $r(k)$. In this case the power spectrum, $S_{xx}(z)$, has quadruplet sets of poles and zeros because of the presence of conjugate pairs at $z = exp(\pm\alpha_m \pm \omega_m)$ and $z = exp(\pm\beta_m \pm \Psi_m)$.

Anderson et. al.[2] have derived the general form of the solution to (9) for input signal with rational power spectra such as that described by (11). In this case, the LeSF weights are given by,

$$w(k) = \sum_{m=1}^{M} \left(B_m e^{-\beta_m k + j\Psi_m k} + C_m e^{+\beta_m k + j\Psi_m k} \right)$$

$$(12)$$

As can be seen, LeSF consists of an exponentially decaying term and an exponentially growing term attributed to reflection [8], that occurs due to finite filter length L. The value of the coefficients B_m and C_m can be determined by solving the set of coupled equations obtained by substituting the expression for $w(k)$ given in (12) into (9).

To be able to use the general form of the solution of the LeSF filter as in (12), we need a pole-zero model of the input autocorrelation in the form as described in (11). For sufficiently large frame length N, such that filter length $L \ll N$, we can make the following approximation.

$$(N - k) \simeq N e^{-k/N} \qquad (13)$$

$$k \in [0, 1, 2, \ldots, L] \text{ and } L \ll N$$

Using this approximation in (8), we get,

$$r(k) = N e^{-k/N} \sum_{i=1}^{M} A_i^2 \cos(\omega_i k) + N\sigma^2 \delta(k) \qquad (14)$$

In this form, $r(k)$ corresponds to a sum of multiple decaying exponential sequences and its z transform takes up the form,

$$S_{xx}(z) = \sum_{m=1}^{M} \frac{N A_i^2 (1 - e^{-2\alpha})}{2} \times$$

$$\left(\frac{1}{(z - e^{-\alpha_m + j\omega_m})(z^{-1} - e^{-\alpha_m - j\omega_m})} \right.$$

$$\left. + \frac{1}{(z - e^{-\alpha_m - j\omega_m})(z^{-1} - e^{-\alpha_m + j\omega_m})} \right) + N\sigma^2$$

$$\text{where } \alpha_m = 1/N \ \forall \, m \in [1.M]$$

$$(15)$$

Under the approximation that the decaying exponentials are widely spaced along the unit circle, the power spectrum $S_{xx}(z)$ in (15) that consists of sum of certain terms can be approximated by a ratio of the product of terms (of the form $(z - e^{\rho + j\theta})$), leading to a rational 'z' transform. Specifically, as explained in [1,2] and making the following assumptions,

- The pole pairs in (15) lie sufficiently close to the unit circle (easily satisfied as $\alpha \simeq 0$.)
- All the frequency pairs (ω_i, ω_j) in (15) are sufficiently separated from each other such that their contribution to the total power spectrum do not overlap significantly.

the z transform of the total input can be expressed as,

$$S_{xx}(z) = \sigma^2 \frac{\prod_{m=1}^{M}(z - e^{-\beta_m + j\omega_m})(z - e^{+\beta_m + j\omega_m})}{\prod_{m=1}^{M}(z - e^{-\alpha_m + j\omega_m})(z - e^{+\alpha_m + j\omega_m})}$$
$$\times \frac{(z - e^{+\beta_m - j\omega_m})(z - e^{-\beta_m - j\omega_m})}{(z - e^{+\alpha_m - j\omega_m})(z - e^{-\alpha_m - j\omega_m})} \tag{16}$$

where $\alpha_m = 1/N$

Corresponding to each of the sinusoidal component in the input signal there are four poles at locations $z = e^{\pm \alpha} \pm \omega_m$ and there are four zeros on the same radial lines as the signal poles but at different distances away from the unit circle. Using the general solution described in (12), which has been derived at length in [2], the solution of the LeSF weight vector to the present problem is,

$$w(n) = \sum_{m=1}^{M} \left(B_m e^{-\beta_m n} + C_m e^{+\beta_m n} \right) \cos \omega_m (n + P) \tag{17}$$

The values of β_m, B_m and C_m can be determined by substituting (17) and (14) in (9). The lth equation in the linear-system described in (9) has terms with coefficients $exp(-\beta_m l)$, $exp(+\beta_m l)$, $exp(-\alpha l) \cos(\omega_m (l+P))$ and $exp(\alpha l) \cos(\omega_m (l+P))$. Besides these, there are two other kind of terms that can be neglected.

- "Non-stationary" terms that are modulated by a sinusoid at frequency $2\omega_m$ where $m \in [1, M]$. For $\omega_m \neq 0$, $\omega_m \neq \pi$, their total contribution is approximately zero.[1]
- Interference terms that are modulated by a sinusoid at frequency $\Delta\omega = (\omega_i - \omega_j)$ where $(i, j) \in [1, \ldots, M]$. If filter length $L \gg 2\pi/\Delta\omega$, these interference terms approximately sum up to zero and hence can be neglected.

The coefficients of the terms $exp(-\beta_m l)$, $exp(+\beta_m l)$ are the same for each of the L equations and setting them to zero leads to just one equation which relates β_m to α and the SNR. Let ρ_i denote the "partial" SNR of the sinusoid at frequency ω_i i.e $\rho_i = A_i^2/\sigma^2$ and the complementary signal SNR be denoted as $\gamma_i = (\sum_{m=1, m\neq i}^{M} A_i^2)/\sigma^2$. Then we have the following relation,

$$\cosh \beta_i = \cosh \alpha + \frac{\rho_i}{2\gamma_i + \rho_i + 2} \sinh \alpha \tag{18}$$

There are two interesting cases. First case is when the sinusoid at frequency ω_i is significantly stronger than other sinusoids such that γ_i is quite low. This is

---

[1] Due to self cancelling positive and negative half periods of a sinusoid.

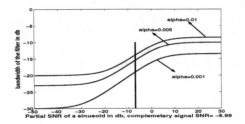

Fig. 2. Plot of the filter bandwidth β_i centered around frequency ω_i as a function of partial sinusoid SNR ρ_i for a given complementary signal SNR $\gamma_i = -6.99db$ and "effective" input bandwidth $\alpha(alpha) = 0.01, 0.005, 0.001$ respectively. The vertical line meets the three curves when $\rho_i = \gamma_i$.

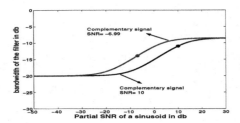

Fig. 3. Plot of the filter bandwidth β_i centered around frequency ω_i as a function of partial sinusoid SNR ρ_i for given complementary signal SNRs $\gamma_i = -6.99db, 10db$ respectively. The "effective" input bandwidth $\alpha(alpha) = 0.01$ for both the curves. The two dots correspond to the cases when the partial SNR ρ_i is equal to complementary signal SNR γ_i.

illustrated in figure (2), where we plot the bandwidth β_i of the LeSF's pass-band that is centered around ω_i as a function of the partial SNR of the ith sinusoid, ρ_i. The complementary signal's SNR is quite low at $\gamma_i = -6.99db$. We plot curves for different "effective" input sinusoid's bandwidth α. From (15), we note that α is reciprocal of frame length N. The vertical line in figure (2) corresponds to the case when $\rho_i = \gamma_i$. We note that for a given partial SNR ρ_i, the LeSF bandwidth becomes narrower as the frame length N increases, indicating a better selectivity of the LeSF filter.

In figure (3), we plot the bandwidth β_i as a function of ρ_i for the cases when complementary signal SNR is high at $\gamma_i = 10db$ and is low at $\gamma_i = -6.99db$. The two dots correspond to the case when $\rho_i = \gamma_i$. We note that $\gamma_i = 10db$ corresponds to a signal with high overall SNR[2]. Therefore the cross-over point $(\gamma_i = \rho_i)$ for low γ_i occurs at narrower bandwidth as compared to high γ_i case. This is so because in the former case the overall signal SNR is low and thus the LeSF filter has to have narrower pass-bands to reject as much of noise as possible.

---

[2] As overall SNR of the signal $= 10 \log_{10}(10^{10\gamma_i} + 10^{10\rho_i})$.

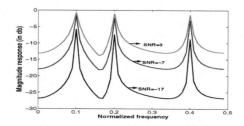

Fig. 4. Plot of the magnitude response of the LeSF filter as a function of the input SNR. The input consists of three sinusoids at normalized frequencies (0.1, 0.2, 0.4) with relative strength (1 : 0.6 : 0.4) respectively.

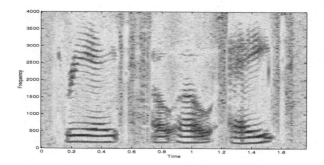

Fig. 5. Clean spectrogram of an utterance from the OGI Numbers95 database

B_i and C_i in (17) are determined by equating their respective coefficients. The "non-stationary" interference terms between all of the pairs of the frequency (ω_i, ω_j), can be neglected if $(\omega_i - \omega_j) >> 2\pi/L$. This requires that LeSF's frequency resolution $(2\pi/L)$ should be able to resolve the constituent sinusoids.

$$B_i = \frac{2e^{-\beta_i}e^{-\alpha P}(\alpha + \beta_i)^2(\beta_i - \alpha)}{((\alpha + \beta_i)^2 - e^{-2\beta_i L}(\beta_i - \alpha)^2)}$$

$$C_i = \frac{2e^{-\beta_i(2L+1)+1}e^{-\alpha P}(\alpha + \beta_i)(\beta_i - \alpha)^2}{((\alpha + \beta_i)^2 - e^{-2\beta_i L}(\beta_i - \alpha)^2)} \tag{19}$$

We note from (18) that the various sinusoids are coupled with each other through the dependence of their bandwidth β_i on the complementary signal SNR γ_i. As a consequence of that B_i, C_i are also indirectly dependent on the powers of the other sinusoids through β_i.

In Fig.4, the magnitude response of the LeSF filter is plotted for various SNR. The input in this case consist of three sinusoids at normalized frequencies (0.1, 0.2, 0.4). The frame length is $N = 500$ and filter length is $(L = 100)$. As the signal SNR decreases, the bandwidth of the LeSF filter starts to decrease in order to reject as much of noise as possible. The LESF filter's gain decreases with decreasing SNR. Similar results were reported in [2,3] for the case of stationary inputs.

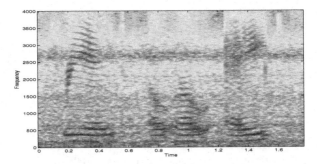

Fig. 6. Spectrogram of the utterance corrupted by F16-cockpit noise at 6dB SNR

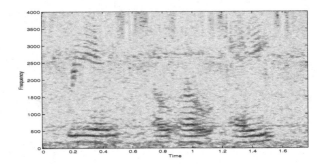

Fig. 7. Spectrogram of the noisy utterance enhanced by a ($L = 100$) tap LeSF filter that has been estimated over blocks of length ($N = 500$)

In Fig. 5, we plot the spectrograms of a clean speech utterance. Fig. 6 and Fig. 7 display the same utterance embedded in F16-cockpit noise at SNR 6dB and its LeSF enhanced version respectively. As can be seen from the spectrograms, the LeSF filter has been able to reject significant amount of additive F-16 cockpit noise [20] from the speech signal.

4 Experiments and Results

In order to assess the effectiveness of the proposed algorithm, speech recognition experiments were conducted on the OGI Numbers[19] corpus. This database contains spontaneously spoken free-format connected numbers over a telephone channel. The lexicon consists of 31 words[3]. The train-set and the test-set consist of 3233 and 1206 utterances respectively. Speech signals were blocked into frames of 500 samples (62.5ms) each and a 100 tap LeSF filter was derived using (4) for each frame. Noting that the autocorrelation coefficients of a periodic signal are themselves periodic with the same period (hence they do not decay with the increasing lag), Sambur[5] has used a bulk delay equal to the pitch period

---

[3] With confusable numbers like 'nine', 'ninety', 'nineteen' and so on.

of the voiced speech for its enhancement. However, for the un-voiced speech a high bulk delay will result in a significant distortion by the LeSF filter as its autocorrelation coefficients decay quite rapidly for the higher lags. Therefore, we kept the bulk delay at '$P = 1$' as a good choice for enhancing both the voiced and un-voiced speech frames. However, we note that the LeSF filter is inherently more suitable for enhancing the voiced speech as in this case we can represent the speech frame as a sum of small number of sinusoids as in (7). The relatively high order ($L = 100$) of the LeSF filter is required to be able to have sufficiently high frequency resolution ($2\pi/L$) to resolve the constituent sinusoids. Each speech frame was then filtered through its corresponding LeSF filter to derive an enhanced speech frame. Finally MFCC feature vector was computed from the enhanced speech frame. These enhanced LeSF-MFCC were compared to the baseline MFCC features and noise robust JRASTA-PLP[4] features with the same window size (62.5ms). The MFCC feature vector computation is the same for the baseline and the LeSF-MFCC features. The only difference is that the MFCC baseline features are computed directly from the noisy speech while the LeSF-MFCC features are computed from LeSF enhanced speech signal. Hidden Markov Model and Gaussian Mixture Model (HMM-GMM) based speech recognition systems were trained using public domain software HTK[18] on the clean training set from the original Numbers corpus. The system consisted of 80 tied-state triphone HMM's with 3 emitting states per triphone and 12 mixtures per state.

Table 1. Word error rate results for factory noise. Parameters of the LeSF filter, L=100 and N=500.

SNR	MFCC	PLP-JRASTA	LeSF MFCC
Clean	5.7	7.8	6.8
12 dB	12.3	12.2	11.9
6 dB	27.1	23.8	21.0
0 db	71.0	59.8	42.6

Table 2. Word error rate results for F16-cockpit noise. Parameters of the LeSF filter, L=100 and N=500.

SNR	MFCC	PLP-JRASTA	LeSF MFCC
Clean	5.7	7.8	6.8
12 dB	13.6	14.2	12.4
6 dB	28.4	25.3	20.6
0 db	72.3	59.2	41.2

To verify the robustness of the features to noise, the clean test utterances were corrupted using Factory and F-16 cockpit noise from the Noisex92 [20] database. The speech recognition results for the baseline MFCC, RASTA-PLP and the proposed LeSF-MFCC, in various levels of noise are given in Tables 1 and 2. Cepstral mean subtraction was performed on all the reported features.

The proposed LeSF processed MFCC performs significantly better than others in all noise conditions. The slight performance degradation of the LeSF-MFCC in the clean is due to the fact that the LeSF filter being an all-pole filter does not model the valleys of the clean speech spectrum well. As a result, the LeSF filter sometimes amplifies the low spectral energy regions of the clean spectrum.

5   Conclusion

We consider a class of non-stationary signals as input that are composed of multiple sinusoids whose frequencies and the amplitudes may vary from block to block and which are embedded in the white noise. We have derived the analytical expressions for the impulse response of the L-weight least squares filter (LesF) as a function of the input SNR (computed over the current frame), effective bandwidth of the signal (due to finite frame length), filter length 'L' and frame length 'N'. Recognizing that such a time-varying sinusoidal model[7] is a reasonable approximation to the speech waveforms, we have applied the block estimated LeSF filter for de-noising speech signals embedded in the realistic[20] broadband noise as commonly encountered on a factory floor and an aircraft cockpit. The proposed technique leads to a significant improvement in ASR performance as compared to noise robust JRASTA-PLP[4] and the MFCC features computed from the unprocessed noisy signal.

Acknowledgements

This work has been supported by the EU 6th Framework Programme, under contract number IST-2002-002034 (DIVINES project).

References

1. E. Satorius, J. Zeidler and S. Alexander, " Linear predictive digital filtering of narrowband processes in additive broad-band noise, " Naval Ocean Systems Center, San Diego, CA, Tech. Rep. 331, Nov. 1978.
2. C. M. Anderson, E. H. Satorius and J. R. Zeidler, " Adaptive Enhancement of Finite Bandwidth Signals in White Gaussian Noise, " In IEEE Trans. on ASSP, Vol. ASSP-31, No.1, February 1983.
3. J. R. Zeidler, E. H. Satorius, D. M. Chabries and H. T. Wexler, " Adaptive Enhancement of Multiple Sinusoids in Uncorrelated Noise, " In IEEE Trans. on ASSP, Vol. ASSP-26, No. 3, June 1978.
4. H. Hermansky, N. Morgan, " Rasta Processing of Speech," IEEE Trans. on SAP, vol.2, no.4, October 1994.
5. M. R. Sambur, " Adaptive noise canceling for Speech signals," In IEEE Trans. on ASSP, vol. ASSP-26, No.5, October 1978.
6. S. Haykin, Adaptive Filter Theory, Prentice-Hall Publishers, N.J., USA, 1993.
7. R. J. McAulay and T. F. Quatieri, " Speech Analysis/Synthesis Based on a Sinusoidal Representation, " In IEEE Trans. on ASSP, Vol. ASSP-34, No. 4, August 1986.

8. B Widrow et. al., " Adaptive noise cancelling: Principles and applications, " Proc. IEEE, vol.65, pp 1692-1716, Dec 1975.
9. M. Sondhi and D. Berkley, " Silencing echoes on the telephone network," Proc. of IEEE, vol.68, pp948-963, Aug. 1980.
10. A Gersho, " Adaptive equalization of highly dispersive channels for data transmission, " Bell Syst. Tech. J., vol.48, pp.55-70, Jan. 1969.
11. E. Satorius and S. T. Alexander, " Channel equalization using adaptive lattice algorithms, " IEEE Trans. Commun. vol. 27, pp.899-905, June 1979.
12. E. Satorius and J. Pack, " Application of least squares lattice algorithms for adaptive equalization, " IEEE Trans. on Commun. vol. COM-29, pp.136-142, Feb. 1981.
13. N. Bershad, P. Feintuch, F. Reed and B. Fisher, " Tracking characteristics of the LMS adaptive line-enhancer -Response to a linear chirp signal in noise, " IEEE Trans. on ASSP, vol. ASSP-28, pp504-517, Oct. 1980
14. L. J. Griffiths, " A simple adaptive algorithm for real time processsing in antenna arrays, " Proc. of IEEE, vol. 57, pp.1696-1704, Oct. 1969.
15. O.L. Frost, " An algorithm for linearly constrained adaptive array processing , " Proc. of IEEE, vol. 60, pp.926-935, Aug. 1972.
16. L. Marple, " Efficient least squares FIR system identification, " IEEE Trans. on ASSP, vol.ASSP-29, pp.62-73, Feb. 1981.
17. S. B. Davis and P. Mermelstein, "Comparison of Parametric Representation for Monosyllabic Word Recognition in Continuously Spoken Sentences, " IEEE Trans. on ASSP, Vol. ASSP-28, No. 4, August 1980.
18. S. Young, J. Odell, D. Ollason, V. Valtchev, and P. Woodland, The HTK Book, Cambridge University, 1995.
19. R. A. Cole, M. Fanty, and T. Lander, "Telephone speech corpus at CSLU," Proc. of ICSLP, Yokohama, Japan, 1994.
20. A. Varga, H. Steeneken, M. Tomlinson and D. Jones, " The NOISEX-92 study on the effect of additive noise on automatic speech recognition, " Technical report, DRA Speech Research Unit, Malvern, England, 1992.

A Variable-Scale Piecewise Stationary Spectral Analysis Technique Applied to ASR

Vivek Tyagi[1,3], Christian Wellekens[1,3], and Hervé Bourlard[2,3]

[1] Institute Eurecom, Sophia-Antipolis, France
[2] IDIAP Research Institute, Martigny, Switzerland
[3] Swiss Federal Institute of Technology (EPFL), Lausanne, Switzerland
vivek.tyagi@eurecom.fr, christian.welleken@eurecom.fr,
herve.bourlard@idiap.ch

Abstract. It is often acknowledged that speech signals contain short-term and long-term temporal properties [15] that are difficult to capture and model by using the usual fixed scale (typically 20ms) short time spectral analysis used in hidden Markov models (HMMs), based on piecewise stationarity and state conditional independence assumptions of acoustic vectors. For example, vowels are typically quasi-stationary over 40-80ms segments, while plosives typically require analysis below 20ms segments. Thus, a fixed scale analysis is clearly sub-optimal for "optimal" time-frequency resolution and modeling of different stationary phones found in the speech signal. In the present paper, we investigate the potential advantages of using variable size analysis windows towards improving state-of-the-art speech recognition systems. Based on the usual assumption that the speech signal can be modeled by a time-varying autoregressive (AR) Gaussian process, we estimate the largest piecewise quasi-stationary speech segments, based on the likelihood that a segment was generated by the same AR process. This likelihood is estimated from the Linear Prediction (LP) residual error. Each of these quasi-stationary segments is then used as an analysis window from which spectral features are extracted. Such an approach thus results in a variable scale time spectral analysis, adaptively estimating the largest possible analysis window size such that the signal remains quasi-stationary, thus the best temporal/frequency resolution tradeoff. The speech recognition experiments on the OGI Numbers95 database[19] show that the proposed variable-scale piecewise stationary spectral analysis based features indeed yield improved recognition accuracy in clean conditions, compared to features based on minimum cross entropy spectrum [1] as well as those based on fixed scale spectral analysis.

1 Introduction

Most of the Automatic Speech Recognition (ASR) acoustic features, such as Mel-Frequency Cepstral Coefficient (MFCC)[16] or Perceptual Linear Prediction (PLP)[17], are based on some sort of representation of the smoothed spectral envelope, usually estimated over fixed analysis windows of typically 20ms to

S. Renals and S. Bengio (Eds.): MLMI 2005, LNCS 3869, pp. 274–284, 2006.
© Springer-Verlag Berlin Heidelberg 2006

30ms of the speech signal [16,15]. Such analysis is based on the assumption that the speech signal can be assumed to be quasi-stationary over these segment durations. However, it is well known that the voiced speech sounds such as vowels are quasi-stationary for 40ms-80ms while, stops and plosive are time-limited by less than 20ms [15]. Therefore, it implies that the spectral analysis based on a fixed size window of 20ms-30ms has some limitations, including:

- The frequency resolution obtained for quasi-stationary segments (QSS) longer than 20ms is quite low compared to what could be obtained using larger analysis windows.
- In certain cases, the analysis window can span the transition between two QSSs, thus blurring the spectral properties of the QSSs, as well as of the transitions. Indeed, in theory, Power Spectral Density (PSD) cannot even be defined for such non stationary segments [9]. Furthermore, on a more practical note, the feature vectors extracted from such transition segments do not belong to a single unique (stationary) class and may lead to poor discrimination in a pattern recognition problem.

In this work, we make the usual assumption that the piecewise quasi-stationary segments (QSS) of the speech signal can be modeled by a Gaussian AR process of a fixed order p as in [2,4,10,11]. We then formulate the problem of detecting QSSs as a Maximum Likelihood (ML) detection problem, defining a QSSs as the longest segment that has most probably been generated by the same AR process.[1] As is well known, given a pth order AR Gaussian QSS, the Minimum Mean Square Error (MMSE) linear prediction (LP) filter parameters $[a(1), a(2), ... a(p)]$ are the most "compact" representation of that QSS amongst all the pth order all pole filters [9]. In other words, the normalized "coding error"[2] is minimum amongst all the pth order LP filters. When erroneously analyzing two distinct p^{th} order AR Gaussian QSSs in the same non-stationary analysis window, it can be shown that the "coding error" will then always be greater than the ones resulting of QSSs analyzed individually in stationary windows[14]. This is intuitively satisfying since, in the former case, we are trying to encode '$2p$' free parameters (the LP filter coefficients of each of the QSS) using only p parameters (as the two distinct QSS are now analyzed within the same window). Therefore, higher coding error is expected in the former case as compared to the optimal case when each QSS is analyzed in a stationary window. As further explained in the next sections, this forms the basis of our criteria to detect piecewise quasi-stationary segments. Once the "start" and the "end" points of a QSS are known, all the speech samples coming from this QSS are analyzed within that window, resulting in (variable-scale) acoustic vectors.

Our algorithm is thus reminiscent of the likelihood ratio test based ML segmentation algorithm derived by Brandt [10] and later on used in [11]. In [11], the author has illustrated certain speech waveforms with segmentation boundaries overlaid. The validity of their algorithm is shown by a segmentation experiment,

---

[1] Equivalent to the detection of the transition point between the two adjoining QSSs.
[2] The power of the residual signal normalized by the number of samples in the window.

which on an average, segments phonemes into 2.2 segments. This result is quite useful as a pre-processor for the manual transcription of speech signals. However, the author in [11] did not discuss or extend the ML segmentation algorithm as a variable-scale quasi-stationary spectral analysis technique suitable for ASR, as done in the present work.

Before proceeding further, however, we feel it necessary to briefly discuss certain inconsistencies between variable-scale spectral analysis and state-of-the-art Hidden Markov models ASR using Gaussian mixture models (HMM-GMM). HMM-GMM systems typically use spectral features based on a constant window size (typically $20ms$) and a constant shift size (typically $10ms$). The shift size determines the Nyquist frequency of the cepstral modulation spectrum [7], which is typically measured by the delta features of the static MFCC or PLP features. In a variable-scale piecewise quasi-stationary analysis, the shift size should preferably be equal to the size of the detected QSS. Otherwise, if the shift size is x% of the duration of the QSS, then the next detected QSS will be the same but of duration $(100 - x)\%$ and the following one will be of duration $(100 - 2x)\%$ and so on until we have shifted past the entire duration of the QSS. This results in the undesirable effect that the same QSS gets analyzed by successively smaller windows, hence increasing the variance of the feature vector of this QSS. On the other hand, the use of a shift size equal to the variable window size will change the Nyquist frequency of the cepstral modulation spectrum [7]. Therefore, the modulation frequency pass-band of the delta filters [7] will vary from frame to frame and may suffer from aliasing for shift sizes in excess of $20ms$.

In [3], Atal has described a temporal decomposition technique to represent the continuous variation of the LPC parameters as a linearly weighted sum of a number of discrete elementary components. These elementary components are designed such that they have the minimum temporal spread (highly localized in time) resulting in superior coding efficiency. However, the relationship between the optimization criterion of "the minimum temporal spread" and the quasi-stationarity is not obvious. Therefore, the discrete elementary components are not necessarily quasi-stationary and vice-versa.

Coifman et al [6] have described a minimum entropy basis selection algorithm to achieve the minimum information cost of a signal relative to the designed orthonormal basis. In [8], Srinivasan et al. have proposed a multi-scale QSS speech enhancement technique based on Coifman's technique [6]. In [4], Svendsen et al have proposed a ML segmentation algorithm using a single fixed window size for speech analysis, followed by a clustering of the frames which were spectrally similar for sub-word unit design. We emphasize here that this is different from the approach proposed here where we use variable size windows to achieve the objective of piecewise quasi-stationary spectral analysis. More recently, Achan et al [13] have proposed a segmental HMM for speech waveforms which identifies waveform samples at the boundaries between glottal pulse periods with applications in pitch estimation and time-scale modifications.

Our emphasis in this paper is on better spectral modeling of the speech signal rather than achieving better coding efficiency or reduced information cost.

Nevertheless, we believe that these two objectives are somewhat fundamentally related. The main contribution of the present paper is to demonstrate that the variable-scale QSS spectral analysis technique can possibly improve the ASR performance as compared to the fixed scale spectrum analysis. We identify the above mentioned problems and make certain engineering design choices to overcome these problems. Moreover, we show the relationship between the maximum likelihood QSS detection algorithm and the well known spectral matching property of the LP error measure [5]. Finally, we do a comparative study of the proposed variable-scale spectrum based features and the minimum cross-entropy time-frequency distributions developed by Loughlin et al [1].

In the sequel of this paper, Section 2 formulates the ML detection problem for identifying the transition points between QSS. In Section 3, we illustrate an analogy of the proposed technique with spectral matching property of the LP error measure. Finally, the experimental setup and results are described in Section 4.

2   ML Detection of the Change-Point in an AR Gaussian Random Process

Consider an instance of a pth order AR Gaussian process, $\mathbf{x[n]}, n \in [1, N]$ whose generative LP filter parameters can either be $\mathbf{A}_0 = [1, a_0(1), a_0(2)....a_0(p)]$ or can change from $\mathbf{A}_1 = [1, a_1(1), a_1(2)....a_1(p)]$ to $\mathbf{A}_2 = [1, a_2(1), a_2(2)....a_2(p)]$ at time n_1 where $n_1 \in [1, N]$. As usual, the excitation signal is assumed to be drawn from a white Gaussian process and its power can change from $\sigma = \sigma_1$ to $\sigma = \sigma_2$. The general form of the Power Spectral Density (PSD) of this signal is then known to be

$$P_{xx}(f) = \frac{\sigma^2}{|1 - \sum_{i=1}^{p} a(i) \exp(-j2\pi i f)|^2} \tag{1}$$

where $a(i)$s are the LPC parameters. The hypothesis test consists of:

- $\mathbf{H}_0$: No change in the PSD of the signal $x(n)$ over all $n \in [1, N]$, LP filter parameters are $\mathbf{A}_0$ and the excitation (residual) signal power is σ_0.
- $\mathbf{H}_1$: Change in the PSD of the signal $x(n)$ at n_1, where $n_1 \in [1, N]$, LP filter parameters change from $\mathbf{A}_1$ to $\mathbf{A}_2$ and the excitation(residual) signal power changes from σ_1 to σ_2.

Let, $\hat{\mathbf{A}}_0$ denote the maximum likelihood estimate (MLE) of the LP filter parameters and $\hat{\sigma}_0$ denote the MLE of the residual signal power under the hypothesis $\mathbf{H}_0$. The MLE estimate of the filter parameters is equal to their MMSE estimate due to the Gaussian distribution assumption [2] and, hence, can be computed using the Levinson Durbin algorithm [9] without significant computational cost.

Let $\mathbf{x}_1$ denote $[x(1), x(2), ...x(n_1)]$ and $\mathbf{x}_2$ denote $[x(n_1 + 1), ...x(N)]$. Under hypothesis $\mathbf{H}_1$, $(\hat{\mathbf{A}}_1, \hat{\sigma}_1)$ are the MLE of $(\mathbf{A}_1, \sigma_1)$ estimated on $\mathbf{x}_1$, and $(\hat{\mathbf{A}}_2, \hat{\sigma}_2)$ are the MLE of $(\mathbf{A}_2, \sigma_2)$ estimated on $\mathbf{x}_2$, where $\mathbf{x}_1$ and $\mathbf{x}_2$ have been assumed to be independent of each other. A Generalized Likelihood Ratio Test (GLRT) [14] would then pick hypothesis $\mathbf{H}_1$ if

$$\log L(\mathbf{x}) = \log(\frac{p(\mathbf{x}_1|\hat{\mathbf{A}}_1, \hat{\sigma}_1)p(\mathbf{x}_2|\hat{\mathbf{A}}_2, \hat{\sigma}_2)}{p(\mathbf{x}|\hat{\mathbf{A}}_0, \hat{\sigma}_0)}) > \gamma \tag{2}$$

where γ is a decision threshold that will have to be tuned on some development set. Given that the total number of samples in $\mathbf{x}_1$ and $\mathbf{x}_2$ are the same as in $\mathbf{x}_0$, their likelihoods can be compared directly in (2). Under the hypothesis $\mathbf{H}_0$ the entire segment $\mathbf{x} = [x(1)...x(N)]$ is considered stationary and the MLE $\hat{\mathbf{A}}_0$ is computed via the Levinson-Durbin algorithm using all the samples in segment $\mathbf{x}$. It can be shown that the MLE $\hat{\sigma}_0$ is the power of the residual signal [2,14]. Under $\mathbf{H}_1$, we assume that there are two distinct QSS, namely $\mathbf{x}_1$ and $\mathbf{x}_2$. The MLE $\hat{\mathbf{A}}_1$ and $\hat{\mathbf{A}}_2$ are computed via the Levinson-Durbin algorithm using samples from their corresponding QSS. MLE $\hat{\sigma}_1$ and $\hat{\sigma}_2$ are computed as the power of the corresponding residual signals. In fact, $p(\mathbf{x}|\hat{\mathbf{A}}_0, \hat{\sigma}_0)$ is equal to the probability of residual signal reconstructed using filter parameters $\hat{\mathbf{A}}_0$, yielding:

$$p(\mathbf{x}|\hat{\mathbf{A}}_0, \hat{\sigma}_0) = \frac{1}{(2\pi\hat{\sigma}_0^2)^{N/2}} \exp\left[\frac{-1}{2\hat{\sigma}_0^2} \sum_{n=1}^{N}(e_0^2(n))\right] \tag{3}$$

where $e_0(n)$ is the residual error and

$$e_0(n) = x(n) - \sum_{i=1}^{p} a_0(i)x(n-i), \ \ n \in [1, N]$$

and

$$\hat{\sigma}_0^2 = \frac{1}{N} \sum_{n=1}^{N} e_0^2(n)$$

Similarly, $p(\mathbf{x}_1|\hat{\mathbf{A}}_1, \hat{\sigma}_1)$ and $p(\mathbf{x}_2|\hat{\mathbf{A}}_2, \hat{\sigma}_2)$ are the likelihoods of the residual signal vectors of the AR models $\mathbf{A}_1$ and $\mathbf{A}_2$, respectively, and have the same functional forms as above. Substituting these expressions into (2) yields

$$\log L(\mathbf{x}) = \frac{1}{2} \log\left[\frac{\hat{\sigma}_0^N}{\hat{\sigma}_1^{n_1}\hat{\sigma}_2^{(N-n_1)}}\right] \tag{4}$$

In the present form, the GLRT $\log L(\mathbf{x})$ has now a natural interpretation. Indeed, if there is a transition point in the segment $\mathbf{x}$ then it has, in effect, $2p$ degrees of freedom. Under hypothesis $\mathbf{H}_0$, we encode $\mathbf{x}$ using only p degrees of freedom (LP parameters $\hat{\mathbf{A}}_0$) and, therefore, the coding (residual) error $\hat{\sigma}_0^2$ will be high. However, under hypothesis $\mathbf{H}_1$, we use $2p$ degrees of freedom (LP parameters $\hat{\mathbf{A}}_1$ and $\hat{\mathbf{A}}_2$) to encode $\mathbf{x}$. Therefore, the coding (residual) errors $\hat{\sigma}_1^2$ and $\hat{\sigma}_2^2$ can be minimized to reach the lowest possible value.[3] This will result in

---

[3] When $\hat{\mathbf{A}}^1$ and $\hat{\mathbf{A}}^2$ are estimated, strictly based on the samples from the corresponding quasi-stationary segments.

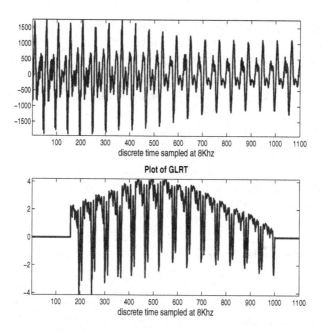

Fig. 1. Typical plot of the Generalized log likelihood ratio test (GLRT) for a speech segment. The sharp downward spikes in the GLRT are due to the presence of a glottal pulse at the beginning of the right analysis window ($\mathbf{x}_2$). The GLRT peaks around the sample 500 which marks as a strong AR model switching point.

$L(\mathbf{x}) > 1$. On the other hand, if there is no AR switching point in the segment $\mathbf{x}$ then it can be shown that, for large n_1 and N, the coding errors are all equal ($\hat{\sigma}_0^2 = \hat{\sigma}_1^2 = \hat{\sigma}_2^2$). This will result in $L(\mathbf{x}) \simeq 1$.

An example is illustrated in Figure 1. The top pane shows a segment of a voiced speech signal. In the bottom figure, we plot the GLRT as the function of the hypothesized change over point n. Whenever, the right window i.e the segment $\mathbf{x}_2$ spans the glottal pulse in the beginning of the window, the GLRT exhibits strong downward spikes which is due to the fact that the LP filter cannot predict large samples in the beginning of the window. However, these downward spikes do not influence our decision significantly as we are interested in large positive value of the GLRT to detect a model change over point. The minimum sizes of the left and the right windows are 160 and 100 samples respectively. This explains the zero value of the GLRT at the beginning and the end of the whole test segment. The GLRT peaks around sample 500 which marks a strong AR model switching point.

3 Relation of GLRT to Spectral Matching

As is well known the LP error measure possesses the spectral matching property [5]. Specifically, given a speech segment $\mathbf{x}$, let its power spectrum (periodogram) be denoted by $\mathbf{X}(e^{j\omega})$. Let the all pole model spectrum of the segment $\mathbf{x}$ be denoted as $\hat{\mathbf{X}}_0(e^{j\omega})$. Then it can be shown that the MMSE error σ_0^2 of the LP filter estimated over the entire segment $\mathbf{x}$ is given by [5]

$$\sigma_0^2 = \int_{-\pi}^{\pi} \frac{\mathbf{X}(e^{j\omega})}{\hat{\mathbf{X}}_0(e^{j\omega})} d\omega \text{ where,} \tag{5}$$

$$\hat{\mathbf{X}}_0(e^{j\omega}) = \frac{1}{|1 - \sum_{i=1}^{p} a_0(i) \exp(-j2\pi i f)|^2} \tag{6}$$

Therefore minimizing the residual error σ_0^2 is equivalent to the minimization of the integrated ratio of the signal power spectrum $\mathbf{X}(e^{j\omega})$ to its approximation $\hat{\mathbf{X}}_0(e^{j\omega})$ [5]. Substituting (5) in (4) we obtain,

$$\log L(\mathbf{x}) = \frac{1}{2} \log \frac{\left(\int_{-\pi}^{\pi} \frac{\mathbf{X}(e^{j\omega})}{\hat{\mathbf{X}}_0(e^{j\omega})} d\omega\right)^N}{\left(\int_{-\pi}^{\pi} \frac{\mathbf{X}_1(e^{j\omega})}{\hat{\mathbf{X}}_1(e^{j\omega})} d\omega\right)^{n_1} \left(\int_{-\pi}^{\pi} \frac{\mathbf{X}_2(e^{j\omega})}{\hat{\mathbf{X}}_2(e^{j\omega})} d\omega\right)^{N-n_1}} \tag{7}$$

where, $\mathbf{X}(e^{j\omega})$, $\mathbf{X}_1(e^{j\omega})$ and $\mathbf{X}_2(e^{j\omega})$ are the power spectra of the segments $\mathbf{x}$, $\mathbf{x}_1$ and $\mathbf{x}_2$ respectively. Similarly $\hat{\mathbf{X}}_0(e^{j\omega})$, $\hat{\mathbf{X}}_1(e^{j\omega})$ and $\hat{\mathbf{X}}_2(e^{j\omega})$ are the MMSE p^{th} order all-pole model spectra estimated over the segments $\mathbf{x}$, $\mathbf{x}_1$ and $\mathbf{x}_2$ respectively. Therefore, $\hat{\mathbf{X}}_0(e^{j\omega})$, $\hat{\mathbf{X}}_1(e^{j\omega})$ and $\hat{\mathbf{X}}_2(e^{j\omega})$ are the best spectral matches to their corresponding power spectra. One way of interpreting (7) is that it is a measure of the relative goodness between the best spectral match achieved by modeling $\mathbf{x}$ as a single QSS and the best spectral matches obtained by assuming $\mathbf{x}$ to consist of two distinct QSS, namely $\mathbf{x}_1$ and $\mathbf{x}_2$. This is further explained as follows. If $\mathbf{x}_1$ and $\mathbf{x}_2$ are indeed two distinct QSS, then $\mathbf{X}_1(e^{j\omega})$ and $\mathbf{X}_2(e^{j\omega})$ will be quite different and $\mathbf{X}(e^{j\omega})$ will be a gross average of these two spectra. In other words, the frequency support of $\mathbf{X}(e^{j\omega})$ will be a union of those of the $\mathbf{X}_1(e^{j\omega})$ and $\mathbf{X}_2(e^{j\omega})$. $\hat{\mathbf{X}}_1(e^{j\omega})$ and $\hat{\mathbf{X}}_2(e^{j\omega})$, having p poles each, will match

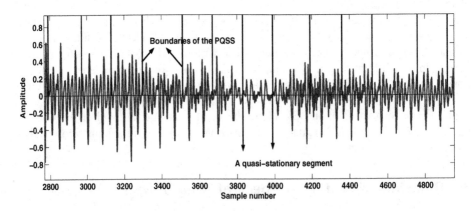

Fig. 2. Quasi stationary segments (QSS) of a speech signal as detected by the algorithm with $\gamma = 3.5$ and LP order $p = 14$

their corresponding power spectra reasonably well, resulting in a lower value of the denominator in (7). However, $\hat{\mathbf{X}}_0(e^{j\omega})$ will be a relatively poorer spectral match to $\mathbf{X}(e^{j\omega})$ as it has only p poles to account for the wider frequency support. Therefore we incur a higher spectral mismatch by assuming $\mathbf{x}$ to be a single QSS when in fact it is composed of two distinct QSS $\mathbf{x}_1$ and $\mathbf{x}_2$. This results in the GLRT $\log L(\mathbf{x})$ taking up a high value. Whereas if $\mathbf{x}_1$ and $\mathbf{x}_2$ are the instances of the same quasi-stationary process, then so is $\mathbf{x}$. Therefore $\mathbf{X}_1(e^{j\omega})$, $\mathbf{X}_2(e^{j\omega})$ and $\mathbf{X}(e^{j\omega})$ are nearly the same with similar all-pole models, resulting in a value of the GLRT close to zero. The above discussion points out the fact that the QSS analysis based on the proposed GLRT is constantly striving to achieve a better time varying spectral modeling of the underlying signal as compared to single fixed scale spectral analysis.

4   Experiments and Results

We have used the GLRT $L(\mathbf{x})$ in (4) to perform QSS spectral analysis of speech signals for ASR applications. We initialize the algorithm with a left window size $\mathtt{W\_L} = 20$ms and a right window size $\mathtt{W\_R} = 12.5$ms. We compute their corresponding MMSE residuals and the MMSE residual of the union of the two windows. Then, the GLRT is computed using (4) and is compared to the threshold. The choice of the threshold $\gamma = 3.5$ was obtained by a visual inspection of the quasi-stationarity of the segmented speech signal as returned by the algorithm. In figure (2), we illustrate the boundaries of the QSS as detected by the algorithm with $\gamma = 3.5$. Realizing that the resulting segmentation corresponded to reasonably quasi-stationary segments, we adopted the threshold value $\gamma = 3.5$ for all the experiments reported in this paper. In general, the ASR results are slightly sensitive to the threshold, although not in a huge way. If the GLRT is greater than the threshold γ, $\mathtt{W\_L}$ is considered the largest possible QSS and we obtain a spectral estimate using all the samples in $\mathtt{W\_L}$. Otherwise,$\mathtt{W\_L}$ is incremented by $\mathtt{INCR}=1.25$ms and the whole process is repeated until GLRT exceeds γ or $\mathtt{W\_L}$ becomes equal to the maximum window size $\mathtt{WMAX}=60ms$. The computation of a MFCC feature vector from a very small segment (such as 10ms) is inherently very noisy.[4] Therefore, the minimum duration of a QSS as detected by the algorithm was constrained to be $20ms$. Throughout the experiments, a fixed LP order $p = 14$ was used.

The likelihood ratio test is quite widely used for speaker segmentation [12] where the average length of a single speaker segment may last from 1sec to several seconds. This provides a relatively large amount of samples to estimate the parameters of the probability density functions as compared to the present problem where we have to detect stationarity change over point within 20ms to 60ms. As a result, the GLRT in (4) is quite noisy and a criterion such as local maxima of the GLRT cannot be used. However, when the model change occurs over longer time scales (e.g. speaker change detection where the smallest segment is of the order of a second), Ajmera et al. [12] have successfully used

---

[4]   Due to very few samples involved in the Mel-filter integration.

a local maximmum of the GLRT as a speaker change point detector, thereby, avoiding the use of a threshold.

To avoid fluctuating Nyquist frequency of the cepstral modulation spectrum[7], a fixed shift size of $12.5ms$ was used in the algorithm. As explained in the Section (1), this sometime resulted in the undesirable effect that the same QSS gets analyzed by progressively smaller windows. To alleviate this problem, the zeroth cepstral coefficient $c(0)$, which is a non-linear function of the windowed signal energy and, hence, of the window size, was normalized such that its dependence on the window size is minimized.

In order to assess the effectiveness of the proposed algorithm, speech recognition experiments were conducted on the OGI Numbers corpus [19]. This database contains spontaneously spoken free-format connected numbers over a telephone channel. The lexicon consists of 31 words. Figure (3) illustrates the distribution of the QSSs as detected by the proposed algorithm. Nearly 47% segments were analyzed with the smallest window size of $20ms$ and they mostly corresponded to short-time limited segments. However, voiced segments and long silences were mostly analyzed by using longer windows in the range $30ms - 60ms$. The short peak at 60ms is due to the accumulated value over all the segments that should have been longer than 60ms but were constrained by our choice of the largest window size.

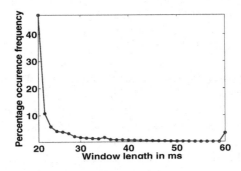

Fig. 3. Distribution of the QSS window sizes detected and then used in the training set

Throughout the experiments, MFCC coefficients and their temporal derivatives were used as speech features. However, five feature sets were compared:

1. [39 dim. MFCC:] computed over a fixed window of length 20ms.
2. [39 dim. MFCC:] computed over a fixed window of length 50ms.
3. [78 dim. Concatenated MFCC:] a concatenation of the above two feature vectors.
4. [Minimum cross entropy,39 dim MFCC:] MFCC computed from the geometric mean of the power spectra computed from 20ms, 30ms, 40ms and 50ms long windows.

5. [Variable-scale QSS MFCC+Deltas:] For a given frame, the window size is dynamically chosen using the proposed algorithm ensuring that the windowed segment is quasi-stationary.

In [1], Loughlin et al proposed using a geometric mean of multiple spectrograms of different window sizes to overcome the time-frequency limitation of any single spectrogram. They showed that combining the information content from multiple spectrograms in form of their geometric mean is optimal for minimizing the cross entropy between the multiple spectra. We have followed their approach to derive MFCC features from the geometric mean of the multiple power spectra computed over varying window sizes, specifically 20ms, 30ms, 40ms and 50ms.

Hidden Markov Model and Gaussian Mixture Model (HMM-GMM) based speech recognition systems were trained using public domain software HTK [18] on the clean training set from the original Numbers corpus. The speech recognition results in clean conditions for various spectral analysis techniques are given in table 1. The fixed scale MFCC features using 20ms and 50ms long analysis windows have 5.8% and 5.9% word error rate (WER) respectively. The concatenation of MFCC feature vectors derived from 20ms and 50ms long windows has a 5.7% WER and it has twice the number of HMM-GMM parameters as compared to the rest of the systems[5]. The slight improvement in this case may be due to the multiple scale information present in this feature, albeit in an ad-hoc way. The minimum cross-entropy MFCC features which were derived from the geometric mean of the power spectra computed over 20ms, 30ms, 40ms and 50ms long analysis windows, have a WER of 5.7%. The proposed variable-scale system which adaptively chooses a window size in the range [20ms, 60ms], followed by the usual MFCC computation, has a 5.0% WER. This corresponds to a relative improvement of more than 10% over the rest of the techniques

Table 1. Word error rate in clean conditions

MFCC 20ms	5.8
MFCC 50ms	5.9
Concat. MFCC (20ms, 50ms)	5.7
Min. Cross entropy based MFCC	5.7
Proposed Variable-scale QSS MFCC	5.0

5 Conclusion

We have demonstrated that the variable-scale piecewise quasi-stationary spectral analysis of speech signal can possibly improve the state-of-the-art ASR. Such a technique can overcome the time-frequency resolution limitations of the fixed scale spectral analysis techniques. Comparisons were drawn with the other competing multi-scale techniques such as the minimum cross-entropy spectrum. The proposed technique led to the minimum WER as compared to the rest of the techniques.

---

[5] Due to twice the feature dimension as compared to the rest of the systems.

Acknowledgements

This work has been supported by the EU 6th Framework Programme, under contract number IST-2002-002034 (DIVINES project).

References

1. P. Loughlin, J. Pitton and B. Hannaford, "Approximating Time-Frequency Density Functions via Optimal Combinations of Spectrograms," IEEE Signal Processing Letters, vol.1, No.12, December 1994.
2. F. Itakura, " Minimum Prediction Residual Principle Applied to Speech Recognition, " IEEE Trans. on ASSP, Vol.23, no.1, February 1975.
3. B. S. Atal, "Efficient coding of LPC parameters by temporal decomposition, " In the Proc. of IEEE ICASSP, Boston, USA, 1983.
4. T. Svendsen, K. K. Paliwal, E. Harborg, P. O. Husoy, "An improved sub-word based speech recognizer," Proc. of IEEE ICASSP, 1989.
5. J. Makhoul, "Linear Prediction: A Tutorial Review, " In the Proc. of IEEE, vol.63, No.4, April 1975.
6. R. R. Coifman and M. V. Wickerhauser, " Entropy based algorithms for best basis selection, " IEEE Trans. on Information Theory, Vol.38, Issue:2, March 1992.
7. V. Tyagi, I McCowan, H. Bourlard, H. Misra, " Mel-Cepstrum Modulation Spectrum (MCMS) features for Robust ASR, " In the Proc. of IEEE ASRU 2003, St. Thomas, Virgin Islands, USA.
8. S. Srinivasan and W. B. Kleijn, "Speech Enhancement Using Adaptive time-domain Segmentation, " In the Proc. of ICSLP 2004, Jeju, S. Korea.
9. S. Haykin, Adaptive Filter Theory, Prentice-Hall Publishers, N.J., USA, 1993.
10. A. V. Brandt, "Detecting and estimating the parameters jumps using ladder algorithms and likelihood ratio test," in Proc. of ICASSP, Boston, MA, 1983,pp. 1017-1020.
11. R. A. Obrecht, "A new Statistical Approach for the Automatic Segmentation of Continuous Speech Signals, " IEEE Trans. on ASSP, vol.36, No.1, January 1988.
12. J. Ajmera, I. McCowan and H. Boulard, "Robust Speaker Change Detection," IEEE Signal Processing Letters, vol.11, No. 8, August 2004.
13. K. Achan, S. Roweis, A. Hertzmann and B. Frey, "A Segmental HMM for Speech Waveforms, " UTML Techical Report 2004-001, Dept. of Computer Science, Univ. of Toronto, May 2004.
14. S. M. Kay, Fundamentals of Statistical Signal Processing: Detection Theory, Prentice-Hall Publishers, N.J., USA, 1998.
15. L. Rabiner and B. H. Juang, Fundamentals of Speech Recognition, Prentice-Hall, N.J., USA, 1993.
16. S. B. Davis and P. Mermelstein, "Comparison of Parametric Representation for Monosyllabic Word Recognition in Continuously Spoken Sentences, " IEEE Trans. on ASSP, Vol. ASSP-28, No. 4, August 1980.
17. H. Hermansky, "Perceptual linear predictive (PLP) analysis of speech, " J. Acoust. Soc. Am., vol.87:4, April 1990.
18. S. Young, J. Odell, D. Ollason, V. Valtchev, and P. Woodland, The HTK Book, Cambridge University, 1995.
19. R. A. Cole, M. Fanty, and T. Lander, "Telephone speech corpus at CSLU," Proc. of ICSLP, Yokohama, Japan, 1994.

Accent Classification for Speech Recognition

Arlo Faria

International Computer Science Institute, Berkeley CA 94704, USA
arlo@icsi.berkeley.edu

Abstract. This work describes classification of speech from native and non-native speakers, enabling accent-dependent automatic speech recognition. In addition to the acoustic signal, lexical features from transcripts of the speech data can also provide significant evidence of a speaker's accent type. Subsets of the Fisher corpus, ranging over diverse accents, were used for these experiments. Relative to human-audited judgments, accent classifiers that exploited acoustic and lexical features achieved up to 84.5% classification accuracy. Compared to a system trained only on native speakers, using this classifier in a recognizer with accent-specific acoustic and language models resulted in 16.5% improvement for the non-native speakers, and a 7.2% improvement overall.

1 Introduction

Automatic speech recognition systems are highly susceptible to speaker variability. Statistical analysis reveals that – after gender – the principal component of this inter-speaker variation is accent [2]. Recognition models trained on one type of accent fare poorly when evaluated on a mismatched test condition. For this reason, most speech technology research is restricted to North American dialects of English, while the collected corpora mostly comprise native speakers.

With improving performance of speech recognizers and their expanding applications, the need to address non-native speakers has gained importance. Two recent speech corpora reflect the necessity of this research. The massive Fisher corpus[1] includes a considerable number of recruited subjects who speak English as a second language; meanwhile, the European Commission's AMI Project[2] is collecting data from meetings with many non-native English-speaking participants, as well as native speakers of non-American varieties of English.

To address the problems that non-native speakers present to speech recognizers, previous work has relied upon non-native accented training data. Adapting and retraining acoustic models from an accented corpus improved recognition of Japanese-accented English [8], and similarly with a Hispanic-English corpus [3]. Acoustic model adaptation can also be derived from a speaker's source language [5], data which is potentially more accessible. Alternatively, lexicon adaptation [9] can be utilized to reflect the phonology of non-native pronunciation.

---

[1] http://www.ldc.upenn.edu/Projects/EARS
[2] http://www.amiproject.org

S. Renals and S. Bengio (Eds.): MLMI 2005, LNCS 3869, pp. 285–293, 2006.
© Springer-Verlag Berlin Heidelberg 2006

This work presents an integrated accent-dependent speech recognition architecture that is analogous to gender-dependent systems. An accent classifier divided training data into native and non-native sets, from which recognition models were estimated; test data was similarly split and recognized with the corresponding accent-specific models.

We give careful consideration to the lexical aspects of non-native speech. Exploratory language modeling experiments suggested that the word structure of non-native language can be distinctly different from the native variety. Thus, in addition to the acoustic signals, text transcripts of the speech data were also used for accent classification.

To maximize the amount of data, non-native speakers were considered as a whole, rather than working with just one specific accent group. This treatment was partly justified by the better performance of a lexical classifier compared to an acoustic classifier. While non-native accents might sound quite different from each other, the words that these speakers generate tend to be characteristic of their non-native identity.

2   Data Preparation

These experiments were performed using a subset of the Fisher collection:

- **Speakers**: 948 speakers; 540 male, 408 female
- **Duration**: 158 hours = 948 speakers × 10-minute sides
- **Words**: 843 words per speaker, on average
- **Segments**: 90.5 segments per speaker, on average

The audio speech signals were recorded over 8 kHz telephone channels, and were accompanied by human-generated word-level reference transcripts. An acoustic speech segmentation tool automatically created segments without regard to sentence or phrase structure, although these segments were treated like sentences for language modeling purposes (i.e., affixed with the boundary tags <s> and </s>).

Self-reported participant information was gathered to describe speaker demographics, and trained human auditors rated each speaker's accent as *American* or *Other*. For these experiments, the non-native speakers were those whose native language was not reported as English and whose accents were audited as *Other*. The set of native speakers reported English as a native language and had accents audited as *American*[3]; a subset was selected to match the size and gender proportions of the non-native set. Normalizing the amount of data per speaker, we used just one 10-minute conversation side for each speaker.

Table 1 gives the composition of the native and non-native accented sets. Native speakers are grouped by place of birth, with many locally recruited participants originating from the American Northeast. The non-native portion is categorized by speakers' self-reported native languages. These groupings are only

---

[3] The Fisher collection explicitly excluded British speakers from participation.

Table 1. Fisher corpus demographics

Accent Type	Speakers	Male	Female	Accent Type	Speakers	Male	Female
Non-native	474	270	204	American English	474	270	204
Indian	116	85	31	Pennsylvania	60	39	21
Chinese	102	50	52	New York	56	36	20
Russian	61	23	38	California	53	32	21
Spanish	60	36	24	Texas	21	11	10
German	26	13	13	New Jersey	18	10	8
French	20	7	13	Ohio	19	11	8
Other	89	56	33	Other	247	131	116

for description of the data sets; in this paper, only the native versus non-native distinction is considered.

In Table 1, the non-native accents are grouped as follows:

- **Indian** is primarily Hindi. Also: Tamil, Farsi, Urdu, Telegu, Bengali, Marathi, Gujarati, Malayalam, Kannada, Punjabi, and Sindhi.
- **Chinese** includes Mandarin and Cantonese.
- **Russian** comprises Russian, Bulgarian, Hungarian, Polish, Czech, Armenian, Serbian, Croatian, Bosnian, Slovak, and Latvian.
- **Spanish** speakers are mainly Hispanic and Latin Americans. Also included are the West Iberian languages: Portuguese and Galego.
- **German** comprises mostly Germanic languages: German, Danish, Dutch, Swedish, and Afrikaans.
- **French** speakers are from France, Canada, and Switzerland.
- **Other** languages (with four or more speakers): Arabic, Turkish, Korean, Creole, Yoruba, Romanian, Japanese, Hebrew, Greek.

Test and training sets of 100 and 374 speakers, respectively, were selected from the native and non-native sets above, ensuring that the composition of each subset reflected the proportions given in Table 1.

3 Accent Classification

3.1 Acoustic GMM Classifier

Given accent-specific acoustic models λ_a that assign probability to acoustic observations X, we can invoke the maximum likelihood criterion to determine the accent classification $\hat{a}$:

$$\hat{a} = \arg \max_a \mathrm{P}(X|\lambda_a)$$

Ideally, the acoustic models in this computation would be a set of accent-specific phone HMMs used for recognition; however, then it is usually necessary to align X to a phone sequence determined in an earlier decoding pass. A more efficient solution implements λ_a as a Gaussian Mixture Model: a global distribution of speech frames, independent of sequence. This application of GMMs is fairly standard in other speech classification tasks such as speech detection, gender classification, speaker identification, and warp factor selection for vocal tract length normalization.

Accent-specific acoustic GMMs were built from the native and non-native training data; each was a mixture 256 Gaussians trained for 10 iterations of EM. Acoustic observations were standard ASR features: 12 mel-frequency cepstral coefficients and energy, plus their first and second order derivatives. Features were transformed with speaker-based cepstral mean/variance normalization, and also with vocal tract length normalization to counteract the models' gender independence.

3.2   Lexical SVM Classifiers

Non-native accented speakers of English are often distinguished by acoustic divergence from the standard pronunciation of native speakers. Beyond the phonetics and phonology, however, non-native speakers generally have a weaker command of the language and consequently produce sequences of words that a native speaker would be less likely to utter. The motivation for using lexical features for accent classification is based upon this hypothesis that non-native speakers produce word sequences that are fundamentally different from the language produced by native speakers. Before attempting to work with lexical features, however, it would be reassuring to test this hypothesis with some simple language modeling experiments.

Language models were built from each of the accented training sets (about 300K words each), and the perplexity was calculated for each of the accented test sets (about 100K words). These open-vocabulary trigram models were smoothed using Chen and Goodman's modified Kneser-Ney discounting scheme, implemented in the SRI Language Modeling Toolkit [6]. Table 2 demonstrates the results of training and testing language models on various combinations of the native and non-native sets. There is a clear correlation between matched accent conditions and lower perplexity. Because non-native word sequences are better predicted by training on non-native speakers, this suggests that there is a distribution of characteristic words and phrases that differs from the native set's. Additionally, the non-native test set had a significantly lower out-of-vocabulary rate, reflecting the understandably smaller vocabulary size of speakers who have had less exposure to the English language.

Table 3 provides more evidence supporting the hypothesis that language generated by non-native speakers is different. A rule-based tagger trained from WSJ

Table 2. Perplexity and out-of-vocabulary rate

	Native train	Non-native train
Native test	143	153
	1.78%	2.31%
Non-native test	146	135
	1.53%	1.68%

Table 3. Perplexity of a POS sequence model

	Native train	Non-native train
Native test	14.09	14.31
Non-native test	14.28	14.05

data [1] assigned Penn Treebank part-of-speech tags to all the data, allowing the estimation of a part-of-speech trigram model. Again there is a correlation between matched accent conditions and better predictability of tag sequences. This might be attributed to a preference for certain syntactic forms and tenses. Or it is possibly related to grammatical errors committed by language learners: auxiliary and function words tend to be misused; if POS tags convey some morphological information, it would also be possible to detect errors of agreement.

Given these results, two kinds of word-based features were investigated for accent classification:

- Word n-grams. The distribution of words and word sequences is different for each accent group, so n-gram counts could be good features for categorization of speaker accents given their text transcripts.
- POS n-grams. There are probably some sequences of part-of-speech tags that native speakers rarely produce, but are more commonly misused by non-native speakers.

The integral counts of these n-grams were provided as input features for text categorization with Support Vector Machines, using the SVM-Lite toolkit [4] with a linear kernel. The training algorithm was presented with 748 accent-labeled data points, one for each conversation side.

3.3   Comparison of Accent Classifiers

For the accent classifiers described, performance on the test set of 200 speakers was evaluated by comparing to the reference judgments made by human auditors

Table 4. Accuracy of accent classification

Feature type	Classifier type	Classification accuracy
Acoustic MFCCs	GMM	69.5%
Word Unigrams	SVM	74.5%
Word Bigrams	SVM	75.0%
Word Trigrams	SVM	76.5%
POS Unigrams	SVM	68.5%
POS Bigrams	SVM	70.5%
POS Trigrams	SVM	72.5%
All Lexical	Interpolated	77.5%
All Lexical + Acoustic	Interpolated	82.0%
Word Trigram + Acoustic	Interpolated	81.5%

Table 5. Lexical features from reference and recognized transcripts

Feature type	Classifier type	Classification accuracy
Word Trigrams with reference transcripts	SVM	76.5%
Word Trigrams with recognized hypotheses	SVM	79.0%
Word Trigrams (ref trans) + Acoustic	Interpolated	81.5%
Word Trigrams (rec hyps) + Acoustic	Interpolated	84.5%

of the Fisher corpus. As a baseline, the prior probability of each accent (native or non-native) was exactly 50%.

Two types of classifiers were used: a maximum-likelihood GMM for the acoustic features, and a SVM for the lexical features. Neither classifier returned normalized probabilities, so the combination of these scores was accomplished by linear interpolation (summation of weighted scores), tuned with a grid search over the mixing weights[4].

The performance of all the classifiers is given in Table 4, where the optimal combination of all features achieved 82% accuracy; combining the SVM score for word trigrams with the acoustic GMM score was sufficient for 81.5% accuracy, and for simplicity this was the scheme chosen for the experiments in the next section.

In all experiments described thus far, lexical features were extracted from human-annotated reference transcripts. In the next section, we will describe ASR architectures that use accent classifiers with lexical features extracted from 1st-pass recognition hypotheses. Despite the high word error rate, the accent classification accuracy actually improves, as shown in Table 5. This convenient result suggests that the errors made by the recognizer are perhaps also correlated to a speaker's accent.

4   Accent-Dependent Speech Recognition

An accent classification system is not very practical on its own, and in this project its intended application is to pre-process the data used in an accent-dependent speech recognition system. Using accent-specific models can greatly improve recognition performance, but relies upon a good accent classifier to appropriately select which models to apply.

Several ASR systems were built and tested with SRI's DECIPHER [7]. The resulting performance was suboptimal because many compromises were made to allow for rapid training and testing of the systems, as well as to provide a carefully controlled experiment. In particular, the gender-independent acoustic models (genonic HMMs) were trained on a relatively small amount of data: about 60 hours of the quickly annotated Fisher corpus, rather than hundreds of hours of precisely transcribed speech. The language models were exclusively trained on the small subsets of the Fisher data: bigrams can be rather sparse with only

---

[4] This was a "cheating" experiment: tuned on the test set. However, there was not a sharp peak at the optimal interpolation weight

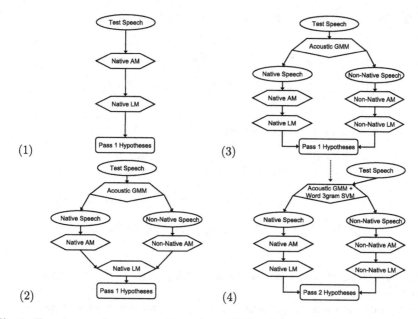

Fig. 1. Four types of system architectures: (1) Baseline system using native models; (2) Accent-specific acoustic models; (3) Accent-specific acoustic and language models; (4) Two-pass system using lexical and acoustic features for accent classification

300K words of training text. Also, there was no speaker adaptation of acoustic models – only VTLN in the front-end feature extraction. These optimizations allowed very fast run-time performance, as the recognizer processed speech data in less than 3x real-time on a 2.4GHz Pentium machine.

Figure 1 depicts various accent-dependent architectures. In System (2), an acoustic GMM classifier selects the accent-specific acoustic models. System (3) is similar, but the language models are also accent-specific. The first-pass recognition hypotheses from System (3) are utilized in System (4) to classify accents using acoustic and lexical features.

4.1 Results of Recognition Experiments

We first consider the separation of native and non-native speakers according to the judgments of the human auditors. Table 6 describes the performance of accent-dependent recognizers when models are matched and mis-matched to the test accents. The first column represents a system trained only on native speakers, System (1). The rightmost column represents a gold-standard system, if it could use the human auditors to select which accent-specific recognition models to employ.

Results of the recognition experiments are summarized in Table 7, demonstrating how an automatic speech recognition system can improve performance by identifying non-native speakers with lexical information, as well as acoustic, and recognizing those speakers with non-native models. These results again sup-

Table 6. Combinations of accent-specific models: Word Error Rate %

	Native models	Non-native models	Accent-matched models
Native Test	**50.72**	59.30	**50.72**
Non-native Test	64.40	**52.79**	**52.79**
Overall	57.20	56.22	**51.70**

Table 7. Results of speech recognition experiments: Word Error Rate %

System	Native	Non-native	Overall
(1)	50.72	64.40	57.20
(2)	53.76	53.45 (-17.0%)	53.62 (-6.3%)
(3)	53.73	53.32 (-17.2%)	53.55 (-6.4%)
(4)	52.64	53.75 (-16.5%)	53.08 (-7.2%)
Gold Standard	50.72	52.79 (-18.0%)	51.70 (-9.6%)

port the hypothesis that non-native speakers differ in the lexical aspects of their language use.

In retrospect, it would have been informative to compare these results to an accent-independent system with models trained on all the data, not just the native set. Models trained on twice as much data would be less sparse; however, combining the accents would also make the distributions less sharp. This is a possibility for future experimentation.

5   Conclusion

This work described a series of experiments using subsets of native and non-native speakers drawn from the Fisher corpus. An investigation of the word and part-of-speech sequence models gave evidence that speaker accents are more than simply acoustic differences. Lexical features proved useful for accent classification, even when extracted from relatively poor recognition hypotheses. Lastly, accent classifiers were integrated into an accent-dependent speech recognition architecture which significantly outperformed a system trained only on native speakers.

Similar to physiological factors such as gender, accents contribute to the general problem of speaker variability. As speech recognition systems evolve to address these challenges, the utility of the technology increases and it becomes more accessible to diverse populations. In this global perspective, modern speech recognizers must be designed to perform for all kinds of accents, and not exclusively native speakers.

Acknowledgements

Thanks to Barbara Peskin and Dan Klein for advising this work; Andreas Stolcke, Kofi Boakye, and Andy Hatch provided invaluable technical support with the implementation; also, Javier Macías-Guarasa's accent adaptation work was a strong inspiration.

This work was partly supported by the European Union 6th FWP IST Integrated Project AMI (Augmented Multi-party Interaction, FP6-506811).

References

1. E. Brill. A report of recent progress in transformation-based error-driven learning. In *AAAI*, 1994.
2. C. Huang, E. Chang, and T. Chen. Accent issues in large vocabulary continuous speech recognition. Technical Report MSR-TR-2001-69, Microsoft Research China, Beijing, China, 2001.
3. A. Ikeno et al. Issues in recognition of Spanish-accented spontaneous english. In *Proceedings of IEEE/ISCA Workshop on Spontaneous Speech Processing and Recognition*, Tokyo, Japan, 2003.
4. T. Joachims. Text categorization with Support Vector Machines: Learning with many relevant features. In *Proc. of European Conference on Machine Learning*, 1998.
5. L. W. Kat and P. Fung. MLLR-based accent model adaptation without accented data. In *Proceedings of ICSLP*, 2000.
6. A. Stolcke. SRILM – an extensible language modeling toolkit. In *Intl. Conf. on Spoken Language Processing*, 2002.
7. A. Stolcke et al. The SRI March 2000 Hub-5 conversational speech transcription system. In *Proc. NIST Speech Transcription Workshop*, University of Maryland, May 2000.
8. L. M. Tomokiyo. *Recognizing Non-native Speech: Characterizing and Adapting to Non-native Usage in LVCSR*. PhD thesis, Carnegie Mellon University, 2001.
9. W. Ward et al. Lexicon adaptation for LVCSR: Speaker idiosyncracies, non-native speakers, and pronunciation choice. In *Proceedings of the PMLA Workshop*, Estes Park, Colorado, 2002.

Hierarchical Multi-stream Posterior Based Speech Recognition System

Hamed Ketabdar[1,2], Hervé Bourlard[1,2], and Samy Bengio[1]

[1] IDIAP Research Institute, Martigny, Switzerland
[2] Ecole Polytechnique Fédérale de Lausanne (EPFL), Switzerland

Abstract. In this paper, we present initial results towards boosting posterior based speech recognition systems by estimating more informative posteriors using multiple streams of features and taking into account acoustic context (e.g., as available in the whole utterance), as well as possible prior information (such as topological constraints). These posteriors are estimated based on "state gamma posterior" definition (typically used in standard HMMs training) extended to the case of multi-stream HMMs.This approach provides a new, principled, theoretical framework for hierarchical estimation/use of posteriors, multi-stream feature combination, and integrating appropriate context and prior knowledge in posterior estimates. In the present work, we used the resulting gamma posteriors as features for a standard HMM/GMM layer. On the OGI Digits database and on a reduced vocabulary version (1000 words) of the DARPA Conversational Telephone Speech-to-text (CTS) task, this resulted in significant performance improvement, compared to the state-of-the-art Tandem systems.

1 Introduction

Using posterior probabilities for Automatic Speech Recognition (ASR) has become popular and frequently investigated in the past decade. Posterior probabilities have been mainly used either as features or as local scores (measures) in speech recognition systems. Hybrid Hidden Markov Model / Artificial Neural Network (HMM/ANN) approaches [1] were among the first ones to make use of posterior probabilities as local scores. In these approaches, ANNs and more specifically Multi-Layer Perceptrons (MLPs) are used to estimate the emission probabilities required in HMM. Hybrid HMM/ANN method allows for discriminant training, as well as for the possibility of using short acoustic context by presenting several frames at MLP input. Posterior probabilities have also been used as local scores for word lattice rescoring [2], beam search pruning [3] and confidence measures estimation [4]. Regarding the use of posterior probabilities as features, one successful approach is Tandem [5]. In Tandem, a trained MLP is used for estimating local phone posteriors. These posteriors, after some transformations, can be used alone or appended to standard features (such as MFCC or PLP) as input features to HMMs. Tandem technique takes the advantage of discriminative acoustic model training, as well as being able to use the techniques

S. Renals and S. Bengio (Eds.): MLMI 2005, LNCS 3869, pp. 294–306, 2006.

developed for standard HMM systems. In both hybrid HMM/ANN and Tandem approaches, local posteriors (i.e., posteriors estimated using only local frame or limited number of local frames as context) are used.

In [6], a method was presented to estimate more informative posterior probabilities based on "state gamma posterior" definition (as usually referred to in HMM formalism) to generate posteriors taking into account all acoustic information available in each utterance, as well as prior knowledge, possibly formulated in terms of HMM topological constraints. In their approach, posterior probabilities are estimated based on state gamma posterior definition in a HMM configuration, which, after some transformations, are fed as features into a second layer consisting of standard HMM/Gaussian Mixture Models (HMM/GMM). Such an approach was shown to yield significant performance improvement over Tandem approach. In [7], these posteriors are used as local scores for a Viterbi decoder. It also showed improvement over hybrid HMM/ANN approach which uses local posteriors as local scores.

Building upon the idea of multi-stream HMMs [8,9], in this paper we present initial investigations towards extending the mentioned posterior estimation method to multi-stream case. We show that the posterior probabilities can be estimated through a multi-stream HMM configuration based on multi-stream state gamma definition, thus giving the estimate of posteriors by combining multiple streams of input features and also taking into account whole context in each stream as well as prior knowledge encoded in the model. Our hierarchical approach is as follows: The input feature streams are PLP cepstral [10] and TRAP temporal [11] features which are known to have some complementary information. We estimate the posteriors based on state gamma posterior definition through a multi-stream HMM configuration. These posteriors are used after some transformations as features for a standard HMM/GMM layer. This hierarchical approach provides a new, principled, theoretical framework for combining different streams of features taking into account context and model knowledge. We show that this method gives significant performance improvement over baseline PLP-TANDEM [5] and TRAP-TANDEM [11] techniques and also entropy based combination method [12] on OGI digits [13] and a reduced vocabulary version (1000 words) of CTS [6] databases.

In the present paper, Section 2 reviews single stream gamma posterior estimation method. The extension of this method to multi-stream case is explained in Section 3. Section 4 explains the configuration of our hierarchical multi-stream posterior based ASR system. Experiments and results are presented in Section 5. Conclusions and future work plans are discussed in Section 6.

2 Single Stream "Gamma Posterior" Estimation

In this section, we show how posterior probabilities can be estimated taking into account whole context in a stream and prior knowledge (e.g. topological constraints) encoded in the model. These posteriors are estimated based on "state gamma posterior" definition (as it is referred to in HMM formalism) through an HMM configuration.

In phone based speech recognition systems, phones are usually modeled by a few number of states. The posteriors are first estimated for each state (called "state gamma posteriors" as referred to in HMM formalism and used in HMM training), which then can be integrated to phone or higher level posteriors.

According to standard HMM formalism, the state gamma posterior $\gamma(i, t|M)$ is defined as the probability of being in state i at time t, given the whole observation sequence $x_{1:T}$ and model M encoding specific prior knowledge (topological/temporal constraints):

$$\gamma(i, t|M) \triangleq p(q_t = i|x_{1:T}, M) \tag{1}$$

where x_t is a feature vector at time t, $x_{1:T} = \{x_1, \ldots, x_T\}$ is an acoustic observation sequence of size T and q_t is HMM state at time t, which value can range from 1 to N_q (total number of possible HMM states). In the following, we will drop all the dependencies on M, always keeping in mind that all recursions are processed through some prior (Markov) model M.

In standard likelihood-based HMMs, the state gammas $\gamma(i, t)$ can be estimated by using forward α and backward β recursions (as referred to in HMM formalism) [14] using local emission likelihoods $p(x_t|q_i = t)$ (e.g., modeled by GMMs):

$$\begin{aligned} \alpha(i, t) &\triangleq p(x_{1:t}, q_t = i) \\ &= p(x_t|q_t = i) \sum_j p(q_t = i|q_{t-1} = j) p(x_{1:t-1}, q_{t-1} = j) \\ &= p(x_t|q_t = i) \sum_j p(q_t = i|q_{t-1} = j) \alpha(j, t-1) \end{aligned} \tag{2}$$

$$\begin{aligned} \beta(i, t) &\triangleq p(x_{t+1:T}|q_t = i) \\ &= \sum_j p(x_{t+1}|q_{t+1} = j) p(q_{t+1} = j|q_t = i) p(x_{t+2:T}|q_{t+1} = j) \\ &= \sum_j p(x_{t+1}|q_{t+1} = j) p(q_{t+1} = j|q_t = i) \beta(j, t+1) \end{aligned} \tag{3}$$

thus yielding the estimate of $p(q_t = i|x_{1:T})$:

$$\gamma(i, t) \triangleq p(q_t = i|x_{1:T}) = \frac{\alpha(i, t)\beta(i, t)}{\sum_j \alpha(j, t)\beta(j, t)} \tag{4}$$

As mentioned above, we recall that the α and β recursions are processed through a specific HMM, which is used to represent prior knowledge.

Similar recursions, also yielding "state gamma posteriors" and using the same assumptions as the case of likelihood based recursions, can be developed for local posterior based systems such as hybrid HMM/ANN systems using MLPs to estimate HMM emission probabilities [6]. In standard HMM/ANN systems, these local posteriors are usually turned into "scaled likelihoods" by dividing MLP outputs $p(q_t = i|x_t)$ by their respective prior probabilities $p(q_t = i)$, i.e.: $\frac{p(x_t|q_t=i)}{p(x_t)} = \frac{p(q_t=i|x_t)}{p(q_t=i)}$. These scaled likelihoods can be used in "scaled alpha" α_s and "scaled beta" β_s recursions to yield gamma posterior estimates [6]. These recursions are similar to the previous recursions except that the likelihood term is replaced by the scaled likelihood:

$$
\begin{aligned}
\alpha_s(i,t) &\triangleq \frac{p(x_{1:t}, q_t = i)}{\prod_{\tau=1}^{t} p(x_\tau)} \\
&= \frac{p(x_t|q_t = i)}{p(x_t)} \sum_j p(q_t = i|q_{t-1} = j)\alpha_s(j, t-1) \\
&= \frac{p(q_t = i|x_t)}{p(q_t = i)} \sum_j p(q_t = i|q_{t-1} = j)\alpha_s(j, t-1)
\end{aligned} \tag{5}
$$

$$
\begin{aligned}
\beta_s(i,t) &\triangleq \frac{p(x_{t+1:T}|q_t = i)}{\prod_{\tau=t+1}^{T} p(x_\tau)} \\
&= \sum_j \frac{p(x_{t+1} = j|q_{t+1} = j)}{p(x_{t+1} = j)} p(q_{t+1} = j|q_t = i)\beta_s(j, t+1) \\
&= \sum_j \frac{p(q_{t+1} = j|x_{t+1})}{p(q_{t+1} = j)} p(q_{t+1} = j|q_t = i)\beta_s(j, t+1)
\end{aligned} \tag{6}
$$

$$
\gamma(i,t) \triangleq p(q_t = i|x_{1:T}) = \frac{\alpha_s(i,t)\beta_s(i,t)}{\sum_j \alpha_s(j,t)\beta_s(j,t)} \tag{7}
$$

subscript s indicates that the recursion is based on scaled likelihood. In the above equations, exactly the same independence assumptions as standard HMMs are used, beside the fact that the local correlation may be better captured if the ANN is presented with acoustic context.

3   Multi-stream "Gamma Posterior" Estimation

In multi-stream HMM configuration, the definition of the state gamma posterior is extended to the probability of being in specific state i at specific time t, given the whole observation sequences for *all* streams, and model M encoding specific prior knowledge:

$$
\gamma(i,t) \triangleq p(q_t = i|x_{1:T}^1, x_{1:T}^2, ..., x_{1:T}^N, M) \tag{8}
$$

where superscript n indicates the stream number. We call the state gamma posterior estimated using multiple streams of features as "multi-stream state gamma". As we show in this section, multi-stream state gammas can be estimated using multi-stream forward α and backward β recursions. The multi-stream α and β recursions can also be written based on individual stream α^n and β^n recursions. In this work, we focus on the posterior based systems, therefore all the recursions are written using scaled likelihoods. The same multi-stream recursions but for likelihood based systems has been explained in [15].

We start with individual stream forward α^n and backward β^n recursions:

$$\alpha_s^n(i,t) \triangleq \frac{p(x_{1:t}^n, q_t = i)}{\prod_{\tau=1}^t p(x_\tau^n)}$$

$$= \frac{p(q_t = i|x_t^n)}{p(q_t = i)} \sum_j p(q_t = i|q_{t-1} = j)\alpha_s^n(j, t-1) \tag{9}$$

$$\beta_s^n(i,t) \triangleq \frac{p(x_{t+1:T}^n|q_t = i)}{\prod_{\tau=t+1}^T p(x_\tau^n)}$$

$$= \sum_j \frac{p(q_{t+1} = j|x_{t+1}^n)}{p(q_{t+1} = j)} p(q_{t+1} = j|q_t = i)\beta_s^n(j, t+1) \tag{10}$$

where $\alpha_s^n(i,t)$ and $\beta_s^n(i,t)$ show the forward and backward recursions for stream n. Subscript s indicates that the recursion is written using scaled likelihoods.

We note here that we need to estimate $p(q_t = i)$, which can be done recursively as follows:

$$p(q_t = i) = \sum_j p(q_t = i|q_{t-1} = j)p(q_{t-1} = j) \tag{11}$$

Using individual stream forward recursions α_s^n and applying the usual HMM assumptions, we can write multi-stream forward α_s recursion as follows:

$$\alpha_s(i,t) \triangleq \frac{p(x_{1:t}^1, x_{1:t}^2, ..., x_{1:t}^N, q_t = i)}{\prod_{\tau=1}^t p(x_\tau^1) \prod_{\tau=1}^t p(x_\tau^2)... \prod_{\tau=1}^t p(x_\tau^N)} \tag{12}$$

$$= \frac{p(x_{1:t}^1, x_{1:t}^2, ..., x_{1:t}^N|q_t = i)p(q_t = i)}{\prod_{\tau=1}^t p(x_\tau^1) \prod_{\tau=1}^t p(x_\tau^2)... \prod_{\tau=1}^t p(x_\tau^N)} \tag{13}$$

$$= \frac{p(x_{1:t}^1|q_t = i)p(x_{1:t}^2|q_t = i)...p(x_{1:t}^N|q_t = i)p(q_t = i)}{\prod_{\tau=1}^t p(x_\tau^1) \prod_{\tau=1}^t p(x_\tau^2)... \prod_{\tau=1}^t p(x_\tau^N)} \tag{14}$$

$$= \frac{\frac{p(x_{1:t}^1, q_t=i)}{\prod_{\tau=1}^t p(x_\tau^1)}}{p(q_t = i)} \frac{\frac{p(x_{1:t}^2, q_t=i)}{\prod_{\tau=1}^t p(x_\tau^2)}}{p(q_t = i)} ... \frac{\frac{p(x_{1:t}^N, q_t=i)}{\prod_{\tau=1}^t p(x_\tau^N)}}{p(q_t = i)} p(q_t = i) \tag{15}$$

$$= \frac{\alpha_s^1(i,t)}{p(q_t = i)} \frac{\alpha_s^2(i,t)}{p(q_t = i)} ... \frac{\alpha_s^N(i,t)}{p(q_t = i)} p(q_t = i) \tag{16}$$

$$= \frac{\prod_{n=1}^N \alpha_s^n(i,t)}{p(q_t = i)^{N-1}} \tag{17}$$

when going form (13) to (14), we add the following reasonable assumption:

$$p(x_{1:t}^1, x_{1:t}^2, ..., x_{1:t}^N|q_t = i) = \tag{18}$$
$$p(x_{1:t}^1|q_t = i)p(x_{1:t}^2|q_t = i)...p(x_{1:t}^N|q_t = i)$$

while (14) is rewritten as (15) simply by applying Bayes rule.

The multi-stream β_s recursion can also be written using individual stream β_s^n recursions:

$$\beta_s(i,t) \triangleq \frac{p(x_{t+1:T}^1, x_{t+1:T}^2, ..., x_{t+1:T}^N | q_t = i)}{\prod_{\tau=t+1}^T p(x_\tau^1) \prod_{\tau=t+1}^T p(x_\tau^2)... \prod_{\tau=t+1}^T p(x_\tau^N)} \tag{19}$$

$$= \frac{p(x_{t+1:T}^1 | q_t = i)p(x_{t+1:T}^2 | q_t = i)...p(x_{t+1:T}^N | q_t = i)}{\prod_{\tau=t+1}^T p(x_\tau^1) \prod_{\tau=t+1}^T p(x_\tau^2)... \prod_{\tau=t+1}^T p(x_\tau^N)} \tag{20}$$

$$= \frac{p(x_{t+1:T}^1 | q_t = i)}{\prod_{\tau=t+1}^T p(x_\tau^1)} \frac{p(x_{t+1:T}^2 | q_t = i)}{\prod_{\tau=t+1}^T p(x_\tau^2)} ... \frac{p(x_{t+1:T}^N | q_t = i)}{\prod_{\tau=t+1}^T p(x_\tau^N)} \tag{21}$$

$$= \beta_s^1(i,t)\beta_s^2(i,t)...\beta_s^N(i,t) \tag{22}$$

$$= \prod_{n=1}^N \beta_s^n(i,t) \tag{23}$$

Note that (19) is rewritten as (20) assuming

$$p(x_{t+1:T}^1, x_{t+1:T}^2, ..., x_{t+1:T}^N | \ q_t = i) = \tag{24}$$
$$p(x_{t+1:T}^1 | q_t = i)p(x_{t+1:T}^2 | q_t = i)...p(x_{t+1:T}^N | q_t = i)$$

The multi-stream state gamma $\gamma(i,t)$ can then be obtained using multi-stream α_s and β_s recursions:

$$\gamma(i,t) \triangleq p(q_t = i | x_{1:T}^1, x_{1:T}^2, ..., x_{1:T}^N)$$

$$= \frac{p(x_{1:T}^1, x_{1:T}^2, ..., x_{1:T}^N, q_t = i)}{p(x_{1:T}^1, x_{1:T}^2, ..., x_{1:T}^N)}$$

$$= \frac{p(x_{1:t}^1, x_{t+1:T}^1, x_{1:t}^2, x_{t+1:T}^2, ..., x_{1:t}^N, x_{t+1:T}^N, q_t = i)}{\sum_j p(x_{1:t}^1, x_{t+1:T}^1, x_{1:t}^2, x_{t+1:T}^2, ..., x_{1:t}^N, x_{t+1:T}^N, q_t = j)}$$

$$= \frac{p(x_{1:t}^1, x_{1:t}^2, ..., x_{1:t}^N, q_t = i)p(x_{t+1:T}^1, x_{t+1:T}^2, ..., x_{t+1:T}^N | q_t = i)}{\sum_j p(x_{1:t}^1, x_{1:t}^2, ..., x_{1:t}^N, q_t = j)p(x_{t+1:T}^1, x_{t+1:T}^2, ..., x_{t+1:T}^N | q_t = j)}$$

$$= \frac{\frac{p(x_{1:t}^1, x_{1:t}^2, ..., x_{1:t}^N, q_t=i)p(x_{t+1:T}^1, x_{t+1:T}^2, ..., x_{t+1:T}^N | q_t=i)}{\prod_{n=1}^N \prod_{\tau=1}^T p(x_\tau^n) \prod_{n=1}^N \prod_{\tau=t+1}^T p(x_\tau^n)}}{\sum_j \frac{p(x_{1:t}^1, x_{1:t}^2, ..., x_{1:t}^N, q_t=j)p(x_{t+1:T}^1, x_{t+1:T}^2, ..., x_{t+1:T}^N | q_t=j)}{\prod_{n=1}^N \prod_{\tau=1}^t p(x_\tau^n) \prod_{n=1}^N \prod_{\tau=t+1}^T p(x_\tau^n)}}$$

$$= \frac{\alpha_s(i,t)\beta_s(i,t)}{\sum_j \alpha_s(j,t)\beta_s(j,t)} \tag{25}$$

We remind that all multi-stream recursions are processed through a (Markov) model M encoding some prior knowledge (e.g. topological constraints).

3.1   Ergodic HMM with Uniform Transition Probabilities

As already mentioned above, all single stream, as well as multi-stream α and β recursions are applied through a given HMM topology representing some prior knowledge. When no specific prior knowledge is available, the simplest solution consists in using ergodic HMM with uniform transition probabilities, i.e. $p(q_t = i|q_{t-1} = j) = K$. In this case, the multi-stream gamma estimation equation (25) can be rewritten as follows:

$$
\begin{aligned}
\gamma(i,t) &= p(q_t = i|x^1_{1:T}, x^2_{1:T}, ..., x^N_{1:T}) \\
&= \frac{\alpha_s(i,t)\beta_s(i,t)}{\sum_j \alpha_s(j,t)\beta_s(j,t)} \\
&= \frac{\frac{\prod_{n=1}^N \alpha_s^n(i,t)}{p(q_t=i)^{N-1}}\beta_s(i,t)}{\sum_j \frac{\prod_{n=1}^N \alpha_s^n(j,t)}{p(q_t=j)^{N-1}}\beta_s(j,t)} \\
&= \frac{\prod_{n=1}^N \frac{p(q_t=i|x_t^n)}{p(q_t=i)} \frac{\sum_k p(q_t=i|q_{t-1}=k)\alpha_s^n(k,t-1)}{p(q_t=i)^{N-1}}\beta_s(i,t)}{\sum_j \prod_{n=1}^N \frac{p(q_t=j|x_t^n)}{p(q_t=j)} \frac{\sum_k p(q_t=j|q_{t-1}=k)\alpha_s^n(k,t-1)}{p(q_t=j)^{N-1}}\beta_s(j,t)}
\end{aligned}
\tag{26}
$$

Assuming ergodic uniform transition probabilities, the sum over k factors in above numerator and denominator and also β_s factors are identical and can thus be droped. Moreover, the state prior $p(q_t = i)$ is constant, thus yielding:

$$
\gamma(i,t) = \frac{\prod_{n=1}^N p(q_t = i|x_t^n)}{\sum_j \prod_{n=1}^N p(q_t = j|x_t^n)}
\tag{27}
$$

Therefore, the multi-stream state gamma is the normalized product of posteriors (MLP outputs) and gammas do not capture context and specific prior knowledge. In this case, the multi-stream gamma estimation method can be interpreted as a principled way to combine two streams of features.

3.2   Higher Level Posterior Estimation

In case of having phone-based ASR system and modeling each phone with more than one state, state gamma posteriors should be integrated to phone level posteriors. In the following, we call these phone posteriors as "phone gammas" $\gamma_p(i,t)$, which can be expressed in terms of state gammas $\gamma(i,t)$ as follows:

$$
\begin{aligned}
\gamma_p(i,t) &\triangleq p(p_t = i|x^1_{1:T}, x^2_{1:T}, ..., x^N_{1:T}) = \sum_{j=1}^{N_q} p(p_t = i, q_t = j|x^1_{1:T}, x^2_{1:T}, ..., x^N_{1:T}) \\
&= \sum_{j=1}^{N_q} p(p_t = i|q_t = j, x^1_{1:T}, x^2_{1:T}, ..., x^N_{1:T})p(q_t = j|x^1_{1:T}, x^2_{1:T}, ..., x^N_{1:T}) \\
&= \sum_{j=1}^{N_q} p(p_t = i|q_t = j, x^1_{1:T}, x^2_{1:T}, ..., x^N_{1:T})\gamma(j,t)
\end{aligned}
\tag{28}
$$

where p_t is a phone at time t. Probability $p(p_t = i|q_t = j, x^1_{1:T}, x^2_{1:T}, ..., x^N_{1:T})$ represents the probability of being in a given phone i at time t knowing to be in the state j at time t. If there is no parameter sharing between phones, this is deterministic and equal to 1 or 0. Otherwise, this can be estimated from the training data. In this work, we model each phone with one state in the multi-stream HMM, therefore in this particular case, state gammas are equal to phone gammas and we do not need to integrate state gammas to phone gammas.

4 Hierarchical Multi-stream Posterior-Based ASR

In this section, the configuration of our hierarchical multi-stream speech recognition system is explained. The main idea is to combine N (two in our case) streams of features which have complementary information by estimating gamma posteriors through a multi-stream HMM configuration. These posteriors capture the whole context in all streams as well as prior knowledge (e.g. topological constraints) encoded in the model, thus they are expected to be more informative than individual streams of features before the combination. Figure 1 shows our hierarchical multi-stream posterior based ASR system. This hierarchical system consists of three layers: The first layer gets two streams of raw features (PLPs and TRAPs) extracted from speech signal, and estimates two streams of posteriors using MLPs. This is called "single stream posterior estimation". These streams of posteriors are used after turning to scaled likelihoods in the second layer of hierarchy, which is a multi-stream posterior based HMM to obtain the estimates of multi stream state gammas. The state gammas are then used as features after some transformations (KLT) for the third layer of hierarchy which is a standard HMM/GMM train/inference back-end. In the following, some issues related to the system is explained in more details:

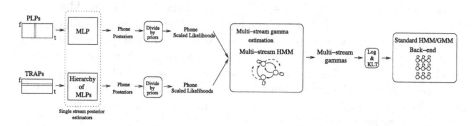

Fig. 1. Hierarchical multi-stream posterior based ASR: Two streams of posteriors are estimated form PLP and TRAP features using MLPs, then these posteriors are turned into scaled likelihoods by dividing by the priors. The resulting two streams of scaled likelihoods are fed to the multi-stream HMM. The multi-stream gammas are estimated using multi-stream forward α_s and backward β_s recursions as explained in Section 3. These multi-stream gamma posteriors are used after some transformations (KLT) as features for a standard HMM/GMM back-end system.

4.1 Input Streams of Features

The first step in developing the system is to choose two sets of features having complementary information. Spectral (cepstral) features and features having long temporal information are suitable candidates. We used PLP cepstral features[1] [10] and TRAPs temporal features [11] as input feature streams for the system. TRAP features represent temporal energy pattern for different bands over a long context, while PLPs represent full short-term spectrum (possibility with very short time context).

4.2   Single Stream Posterior Estimation

In the first layer of hierarchy, the two input feature streams (PLPs and TRAPs) are processed by MLPs to estimate posterior probabilities of context-independent phones. For PLP cepstral features, usually 9 frames of PLP coefficients and their first and second order derivatives are concatenated as the input for a trained MLP to estimate the posterior probabilities of context-independent phones [5]. The phonetic class is defined with respect to the center of 9 frames. For the case of TRAPs, different bands temporal energy pattern over 0.5 to 1 second TRAP temporal vector are first processed by band classifier MLPs, then the outputs of these band classifiers are fed as inputs for a merger MLP [11]. The Merger MLP outputs gives the posterior estimate for context-independent phones. Again, phonetic class is defined with respect to the center of 0.5-1 second temporal vector. In the reminder of the paper, we call these single stream posterior estimates as PLP and TRAP posteriors.

4.3   Multi-stream Posterior Estimation

Having two stream of posteriors estimated from PLP and TRAP features using MLPs, the next step in the hierarchy is to estimate state gammas through the multi-stream HMM configuration. Posteriors are first divided by priors to obtain scaled likelihoods, i.e.: $\frac{p(x_t^n|q_t=i)}{p(x_t^n)} = \frac{p(q_t=i|x_t^n)}{p(q_t=i)}$, and then these scaled likelihoods are used in multi-stream forward α_s and backward β_s recursions according to (17, 23) to obtain estimates of state gammas. In this work, we model each phone with one state, thus state gammas are equal to phone gammas. Moreover, we assume ergodic uniform transition probabilities between phones, therefore as explained in Section 3.1, the multi-stream state gamma estimation can be interpreted as a probabilistic principled way to combine different streams of features which have complementary information.

5   Experiments and Results

Results are presented on OGI digits [13] and a reduced vocabulary version of the DARPA Conversational Telephone Speech-to-text (CTS) task (1'000 words) databases [6]. We used PLP and TRAP features as input streams to our system.

The PLP cepstral coefficients [10] are extracted using 25-ms window with 10-ms shifts. At each frame, 13 PLP coefficients, their first-order and second-order derivatives are extracted and concatenated to make one feature vector.

---

[1] In the reminder of the paper, "PLP cepstral features" stands for PLP cepstral coefficients and their first and second order derivatives.

For extracting TRAP features, the short-term critical band spectrum is computed in 25-ms windows with 10-ms shifts and the logarithm of the estimated critical band spectral densities are taken. There are 15 bands. For each band, 50 frames before and after the center of analysis is taken resulting in 101 points long temporal TRAP vector [11].

In this work, each phone is modeled by one state in the multi-stream HMM and we assume ergodic uniform transition probabilities between phones.

5.1   OGI Digits

The task is recognition of eleven words (American English Digits). The test set was derived from the subset of CSLU Speech Corpus [13], containing utterances of connected digits. There are 2169 utterances (12437 words, about 1.7 hours) in the test set. Training set contains 2547 utterances (about 1.2 hours). This set is also derived from CSLU Speech Corpus and utterances containing only connected digits are used. Standard HMM/GMM train/inference back-end system is based on HTK. There are 29 context-independent phonetic classes. The subset of OGI stories [16] plus a subset of OGI numbers [13] was used for training MLPs for single stream posterior estimation. This set has in total 3798 utterances with total length about 4.5 hours.

Two streams of posteriors (one from PLP features and the other one from TRAP features) are estimated as explained in Section 4.2 for the test and training set. They are then turned into scaled likelihoods and used in the multi-stream HMM layer to get the estimates of state (phone) gammas. These gamma posteriors are fed as features (after gaussianization and decorrelation through log and KL transform) to the standard HMM/GMM layer. For comparison purposes, we also run the standard HMM/GMM system using single stream posterior estimates as features (after log and KLT) in order to obtain the baseline performance of single stream PLP and TRAP posteriors before the combination (This corresponds to PLP-TANDEM and TRAP-TANDEM methods). Moreover, we used an inverse entropy based combination method [12] to combine PLP and TRAP posteriors, and compare the combination performance with our method. Table 1 shows the result of recognition studies.The first column shows the features (after log and KLT) which are fed to standard HMM/GMM layer. The second column shows word error rate (WER). The first row shows the baseline performance of posteriors estimated using PLP features (the first stream). The second row shows the baseline performance of posteriors estimated using TRAP features

Table 1. Word error rates (WER) on OGI Digits task

Features	WER
PLP posteriors	3.6%
TRAP posteriors	4.8%
Inverse entropy combination	3.5%
Multi-stream gammas	**2.9%**

(the second stream). The third row shows the performance of features obtained by inverse entropy combination of PLP and TRAP posteriors and the fourth row shows the performance of our system which uses multi-stream gamma posteriors obtained by combining the mentioned streams of PLP and TRAP posteriors through the multi-stream HMM. The system using multi-stream gamma posteriors performs significantly better than the systems using baseline single stream posteriors before the combination and also inverse entropy based combination.

5.2   DARPA CTS Task

The use of multi-stream gamma estimation method was further evaluated on a conversational telephone speech (CTS) recognition task. The training set for this task contained 15011 utterances (about 15.9 hours) and the test set contained 951 utterances (about 0.6 hour) of male speakers CTS speech randomly selected from the Fisher Corpus and the Switchboard Corpus. There were 46 context-independent phonetic classes in this task. The layer estimating single stream posteriors were trained on the same training set using PLP and TRAP features. The standard HMM/GMM system is based on HTK. A 1000 word dictionary with multi-words and multi-pronunciations was used for decoding, using a bigram language model.

Similar experiments as the case of OGI Digits database was repeated. Table 2 shows the recognition results. Again, multi-stream gamma combination gives significant improvement over PLP and TRAP posteriors before the combination and also inverse entropy combination.

Table 2. Word error rates (WER) on CTS task

Features	WER
PLP posteriors	48.7%
TRAP posteriors	55.1%
Inverse entropy combination	48.7%
Multi-stream gammas	**46.8%**

6   Conclusions and Future Work

In this paper, we proposed a new, principled, theoretical framework for hierarchical estimation/use of posteriors and multi-stream feature combination, and we presented initial results for this theory. We explained how the posterior estimation can be enhanced by combining different streams of features and taking into account all possible information present in the data (whole acoustic context), as well as possible prior information (e.g. topological constraints). We used these posteriors as features for a standard HMM/GMM system. We showed our system performs significantly better as compared to the PLP-TANDEM and TRAP-TANDEM baseline systems and inverse entropy combination method on two different ASR tasks. This theoretical framework allows designing optimal hierarchical multi-stream systems since it proposes a principled way for combining different streams of features by hierarchical posterior estimation and introducing context and prior knowledge to get better evidences in the form of posteriors.

In this work, we investigated the particular case of assuming ergodic uniform transition probabilities. We will further investigate this method by introducing prior knowledge encoded in appropriate model to get better estimates of posteriors. The state gammas can be also used for reestimating MLP parameters in the single stream posterior estimation layer. In this case, the MLPs used for estimating single stream phone posteriors from acoustic features are retrained with multi-stream phone gamma posteriors as new labels.

Acknowledgments

This project was jointly funded by the European AMI and PASCAL projects and the IM2 Swiss National Center of Competence in Research. The authors want to thank Petr Fousek for providing PLP and TRAP features and Hynek Hermansky for helpful discussions.

References

1. Bourlard, H. and Morgan, N., "Connectionist Speech Recognition – A Hybrid Approach", Kluwer Academic Publishers, 1994.
2. Mangu, L., Brill, E., and Stolcke, A., "Finding consensus in speech recognition: word error minimization and other applications of confusion networks", *Computer, Speech and Language*, Vol. 14, pp. 373-400, 2000.
3. Abdou, S. and Scordilis, M.S., "Beam search pruning in speech recognition using a posterior-based confidence measure", *Speech Communication*, pp. 409-428, 2004.
4. Bernardis, G. and Bourlard, H., "Improving posterior confidence measures in hybrid HMM/ANN speech recognition system", *Proc. ICSLP*, pp. 775-778, 1998.
5. Hermansky, H., Ellis, D.P.W., and Sharma, S., "Connectionist Feature Extraction for Conventional HMM Systems", *Proc. ICASSP*, 2000.
6. Bourlard, H., Bengio, S., Magimai Doss, M., Zhu, Q., Mesot, B., and Morgan, N., "Towards using hierarchical posteriors for flexible automatic speech recognition systems", *DARPA RT-04 Workshop*, November 2004, also IDIAP-RR 04-58.
7. Ketabdar, H., Vepa, J., Bengio, S., and Bourlard, H., "Developing and enhancing posterior based speech recognition systems", *IDIAP RR 05-23*, 2005.
8. Bourlard, H. and Dupont, S., "Sub-band-based speech recognition", *Proc. IEEE Intl. Conf. on Acoustics, Speech and Signal Processing*, pp. 1251-1254, 1997.
9. Dupont, S. and Luettin, J., "Audio-visual speech modeling for continuous speech recognition", *IEEE Transactions on Multimedia*, vol. 2. no. 3, pp. 141-151, 2000.
10. Hermansky, H., "Perceptual linear predictive (PLP) analysis of speech". *J. Acoust. Soc. Am.*, vol. 87, no. 4, pp. 1738-1752, 1990.
11. Hermansky, H., Sharma, S., "TRAPs: classifiers of TempoRAl Patterns", *Proc. ICSLP-98*, Australia, November 98.
12. Misra, H., Bourlard, H. and Tyagi V., "New entropy based combination rules in HMM/ANN multi-stream ASR", *Proc. ICASSP*, 2003.

13. Cole, R., Fanty, M., Noel, M. and Lander T. "Telephone Speech Corpus Development at CSLU", In Proc. of ISCLP (Yokohama, Japan, 1994), pp. 1815-1818.
14. Rabiner, L. R., "A tutorial on hidden Markov models and selective applications in speech recognition", *Proc. IEEE*, vol. 77, pp. 257-286, 1989.
15. Bengio, S., "Joint training of multi-stream HMMs", *to be published as IDIAP-RR 05-22*, 2005.
16. Cole, R., Noel, M., Lander T. and Durham T. "New Telephone Speech Corpora at CSLU", In Proc. of EUROSPEECH (Madrid, Spain, 1995), pp. 821-824.

Variational Bayesian Methods for Audio Indexing

Fabio Valente and Christian Wellekens

Institut Eurecom,
Sophia Antipolis, France
{fabio.valente, christian.wellekens}@eurecom.fr

Abstract. In this paper we aim to investigate the use of Variational Bayesian methods for audio indexing purposes. Variational Bayesian (VB) techniques are approximated techniques for fully Bayesian learning. Contrarily to non Bayesian methods (e.g. Maximum Likelihood) or partially Bayesian criterion (e.g. Maximum a Posteriori), VB benefits from important model selection properties. VB learning is based on the Free Energy optimization; Free Energy can be used at the same time as an objective function and as a model selection criterion allowing simultaneous model learning/model selection. Here we explore the use of VB learning and VB model selection in a speaker clustering task comparing results with classical learning techniques (ML and MAP) and classical model selection criteria (BIC). Experiments are run on the evaluation data set NIST-1996 HUB-4 and results show that VB can outperform classical methods.

1   Introduction

Model selection is a main issue in many machine learning problems. In different real data applications an hypothesis on the model is done before proceeding with the learning task. If the hypothesized model does not respect the structure of experimental data, the effectiveness of the learning is strongly affected. Here the need comes for techniques that can select the model that best fit to data.

The probabilistic framework is largely used for model selection. It considers probabilities over different models and assumes that the best model is the one that maximizes model probability given the observed data i.e. given a model m and an observation data set D , best model maximizes $P(m|D)$. Depending on the model complexity, $P(m|D)$ cannot always be obtained in close form and approximated techniques must be considered instead. The most used approximations (e.g. BIC [1]) are sometimes inappropriate according to the considered application and need heuristic tuning to be effective. In this paper we discuss a new type of approximated method called Variational Learning (a.k.a. Ensemble Learning) that allows an approximated close form solution to the model selection problem. The key of Variational methods is the replacement of real unknown parameter distributions with approximated distributions (Variational distributions) that permit an analytical tractability of the solution. Obviously

S. Renals and S. Bengio (Eds.): MLMI 2005, LNCS 3869, pp. 307–319, 2006.
© Springer-Verlag Berlin Heidelberg 2006

the effectiveness of this approach depends on how close the approximated distributions are to real distributions.

We investigate here the use of Variational techniques in a speaker clustering task. This task often represents the first processing step in many audio indexing and speech recognition systems. Speaker clustering is formulated as a model selection problem in which the speaker number must be estimated. The most popular solution uses the BIC (see [2],[3]) that is actually true only asymptotically. In order to obtain reasonable results in the limited data case, an heuristic adjustment of the model selection criterion is done. It often gives serious tuning problems and final result is strongly affected. Variational methods are a finer approximation of the Bayesian integral and result more effective than BIC in many model selection tasks. Furthermore they allows simultaneous model learning and model selection in a fully Bayesian fashion.

The paper is organized as follows: in section 2 we discuss model selection problems, in section 3 we present the Variational Bayesian framework, in section 4 we present the speaker clustering model and experiments that compare VB and MAP/BIC, ML/BIC systems.

2   Model Selection

Let us consider a data set D and model set $Model = \{m\}$. In a probabilistic framework, model that fits data in the best way is the model that maximizes $P(m|D)$ i.e. the model probability given the data. Applying Bayes rule, we obtain:

$$P(m|D) = \frac{P(D|m)P(m)}{P(D)} \qquad (1)$$

where $P(D) = \sum_m P(D|m)P(m)$ does not depend on m. If prior probability over model $P(m)$ is uniform (i.e. no prior information over the model is available), the best model is the model that maximizes data evidence i.e. $P(D|m)$. Let us designate with θ the model parameter set and with $p(\theta|m)$ parameter set distribution. The data evidence can be obtained marginalizing model parameters w.r.t. their distributions i.e.

$$p(D|m) = \int p(D|\theta, m)\, p(\theta|m) d\theta \qquad (2)$$

Expression (2) is known as marginal-likelihood.

Marginal likelihood has the interesting property of penalizing models that have too many degree of freedom not necessary for modeling experimental data. This is also known as the Occam razor property (e.g. see [4]). The idea is that models with more free parameters can model a larger data set, resulting in a parameter probability $p(\theta|m)$ more spread over the parameter domain.

Unfortunately for many currently used models like Hidden Markov Models (HMM) or Gaussian Mixture Models (GMM), no close form solution is possible for marginal likelihood because of hidden variables. A common choice for overcoming this problem consists in simply ignoring the integral in (2); in this way the classical Maximum a Posteriori parameter estimation can be recovered i.e.

$$\theta_{MAP} = argmax_\theta \, p(D|\theta, m)p(\theta|m) \qquad (3)$$

The MAP approach is tractable but not fully Bayesian because it is a point estimation that just considers parameters instead of distributions over parameters.
Using a metaphor coming from physics, MAP just considers the 'density' instead
of the 'mass' of the distribution. MAP becomes a reasonable approximation when
parameter distribution is extremely peaked and the 'mass' of the distribution is
concentrated around the maximum but in general cases it can neglect important
contributions to the integral. On the other hand MAP criterion has no model
selection properties and approximation of the integral mass must be considered.
The most popular approximation technique is the Bayesian Information Criterion (BIC). BIC was first derived by Schwartz in [1]. It can be obtained from a
Laplace approximation of the Bayesian integral (2). The Laplace approximation
makes a local Gaussian approximation around the MAP parameter estimate $\hat{\theta}$
and is based on large data limit. Let us suppose that the cardinality of the data
set D is N, and that the number of free parameters θ is p, in this case the
BIC is:

$$log\,p(D|m)_{BIC} = log\,p(D|\hat{\theta}, m) - \frac{p}{2}ln\,N \qquad (4)$$

Expression (4) has an intuitive explanation: a more complicated model i.e. a
model with many free parameters p will result in a larger penalty term $\frac{p}{2}log\,N$
respect to a model with a smaller number of free parameters. BIC is a very
rude approximation of the Bayesian integral but presents many tractability advantages because it can be easily computed as long as a MAP estimation of
model parameter is available. As previously outlined BIC is based on a large
data limit that is rarely meet in real data problems. To overcome this limitation
and to make the criterion more effective in different situations, the penalty term
is generally multiplied by a threshold λ that is heuristically determined depending on the application. For example in audio indexing problems, a huge gain
in the model selection task is obtained manually modifying the penalty term
(see [3]) or using some validation data to find the optimal λ for a given data
set.

3   Variational Learning

Variational learning is a relatively new technique based on the use of approximated distributions instead of real distributions in order to obtain a tractable
learning task. Variational methods assume that the unknown posterior distri-
bution over parameter $p(\theta|D, m)$ can be approximated by another distribution
$q(\theta|D, m)$ that is actually the variational posterior distribution (or simply variational distribution) derived from data. Considering Jensen inequality it is possible to write:

$$log\,p(D|m) = log\int d\theta q(\theta|D, m)\frac{p(\theta|m)p(D, \theta|m)}{q(\theta|D, m)} \geq \int d\theta q(\theta|D, m)log\frac{p(D, \theta|m)}{q(\theta|D, m)} = F(\theta)$$

$$(5)$$

$F(\theta)$ is called variational free energy or ensemble learning energy and is a lower bound on the marginal log likelihood; variational learning aims to optimize the free energy w.r.t. variational distributions instead of the intractable marginal log likelihood $log\,p(D|m)$. One of the key point in this framework is the choice of the form for distribution $q(\theta|D, m)$ that must be close enough to the real unknown parameter distribution $p(\theta|D, m)$ and still of a tractable form. The difference between marginal log-likelihood and free energy is:

$$log\,p(D|m) - F(\theta) = KL(q(\theta|D, m)||p(\theta|D, m)) = - \int q(\theta|D, m)log\frac{p(\theta|D, m)}{q(\theta|D, m)}$$
(6)

Equation (6) means that variational learning actually minimizes the distance between the true posterior distribution and the variational posterior distributions. In the limit case, if $q(\theta|D, m) = p(\theta|D, m)$ the free energy is equal to the log-marginal likelihood.

3.1   Learning with Hidden Variables

A very appealing property of variational learning is its capacity of handling hidden variables. In fact hidden variables can be simply seen as stochastic variables (as parameters) with their own distributions. In some variational learning systems there is no difference between the way parameters and hidden variables are considered (e.g. see [6]). Let us define X the hidden variable set, it is possible to introduce a joint variational distribution over hidden variables and parameters $q(X, \theta|D, m)$ and applying again Jensen inequality we obtain:

$$log\,p(D|m) = \int p(D, X, \theta|m)\,d\theta\,dX \geq \int q(X, \theta|D, m)log\frac{p(D, X, \theta|m)}{q(X, \theta|D, m)} = F(\theta, X)$$
(7)

At this point another further approximation must be done in order to obtain a tractable form: in fact considering the joint variational distribution $q(\theta, X|D, m)$ of parameters and hidden variables can be a prohibitive task when the number of hidden variables is large. For this reason the independence between hidden variables and parameters is assumed i.e. $q(\theta, X|D, m) = q(\theta|D, m)q(X|D, m)$. Under this hypothesis, optimal variational posterior distributions that maximizes the free energy can be found using an EM-like algorithm (see [8]) also known as VBEM algorithm. In fact simply deriving the free energy w.r.t. $q(\theta|D, m)$ and $q(X|D, m)$, it is possible to obtain an iterative update equation system that will converge in a local maximum of the free energy. The equation system consists of an E-like step :

$$q(X|D, m) \propto e^{<log\,p(D, X|\theta, m)>_\theta}$$
(8)

and an M-like step:

$$q(\theta|D, m) \propto e^{<log\,p(D, X|\theta, m)>_X}p(\theta|m)$$
(9)

where $< . >_z$ means average w.r.t. z. This EM-like algorithm does not estimate any parameter (contrarily to MAP) but just parameter distributions. Under the factorization hypothesis it is possible to rewrite the free energy as follows:

$$F(\theta, X) = \int d\theta dX q(X|D, m)q(\theta|D, m)log[\frac{p(D, X, \theta|m)}{q(X|D, m)q(\theta|D, m)}]$$

$$= < log \frac{p(D, X|\theta, m)}{q(X|D, m)} >_{X,\theta} -KL[q(\theta|D, m)||p(\theta|m)] \quad (10)$$

The free energy can be seen as composed of two terms: a first term depending on data and variational distributions (over both parameters and hidden variables) and a second term that is the KL divergence between the variational distribution over parameters $q(\theta|D, m)$ and the prior distribution over parameters $p(\theta|m)$. By definition we have $KL[q(\theta|Y, m)||p(\theta|m)] \geq 0$ with equality when $q(\theta|Y, m) = p(\theta|m)$; this term acts like a sort of penalty term that penalizes models with more parameters. In fact models with many parameters will result in a sum of KL divergence term for each parameter. It is very interesting to notice that VB does not simply consider the number of parameters (like in the BIC) but it explicitly considers the divergence between posterior distributions and prior distributions. It can be shown that in large data limit this penalty term converges to the BIC penalty term (see [9]). Intuitively free energy is an interesting quantity for doing model selection as long as it approximates the Bayesian integral, we will consider a more rigorous framework in section 3.2.

Now that an efficient solution for handling hidden variables has been introduced, fully Bayesian learning is possible in many models previously intractable. For example variational learning in Hidden Markov Models is first introduced in [5] and in Gaussian Mixture Models is first introduced in [8]. The applicability of Variational Bayesian EM (VBEM) algorithm to a general model is studied in [7]. VBEM algorithm can be derived for conjugate-exponential models i.e. models that meet the following two conditions: 1) The complete data likelihood is in the exponential family; 2) The parameter prior is conjugate to the complete data likelihood. Many well known models satisfy those two conditions: Gaussian mixture models, Hidden Markov models, Factor Analyzer, Principal Component Analysis, etc.

3.2   Model Selection Using Free Energy

In this section we define a more rigorous framework for model selection using free energy. Let us consider the log marginal likelihood obtained integrating over all possible models $p(D) = \sum_m p(D|m)p(m)$ and let us introduce a variational posterior probability over models $q(m)$. Applying one more time Jensen inequality, it is possible to have:

$$log\, p(D) = log[\sum_m p(D|m)p(m)] \geq \sum_m q(m)[F_m + log\frac{p(m)}{q(m)}] \quad (11)$$

where $p(m)$ is a prior probability over the model and F_m is the free energy for model m. Again a bound on the log marginalized likelihood is derived. Deriving w.r.t. $q(m)$ and solving we obtain for the optimal variational distribution over models:

$$q(m) \propto exp\{F_m\}p(m) \tag{12}$$

that means that optimal posterior over model is proportional to the exponential of the free energy times the prior probability. If prior probability over models is uniform, $q(m)$ will depend on free energy only. It means that the free energy can be used for doing model selection instead of the real log marginal likelihood.

4   Variational Bayesian Speaker Clustering

The most popular approach to speaker clustering task consists in the use of an ergodic HMM [10] in which each state represents a speaker. Our system is based as well on a fully connected HMM with emission probabilities modeled by GMMs. In order to obtain a non-spare solution a duration constraint of D frames on the emission probabilities is imposed. Furthermore we assume that the probability of transition to state j is the same regardless the initial state i.e. $\alpha_{rj} = \alpha_{r'j} \; \forall r, r'$, where $j = \{1, ..., S\}$ with S the total number of states. To summarize let us designate $[O_1, ..., O_T]$ a sequence of T blocks of D consecutive frames $[O_{t1}, ..., O_{tD}]$ where D is the duration constraint. It is then possible to write the log-likelihood :

$$log\,P(O|\theta, m) = \sum_{t=1}^{T} log\,[\sum_{j=1}^{S} \alpha_j \{\prod_{p=1}^{D} \sum_{i=1}^{M} \beta_{ij} N(O_{tp}, \mu_{ij}, \Gamma_{ij})\}] \tag{13}$$

where S represents the number of states (that represent speakers), M Gaussian component that models each speaker, and $\theta = \{\beta_{ij}, \mu_{ij}, \Gamma_{ij}\}$ represents mixture model parameters (weights, means and Gaussians). If the state number S is known, model (13) can be learned using the Expectation-Maximization algorithm for both MAP and ML criteria.

As long as the number of speakers (i.e. states) is unknown, it must be estimated using a model selection criterion. Generally the BIC criterion is used. We consider here the Variational Bayesian framework for both model learning and model selection at the same time.

In VB methods prior distributions over parameters must be chosen; according to the discussion of section 3 we set those distributions as belonging to the conjugate exponential family. Let us consider now model in expression (13) and let us define following probability distributions over parameters:

$$P(\alpha_j) = Dir(\lambda_{\alpha 0}) \; P(\beta_{ij}) = Dir(\lambda_{\beta 0})$$
$$P(\mu_{ij}|\Gamma_{ij}) = N(\rho_0, \xi_0\Gamma_{ij}) \; P(\Gamma_{ij}) = W(\nu_0, \Phi_0) \tag{14}$$

where $Dir()$, $N()$, $W()$ are respectively Dirichlet, Normal, Wishart distributions and $\{\lambda_{\alpha 0}, \lambda_{\beta 0}, \rho_0, \xi_0, \nu_0, \Phi_0\}$ are hyperparameters. We assume here a fully tied prior distributions i.e. $\lambda_{\alpha 0} = \lambda_{\beta 0} = \xi_0 = \nu_0 = \tau$, $\Phi_0 = \tau \times I$ where I is an identity matrix and $\rho = \bar{y}$ where $\bar{y}$ is the average of all file observations. Parameter τ is also known as relevance factor.

Model (13) with prior distribution (14) belongs to the conjugate-exponential family so the EM-like algorithm can be applied. Variational posterior distributions have the same form of prior distributions with updated hyperparameters i.e.:

$$P(\alpha_j) = Dir(\lambda_{\alpha\,j}) \ \ P(\beta_{ij}) = Dir(\lambda_{\beta\,ij})$$
$$P(\mu_{ij}|\Gamma_{ij}) = N(\rho_{ij}, \xi_0\Gamma_{ij}) \ \ P(\Gamma_{ij}) = W(\nu_{ij}, \Phi_{ij}) \tag{15}$$

Once variational posterior are estimated, a close form for the free energy can be obtained and used for model selection purposes. The EM-like algorithm for model (13) is derived in the appendix.

4.1 Experiments

In this section we compare experimentally VB system, ML/BIC system and MAP/BIC system in a speaker clustering task on the evaluation data set NIST-1996 HUB-4. Acoustic features consist of 12 MFCC coefficients. The training procedure uses the following algorithm: the system is initialized with a large speaker number $M_{initial}$ then optimal parameters are learned using three criteria (VB,ML,MAP). Initial speaker number is then reduced progressively from $M_{initial}$ to 1 and parameter learning is done for each new initial speaker number. Optimal speaker number is estimated scoring different models with VB free energy (that was used as objective function in the training step) and with the BIC (for MAP and VB). It is important to outline that when $M_{initial}$ is big VB prunes models to a smaller number of final speaker.

In order to evaluate the quality of clustering we use concepts of cluster purity and speaker purity introduced respectively in [11] and [12]. We consider in all our tests an additional cluster for non-speech events. Using the same notation of [12], let us define:

- R: number of speakers
- S: number of clusters
- n_{ij}: total number of frames in cluster i spoken by speaker j
- $n_{j.}$: total number of frames spoken by speaker j, $j = 0$ means non-speech frames
- $n_{.i}$: total number of frames in cluster i
- N: total number of frames in the file
- N_s: total number of speech frames

It is now possible to define the cluster purity p_i and the speaker purity q_j:

$$p_i = \sum_{j=0}^{R} \frac{n_{ij}^2}{n_{.i}^2} \ \ q_j = \sum_{i=0}^{S} \frac{n_{ij}^2}{n_{j.}^2} \tag{16}$$

Definitions of *acp (average cluster purity)* and *asp (average speaker purity)* follow:

$$acp = \frac{1}{N} \sum_{i=0}^{S} p_i \, n_{.i} \quad asp = \frac{1}{N_s} \sum_{j=1}^{R} q_j \, n_{.j} \tag{17}$$

In order to define a criterion that takes care of both *asp* and *acp*, the geometrical mean is used:

$$K = \sqrt{asp \cdot acp} \tag{18}$$

We present three different scores for each system: a score obtained initializing the system with the real speaker number obtained from labels (designed as (known)), the best score obtained (designed as (best))and the score of the selected model given by BIC or VB score (designed as (selected)).

Table 1. Results on NIST 1996 HUB-4 evaluation test for speaker clustering: ML/BIC vs. VB with non-informative priors

File	File 1				File 2				File 3				File 4			
	N_c	acp	asp	K	N_c	acp	asp	K	N_c	acp	asp	K	N_c	acp	asp	K
(a) ML (known)	8	0.60	0.84	0.71	14	0.76	0.67	0.72	16	0.75	0.74	0.75	21	0.72	0.65	0.68
(b) ML (best)	10	0.80	0.86	0.83	9	0.72	0.77	0.74	15	0.77	0.83	0.80	12	0.63	0.80	0.71
(c) ML (selected)	13	0.80	0.86	0.83	16	0.84	0.63	0.73	15	0.77	0.83	0.80	21	0.76	0.60	0.68
(d) VB (known)	8	0.70	0.91	0.80	14	0.75	0.82	0.78	16	0.68	0.86	0.76	21	0.60	0.80	0.69
(e) VB (best)	12	0.85	0.89	0.87	14	0.84	0.81	0.82	14	0.75	0.90	0.82	13	0.63	0.80	0.71
(f) VB (selected)	15	0.85	0.89	0.87	14	0.84	0.81	0.82	14	0.75	0.90	0.82	13	0.64	0.72	0.68

Let us consider at first results of ML/BIC and VB. In order to compare them in fairest way VB priors are initialized as non-informative priors (i.e. small relevance factor τ that brings no information). The system is initialized with $M_{initial} = 35$ speakers modeled by a 15 components GMM. Results are shown in table 1. First of all, VB baseline and best results (lines d-e) are higher than the ML/BIC results (lines a-b) on the first three files while they are almost similar on the last one. It is very important to notice that on the first three files the VB selected model corresponds to the best model; this shows the fact that the VB bound is a very effective metrics for performing model selection. Results in table 1 for ML/BIC refers to values selected using $\lambda = 2$: for this threshold value, BIC selected models are near to the best ML model (even if their K score are lower compared to VB scores). Anyway results in the ML/BIC system are extremely sensitive to the value of λ. In File 1 inferred speaker number is far away from the real speaker number probably because of the fact that a big part of the file is non-speech events that are clustered in many different clusters: anyway final K is high. In File 2 and File 3 inferred speaker number is near to real speaker number (File 2 contains very few non-speech parts). Finally in File 4 BIC infers the right cluster number while VB does not: anyway final K score is the same for BIC and ML. As we outlined in section 3.2, VB should infer the best Gaussian component number per cluster together with the best speaker number.

Figure 1 plots on a double Y axis graph final Gaussian components (left Y axis) and observation number assigned to a cluster (right Y axis). It is easy to notice that small amount of data assigned to a cluster results in a smaller number of final Gaussian components; on the other hand a large amount of data results in a model that keeps all Gaussian components (15 in our case). In Figure 2 free energy and score K are plotted on the same graph w.r.t. number of speakers for file 1. The free energy follows closely the score K for all considered number of speakers resulting in an extremely useful criterion for inferring the best system (similar graphs can be obtained for the other 3 files). As final remark we can notice that the best score never corresponds to the score obtained initializing the system with the real speaker number.

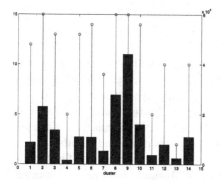 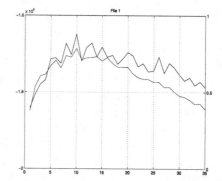

Fig. 1. Thick line (left Y axis): final Gaussian components vs. cluster number; big line (right Y axis): observation number assigned to a cluster vs. cluster number

Fig. 2. Blue line (right Y axis): free energy vs. number of clusters (states); Green line (left Y axis): K vs. number of clusters; Free energy follows the clustering score

Another interesting result can be obtained comparing the VB method with another partially Bayesian method like the MAP. In fact MAP needs as well prior distributions but does not produce any posterior distributions contrarily to VB. MAP and VB can be initialized with the same prior distributions that can be obtained from some previous knowledge on the data. This is the idea of all adaptation methods that initialize prior distributions with a general speaker model called Universal Background Model (UBM). We want to compare here the adaptation obtained with the MAP criterion with the adaptation obtained with the VB criterion. In the MAP system the model selection is the BIC while in the VB system the free energy is used. The UBM used is a 32 component GMM estimated from the BN96 HUB4 training data set. The system is initialized with $M_{initial} = 35$ speakers and results are again provided in terms of average cluster purity, average speaker purity and $K = \sqrt{acp \cdot asp}$.

Table 2 shows results on the four files. Line (a) shows MAP results when the speaker number is a priori known, line (b) shows the best score obtained by the MAP system changing speaker number from $M_{initial} = 35$. Line (c) shows

Table 2. Results on NIST 1996 HUB-4 evaluation test for speaker clustering: MAP/BIC vs. VB with informative priors

File	File 1				File 2				File 3				File 4			
	N_c	acp	asp	K	N_c	acp	asp	K	N_c	acp	asp	K	N_c	acp	asp	K
(a) MAP (known)	8	0.52	0.72	0.62	14	0.68	0.78	0.73	16	0.71	0.77	0.74	18	0.65	0.69	0.67
(b) MAP (best)	20	0.81	0.84	0.83	22	0.84	0.80	0.82	29	0.78	0.74	0.76	18	0.65	0.69	0.67
(c) MAP (selected)	15	0.80	0.81	0.81	18	0.78	0.85	0.81	16	0.69	0.77	0.73	20	0.63	0.64	0.64
(d) VB (known)	8	0.68	0.88	0.77	14	0.69	0.80	0.74	16	0.74	0.83	0.78	21	0.67	0.73	0.70
(e) VB (best)	22	0.83	0.85	0.84	18	0.85	0.87	0.86	22	0.82	0.82	0.82	20	0.69	0.72	0.70
(f) VB (selected)	22	0.83	0.85	0.84	19	0.87	0.80	0.83	16	0.78	0.79	0.79	19	0.67	0.73	0.70

results for MAP system with BIC selection. Lines (d),(e) and (f) are analogous to lines (a), (b) and (c) but model learning and model selection is done using VB learning. We actually present in line (c) the best results obtained with an empirical threshold set to $\lambda = 0.4$.

First of all we can notice that on the three considered situation VB always outperforms the MAP/BIC framework. Probably the most interesting result comes from best results obtained from the two approaches (lines (b) and (e)) that shows that VB does not simply make selection better than MAP but can also adapt a model that holds a higher score. Results with informative priors are still comparable to results with non-informative priors described in table 1.

Inferred cluster number is near to real speaker number for file 3 and file 4 while it is definitely far from reality in file 1 and file 2. Actually final cluster number obtained with informative priors is always higher than the one obtained using non-informative priors described in table 1. It can easily explained considering the fact that models are adapted from a background model giving origin to some small spurious clusters that are not merged together. For instance in file 1 the real cluster number is 8 while the inferred cluster number is 22, anyway values of *acp* and *asp* are high showing a good clustering; this is probably due to the fact there are many small clusters of speech and non-speech that are not merged together.

The use of informative priors (i.e. a background model) for speaker clustering presents the advantage that robust models can be obtained with small amount of data. Sometimes a speaker does not provide enough speech to generate a model and in systems without prior information it is simply clustered together with other speakers: that explains the fact in our previous non-informative prior system (see table 1), inferred cluster number is smaller. Anyway a drawback comes from the quality of the background model: if for any reason it is not a good prior model for the current speech, the same speaker may be split in more clusters. This is a very important issue in Broadcast news segmentation because speech is often corrupted by many noise sources (e.g. music, background speech, various noises) that are obviously unpredictable by the background model; in those cases an absence of prior information may be more efficient (for clustering) than a wrong prior information. For this reason the system would definitively benefits of a preliminary step of speech/non-speech discrimination.

5   Conclusions

In this paper we have studied a speaker clustering system based on the VB framework for model learning and model selection with non-informative and informative (i.e. an UBM model is used for prior distributions initialization). We compared results with a ML/BIC system and a MAP/BIC system. VB outperforms both approaches both in model learning and in model selection.

References

[1] Schwartz G., "Estimation of the dimension of a model",Annals of Statistics, 6, 1978.

[2] Chen S. and Gopalakrishnan P. "Speaker, environment and channel change detection and clustering via the Bayesian Information Criterion", Proceedings of the DARPA Workshop,1998.

[3] Tritschler A. and Gopinath R,"Improved speaker segmentation and segments clustering using the Bayesian information criterion",Proceedings of Eurospeech'99,679–682,1999.

[4] MacKay D. J. C., "Probable networks and plausible predictions-a review of practical Bayesian methods for supervised neural networks",Network:Comput. Neural Syst.,6,469–505,1995.

[5] MacKay D. J. C. "Ensemble Learning for Hidden Markov Models",/www.inference.phy.cam.ac.uk/mackay/abstracts/ensemblePaper.html1997.

[6] Bishop C. M. and Winn J.,"Structured variational distributions in VIBES", Proceedings Artificial Intelligence and Statistics,C. M. Bishop and B. Frey editors,Society for Artificial Intelligence and Statistics,2003.

[7] Beal M.,"Variational Algorithm for Approximate Bayesian Inference",2003,PhD thesis, The Gatsby Computational Neuroscience Unit, University College London

[8] Attias H. "A variational Bayesian framework for graphical models",Advances in Neural Information Processing Systems,12,2000,209–215.

[9] Attias H.,"Inferring parameters and structures of latent variable models by Variational Bayes",Proceedings of the 15th Conference on Uncertainty in Artificial Intelligence,21–30,1999.

[10] Olsen J. O., "Separation of speakers in audio data", EUROSPEECH 1995, pp. 355-358.

[11] Solomonoff A., Mielke A., Schmidt, Gish H.," Clustering speakers by their voices", ICASSP 98, pp. 557-560

[12] Lapidot I. "SOM as Likelihood Estimator for Speaker Clustering",EUROSPEECH 2003.

Appendix

In this appendix we give details the EM-like algorithm for variational Bayesian learning for model 13. Two kinds of latent variables x and z must be considered here: a variable x that designate the speaker (or equivalent state) that is speaking, and z (conditioned to x) that designate the Gaussian component that has emitted the observation. We assume prior distributions as (14). The E-like step i.e. expression (8) for hidden variables x and z can be written as:

$$q(x_t, z_{tp}|O_{tp}) = q(z_{tp}|O_{tp}, x_t)q(x_t|O_{tp})$$
$$\propto exp\{< log\alpha_{x_t} > + < log\beta_{x_t,z_{tp}} > + < logP(O_{tp}|x_t, z_{tp}) >\} \tag{19}$$

Developing (19), it is possible to derive $\tilde{\gamma}_{x_t=j} = q(x_t|O_{tp})$ and $\tilde{\gamma}_{z_{tp}=i|x_t=j} = q(z_{tp}|O_{tp}, x_t)$ where j is the hidden state and i is the hidden Gaussian.

$$\tilde{\gamma}^*_{z_{tp}=i|x_t=j} = \tilde{\beta}_{ij}\, \tilde{\Gamma}_{ij}^{1/2}\, exp\{-E\}\, exp\{\frac{-g}{2\nu_{ij}}\} \text{ with } E = \frac{1}{2}(O_{tp} - \rho_{tp})^T \bar{\Gamma}_{ij}(O_{tp} - \rho_{tp}) \tag{20}$$

$$\tilde{\gamma}_{z_{tp}=i|x_t=j} = q(\gamma_{z_{tp}} = i|\gamma_{x_t} = j) = \frac{\tilde{\gamma}^*_{z_{tp}=i|x_t=j}}{\sum_i \tilde{\gamma}^*_{z_{tp}=i|x_t=j}} \tag{21}$$

$$\tilde{\gamma}^*_{x_t=j} = \tilde{\alpha}_j \prod_{p=1}^{D} \sum_{i=1}^{M} \tilde{\gamma}^*_{z_{tp}=i|x_t=j} \tag{22}$$

$$\tilde{\gamma}_{x_t=j} = q(\gamma_{x_t} = j) = \frac{\tilde{\gamma}^*_{x_t=j}}{\sum_j \tilde{\gamma}^*_{x_t=j}} \tag{23}$$

where g is the dimension of acoustic vectors. Parameters expected values can be computed as follows:

$$log\, \tilde{\alpha}_j = \Psi(\lambda_{\alpha_j}) - \Psi(\sum_j \lambda_{\alpha_j}); \quad log\, \tilde{\beta}_{ij} = \Psi(\lambda_{\beta_{ij}}) - \Psi(\sum_j \lambda_{\beta_{ij}}); \tag{24}$$

$$log\, \tilde{\Gamma}_{ij} = \sum_{i=1}^{g} \Psi((\nu_{ij} + 1 - i)/2) - log|\Phi_{ij}| + glog2; \quad \bar{\Gamma}_{ij} = \nu_{ij}\Phi_{ij}^{-1}; \tag{25}$$

where Ψ is the digamma function. In the M step, we know that posterior distributions will have the same form of prior distributions i.e. distributions (15). Re-estimation formulas for parameters are given by:

$$\alpha_j = \frac{\sum_{t=1}^{T} \tilde{\gamma}_{x_t=j}}{T} \tag{26}$$

$$\beta_{ij} = \frac{\sum_{t=1}^{T} \sum_{p=1}^{D} \tilde{\gamma}_{x_t=j}\tilde{\gamma}_{z_{tp}=i|x_t=j}}{\sum_{t=1}^{T} \sum_{p=1}^{D} \tilde{\gamma}_{x_t=j}} \tag{27}$$

$$\mu_{ij} = \frac{\sum_{t=1}^{T} \sum_{p=1}^{D} \tilde{\gamma}_{x_t=j}\tilde{\gamma}_{z_{tp}=i|x_t=j}O_{tp}}{\sum_{t=1}^{T} \sum_{p=1}^{D} \tilde{\gamma}_{x_t=j}\tilde{\gamma}_{z_{tp}=i|x_t=j}} \tag{28}$$

$$\Gamma_{ij} = \frac{\sum_{t=1}^{T} \sum_{p=1}^{D} \tilde{\gamma}_{x_t=j}\tilde{\gamma}_{z_{tp}=i|x_t=j}(O_{tp} - \mu_{ij})^T(O_{tp} - \mu_{ij})}{\sum_{t=1}^{T} \sum_{p=1}^{D} \tilde{\gamma}_{x_t=j}\tilde{\gamma}_{z_{tp}=i|x_t=j}} \tag{29}$$

and hyperparameter re-estimation formulas are given by:

$$\lambda_{\alpha_j} = \sum_{t=1}^{T} N_j + \lambda_{\alpha 0}; \quad \lambda_{\beta_{ij}} = N_{ij} + \lambda_{\beta 0}; \quad \rho_{ij} = \frac{N_{ij}\,\mu_{ij} + \xi_0\,\rho_0}{N_{ij} + \rho_0}; \quad (30)$$

$$\Phi_{ij} = N_{ij}\,\Gamma_{ij} + \frac{N_{ij}\xi_0(\mu_{ij} - \rho_0)(\mu_{ij} - \rho_0)^T}{N_{ij} + \rho_0} + \Phi_0; \quad (31)$$

$$\nu_{ij} = N_{ij} + \nu_0; \quad \xi_{ij} = N_{ij} + \xi_0; \quad (32)$$

$$(33)$$

where $N_{ij} = \sum_{t=1}^{T} \sum_{p=1}^{D} \tilde{\gamma}_{x_t=j}\tilde{\gamma}_{z_{tp}=i|x_t=j}$ and $N_j = \sum_{t=1}^{T} \tilde{\gamma}_{x_t=j}$.

Microphone Array Driven Speech Recognition: Influence of Localization on the Word Error Rate*

Matthias Wölfel, Kai Nickel, and John McDonough

Institut für Theoretische Informatik, Universität Karlsruhe (TH),
Am Fasanengarten 5, 76131 Karlsruhe, Germany
{wolfel, nickel, jmcd}@ira.uka.de

Abstract. Interest within the *automatic speech recognition* (ASR) research community has recently focused on the recognition of speech captured with one or more microphones located in the far field, rather than
being mounted on a headset and positioned next to the speaker's mouth.
Far field ASR is a natural application for beamforming techniques using
an array of microphones. A prerequisite for applying such techniques,
however, is a reliable means of speaker localization. In this work, we
compare the accuracy of source localization systems based on only audio features, only video features, as well as a combination of audio and
video features using speech data collected during seminars held by actual
speakers. We also investigate the influence of source localization accuracy
on the *word error rate* (WER) of a far field ASR system, comparing the
WERs obtained with position estimates from several automatic source
localizers with those obtained from true speaker positions. Our results
reveal that accurate speaker localization is crucial for minimizing the
error rate of a far field ASR system.

1 Introduction

Interest within the *automatic speech recognition* (ASR) research community has
recently focused on the recognition of speech captured with one or more microphones located in the far field, rather than being mounted on a headset and
positioned next to the speaker's mouth. Far field ASR is a natural application for
beamforming techniques using an array of microphones, which has been shown
to provide superior sound capture capability with respect to a single microphone
both in terms of *signal-to-noise ratio* (SNR) and *word error rate* (WER). A pre-
requisite for applying such techniques, however, is a reliable means of speaker
localization. In prior work, we used an extended Kalman filter to directly update
position estimates in an audio only speaker localization system based on time
delay of arrival [1]. In other work, we enhanced our Kalman filter-based audio
localizer with video information to obtain more accurate position estimates [2].

---

* This work was sponsored by the European Union under the integrated project CHIL,
Computers in the Human Interaction Loop, contract number 506909.

S. Renals and S. Bengio (Eds.): MLMI 2005, LNCS 3869, pp. 320–331, 2006.

We have also proposed an audio-video source localizer based on a particle filter [3], which for some applications has several advantages as compared to the conventional Kalman filter. In this work, we compare the accuracy of source localization systems using only audio features, only video features, as well as a combination of audio and video features. We also investigate the influence of source localization accuracy on the WER of a far field ASR system, comparing the WERs obtained with position estimates from several automatic source localizers with those obtained from true speaker positions. To provide a baseline, we also compare the performance of our far field ASR system with the performance from a *close-talking microphone* (CTM).

The speech material used in our empirical studies was collected as part of the European Union integrated project CHIL [4], *Computers in the Human Interaction Loop*, which aims to make significant advances in the fields of speaker localization and tracking, speech activity detection and far field ASR. The corpus is comprised of seminars and oral presentations collected with both near and far field microphones. In addition to the audio sensors, the seminars were recorded by calibrated video cameras. This simultaneous audio-visual data capture enables the realistic evaluation of component technologies as was never possible with earlier data bases. One of the long term goals of the CHIL project is the reliable recognition of speech in a real reverberant environments, without any constraint on the number of simultaneously active sound sources. This problem is surpassingly difficult, given that speech recorded with far field microphones is generally degraded by both background noise and reverberation. Moreover, our speech material is challenging for other reasons: The style of the speech varies greatly, from spontaneous to read, and contains many of the artifacts seen in spontaneous speech, such as filled pauses, restarts and hyper articulation. Although the seminars were held in English, many of the speakers are non-native and hence speak with pronounced European accents. In addition, the seminars are most often concerned with automatic speech recognition and related topics, which implies that recognition vocabularies and language models built with the standard corpora of training text are poorly matched to this recognition task.

The remainder of this article is organized as follows. Section 2 describes the development of a baseline system at the Universität Karlsruhe (TH) including data collection and labeling, speaker localization, beamforming, language model training and acoustic training and adaptation. Section 3 presents a variety of source localization and ASR experiments using different types of acoustic source localization schemes. Finally, Section 4 concludes the presented work and give plans for future work.

2   Baseline System

The CHIL seminar data present significant challenges to both modeling components used in ASR, namely the language and acoustic models. With respect to the former, the currently available CHIL data primarily concentrates on technical topics with focus on speech research. This is a very specialized task that contains many acronyms and therefore is quite mismatched to typical language models currently used in the ASR literature. Furthermore, large portions of the data contain spontaneous, disfluent, and interrupted speech, due to the interactive nature of seminars and the varying degree of the speakers' comfort with their topics. On the acoustic modeling side, and in addition to the latter difficulty, the seminar speakers exhibit moderate to heavy German or other European accents in their English speech. The above problems are compounded by the fact that, at this early stage of the CHIL project, not enough data is available for training new language and acoustic models matched to this seminar task, and thus one has to rely on adapting existing models that exhibit gross mismatch to the CHIL data. Clearly, these challenges present themselves in both close-talking microphone data, as well as the far-field data captured using the *microphone array* (MA).

2.1   Data Collection and Labeling

The data used for the experiments described in this work was collected during a series of seminars held by students and visitors at the Universität Karlsruhe (TH), Germany, since Fall 2003. The students and visitors spoke English, but mainly with German or other European accents, and with varying degrees of fluency. This data collection was done in a very natural setting, as the students were far more concerned with the content of their seminars, their presentation in a foreign language and the questions from the audience than with the recordings themselves. Moreover, the seminar room is a common work space used by other students who are not seminar participants. Hence, there are many "real world" events heard in the recordings, such as door slams, printers, ventilation fans, typing, background chatter, and the like.

The seminar speakers were recorded with a Sennheiser CTM, a 64-channel Mark III MA developed at NIST (National Institute of Standards and Technologies) mounted on the wall, four T-shaped MAs with four elements mounted on the four walls of the seminar room and three Shure Microflex table-top microphones located on the work table where the position was not fixed. A diagram of the seminar room is shown in Figure 1. All audio files have been recorded at 44.1 kHz with 24 bits per sample. The high sample rate is preferable to permit more accurate position estimations, while the higher bit depth is necessary to accommodate the large dynamic range of the far field speech data. For the recognition process the speech data was down-sampled to 16 kHz with 16 bits per sample. In addition to the audio data capture, the seminars were simultaneously recorded with four calibrated video cameras that are placed at a height of 2.7 m in the room corners. Their joint field of view covers almost the entire room. The images are captured at a resolution of 640x480 pixels and a framerate of 15 frames per second, and stored as jpg-files for offline processing.

The data from the CTM was manually segmented and transcribed. The data from the far distance microphones was labeled with speech and non-speech regions. The location of the centroid of the speaker's head in the images from the four calibrated video cameras was manually marked every 0.7 second. Based

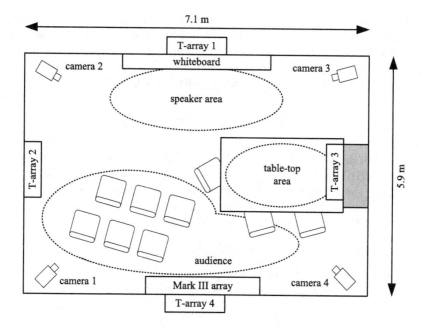

Fig. 1. The CHIL seminar room layout at the Universität Karlsruhe (TH)

on this marks the true position of the speaker's head (ground truth) in three dimensions could be calculated within an accuracy of approximately 10 cm [5].

2.2 Speaker Localization: Audio Features

The lecturer is the person that is normally speaking, therefore we can use audio features using multiple microphones to detect the speaker position.

Consider the j-th pair of microphones, and let $\mathbf{m}_{j1}$ and $\mathbf{m}_{j2}$ respectively be the positions of the first and second microphones in the pair. Let $\mathbf{x}$ denote the position of the speaker in a three dimentional space. Then the *time delay of arrival* (TDOA) between the two microphones of the pair can be expressed as

$$T_j(\mathbf{x}) = T(\mathbf{m}_{j1}, \mathbf{m}_{j2}, \mathbf{x}) = \frac{\|\mathbf{x} - \mathbf{m}_{j1}\| - \|\mathbf{x} - \mathbf{m}_{j2}\|}{c} \tag{1}$$

where c is the speed of sound. To estimate the TDOAs a variety of well-known techniques [6,7] exist. Perhaps the most popular method is the *phase transform* (PHAT), which can be expressed as

$$R_{12}(\tau) = \frac{1}{2\pi} \int_{-\infty}^{\infty} \frac{X_1(e^{j\omega\tau})X_2^*(e^{j\omega\tau})}{|X_1(e^{j\omega\tau})X_2^*(e^{j\omega\tau})|} \, e^{j\omega\tau} \, d\omega \tag{2}$$

where $X_1(\omega)$ and $X_2(\omega)$ are the Fourier transforms of the signals of a microphone pair in a microphone array. Normally one would search for the highest peak in the PHAT to estimate the TDOA. As we are using a particle filter framework, described in Section 2.4, we need to calculate the probability of the acoustic observation A given that the state of the system is characterized by the current particle s_i. We decompose the acoustic observation A into m pairs of microphones (in our case 12), such that the total probability is given by

$$p(A|\mathbf{s}_i) = \frac{1}{m} \sum_{j=1}^{m} p(A^j|\mathbf{s}_i) \tag{3}$$

In order to obtain a (pseudo) probability score for each microphone pair j, we consider the PHAT value at the time delay position $T_j(\mathbf{x} = s_i)$ given a particular particle s_i. As the values returned by the PHAT can be negative, but probability density functions must be strictly nonnegative, we found that setting all negative values of the PHAT to zero yielded the best results.

$$p(A^j|\mathbf{s}_i) = \max(R_j(T_j(\mathbf{x} = s_i)), 0) \tag{4}$$

To get the final probability distribution which tells us how likely the acoustic observation A is produced by a particle s_i, we must normalize over all particles:

$$\bar{p}(A|\mathbf{s}_i) = \frac{p(A|\mathbf{s}_i)}{\sum_i p(A|\mathbf{s}_i)} \tag{5}$$

2.3   Speaker Localization: Video Features

For the task of person tracking in video sequences, there is a variety of features to choose from. In our lecture scenario, the problem comprises both locating the lecturer and disambiguating the lecturer from the people in the audience. As lecturer and audience cannot be separated reliably by means of fixed spatial constraints as, e.g., a dedicated speaker area, we have to look for features that are more specific for the lecturer than for the audience.

Intuitively, the lecturer is the person that is standing and moving (walking, gesticulating) most, while people from the audience are generally sitting and moving less. In order to exploit this specific behavior, we decided to use dynamic foreground segmentation based on adaptive background modeling as primary feature, a detailed explanation can be found in [3]. In order to support the track indicated by foreground segments, we use detectors for face and upper body, also described in [3]. Both features (foreground F and detectors D) are linearly combined using a mixing weight β (for our experiments β was fixed to 0.7, this value was optimized on a development set), so that the particle weights for view j are given by

$$p(V^j|s_i) = \beta \cdot p(D^j|s_i) + (1 - \beta) \cdot p(F^j|s_i) \tag{6}$$

To combine the different views, we sum over the weights from the v different cameras in order to obtain the total weight of the visual observation of the particular particle:

$$p(V|s_i) = \frac{1}{v} \sum_{j=1}^{v} p(V^j|s_i) \tag{7}$$

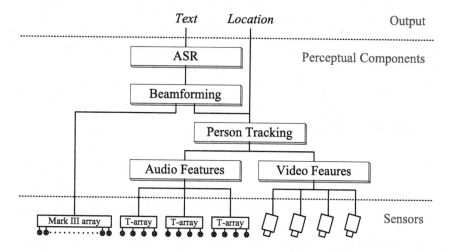

Fig. 2. Components of the system

To get a (pseudo) probability value which tells us how well the particle s_i explains the visual observation V we have to normalize over all values:

$$\bar{p}(V|s_i) = \frac{p(V|s_i)}{\sum_i p(V|s_i)} \tag{8}$$

2.4   Data Fusion with Particle Filter

Particle filters [8] represent a generally unknown probability density function by a set of random samples $\{s_i\}$. Each of these particles is a vector in state space and is associated with an individual weight π_i. The evolution of the particle set is a two-stage process which is guided by the observation and the motion model:

1. *The prediction step:* From the set of particles from the previous time instance, an equal number of new particles is generated. In order to generate a new particle, a particle of the old set is selected randomly in consideration of its weight, and then propagated by applying the motion model. In the simplest case, this can be additive Gaussian noise, but higher order motion models can also be used.
2. *The measurement step:* In this step, the weights of the new particles are adjusted with respect to the current observation. This means, the probability $p(z_t|s_i)$ of the observation z_t needs to be computed, given that the state of particle s_i is the true state of the system.

As we want to track the lecturer's head centroid, each particle $s_i = (x, y, z)$ represents a coordinate in space. The ground plane is spanned by x and y, the height is represented by z. The particles are propagated by simple Gaussian diffusion, thus representing a coarse motion model:

$$s'_i = s_i \cdot (N_{\sigma=0.2m}, N_{\sigma=0.2m}, N_{\sigma=0.1m}) \tag{9}$$

Using the features as described before in Sections 2.2 and 2.3, we can calculate a weight π_i for each particle at the current time instance by combining the probability of the current acoustical observation A and the visual observation V using a weighting factor α:

$$\pi_i = \alpha \cdot \bar{p}(A|s_i) + (1 - \alpha) \cdot \bar{p}(V|s_i) \tag{10}$$

The weighting factor α was set by

$$\alpha = \frac{m_0}{m} \cdot 0.6 \tag{11}$$

where m is the total number of microphone pairs and m_0 the number of values above 0. The average value of α was approximately 0.4. Therefore, more weight was given to the video features.

A particle's weight is set to 0 if the particle leaves the lecture room[1] or if its z-coordinate leaves the valid range for a standing person ($1.2m < z < 2.1m$). The final hypothesis about the lecturer's location over the whole particle set $1 \ldots q$ (in our case $q = 300$) can be derived by a weighted summation over the individual particle locations $s_{i,t}$ at time t:

$$\Lambda_t = \frac{1}{q} \sum_{i=1}^{q} \pi_{i,t} \cdot s_{i,t} \tag{12}$$

Sampled Projection Instead of Triangulation

A common way to obtain the 3D position of an object from multiple views is to locate the object in each of the views and then to calculate the 3D position by using triangulation. This approach, however, has several weak points: Firstly, the object must be detected in at least two different views at the same time. Secondly, the quality of triangulation depends on the points of the object's images that are chosen as starting points for the lines-of-sight; if they do not represent the same point of the physical object, there will be a high triangulation error. Thirdly, searching for the object in each of the views separately—without incorporating geometry information—results in an unnecessarily large search space.

In the method proposed here, we avoid the aforementioned problems by not using triangulation at all. Instead, we make use of the particle filter's capacity to predict the object's location as a well-distributed set of hypotheses; i.e., many particles cluster around likely object locations, and fewer particles populate the space between. As the particle set represents a probability distribution of the predicted object's location, we can use it to narrow down the search space. So instead of searching a neighborhood exhaustively, we only look for the object at the particles' positions.

---

[1] We restrict the particles to be within the full width of the room's ground plane ($0 < y < 7.1m$) and half of the depth ($0 < x < 3m$).

When comparing the proposed method to Kalman filter-based tracking, the following advantage becomes apparent: A particle filter is capable of modeling multi-modal distributions. That means in particular, that no single measurement has to be provided and no information is lost by suppressing all but the strongest measurement, as it is the case for Kalman filter. Furthermore, there is no data-association problem such as would be encountered when trying to match object candidates from different views in order to perform explicit triangulation.

2.5 Beamforming

In this work, we used a simple delay and sum beamformer implemented in the subband domain. Subband analysis and resynthesis was performed with a cosine modulated filter bank [9, §8]. In the complex subband domain, beamforming is equivalent to a simple inner product

$$y(\omega_k) = \mathbf{v}^H(\omega_k)\mathbf{X}(\omega_k)$$

where ω_k is the center frequency of the kth subband, $\mathbf{X}(\omega_k)$ is the vector of subband inputs from all channels of the array, and $y(\omega_k)$ is the beamformed subband output. The speaker position comes into play through the *array manifold vector* [10, §2]

$$\mathbf{v}^H(\omega_k) = \left[e^{j\omega_k\tau_0(\mathbf{X})}\ e^{j\omega_k\tau_1(\mathbf{x})}\ \cdots\ e^{j\omega_k\tau_{N-1}(\mathbf{x})}\right]$$

where $\tau_i(\mathbf{x}) = \|\mathbf{x} - \mathbf{m}_i\|/s$ is the propagation delay for the i-th microphone located at $\mathbf{m}_i$.

2.6 Language Model Training

To train *language models* (LM) for LM interpolation we used corpora consisting of broadcast news (160M words), *proceedings* (17M words) of conferences such as ICSLP, Eurospeech, ICASSP or ASRU and *talks* (60k words) by the Translanguage English Database. Our final LM was generated by interpolating a 3-gram LM based on broadcast news and proceedings, a class based 5-gram LM based on broadcast news and proceedings and a 3-gram LM based on the talks. The perplexity is 144 and the vocabulary contains 25,000 words plus multi-words and pronunciation variants.

2.7 Acoustic Model Training

As relatively little supervised data is available for acoustic modeling of the recordings the acoustic model has been trained on *Broadcast News* [11] and merged with the close talking channel of meeting corpora [12,13] summing up to a total of 300 hours of training material.

The speech data was sampled at 16kHz. Speech frames were calculated using a 10 ms Hamming window. For each frame, 13 *Mel-Minimum Variance Distortionless Response* (Mel-MVDR) cepstral coefficients were obtained through a discrete cosine transform from the Mel-MVDR spectral envelope [14]. There-after, linear discriminant analysis was used to reduce the utterance based cepstral mean normalized features plus 7 adjacent to a final feature number of 42. Our baseline model consisted of 300k Gaussians with diagonal covariances organized in 24k distributions over 6k codebooks.

2.8   Acoustic Adaptation: Close Talk Speech

The adaptation of the close talking acoustic model was done in consecutive steps:

1. A supervised Viterbi training of the CHIL adaptation speakers followed by a *maximum a posteriori* (MAP) combination of this model with the acoustic model of the original system: To find the best mixing weight, a grid search over different mixing weights was performed. The weight, which reached the best likelihood on the hypotheses of the first pass of the unadapted speech recognition system, was chosen as the final mixing weight.
2. A supervised *maximum likelihood linear regression* (MLLR) in combination with *feature space adaptation* (FSA) and *vocal track length normalization* (VTLN) on the close talking CHIL development set: This step adapts to the speaking style of the lecturer and the channel. In the case of non-native speakers the adaptation should also help to cover some 'non nativeness'.
3. A second, now unsupervised MLLR, FSA and VTLN adaptation based on the hypothesis of the first recognition run: this procedure aims at adapting to the particular speaking style of a speaker and to changes within the channel.

2.9   Acoustic Adaptation: Far Distance Speech

The adaptation of the far distance acoustic model was done in consecutive steps:

1. Four iterations of Viterbi training on far distance data from NIST [15] and ICSI [16] over all channels on top of the acoustic trained models to better adjust the acoustic models to far distance.
2. A supervised MLLR in combination with FSA and VTLN on the far distance (single distance or MA processed) CHIL development set: This step adapts to the speaking style of the lecturer and the channel (in particular to the room reverberation). In the case of non-native speakers the adaptation should also help to cover some non-native speech.
3. A second, now unsupervised MLLR, FSA and VTLN adaptation based on the hypothesis of the first recognition run: this procedure aims at adapting to the particular speaking style of a speaker and to changes within the channel.

3   Experiments

In order to evaluate the performance of the described system, we ran experiments on recordings as described before on five seminars/speakers providing a total of approximately 130 minutes speech material with 16.395 words.

3.1   Source Localization

The error measure used for source localization is the average Euclidean distance between the hypothesized head coordinates and the labeled ones.

It can be seen, Table 1, that even though the video only tracker performs considerably better than the audio only tracker, the performance can still be significantly increased by combining both modalities. This effect is particularly distinctive during one recording in which the lecturer is standing most of the time in one dark corner of the room, thus being hard to find using solely video features (116cm mean error). While the video only tracker has the same performance for all frames and speech only frames, the precision of the audio only and the combined tracker is higher for the frames where speech is present compared to the precision over all frames.

Table 1. Averaged error in 3D head position estimation of a lecturer over all frames (approximately 130 Minutes) and frames where speech was present (approximately 105 Minutes)

Tracking mode	Average error (cm)	
	all frames	*speech frames*
Audio only	46.1	41.7
Video only	36.3	36.5
Video & Audio	30.5	29.1

3.2   Speech Recognition

The speech recognition experiments described below were conducted with the *Janus Recognition Toolkit* (JRTk), which was developed and is maintained jointly by the Interactive Systems Laboratories at the Universität Karlsruhe (TH), Germany and at the Carnegie Mellon University in Pittsburgh, USA. All tests used the language and acoustic models described above for decoding.

As mentioned before the big advantage of the MA is the big gain in WER over a single channel, compare the numbers in Table 2. Infact using a MA with an estimated speaker position over a single far distance channel we gain back 26.9% of the accuracy compared to the CTM.

Table 2. *Word error rates* (WER)s for a close talking microphone and a single microphone of the array and the microphone array with different position estimates

Tracking mode	WER
Close Talking Microphone	34.0%
Microphone Array	
single microhone	66.5%
estimated position (Audio only)	59.8%
estimated position (Video only)	59.1%
estimated position (Audio & Video)	58.4%
labeled position	55.8%

3.3   Source Localization vs. Speech Recognition

Figure 3 compares the average position error of the source localization to the WER. If the error of the labeled position to the ground truth is around 15 cm (our calculatinon of the accuracy is approximately 10 cm), then a linear relationship can be seen.

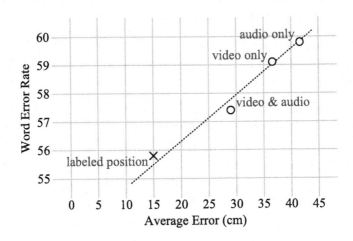

Fig. 3. Plot comparing the average position error to the word error rate

4   Conclusions

We have compared the WER on different approached for person tracking using multiple cameras and multiple pairs of microphones. The core of the tracking algorithm is a particle filter that works with estimating the 3D location by sampled projection, thus benefiting from each single view and microphone pair. The video features used for tracking are based on adaptive foreground segmentation and the response of detectors for upper body, frontal face and profile face. The audio features are based on the TDOA between pairs of microphones, and are estimated with a PHAT function.

The tracker using audio and video input clearly outperforms both the audio- and video-only tracker on the accuracy of the estimate resulting in a decrease of WER. One reason for this is that the video and audio features described in this paper complement one another well: the comparatively coarse foreground feature along with the audio feature guide the way for the face detector, which in turn gives very precise results as long as it searches around the true head position. Another reason for the benefit of the combination is that neither motion and face detection nor acoustic source localization responds exclusively to the lecturer and not to people from the audience – so the combination of both increases the chance of actually tracking the lecturer and therefore a decrease in WER.

In the future we want to use advanced techniques such as cepstral domain maximum likelihood beamformer [17] for the MA. For the fusion weight we want to define a criteria which depends on voice activity detection to give more weight to the audio in the case of speech and vice versa.

References

1. U. Klee, T. Gehrig, and J. McDonough, "Kalman filters for time delay of arrival-based source localization," *Proc. Eurospeech*, 2005.
2. T. Gehrig, K. Nickel, H. K. Ekenel, U. Klee, and J. McDonough, "Kalman filters for audio-video source localization," in *Proc. IEEE Workshop on Applications of Signal Processing to Audio and Acoustics*, 2005.
3. K. Nickel, T. Gehrig, R. Stiefelhagen, and J. McDonough, "A joint particle filter for audiovisual speaker tracking," *7th Intl. Conference on Multimodal Interfaces*, 2005.
4. H. Steusslof, A. Waibel, and R. Stiefelhagen, "Computers in the human interaction loop," *http://chil.server.de*.
5. D. Focken and R. Stiefelhagen, "Towards vision-based 3-d people tracking in a smart room," *IEEE Int. Conf. Multimodal Interfaces*, 2002.
6. M. Omologo and P. Svaizer, "Acoustic event localization using a crosspower-spectrum phase based technique," *Proc. ICASSP*, vol. II, pp. 273–6, 1994.
7. J. Chen, J. Benesty, and Y. A. Huang, "Robust time delay estimation exploiting redundancy among multiple microphones," *IEEE Trans. Speech Audio Proc.*, vol. 11, no. 6, pp. 549–57, November 2003.
8. M. Isard and A. Blake, "Condensation–conditional density propagation for visual tracking," *International Journal of Computer Vision*, vol. 29, no. 1, pp. 5–28, 1998.
9. P. P. Vaidyanathan, *Multirate Systems and Filter Banks*. Englewood Cliffs: Prentice Hall, 1993.
10. H. L. Van Trees, *Optimum Array Processing*. New York: Wiley-Interscience, 2002.
11. Linguistic Data Consortium (LDC), "English broadcast news speech (Hub-4)," www.ldc.upenn.edu/Catalog/ LDC97S44.html.
12. F. Metze, C. Fügen, Y. Pan, T. Schultz, and H. Yu, "The ISL rt-04s meeting transcription system," in *Proc. ICASSP-2004 Meeting RecognitionWorkshop. Montreal; Canada: NIST*, 2004.
13. S. Burger, V. Maclaren, and H. Yu, "The isl meeting corpus: The impact of meeting type on speech style," *ICSLP*, 2002.
14. M. Wölfel, J. McDonough, and A. Waibel, "Warping and scaling of the minimum variance distortionless response," *ASRU*, 2003.
15. V. Stanford, C. Rochet, M. Michel, and J. Garofolo, "Beyond close-talk - issues in distant speech acquisition, conditioning classification, and recognition," *ICASSP 2004 Meeting Recognition Workshop*, 2004.
16. A. Janin, J. Ang, S. Bhagat, R. Dhillon, J. Edwards, N. Morgan, B. Peskin, E. Shriberg, A. Stolcke, C. Wooters, and B. Wrede, "The icsi meeting project: Resources and research," *ICASSP 2004 Meeting Recognition Workshop*, 2004.
17. D. Raub, J. McDonough, and M. Wölfel, "A cepstral domain maximum likelihood beamformer for speech recognition," *ICSLP*, 2004.

Automatic Speech Recognition and Speech Activity Detection in the CHIL Smart Room

Stephen M. Chu, Etienne Marcheret, and Gerasimos Potamianos

Human Language Technologies, IBM T.J. Watson Research Center,
Yorktown Heights, New York 10598, USA
{schu, etiennem, gpotam}@us.ibm.com

Abstract. An important step to bring speech technologies into wide deployment as a functional component in man-machine interfaces is to free the users from close-talk or desktop microphones, and enable far-field operation in various natural communication environments. In this work, we consider far-field automatic speech recognition and speech activity detection in conference rooms. The experiments are conducted on the smart room platform provided by the CHIL project. The first half of the paper addresses the development of speech recognition systems for the seminar transcription task. In particular, we look into the effect of combining parallel recognizers in both single-channel and multi-channel settings. In the second half of the paper, we describe a novel algorithm for speech activity detection based on fusing phonetic likelihood scores and energy features. It is shown that the proposed technique is able to handle non-stationary noise events and achieves good performance on the CHIL seminar corpus.

1 Introduction

Speech is one of the most effective means of communication for humans. It is therefore an essential modality in multimodal man-machine interactions. Speech-enabled interfaces are desirable because they promise hands-free, natural, and ubiquitous access to the interacting device. Much progress in speech technologies has been made in recent years. However, the majority of the successful applications to date, e.g. call-center automation, broadcast news transcription, and desktop dictation, all but confine the speaker to a nearby microphone.

An important step to bring speech technologies into wide deployment as a functional component in man-machine interfaces is to free the users from close-talk or desktop microphones, and enable far-field operation in various natural communication environments. In this work, we consider two related aspects of speech technologies, automatic speech recognition (ASR) and speech activity detection (SAD), in a far-field scenario. The experiments are carried out on the *smart room* platform provided by the European Commission integrated project: Computers in the Human Interaction Loop (CHIL). The CHIL *smart room* is a conference room equipped with multiple audio and visual sensors to facilitate intelligent multimodal interactions. On

S. Renals and S. Bengio (Eds.): MLMI 2005, LNCS 3869, pp. 332–343, 2006.

the acoustic side, the main far-field input is provided by linear microphone arrays. In addition to the linear arrays, T microphone arrays, desktop microphones, as well as close talk microphones may also be available. On the visual side, video cameras with wide-angle lens provide coverage of the entire space; active pan-tilt-zoom (PTZ) cameras allow close-up shots of the subjects in the room. In this paper, we shall concentrate on experiments using only the audio sensors. Note that the concept of *smart room* is not restricted to the context of CHIL. Research results obtained here can be readily extended to other interactive environments where multimodal *ambient intelligence* is sought.

Far-field ASR in conference rooms is a challenging task. Because of reverberation, it would be extremely difficult for a single distant microphone to give satisfactory recognition results, unless the training and testing conditions in terms of acoustic environment, speaker location, and microphone placement are perfectly matched. A promising way of improving far-field ASR performance is to use an array of microphones [1]. Microphone arrays are able to acquire higher quality signal because of the high directivity achieved by beam-forming algorithms, which typically assume that the geometry of the array is regular and known. Ultimately, we would like to have systems that can take advantage of an arbitrary set of distributed acoustic sensors. In such cases, it becomes necessary to look beyond the conventional beam-forming algorithms and consider alternative ways to fuse the information provided by the multiple microphones. Instead of operating in the signal level, it is also possible to carry out the fusion in the hypothesis domain. Through the subsequent experiments, we aim to gain some preliminary understandings of the potentials of the proposed high-level fusion by comparing the recognition performance of single microphone, beam-forming, and hypothesis combination.

Speech activity detection is a crucial aspect in *smart room* applications. Not only does it play an essential role as a front-end step to the ASR process, but also provides important cues to speaker localization and acoustic scene analysis algorithms. Most existing SAD algorithms build classifiers directly on the features extracted from the acoustic signal [2]-[4]. The features may be straight forward energy coefficients or more complex frequency domain representations. The common choice of classifiers ranges from adaptive thresholds to linear discriminants, regression trees, and Gaussian mixture models (GMM). In general, energy-based speech detection is computationally efficient and simple to implement, but lacks robustness to noise. Although performance can be improved by using adaptive thresholds or appropriate filtering of the energy estimates, it remains difficult to address non-stationary noise effectively. It has been shown that frequency based speech features, such as Mel-frequency cepstral coefficients (MFCC), are necessary for further improvement in noise robustness. In this paper, we propose to employ such features indirectly, through the acoustic model that is assumed to have generated them. The resulting acoustic phonetic features are extracted based on the phonetic class conditional MFCC observation vector likelihoods by the acoustic model, and are used to augment baseline energy based features. The two types of features are fused and subsequently considered for speech/silence detection using a GMM classifier.

The rest of the paper is organized as follows. In the next section, we first describe the sensor configuration in the CHIL smart room and the CHIL seminar corpus. Section 3 addresses the development of speech recognition systems for the seminar transcription task. In particular, we look into the effect of combining parallel recognizers in both single-channel and multi-channel settings. Section 4 introduces the proposed SAD algorithm based on fusing phonetic likelihood scores and energy features. Instead of putting ASR and SAD results together in a separate section, we shall cover the experimental results in their respective sections immediately after the algorithms are introduced. Finally, conclusions and future work are discussed in section 5.

2 CHIL Seminar Corpus

The speech data used in the experiments are collected in the CHIL smart room at the Universität Karlsruhe in Karlsruhe, Germany. The corpus consists of two parts.

The first part was recorded in the fall of 2003 and made available for the June 2004 evaluation, thus shall be refereed to as the June'04 dataset in the remainder of the paper. The content of the speech data contains technical seminars given by students of the university. There are seven seminars and seven distinct speakers with varying degree of fluency in English. During each session, both close talk and far-field recordings are made concurrently, the former through a Sennheiser close talk microphone (CTM), and the latter by two linear eight-channel microphone arrays. The signal is sampled at 16 KHz with 16-bit resolution. The total duration of the recording is 137 minutes. The data is further partitioned into two subsets: a development set with 68 minutes and 3971 utterances, and a test set with 69 minutes and 3077 utterances. All seven speakers appear in both of the subsets.

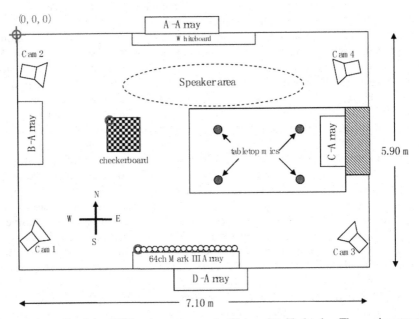

Fig. 1. Schematic of the CHIL smart room at the Universität Karlsruhe. The environment as shown was used to collect the Jan'05 dataset.

The second part of the corpus was recorded after a series of hardware updates were made to the smart room. In particular, the Sennheiser CTM is replaced by a Countryman E6 microphone; and a new 64-channel Mark III microphone array developed by the National Institute of Standards and Technology (NIST) is now providing the far-field data. The signal is sampled at 44.1 KHz with 24 bits per sample. The schematic of the updated CHIL seminar room is shown in Figure 1. The data was made available for the January 2005 evaluation, and shall be referred to as the Jan'05 dataset here on.

There are five seminars and five speakers in this collection. Among the speakers, one also appeared in the June'04 dataset. The development set contains 46 minutes of speech segmented into 1395 utterances; the test set contains 133 minutes of data and 1764 utterances. Two speakers are found in the development set, including the one shared with the June'04 dataset. In addition to those two speakers, the test set also has three speakers unseen in the development set.

Both the June'04 dataset and the Jan'05 set were manually segmented and transcribed. For the far-field data, speech and non-speech regions are also labeled to provide ground truth for the SAD experiments.

3 ASR Experiments

To develop an effective speech recognition system for the CHIL seminar transcription, the following characteristics of the task must be considered.

First, the amount of available training data is limited. Given that the total duration of the development set is less than two hours, it is therefore unfeasible to train a large vocabulary continuous speech recognizer (LVCSR) from scratch. A more plausible approach is to start from a set of acoustic models trained on other much larger speech corpora, and then refine these models using the CHIL development data through adaptation.

Second, the smart room environment, the seminar scenario, and the mostly European speaker set make this collection distinct from most of the existing large speech corpora/tasks. Therefore, a system based solely on one of the existing databases is unlikely to give the optimal performance. In our work, we aim to take advantage of different speech datasets by running three systems developed separately on three very different corpora in parallel, and combining the word hypotheses generated by the systems to give the final output.

Lastly, because the domain of the speech content is well defined, further reduction in recognition error can be achieved by developing a domain specific language model. In the June 2003 CHIL evaluation [5], we first experimented using the text from in-domain technical publications for language model development. The merit of the approach was clearly demonstrated in the evaluation results. In this work, we shall continue to use the same method.

3.1 System Description

The three parallel recognition systems considered here are: (1) a wide-band dictation system, (2) a wide-band dialogue system with German accent [6], and (3) a narrowband conversational system. The front-end specifications and the configurations of the acoustic models are summarized in Fig. 2.

In both the first and the second system, supervised *maximum a posteriori* (MAP) adaptation was performed using the development set (joint set of the June'04 and Jan' 05 development data). In the third system, supervised MLLR was applied. Note that these adaptations were speaker-independent. In addition to MLLR, the third system also performs speaker-dependent VTLN and feature-level minimum phone error (fMPE) [7] adaptation. These operations are carried out at run-time and are unsupervised.

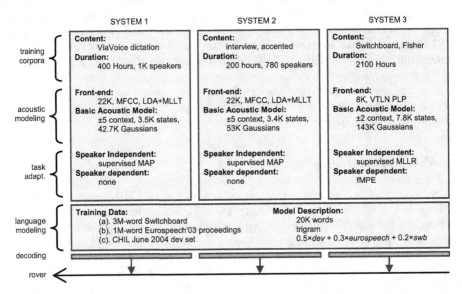

Fig. 2. The IBM CHIL ASR system is composed of three parallel large vocabulary speech recognizers. The acoustic models in each of the individual systems are trained on different speech corpora and adapted to the CHIL seminar transcription task using the development data. The three systems share the same language model. The word hypotheses are combined using ROVER to give the final recognition result.

The language model is developed on three datasets: the CHIL development set, a three million word set from the Switchboard corpus, and a one million word set derived from Eurospeech '03 proceedings using automated PDF to ASCII conversion. The 20k vocabulary contains the following words: all words in the CHIL development set, words in the Switchboard set with 5+ counts, words in the Eurospeech set with 2+ counts. A trigram model is built on each of the three corpora with modified Kneser-Ney smoothing. The final language model is obtained through the following interpolation,

$$0.5 \times chil + 0.3 \times eurospeech + 0.2 \times switchboard \tag{1}$$

The language model is shared by all three recognition systems. During testing, the input speech is first decoded separately by the three individual systems. Then the outputs are combined using the NIST ROVER [8] system to produce the final hypothesis.

3.2 Experimental Results

To establish appropriate benchmarks for the multi-channel far-field experiments, we first test the recognition system with the CTM recording and data from a single channel in the microphone array. Adaptations are applied to the basic acoustic models using the development data from the corresponding channels. With respect to the given system, the CTM result should give an upper bound for the multi-channel far-field performance; while the single channel result should provide an estimate of the baseline.

We also compare the performance from the current recognition system with an earlier system (06/04), which is essentially *system 2* in Fig. 2, adapted with only the June'04 development set. The benchmark results are summarized in Table 1.

Table 1. Recognition results in word error rate for the close talk and far field microphones. The results from the 06/04 system and the 01/05 system are compared.

Test set : system	close talk	far field
06/04 : 06/04	35.1%	64.5%
06/04 : 01/05	31.5%	63.2%
01/05 : 01/05	36.9%	70.8%

The results clearly show the difficulty posed by far-field ASR. In all three cases, the word error rates (WER) for the single far-field microphone are approximately doubled compared with the corresponding CTM performance. The results also confirm the benefit of parallel decoding using diverse acoustic models. On the same June'04 test set, the parallel system is able to reduce the WER from 35.1% to 31.5%, which translates to a 10.3% relative reduction. The differences are illustrated in Fig. 3.

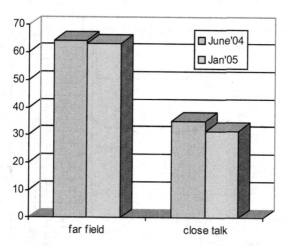

Fig. 3. Benchmark results of the ASR systems using data from CTM and single channel far-field microphone. On the June'04 test set, the Jan'05 system employing three parallel acoustic models gives superior recognition performance to the June'04 system.

Two multi-channel far-field ASR experiments are carried out. Both use the same 16 channels of microphone array data found in the June'04 dataset. In the first experiment, beam-forming is applied to the multiple outputs of the microphone array to generate a single channel of acoustic signal. The signal is then passed to the ASR system for adaptation and recognition. In the second experiment, each channel of the microphone array is first processed independently. For a given utterance, 16 word-level hypotheses with word confidence scores are generated. These hypotheses are then combined using the ROVER program to give the final word sequence.

The results of the multi-channel ASR experiments are shown in Fig. 4. In addition to the beam-forming and hypothesis-combination results, the single-channel WERs for all 16 channels are also listed. The single-channel WER is used to create a ranked list of the channels; and hypothesis integration experiments are repeated for top n channels for $n = 1, 2, \ldots, 16$.

Decoding the beam-formed signal gives a WER of 58.5%. This is a clear improvement over the single-channel results, which has an average WER of 64% approximately. The lowest WER achieved by hypothesis integration is 59.5%, which is not far behind the beam-forming performance. This is indeed encouraging considering the facts that the beam-forming algorithm explicitly relies on the known geometry of the array, and that the hypothesis integration approach is able to attain more than 80% of the gain without the advantage of this prior knowledge. Therefore, in the situation where the sensor configuration is not known, hypothesis integration can serve as a viable alternative to signal domain algorithms.

One disadvantage of running multiple recognition engines is the increased demand on computational resource. However, from Fig. 4, it can be observed that in this particular experiment, most of the gain occurs when the first few channels are added. If this observation is true in general, then the computational load of the approach can be significantly reduced. Further experiments are still required.

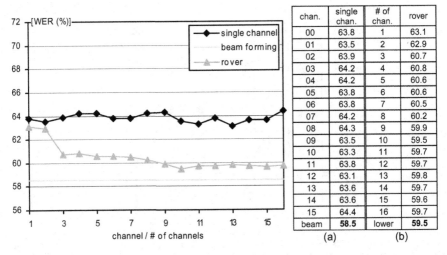

Fig. 4. Comparing the recognition results on the microphone array data. (a). results for each individual channel and the beam-forming signal; (b). Rover top n channels according to (a).

In essence, array-processing is an information fusion problem. The fusion problem arises when different observations about the same underlying process are available from multiple sources. The goal then is to find the optimal way to integrate the sources so that the generating process can be inferred. In a conventional beam-forming algorithm, the information is integrated at a very low-level in the signal do-main; whereas in the rather straight-forward alternative approach taken in the second experiment, the fusion takes place at a much higher level in the hypothesis space. In fact, it is worthwhile to look into mechanisms for multi-channel ASR that permit intermediate level fusion.

4 Speech Activity Detection Experiments

The proposed SAD system operates on two types of features, the energy features generated directly from the signal, and the acoustic phonetic features defined from observations generated by the ASR acoustic model. The energy features are five-dimensional vectors computed from band-passed signals. Conceptually, the five components track the energy envelope of the waveform with different sensitivities, thus providing evolving statistics about the signal. The details of the computations can be found in [9], and are omitted here for brevity. The emphasis will be given to the acoustic phonetic features proposed in this work.

4.1 Acoustic Phonetic Features for SAD

The acoustic phonetic feature space employed for speech activity detection is de-rived from the acoustic model used for ASR. The acoustic model is generated from partitioning the acoustic space by context-dependent phonemes with the context defined in this work as plus and minus five phonemes, cross-word to the left only. The context-dependent phoneme observation generation process is modeled as a GMM within the hidden Markov model (HMM) framework, and in typical large-vocabulary ASR systems, this leads to more than 40k Gaussian mixture compo-nents. Calculating all HMM state likelihoods from all Gaussians at each frame would preclude real-time operation. Therefore, we define a hierarchical structure for the Gaussians, where it is assumed that only a small subset of them is significant to likelihood computation at any given time. The hierarchical structure takes ad-vantage of the sparseness by surveying the Gaussian pool in multiple resolutions given an acoustic feature vector $\mathbf{x}$. As part of the training process, the complete set of available Gaussian densities is clustered into a search tree, in which the leaves correspond to the individual Gaussians, and a parent node is the centroid of its chil-dren for a defined distance metric. At the bottom of this tree resides a many-to-one mapping, collapsing the individual Gaussians to the appropriate HMM state. There-fore, the HMM state conditional likelihood of a given observation vector $\mathbf{x}$ at time t is computed as

$$p(\mathbf{x} \mid s) = \sum_{g \in G(s)} p(g \mid s) p(\mathbf{x} \mid g) \qquad (2)$$

where $G(s)$ is the set of Gaussians that make up the GMM for state s. Traversing the tree will yield a subset of active Gaussians, denoted by Y. Based on Y and the many-to-one mapping, the conditional likelihood of a state is approximated as

$$p(\mathbf{x} \mid s) = \max_{g \in Y \cap G(s)} p(g \mid s) p(\mathbf{x} \mid g) \tag{3}$$

If no Gaussian from a state is present in Y, a default floor likelihood is then assigned to that state.

To define the acoustic phonetic space used for speech activity detection, we apply an additional many-to-one mapping to the pruned result of the hierarchical tree. This function maps phonemes into three broadly defined classes: (i) the pure silence phoneme, trained from non-speech; (ii) the disfluent phonemes, which are noise like phonemes, namely the unvoiced fricatives and plosives, i.e., the ARPAbet subset {/b/, /d/, /g/, /k/, /p/, /t/, /f/, /s/, /sh/}; and (iii) all the remaining phonemes, such as the vowels and voiced fricatives. The three classes will be denoted by c_1, c_2, and c_3. From the acoustic feature $\mathbf{x}$, which is used to traverse the acoustic model hierarchy, we can form the speech detection class posteriors for the three speech detection classes as,

$$P(c_i \mid \mathbf{x}) = \frac{\displaystyle\sum_{g \in Y \cap G(c_i)} p(\mathbf{x} \mid g) p(g \mid c_i)}{\displaystyle\sum_{i=1}^{3} \left\{ \sum_{g \in Y \cap G(c_i)} p(\mathbf{x} \mid g) p(g \mid c_i) \right\}}, \tag{4}$$

where $G(c_i)$ is the set of Gaussians defined by the mapping from the phonemes to the speech detection class c_i.

Pruning at each level of the hierarchical acoustic model is accomplished by using a threshold relative to the maximum scoring likelihood for that level. As a result, the sharper the drop-off in Gaussian likelihoods, the more aggressive the pruning becomes. Therefore, both SNR and the phoneme being pronounced impact the pruning. Features extracted from vowels and other voiced phonemes will result in more aggressive pruning than unvoiced fricatives, plosives and silence phonemes. This pruning will remain relative to SNR, with increasing SNR resulting in an overall more aggressive pruning.

The above observation results in additional speech detection features based on class-normalized Gaussian counts. Let's denote the number of Gaussians after hierarchical pruning that map to speech detection class c_i, n_{c_i}, and consider the normalized counts

$$\bar{n}_{c_i} = n_{c_i} \bigg/ \sum_{j=1}^{3} n_{c_j}, \text{ for } i = 1,2,3 \tag{5}$$

as additional features. Combining (4) and (5), we obtain the six-dimensional acoustic phonetic feature vector

$$v_a = \begin{bmatrix} v_{a1} \\ v_{a2} \\ v_{a3} \end{bmatrix}, \quad v_{ai} = \begin{bmatrix} \log(P(c_i \mid x) \\ \log(n_{c_i}) \end{bmatrix}. \tag{6}$$

Finally, the five-dimensional energy features and the acoustic phonetic features are concatenated to form an 11-dimensional feature vector.

4.2 Training and Classification

The joint energy and acoustic phonetic feature vectors are projected to an eight-dimensional feature space using PCA, on which a three-class GMM classifier is built. For each class eight Gaussian densities with diagonal covariance matrices are used.

The class labels for the training data is inferred through Viterbi alignment using the ASR acoustic model and the transcripts of the corresponding utterances. Once the phone-level alignment is computed, the class identity of a frame can be readily obtained via the phoneme-to-class mapping described earlier.

During classification, the likelihood scores of a frame given the three GMMs are first evaluated. The scores are then smoothed over time to give the classification result. As a final step, the three classes are mapped to speech/non-speech according to the following rules.

1. $c_1 \rightarrow$ non-speech
2. $c_3 \rightarrow$ speech
3. $c_2 \rightarrow$ speech, if the one of the two neighboring frames is c_1, and the other is c_3; otherwise $c_2 \rightarrow$ non-speech

This mapping allows the system to correctly handle both consonant-vowel-consonant transitions and non-stationary noise events.

4.3 Experimental Results

The far-field performance of the SAD system is evaluated using the first channel of the linear microphone array in the CHIL June'04 dataset.

The basic acoustic models used to compute the acoustic phonetic features are the same as the ones in *system* 1 described in the ASR experiments. Specifically, they consist of 3.5K HMM states and 43K Gaussian mixtures, trained on 400 hours of data from 1000 speakers. The acoustic models use 40-dimentional features derived from 24-dimensional MFCCs through LDA/MLLT. Supervised MAP adaptation is applied on top of the basic acoustic models using the development set.

Three metrics are used to evaluate the SAD performance. They are defined as follows,

- Speech detection error rate (SDER) = time of incorrect decisions at speech segments / time of speech segments
- Non-speech detection error rate (NDER) = time of incorrect decisions at non-speech segments / time of non-speech segments
- Average detection error rate (ADER) = (SDER + NDER) / 2.

In our experiments, the operating points of the SAD are chosen such that the following condition is satisfied,

$$|SDER - NDER| / (SDER + NDER) \leq 0.1 \tag{7}$$

The SAD results using both the basic and the adapted acoustic models are shown in Table 2. As expected, the performance of the adapted system is significantly better than the system using baseline acoustic models.

Table 2. Speech activity detection results on the June'04 CHIL seminar dataset. The system uses joint energy and acoustic phonetic features and Gaussian mixture models for classification.

metric	baseline	MAP adaptation
SDER	16.70%	10.01%
NDER	16.43%	11.92%
ADER	16.57%	10.96%

The reported performance of the adapted system was superior to all five other systems evaluated by the CHIL consortium [10], achieving 4% to 36% relative ADER reduction. All other submitted systems built classifiers directly on the energy or other speech features. The results clearly demonstrate the strength of the acoustic phonetic based approach to speech activity detection.

5   Conclusions

In this work, we consider far-field automatic speech recognition and speech activity detection in the CHIL smart room. In particular, we look into the effect of combining parallel recognizers in both single-channel and multi-channel settings for far-field ASR. Experiments show that for microphone array-based ASR, word-level hypothesis combination is able to achieve recognition performance comparable to conventional beam-forming algorithms. For speech activity detection, a novel algorithm based on fusing acoustic phonetic features and energy features is proposed and successfully evaluated on the CHIL seminar corpus.

Acknowledgements

The work is supported by the European Commission under the integrated project CHIL, "Computers in the Human Interaction Loop," contract number 506909.

References

1. M. Brandstein and D. Ward, Ed., *Microphone Arrays*, Berlin: Springer Verlag, 2000.
2. Q. Li, J. Zheng, Q. Zhou, and C.-H. Lee, "A robust, real-time end-point detector with energy normalization for ASR in adverse environments," in *Proceedings of IEEE International Conference on Acoustics, Speech, and Signal Processing*, 2001, pp. 233-236.

3. A. Martin, D. Charlet, and L. Mauuary, "Robust speech/non-speech detection using LDA applied to MFCC," in *Proceedings of IEEE International Conference on Acoustics, Speech, and Signal Processing*, 2001, pp. 237-240.
4. J. Padrell, D. Macho, and C. Nadeu, "Robust speech activity detection using LDA applied to FF parameters," in *Proceedings of IEEE International Conference on Acoustics, Speech, and Signal Processing*, 2005.
5. D. Macho et al., "Automatic speech activity detection, source localization, and speech recognition on the CHIL seminar corpus," to be presented at IEEE International Conference on Multimedia & Expo, Amsterdam, Netherlands, 2005.
6. B. Ramabhadran, J. Huang, and M. Picheny, "Towards automatic transcription of large spoken archives – English ASR for the MALACH project," in *Proceedings of IEEE International Conference on Acoustics, Speech, and Signal Processing*, 2003.
7. D. Povey, B. Kingsbury, L. Mangu, G. Saon, H. Soltau, and G. Zweig, "fMPE: discriminatively trained features for speech recognition," in *Proceedings of IEEE International Conference on Acoustics, Speech, and Signal Processing*, 2005, vol. 1, pp. 961-964.
8. J. G. Fiscus, "A post-processing system to yield reduced word error rates: recognizer output voting error reduction (ROVER)," in *Proceedings of the 1997 IEEE Workshop on Automatic Speech Recognition and Understanding*, pp. 347-354.
9. M. Monkowski, "Automatic gain control in a speech recognition system," U.S. Patent 6,314,396, November 6, 2001.
10. D. Macho, "Speech activity detection: summary of CHIL evaluation run #1," January 2005, http://chil.server.de/servlet/is/3870/.

The Development of the AMI System for the Transcription of Speech in Meetings

Thomas Hain[1], Lukas Burget[2], John Dines[3], Iain McCowan[3], Giulia Garau[4], Martin Karafiat[2], Mike Lincoln[4], Darren Moore[3], Vincent Wan[1], Roeland Ordelman[5], and Steve Renals[4]

[1] Department of Computer Science,
University of Sheffield, Sheffield S1 4DP, UK
[2] Faculty of Information Engineering,
Brno University of Technology, Brno, 612 66, Czech Republic
[3] IDIAP, CH-1920 Martigny, Switzerland
[4] Centre for Speech Technology Research,
University of Edinburgh, Edinburgh EH8 9LW, UK
[5] Department of Electrical Engineering,
University of Twente, 7500AE Enschede, The Netherlands

Abstract. The automatic processing of speech collected in conference style meetings has attracted considerable interest with several large scale projects devoted to this area. This paper describes the development of a baseline automatic speech transcription system for meetings in the context of the AMI (Augmented Multiparty Interaction) project. We present several techniques important to processing of this data and show the performance in terms of word error rates (WERs). An important aspect of transcription of this data is the necessary flexibility in terms of audio pre-processing. Real world systems have to deal with flexible input, for example by using microphone arrays or randomly placed microphones in a room. Automatic segmentation and microphone array processing techniques are described and the effect on WERs is discussed. The system and its components presented in this paper yield competitive performance and form a baseline for future research in this domain.

1 Introduction

Many people spend a considerable time in their working life in meetings, however the efficiency of meetings is often low and hence approaches for streamlining the process and for retaining and crystallising the right information have been developed. So far computers are rarely used to aid this process. Projects like AMI (which stands for Augmented Multiparty Interaction) aim to investigate to use of machine based techniques to aid people in and outside of meetings to gain efficient access to information. Meetings are an audio visual experience by nature, information is presented for example in the form of presentation slides, drawings on boards, and of course by verbal communication. The latter forms the backbone of most meetings. The automatic transcription of speech in

S. Renals and S. Bengio (Eds.): MLMI 2005, LNCS 3869, pp. 344–356, 2006.
© Springer-Verlag Berlin Heidelberg 2006

meetings is of crucial importance for meeting analysis, content analysis, summarisation, and analysis of dialogue structure. Widespread Work on automatic recognition of speech in meetings started with yearly performance evaluations by the U.S. National Institute of Standards and Technology (NIST) [19]. Work on meeting transcription was initially facilitated by the collection of the ICSI meeting corpus [13] which was followed by trail NIST meeting transcription evaluations in Spring 2002. Further meeting resources were made available by NIST [9], Interactive System Labs (ISL) [3] and the Linguistic Data Consortium RT04s Meeting evaluations [19].

As the number of speech resources for meetings is still relatively small, similar to work presented in [22], a recognition system for conversational telephone speech (CTS) forms the starting point for our work on meetings. This approach was preferred to bootstrapping from Broadcast News (BN) systems (as for example in [21]) as the meeting style is expected to be colloquial rather than presentational. In the following we give a description of meeting resources followed by a description of our CTS baseline system. This is followed by an analysis of meeting vocabulary and linguistic context followed by experimental results with various approaches to acoustic modelling.

2   Meeting Resources

The ICSI Meeting corpus [13] is the largest meeting resource available consisting of 70 technical meetings at ICSI with a total of 73 hours of speech. The number of participants is variable and data is recorded from head-mounted and a total of four table-top microphones. A 3.5 hour subset of this corpus covering 30 minute extracts of 7 meetings was set aside for testing (icsidev). Further meeting corpora were collected by NIST [9] and ISL [3], with 13 and 10 hours respectively.Both NIST and ISL meetings have free content (e.g. people playing games or discussing sales issues) and number of participants. We also make use of the RT04s NIST evaluation set (rt04seval) which also includes meetings recorded by the LDC.

As part of the AMI project a major collection and annotation effort of the AMI meeting corpus[4] is currently underway. Data is collected from three different model meeting rooms in Europe (mostly Edinburgh and IDIAP at the moment). Overall more than 100 hours of speech are to be transcribed. The meeting language is English. Each meeting normally has four participants and the corpus will be split into a *scenario* portion and individual meetings. The scenario portion will involve the same participants over multiple meetings on one specific task. The data used in this paper only originates from scenario meetings. An additional development set (amidev) consisting of 8 meetings from 2 locations is used for testing.

3   The AMI CTS System

All systems in this paper are based on standard speech recognition technology such as HMM based acoustic models and N-gram based language models. In the following we briefly outline the front-end and acoustic modelling, dictionary consruction, and language modelling on this task.

3.1   Acoustic Modelling

Font-ends make use of 12 MF-PLP [24,12] coefficients and the 0th cepstral coefficient c_0. These are derived from a reduced bandwidth of 125-3800Hz. First and second order derivatives are added to form a 39 dimensional feature vector. Cepstral mean and variance normalisation is performed on complete conversation sides and hence are implicitly speaker specific. Acoustic models are phonetic decision tree state clustered triphone models with standard left-to-right 3-state topology. They were obtained using standard HTKmaximum likelihood training procedures (see for example [11]). The system uses approximately 7000 states where each state is represented as a mixture of 16 Gaussians. Speaker adaptive training is performed in the form of vocal tract length normalisation (VTLN) both in training and test. Warp factors are estimated using a parabolic search procedure, a piecewise linear warping function and a maximum likelihood criterion[11]. Speaker adaptation is perfermed using maximum likelihood linear regression (MLLR) of the means and variances[8].

Feature transformation is applied in the form of smoothed heteroscedastic linear discriminant analysis (SHLDA) [17]. SHLDA is used to reduce a 52 dimensional formed by the standard feature vector plus third derivatives to 39 dimensions. HLDA estimation procedure[16] requires the estimation of full covariance matrices per Gaussion. SHLDA uses smoothing of the covariance estimates by interpolating with standard LDA type with-in class covariances.

$$\Sigma_{sm} = \alpha\Sigma + (1 - \alpha)\Sigma_{WC} \tag{1}$$

Σ_{sm} is the smoothed estimate of the covariance matrix and Σ_{WC} is the LDA type within-class matrix estimate based on an occupancy weighted average. Values for α of $0.8 - 0.9$ were found to yield satisfactory results.

3.2   Dictionaries

The UNISYN pronunciation lexicon [7] forms the basis of dictionary development with pronunciations mapped to the General American accent. Normalisation of lexicon entries to resolve differences between American and British derived spelling conventions was performed yielding a 115k word base dictionary. Pronunciations for a further 11500 words were generated manually to ensure coverage of training data. For consistency and a simplified manual pronunciation generation process hypotheses generation procedures have been developed. Pronunciations for partial words are automatically derived from the baseform dictionary. Hypotheses for standard words were generated using CART based letter-to-sound rules. The CART based letter-to-sound prediction module was trained on the UNISYN dictionary using tools provided with the Festival speech synthesis software [1] using left and right context of five letters and left context of

Table 1. Size of various text corpora in million words (MW)

Corpus name	#words (MW)
Swbd/CHE	3.5
Fisher	10.5
Web (Switchboard)	163
Web (Fisher)	484
Web (Fisher topics)	156
BBC - THISL	33
HUB4-LM96	152
SDR99-Newswire	39
Enron email	152
ICSI meeting	1
Web (meetings)	128

two phones. This gave 98% phone accuracy and 89% word accuracy on the base dictionary., for manually generated pronunciations the error rates were 89% and 51% respectively. Although the word accuracy is quite low on new words (many of which were proper names, partial words etc.), the phone accuracy remains relatively high.

3.3   Language Modelling and Vocabulary

Selection of vocabulary for recognition is based on a collection of in-domain words. However, in the case of insufficient data it is beneficial to augment this list with the most frequent words from other sources, for example Broadcast News (BN) corpora. This "padding" technique was used for all dictionaries in this paper unless stated otherwise. The target dictionary size was 50000 words and the source of words was BBC news data, the Broadcast News 1996 Hub4 corpus (HUB4-LM96), and Enron data[14] (see table 2).

Language model training data for conversational speech is sparse. Hence models are constructed from other sources and interpolated (as in e.g. [11]). This is true for both CTS and meeting data. Hence we have processed a large number of different corpora to form the basis of our language models. The most important corpora are listed in Table 1. A full discussion of all source material would go beyond the scope of this paper. The most important non-standard data was found to be the the Web collected resources [2] and ICSI meetings. In total more than 1300 MW of text are used. Each corpus was normalised using identical processes. Apart from standard cleanup we tried to ensure normalised spelling

Table 2. Perplexities on the NIST Hub5E 1998/2001/2002 evaluation test sets (CTS)

Hub5e eval sets	Bigram	Trigram	4-gram
Swbd	104.53	85.97	84.12
Swbd + HUB4	95.00	72.55	69.04
Swbd + HUB4 + Web	90.89	66.75	61.59

and uniform hyphenations across all corpora. For the training and testing of language models the SRI LM toolkit [23] was used to train models with Kneser-Ney discounting and Backoff. Table 2 shows perplexity results on the NIST Hub5e evaluation sets. Note the substantial reduction in perplexity by the additional web resources.

3.4   Decoding and Overall System Performance

Decoding operates in three passes. The Cambridge University speech decoder HDecode is used for recognition with trigram language models. Table 3 shows results for each pass. The first pass yields a first level transcription which is used or VTLN warp factor estimation. In the second pass improved output is generated using VTLN trained models. The final output is obtained after MLLR adaptation using transforms for speech and silence. The table also gives a comparison of results with and without SHLDA. Trigram language models as described above were used in the experiments. A significant reduction in word error rate (WER) from both VTLN and SHLDA is observed.

Table 3. %WER results on the NIST Hub5E 2001 evalution set

eval01	VTLN	MLLR	non-HLDA	SHLDA
pass1			37.2	35.0
pass2	×		33.8	32.1
pass3	×	×	32.1	30.6

4   Language in Meetings

Even though of general conversational nature, meeting data differs substantially from CTS. First of all the acoustic recoding condition is usually more complex as the speaker has no feedback on the recording quality. Speech signals of close-talking microphones are distorted by heavy breathing, head-turning and cross-talk. Table 4 shows raw statistics on several meeting corpora. Average utterance durations are larger than on CTS, however with great variation. We can also observe that corpus size is not a good predictor for the number of unique words in the corpus and hence complexity.

Table 4. Statistics for meeting corpora

	ICSI	NIST	ISL	AMI
Avg. Dur (sec)	2.42	3.98	3.21	3.95
#words	823951	157858	119184	154249
#unique wds	11439	6653	5622	4801

4.1 Vocabulary

We shall loosely define a domain as a set of sub-corpora that, when used in a combined non-discriminative fashion, yield better performing models than the parts. This definition is not strict and will show a tendency to combine small corpora. However for the purpose of model training the question of how to use data is most important. Table 5 shows on the left hand side Out Of Vocabulary (OOV) rates using vocabulary derived from each meeting corpus. The OOV rates do not correlate perfectly with vocabulary sizes (Table 4). On the right hand side the wordlists are padded as described in section 3.3 (this includes removal of obvious typographic errors). It is evident that overall the effect of vocabulary mismatch is greatly reduced uniformly for all cases. This suggest that only a very small amount of meeting specific vocabulary is necessary. Hence padding was used in all further experiments.

Table 5. %OOV rates of meeting resource specific vocabularies. Columns denote the word list source, rows the test domain.

	No padding				Padding to 50k			
	ICSI	NIST	ISL	AMI	ICSI	NIST	ISL	AMI
ICSI	0.00	4.95	7.11	6.83	0.01	0.47	0.58	0.57
NIST	4.50	0.00	6.50	6.88	0.43	0.09	0.59	0.66
ISL	5.12	5.92	0.00	6.68	0.41	0.37	0.03	0.57
AMI	4.47	4.39	5.41	0.00	0.53	0.53	0.58	0.30
COMB	1.60	4.35	6.15	5.98	0.16	0.42	0.53	0.55

4.2 Content

Apart from the raw word difference it is important understand the effect of the wide range of topics covered in the various meetings. A set of experiments was conducted to compare meeting resource optimised language models on the basis of the meeting resource specific (MRS) padded vocabularies. Language models are obtained by optimisation of interpolation weights for the components outlined in Table 1. Table 6 shows perplexities on all corpora. In all cases that the best perplexities are achieved on the originating corpus, however with little margin. Note also that the MRS LMs significantly outperform the generic LMs

Table 6. Cross meeting room perplexities on subsets of rt04seval and rt05samidev. COMB denotes training or testing using all meeting data.

Test Corpus	ICSI	NIST	ISL	AMI	COMB
ICSI	68.17	74.57	73.76	77.14	67.97
NIST	105.91	100.87	102.01	105.95	101.25
iSL	104.68	99.45	98.45	106.39	102.86
AMI	115.56	114.26	114.41	88.91	94.08
LDC	97.78	90.66	88.87	92.44	93.84
COMB	107.46	105.93	105.73	90.62	92.74

only in the case of ISL and AMI. In general the perplexity of ICSI test data is very low. This appears to be a property of this data set.

5   Meeting Transcription

Common for all meeting rooms is that audio is recorded either by close-talking microphones or via single or multiple distant microphones. The latter may be arranged in a fixed array configuration. Due to interaction between speakers the system must be capable of speech detection and and speaker grouping as well as recognition. In the following we first outline techniques for audio segmentation and microphone array processing, followed by a description of model training procedures and recognition results.

5.1   Automatic Segmentation

Speech activity detection (SAD) for close talking microphones poses a significant challenge. The high levels of cross-talk and non-speech noise (such as breath or contact noise) prohibit the use of threshold based techniques, the standard in more 'friendly' recording conditions. The system used here is a straight-forward statistical based approach with additional components to control cross-talk between channels. Statistical approaches to SAD typically use HMM or GMM based classifiers with special feature vectors such as channel cross-correlation and kurtosis (e.g. [20,25]). A 14 dimensional PLP [12] feature vector is used to train a Multi-Layer-Perceptron (MLP) classifier with a 101 frame input layer, a 20 unit hidden layer and an output layer of two classes. Parameters are trained on 10 meetings from each meeting resource totalling around 20 hrs of data. Further 5 meetings from each corpus are used to determine early stopping of the parameter learning. The utterance segmentation uses Viterbi decoding and scaled likelihoods derived from the MLP and a minimum segment duration of 0.5 seconds.

Cross talk suppression is performed at the signal level using adaptive-LMS echo cancellation [18]. Additons to the basic system are: the use of multiple reference channels in cancellation; automatic channel delay estimation and offsetting of reference signals to account for this delay; automatic cross-talk level estimation; and ignoring of channels which produce low levels of cross-talk. Updates are further made on a per sample basis to account for non-stationary 'echo' path. On the classifier level additional features were introduced to aid the detection of cross-talk:

$$\mathrm{RMS}_{norm}\left(x_{t-L}^{t+L}(i)\right) = \log\left(\mathrm{RMS}\left(x_{t-L}^{t+L}(i)\right)\right) - \log\left(\sum_{j=1}^{N}\mathrm{RMS}\left(x_{t-L}^{t+L}(j)\right)\right), \quad (2)$$

$$Kur\left(x_{t-L}^{t+L}\right) = \frac{E\left\{\left(x_{t-L}^{t+L} - E\left\{x_{t-L}^{t+L}\right\}\right)^{4}\right\}}{E\left\{\left(x_{t-L}^{t+L} - E\left\{x_{t-L}^{t+L}\right\}\right)^{2}\right\}^{2}}, \quad (3)$$

$$Cep\left(x_{t-L}^{t+L}\right) = \max_{t=P_l-P_h}\left(\mathcal{F}\left(\log\left(\mid\mathcal{F}\left(x_{t-L}^{t+L}\right)\mid\right)\right)\right). \quad (4)$$

where x_{t-L}^{t+L} is the signal x windowed over $2 \cdot L$ samples and P_l and P_h are the minimum and maximum pitch period over which peak picking is carried out (corresponding to 50-300Hz). Eq. 2 describes across-meeting normalised RMS energy, Eq. 3 signal and spectrum kurtosis, and Eq. 4 as a voicing strength measure based on the maximum amplitude in the speech cepstrum in the range of frequencies 50-300Hz.

5.2   Microphone Array Processing

Audio from multiple distant microphones (MDMs) can be used in variety of ways. The AMI baseline system uses an enhancement based approach. Recordings from a number of microphones placed in the meeting rooms are combined to arrive at a single, enhanced output file that is then used as input for recognition. The system is required to cope with a number of unknown variables: varying numbers of microphones; unknown microphone placement; unknown numbers of talkers; time variant skew between input channels introduced by the recording system; and different room geometry and acoustic conditions.

The MDM processing operates in a total of four stages. First gain calibration is performed by normalising the maximum amplitude level of each of the input files. Then a noise estimation and removal procedure is run. This in itself is a two pass process. On the first pass the noise spectrum $\Phi_{nn}(f)$ of each input channel is estimated as the noise power spectrum of the M lowest energy frames in the file ($M = 20$ was used for the current experiments). On the second pass a Wiener filter with transfer function $\frac{\Phi_{xx}(f) - \Phi_{nn}(f)}{\Phi_{xx}(f)}$ (where $\phi_{xx}(f)$ is the input signal spectrum) is applied to each channel to remove stationary noise. The noise coherence matrix Q, estimated over the M lowest energy frames, is also output at this time. In the third stage delay vectors between each channel pair are calculated for every frame in the input sample. The delay between two channels is the time difference between the arrival of the dominant sound source and is calculated by finding the peak in the Generalised Cross Correlation [15] between input frames across two channels. The delay vector is given as the delays for all pairs with respect to a single reference channel - there are therefore N delays in each vector, with the delay for the reference channel equal to 0. Further a vector of relative scaling factors is calculated, corresponding to the ratio of of frame energies between each channel and the reference channel. The start and end times in seconds, along with the delay and scaling factors are output for each frame. Finally The delay and scaling vectors are then used to calculate beamforming filters for each frame using the standard superdirective technique [5,6]. The superdirective formulation requires knowledge of the noise coherence matrix. However this is not available as the microphone positions are not known. Either a unity coherence matrix may be used (leading to delay-sum filters) or the Q matrix estimate in the second stage may be used. Each frame is then beamformed using the appropriate filters and the output subsequently used for recognition.

5.3   Model Building

As outlined above the the fact that meeting resources are still comparatively small, bootstrapping from CTS models was used. However, as CTS data is only available at a bandwidth of 4kHz this poses additional questions on the initialisation and training procedure.

Bandwidth and Adaptation. Table 7 shows recognition performance on the icsidev test set using various model training strategies. The baseline CTS systems yield a still reasonable error rate. Training on 8kHz-limited (NB) ICSI training data yields a WER of 27.1%. Using the full bandwidth (WB) reduces the WER by 1.8%. The standard approach for adaptation to large amounts of data is MAP [10]. As CTS is NB only, adaptation to WB ICSI data was performed using MAP adaptation in an iterative fashion. However the performance of the adapted NB system was still poorer than that of the system trained on WB data. The results show that MAP adaptation from CTS models while using wideband data is desirable. In our implementation the adaptation model set is used for two purposes: for computation of state level posteriors and to serve as a prior. Even if the former is performed well, NB models cannot be used to serve as prior directly. In order to overcome this problem the means of the CTS models were modified using block-diagonal MLLR transforms. One transform for speech and one for silence was estimated on the complete ICSI corpus using models trained on ICSI NB data. After an initial step with MLLR-adapted CTS models iterative MAP adaptation is resumed as before. The use of more detailed modelling of the transition from NB to WB by the use of more transforms was not found to yield a significant performance improvement. After 8 iterations a further 0.9% reduction in WER is obtained.

Table 7. %WER results on icsidev for several different training strategies and a trigram LM optimised for the ICSI corpus

Data	Bandwidth	Adaptation	#Iter	%WER
CTS	NB	-	-	33.3
ICSI	NB	-	-	27.1
ICSI	WB	-	-	25.3
ICSI	NB	MAP	1	26.5
ICSI	NB	MAP	8	25.8
ICSI	WB	MLLR + MAP	8	24.6
ALL	WB	MLLR + MAP	8	25.8

Meeting Resource Specific Language Modelling. The language and vocabulary in meetings differs substantially. We have found evidence that his is also true for the acoustics However the advantage of having more data outweighs the differences. Hence we use acoustic models trained on the all meeting resources. Table 8 shows WER results using acoustic models trained on the complete meeting data and specific language models. An initial observation makes clear that on average the best strategy is to combine all the resources (similar

Table 8. %WER on the rt04eval sets . TOT gives WERs overall, while MRS denotes the use of language models focusing on specific meeting rooms.

	TOT	ISL	ICSI	NIST	LDC
MRS ISL	40.2	44.7	25.8	34.1	53.8
MRS ICSI	40.2	45.2	25.1	34.7	53.5
MRS NIST	40.2	44.6	26.2	34.1	53.6
MRS AMI	41.0	45.1	26.9	35.8	54.2
COMBINED	40.0	44.5	25.6	34.4	53.4

to the acoustics). Further the variation of scores is modest whereby AMI data is distinct from all other resources. A moderate beneficial effect can be observed from using meeting room specific language models.

Independent Headset Microphone (IHM) Processing. The sections above gave an outline of the components required for a baseline system on meeting transcription. The task of combining the components in a sensible complex. For optimal performance many of the techniques cannot just simply be "plugged" together. Table 9 shows WER results using various model building techniques. Models are trained on a total of 96 hours of meeting speech. The baseline model yields 40% overall. By far the best performance is achieved on the ICSI portion of the data and performance is roughly gender balanced. Similar to CTS the use of VTLN yields a substantial improvement. Comparing the systems VTLN1 and VTLN2, the gain from CTS-adaptation remains even in conjunction with VTLN. The next part of the table shows the use of echo-cancelled (EC) data (as used for segmentation). Virtually no effect on recognition performance can be observed. The last section shows results with automatic segmentation (all other results are based on reference segmentation). The SEG1 system only makes use of the basic configuration, i.e. using an MLP only trained on PLP features.

Table 9. %WER on the rt04eval set using a combined tigram language model. CTS denotes CTS-adapted, EC echo cancellation.The table shows gender specific results (F/M) and results per meeting room . In the first section the reference segmentation of the data is used.

System	CTS	VTLN	EC	TOT	F	M	ISL	ICSI	LDC	NIST
BASE	×			40.0	39.4	40.4	44.5	25.6	53.4	34.4
VTLN1	×	×		36.9	36.4	37.2	42.0	22.4	50.3	30.5
VTLN2		×		37.6	36.0	38.4	42.7	23.3	51.3	30.1
VTLN1 - SHLDA	×	×		36.0	35.1	36.5	41.0	21.8	50.5	27.4
EC1	×		×	40.3	39.5	40.7	44.7	25.9	54.8	33.1
VTLN-EC1	×	×	×	37.0	36.1	37.5	41.2	22.9	50.8	30.9
SEG1	×			50.8	51.1	50.6	50.4	38.2	73.3	37.4

MDM Processing. Almost all meeting corpora used a different approach to record speech with remote microphones. In the ICSI corpus microphones are not in fixed array configuration, the ISL corpus only uses one distant microphone,

Table 10. %WER on rt04seval and rt05samidev-n when training on various meeting resource combinations

Combination		rt05seval					rt05samidev-n		
	TOT	ISL	ICSI	LDC	NIST	TOT	UEDIN	IDIAP
ICSI,NIST	50.4	56.2	24.1	61.1	36.9	59.1	60.2	58.4
ICSI,NIST,ISL	50.6	56.2	22.9	61.8	37.2	59.1	60.0	57.6
ICSI,NIST,ISL,AMI	50.3	54.5	27.4	61.3	36.2	57.3	59.0	54.5

Table 11. %WER on rt04seval and rt05samidev-n with different amounts of traiing data. ms0, ms10,and wb describe data preparation (see text).

System		rt05seval					rt05samidev-n		
	TOT	CMU	ICSI	LDC	NIST	TOT	UEDIN	IDIAP
ms0	51.0	55.4	26.4	63.4	34.9	57.4	58.9	55.0
ms10	51.0	54.3	25.9	63.6	37.0	56.4	58.0	54.0
wb	50.7	56.5	24.3	61.9	36.4	56.3	58.2	53.4
VTLN - wb	47.2	51.4	20.6	60.2	31.3	-	-	-
wb icsiseg	55.2	59.5	32.2	66.7	40.5	-	-	-

AMI uses a circular microphone array. Table 10 shows performance results with models trained on specific corpora. Overall the size and type of data used appears to have little impact on performance. Only the use of AMI training data appears to aid recognition on the AMI test set. The enhancement based approach described in section 5.2 has the disadvantage that it cannot cope with overlapped speech. Since straight-forward removal of overlapping segments however would be far to restrictive. Instead word timings from forced alignment were used to identify overlaps. Speech segments were split, either at point of at least 100ms silence (ms10), of silence occurrence(ms0), or at arbitrary word boundaries (wb). These approaches reduce the original training set size of 96 hours to 56, 63 or 66 hours respectively. Table 11 shows associated WER results. Only a minor preference of an increase in training set size is evident. However training set size has an impact on the effect of channel based normalisation schemes. Table 11 shows the performance after VTLN in both training and test, yielding improvements comparable to IHM. Finally table 11 shows results for use of automatic segments as generated by the ICSI segmenter[22] which results in 5% absolute reduction in WER, mostly driven by an increase in the deletion rate. note that the greatest degradation was on the ICSI corpus.

6   Conclusions

In this paper the components of the AMI meeting transcription system were described. So far the system is equipped with baseline compomen ts that allow the processing of the highly variable data. We have shown: the feasibility to use the Edinburgh UNISYN dictionary for speech recognition, the effective use of language model data for meetings collected from the internet; the effective use of

SHLDA and VTLN on CTS and meetings, both in IHM and MDM recorddings; the language properties of meeting rooms; and effective data preparation for this domain. We have further presented initial transcription results on the AMI meeting corpus.

Acknowledgements

This work was partly supported by the European Union 6th FWP IST Integrated Project AMI (Augmented Multi-party Interaction, FP6-506811). The authors thank the rest of the AMI-ASR team for their valuable contributions: Barbara Peskin, Jan Czernocky, Jithendra Vepa, and Chuck Wooters. Thanks to Andreas Stolcke and ICSI for providing the segments and speaker labels for MDM data. We also thank Cambridge University Engineering Department for providing the h5train03 CTS training set and for the right to use Gunnar Evermann's HDecode at the University of Sheffield.

References

1. A.W. Black, P. Taylor and R. Caley (2004). The Festival Speech Synthesis System, Version 1.95beta. CSTR, University of Edinburgh, Edinburgh.
2. I. Bulyko, M. Ostendorf and A. Stolcke. Getting More Mileage from Web Text Sources for Conversational Speech Language Modeling using Class-Dependent Mixtures. in Proc HLT'03.
3. S. Burger, V. MacLaren, H. Yu (2002). The ISL Meeting Corpus: The Impact of Meeting Type on Speech Style. In Proc. ICSLP'2002.
4. J. Carletta,S. Ashby, S. Bourban, M. Guillemot M. Kronenthal, G. Lathoud, M. Lincoln, I. McCowan, T. Hain, W. Kraaij, W. Post, J. Kadlec, P. Wellner, M. Flynn, D. Reidsma (2005. The AMI Meeting Corpus. Submitted to MLMI'05.
5. H. Cox, R. Zeskind, and I. Kooij (1986). Practical supergain. IEEE Transactions on Acoustics, Speech and Signal Processing, ASSP-34(3):393–397.
6. H. Cox, R. Zeskind, and M. Owen (1987). Robust adaptive beamforming. IEEE Transactions on Acoustics, Speech and Signal Processing, ASSP-35(10):1365–1376.
7. S. Fitt (2000). Documentation and user guide to UNISYN lexicon and post-lexical rules, Tech. Rep., Centre for Speech Technology Research, Edinburgh.
8. M.J.F. Gales & P.C. Woodland (1996). Mean and Variance Adaptation within the MLLR Framework. *Computer Speech & Language*, Vol. 10, pp. 249–264.
9. J.S. Garafolo, C.D. Laprun, M. Michel, V.M. Stanford, E. Tabassi (2004). In Proc. 4th Intl. Conf. on Language Resources and Evaluation (LREC'04).
10. J.L. Gauvain, C. Lee (1994). MAP estimation for multivariate Gaussian mixture observation of Markov Chains, IEEE Tr. Speech& Audio Processing, 2, pp. 291-298.
11. T. Hain, P. Woodland, T. Niesler, and E. Whittaker (1999). The 1998 HTK system for transcription of conversational telephone speech. Proc. IEEE ICASSP, 1999.
12. H. Hermansky (1990). Perceptual Linear Predictive (PLP) analysis of speech. Acoustical Society of America, 87(4):1738–1752.
13. A. Janin, D. Baron, J. Edwards, D. Ellis, D. Gelbart, N. Morgan, B. Peskin, T. Pfau, E. Shriberg, A. Stolcke, C. Wooters (2003). The ICSI Meeting Corpus. ICASSP'03, Hong Kong.

14. B. Klimt, Y. Yang (2004). Introducing the Enron Corpus, Second Conference on Email and Anti-Spam, CEAS 2004.
15. C. H. Knapp and G. C. Carter (1976). The generalized correlation method for estimation of time delay/ IEEE Transactions on Acoustics, Speech and Signal Processing, ASSP-24:320–327, August 1976.
16. N. Kumar (1997), Investigation of Silicon-Auditory Models and Generalization of Linear Discriminant Analysis for Improved Speech Recognition.PhD thesis, John Hopkins University, Baltimore.
17. L. Burget (2004), Combination of Speech Features Using Smoothed Heteroscedastic Linear Discriminant Analysis. in Proc. ICSLP'04, Jeju island, KR, 2004, p. 4.
18. D. Messerschmitt, D. Hedberg, C. Cole, A. Haoui, and P. Winship (1989). Digital voice echo canceller with a TMS32020. Appl. Rep. SPRA129, Texas Instruments.
19. Spring 2004 (RT04S) Rich Transcription Meeting Recognition Evaluation Plan. NIST, US. Available at http://www.nist.gov/speech.
20. T. Pfau and D.P. W. Ellis (2001). Hidden markov model based speech activity detection for the ICSI meeting project. Eurospeech'01.
21. T. Schultz, A. Waibel, M. Bett, F. Metze, Y. Pan, K. Ries, T. Schaaf, H. Soltau, M. Westphal, H. Yu, and K. Zechner (2001). The ISL Meeting Room System. In Proc. of the Workshop on Hands-Free Speech Communication (HSC-2001), Kyoto.
22. A. Stolcke, C. Wooters, N. Mirghafori, T. Pirinen, I. Bulyko, D. Gelbart, M. Graciarena, S. Otterson, B. Peskin, and M. Ostendorf (2004). Progress in Meeting Recognition: The ICSI-SRI-UW Spring 2004 Evaluation System. NIST RT04 Workshop.
23. The SRI Language Modelling Toolkit (SRILM). http://www.speech.sri.com/projects/srilm, SRI international, California.
24. P.C. Woodland, M.J.F. Gales, D. Pye & S.J. Young (1997). Broadcast News Transcription using HTK. In *Proc. ICASSP'97*, pp. 719-722, Munich.
25. S. Wrigley, G. Brown, V. Wan, and S. Renals (2005). Speech and crosstalk detection in multichannel audio. IEEE Trans. Speech& Audio Proc., 13(1):84–91.

Improving the Performance of Acoustic Event Classification by Selecting and Combining Information Sources Using the Fuzzy Integral

Andrey Temko, Dušan Macho, and Climent Nadeu

TALP Research Center, Universitat Politècnica de Catalunya, Campus Nord, Edifici D5,
Jordi Girona 1-3, 08034 Barcelona, Spain
{temko, dusan, climent}@talp.upc.es

Abstract. Acoustic events produced in meeting-room-like environments may carry information useful for perceptually aware interfaces. In this paper, we focus on the problem of combining different information sources at different structural levels for classifying human vocal-tract non-speech sounds. The Fuzzy Integral (FI) approach is used to fuse outputs of several classification systems, and feature selection and ranking are carried out based on the knowledge extracted from the Fuzzy Measure (FM). In the experiments with a limited set of training data, the FI-based decision-level fusion showed a classification performance which is much higher than the one from the best single classifier and can surpass the performance resulting from the integration at the feature-level by Support Vector Machines. Although only fusion of audio information sources is considered in this work, the conclusions may be extensible to the multi-modal case.

1 Introduction

In context-aware systems such as smart-rooms or intelligent personal devices, acoustic event classification (AEC) can provide support for a high-level analysis of the underlying acoustic scene. On the other hand, AEC can also offer useful information to peer technologies like speech enhancement or acoustic source localization to improve their performance. In this paper, we focus on the classification of a particular type of acoustic events, a set of human vocal-tract non-speech sounds, since they were found responsible for a large part of errors in classification of meeting-room acoustic events [1]. In fact, those sounds contributed with a 70% to the total classification error, in spite of accounting only for 30% of the acoustic events. Additionally, as it was also observed in [1], they are mainly confused among themselves.

In [1], we build and tested several feature sets by combining features used in speech recognition with other perceptual features. Also, several classifiers were tested, which were based on either Gaussian mixture models (GMM) or support vector machines (SVM) [2]. In our tests, the latter approach showed significantly higher classification accuracies. Actually, SVMs are discriminant classifiers and they do not need a training database as large as generative classifiers like GMMs do. Furthermore, we could say that they are not so sensitive to the presence of irrelevant features [3], so it is appropriate to use them with a large and diverse feature set, as it was done in those tests.

S. Renals and S. Bengio (Eds.): MLMI 2005, LNCS 3869, pp. 357–368, 2006.

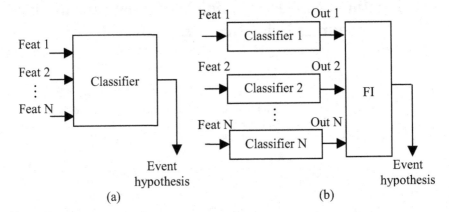

Fig. 1. Fusion at the feature (a) and decision (b) levels

In this paper, we present some preliminary attempts to improve the performance achieved in [1] for the above-mentioned subset of human sounds, by focusing on both feature selection and combination of classifiers, and using concepts and tools from fuzzy theory; concretely, the fuzzy integral (FI) [4,5,6] and the fuzzy measure (FM).

Over the past several years there have been a number of successful applications of fuzzy integral in multi-criteria decision-making and pattern recognition (e.g. [7,8,9]). In AEC, different acoustic features are extracted from the audio signal with an objective to obtain different kinds of information sources. These features are then used to feed a classifier or several classifiers. In this work we compare the fusion of the information sources at the feature-level (early integration, see Figure 1 (a)) with the fusion at the decision-level (late integration, see Figure 1 (b)) using Fuzzy Integral approach.

It is assumed that each feature represents an equally contributing and independent source of information; in praxis, however, the contribution of individual features is not obvious and apparently diverse features can be highly correlated. When performing the feature-level fusion, the created feature space may be of very high dimension and thus be susceptible to the curse of dimensionality [10]. On the other hand, at the decision-level, since the media sources are treated separately, the interdependencies among the different sources are usually left unexplored. Simple fusion methods (e.g. sum, product, minimum, maximum, weighted arithmetical mean (WAM), etc [7,11,12]) are not able to model in any understandable way an interaction among various sources of information and thus are not suitable for aggregation of interacting criteria. In order to obtain a flexible representation of correlation among information sources, it is useful to define the weights according to the FM, based not only on each criterion but also on each subset of criteria. From a given FM, it is possible to extract information that may give an insight into the behaviour of FI: importance and interaction of information sources, tolerance and uncertainty of the decision-maker, etc.

Both the feature-level fusion and the decision-level fusion are compared in this work by performing AEC experiments. As a default classifier we use SVMs, which helps to overcome the problem of the high-dimensionality of the input space of features. The results indicate that the decision-level fusion by FI outperforms WAM and has similar or better results than feature-level fusion with SVM. We also observed that the fact of decreasing the number of information sources negatively influences the results from decision-level fusion with FI, but leads to an improvement for feature-level fusion by SVM. The FI aggregation may be appropriate when the feature-level fusion is difficult (e.g. due to the different nature of the involved features), or when it is beneficial to preserve the application or technique dependence (e.g. when fusing well established feature-classifier configurations). For that reason, we have also conducted experiments to combine Hidden Markov Models (HMM) that use frame-level features with SVM using signal-level features and witnessed an additional improvement.

The rest of the paper is organized as follows: Section 2 gives the basics of FI and FM. Section 3 presents the description of the experiments, the database, the features, the classifier setup, and the metrics used throughout the work, along with test results and discussions. Finally, conclusions are given in Section 4.

2   Fuzzy Integral and Fuzzy Measure

We are searching for a suitable fusion operator to combine a finite set of information sources $Z = \{1,...,z\}$. Let $D = \{D_1, D_2,..., D_z\}$ be a set of trained classification systems and $\Omega = \{c_1, c_2,..., c_N\}$ be a set of class labels. Each classification system takes as input a data point $x \in \Re^n$ and assigns it to a class label from Ω. Alternatively, each classifier output can be formed as a N-dimensional vector that represents the degree of support of that classification system to each of N classes. Suppose also that these evaluations are commensurable, i.e. defined on the same measurement scale (most often the outputs of classification systems are posterior probabilities-like). Thus, consider h_i, $i=1,...,z$, the output scores of z classification systems for class c_n (the supports for class c_n). Before defining how FI combines information sources, let's look to a conventional weighted arithmetical mean (WAM) operator. A final support measure for class c_n using WAM can be defined as:

$$M_{WAM} = \sum_{i \in Z} \mu(i) h_i \tag{1}$$

where $\sum_{i \in Z} \mu(i) = 1$ (additive), $\mu(i) \geq 0 \ for\ all\ i \in Z$

The WAM operator combines the score of z competent information sources through the weights of importance expressed by $\mu(i)$. The main disadvantage of the WAM operator is that it implies preferential independence of the information sources [12].

Let's denote with $\mu(i, j) = \mu(\{i, j\})$ the weight of importance corresponding to the couple of information sources i and j from Z. If μ is not additive, i.e. $\mu(i, j) \neq [\mu(i) + \mu(j)]$ for a given couple $\{i, j\} \subseteq Z$, we must take into account some interaction among the information sources. Therefore, we can build an aggregation operator starting from the WAM, adding the term of "second order" that involves the corrective coefficients $\mu(i, j) - [\mu(i) + \mu(j)]$, then the term of "third order", etc. In this way, we arrive to the definition of the FI: assuming the sequence h_i, $i=1,...,z$, is ordered in such a way that $h_1 \leq ... \leq h_z$, the Choquet *fuzzy integral* [5,6,12] can be computed as

$$M_{FI}(\mu,h) = \sum_{i=1}^{z} [\mu(i,...,z) - \mu(i+1,...,z)] \, h_i \qquad (2)$$

where $\mu(z+1) = \mu(\emptyset) = 0$. $\mu(S)$ can be viewed as a weight related to a subset S of the set Z of information sources. It is called *fuzzy measure* and has to meet the following conditions:

$\mu(\emptyset) = 0, \mu(Z) = 1$,   Boundary

$S \subseteq T \Rightarrow \mu(S) \leq \mu(T)$,   Monotonicity

where $S, T \subseteq Z$.

To illustrate the FI, let us consider a case of two information sources with outputs h_1 and h_2, and assume that $h_1 < h_2$. Consequently, we have corrective coefficients of the second order only: $\mu(1,2) - [\mu(1) + \mu(2)]$. According to (2), FI is computed as

$$M_{FI}(\mu,h) = [\mu(1,2) - \mu(2)] \, h_1 + \mu(2) \, h_2$$

which, after a slight manipulation, results in

$$M_{FI}(\mu,h) = [\mu(1,2) - (\mu(2) + \mu(1))] \, h_1 + \mu(1) \, h_1 + \mu(2) \, h_2$$

where the first term corresponds to the "second order" correction mentioned above.

As was mentioned in [12], FI has very good properties for aggregation: it is continuous, non-decreasing, ranges between a minimum and a maximum value, and coincides with WAM (discrete Lebesgue integral) as long as the FM is additive. Actually, it was shown in [12] that the ordered weighted average, the WAM, and the partial minimum and maximum operators are all particular cases of FI with special FM. In fact, FI can be seen as a compromise between the evidence expressed by the outputs of the classification systems and the competence represented by the FM [7].

Indeed, the large flexibility of the FI aggregation operator is due to the use of FM that can model interaction among criteria. And although the FM $\mu(i)$ provides an initial view about the importance of information source i, all possible subsets of Z that include that information source should be analysed to give a final score. For instance, we may have $\mu(i) = 0$, suggesting that element i, $i \notin T$, is not important; but if, at the same time, $\mu(T \cup i) \gg \mu(T)$, this actually indicates i is an important element for the decision. For calculating the *importance* of the information source i, the Shapley score [6,12] is used. It is defined as:

$$\phi(\mu,i) = \sum_{T \subseteq Z \setminus i} \frac{(|Z| - |T| - 1)! |T|!}{|Z|!} [\mu(T \cup i) - \mu(T)] \qquad (3)$$

Generally, (3) calculates a weighted average value of the marginal contribution $\mu(T \cup i) - \mu(T)$ of the element i over all possible combinations. It can be easily shown that the information source importance sums to one.

Another interesting concept is interaction among information sources. As long as the fuzzy measure is not additive, there exists some correlation among information sources. When $\mu(i, j) < \mu(i) + \mu(j)$ the information sources i and j express negative synergy and can be considered redundant. On the contrary, when $\mu(i, j) > \mu(i) + \mu(j)$, the information sources i and j are complementary and express positive synergy. For calculating the interaction indices, instead of the marginal contribution of element i in (3), the contribution of a pair of information sources i and j is defined as the difference between the marginal contribution of the pair and the addition of the two individual marginal contributions, or equivalently:

$$(\Delta_{i,j}\mu)(T) = \mu(T \cup i, j) - \mu(T \cup i) - \mu(T \cup j) + \mu(T) \tag{4}$$

and the *interaction indices* are calculated as:

$$I(\mu; i, j) = \sum_{T \subseteq Z \setminus i, j} \frac{(|Z| - |T| - 2)! |T|!}{(|Z| - 1)!} (\Delta_{i,j}\mu)(T)] \tag{5}$$

We can see the index is positive as long as i and j are negatively correlated (complementary) and negative when i and j are positively correlated (competitive).

As the FM is a generalization of a probability measure, we can calculate a measure of uncertainty associated to FM analogously to the way the entropy is computed from the probability [13], that is:

$$H(\mu) = \sum_{i=1}^{z} \sum_{T \subseteq Z \setminus i} \gamma_T \, g[\mu(T \cup i) - \mu(T)] \tag{6}$$

where $\gamma_T = (|Z| - |T| - 1)! |T|! / |Z|!$, $g(x) = -x \ln x$, and $0 \ln 0 = 0$ by convention.

When normalized by $\ln|Z|$, $H(\mu)$ measures the extent to which the information sources are being used in calculating the aggregation value of $M_{FI}(\mu, h)$. When that *entropy* measure is close to 1, all criteria are used almost equally; when it is close to 0, the FI concentrates almost on only one criterion [14].

It is obvious that FI completely relies on the FM. The better the FM describes the real competence and interaction among all classification systems, the more accurate results can be expected. There are two methods of calculating the FM known to the authors (if it is not provided by an expert knowledge): one based on fuzzy densities [7], and the other based on learning the FM from training data [8][9]. In our work, we have used the latter method: a supervised, gradient-based algorithm of learning the FM, with additional steps for smoothing the unmodified nodes.

3 Experiments and Discussion

3.1 Experimental Setup

3.1.1 Database
Due to the lack of an acceptable corpus, the acoustic event database used in this work has been assembled using different sources. Part of the database was taken from the seminar recordings employed within the CHIL project [15]. The other part has been found in a large number of Internet websites. All sounds were down-sampled to 8

kHz. The fact that the acoustic events were taken from different sources makes the classification task more complicated due to the presence of several (sometimes unknown) environments and recording conditions.

Table 1. Sound classes and number of samples per class

	Event	Number
A	Cough & Throat	119
B	Laughter	37
C	Sneeze	40
D	Sniff	37
E	Yawn	12

Table 1 shows the five acoustic classes considered in this work. There is a high variation in the number of samples per class, which represents an additional difficulty. In order to achieve a reasonable testing scenario, the data has been approximately equally split into the training and testing parts in such a way that there was the same number of representatives from the two data sources in the training and testing part. 10 runs were done in all the experiments.

3.1.2 Audio features
Although the best feature sets for AEC in [1] consisted of combinations of features used in automatic speech recognition and other perceptual features, in the current work we only focus on the latter, since their contribution to vocal-tract sounds is not so well-established. 10 types of features were chosen with a substantial degree of redundancy in order to find out, with the FM, their relative importance and their degree of interaction. The following types of frame-level acoustic features are investigated (with the number of features per frame in parenthesis):

1. Zero crossing rate (1)
2. Short-time energy (1)
3. Fundamental frequency (1)
4. Sub-band log energies (4)
5. Sub-band log energy distribution (4)
6. Sub-band log energy correlations (4)
7. Sub-band log energy time differences (4)
8. Spectral centroid (1)
9. Spectral roll-off (1)
10. Spectral bandwidth (1)

Thus, 22 acoustical measures are extracted from each frame, using 16ms/8ms frame length/shift. Then, from the whole time sequence of each acoustical measure in an event, four statistical parameters are computed: mean, standard deviation, autocorrelation coefficient at the second lag, and entropy. Those four statistical values per acoustical measure are used to represent the whole event.

3.1.3 SVM Setup

In experiments with SVM we use the Gaussian kernel. Leave-one-out cross validation [2] was applied to search for optimal kernel parameter σ. To cope with data unbalance we introduce different generalization parameters (C_+ and C_-) for positively- and negatively-labeled training samples [1]. MAX WINS scheme was used to extend SVM to the task of classifying several classes.

3.1.4 Metrics

For comparison of the results, three metrics are used. One is the overall system accuracy, which is computed as the quotient between the number of correct hypothesis (outputs) given by the classifier for all the classes and the total number of instances in the testing set. The other two metrics are the mean per class recall and the mean per class precision, which are defined as:

$$\text{Rec} = \frac{1}{|C|} \sum_{c \in C} \frac{|h_{corr}(c)|}{|r(c)|}, \qquad \text{Prec} = \frac{1}{|C|} \sum_{c \in C} \frac{|h_{corr}(c)|}{|h(c)|} \qquad (7)$$

where $|.|$ denotes cardinality of a set, C is the set of classes, c is a specific class, $r(c)$ is the number of reference (manually-labeled testing) instances and $h(c)$ is the number of hypothesis instances for class c. The subscript $_{corr}$ refers to a correct hypothesis. Due to the unbalance in amount of data per class, we think that the recall measure is more meaningful than the overall accuracy, but we use both of them for our comparisons, together with the precision measure.

3.2 Feature and Decision-Level Information Fusion

In this section, the two ways of information fusion mentioned in the Introduction are compared. For the feature-level fusion (see Fig.1 (a)), all ten types of features were used to feed the input of one SVM classifier. For the decision-level fusion (see Fig 1 (b)), ten independent SVM-based classifiers were trained, one for each feature type. The ten input criteria, represented by these ten classifiers, were then combined by WAM operator and FI with learned FM. For the weights in WAM operator we use uniform class noise model with the weights computed as $\mu_i = E_i^{E_i}(1 - E_i)^{1-E_i}$ where E_i is the training error of class c_i [16]. As we can see from Figure 2, both fusion approaches show a strong improvement in comparison to SVM with the best single feature type (number 4). As expected, feeding all the features to the SVM classifier also increased significantly the performance (SVM, 10 feature types). Interestingly enough, the fusion at the decision-level by FI showed comparable results to the powerful SVM classifier, which uses all the features. To gain an insight into the way FI works, we compare in Table 2 the individual recall score of the best feature type (column 2) for a given class, and the FI score (column 3) for the same class. Notice that, for the most represented class (A), the FI performance is lower, whereas for two less represented classes (C and D) it is higher. As the FM was trained using the errors of the particular classes as cost functions, we observe that, at the expense of accepting more errors for the most represented classes, the FI can recover a few errors for infrequent classes and thus obtain higher recall.

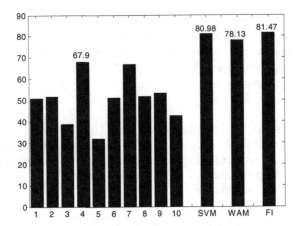

Fig. 2. Recall measure for: the 10 SVM systems running on each feature type, the combination of the 10 features at the feature-level with SVM, and the fusion on the decision-level with WAM and FI operators

However, the accuracy and precision measures for both FI and WAM were slightly worse than that of SVM. Notice also that FI fusion has approximately 10 times higher computation cost (10 independent SVM classifiers vs. one), and therefore the SVM feature-level fusion is preferable in this case.

Table 2. Comparison of individual recall scores for each class

Class	Best score	FI
A(119)	0.85	0.81
B(37)	0.61	0.61
C(40)	0.95	1.00
D(37)	0.77	1.00
E(12)	0.67	0.67

3.3 Feature Ranking and Selection

In the context of pattern recognition, the variable part of a classification system can be either features or classifiers. If we set classifiers to be the same, we can interpret the FM as the importance of features for the given classification task and we can use it for feature ranking and selection.

The information about both the importance of each feature type and the interaction among different feature types can be extracted applying the Shapley score to the FM. Using this approach, Figure 3 (a) shows that in our case the feature type 6 is the most important, followed by the feature type 7. As both feature types measure the changes of the spectral envelope along the time, we can conclude that that information is of high importance. The only other feature type with importance score above the average is number 4.

On the other hand, Figure 3 (b) shows the interaction among the feature types in our task; it can be seen that feature types 6 and 7 express a negative interaction, which coincide with their similar character. As an extreme case, the light cell (4,5) has a large negative value and thus indicates a high competitiveness (redundancy) of the mentioned feature types. That witnesses that those features are better to be considered separately. Actually, the feature type 4 (SBE) and the feature type 5 (Sp.Dist) become roughly the same feature after using the SVM normalization. In a similar way, as feature types 1 and 8 are both targeting the "main" frequency, their cell is also rather light. Also, from the two lighter cells in the bottom of the Figure 3 (b), one can conclude that feature type 9 is redundant if feature types 8 and 10 are considered. On the contrary, feature types 4 and 6, or 4 and 7, or 4 and 10 seem to be highly complementary, and thus are preferable to be considered together.

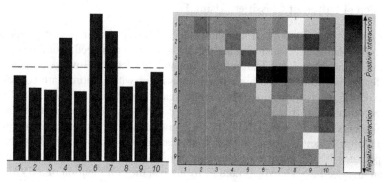

Fig. 3. Importance (a) and interaction (b) of features extracted from FM. Dashed line in part (a) shows the average importance level.

In the following AEC tests, we use the information from Figure 3 to perform the feature selection. In the first test, we select the 5 best feature types according to the individual feature type importance (Method 1), while to select the 5 best features in the second test, both the individual feature type importance and the interaction indices are used (Method 2, see [17] for a detailed description). The selected features are then fed to the SVM classifier. The performance of SVM with all features is considered as a baseline in this part. It can be seen from the results in Table 3 that Method 1 did not lead to a better performance, while Method 2 obtained a slight improvement over the baseline.

The last column in Table 3 shows that the FI scores resulting from using the feature types chosen by Method 2 are clearly worse than the SVM ones. Actually, the recall score is much lower than the one shown in Figure 2 for the FI technique when using the whole set of features. The measure of uncertainty defined in (6) helps us to understand that behaviour of the FI on the reduced set of criteria. In fact, for 10 features it is 0.86, meaning that to achieve the results shown in Figure 2, the FI operator uses in average 86% of the information contained in its 10 criteria, so preserving only

50% of all features is not sufficient. Consequently, we can conclude that, whereas an increment in the number of features may not be beneficial for techniques like SVM that cannot handle interactions among criteria, the FI can take advantage of the interactions between information sources (associated to features) to get a substantial gain in performance.

Table 3. Classification results using feature selection based on FM

	Support Vector Machines			FI
	Baseline	**Method 1**	**Method 2**	
Features	10 (all)	5(1,4,6,7,10)	5(4,6,7,8,10)	Method 2
Prec	84.50	82.76	**86.14**	81.74
Rec	**80.98**	75.31	80.14	74.79
Acc	84.83	83.97	**85.86**	83.79

3.4 Fusion of Different Classifiers Using FI

In previous sections we showed that the FI decision-level fusion obtains comparative results to the feature-level fusion using the SVM classifier. Indeed, from the computational cost point of view the feature-level fusion is preferred. However, when the resulting feature space has a too high dimensionality or when features are conveyed by different data types (strings, matrices, etc) the feature-level fusion is not an option.

On the other hand, it may be beneficial to combine the outputs of different well-established classification configurations for a given task; for example, the output of a SVM classifier which is discriminative but uses features from the whole signal with the output of a HMM generative classifier which considers time localized features. Based on that, we have tested with the FI formalism the combination of a SVM classifier that uses statistical (event-level) features with a HMM classifier that uses acoustic (frame-level) features. In these experiments, the best 5 feature types selected in the previous subsection by Method 2 are used with the SVM classifier. For HMM, we use a standard configuration coming from speech recognition: a 3 state left-to-right continuous density HMM model per class, with 8 Gaussians per state, and 13 frequency-filtered filter-bank energies (FFBE) [18] as features. Table 4 shows the results with and without time derivatives (ΔFFBE).

Table 4. HMM performance with and without time derivatives

	HMM-FFBE	**HMM-FFBE+ΔFFBE**
Prec	69.28	66.70
Rec	67.36	59.31
Acc	84.48	79.17

Given the low scores in Table 4 it is clear that the amount of data we use is not enough to train the 26 dimensional data well. Thus, we decided to fuse 3 criteria: SVM, HMM-FFBE and HMM-ΔFFBE. Results of the individual classifiers and the FI

Table 5. Individual and FI performance scores

	SVM	HMM-FFBE	HMM-ΔFFBE	FI
Prec	86.14	69.28	51.06	89.47
Rec	80.14	67.36	60.73	82.43
Acc	85.86	84.48	52.59	87.93

decision fusion system are presented in Table 5 where an improvement can be observed by FI fusion of the SVM output with two information sources which give much lower individual performances, but use different features.

Unfortunately, we could not see any clear dependence of the ensemble performance on the diversity of the classification systems [16].

Note from Figure 2 that a much higher improvement was observed by fusing a larger number of information sources (10). However, the difficulty of learning FM increases with the number of information sources.

4   Conclusion

In this work, we have carried out a preliminary investigation about the fusion of several information sources with the fuzzy integral approach to improve the performance of the baseline SVM approach in the task of classifying a small set of human vocal-tract non-speech sounds. By interpreting an information source as a specific combination of a classifier and a set of features, we have been able to carry out different types of tests.

In the experiments, fusion of several information sources with the FI formalism showed a significant improvement with respect to the score of the best single information source. Moreover, the FI decision-level fusion approach showed comparable results to the high-performing SVM feature-level fusion. We have also observed that the importance and the degree of interaction among the various feature types given by the FM can be used for feature selection, and gives a valuable insight into the problem. The experimental work also indicates that the FI is a good choice when feature-level fusion is not an option.

Acknowledgements

The authors wish to thank Enric Monte for his valuable help and encouraging discussions. This work has been partially sponsored by the EU-funded project CHIL, IP506909, and the Spanish Government-funded project ALIADO.

References

1. A. Temko, C. Nadeu, "Meeting room acoustic event classification by support vector machines and variable-feature-set clustering", *ICASSP 2005*, Philadelphia, Mar., 2005.
2. B. Schölkopf, A. Smola, *Learning with Kernels*, MIT Press, Cambridge, MA, 2002.

3. J. Weston, J. Mukherjee, O. Chapelle, M. Pontil, T. Poggio, V. Vapnik: "Feature Selection for SVMs", *Proc. of NIPS*, 2000.
4. M. Sugeno, *Theory of fuzzy integrals and its applications*, PhD thesis, Tokyo Institute of Technology, 1974.
5. M. Grabisch, "The Choquet integral as a linear interpolator", *10th Int. Conf. on Information Processing and Management of Uncertainty in Knowledge-Based Systems (IPMU 2004)*, Perugia (Italy), pp.373-378, July 2004
6. M. Grabisch, "Fuzzy integral in multi-criteria decision-making", *Fuzzy Sets & Systems* 69, pp. 279-298, 1995
7. L. Kuncheva, "'Fuzzy' vs 'Non-fuzzy' in combining classifiers designed by boosting", *IEEE Transactions on Fuzzy Systems*, 11 (6), pp. 729-741, 2003.
8. S. Chang and S. Greenberg, "Syllable-proximity evaluation in automatic speech recognition using fuzzy measures and a fuzzy integral", *Proc. of the 12th IEEE Fuzzy Systems Conf.*, pp. 828- 833 2003.
9. M. Grabisch, "A new algorithm for identifying fuzzy measures and its application to pattern recognition". *Proc. of 4th IEEE Int. Conf. on Fuzzy Systems*, Yokohama, Japan, pp.145-50, 1995
10. Y. Wu, E. Chang, K. Chang, J Smith., "Optimal Multimodal Fusion for Multimedia Data Analysis", *Proc. ACM Int. Conf. on Multimedia*, New York, pp.572-579, Oct. 2004.
11. L. Kuncheva, "Combining classifiers: Soft computing solutions", *Lecture Notes in Pattern Recognition*, World Scientific Publishing Co., Singapore, pp. 427-452, 2001.
12. J-L. Marichal, "Behavioral analysis of aggregation in multicriteria decision aid, Preferences and Decisions under Incomplete Knowledge", *Studies in Fuzziness and Soft Computing,* Vol. 51 (Physica Verlag, Heidelberg), pp. 153-178, 2000.
13. J-L. Marichal, "Entropy of discrete Choquet capacities", *European Journal of Operational Research,* 137 (3), pp. 612-624, 2002.
14. I. Kojadinovic, J-L. Marichal, M. Roubens, "An axiomatic approach to the definition of the entropy of a discrete choquet capacity", *9th Int. Conf. on Information Processing and Management of Uncertainty in Knowledge-Based Systems (IPMU 2002),* Annecy (France), pp.763–768, 2002.
15. "Evaluation Packages for the First CHIL Evaluation Campaign", CHIL project Deliverable D7.4, downloadable from http://chil.server.de/servlet/is/2712/, Mar. 2005.
16. L. Kuncheva, *Combining Pattern Classifiers*, John Wiley & Sons, Inc, 2004.
17. L. Mikenina, H. Zimmermann, "Improved feature selection and classification by the 2-additive fuzzy measure", *Fuzzy Sets and Systems*, 107:2, pp.197-218, 1999.
18. C. Nadeu, J. Hernando, M. Gorricho, "On the decorrelation of filter-bank energies in speech recognition", *Proc. Eurospeech'95*, pp. 1381-1384, 1995.

The Rich Transcription 2005 Spring Meeting Recognition Evaluation

Jonathan G. Fiscus[1], Nicolas Radde[1], John S. Garofolo[1], Audrey Le[1],
Jerome Ajot[1], and Christophe Laprun[1,2]

[1] National Institute of Standards and Technology, 100 Bureau Drive Stop 8940,
Gaithersburg, MD 20899
[2] Systems Plus, Inc., 1370 Piccard Drive, Suite 270, Rockville, MD 20850
{jfiscus, nradde, jgarofolo, ajot, claprun}@nist.gov

Abstract. This paper presents the design and results of the Rich Transcription
Spring 2005 (RT-05S) Meeting Recognition Evaluation. This evaluation is the
third in a series of community-wide evaluations of language technologies in the
meeting domain. For 2005, four evaluation tasks were supported. These included a speech-to-text (STT) transcription task and three diarization tasks:
"Who Spoke When", "Speech Activity Detection", and "Source Localization."
The latter two were first-time experimental proof-of-concept tasks and were
treated as "dry runs". For the STT task, the lowest word error rate for the multiple distant microphone condition was 30.0% which represented an impressive
33% relative reduction from the best result obtained in the last such evaluation -
- the Rich Transcription Spring 2004 Meeting Recognition Evaluation. For the
diarization "Who Spoke When" task, the lowest diarization error rate was
18.56% which represented a 19% relative reduction from that of RT-04S.

1 Motivation

The National Institute of Standards and Technology (NIST) has been working with
the speech recognition community since the mid 1980s to improve the state-of-the-
art in technologies for transforming speech into text. To facilitate progress, NIST
has worked with the community to make training/development data collections
available for several speech domains. NIST collaborated with the research community to define performance metrics and create evaluation tools so that technology developers can perform hill-climbing experiments and self-evaluate their progress. NIST also coordinates periodic community-wide benchmark tests and
technology workshops to inform the research community and Government spon-
sors of progress and to promote technical exchange. The test suites used in these
benchmark tests are generally made available to the community as development
tools after the formal evaluations.

NIST's evaluations have demonstrated great progress in the state-of-the-art in
speech-to-text (STT) transcription systems. STT systems in the late 80s focused on

S. Renals and S. Bengio (Eds.): MLMI 2005, LNCS 3869, pp. 369–389, 2006.
© Springer-Verlag Berlin Heidelberg 2006

read speech from artificially-constrained domains. As the technology improved, the NIST evaluations focused the research community on increasingly difficult challenges with regard to speech modality, speaker population, recording characteristics, language, vocabulary, etc. Now that English Broadcast News word error rates are below 10% and English Conversational Telephone Speech word error rates are nearing 15% [1], it is apparent that the research community is ready for the next challenge.

The meeting domain presents several challenges to the technology which aren't represented in the broadcast news and conversational telephone speech domains. These include varied forums and an infinite number of topics, spontaneous highly interactive and overlapping speech, varied recording environments, varied/multiple microphones, multi-modal inputs, participant movement, and far field speech effects like ambient noise and reverberation. In order to properly study these challenges, laboratory-quality experiment controls must be available to enable systematic research. The meeting domain provides a unique environment to collect naturally-occurring spoken interactions under controlled sensor conditions.

The Rich Transcription Spring 2005 (RT-05S) Meeting Recognition evaluation is part of the NIST Rich Transcription (RT) series of language technology evaluations [1] [2]. These evaluations have moved the technology focus from a strictly word-centric approach to an integrated approach where the focus is on creating richly annotated transcriptions of speech, of which words are only one component. The goal of the RT series is to create technologies to generate transcriptions of speech which are fluent and informative and which are readable by humans and usable in downstream processing by machines. To accomplish this, lexical symbols must be augmented with important informative non-orthographic metadata. These resulting metadata enriched transcripts are referred to as "rich transcriptions." This approach was originated in the DARPA Effective, Affordable, Reusable Speech-to-Text (EARS) Program[1] and is being continued by NIST and other research communities. These metadata can take many forms (e.g., which speakers spoke which words, topic changes, syntactic boundaries, named entities, speaker location, etc.)

The RT-05S evaluation is the result of a multi-site/multi-national collaboration. In addition to NIST, the organizers and contributors included: the Augmented Multiparty Interaction (AMI) program, the Computers in the Human Interaction Loop (CHIL) program, Carnegie Mellon University (CMU), Evaluations and Language resources Distribution Agency (ELDA), International Computer Science Institute and SRI International (ICSI/SRI), The Center for Scientific and Technological Research (ITC-irst), Karlsruhe University (KU), the Linguistic Data Consortium (LDC), and Virginia Tech (VT). AMI, CMU [9], ICSI [7], NIST [8], and VT each donated two meetings recorded at their labs to the evaluation. Excerpts from these meetings were selected to comprise the RT-05 conference room test set which is similar in design to the RT-04S test set. KU donated sixteen meetings to make a separate lecture room test set. CMU, ITC-irst, KU, LDC, and ELDA collaborated to prepare the reference transcripts and annotations.

---

[1] http://www.darpa.mil/ipto/Programs/ears/index.htm

2 Rich Transcription Spring 2005 Meeting Recognition Evaluation

The RT-05S evaluation broke ground on four fronts. First, new audio sensors and digital microphone arrays were added to the test conditions. Second, a new STT evaluation tool developed at NIST was released to the participants to score transcriptions of simultaneous overlapping speech. Third, two test sets were prepared for the evaluation, each representing two meeting sub-domains: small conference room meetings and lectures. Fourth, the conference room test set contained two meetings from Virginia Tech for which no training data was available.

All participating teams were required to submit a single primary system on the required task-specific evaluation condition. The primary systems are expected, by the developers, to be their best performing systems. NIST's analysis focuses on these primary systems.

The Rich Transcription Spring 2005 Evaluation plan [3] documents the Rich Transcription Spring 2005 (RT-05S) Meeting Recognition evaluation. The evaluation plan describes in detail the evaluation tasks, data sources, microphone conditions, system input and output formats, and evaluation metrics employed in the evaluation. This section summarizes the evaluation plan and covers the meeting sub-domains represented in the test set, the audio input conditions supported by the test corpora, and the evaluation task definitions

2.1 Meeting Sub-domains: Conference Room vs. Lecture Room

The meeting domain is highly variable along several dimensions. In the broad sense, any interaction between 2 more people may be considered a meeting. As such, meetings can range from brief informal exchanges to extremely formal proceedings with many participants following specific rules of order. There are a number of factors that shape how the participants interact with each other. Further, it is well known that the type, number, and placement of sensors have a significant impact on the performance of recognition tasks. The variability is so large that it would be impossible to build either a training or testing corpus that encompasses all of these factors. To make the problem tractable, the RT evaluations have attempted to constrain the definition to two specific sub-domains: small conference room meetings (also occasionally referred to as "board room" meetings) and "lecture room" meetings. The two sub-domains are used to differentiate between two very different participant interaction modes as well as two different sensor setups. The RT-05S evaluation includes a separate test set for each of these two sub-domains, labeled "confmtg" and "lectmtg."

In addition to differences in room and sensor configuration, the primary difference between the two sub-domains is in the group dynamics of the meetings. The RT conference meetings are primarily goal-oriented decision-making exercises and are either moderated or lead by one member of the meeting. As such, these meetings are highly-interactive and multiple participants contribute to the information flow and decisions made. In contrast, lecture meetings are educational events where a single lecturer is briefing the audience on a particular topic. While the audience occasionally participates in question and answer periods, it rarely controls the direction of the interchange or the outcome.

Section 2.4 describes the corpora used for both the *lectmtg* and *confmtg* domains in the RT-05S evaluation.

2.2 Microphone Conditions

As with RT-04S, three core input conditions were supported for RT-05S: multiple distant microphones (MDM), single distant microphone (SDM), and individual head microphones (IHM). The troika of audio input conditions makes a very powerful set of experimental controls for black box evaluations. The MDM condition provides a venue for the demonstration of multi-microphone input processing techniques. It lends itself to experimenting with simple beamforming and noise abatement techniques to address room acoustic issues. The SDM input condition provides a control condition for testing the effectiveness of multi-microphone techniques. The IHM condition provides two important contrasts: first, it effectively eliminates the effects of room acoustics, background noise, and overlapping simultaneous speech, and second it is most similar to the Conversational Telephone Speech (CTS) domain [1] and may be compared to results in comparable CTS evaluations.

The enumeration below contains definitions of the three previously mentioned audio input conditions and three new microphone sources for the RT-05S evaluation: multiple Mark III microphone arrays, multiple beamformed signals, and multiple source localization arrays.

- Multiple distant microphones: (MDM) This evaluation condition includes the audio from at least 3 omni-directional microphones placed (generally on a table) between the meeting participants. This condition was supported in both the *confmtg* and *lectmtg* datasets.
- Single distant microphone: (SDM) This evaluation condition includes the audio of a single, centrally located omni-directional microphone for each meeting. This microphone channel is selected from the microphones used for the MDM condition. Based on metadata provided with the recordings, it is selected so as to be the most centrally-located omni-directional microphone. This condition was supported in both the *confmtg* and *lectmtg* datasets.
- Individual head microphone: (IHM) This evaluation condition includes the audio recordings collected from a head mounted microphone positioned very closely to each participant's mouth. The microphones are typically cardioid or super cardioid microphones[2] and therefore the best quality signal for each speaker. Since the IHM condition is a contrastive condition, systems can also use any of the microphones used for the MDM condition. This condition was supported in both the *confmtg* and *lectmtg* datasets.
- Multiple Mark III microphone arrays: (MM3A) This evaluation condition includes audio from all the collected Mark III microphone arrays. The *lectmtg* dataset con-

---

[2] After the evaluation began, NIST discovered some of their head microphones were omni-directional.

tains the data from each channel of one Mark-III microphone array per meeting. In addition, the NIST subset of the *confmtg* data contains the data from each channel of three Mark-III microphone arrays per meeting. Due to time constraints, no results were submitted using these data.

- Multiple Source Localization microphone arrays (MSLA): This evaluation condition includes the audio from all the CHIL source localization arrays (SLA). An SLA is a 4-element digital microphone array arranged in an upside down 'T' topology [4]. The lecture room meeting recordings include four SLAs, one mounted on each wall of the room.

2.3 Evaluation Tasks

Four evaluation tasks were supported for the RT-05S evaluation: a Speech-To-Text transcription task and three diarization tasks: "Who Spoke When", "Speech Activity Detection", and "Source Localization." The latter two tasks were proposed for inclusion by the CHIL program and they were considered dry run tasks for the RT-05S evaluation. The following is a brief description of each of the evaluation tasks:

Speech-To-Text (STT) Transcription: STT systems are required to output a transcript of the words spoken by the meeting participants along with the start and end times for each recognized word. For this task, no speaker designation is required. Therefore, the speech from all participants is to be transcribed as a single word output stream.

Systems were evaluated using the Word Error Rate (WER) metric. WER is defined to be the sum of system transcription errors, (word substitutions, deletions, and insertions) divided by the number of reference words and expressed as a percentage. It is an error metric, so lowers scores indicate better performance. The score for perfect performance is zero. Since insertion errors are counted, it is possible for WER scores to exceed one hundred percent.

WER is calculated by first harmonizing the system and reference transcript through a series of normalization steps. Then the system and reference words are aligned using a Dynamic Programming solution. Once the alignment mapping between the system and reference words is determined, the mapped words are compared to classify them as either correct matches, inserted system words, deleted reference words, or substituted system words. The errors are counted and statistics are generated.

The MDM audio input condition was the primary evaluation condition for the STT task for both meeting sub domains. The *confmtg* data supported two contrastive conditions, SDM and IHM, and the *lectmtg* data supported four contrastive conditions, SDM, IHM, MSLA, and MM3A. Participants could submit systems for the *confmtg* domain, the *lectmtg* domain, or both the sub domains. Systems could use the knowledge of the domain as side information and therefore configure their systems for each sub domain.[3]

---

[3] All systems, for all tasks, were privy to side information about the data being processed. The evaluation plan enumerates these in detail.

Diarization "Who Spoke When" (SPKR) SPKR: Systems are required to annotate a meeting with regions of time indicating when each meeting participant is speaking and clustering the regions by speaker. It is a clustering task as opposed to an identification task since the system is not required to output a name for the speakers – only a generic id.[4]

The Diarization Error Rate (DER) metric is used to assess SPKR system performance. DER is the ratio of incorrectly attributed speech time, (either falsely detected speech, missed detections of speech, or incorrectly clustered speech) to the total amount of speech time, expressed as a percentage. As with WER, a score of zero indicates perfect performance and higher scores indicate poorer performance than lower scores.

DER is calculated by first computing a 1:1 mapping between the system-generated speaker clusters and the segment clusters in the reference transcript using the Hungarian solution to a bipartite graph[5]. Once the mapping is found, system segments not attributed to the mapped reference speaker cluster are declared incorrectly clustered speech. Falsely detected speech and missed detections of speech are calculated by simple accumulating the amount of time for each class of error.

For 2005, the primary measure of DER was calculated for non-overlapping speech only in order to be comparable with previous evaluations of speaker diarization. However, given the shifting focus to evaluation of all speech (including overlapping speech), the DER was also computed for overlapping speech segments. Both sets of scores are provided. In future such evaluations, the primary measure will focus on all speech.

Inherent ambiguities in pinpointing speech boundaries in time and annotator variability result in a small degree of inconsistency in the time annotations in the reference transcript. As such, a 0.25 second collar around each reference segment is not scored. This collar effectively minimizes the amount of DER error due to reference annotation inconsistencies.

Another challenge is in determining how large a pause in speech must be to cause a segment break. Although somewhat arbitrary, the cutoff value of 0.3 seconds was empirically determined to be a good approximation of the minimum duration for a pause in speech resulting in an utterance boundary. As such, segments that are closer than 0.3 seconds apart are merged in both the reference and system output transcripts.

The MDM audio input condition was the primary evaluation condition for the SPKR task for both meeting sub domains. The *confmtg* data supported one contrastive condition, SDM, and the *lectmtg* data supported three contrastive conditions, SDM, MSLA, and MM3A. Participants could submit systems for the *confmtg* domain, the

---

[4] In a real meeting transcription application, it is likely that the SPKR and STT system outputs would be merged to attribute each transcribed word to a particular meeting participant. The decision was made to not yet evaluate an integrated STT/SPKR task since, at this early stage, it is important to understand how each of the core components of such a system behaves. It's anticipated that such an integrated task will be included in the RT evaluations in the future.

[5] http://www.nist.gov/dads/HTML/HungarianAlgorithm.html

lectmtg domain, or both the sub domains. Systems could use the knowledge of the domain as side information and therefore configure their systems for each sub domain.[6]

Diarization "Speech Activity Detection" (SAD): SAD systems are required to annotate a meeting with regions of time indicating when at least one person is talking. The SAD task is therefore a simplified version of the SPKR task because no speaker clustering is performed by the system. The task was introduced to lower barriers for participation and to gauge the contribution of SAD errors to the SPKR and STT tasks. Since this is the first time the SAD task has been included in the RT evaluations, it was treated as an experimental dry run.

Because SAD is viewed as a simplification of the SPKR task, the SPKR DER scoring metric is also used to score the SAD task. The same no-score collar, 0.25 seconds, was applied during scoring and the same smoothing parameter, 0.3 seconds, was applied to the reference files. The reference files were derived from the SPKR reference files by simply merging the reference speaker clusters into a single cluster and then merging segments that either overlap or were within the 0.3 second smoothing parameter.

The MDM audio input condition was the primary evaluation condition for the SAD task for both meeting sub domains. The *confmtg* data supported two contrastive conditions, SDM and IHM, and the *lectmtg* data supported four contrastive conditions, SDM, IHM, MSLA, and MM3A. Participants could submit systems for the *confmtg* domain, the *lectmtg* domain, or both the sub domains. Systems could use the knowledge of the domain as side information and therefore configure their systems for each sub domain.[7]

The SAD task using IHM data is not directly comparable to SAD on distant microphone data, (i.e., MDM, SDM, MSLA, or MM3A data). An IHM channel includes both the wearer's speech and cross talk for other meeting participants. This cross talk is not considered detectable speech even though it was human generated. Not only must IHM SAD systems detect speech, but also detect when the speech is cross talk. This of course is a much harder problem.

One issue arose during this evaluation regarding meeting participants who speak very little. Since the DER was measured separately for each close-talking microphone and since the denominator of the DER metric is the amount of speech uttered, the DER for quiet speakers may be dominated by falsely detected speech errors. Time did not permit us to examine alternative scoring techniques which would minimize this effect prior to the MLMI workshop.

Diarization "Source Localization" (SLOC): SLOC systems are required to emit the three-dimensional position (in millimeters) of each person who is talking. The labels do not include the speaker's identity, but systems must be able to distinguish between time periods with speech and without speech. As such, this task is similar to the SAD task with the additional requirement of speaker location. The RT-05S instantiation of

---

[6] All systems, for all tasks, were privy to side information about the data being processed. The evaluation plan enumerates these in detail.

[7] All systems, for all tasks, were privy to side information about the data being processed. The evaluation plan enumerates these in detail.

the SLOC task is a simplified proof-of-concept version of this task. For RT-05S, the task was constrained to segments which contained only a single speaker -- a lecturer in the CHIL lecture room data. Therefore, SLOC for overlapping speakers was not addressed.

In order to infer location from the audio stream, SLOC systems use the source localization array audio data. The three dimensional position of the each SLA microphone element has been computed and given to the systems and from that information; the SLOC systems infer the location of the speaker.

The primary, and only, evaluation condition for the SLOC task is the MSLA audio input condition for the *lectmtg* data. No other audio input conditions were supported for this task and none of the *confmtg* data has SLA recordings.

The definition of the task and evaluation metrics are documented in the CHIL "Speaker Localization and Tracking – Evaluation Criteria" document [4]. The metric used to evaluate the SLOC task was the Root-Mean-Squared of Localization Error (RMSE). The EVAL_IRST_SP_LOC scoring software was developed by ITC-irst and contributed to NIST in scoring the results of the evaluation. The RMSE metric determines the Euclidean distance between the reference speaker position and the system-hypothesized speaker position every 10 milliseconds. The task was added to the evaluation at the request of the CHIL program participants and was supported in large part by the CHIL Program.

2.4 RT-05S Evaluation Corpora Details

As indicated previously, the RT-05S evaluation data consisted of two test sets: a conference room meeting (*confmtg*) test set and a lecture room meeting (*lectmtg*) test set. The recordings were sent to participants as either down sampled 16-bit, 16Khz NIST Speech Header Resources (SPHERE) files or in the original sample format 24-bit, 44.1 Khz WAV and headerless raw files. The recordings of the meetings in the *confmtg* data set were distributed in their entirety while only the selected excerpts from the *lectmtg* data were distributed.[8] Some of the meeting recordings also included video recordings. However, they were not distributed for the evaluation since none of the evaluation participants planned to implement multi-modal experiments this year. The video recordings may be made available at a later date for future multi-modal system development.

Conference Room Meetings: The confmtg test set consisted of nominally 120 minutes of meeting excerpts from ten different meetings. Five sites each provided two meetings for the evaluation test set and NIST selected a twelve minute excerpt from each meeting to be evaluated. The five contributing sites were the Augmented Multi-party Interaction (AMI) Project, Carnegie Mellon University (CMU), the International Computer Science Institute (ICSI), the National Institute of Standards and Technology (NIST), and Virginia Tech (VT). The Linguistic Data Consortium (LDC) transcribed the test set according to the "Meeting Data Careful Transcription Specification - V1.2" guidelines [5]. Table 1 gives the salient details concerning the confmtg evaluation corpus.

---

[8] The 1.2 terabytes of lecture meeting data proved too large to distribute within the evaluation time constraints.

Each meeting recording evaluation excerpt met minimum sensor requirements. Each meeting participant wore a head-mounted close talking microphone and there were at least three table top microphones placed on a table between the meeting participants. The only exception to this is meeting NIST_20050412-1303 from NIST in which a meeting participant was talking over a conference phone. In addition to these sensors, the AMI meetings included an eight-channel circular microphone array placed on the table between the meeting participants, and the NIST meetings included three Mark III arrays mounted on the walls.

Table 1. Summary of Conference Room Meeting evaluation corpus

Meeting ID	Duration (minutes)	Number of Participants	Notes
AMI_20041210_1052	12.2	4	Remote control design
AMI_20050204_1206	11.9	4	Remote control design
CMU_20050228_1615	12.0	4	Data collection for translation
CMU_20050301-1415	12.0	4	Transcription convention discussion
ICSI_20010531-1030	12.2	7	Meeting data collection
ICSI_20011113-1100	12.0	9	Staff meeting
NIST_20050412-1303	12.1	10	NIST ITL Diversity Committee meeting
NIST_20050427-0939	11.9	4	NIST computer support staff meeting
VT_20050304-1300	12.0	5	Tsunami relief planning
VT_20050318-1430	12.1	5	Scholarship selection committee
Total	120.4	56	
Unique speakers		46	

Lecture Room Meetings: The *lectmtg* test set consisted of 150 minutes of lecture meeting excerpts from 16 different lectures recorded at Karlsruhe University[4]. The lectures were all technical language technology talks given by invited lecturers. Two types of excerpts were selected and transcribed by CMU: lecturer excerpts where the lecturer was the primary talker, and question/answer (Q&A) excerpts where the lecturer fielded questions from the audience. There were seventeen lecturer excerpts[9] accounting for 89 minutes of data and twelve Q&A excerpts accounting for 61 minutes of data. Once the excerpts were selected, ELDA, KU and ITC-irst collaborated to annotate the data for the source localization task.

The audio sensors used in the *lectmtg* data were configured differently than the *confmtg* data. Only the lecturer and up to two audience members wore head-mounted, close-talking microphones. The rest of the audience was audible on the distant microphones. Four microphones were placed on the table in front of the lecturer and a fifth

---

[9] Two excerpts were selected from one of the meetings.

tabletop microphone was placed in the corner of the room. Four source localization arrays were mounted on each of the four walls of the room. Finally, a NIST Mark III array was placed directly in front of the lecturer.

2.5 Simultaneous Speech: STT Scoring

As previously noted, people often talk at the same time during meetings. The resulting overlapping speech represents a large challenge for speech technologies. Figure 1 is a cumulative histogram of the time within the test sets as a function of the number of active speakers[10]. It is evident from the graph that a large fraction of the time in each test set (~30% and 8% for the *confmtg* and *lectmtg* data sets respectively) involves simultaneous speech[11].

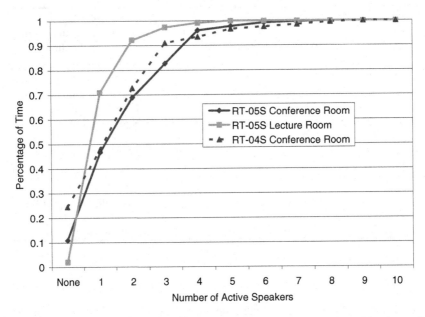

Fig. 1. Cumulative histogram of testable time as a function of active speakers. The data points labeled '*None*' indicate time in the test set where no one is talking.

During the RT-04S evaluation, a prototype method was developed at NIST [2] to perform multi-stream STT scoring. For the RT-05S evaluation, a new alignment tool ASCLITE was developed in C++ and distributed to sites for use in the evaluation as part if the SCTK [6] toolkit. The techniques used by ASCLITE are described in [2]. The previous instantiation of SCLITE required a single reference and output word

---

[10] Active speakers calculated by segmenting the test set into independent regions for alignment where each region has no speakers crossing the region boundaries.

[11] Estimates published in 2004 for the RT-04S test set [2] were higher because silence regions in the test set were not included in the estimate.

stream for alignment. ASCLITE represents an extension to support the alignment of multiple reference word streams (one for each speaker) to a single output word stream. Using this technique, system words are allowed to map to any reference word while maintaining the sequential ordering of words. This evaluation protocol enables the evaluation of single-stream STT systems using a multiple-speaker test set. Using ASCLITE, these systems can now be evaluated over segments of overlapping speech.

In order to limit the combinatorial explosion, the set of legal alignments is constrained to disallow the mapping of two reference words to each other. Even with this constraint, state-of-the-art computer system memory limits are exceeded. Experiments with the RT-04S and RT-05S test sets indicated that up to five simultaneous reference streams could be scored without exceeding memory limitations. Therefore, segments with greater than 5 simultaneous speakers were not evaluated. However, not much data was lost in this constraint. The majority of the test sets (98%, 97% and 100% of the RT-05S *confmtg*, RT-04S *confmtg*, and RT-05S *lectmtg* respectively) were able to be evaluated.

3   Results of the RT-05S Evaluation

3.1   RT-05S Evaluation Participants

The following table lists the RT-05S participants and the evaluation tasks each site took part in. In total there were nine sites submitting with three sites participating in two tasks.

Table 2. Summary of evaluation participants and the tasks for which systems were submitted

Site ID	Site Name	STT	SPKR	SAD	SLOC
AMI	Augmented Multiparty Interaction Program	X			
ICSI/SRI	International Computer Science Institute and SRI International	X	X		
ITC-irst	Center for Scientific and Technological Research				X
KU	Karlsruhe Univ.				X
ELISA Consortium	Laboratoire Informatique d'Avignon (LIA), Communication Langagière et Interaction Personne-Système (CLIPS), and LIUM		X	X	
MQU	Macquarie Univ.		X		
Purdue	Purdue Univ.			X	
TNO	The Netherlands Organisation for Applied Scientific Research		X	X	
TUT	Tampere Univ. of Technology				X

3.2 Speech-To-Text (STT) Results

Two sites participated in the STT task, ICSI/SRI and AMI. They both ran their systems on both the confmtg and lectmtg data. While it is disappointing to see only two participants for this task, these two submissions represent many people's efforts across multiple research sites.

Appendix A contains the system performance graphs for the STT task Figure 2 shows the WERs for the confmtg data set under the MDM audio input conditions as 46.9% and 38.4% for AMI and ICSI/SRI respectively. For ICSI/SRI, this represents a 33% relative reduction in WER from last year in which ICSI/SRI achieved a 53.4% WER (Figure 5). While the AMI WER was higher, this was the first public evaluation for the AMI system and a very good first showing. The lowest IHM WER was 25.9% compared to last year's 32.7% (Figure 5) which is a 20% relative reduction.

From Figure 2 The lectmtg data appears to be slightly harder than the confmtg data (13% and 40% relative for AMI and ICSI/SRI respectively) for the MDM microphone condition. However, the error rates comparing confmtg and lectmtg IHM systems are similar indicating that while the language difficulty may be equal, perhaps the challenges of distant microphones may not.

In Figure 4, the confmtg WERs by meeting shows no obvious performance outliers. However for the VT meetings, which are blind test data for the systems, ICSI/SRI did well on the VT meetings while AMI did not.

ICSI/SRI ran their system on the MSLA audio input condition on the lectmtg data. They achieved a 46.3% WER which is a 14% relative reduction from their MDM result. This is encouraging result. It is our opinion that as even more audio channels are used to record the speech, WERs will be reduced even further although the exact benefit can only be determined through experimentation.

When the lectmtg data is split into lecturer and Q&A subsets, there is no difference in performance for AMI. However ICSI/SRI did slightly better on the lecturer speech 51% as opposed to 58% on the Q&A speech.

3.3 Diarization "Who Spoke When" (SPKR) Results

Four sites participated in the SPKR task, the ELISA Consortium, ICSI/SRI, MQU and TNO. Appendix B contains the performance graphs for the SPKR task. The lowest DER for the primary systems on the confmtg data was 18.5% and 15.3% for the MDM and SDM audio input conditions respectively (Figure 6). Both scores were achieved by ICSI/SRI. These scores represent 20% and 32% relative reductions compared to RT-04S (Figure 10).

Oddly, this year's SDM error rates are lower than the MDM error rates. The difference is predominantly caused by the VT meetings where the SDM error rates are 64% and 24% lower than matched MDM DERs. For the rest of the meetings, the MDM and SDM scores are, by a sign test, not statistically different.

Figure 8 plots the MDM primary systems performance on the confmtg data set as a function of meeting id. The VT-20050318 meeting had the highest DER for all systems. Since the VT meetings are blind test data, this may be an indication of over - fitting to development data or, when coupled with the aforementioned low SDM error rates for the VT meetings, this may be an indication of differences in recording conditions. Neither can be proven with the existing data.

Like last year, the error rates for the full test set (the diamonds in Figure 7) are higher than just the non-overlapping speech.

The DERs for the lectmtg data set are in general lower than DERs for the confmtg data set. The best primary submission for all three audio input conditions is 12.2% for the ICSI/SRI team (Figure 6). This impressive result was achieved by declaring all testable speech as a single speaker without looking at the audio data. While the baseline is low, ICSI/SRI achieved a lower DER of 10.4% with a real system (Figure 7). In fact, most sites had contrastive systems with lower DERs so Figure 7 uses the lowest achieved DER for each data set/site/audio condition combination.

Not surprisingly, Figure 9 shows a marked difference in performance between the lecturer speech and the Q&A subset of the lectmtg data. System performance on the Q&A subset of the data is commensurate with the ELISA confmtg MDM results, but 27% higher for the ICSI/SRI system on the confmtg MDM data. It is difficult to say from the results whether or not the data was harder or if there was insufficient time for system development.

3.4 Diarization "Speech Activity Detection" (SAD) Results

Three sites participated in the SAD task: the ELISA consortium, Purdue and TNO. The lowest DER (from Figure 11) for the MDM condition on the confmtg data was 5.04% by TNO while ELISA's error rate was 7.42%. These error rates are commensurate with the SPKR systems scored with the SAD evaluation criterion shown inFigure 7. ELISA achieved a 6.59% DER for the lectmtg data, MDM audio condition and the error rates for lecturer vs. Q&A subsets were roughly equal with 6.67% and 6.47% respectively

Purdue [383] was the only site to participate in the IHM audio input condition on the confmtg data. They achieved an SAD DER of 26.9%. As expected, SAD DERs are demonstrably higher for IHM than MDM or SDM conditions.

The SAD dry run was successful in that a system was built and tested with the evaluation infrastructure. However, the community is looking towards more challenging tasks, like the SPKR task, so SAD will not be an evaluation task in 2006.

3.5 Diarization "Source Localization" (SLOC) Results

Three sites participated in the SLOC task: ITC-irst, KU and TUT. The RMSE Error rates for the three systems were 309mm, 569mm, and 851mm respectively on the lecturer subset of the *lectmtg* test set.

The lowest error rate is impressive for the initial benchmark of this technology. The dry run was successful in that systems could be built to tackle the task and the evaluation methodology effectively measured system performance. However this level of performance is likely not sufficient for two reasons: (1) the systems were given lecturer-only speech, and (2) the required accuracy is likely to be lower than current performance.

These systems were given speech from a single talker, the lecturer. There was little competing speech and the lecturer's movements were typically constrained to the front of the room. As additional talkers are active and they move throughout the meeting space, error rates will degrade.

The community needs a good method to determine what constitutes sufficient accuracy; is it defined by geometrically measuring the person's location or by error rate reductions for consumers of SLOC system output? The current performance level is not sufficient for determining the exact person location. The average human male's neck to shoulder size is 235 mm[12] meaning the average error is beyond the person's body. The community is starting to research the uses of SLOC systems and the field has exciting possibilities.

4   Conclusions and Future Evaluations

In our opinion, the primary lesson learned from the RT-05S evaluation was that systems will do better as more sensors are collected; addition sensors will enable new tasks, like SLOC, and improve performance of existing tasks, like ICSI's WER reduction from additional distant microphones. The additional sensors also provide a rich opportunity for multimodal systems that blend the strengths of audio-based processing with video processing strengths. Indeed, this should be a new thrust in the meeting domain to support and experiment with sensor fusion techniques.

The successful evaluation of overlapping, simultaneous speech for the STT task is an indication that it is time to push for stream-based STT in the meeting domain. While it is invaluable to work on component technologies for a while, merging STT and SPKR is starting to make sense just like merging STT and segmentation in the early stages of the Broadcast News domain. With the advent of a plethora of audio channels, blind source separation (BSS) could easily support this task without modification to existing STT systems since BSS will deliver a single speaker's speech to the STT system.

The meeting recognition community is largely a volunteer group and therefore not encumbered with demands of program goals. The community should consider tackling unsolved problems in the STT field such as out-of-vocabulary (OOV) word detection. All of today's STT systems have finite vocabularies and including the capability of detecting OOVs would improve the usefulness of rich transcriptions to downstream users.

It is clear that the meeting recognition community is a vibrant and growing community. This year's goal should be to broaden the research base for technologies to pull in new participants with new ideas and energy.

---

[12] The maximum shoulder width for a man's X-Large shirt according to the "Standards and Guidelines for Crochet and Knitting" by the Craft Yarn council of America, http://www.yarnstandards.com/s-and-g.pdf.

Acknowledgements

NIST would like to thank everyone who donated meeting recordings for the evaluation, AMI, CMU, ICSI/SRI, VT and KU. Special thanks go to the sites that prepared the reference transcriptions and annotations: CMU, ELDA, KU, and LDC.

Disclaimer

These tests are designed for local implementation by each participant. The reported results are not to be construed, or represented, as endorsements of any participant's system, or as official findings on the part of NIST or the U. S. Government.

References

1. Fiscus et. al., "Results of the Fall 2004 STT and MDE Evaluation", RT-04F Evaluation Workshop Proceedings, November 7-10, 2004.
2. Garofolo et. al., "The Rich Transcription 2004 Spring Meeting Recognition Evaluation", ICASSP 2004 Meeting Recognition Workshop, May 17, 2004
3. Spring 2005 (RT-05S) Rich Transcription Meeting Recognition Evaluation Plan, http://www.nist.gov/speech/tests/rt/rt2005/spring/rt05s-meeting-eval-plan-V1.pdf
4. Speaker Localization and Tracking – Evaluation Criteria, http://www.nist.gov/speech/tests/rt/t2005/spring/sloc/CHIL-IRST_SpeakerLocEval-V5.0-2005-01-18.pdf
5. LDC Meeting Recording Transcription, http://www.ldc.upenn.edu/Projects/Transcription/NISTMeet
6. SCTK toolkit, http://www.nist.gov/speech/tools/index.htm
7. "The ICSI Meeting Project: Resources and Research" A. Janin, J. Ang, S. Bhagat, R. Dhillon, J. Edwards, J. Macias-Guarasa, N. Morgan, B. Peskin, E. Shriberg, A. Stolcke, C. Wooters and B. Wrede, NIST ICASSP 2004 Meeting Recognition Workshop, Montreal
8. "The NIST Meeting Room Pilot Corpus", John S. Garofolo, Christophe D. Laprun, Martial Michel, Vincent M. Stanford, Elham Tabassi, LREC 2004
9. "The ISL Meeting Corpus: The Impact of Meeting Type on Speech Style", Susanne Burger, Victoria MacLaren, Hua Yu, ICSLP-2002
10. "Speech Activity Detection on Multichannels of Meeting Recordings", Zhongqiang Huang and Mary P. Harper, Proceedings from the RT-05 Workshop at MLML-05.

Appendix A: Speech-To-Text Results

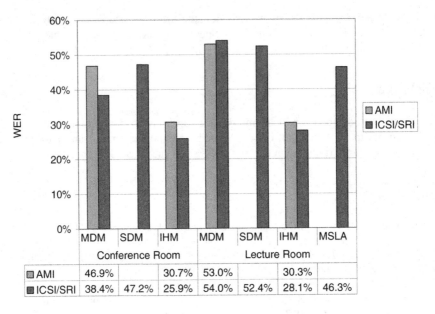

	MDM	SDM	IHM	MDM	SDM	IHM	MSLA
AMI	46.9%		30.7%	53.0%		30.3%	
ICSI/SRI	38.4%	47.2%	25.9%	54.0%	52.4%	28.1%	46.3%

Fig. 2. WERs for primary STT systems across test sets and audio input conditions

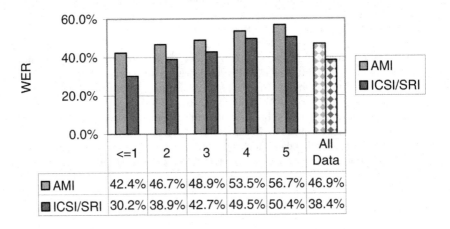

	<=1	2	3	4	5	All Data
AMI	42.4%	46.7%	48.9%	53.5%	56.7%	46.9%
ICSI/SRI	30.2%	38.9%	42.7%	49.5%	50.4%	38.4%

Fig. 3. WERs for primary MDM STT systems as a function of the number of active speakers in a segment. The bars for <=1 include regions were no one is talking and the final column "All Data" is the cumulative WER from Figure 2.

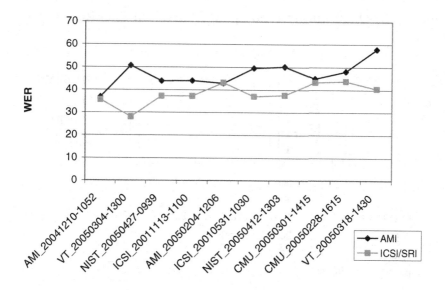

Fig. 4. WERs for primary MDM STT systems broken down by meeting. Meetings are sorted by average WER.

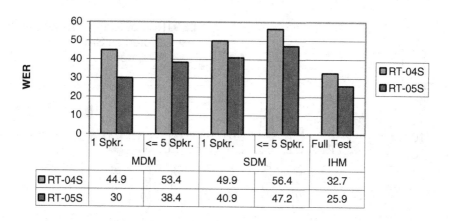

	1 Spkr.	<= 5 Spkr.	1 Spkr.	<= 5 Spkr.	Full Test
	MDM	MDM	SDM	SDM	IHM
RT-04S	44.9	53.4	49.9	56.4	32.7
RT-05S	30	38.4	40.9	47.2	25.9

Fig. 5. WERs for the best MDM and SDM STT systems from RT-04S and RT-05S. MDM and SDM results are broken down by *"1 Spkr."* for non-overlapping speech, *'<=5 Spkr.'* which includes simultaneous speech, or *'Full Test'* for the complete test set. The RT-04S systems were re-scored with ASCLITE.

Appendix B: Diarization "Who Spoke When" (SPKR) Result

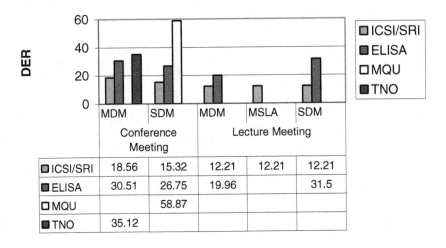

	MDM	SDM	MDM	MSLA	SDM
▣ ICSI/SRI	18.56	15.32	12.21	12.21	12.21
▣ ELISA	30.51	26.75	19.96		31.5
▢ MQU		58.87			
▪ TNO	35.12				

Fig. 6. DERs for primary SPKR systems across test sets and audio input conditions

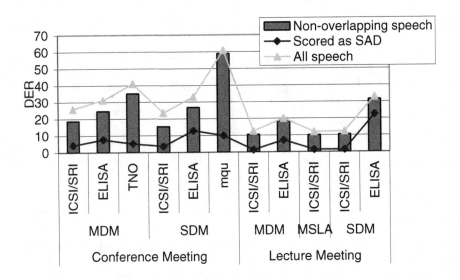

Fig. 7. DERs for "Lowest Error Rate" systems from each site across test sets and audio input conditions. The *triangles* mark the DERs over all data including simultaneous speech. The *diamonds* mark the error rate of SPKR systems scored as SAD systems.

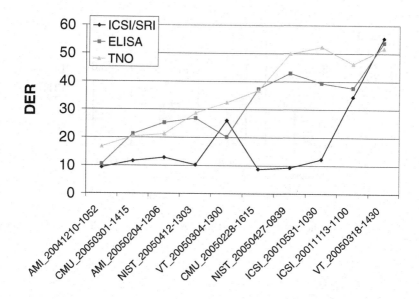

Fig. 8. DERs for primary MDM SPKR systems broken down by meeting id. Meetings are sorted by average DER.

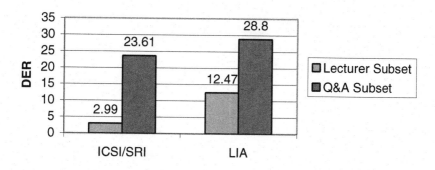

Fig. 9. DERs for "Lowest Error Rate" systems from each site for the lectmtg data broken down by the *lecturer* and *Q&A* subsets

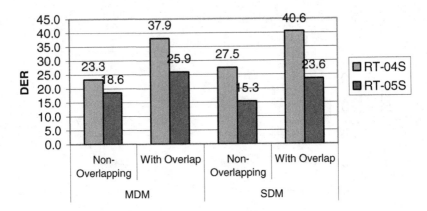

Fig. 10. DERs for the best MDM and SDM SPKR systems from RT-04S and RT-05S

Appendix C: Diarization "Speech Activity Detection" Results

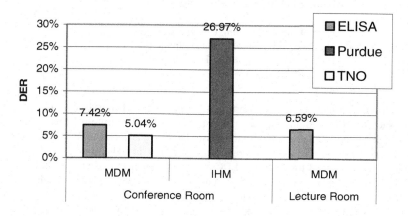

Fig. 11. DERs for primary SAD systems across test sets and audio input conditions

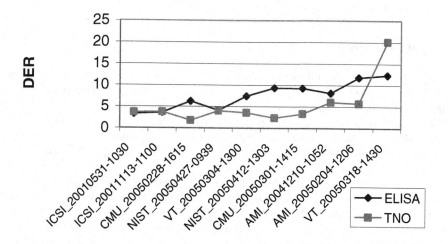

Fig. 12. DERs for primary MDM SAD systems broken down by meeting id. Meetings are sorted by average DER.

Linguistic Resources for Meeting Speech Recognition

Meghan Lammie Glenn and Stephanie Strassel

Linguistic Data Consortium, University of Pennsylvania,
3600 Market Street, Suite 800, Philadelphia, PA 19104 USA
{mlglenn, strassel}@ldc.upenn.edu
http://www.ldc.upenn.edu

Abstract. This paper describes efforts by the University of Pennsylvania's Linguistic Data Consortium to create and distribute shared linguistic resources – including data, annotations, tools and infrastructure – to support the Rich Transcription 2005 Spring Meeting Recognition Evaluation. In addition to distributing large volumes of training data, LDC produced reference transcripts for the RT-05S conference room evaluation corpus, which represents a variety of subjects, scenarios and recording conditions. Careful verbatim reference transcripts including rich markup were created for all two hours of data. One hour was also selected for a contrastive study using a quick transcription methodology. We review the two methodologies and discuss qualitative differences in the resulting transcripts. Finally, we describe infrastructure development including transcription tools to support our efforts.

1 Introduction

Linguistic Data Consortium was established in 1992 at the University of Pennsylvania to support language-related education, research and technology development by creating and sharing linguistic resources, including data, tools and standards. Human language technology development in particular requires large volumes of annotated data for building language models, training systems and evaluating system performance against a human-generated gold standard. LDC has directly supported NIST's Rich Transcription evaluation series by providing both training and evaluation data and related infrastructure. For the Rich Transcription 2005 Spring Meeting Recognition Evaluation, LDC provided large quantities of training data from a variety of domains to program participants. Additionally, LDC produced both quick and careful reference transcripts of evaluation data to support automatic speech-to-text transcription, diarization, and speaker segmentation and localization in the meeting domain. Finally, in the context of this program LDC has undertaken creation of specialized annotation software that supports rapid, high-quality creation of rich transcripts, both in the meeting domain and in a wide variety of other genres.

2 Data

2.1 Training Data

To enhance availability of high-quality training data for RT-05S, LDC distributed twelve corpora that are part of the LDC catalog for use as training data by evaluation

S. Renals and S. Bengio (Eds.): MLMI 2005, LNCS 3869, pp. 390–401, 2006.

participants. The data included not only three corpora in the meeting domain, but also two large corpora of transcribed conversational telephone speech (CTS) as well as one corpus of transcribed broadcast news (BN). All data was shipped directly to registered evaluation participants upon request, after sites had signed a user agreement specifying research use of the data. The distributed training data is summarized in the table below.

RT-05S Training Data Distributed by LDC

Title	Speech	Transcripts	Volume	Domain
Fisher English Training Part 1	LDC2004S13	LDC2004T19	750+ hours	CTS
Fisher English Training Part 2	LDC2005S13	LDC2005T19	750+ hours	CTS
ICSI Meeting Corpus	LDC2004S02	LDC2004T04	72 hours	Meeting
ISL Meeting Corpus	LDC2004S05	LDC2004T10	10 hours	Meeting
NIST Meeting Pilot Corpus	LDC2004S09	LDC2004T13	13 hours	Meeting
TDT4 Multilingual Corpus	LDC2005S11	LDC2005T16	300+ hours	BN

2.2 Evaluation Data

In addition to training data, LDC developed a portion of the benchmark test data for this year's evaluation. The RT-05S conference room evaluation corpus includes ten meeting sessions contributed by five organizations or consortia: AMI (Augmented Multi-Party Interaction Project), CMU (Carnegie Mellon Institute), ICSI (International Computer Science Institute), NIST (National Institute of Standards and Technology), and VT (Virginia Tech). The sessions contain an average of six participants. In all but one case, head-mounted microphone recordings were available; the one exception is a speaker participating in the recording session by teleconference. The meetings represent a variety of subjects, scenarios and recording conditions. The RT-04 meeting evaluation corpus, also transcribed by LDC, covered a broader set of meeting activities, including simulated meetings and game playing (for instance a game of Monopoly or role playing games). The RT-05S conference room corpus on the other hand contains more typical business meeting content [1]. As a result, LDC transcribers found the RT-05S corpus easier to transcribe.

3 Transcription

3.1 Careful Transcription (CTR)

For purposes of evaluating transcription technology, system output must be compared with high-quality manually-created verbatim transcripts. LDC has already defined a careful transcription (CTR) methodology to ensure a consistent approach to the creation of benchmark data. The goal of CTR is to create a reference transcript that is as good as a human can make it, capturing even subtle details of the audio signal and providing close time-alignment with the corresponding transcript. CTR involves multiple passes over the data and rigorous quality control. Some version of LDC's current CTR specification has been used to produce test data for several speech technology evaluations in the broadcast news and conversational telephone speech domains in English, Mandarin, Modern Standard and Levantine Arabic as well as other languages over the past decade. The CTR methodology was extended to the meeting domain in 2004 to support the RT-04 meeting speech evaluation, and was used in producing this year's conference room evaluation corpus [2].

Working with a single speaker channel at a time (using head-mounted microphone recordings where available), annotators first divide the audio signal into virtual segments containing speaker utterances and noise. At minimum, the audio is divided into individual speaker turns, but long speaker turns are segmented into smaller units. Speaker turns can be difficult to define in general and are particularly challenging in the meeting domain due to the frequency of overlapping speech and the prevalence of side conversations that occur simultaneously with the main thread of speech. Further, speakers may utter comments under the breath that are difficult to distinguish from non-speech sounds, even when listening to a head-mounted microphone signal. Transcribers are therefore generally instructed to place segment boundaries at natural breakpoints like breath groups and pauses, typically resulting in segments of three to eight seconds in duration. In placing segment boundaries, transcribers listen to the entire audio file in addition to visually inspecting the waveform display, capturing any region of speech (no matter how minimal) as well as isolating certain speaker noises including coughs, sneezes, and laughter. Breaths are not specifically captured unless they occur around a speaker utterance. Transcribers are instructed to leave several milliseconds of silence padding around each segment boundary, and to be cautious about clipping off the onset of voiceless consonants or the ends of fricatives. Meeting segmentation practices do not differ substantially from those for other domains, but additional care is taken to create segment boundaries that respect the natural flow of the conversation, particularly with respect to the speaker turn issues mentioned above.

After accurate segment boundaries are in place, annotators create a verbatim transcript by listening to each segment in turn. Because segments are typically around five seconds, it is usually possible to create a verbatim transcript in one listen; but difficult regions that contain speaker disfluencies or other phenomena may warrant several reviews. No time limit is imposed, but annotators are instructed to utilize the "uncertain transcription" convention if they need to review a segment three or more times. A second pass checks the accuracy of the segment boundaries and transcript itself, revisits sections marked as uncertain, and adds information like speaker identity, background noise conditions, plus special markup for mispronounced words, proper names, acronyms, partial words, disfluencies and the like. A final pass over the transcript is conducted by the team leader to ensure accuracy and completeness. The individual speaker channels that have been transcribed separately are then merged together. Senior annotators listen to the merged files and use the context of the full meeting to verify specific vocabulary, acronyms and proper nouns as required. Further automatic and manual scans over the data identify regions of missed speech, correct common errors, and conduct spelling and syntax checks, which identify badly formatted regions of each file.

3.1.1 Quality Control

The meeting domain presents a number of unique challenges to the production of highly accurate verbatim transcripts, which motivates the application of quality control procedures as a part of the multi-pass strategy described above. One such challenge is the prevalence of overlapping speech. In meetings, overlap is extremely frequent, accounting for well over half the speech on average. Even when transcribing from the individual speaker recordings, capturing overlapping speech is difficult. Other speakers are typically audible on close-talking microphone channels, and transcribers must focus their attention on a single speaker's voice while simultaneously considering the context of the larger conversation to understand what is being said. During all stages of transcription, transcribers and team leaders devote extra attention to overlapping speech regions.

Transcription starts with the individual head-mounted microphone recordings, which facilitates the accuracy of basic transcription. Senior annotators listen to all untranscribed regions of individual files, identifying any areas of missed speech or chopped segments using a specialized interface. Some meetings contain highly specialized, technical terminology and names that may be difficult for transcribers to interpret. To resolve instances of uncertainty, final quality checks are conducted on a merged file, which conflates all individual speaker transcripts into a single session that is time-aligned with a mixed recording of all head-mounted channels, or a distant or table-top microphone channel. This merged view provides a comprehensive check over the consistency of terminology and names across the file, and is conducted by a senior annotator who has greater access to and knowledge of technical jargon. Senior annotators also check for common errors and standardize the spelling of proper nouns and representation of acronyms in the transcript. Transcription ends with multiple quality assurance scans, which include spell checking, syntax checking, which identifies portions of the transcript that are poorly formatted (for example, conflicting markup of linguistic features), and expanding contractions.

3.2 Quick Transcription

The careful transcription process described above was used to prepare benchmark data for purposes of system evaluation. In addition, LDC selected a one-hour subset of the evaluation data for transcription using Quick Transcription (QTR) methodology. The goal of the QTR task is simply to "get the words right" as quickly as possible; to that end, the QTR methodology automates some aspects of the transcription process and eliminates most feature markup, permitting transcribers to complete a verbatim transcript in a single pass over the data. The QTR approach was adopted on a limited scale for English conversational telephone speech data within the DARPA EARS program [3], with real-time transcription rates of seven to ten times real-time. Automatic post-processing includes spell checking, syntax checking and scans for common errors. Team leaders monitor annotator progress and speed to ensure that transcripts are produced within the targeted timeframe. The resulting quick transcription quality is naturally lower than that produced by the careful transcription methodology. Speeding up the process inevitably results in missed or mis-transcribed speech; this is particularly true for disfluent or overlapping regions of the transcript. However, the advantage of this approach is undeniable. Annotators work, on average, ten times faster using this approach than they are able to work within the careful transcription methodology.

Manual audio segmentation is an integral part of careful transcription, but is very costly, accounting for 1/4 or more of the time required to produce a highly-accurate verbatim transcript. To reduce costs in QTR, we developed AutoSegmenter, a process that pre-segments a speech file into reasonably accurate speaker segments by detecting pauses in the audio stream. AutoSegmenter achieves relatively high accuracy on clean audio signals containing one speaker, and typically produces good results on the head-mounted microphone channels. If the audio is degraded in any way, however, the quality of automatic segmentation falls dramatically, leading to large portions of missed speech, truncated utterances, and false alarm segments – segments that may have been triggered by noise, distortion, or other meeting participants. In the QTR method, segment boundaries produced by AutoSegmenter are taken as ground truth and are not altered or manually verified, since doing so would result in real-time rates far exceeding the target of five times real-time.

3.2.1 Quality Control

Quality assurance efforts are minimized for QTR, since the goal of this approach is to produce a transcript in as little time as possible. A quick quality assurance check was applied to the five transcripts were reviewed in a quick final pass, which involved a spell check, a syntax check and some basic formatting standardization including the removal of "empty" segments – that is, false alarm segments created by AutoSegmenter that contain no speech. (Typically these segments contain background noise or other speaker noise which under QTR is not transcribed.) Additionally, the contractions in each file were expanded. Transcripts were not reviewed for accuracy or completeness.

3.3 CTR vs. QTR: A Contrastive Study

With one hour of the conference room evaluation data transcribed using both the CTR and QTR methods, comparison of the resulting data is possible. Practical constraints of time and funding prevented us from providing a complete quantitative analysis of discrepancies during RT-05. While LDC's transcription toolkit does include processes to automatically compare and calculate agreement rates for multiple transcripts of the same source data, existing infrastructure assumes that segment boundaries are identical for transcripts being compared. The data created for RT-05 does not meet this requirement; CTR files contain manual segment boundaries while QTR files contain autosegments. However, a qualitative comparison is still possible.

In general terms, careful transcription offers maximum transcript accuracy, but it is time consuming and costly. Quick transcription by contrast is much more efficient, but does not maintain the same level of accuracy. Both methods may be called for to suit particular needs (for example, CTR for benchmark evaluation data; QTR for large-volume training data).

Comparison of the CTR- and QTR-produced transcripts of the five sessions reveals discrepancies in both segmentation practices and orthographic completeness. These categories are not orthogonal: many orthographic errors are caused by the automatic assignment of segment boundaries and the time constraints imposed in QTR. The following table shows the most common differences between QTR and CTR transcripts. Highlighting indicates higher accuracy or completeness.

Table 1. Common discrepancies between Quick and Careful transcripts

	QTR	**CTR**
transcription	word substitutions (e.g., **and** instead of **%um**)	careful word transcription
	no indication of speaker restarts, disfluencies	indication of speaker restarts, disfluencies
	lacking some punctuation, capitalization	standard punctuation, capitalization
	lacks special markup (for filled pauses, acronyms, mispronounced words, etc.)	contains special markup (for filled pauses, acronyms, mispronounced words, etc.)
	misinterpreted acronyms	acronyms verified
	misinterpreted, inconsistent transcription of technical jargon	technical jargon verified
segmentation	isolated breaths segmented (captured by AutoSegmenter)	no isolated breaths captured (in accordance with task specification)
	words dropped out of segment	careful word segmentation – no missed words
	split words (1- **it** 2-**'s**)	no split words (it's)

3.3.1 Orthographic Discrepancies

The quality and completeness of orthography and transcription content is necessarily lower with QTR, given the abbreviated real-time rate goals of this method. According to the task definition, QTR is an effort to "get the words right." A quick transcript will contain limited or no special markup, inconsistent capitalization and fewer punctuation marks. Meeting sessions contain specialized and sometimes highly technical content. During the CTR quality control process, senior annotators investigate the meeting context and relevant jargon to resolve any cases of uncertainty on a transcriber's part. However, during the quick transcription process, which targets a transcription rate of five times real-time, no time is allocated to researching specialized vocabulary. As shown in the example below, this can result in mis-

Table 2. Transcription discrepancies in ICSI_20010531-1030

QTR	CTR
689.110 692.550 me013: ((**roar**)) digits and and stuff like that. the me- the meeting meeting 692.790 694.240 me013: is uh later today.	689.075 691.400 me013: @**AURORA** digits, and and stuff like that. 691.400 694.250 me013: The mee- the meeting meeting is %uh later today.

transcribed segments, or the use of the "uncertain transcript" flag, denoted by double parentheses.

It is always possible for two transcribers to interpret non-technical speech differently. In CTR, these errors are typically eliminated through repeated quality assurance passes over the data, which specifically target accuracy and consistency across all speakers in a given session and resolution of cases of transcriber uncertainty. Consider the following example:

Table 3. Common transcription discrepancies in CMU_20050301-1415

QTR	CTR
157.130 161.370 fLDKKLH: I ((**officially**)) I don't know. I thought it was more around forty seconds though for that	156.750 161.325 fLDKKLH: I've usually -- I don't know, I thought it was more around forty seconds though for that.

This and the previous example show how the faster real-time rate in QTR affects transcription quality.

3.3.2 Segmentation Discrepancies

The limitations of automatic segmentation in the meeting domain become abundantly clear when comparing segments in QTR and CTR transcripts. Meeting data introduces its own set of hurdles, such as ambient noise and multiple simultaneous speakers. Adjusting the AutoSegmenter threshold to capture all speech and noise from the targeted speaker, while excluding noises and isolated breaths or other non-transcribed material, is extremely difficult. In light of such challenges, the automatically generated segment boundaries may chop off words, parts of sentences, or eliminate entire utterances. Inaccurate segmentation of the speech signal can change the meaning of

Table 4. Segmentation discrepancies in CMU_20050301-1415

QTR			CTR		
224.810	226.180	fZMW: But uh yeah, I agree.	224.575	226.325	fZMW: That's what I (()) -- yeah. I agree.

the utterance itself, as in this example, where the QTR segment starts approximately .25 seconds later than the CTR segment.

The impact of low amplitude on segmentation and transcription in general can be significant. In the example below, even careful manual segmentation and transcription was made difficult by a weak audio signal. The QTR rendering of the excerpt below is extremely impoverished, lacking approximately 50% of the words captured in the CTR version.

Table 5. Segmentation/transcription discrepancies in VT_20050318-1430

QTR	CTR
800.470 800.980 rehg-g: Wright State.	800.450 804.150 rehg-g: ^Wright State student, he wants to continue at ^Wright State, so that's
801.650 803.310 rehg-g: he wants to continue at Wright State.	804.400 805.800 rehg-g: that's his preference school.
804.580 805.360 rehg-g: That's his preference.	
[missed]	806.650 809.400 rehg-g: %um In biomedical engineering and %uh
[missed]	810.950 813.900 rehg-g: kind of interesting in his write up because he said he wanted to %uh
[missed]	814.800 816.725 rehg-g: design ^Luke ^Skywalker's hand.
[missed]	817.025 817.975 stephen-e: {laugh}
[missed]	817.600 818.525 rehg-g: It's like wow. {laugh}
820.490 821.250 rehg-g: said when whenever	819.325 825.250 rehg-g: Because you know every -- he said when whenever whenever someone asks him what he wants to do, what he's doing that's the easiest way to describe it.
821.510 825.080 rehg-g: Whenever someone asks him what he wants to do or what he's doing that's the easiest way to describe it.	

Another common automatic segmentation error is a form of truncation that occurs when complete utterances are captured by AutoSegmenter but are chopped in half in the presence of short pauses, as in the following example:

Table 6. Segment truncation in CMU_20050301-1415

QTR	CTR
67.640 68.950 fZMW: if it's longer than twenty sec-	67.425 70.350 fZMW: If it's longer than twenty seconds then they have a prob-lem.
67.980 68.930 fLDKKLH: Mhm.	67.875 68.600 fLDKKLH: Mhm.
69.060 70.410 fZMW: -conds then I have a problem.	

In this example, AutoSegmenter detected a 0.1 second pause in the middle of the word "seconds," resulting in a halved word. Where the audio signal is clean and the amplitude is high, AutoSegmentation provides good results:

Table 7. Similarities between CTR and QTR in CMU_20050301-1415

QTR	CTR
131.810 137.910 mVHQQMY: I- is that due to uh speech recognition in general or just with whatever particular system they were using?	131.725 137.750 mVHQQMY: I- is that due to %uh speech recognition in general or just with whatever particular system they were using?
136.450 140.980 fZMW: We never had this problem though I was kind of sur-prised that they went back to this old system.	136.275 141.225 fZMW: We never had this problem though I was kind of sur-prised that they went back to this old system.

The level of accuracy demonstrated in the previous example makes a case in favor adopting a QTR-style approach to at least parts of the transcription process.

3.4 Transcription Rates

A fundamental challenge in transcribing meeting data is simply the added volume resulting from not one or two but a half a dozen or more speakers. A typical thirty-minute telephone conversation will require twenty hours or more to transcribe carefully (30 minutes, two speakers, 20 times real-time per channel). A meeting of the same duration with six participants may require more than 60 hours to produce a transcript of the same quality. LDC careful transcription real-time rates for the RT05S two-hour dataset approached 65 times real-time, meaning that one hour of data required around 65 hours of labor (excluding additional QC provided by the team leader). Examined in light of the number of total channels, however, the real-time rate for careful transcription per channel is around 15 times real-time, comparable with rates for BN and slightly less than that for CTS. Methods like Quick Transcription can cut these times considerably, but the volume of effort required is still substantial. The real-time rate for quick transcription of a one-hour dataset is about 18 times real-time; the real-time rate per channel is around four times real-time.

4   Infrastructure

Specialized software and workflow management tools can greatly improve both efficiency and consistency of transcription, particularly in the meeting domain. The nature of meeting speech transcription requires frequent jumping back and forth from a single speaker to a multi-speaker view of the data, which presents a challenge not only for the transcribers, but for the transcription tools they use. Current transcription tools are not optimized for this approach (or in many cases do not permit it at all). Further, different languages and domains currently require different tools (leading to lack of comparability across results). For the most part existing transcription tools cannot incorporate output of automatic processes, and they lack correction and adjudication modes. Moreover, user interfaces are not optimized for the tasks described above, in particular QTR. To support the demand for rapid, efficient and consistent transcription, LDC has created a next-generation speech annotation toolkit, XTrans, to directly support a full range of speech annotation tasks including quick and careful transcription of meetings. XTrans utilizes the Annotation Graph Toolkit [4, 5] whose infrastructure of libraries, applications and GUI components enables rapid development of task-specific annotation tools. Among the existing features, XTrans

- Operates across languages
- Operates across platforms
- Supports transcription across domains
- Contains customized modules for Quick Transcription, Careful Transcription and Rich Transcription/Structural Metadata markup
- Includes specialized quality control features; for instance speakerID verification to find misapplied speaker labels and silence checking to identify speech within untranscribed regions.
- Contains an "adjudication mode", allowing users to compare, adjudicate and analyze discrepancies across multiple human or machine-generated transcripts

As an added feature of great benefit to meeting transcription, XTrans allows users to easily move back and forth between the multi- and single-speaker views, turning individual channels on and off as required to customize their interaction with the data.

Two Data Views in XTrans

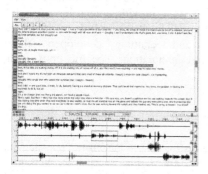

Fig. 1. Global speaker view in XTrans

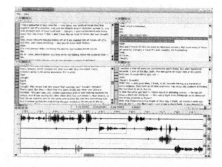

Fig. 2. Individual speaker view in XTrans

XTrans also automates many common annotation tasks, for instance removing the need for repetitive keystrokes and allowing the annotator to speed up audio playback. A timer function will also enforce transcriber efficiency by warning users (and reporting to managers) when transcription rates exceed the targeted real-time rate for a given task. As with LDC's current transcription tools, XTrans will be fully integrated into LDC's existing annotation workflow system, AWS. AWS controls work (project, file) assignment; manages directories and permissions; calls up the annotation software and assigned file(s) for the user; and tracks annotation efficiency and progress. AWS allows for double-blind assignment of files for dual annotation, and incorporates adjudication and consistency scoring into the regular annotation pipeline. Supervisors can query information about progress, efficiency and consistency by user, language, data set, task, and so on.

5 Future Plans and Conclusion

LDC's planned activities include additional transcription in the meeting domain as well as new data collection. Using existing facilities at LDC developed for other research programs, meeting collection is currently opportunistic, with regularly scheduled business meetings being recorded as time allows. Five hours of English meetings, three hours of meetings in Chinese and another two hours in Arabic have already been collected under this model. As new funding becomes available, we also plan to develop our collections infrastructure with additional head-mounted and lavaliere microphones, an improved microphone array, better video capability and customized software for more flexible remote recording control. While the current collection platform was designed with portability in mind, we hope to make it a fully portable system that can be easily transported to locations around campus to collect not only business meetings but also lectures, training sessions and other kinds of scenarios.

Future plans for XTrans include incorporation of video input to assist with tasks like speaker identification and speaker turn detection. We also plan to add a "correction mode" that will allow users to check manual transcripts or verify output of automatic processes including autosegmentation, forced alignment, SpeakerID and automatic speech recognition output. A beta version of XTrans is currently under testing, and the tool will be freely distributed from LDC beginning in late 2005 [6].

Shared resources are a critical component of human language technology development. LDC is actively engaged in ongoing efforts to provide crucial resources for improved speech technology to RT-05 program participants as well as to the larger community of language researchers, educators and technology developers. These resources are not limited to data, but also include annotations, specifications, tools and infrastructure.

References

1. Strassel, S., Glenn, M.: Shared Linguistic Resources for Human Language Technology in the Meeting Domain. Proceedings of the ICASSP 2004 Meeting Recognition Workshop. (2004) http://www.nist.gov/speech/test_beds/mr_proj/icassp_program.html

2. Linguistic Data Consortium: RT-04 Meeting Transcription Guidelines. (2004) http://www. ldc.upenn.edu/Projects/Transcription/NISTMeet/index.html
3. Strassel, S., Cieri, C., Walker, K., Miller, D.: Shared Resources for Robust Speech-to-Text Technology, Proceedings of Eurospeech (2003)
4. Bird, S., Liberman, M.: A formal framework for linguistic annotation. Speech Communication, (2001) 33:23–60.
5. Maeda, K., Strassel, S.: Annotation Tools for Large-Scale Corpus Development: Using AGTK at the Linguistic Data Consortium. Proceedings of the 4th International Conference on Language Resources and Evaluation (2004).
6. http://www.ldc.upenn.edu/Projects/Transcription/Tools

Robust Speaker Segmentation for Meetings: The ICSI-SRI Spring 2005 Diarization System

Xavier Anguera[1,2], Chuck Wooters[1], Barbara Peskin[1], and Mateu Aguiló[1,2]

[1] International Computer Science Institute, Berkeley CA 94704, USA
[2] Technical University of Catalonia, Barcelona, Spain
{xanguera, wooters, barbara, mateu}@icsi.berkeley.edu

Abstract. In this paper we describe the ICSI-SRI entry in the Rich Transcription 2005 Spring Meeting Recognition Evaluation. The current system is based on the ICSI-SRI clustering system for Broadcast News (BN), with extra modules to process the different meetings tasks in which we participated. Our base system uses agglomerative clustering with a modified Bayesian Information Criterion (BIC) measure to determine when to stop merging clusters and to decide which pairs of clusters to merge. This approach does not require any pre-trained models, thus increasing robustness and simplifying the port from BN to the meetings domain. For the meetings domain, we have added several features to our baseline clustering system, including a "purification" module that tries to keep the clusters acoustically homogeneous throughout the clustering process, and a delay&sum beamforming algorithm which enhances signal quality for the multiple distant microphones (MDM) sub-task. In post-evaluation work we further improved the delay&sum algorithm, experimented with a new speech/non-speech detector and proposed a new system for the lecture room environment.

1 Introduction

The goal of a diarization system is to locate homogeneous regions within an audio segment and consistently label them for speaker, gender, music, noise, etc. Within the framework of the Rich Transcription 2005 Spring Meeting Recognition Evaluation, the labels of interest were solely speaker regions. This year's evaluation expands its focus from last year and considers two meeting subdomains: the conference room, as in previous NIST evals, and the lecture room, with seminar-like meetings. In each subdomain a test set of about two hours was distributed. Participants' systems were asked to answer the question "Who spoke when?" The systems were not required to identify the actual speakers by name, but just to consistently label segments of speech from the same speaker. Performance was measured based on the percentage of audio that was incorrectly assigned.

This year is the first time that we participated in the Diarization task for the Meetings environment. The clustering system used is based on our agglomerative clustering system originally developed by Ajmera et al. (see [1] [2] [3] [4]). Its primary advantage is that it requires no pre-trained acoustic models and therefore

S. Renals and S. Bengio (Eds.): MLMI 2005, LNCS 3869, pp. 402–414, 2006.

is robust and easily portable to new tasks. One new feature we have added to the system is a purification step during the agglomerative clustering process. The purification process attempts to split clusters that are not acoustically homogeneous. Another new feature we have added is multi-channel signal enhancement. For the conditions where multiple microphones are available, we combine these multiple signals into a single enhanced signal using delay&sum beamforming. The resulting system performed well in the meetings environment, achieving official scores of 18.56% and 15.32% error for the Multiple Distant Microphones (MDM) and Single Distant Microphone (SDM) conference room conditions[1], and 10.41%, 10.43% and 9.98% error for the lecture room MDM, SDM and Multiple Source Localization Array (MSLA) conditions[2].

In Section 2 we present the detailed description of the different parts in our system. In Section 3 we describe the systems submitted in the evaluation and their performance. In Section 4 we describe some improvements to the system that were made after the evaluation was submitted. Finally, ongoing and future work are presented in Section 5.

2   System Description

The system this year has two parts that are combined to adapt to the different tasks and data available. The first part consists of an acoustic fusion of all the available channels (when they exist) into a single enhanced channel via the delay-and-sum beamforming algorithm. The second part is our basic speaker diarization system, similar to the system submitted for the Fall 2004 Broadcast News evaluation (RT04f) (see [4]). The main differences in this second part are:

1. the use of an un-biased estimator for the variance together with minimum variance thresholding.
2. a purification algorithm to clean the clusters of non acoustically homogeneous data.
3. a major bug-fix in the core clustering system.

The delay&sum beamforming algorithm is used in some tasks where more than one microphone is available (i.e. MDM and MSLA for Diarization). It uses a sliding analysis window of length 500ms, with an overlap of 50%. At each step, a 500ms segment from each of the different channels is aligned to a reference channel producing a delay for that segment. The delay-adjusted segments are then summed to produce an enhanced output, which becomes the input of the basic diarization system. The delays are computed using GCC-PHAT and special care is taken to maintain continuity in the delays given non-speech and multiple speaker areas. For a more detailed description see section 2.1.

---

[1] After the evaluation we made some simple changes to the delay&sum algorithm that considerably changed these results.

[2] Although these are not the primary submission results, as explained below, these are obtained using the clustering system just described.

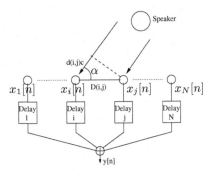

Fig. 1. Delay-and-sum system

The second part of the system is our basic speaker diarization system. This system uses agglomerative clustering and begins by segmenting the data into small pieces. Initially, each piece of data is assigned to a separate cluster. The system then iteratively merges clusters and resegments, stopping when there are no clusters that can be merged. This procedure requires two measures: one to determine which pair of clusters to merge, and a second measure to determine when to terminate the merging process. In our baseline system, we use a modified version of BIC [5] for both of these measures. The modified BIC equation is defined as:

$$\log p(D|\theta) \geq \log p(D_a|\theta_a) + \log p(D_b|\theta_b) \qquad (1)$$

where D_a and D_b represent the data in two clusters and θ_a and θ_b represent the models trained on the data assigned to the two clusters. Finally, D is the data from $D_a \cup D_b$ and θ represents the model trained on D.

Eq. 1 is similar to BIC, except that the model θ is constructed such that the number of parameters is equal to the sum of the number of parameters in θ_a and θ_b. By keeping the number of parameters constant on both sides of the equation, we have eliminated the traditional BIC penalty term. This increases the robustness of the system as there is no need to tune this parameter.

We can compute a merging score for θ_a and θ_b by combining the right and left-hand sides of Eq. 1:

$$\text{MergeScore}(\theta_a, \theta_b) = \qquad (2)$$
$$\log p(D|\theta) - (\log p(D_a|\theta_a) + \log p(D_b|\theta_b))$$

2.1   Delay-and-Sum Beamforming

The delay&sum (D&S) beamforming technique [6] is a simple yet effective way to enhance an input signal when it has been recorded on more than one microphone. It doesn't assume any information about the position of the microphones or their placement. The principle of operation of D&S can be seen in Figure 1.

Given the signals captured by N microphones, $x_i[n]$ with $i = 0 \ldots N-1$ (where n indicates time steps) if we know their individual relative delays $d(0, i)$ (called

Time Delay of Arrival, TDOA) with respect to a common reference microphone x_0, we can obtain the enhanced signal using equation 3.

$$y(n) = x_0[n] + \sum_{i=1}^{N-1} W_i[n]x_i[n - d(0, i)] \tag{3}$$

Where $W_i[n]$ represents individual channel weighting. In the basic delay&sum formulation they are set to 1. By adding together the aligned signals the usable speech adds together and the ambient noise (assuming it is random and has a similar probability function) will be reduced. Using D&S, according to [6], we can obtain up to a 3db SNR improvement each time that we double the number of microphones. We were able to obtain a 15.62% DER using D&S over multiple microphones compared to 21.32% on SDM for the RT04s development set.

In order to estimate the TDOA between two segments from two microphones we used the generalized cross correlation with phase transform (GCC-PHAT) method (see [7]). Given two signals $x_i(n)$ and $x_j(n)$ the GCC-PHAT is defined as:

$$G_{PHAT}(f) = \frac{X_i(f)[X_j(f)]^*}{|X_i(f)[X_j(f)]^*|} \tag{4}$$

where $X_i(f)$ and $X_j(f)$ are the Fourier transforms of the two signals and [ ]* denotes the complex conjugate. The TDOA for these two microphones is estimated as:

$$\hat{d}_{PHAT}(i, j) = \frac{argmax}{d} \left(\hat{R}_{PHAT}(d) \right) \tag{5}$$

where $\hat{R}_{PHAT}(d)$ is the inverse Fourier transform of $G_{PHAT}(f)$. Although the maximum value of $\hat{R}_{PHAT}(d)$ corresponds to the estimated TDOA, we have found it useful to keep the top N values for further processing.

There are two cases where the GCC-PHAT computation can provide inaccurate estimates for speaker clustering. On one hand, as we don't eliminate the regions of non-speech from the signal prior to delay&sum and due to the small size of the analysis window (500ms), when trying to estimate the TDOA from a non-speech region it returns a random delay value with a very small correlation. To avoid this we consider only TDOA estimates with GCC-PHAT values greater than 0.1 (of a normalized maximum value of 1), and carry over the previous estimates to the current segment otherwise. On the other hand, the GCC-PHAT also has problems when there are two or more people talking at the same time. In such cases the estimated TDOA will focus on one or another of the sources, producing an instability and diminishing the quality of the output. To solve this problem we compute the 8 biggest peaks of the GCC-PHAT in each analysis window and select the TDOA that is within a small distance from the previously obtained delay or the bigger one.

2.2   Speech/Non-Speech Detection

In this year's system we continue to use the SRI Speech-to-Text (STT) system's speech/non-speech (SNS) detector to eliminate the non-speech frames from the input to the clustering algorithm. Its use in our speaker diarization system was introduced in last year's RT04f evaluation. The SRI SNS system is a two-class decoder with a minimum duration of 30ms (three frames) enforced with a three-state HMM structure. The features used in the SNS detector (MFCC12) are different from the features used for the clustering. The resulting speech segments are merged to bridge short non-speech regions and padded. The speech/non-speech detector used in RT05s has been trained on meetings data (RT-02 devset data and RT-04s training data). The parameters of the detector were tuned on the RT05s meetings development data to minimize the combination of Misses and False Alarms as reported by the NIST mdeval scoring tool.

2.3   Signal Processing and System Initialization

For our system this year, we used 19 MFCC parameters, with no deltas. The MFCCs were computed over a 30 millisecond analysis window, stepping at 10 millisecond intervals. Before computing the features for each meeting, we extracted just the region of audio specified in the NIST input Unpartitiones Evaluation Map (UEM) files. The features are then calculated over this extracted region.

The first step in our clustering process is to initialize the models. This requires a "guess" at the maximum number of speakers (K) that are likely to occur in the data. We used K=10 for the conference room data and K=5 for the lecture room data. The data is then divided into K equal-length segments and each segment is assigned to one model. Each model's parameters are then trained using its assigned data. To model each cluster we use mixtures of gaussians with diagonal covariance matrix starting with 5 gaussians per model. These are the models that seed the clustering and segmentation processes described next.

2.4   Clustering Process

The procedure for segmenting the data consists of the following steps:

1. Run the SRI Meetings SNS detector.
2. Extract 19 MFCCs every 10ms.
3. Discard the non-speech frames.
4. Create the initial models as described above in Section 2.3.
5. The iterative merging process consists of the following steps:
   (a) Run a Viterbi decode to re-segment the data.
   (b) Retrain the models using the segmentation from (a).
   (c) Select the pair of clusters with the largest merge score (Eq. 2) that is > 0.0. (Since Eq. 2 produces positive scores for models that are similar, and negative scores for models that are different, a natural threshold for the system is 0.0.)
   (d) If no pair of clusters is found, stop.
   (e) Merge the pair of clusters found in (c). The models for the individual clusters in the pair are replaced by a single, combined model.
   (f) Run the purification algorithm (see section 2.5 for details) if the number of merging iterations is less than the initial number of clusters.
   (g) Go to (a).

2.5   Purification Algorithm

We have observed that the performance of our system is significantly affected by the way the models get initialized. Even though the initial models are re-segmented and retrained a few times during the clustering process, there are "impure" segments of audio that remain in a model in which they don't belong and negatively affect the final performance of the system. Such segments are either non-speech regions not detected by the SNS detector, or actual speech.

A particular segment of the audio that is quite dissimilar to the other segments in that model may not get assigned to any other model due to: a) the current model over-fitting that data, or b) there is not another model that provides a better match.

The purification algorithm is a post-merging step designed to find these segments and extract them, thus "purifying" the cluster. The segments considered are continuous intervals as found in the Viterbi segmentation step. The algorithm that we use to do the purification is applied after each cluster merge as follows:

1. For each cluster, we compute the normalized likelihood (dividing the total likelihood by the number of frames) of each segment in the cluster given the cluster's model. The segment with the highest likelihood is selected as the one that best fits the model.
2. For each cluster, we compute the modified BIC score (as seen in eq. 2) between the best fitting segment (as found in the previous step) and each of the other segments. If all comparisons give a positive value, the cluster is assumed to be pure, and is not considered a candidate for purification.
3. The segment with the lowest score below a certain threshold (-50 in our system) is extracted from the cluster and is re-assigned to its own cluster.

The source cluster keeps the same number of gaussians; therefore the purification process increases the total number of gaussians in the system (because a new cluster is created in the last step above). The purification algorithm is executed at most only on the first K iterations of the resegmentation-merging processing. We observed an improvement of approx. 2% absolute using this technique on a development data set built from the RT04s data sets and AMI meetings.

3   Evaluation Performance

For the evaluation we used different combinations of the pieces presented above. Almost all of these combinations share several common attributes:

- 19th order MFCC, no deltas, 30 msec analysis window, 10 msec step size.
- Each initial cluster begins with five gaussians.
- Iterative segmentation/training.
- Cluster purification.

3.1   Conference Room Systems

For the conference room environment we submitted one primary system in each of the MDM and SDM conditions. The MDM system uses delay&sum to acoustically fuse all the available channels into one enhanced channel. Then it applies the clustering to this enhanced channel. The SDM condition skips the delay&sum processing, as the system's input is already a single channel (from the most centrally located microphone according to NIST).

3.2   Lecture Room System

In the lecture room environment we submitted primary systems for the tasks MDM, SDM and MSLA, and contrastive systems for MDM (two systems), SDM and MSLA (two systems). Following is a brief description for each of these systems and their motivation:

- MDM, SDM and MSLA primary condition (MDM/SDM/MSLA_p-omnione): We observed in the development data that on many occasions we were able to obtain the best performance by just guessing one speaker for the whole duration of the lecture. This is particularly true when the meeting excerpt consists only of the lecturer speaking, but is often also achieved in the question-and-answer section since many of the excerpts in the development data consisted of very short questions followed by long answers by the lecturer. We therefore presented these systems as our primary submissions, serving also as a baseline score for the lecture room environment. Contrary to what we observed in the development data, our contrastive ("real") systems outperformed our primary ("guess one speaker") submissions on the evaluation data.
- MDM using speech/non-speech detection (mdm_c-spnspone): This differs from the primary submission only on the use of the SNS detector to eliminate the areas of non-speech.
- MDM using the TableTop microphone (mdm_c-ttoppur): From the available five microphones in the lecture room, the TableTop microphone is clearly of much better quality than all the others. We find it using an SNR estimator and the standard clustering is used on it.
- SDM using the SDM channel with a minimum duration of 12 seconds for each cluster (sdm_c-pur12s): This uses our clustering system on the SDM channel.
- MSLA with standard delay&sum (msla_c-nwsdpur12s).
- MSLA with weighted delay&sum (msla_c-wsdpur12s).

3.3   Scores

The DER scores on non-overlapped speech for this year's evaluation as they were released by NIST are shown in the ninth column of table 1, together with a summary of each system's characteristics. The numbers in the tenth column

Table 1. Systems summary description and DER on the evaluation set for RT05s

System ID	room type	Task	Submission	Delay &sum	# Initial clusters	Acoustic min. dur.	Mics used	DER	post-eval DER
p-dspursys	Conf.	MDM	Primary	YES	10	3 sec	All	18.56%	16.33%
p-pursys	Conf.	SDM	Primary	NO	10	3 sec	SDM	15.32%	—
p-omnione	Lect.	MDM	Primary	NO	n/a	n/a	n/a	12.21%	—
c-spnspone	Lect.	MDM	Contrast	NO	n/a	n/a	n/a	12.84%	—
c-ttoppur	Lect.	MDM	Contrast	NO	5	5 sec	Tabletop	10.41%	10.21%
p-omnione	Lect.	SDM	Primary	NO	n/a	n/a	n/a	12.21%	—
c-pur12s	Lect.	SDM	Contrast	NO	5	12 sec	SDM	10.43%	10.47%
p-omnione	Lect.	MSLA	Primary	NO	n/a	n/a	n/a	12.21%	—
c-nwsdpur12s	Lect.	MSLA	Contrast	YES	5	12 sec	All	9.98%	9.66%
c-wsdpur12s	Lect.	MSLA	Contrast	YES [1]	5	12 sec	All	9.99%	9.78%

reflect improvements after small bug fixes and serve as the baseline scores used in the remainder of this paper. In the systems using delay&sum, an improvement comes from fixing a small bug in our system that we detected after the eval (the 2% difference in conference room MDM is mainly due to the meeting VT_20050318-1430). In the (non trivial) lecture room systems, the improvement comes from using an improved UEM file for the show CHIL_20050202-0000-E2.

The use of delay&sum to enhance the signal before doing the clustering turned out to be a bad choice for the conference room systems, as the SDM DER is smaller than the MDM. In section 4.1 we consider what the possible problem could be and propose two solutions.

4 Post-evaluation Improvements

In this section we present several improvements to the system that were introduced after the evaluation.

4.1 Individual Channel Weighting

After the conference room evaluation, we observed that the straightforward delay&sum processing we had performed using all available distant channels was suboptimal. We found that the quality of the delay&summed output was negatively affected when the channels are of different types or they are located far from each other in the room.

In the formulation of the delay&sum processing, the additive noise components on each of the channels are expected to be random processes with very similar probability distributions. This allows the noise on each channel to be minimized when the delay-adjusted channels are summed. In standard beam-forming systems, this noise cancellation is achieved through the use of identical microphones placed only a few inches apart from each other.

---

[1] This system uses a weighted version of delay&sum using correlations, as explained in 4.1.

In the meetings room we assume that all of the distant microphones form a microphone array. However, having different types of microphones changes the impulse response of the signal being recorded and therefore changes the probability distributions of the additive noise. Also when two microphones are far from each other the speech they record will be affected by noise of a different nature, due to the room's impulse response.

After the conference room evaluation we began working on different ways to individually weight the channels according to the quality of the signal. Here we present two techniques we have tried, plus their combination:

SNR based weighting: A well known measure of the quality of a speech signal is its Signal-to-Noise ratio (SNR). We estimate the SNR value for each channel for all of the evaluated portion of the meeting and we apply a constant weight to each segment of each channel upon summation. The SNR is computed according to [8].

Correlation based weighting: The weighting value is adapted continuously during the duration of the meeting. This is inspired by the fact that the different channels will have different quality depending on their relative distance to the person speaking, which can change constantly during a recording. The weight for channel i at step n ($\mathcal{W}_i[n]$) is computed in the following way:

$$\mathcal{W}_i[n] = \begin{cases} \frac{1}{\#\text{Channels}} & n = 0 \\ (1 - \alpha) \cdot \mathcal{W}_i[n-1] + \alpha \cdot \text{xcorr}(i, \text{ref.}) & \text{otherwise} \end{cases} \quad (6)$$

where $xcorr(i, ref.)$ is the cross-correlation between the delay-adjusted segment for channel i and the reference channel. When i=reference, it is just the power of the reference channel. If the cross-correlation becomes negative it is set to 0.0. By experimenting on the development set we set $\alpha = 0.05$.

Combination of both techniques: We use the SNR to rank the channels and select the best as the reference channel. Then the process is identical to the correlation weighting.

In table 2 we can see the results of running these three proposed techniques on some of the multiple distant microphone conditions.

Table 2. Effect of channel weighting on Eval DER scores

Submission Desc.	Baseline	SNR Weight	Xcorr Weight	SNR+Xcorr
MDM Conference room	16.33%	17.02%	16.17%	14.81%
MSLA Lecture Room	9.66%	8.94%	9.78%	9.83%

For Conference room data the correlation technique performs better than the SNR, but when combined together they outperform both individual systems. In Lecture room (on MSLA microphones) the SNR constant weights technique works better that variable weighting. In fact, in the Lecture room environment by having most of the time a single speaker we benefit more from a fixed weight, contrary to when multiple speakers intervene, benefitting from variable weights.

In order to isolate the effect of the weighting techniques, we also ran them using perfect speech/non-speech labels, thus minimizing miss and false alarm errors. In table 3 we can see the resulting DER.

Table 3. DER on the evaluation set for RT05s using "perfect" speech/non-speech labels

Submission Desc.	chan. Weights	DER
Conference room SDM	n/a	10.95%
Conference Room MDM	equal	11.55%
Conference Room MDM	correlation	10.50%
Conference Room MDM	SNR	10.60%
Conference Room MDM	SNR+corr	10.57%

4.2 Energy Based Speech/Non-Speech Detector

In our effort to create a robust diarization system that doesn't require any training data and as few "tunable" thresholds as possible, we are experimenting with an alternative to the SRI speech/non-speech(SNS) detector used in this year's evaluation. By using an energy-based detector we obtain improved results on the test data while eliminating the need of training the speech/non-speech detector.

Given an input signal one minute non overlapping regions are processed. After amplitude normalization a matched filter is applied [9] to emphasize the start and end points of the speech/non-speech regions. The detection is performed using a double threshold (from silence to speech and from speech to silence) as implemented in NIST's Speech Quality Assurance Package, see [10]. It is implemented using a finite state machine.

In table 4 we can observe the speech/non-speech error and the DER scores using this speech/non-speech detector on the different tasks. This test was only performed in the conference room domain as we haven't use a speech/non-speech detector in all our lecture room systems.

Table 4. Energy-based vs. model-based SNS on conference room environment

Submission Desc.	weights	SNS Error		full DER	
		Baseline	Energy-SNS	Baseline	Energy-SNS
SDM Conference room	n/a	4.7%	5.0%	15.32%	14.65%
MDM Conference room	equal	5.30%	3.7%	16.33%	13.93%
MDM Conference room	SNR+corr	5.3%	3.7%	14.81%	13.97%

4.3 Selective Lecture Room Clustering

On the lecture room data the submitted systems didn't make use of the information regarding the kind of excerpt that was being clustered. As noted by

NIST, the excepts ending with E1 and E3 have only the lecturer speaking in them; therefore guessing that only one speaker speaks all the time consistently achieves the best performance. On the other hand, the excerpts ending with E2 belong to the Q&A sections, with more speakers and a structure that more closely resembles the conference room environment.

After the evaluation, we constructed a system to take advantage of this information. The system parses the lecture file name before processing and proceeds assigns one speaker all the time if it contains E1 or E3, or uses "normal" clustering when it has E2. In table 5 we present the results of running this system for the different possible sets of microphones.

Table 5. Selective Lecture room clustering DER

Submission Desc.	Baseline DER	Sel. clust. DER
SDM Lecture room	10.47%	9.60%
MDM Lecture room	10.21%	8.75%
MSLA Lecture room	9.66%	9.38%

5   Future Work

Our future work will continue to focus on the use of techniques that require no pre-trained models and as few "tunable" parameters as possible. Signal processing related improvements include:

- Improve SNS without external training data. We will continue work on our energy-based SNS detector, specifically focusing on robustness to different environments including: Broadcast News, Meetings, and Conversational Telephone Speech.
- Improve delay&sum processing and use extra information extracted from that processing (TDOA values, correlation weights, relative energy between microphones, etc.).
- Explore the use of alternative front-end signal processing techniques. To date, we have limited our features to MFCC19. We would like to explore alternative front-end features.

Improvements to the clustering algorithm include:

- Improve the cluster purification algorithm to better deal with SNS errors.
- Explore the use of techniques from Speaker ID (modified to conform to our philosophy of "no pre-trained models") in the clustering algorithm.
- Explore the use of alternative stopping and merging criteria.

6   Conclusions

The primary advantage of our speaker diarization system is that it requires no pre-trained acoustic models and therefore is robust and easily portable to new tasks. For this year's evaluation, we added a couple of new features to the system. One new feature is the purification step during the agglomerative clustering process. The purification process attempts to split clusters that are not acoustically homogeneous. Another new feature is multi-channel signal enhancement. For the conditions where multiple microphones are available, we combine these multiple signals into a single enhanced signal using delay&sum beamforming. After the evaluation we experimented with new algorithms that further improved the performance on the test data. In table 6 we show the best results achieved in each evaluation condition.

Table 6. Best performance systems on the RT05s eval data

Room type	Task	Technique	DER
Conf.	SDM	section 4.2	14.65%
Conf.	MDM	section 4.2	13.93%
Lect.	SDM	section 5	9.60%
Lect.	MDM	section 5	8.75%
Lect.	MSLA	section 4.1	8.94%

On the conference room task we obtain the best results using a cross-correlation channel weighting for the MDM condition. For both MDM and SDM it is best to use an Energy based speech/non-speech detector. On the Lecture room task some of the meetings only have one speaker, therefore performing speaker clustering is not suitable for them. We obtain the best results by choosing to perform speaker clustering or just assigning one speaker all the time, depending on the show name.

Acknowledgments

We would like to acknowledge Hans-Guenter Hirsch for his help with the SNR estimation system. This work was partly supported by the European Union 6th FWP IST Integrated Project AMI (Augmented Multi-Party Interaction, FP6-506811).

References

1. J. Ajmera, H. Bourlard, and I. Lapidot, "Improved unknown-multiple speaker clustering using HMM," IDIAP, Tech. Rep., 2002.
2. J. Ajmera, H. Bourlard, I. Lapidot, and I. McCowan, "Unknown-multiple speaker clustering using HMM," in *ICSLP'02*, Denver, Colorado, USA, Sept. 2002.
3. J. Ajmera and C. Wooters, "A robust speaker clustering algorithm," in *ASRU'03*, US Virgin Islands, USA, Dec. 2003.
4. C. Wooters, J. Fung, B. Peskin, and X. Anguera, "Towards robust speaker segmentation: The ICSI-SRI fall 2004 diarization system," in *Rich Transcription Workshop*, New Jersey, USA, 2004.

5. S. Shaobing Chen and P. Gopalakrishnan, "Speaker, environment and channel change detection and clustering via the bayesian information criterion," in *Proceedings DARPA Broadcast News Transcription and Understanding Workshop*, Virginia, USA, Feb. 1998.

6. J. Flanagan, J. Johnson, R. Kahn, and G. Elko, "Computer-steered microphone arrays for sound transduction in large rooms," *Journal of the Acoustic Society of America*, vol. 78, pp. 1508–1518, November 1994.

7. M. S. Brandstein and H. F. Silverman, "A robust method for speech signal time-delay estimation in reverberant rooms," in *ICASSP-97*, Munich, Germany, 1997.

8. H.-G. Hirsch, "HMM adaptation for applications in telecommunication," *Speech Communication*, no. 34, pp. 127–139, 2001.

9. Q. Li and A. Tsai, "A matched filter approach to endpoint detection for robust speaker verification," in *IEEE Workshop on Automatic Identification Advanced Technologies*, New Jersey, USA, october 1999.

10. NIST speech tools and APIs. [Online]. Available: http://www.nist.gov/speech/tools/index.htm

Speech Activity Detection on Multichannels of Meeting Recordings

Zhongqiang Huang and Mary P. Harper

Electrical and Computer Engineering, Purdue University,
West Lafayette, IN 47907-1285
zqhuang@purdue.edu, harper@ecn.purdue.edu

Abstract. The Purdue SAD system was originally designed to identify speech regions in multichannel meeting recordings with the goal of focusing transcription effort on regions containing speech. In the NIST RT-05S evaluation, this system was evaluated in the ihm condition of the speech activity detection task. The goal for this task condition is to separate the voice of the speaker on each channel from silence and crosstalk. Our system consists of several steps and does not require a training set. It starts with a simple silence detection algorithm that utilizes pitch and energy to roughly separate silence from speech and crosstalk. A global Bayesian Information Criterion (BIC) is integrated with a Viterbi segmentation algorithm that divides the concatenated stream of local speech and crosstalk into homogeneous portions, which allows an energy based clustering process to then separate local speech and crosstalk. The second step makes use of the obtained segment information to iteratively train a Gaussian mixture model for each speech activity category and decode the whole sequence over an ergodic network to refine the segmentation. The final step first uses a cross-correlation analysis to eliminate crosstalk, and then applies a batch of post-processing operations to adjust the segments to the evaluation scenario. In this paper, we describe our system and discuss various issues related to its evaluation.

1 Introduction

Recently, the research community has begun to collect audio and audio-visual recordings of meetings in order to investigate more complex human interactions than dialogs. A number of meeting corpora have recently become available from several research sites [1, 2, 3, 4]. In a meeting recording, in addition to using desktop omnidirectional microphones, each participant typically wears a head-mounted microphone to acquire a high quality audio signal. In this paper, we describe our system which automatically segments the audio of each individual channel into transcribable (speech) and non-transcribable (non-speech) portions with the goal of focusing transcriber effort in order to increase the efficiency of producing high quality manual transcriptions.

Manual transcription is a time-consuming task. The total processing time for one hour of audio can be more than ten hours. In a meeting room recording with

S. Renals and S. Bengio (Eds.): MLMI 2005, LNCS 3869, pp. 415–427, 2006.

several participants and strong crosstalk, it is not unusual that audible voice is ubiquitous on a channel throughout the meeting; however, on average only a small percentage of that "speech" should be attributed to the local speaker, and it is only this speech that should be transcribed. With reference to an automatic segmentation containing transcribable and non-transcribable labels, the annotators can focus their effort on the transcribable segments and skim over the remaining non-transcribable segments. Furthermore, an automatic system can help with challenges such as identification of short duration, low intensity local speech surrounded by crosstalk with greater intensity than the local speech, elimination of short spans of crosstalk breaking a longer span of local speech, or identification of boundaries between local speech and cross-talk speech in regions where both occur together. In addition, because the transcribers are able to concentrate on short segments with reference boundaries, they should be able to produce more accurate transcriptions of these segments [5].

The most pressing challenge for multichannel speech activity detection is the crosstalk imposed by neighboring speakers. The existence of crosstalk results in four possible speech activity types including "local speech", "overlap speech", "background speech", and "silence". The audible crosstalk can sometimes be very strong, presenting acoustic characteristics that can be highly confusable with the local speech. In addition, participants are usually untrained in the use of close-talking microphones and may produce breath and/or contact noise.

In the literature, there have been several past approaches focusing on segmentation of multiple channels. These methods fall largely into the category of statistical pattern recognition approaches that require a large training data set to build the reference models and adopt an ergodic network to model the transitions between different speech activity events. In Liu and Kubala's method [6], which was evaluated on two channel telephone speech, channel-specific features and cross-channel features were concatenated to form the features for the four cross-channel events, each of which was modeled by a mixture of Gaussian components. Pfau et al. [7] proposed a speech and non-speech detector for meeting audio segmentation using an ergodic hidden Markov model consisting of speech and non-speech states that were trained separately. The decoding network was traversed separately on each channel and a post-processing step using short-time cross-correlation was applied to identify crosstalk and overlap speech in the regions where more than one channel was active in the hypothesis. Wrigley et al. [8] recently proposed a more sophisticated approach that used a Gaussian mixture model for each of the four speech activity types in meetings and integrated them into an ergodic hidden Markov model to decode each channel in parallel on a network that is constrained to allow only reasonable classifications to occur among the channels.

An issue when producing meeting data is that there is often little or no training data when efforts begin to transcribe meetings. The training methods used by the previous studies may lead to a mismatch (e.g., different participants, microphone types, gain settings, meeting layouts and crosstalk strength, background noise types and strength) between the reference models trained in advance and

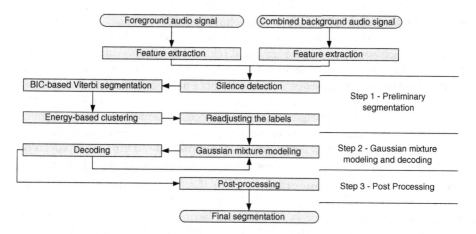

Fig. 1. System Diagram

the distribution of the actual feature space of the new meeting recordings. In our approach, we address this problem by independently training meeting-specific models in an unsupervised way. The system flow chart is shown in Figure 1. A preliminary segmentation is provided by step 1; then in step 2, we train a Gaussian mixture model for each speech activity event. Note that, rather than using the four categories previously used in the literature, in our method, "local speech" and "overlap speech" are modeled together as "local or overlap speech" for the following two reasons: first, the cross talk in "overlap speech" is usually negligible considering the dramatic energy difference between the speech from the local speaker and the background speech from neighboring participants; second, there is often insufficient "overlap speech" in a channel to accurately train a separate model.

This paper is organized as follows. We discuss our system in section 2, focusing on preliminary segmentation in section 2.1, Gaussian mixture modeling in section 2.2, and post processing in section 2.3. In section 3, we describe the experimental data set, the performance of our system at various stages, and issues related to the reference and evaluation metric. The last section concludes this paper.

2   Our Model

2.1   Step 1. Preliminary Segmentation

Preliminary segmentation is an important step for providing the Gaussian mixture modeling process labeled training data. A benefit of the multiple-channel recording scenario is that it enables us to employ mutual information across the channels. It is possible to treat each background channel separately; however, for simplicity we have opted to mix together the audio from the other participants' microphones to form a single combined channel in this study.

Silence Detection: Initially, our algorithm separates "silence" from "speech" (i.e., "local or overlap speech" and "background speech"). Pitch is a good indicator for speech events except for unvoiced regions. A frame is considered to be a "speech frame" if there is a pitch value defined within the corresponding region in either of the two channels or if either channel has a log energy value greater than the mean value of the entire channel, otherwise, it is classified roughly to be a "silence frame". Note that the silence detector produces the same segmentation on the local channel and the composite background channel. The "speech frames" from both channels are concatenated separately to streams of consecutive "speech frames" for the BIC-based Viterbi segmentation described next.

BIC-based Viterbi Segmentation: Here the goal is to divide the "speech frames" of each channel into "local or overlap speech" and "background speech". Average energy in a window is an excellent feature for discriminating between them. A fixed-size window that is shifted by a constant length could be used for this purpose; however, such a window can cover frames of both types when it is placed above a boundary. Chen et al. [9] proposed a Bayesian Information Criterion (BIC) to divide an audio stream into homogeneous segments by maximizing it in a local domain. A point is assumed to be a changing point if the BIC score of a sequence of vectors being modeled by two Gaussian processes against one Gaussian process achieves a maximum that is larger than zero. Inspired by the penalized log-likelihood function and the Viterbi reestimation introduced in [10], we sought to extend the BIC criterion for global optimization. Let $X = X_1^N = \{x_1, \ldots, x_N\}$ be the whole feature vector sequence, and $S = \{s_1, \ldots, s_L\}$ be a potential segmentation. $s_i = \{x_{t_i}, \ldots, x_{t_i+l_i-1}\}$ ($t_1 = 1, t_i+l_i = t_{i+1}, t_L+l_L-1 = N$) where t_i and l_i are the index of the starting vector and the number of samples in segment s_i, respectively. $M = \{m_i, \ldots, m_L\}$ is the model set for $S = \{s_1, \ldots, s_L\}$. The maximum likelihood function of each m_i and s_i pair is given by $L(s_i, m_i)$. Then the global BIC score of X being segmented into S and modeled by M is defined as:

$$BIC(X, S, M) = \sum_{i=1}^{L} \log(L(s_i, m_i)) - \frac{\lambda}{2}\#(M)log(N)$$

where $\#(M)$ is the number of parameters in the model set $M = \{m_1, \ldots, m_L\}$. We assume that the vectors in segment s_i are drawn from a multivariable Gaussian process $m_i = N(\mu_i, \Sigma_i)$ with the maximum log-likelihood function (d is the dimension of the feature space):

$$\log(L(s_i, m_i)) = -\frac{l_i}{2}\log|\Sigma_i| - \frac{d \times l_i}{2}\log(2\pi) - \frac{d \times l_i}{2}$$

The global BIC score now can be written as:

$BIC(X, S, M)$
$= \sum_{i=1}^{L}(-\frac{l_i}{2}\log|\Sigma_i| - \frac{d \times l_i}{2}\log(2\pi) - \frac{d \times l_i}{2}) - \frac{\lambda}{2}\#(M)log(N)$
$= \sum_{i=1}^{L}(-\frac{l_i}{2}\log|\Sigma_i|) - \frac{\lambda}{2}\#(M)log(N) - \frac{d \times N}{2}log(2\pi) - \frac{d \times N}{2}$

The last two terms are constants given a vector sequence, hence removing them will not affect the optimization procedure. Finally, we formulate our objective function as:

$$BIC(X, S, M) = -\sum_{i=1}^{L}(l_i \times \log|\Sigma_i|) - \lambda \#(M)\log(N)$$

In our experiment, the covariance matrix is assumed to be diagonal and the penalty λ is set to 2, based on its ability to produce homogeneous segments of reasonable length on a data set independent of the evaluation data. This final objective function is maximized by searching for the optimal segmentation set $S = \{s_1, \ldots, s_L\}$ through dynamic programming. The whole process is denoted BIC-based Viterbi segmentation.

Energy-based Clustering: BIC-based Viterbi segmentation produces tiny homogeneous segments without type labels. We compute the average log energy of these segments as the clustering feature and then cluster the segments into "local or overlap speech" or "background speech" based on their energy values, with the distance metric defined by the diagonal covariance Mahalanobis.

Readjusting the Labels: At this point, both the time aligned "speech frames" of the local channel and the background channel have their own segment labels. However, a "background speech" frame in the local channel may not have a corresponding "local or overlap speech" frame in the background channel, which conflicts with the cross-channel constraint. We use the following protocol to refine the local speech frame labels. If a frame is located in a "local or overlap speech" segment in the local channel, then it maintains its identity, otherwise, its class will be affected by the label of the corresponding segment in the background channel. When the background channel is a "local or overlap speech" segment, the local frame would maintain its class label as "background speech", however, it should be changed to "local or overlap speech" in case its log-energy is higher than the corresponding "background speech" frame in the background channel. Combining this with the silence detection results, we obtain a preliminary segmentation for the local channel into three classes: "silence", "local or overlap speech", and "background speech".

2.2   Step 2. Gaussian Mixture Modeling

We next train a Gaussian mixture model with 16 components for each of the three events using a conventional EM algorithm. An ergodic network is constructed to model the transitions between events with the topology shown in Figure 2.

Given the network, classification is performed according to the likelihood of a frame being generated by each Gaussian mixture. It outputs a model sequence that refines the segmentation boundaries and re-assigns the feature vectors to one of the three events. These re-assigned labels are used to retrain the GMMs. Four iterations of training and decoding are employed in our system. The purpose of this process is to generalize the feature distributions of the events, which could help to eliminate some outliers and refine the segmentation.

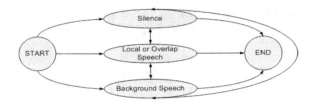

Fig. 2. Ergodic Network

2.3   Step 3. Post-processing

Next, cross-correlation-based post-processing [7] is applied to the 3-class segmentation. Given two one-dimensional zero-mean data series $x[n]$ and $y[n]$, the cross-correlation coefficient is calculated as:

$$CCC(x[n], y[n]) = \frac{E\{x[m]y[m]\}}{\sqrt{E\{x^2[m]\}E\{y^2[m]\}}}$$

We calculate the cross-correlation of cepstra and energy at each dimension and then take the average as the cross-correlation coefficient between two feature vector sequences [6]. That is, assuming $X_i[n]$ and $Y_i[n]$ as the ith dimension of two d-dimensional feature vector sequences $X[n]$ and $Y[n]$, then:

$$CCC(X[n], Y[n]) = \frac{1}{d}\Sigma_{i=1}^d CCC(X_i[n], Y_i[n])$$

To compensate for the time delay between the crosstalk speech and the original speech, a time skew is set to find the maximum cross-correlation coefficient using the following equation:

$$CCC(X[n], Y[n]) = \max_k \frac{1}{d}\Sigma_{i=1}^d CCC(X_i[n + k], Y_i[n])$$

In our system, the window size and the maximum time skew are set to 41 frames and ±5 frames, respectively. A "local or overlap speech" frame is reclassified to "background speech" if its log energy (normalized to the range -Emin...1.0 as in HTK) is lower than that of the background channel and the average cross-correlation coefficient is higher than 0.35.

A batch of post-processing steps are then applied to refine the resulting segmentation. Given the mean 'm_b' of the unnormalized log energy of the "background speech" frames:

- For each "silence" or "background speech" segment, if its average log energy is greater than that of the background channel and greater than 'm_b', then it is reclassified as a "local or overlap speech" segment. This operation is meant to recover speech that is mistakenly recognized as non-transcribable.
- Then "local or overlap speech" segments shorter than 0.05 seconds are merged into their neighboring segments to avoid noisy and false speech segments.

- Those "local or overlap speech" segments whose length falls in the range from 0.05 seconds to 0.2 seconds and that have an average log energy lower than that of the background channel or 'm_b' are reclassified as "background speech". This operation, as well as subsequent processing, is expected to reduce false alarms.
- Those "local or overlap speech" segments longer than 0.2 seconds that have an average log energy lower than 'm_b' are reclassified as "background speech".
- Merge "silence" and "back speech" segments to silence segments and relabel "local or overlap speech" as speech.
- Merge silence segments shorter than 0.3 seconds with their neighboring speech segments to match the smoothing operation in producing the reference.
- Pad 0.15 seconds to both ends of speech segments that are greater than or equal to 0.7 seconds. Since there is a 0.25 seconds collar during scoring, it is safe to pad a certain amount of silence to prevent cutting off the beginning and ending of words without increasing false alarms. 0.7 seconds is an experimental threshold set to avoid padding false alarm segments, which tend to be short in duration.
- Merge silence segments again to eliminate short pauses after padding.

3   Evaluation Results and Discussion

3.1   The Data

Two meetings from each of the following meeting corpora were used in the NIST RT-05S evaluation: AMI (The AMI Meeting Corpus), CMU (The ISL Meeting Corpus), ICSI (The ICSI Meeting Corpus), NIST (The NIST Meeting Room Pilot Corpus), and VT (The VACE Multimodal Meeting Corpus). The participants in each of these meetings were recorded with head microphones, thus enabling the multichannel speech activity detection task. A summary of some of the properties of the meetings is shown in Table 1.

The meeting domain training and development resources available for this evaluation are described in [11]. Since our system does not require training data for the first two steps, we only used the RT-04S evaluation data to adjust the parameters of our post-processing steps. In our system, for each subject in a meeting, audio streams of the respective background channels are combined together to form a single background stream. 23 Mel-frequency cepstrum coefficients (MFCC) and the log energy are extracted as the main features every 10ms with a 25ms Hamming window. In addition, the pitch value is computed at the same time step, and only those with a value between 75Hz and 600Hz are considered valid.

The data used to evaluate the SAD systems were created in a similar way to that used for the diarization task (i.e., the "who spoke when" task). First, manually transcribed segments were provided by LDC, such that the start and end times of each speech segment were set to the nearest tenth of a second and the pauses longer than 0.5 seconds were separated from the speech segments. The

Table 1. Evaluation data table and results

	AMI	CMU	ICSI	NIST	VT
recording time	20041210 -1052	20050228 -1615	20010531 -1030	20050412 -1303	20050304 -1300
# of participants	4	4	7	9	5
meeting duration (mins)	16	18	60	51	22
evaluated time (mins)	12	12	12	12	12
NIST metric	6.43%	7.48%	94.18%	24.69%	1.77%
contrastive metric	1.45%	2.23%	13.18%	2.58%	0.3%
recording time	20050204 -1206	20050301 -1415	20011113 -1100	20050427 -0939	20050318 -1430
# of participants	4	4	9	4	5
meeting duration (mins)	37	20	57	39	44
evaluated time (mins)	12	12	12	12	12
NIST metric	35.95%	5.07%	58.22%	13.66%	6.99%
contrastive metric	8.96%	1.27%	7.38%	3.42%	0.99%

timing of reference boundaries for the SAD task were derived from these manually transcribed segments. Neighboring segments with no pause of 0.3 seconds or more between them were bridged together into a single continuous segment. Non-lexical vocal noises such as laughter, coughing, sneezing, breaths, and lipsmacks were to be classified as silence when constructing segment boundaries. To account for the timing errors in the reference, no-score time collars of 0.25 seconds were placed around each reference boundary to unscore these regions.

3.2   Analysis of Results

The metric that NIST used for speech activity detection performance involves both miss and false alarm rates given the reference. An overall error score is computed as the fraction of speaker time that is not attributed correctly to a speaker. Table 1 shows the NIST metric score of our system for each meeting, as well as a contrastive metric score computed as the fraction of the scored time that is not classified correctly. The overall NIST error across the meetings was

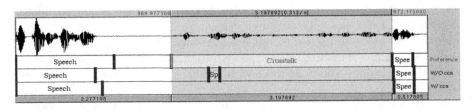

Fig. 3. An example of the impact of cross-correlation analysis (cca) for reducing crosstalk

26.95% (miss rate: 8.07%, false alarm rate: 18.89%) and the overall contrastive metric error was 4.76% (miss rate: 1.41%, false alarm rate: 3.31%).

Our system relies heavily on the performance of the preliminary segmentation. The first simple silence detection algorithm tends to classify any kind of noise as speech if its log energy is greater than the average level on the channel. In subsequent operations, such noise is considered to be equivalent to speech and cannot be eliminated. Hence, breath sounds are a major source of error for our system. Although crosstalk is initially detected as speech in the first step, the large majority of cross talk segments are subsequently reclassified based on the energy-based clustering of the Viterbi segmentation outputs. Crosstalk is further reduced by using the cross-correlation coefficient between the local channel and background channel, as shown in the example in Figure 3. However, some crosstalk that does not have a strong correlation with the background speech remains causing some additional false alarms. The post-processing operations on the segments were intended to reduce some of the classification errors and better match the way in which the data was prepared for evaluation (e.g., by merging short pauses that are included in speech segments in the reference); however, these steps can also introduce errors.

Although there are remaining issues for us to resolve in building a highly effective SAD system for ihm type meeting data, there are also issues that need to be addressed to evaluate such a system most effectively.

The Evaluation Metric: Unlike the SAD task on sdm condition, the percentage of speaking time is quite variable among the channels. Given the focus on speaking time in the NIST metric, across channels the same total amount of error can lead to very different error rates. For example, suppose there is a 10-minute recording, and two channels that contain 1 minute and 9 minutes of speaking time in the audio. If a system produces 2 minutes total error in both cases, regardless of whether it is composed of missed speech or false alarms, the error rate for the first case would be 9 times larger than the second, and twice as large as simply classifying the entire stream as silence. Such a metric can produce an infinite error rate no matter how well a system performs, if the speaking time is zero. For a second example, suppose there are two recordings to be evaluated where the first represents only a small portion of the audio for the second and includes all the speech of the second. In this case, the second segment is far more challenging. Table 2 shows a histogram of the percentage of speaking time across the channels as well as the corresponding error rates obtained by our system using the NIST and contrastive metrics. Although there

Table 2. Error rates given the percentage of speaker time

percentage range	0-100%	0-10%	10-20%	20-30%	30-40%	40-50%	50-60%	60-70%
# of channels	55	**16**	14	15	3	4	2	1
NIST metric	26.95%	**245.56%**	21.4%	18%	5.76%	15.27%	7.67%	2.58%
contrastive metric	4.62%	**7.46%**	2.62%	3.90%	1.96%	6.60%	4.41%	1.66%

are many factors including the percentage of speaking time that can affect the system performance, the trend that the NIST metric has a greater error rate when there is a lower percentage of speaking time is apparent in the table. In contrast, it is more stable to measure the system performance using the contrastive metric. Another alternative to the NIST metric might be separate error rates for detecting speech and non-speech activities.

Long Pauses and Silence Padding: Although most of the evaluation data is comprised of accurate reference boundaries, there are several instances of long pauses (greater than 0.3s) during speech segments and occasional long silence padding (greater than 0.25s). Since pauses and padding are not handled consistently, it is challenging to post-process system outputs to better match the conditions used to produce the reference. A forgiveness collar partially resolves the silence padding problem, but its use also prevents systems from being evaluated near speech boundaries, which should be an important focus of evaluation. Figure 4 depicts a sample of the channel CMU_20050228-1615_h02_mKHNPEA that shows the reference segment and our system segmentation. We have evaluated for this channel how different types of reference boundaries affect the evaluation of our system. Table 3 illustrates the impact of these reference boundaries given our system. One possible way of addressing this is to adopt a stricter sense of where words are and eliminate the use of no-score collars and pause merging. The benefit would be having a better sense of the issues that need to be resolved in building a better algorithm. Forced alignment of the transcripts would be one way of achieving this.

Fig. 4. Long pause and silence padding example

Table 3. Error rates when handling pauses and speech segment boundaries in different ways: the original reference boundaries with no-score collars, close boundaries (obtained by separating pauses from the original speech reference segment and moving the boundaries as close as possible to the word ends (within 0.1s)), and smooth boundaries (obtained by merging neighboring segments within 0.3s of each other given the close boundary reference)

Reference type	scored speaker time	missed speech	false alarms	NIST metric
original boundary	136.79s	19.91s	0.76s	15.15%
close boundary	84.35s	3.43s	3.53s	8.26%
smooth boundary	96.43s	5.04s	2.15s	7.46%

Breath and Other Vocal Noise: For a SAD system, one may wish to locate the words spoken by a person, while ignoring the non-speech noises such as laughter, coughing, sneezing, breath sounds, and lipsmacks. Another alternative is to locate everything attributable to a speaker and then the non-speech events can be eliminated later either manually or automatically. However, it is important that this is handled consistently. Laughter was transcribed and classified as speech in the evaluation. Breath was transcribed and classified as speech when it was near speech, but otherwise not. This leads to a situation where breaths are sometimes classified as speech and sometimes not, making them difficult to address in a consistent manner.

A Focused Performance Analysis: Our system was originally designed for and evaluated on the multiple channel data produced under KDI (captured with boom mics) since we had a high quality ground truth, and then adjustments were made to support transcription of the earliest captured VACE meeting recordings. Since our algorithm has been applied effectively to recording conditions comparable to the two VT meetings in the evaluation set, it is not surprising that our system obtains the best results on them. The VT data contains a significant amount of crosstalk, with some having a strong amplitude challenging to system performance. Here we present the system performance using the contrastive metric at various stages in our multistep approach to highlight the impact of each step. In order to evaluate the intermediate segmentations consistently with the final segmentation, we apply the post-processing operations that follow the cross-correlation analysis described in 2.3 to the intermediate segmentations before we evaluate them.

As shown in the table, at each stage our system finds and refines the boundaries gradually, and finally it reaches an overall error rate of 0.64%. It would be desirable for the missed speech and the false alarms to decrease monotonically; however, we have observed that on some data sets there is a tradeoff between them. The system performance and the capacity of improvement of each step depends heavily on how the reference segments are obtained and how the system is evaluated on the reference.

To get a sense of how the reference and the no-score collar affect system performance, we have evaluated our system on reference segmentations that were obtained after the evaluation by forced-alignment of the transcription[1]. Results appear in Table 5. Although the forced-alignments are not hand-fixed and so are not 100% correct, they provide a relatively more precise gold standard with respect to the location of speech and non-speech activities. Given that the merging and deleting post-processing operations were developed for the NIST

---

[1] Forced-alignment of transcriptions is an important step in creating the VACE Multimodal Meeting Corpus. Transcribable and non-transcribable segmentations of a channel are first produced using the method described in this paper, then transcribers produce transcriptions for the speech segments and make minor adjustment of the segmentation if needed. Automatic forced-alignments are obtained using these transcriptions with careful handling of the OOV words, and only segments containing words are considered as speech.

Table 4. Performance at each stage on the VT meetings

	missed speech	false alarms	contrastive metric
Preliminary segmentation	0.56%	1.38%	1.93%
Gaussian mixture modeling	0.45%	1.33%	1.78%
Post-processing	0.50%	0.14%	0.64%

Table 5. System performance with and without post-processing using different types of references. MS stands for "missed speech", FA for "false alarm", and CM for "contrastive metric". FoA is the reference derived directly from forced-alignments, and REF is the original reference used in the evaluation. The first two rows are evaluated without no-score collars, and the last two rows are evaluated with no-score collars of 0.25 seconds.

	No post-processing			W/ post-processing		
	MS	FA	CM	MS	FA	CM
FoA	1.11%	0.97%	2.09%	0.16%	3.12%	3.27%
REF	4.21%	0.26%	4.47%	1.58%	0.74%	2.32%
FoA with C	0.38%	0.42%	0.80%	0.00%	0.42%	0.42%
REF with C	2.70%	0.22%	2.92%	0.50%	0.14%	0.64%

reference setup, we examine our system performance with and without these steps. We can see that if we use the forced-alignments as the gold standard, then these steps introduce errors, although they do help a lot when the original reference (REF) is used. We also observe that when the no-score collars are added these post-processing operations become essential even for the forced-alignment gold standard.

4   Conclusions

In this paper, we have presented a multichannel speech activity detection algorithm for meeting room recordings. The property that it requires no training data makes it especially useful for dividing audio collections into speech and non-speech segments when preparing to transcribe audio for a new meeting room corpus. We have also discussed several issues related to effective evaluation of a SAD system and have shown the importance of careful development of the gold standard reference and evaluation metrics to support future research. In future work, we will focus on further increasing the accuracy of detecting crosstalk and incorporate methods to better handle non-speech noise.

Acknowledgments

This work was supported in part by NSF under award number 9980054 and ARDA under contract number MDA904-03-C-1788. Part of this work was carried out while the second author was on leave at NSF. Any opinions, findings, and conclusions expressed in this paper are those of the authors and do not necessarily reflect the views of NSF or ARDA. We would also like to acknowledge NIST, without which this evaluation would not exist.

References

[1] Garofolo, J.S., Laprun, C.D., Michel, M., Stanford, V.M., Tabassi, E.: The NIST meeting room pilot corpus. In: Proceedings of the 4th International Conference on Language Resources and Evaluation, Lisbon, Portugal (2004)
[2] Janin, A., Baron, D., Edwards, J., Ellis, D., Gelbart, D., Morgan, N., Peskin, B., Phau, T., Shriberg, E., Stolcke, A., Wooters, C.: The ICSI meeting corpus. In: Proceedings of International Conference on Acoustics, Speech, and Signal Processing. Volume 1. (2003) 364–367
[3] Burger, S., MacLaren, V., Yu, H.: The ISL meeting corpus: The impact of meeting type on speech style. In: Proceedings of International Conference on Spoken Language Processing. (2002) 302–304
[4] Chen, L., Rose, R.T., Parrill, F., Han, X., Tu, J., Huang, Z., Harper, M., Quek, F., McNeill, D., Tuttle, R., Huang, T.: Vace multimodal meeting corpus. In: Proceedings of MLMI-2005 Workshop. (2005)
[5] Chen, L., Maia, E., Liu, Y., Harper, M.P.: Evaluating factors impacting forced alignment in a multimodal corpus. In: Proceedings of the 4th International Conference on Language Resources and Evaluation, Lisbon, Portugal (2004)
[6] Liu, D., Kubala, F.: A cross-channel modeling approach for automatic segmentation of conversational telephone speech. In: Proceedings of IEEE ASRU Workshop. (2003) 333–338
[7] Pfau, T., Ellis, D.P., Stolcke, A.: Multispeaker speech activity detection for the ICSI meeting recorder. In: Proceedings of IEEE ASRU Workshop. (2001) 107–110
[8] Wrigley, S.N., Brown, G.J., Wan, V., Renals, S.: Speech and crosstalk detection in multichannel audio. IEEE Transactions on Speech and Audio Processing (2005) 84–91
[9] Chen, S.S., Gopalakrishnan, P.: Speaker, environment and channel change detection and clustering via the Bayesian information criterion. Technical report, IBM (1998)
[10] Gauvain, J.L., Lamel, L., Adda, G.: The LIMSI broadcast news transcription system. Speech Communication **37** (2002) 89–108
[11] Fiscus, J.: Spring 2005 (RT-05S) Rich Transaction Meeting Recognition Evaluation Plan, http://nist.gov/speech/tests/rt/rt2005/spring/. (2005)

NIST RT'05S Evaluation: Pre-processing Techniques and Speaker Diarization on Multiple Microphone Meetings

Dan Istrate[1], Corinne Fredouille[1], Sylvain Meignier[2],
Laurent Besacier[3], and Jean François Bonastre[1]

[1] LIA-Avignon - BP1228 - 84911 Avignon Cedex 9 - France
[2] LIUM, Avenue Laënnec, 72085 Le Mans Cedex 9
[3] CLIPS-IMAG (UJF & CNRS & INPG) - BP 53 - 38041 Grenoble Cedex 9 - France

Abstract. This paper presents different pre-processing techniques, coupled with three speaker diarization systems in the framework of the NIST 2005 Spring Rich Transcription campaign (RT'05S).

The pre-processing techniques aim at providing a signal quality index in order to build a unique "virtual" signal obtained from all the microphone recordings available for a meeting. This unique virtual signal relies on a weighted sum of the different microphone signals while the signal quality index is given according to a signal to noise ratio.

Two methods are used in this paper to compute the instantaneous signal to noise ratio: a speech activity detection based approach and a noise spectrum estimate. The speaker diarization task is performed using systems developed by different labs: the LIA, LIUM and CLIPS. Among the different system submissions made by these three labs, the best system obtained 24.5 % speaker diarization error for the conference subdomain and 18.4 % for the lecture subdomain.

1 Introduction

The goal of speaker diarization is to segment an N-speaker audio document in homogeneous parts containing the voice of only one speaker and to associate the resulting segments by matching those belonging to the same speaker. In speaker diarization the intrinsic difficulty of the task increases according to the target data: telephone conversations, broadcast news, meeting data.

This paper is related to speaker diarization on meeting data in the framework of the NIST 2005 Spring Rich Transcription (RT'05S) campaign. Meeting data present three main specificities compared to broadcast news data:

- meeting conversations are recorded with multiple microphones which implies redundancies and different qualities of the same speech recording. The use of information from all channels seems to be an important issue;
- the meeting room recording conditions associated with distant microphones lead to noisy recordings, including background noises, reverberations and distant speakers;

S. Renals and S. Bengio (Eds.): MLMI 2005, LNCS 3869, pp. 428–439, 2006.

- the speech is fully-spontaneous, highly interactive and presents a large number of disfluencies as well as speaker segment overlaps.

This paper is focused on the extraction of pertinent information issued from the different multiple microphone recordings in the particular task of speaker diarization. Indeed, signal processing techniques are applied on the different distant microphone signal recordings in order to determine pertinent portions of signal and to build a unique "virtual" signal. This virtual signal is then used as input for the speaker diarization systems. Basically, the unique virtual signal is based on a weighted sum of the multiple microphone signals. The weights of this sum are estimated according to a signal quality index based on a signal to noise ratio estimate.

Two main factors will be studied in this paper. First, the efficiency of the pre-processing techniques to build a unique virtual signal in the context of speaker diarization will be investigated. Then, the focus will be on how well systems that were tuned with broadcast news data only can handle meeting data. Concerning the last point, different speaker diarization systems will be tested in this study. Developed in three different labs: the LIA, LIUM and CLIPS, these systems have been tuned and evaluated during the French ESTER Rich Transcription evaluation campaign. This campaign, organized in January 2005 and sponsored by the French ministry, was dedicated to Broadcast news data [1]. No particular tuning of the systems was made on meeting data in order to evaluate whether a reliable pre-processing on multi-channel recordings may be sufficient in order to maintain performance.

Finally, the RT'05S evaluation campaign has initiated a new task, based on the Speech Activity Detection (SAD). This processing is classically implemented in both the speech transcription and speaker diarization systems but never scored individually. This paper will present the SAD system proposed by the authors for the RT'05S evaluation campaign and their results.

Section 2 presents the Speech Activity Detection algorithm. Section 3 is dedicated to the pre-processing techniques used in order to obtain a unique signal from the multi-channel recordings. In section 4, the LIA, LIUM and CLIPS speaker diarization systems are presented, followed by a brief description of all the systems submitted for the RT'05S evaluation campaign. Section 5 presents the experimental protocols and results, and finally, section 6 concludes this work.

2   Speech Activity Detection Task

Considered until now as only a sub-part of speech transcription or speaker diarization systems, Speech Activity Detection has been evaluated in the RT'05S evaluation campaign as an entire task.

Speech Activity Detection is not trivial in a multiple microphone environment. For instance, the portions of silence might be different from one microphone to another. Besides, energy based SAD systems have some difficulties in dealing with background voices.

The Speech Activity Detection (SAD) system, used by most of the systems presented in this paper, was developed by the LIA. It is based on the ALIZE platform [2] and relies on two passes: (1) to apply a speech activity detector process on each individual channel for a given meeting, provided speech and non-speech segments; (2) to keep the non-speech segments, shared over ALL the channels. The speech activity detector process used in the first pass is based on the speech energy modeling and works as follows:

1. the log spectral energy is computed through at a 10ms rate;
2. The energy values are first normalized using a mean removal and a variance normalization in order to fit a 0-mean and 1-variance distribution;
3. They are then used to train a three component GMM, which aims at selecting speech frames. Indeed, $X\%$ of the most energized frames are selected through the GMM, with: $X = w_1 + (\lambda * \alpha * w_2)$ where: w_1 the weight of the highest (energy) gaussian component, w_2 the weight of the middle component, λ an integer ranging from 0 to 1, α a weighting parameter, empirically fixed to 0.6 on the development set. The value of λ is decided according to the likelihood loss when merging the gaussian components 1 and 2 and the components 2 and 3. If the loss is higher for components 1 and 2, λ is set to 0 else to 1;
4. Once all the frames of a signal are labelled as speech or non-speech and concatenated to form segments according to their labels, a final process is applied in order to refine the speech detection. This last process is based on two morphological rules, which consist in constraining the minimum duration of both the speech and non-speech segments (minimum length is 0.3s).

3   Meeting Pre-processing Algorithms

Meeting signals are recorded in smart rooms i.e. a room equipped with several audio and video captors as well as multimedia output devices (video projectors, multi-stereo audio outputs...). According to the distant microphone position in the table, the quality of signal may hugely differ from one microphone to another. For instance, the main speaker utterances may be caught by one or two distant microphones while the other microphones mainly provide background voices, long silence periods, or background noise only. The aim of this pre-processing system is to use redundant channel information in order to extract pertinent information for an enhanced output virtual signal.

This output signal is a weighted mix of all channels available for a given meeting. For each channel a quality measure (signal to noise ratio - SNR) is estimated in order to adapt channel weights. The sum of weights is equal to 1 and the channel weights w_i are computed following equation (1), where N is the number of channels.

$$w_i = SNR_i / \left(\sum_{j=1}^{N} SNR_j \right) \tag{1}$$

To obtain a reliable quality measure, it is necessary to estimate the noise energy, for which two methods have been considered: the use of a speech activity detector (SAD) and the noise spectrum estimate.

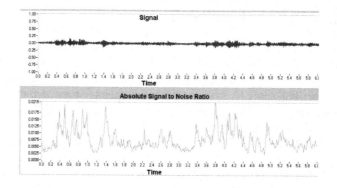

Fig. 1. Example of SNR estimate

If a speech activity detector is used, the labelled *non-speech* segments are used to compute the average noise energy $\overline{E}_{\text{noise}}$ for each channel. The SNR is estimated at each 32ms on frames of 64ms (L=1024 samples) using equation (2).

$$SNR = 10\log_{10}\left(\left(\sum_{i=0}^{L} s_i^2 - \overline{E}_{\text{noise}}\right) / \overline{E}_{\text{noise}}\right) \qquad [dB] \qquad (2)$$

where s_i is a signal sample at instant i.

In the second case, an estimate of the noise spectrum is used in order to discard the speech activity detector errors and to have an instantaneous noise energy value instead of an averaged one. The algorithm is based on a minimum statistics tracking method [3]. Assuming the noisy speech power is the summation of clean speech and background noise power, tracking power spectral minima can provide a fairly accurate estimate of the background noise power and then a good estimate of SNR [4]. Also, by tracking minimum statistics, this algorithm can deal with nonstationary background noise with slowly changing statistical characteristics. The noise spectrum is estimated every 2s using signal power spectrum histogram. An example of signal to noise ratio estimate for a part of channel 1 signal from "NIST 20020305-1007" file is presented in Figure 1.

In this case, the SNR is estimated using the signal power spectrum and noise power spectrum, like in equation (3).

$$SNR = 10 * \log_{10}\left(\sum_{i=0}^{M} \widetilde{S}_i / \sum_{j=0}^{M} \widetilde{N}_j\right) \qquad (3)$$

where $\widetilde{S}_i$ is signal spectral amplitude at frequency i and $\widetilde{N}_j$ is noise spectral amplitude at frequency j.

In order to evaluate the influence of these pre-processing techniques, an unweighted mix ($w_i = \frac{1}{N}$) has also been computed.

4   Speaker Diarization Systems

Three speaker diarization systems are involved in this work, developed by the
LIUM, CLIPS and LIA laboratories individually. Two of them, the LIUM and
CLIPS systems, are based on a classical speaker turn detection followed by a
clustering phase. For the LIA system, both the speaker turn detection and the
speaker clustering are performed simultaneously by using a E-HMM based approach as described in the next section.

   No particular tuning on the meeting data has been carried out for these
systems to participate at the RT'05S evaluation campaign. Indeed, all these
speaker diarization systems have participated at the French Rich Transcription
evaluation campaign ESTER. Testing these systems on meeting data without
any further tuning will allow the evaluation of their robustness to environment
changes, especially if pre-processing techniques are applied beforehand on multiple microphone signals in order to extract pertinent information.

4.1   The LIA System

The LIA speaker diarization system has been entirely developed by using the
ALIZE toolkit (freely available thanks to an open software licence), released by
the LIA and dedicated to speaker recognition [5]. Its performance has been evaluated firstly during the ESTER evaluation campaign on Broadcast News data.
The core of the system is built on a one-step segmentation algorithm implying an
E-HMM (Evolutive HMM) [6, 7]. Each E-HMM state characterizes a particular
speaker and the transitions represent the speaker changes. All possible changes
between speakers are authorized. In this context, the segmentation process has
4 steps:

1. **Initialization:** A first model, named L_0, is estimated on all speech data.
   The HMM has one state, L_0 state.
2. **New speaker detection:** A new speaker is detected in the segments labelled L_0 as follows: a segment is selected among all the L_0 segments according to the likelihood maximization criterion. This selected segment is then
   used to estimate the model of the new speaker, named L_x, which is added
   to the HMM.
3. **Adaptation/Decoding loop:** The objective is to detect all segments belonging to the new speaker L_x. All speaker models are re-estimated through
   an adaptation process according to the actual segmentation. A Viterbi decoding pass is done in order to obtain a new segmentation. This adapta-
   tion/decoding loop is re-iterated while the segmentation is not stable.
4. **Speaker model validation and stop criterion:** The current segmentation is analyzed in order to decide if the new added speaker, L_x, is relevant.
   In this case the decision is made according to heuristical rules on speaker L_x
   segment duration. The stop criterion is reached if there is no more segment
   available in L_0. However, if the contrary, the process goes back to the step 2.

Finally, a resegmentation process is applied, which aims at refining the boundaries and at deleting irrelevant speakers (e.g. speakers with too short speech

segments). This stage is based only on the third step of the segmentation process. A HMM is generated from the segmentation and the adaptation/decoding loop is launched. At the end of each iteration, speakers with too short duration are deleted.

Concerning the front end-processing, the signal is characterized by 20 linear cepstral features (LFCC), computed every 10ms using a 20ms window. The cepstral features are augmented by energy. No frame removal or any coefficient normalization is applied at this stage.

The entire speaker segmentation process is largely described in [8].

4.2   The LIUM System

The LIUM speaker diarization system is based upon a BIC framework similar to [9, 10], composed of three modules:

1. **signal split into small homogeneous segments:** the initial segment boundaries are determined according to a Generalized Likelihood Ratio (GLR) computed over two consecutive windows of 2s sliding over the signal. No threshold is employed, except for the minimal segment length which is set to 2.5s. The signal is over-segmented in order to minimize miss detection of boundaries, but the minimum segment length is set long enough for a correct estimate of a speaker model using a diagonal Gaussian;

2. **speaker clustering without changing the boundaries:** The clustering is based upon a bottom-up hierarchical clustering. In the initial set of clusters, each segment is a cluster. The two closest clusters are then merged at each iteration until the BIC stop criterion is met. The speaker, ie the cluster, is modeled by a full covariance Gaussian as in the segmentation process. The BIC penalty factor is computed over the length of the two candidate clusters instead of the standard penalty computed over the length of the whole signal [11]. To minimize the clustering time, a first pass of clustering is performed only over adjacent clusters. The λ parameter (eq. 4) is fixed to 2 for the first pass and to 7.5 for the second pass;

3. **boundaries adjustment:** a Viterbi decoding is performed to adjust segment boundaries. A speaker is modeled by a one-state HMM containing a diagonal covariance GMM of 8 components learned by EM-ML over the set of speaker segments. The log-penalty of switching between two speakers is fixed experimentally to 100.

Concerning the front end-processing, the signal is characterized by 12 mel cepstral features (MFCC), computed every 10ms using a 20ms window. The cepstral features are augmented by energy. No frame removal or any coefficient normalization is applied at this stage.

4.3   The CLIPS System

The CLIPS system is based on a BIC [12] (Bayesian Information Criterion) speaker change detector followed by a hierarchical clustering. The clustering stop condition is the estimate of the number of speakers using a penalized BIC criterion. Whereas the LIUM system clusters homogeneous segments, the CLIPS system clusters segments, which result from a first speaker change detection pass as follows:

1. **speaker change detection:** a BIC curve is extracted by computing a distance between two 1.75s adjacent windows that go along the signal. Mono-component Gaussian models with diagonal covariance matrices are used to model the two windows. A threshold is then applied on the BIC curve to find the most likely speaker change points which correspond to the local maxima of the curve;

2. **speaker clustering:** Clustering starts by first training a 32 component GMM background model (with diagonal covariance matrices) on the entire test file maximizing a ML criterion thanks to a classical EM algorithm. Segment models are then trained using MAP adaptation of the background model (means only). Next, BIC distances are computed between segment models and the closest segments are merged at each step of the algorithm until N segments are left (corresponding to N speakers in the conversation).

3. **clustering stop criterion:** the number of speakers (N_{Sp}) is estimated using a penalized BIC. The number of speakers is constrained between 1 and 15. The upper limit is related to the recording duration. The number of speakers (N_{Sp}) is selected to maximize equation (4).

$$BIC(M) = \log L(X; M) - \lambda(m/2)N_{Sp} * \log(N_X) \qquad (4)$$

where M is the model composed of the N_{Sp} speaker models, N_X is the total number of speech frames involved, m is a parameter that depends on the complexity of the speaker models and λ is a tuning parameter equal to 0.6.

The signal is characterized by 16 mel Cepstral features (MFCC) computed every 10ms on 20ms windows using 56 filter banks. Then the Cepstral features are augmented by energy. No frame removal or any coefficient normalization is applied here.

The entire speaker segmentation process is largely described in [8].

4.4 Proposed Systems

Different systems have been submitted for the RT'05S campaign. All rely on the following scheme - composition of 3 modules - as summarized in table 1:

1. The pre-processing module can consist in applying:
   - either the *weighted* mix of the multiple microphone signals in which channel weights depend on SNR, estimated either using the speech activity detector (Weighted Mix - SAD) or by applying the noise spectrum algorithm (Weighted Mix - Noise spectrum).
   - or a simple unweighted mix of the multiple microphone signals (Mix).
2. a speaker diarization module, which can be based on the LIA, LIUM or CLIPS systems.

3. the LIA resegmentation process (described in section 4.1) since different studies have shown that a resegmentation phase leads to performance improvement [13, 14, 15, 5].

Table 1. Proposed diarization systems

Systems	Pre-processing	Seg/Re-Seg
WMixSpectrum	Weighted Mix - Noise spectrum	LIA/LIA
WMix	Weighted Mix - SAD	LIA/LIA
MixLIA	Mix	LIA/LIA
MixCLIPS	Mix	CLIPS/LIA
MixLIUM	Mix	LIUM/LIA

5   Experiments

This section presents the protocols and results obtained by the different techniques proposed in this paper and submitted to the RT'05S evaluation campaign.

5.1   Protocols

For RT'05S, the speaker diarization task was evaluated on two subdomains: recordings issued from conference rooms (similar to RT'04S) and from lecture rooms. As for any evaluation campaign, two corpora were available:

- a development corpus: composed of RT'04S development and evaluation corpora (12 meetings of about 10mn each), plus some additional meetings including new recording sites.
- two evaluation corpora, one for each subdomain, composed of 10 meetings of about 10mn each for the conference subdomain and 29 meetings of about 3mn each for the lecture subdomain.

In this paper, only the RT'04S data (development and evaluation) is used as the development corpus, and will be referred to as *dev* corpus in the next sections. On the other hand, the RT'05S evaluation data will be referred to as *eva − conf* for conference data and *eva − lect* for lecture data in the next sections.

Analysis of the different corpora leads to the following observations. Regarding the *dev* corpus, we may note the presence of short silence periods, which implies some difficulties to estimate the noise spectrum or the noise energy, low SNRs (minimum average SNR -5.4 dB; 23.75% of files with SNR < 0 dB and 65% of files with SNR < 3 dB), a variable recording level and a bad use of the input scale (a file with a maximum level of 2% of scale and 58.75% of files with a maximum level <50% of scale), and finally several speakers with overlapped speaking segments.

Some similar observations can be made on the *eva − conf* corpus (same subdomains as the *dev* corpus): short silence periods, with similar consequences, low SNRs (minimum average SNR -1.95 dB; 7.5% of files with SNR < 0 dB and

6.2% of files with SNR < 3 dB), a variable recording level and a bad use of the input scale (a file with a maximum level of 11% of scale and 35% of files with a maximum level <50% of scale), and several speakers with overlapped speaking segments.

Finally, the *eva−lect* corpus reveals some marginal characteristics, enforced by the shortness of the utterances: low SNR (minimum average SNR -2.1 dB; 6.2% of files with SNR < 0 dB and 15.17% of files with SNR < 3 dB), predominantly one speaker per record, and better use of input signal scale.

5.2   Results and Discussion

SAD task. Table 2 shows the performance of the Speech Activity Detection system on the *eva − conf* and *eva − lect* corpora in terms of Missed Speaker Error (MiE) and False Alarm Speaker Error (FaE) rates.

Table 2. Results of SAD on RT'05S

Task	MiE	FaE
eva − conf	5.3	2.1
eva − lect	5.4	1.2

We can observe that the SAD obtains comparable performance on the *eva − conf* and *eva − lect* test sets but presents, on both, large Missed Speaker Error rates ($\approx$5.4%). For comparison, the best SAD system has obtained about 5% in terms of both Missed and False Alarm Speaker error rates during the RT'05S campaign.

Speaker diarization task. Experiments presented in this section aim at comparing the performance of the pre-processing techniques proposed in this paper when combined with the LIA speaker diarization system (*WMixSpectrum*, *WMix* and *MixLIA*) as well as at evaluating the robustness of broadcast news speaker diarization systems on the Meetings recordings (*MixLIA*, *MixCLIPS* and *MixLIUM*).

First, all the submitted speaker diarization systems have been evaluated on the *dev* corpus as presented in Table 3. Here, the system performance is expressed in terms of Missed speaker Error (MiE), False Alarm speaker Error (FaE) and Speaker Diarization Error (SDE) rates (the latter include both the MiE and FaE rates as well as the speaker error rate). Details on each meeting are provided as well as the global performance on the *dev* corpus.

The use of the multi-channel information (*WMixSpectrum* and *WMix*), extracted thanks to the pre-processing techniques does not improve globally the speaker diarization performance on the *dev* corpus but obtains very close results from the baseline system (simple sum of the multiple microphone signals: MixLIA). Nevertheless, signal analysis shows that the pre-processing algorithms improve the global SNR of resulting virtual signals; for example, in the case of

Table 3. Results on development corpus (*dev*)

Meetings	SAD MiE FaE	WMixSpectrum SDE	WMix SDE	MixLIA SDE	MixCLIPS SDE	MixLIUM SDE
CMU 20020319-1400	0.5 5.5	57.9	57.9	57.9	**46.9**	**46.9**
CMU 20020320-1500	0.1 5.3	20.2	20.2	20.2	**18.5**	**18.5**
ICSI 20010208-1430	0.4 3.1	16.5	17.0	19.3	22.5	**13.4**
ICSI 20010322-1450	0.4 1.4	19.6	**13.6**	16.7	17.0	24.6
LDC 20011116-1400	0.4 2.9	**4.5**	15.4	8.0	6.9	7.8
LDC 20011116-1500	0.4 1.6	18.7	12.2	**8.1**	15.8	13.3
NIST 20020214-1148	0.2 8.1	25.4	**16.8**	17.3	22.8	27.2
NIST 20020305-1007	0.0 3.5	33.0	47.8	44.6	**9.4**	19.0
CMU 20030109-1530	0.1 0.7	34.2	34.2	34.2	**27.9**	32.2
CMU 20030109-1600	2.5 1.3	33.5	33.5	33.5	**20.7**	33.5
ICSI 20000807-1000	0.0 3.6	21.2	17.1	**16.2**	17.1	16.3
ICSI 20011030-1030	0.0 3.4	41.4	37.0	**32.3**	51.8	49.4
LDC 20011121-1700	0.0 2.2	32.0	6.7	**3.3**	28.7	39.6
LDC 20011207-1800	0.0 8.6	**26.5**	40.3	44.2	35.7	34.7
NIST 20030623-1409	0.0 1.1	18.9	18.4	24.7	30.5	**11.6**
NIST 20030925-1517	0.4 16.3	64.3	52.0	51.8	70.7	**48.6**
Global performance	0.3 4.1	27.8	26.6	26.2	**25.7**	26.0

LDC 20011121-1700 meeting the unweighted mix leads to a global SNR of -3.88 dB (SNR∈ [-10.1;2]dB) to be compared with -0.1 dB (SNR∈ [-6.2;5.69]dB) for the *Weighted Mix - SAD* algorithm and with -0.59 dB (SNR∈ [-5.0;5.34]dB) for the *Weighted Mix - Noise spectrum* algorithm. The improvement of the SNR on the unique virtual signal does not seem to be helpful for the speaker diarization systems.

Table 4 presents the official results obtained on the RT'05S evaluation corpus for both the conference (*eva − conf* corpus) and lecture room (*eva − lect* corpus) recordings (the *WMixSpectrum* system has not been applied on the conference subdomain test set for the evaluation campaign). The best results have been obtained using the two proposed pre-processing techniques as opposed to the results reached on the RT'04S Meeting data (*dev* corpus). The comparison between the simple unweighted sum method and the weighted ones shows a gain of 15% relative on the *eva − conf* corpus and of 56% on the *eva − lect*. The better quality, in terms of SNR, of RT'05S data can explain the better performance of the systems based on weighted sums. In fact the same SNR gain observed on both RT'04S and RT'05S does not have the same influence in terms of speaker

Table 4. Official results reached for the RT'05S (on *eva-conf* and *eva-lect* corpora)

Show	SAD MiE FaE	WMixSpectrum SDE	WMix SDE	MixLIA SDE	MixCLIPS SDE	MixLIUM SDE
eva-conf	4.0 3.0	-	**24.5**	27.7	25.0	30.5
eva-lect	5.6 1.3	**18.4**	21.4	34.2	35.3	20.0

diarization performance according to the initial signal quality. This result tends to demonstrate the relevance of the proposed strategy: designing a virtual signal based on a weighted sum of the multiple microphone recordings.

Concerning the robustness of the different speaker diarization systems against environment changes, it may be observed that their overall performance has significantly decreased on meeting data (about 21% Speaker Error rate) compared with broadcast news (about 12% Speaker Error rate [1] for the French ESTER evaluation broadcast news corpus), even though it is often difficult to compare results obtained on different databases.

Unfortunately, pre-processing techniques applied on multiple microphone signals do not seem to be sufficient to deal with meeting data issues and to avoid specific speaker diarization systems.

6   Conclusions

This paper is concerned with the speaker diarization task in the specific context of meeting data. More precisely, the focus is made on the handling of multiple microphone signals available per meeting. In this framework, a novel approach is experimented based on the rebuilding of a unique and virtual signal, composed of the most pertinent portions of signals issued from the different multiple microphone recordings. The extraction of these pertinent portions is carried out according to a signal quality index using the signal to noise ratio estimate.

Coupled with different speaker diarization systems developed by three different labs: the LIA, LIUM and CLIPS, the proposed approach has been submitted for the NIST 2005 Spring Rich Transcription evaluation campaign (RT'05S). According to the results obtained on the RT'05S evaluation, the use of this pre-processing strategy, which takes advantage of the multi-channel information, seems to have a slight positive influence on the speaker diarization performance.

This study was also focused on the behavior of speaker diarization systems, tuned on broadcast news and tested on meeting data. One assumption was that the application of the pre-processing techniques and the production of the unique and virtual signal would be sufficient to ensure similar performance between broadcast news and meeting corpora. Nevertheless, the level of performance is quite different between both of them. Even though the pre-processing techniques proposed in this paper may still be improved to provide more pertinent virtual signal, further investigation has to be done to study the other particularities of the meeting data (like spontaneous speech, overlap, ...), which are widely responsible for perturbations of the speaker diarization systems.

References

[1] Galliano, S., Geoffrois, E., Mostefa, D., Choukri, K., Bonastre, J.F., Gravier, G.: The ESTER phase II evaluation campaign for the rich transcription of French broadcast news. In: EuroSpeech'05, Lisboa, Portugal (2005)

[2] Bonastre, J.F., Wils, F., Meignier, S.: ALIZE, a free toolkit for speaker recognition. In: ICASSP'05, Philadelphia, USA (2005)

[3] Cui, X., Bernard, A., Alwan, A.: A noise-robust ASR back-end technique based on weighted viterbi recognition. In: EuroSpeech'03, Geneva, Switzerland (2003)

[4] Hirsh, H.G.: Estimation of noise spectrum and its application to SNR-estimation and speech enhancement. Technical report tr-93-012, ICSI, Berkeley, USA (1993)

[5] Meignier, S., Moraru, D., Fredouille, C., Besacier, L., Bonastre, J.F.: Benefits of prior acoustic segmentation for automatic speaker segmentation. In: ICASSP'04, Montreal, Canada (2004)

[6] Moraru, D., Meignier, S., Fredouille, C., Besacier, L., Bonastre, J.F.: The ELISA consortium approaches in broadcast news speaker segmentation during the NIST 2003 rich transcription evaluation. In: ICASSP'04, Montreal, Canada (2004)

[7] Meignier, S., Bonastre, J.F., Fredouille, C., Merlin, T.: Evolutive HMM for speaker tracking system. In: ICASSP'00, Istanbul, Turkey (2000)

[8] Meignier, S., Moraru, D., Fredouille, C., Bonastre, J.F., Besacier, L.: Step-by-step and integrated approaches in broadcast news speaker diarization. Computer and Speech Language Journal (accepted for publishing in 2005)

[9] Siu, M.H., Rohlicek, R., Gish, H.: An unsupervised, sequential learning algorithm for segmentation of speech waveforms with multi speakers. In: ICASSP'92. Volume 2., San Fransisco, USA (1992) 189–192

[10] Chen, S., Gopalakrishnan, P.: Speaker, environment and channel change detection and clustering via the bayesian information criterion. In: DARPA Broadcast News Transcription and Understanding Workshop, Landsdowne, USA (1998)

[11] Zhu, X., Barras, C., Meignier, S., Gauvain, J.L.: Combining speaker identification and BIC for speaker diarization. In: EuroSpeech'05, Lisboa, Portugal (2005)

[12] Delacourt, P., Wellekens, C.J.: DISTBIC: A speaker based segmentation for audio data indexing. Speech Communication **32** (2000) 111–126

[13] Gauvain, J., Lamel, L., Adda, G.: Audio partitioning and transcription for broadcast data indexation. Multimedia Tools and Applications (2001) 187–200

[14] Reynolds, D.A., Dunn, R.B., Laughlin, J.J.: The Lincoln speaker recognition system: NIST EVAL2000. In: ICSLP'00. Volume 2., Beijing, China (2000)

[15] Adami, A., Kajarekar, S.S., Hermansky, H.: A new speaker change detection method for two-speaker segmentation. In: ICASSP'02. Volume IV., Orlando, USA (2002) 3908–3911

The TNO Speaker Diarization System for NIST RT05s Meeting Data

David A. van Leeuwen

TNO Human Factors,
Postbus 23, 3769 Soesterberg, The Netherlands
david.vanleeuwen@tno.nl

Abstract. The TNO speaker speaker diarization system is based on
a standard BIC segmentation and clustering algorithm. Since for the
NIST Rich Transcription speaker dizarization evaluation measure correct
speech detection appears to be essential, we have developed a speech
activity detector (SAD) as well. This is based on decoding the speech
signal using two Gaussian Mixture Models trained on silence and speech.
The SAD was trained on only AMI development test data, and performed
quite well in the evaluation on all 5 meeting locations, with a SAD error
rate of 5.0 %. For the speaker clustering algorithm we optimized the
BIC penalty parameter λ to 14, which is quite high with respect to
the theoretical value of 1. The final speaker diarization error rate was
evaluated at 35.1 %.

1 Introduction

TNO has been interested in the specific task of speaker diarization for quite
some time, as many of the applications we potentially deal with cannot assume
homogeneous speaker identities in sound recordings. One of our first implementations has been for the domain of Dutch broadcast news, and has been based on
the BIC segmentation algorithms developed by researchers at IBM, specifically
on what Chen and Gopalakrishnan developed for the DARPA sponsored NIST
Broadcast News Transcription benchmark evaluation in 1997 [4] and what later
has been refined in Ref. [15]. Our speaker segmentation implemetation was not
used for speaker adaptation of acoustic models for speech recognition, but rather
for making it possible to have an on-line demonstration of spoken document transcription using our Dutch speech recognition system.[1] Indeed, the demonstration
system has been running autonomously since August 2001, showing online speech
recognition results with a typical latency of about a few minutes. Speaker seg-
mentaton is not only usful for displaying results in more-or-less sensible chunks
of information, but is essential for dealing with a continuous stream of acoustic
information such as a radio broadcast. Moreover, the underlying technology we
used, the Abbot speech recognition system [14], fuses a time-reversed feature
stream processing with the normal feature stream in order to model acoustic

---

[1] See http://speech.tm.tno.nl/radio1/.

S. Renals and S. Bengio (Eds.): MLMI 2005, LNCS 3869, pp. 440–449, 2006.
© Springer-Verlag Berlin Heidelberg 2006

context in both time directions. The feature stream can only be reversed after an endpoint has been defined by a speech segmentation method, and we found it a nice architectural design to use a speaker segmentation system for doing this speech segmentation task.

With TNO's involvement in the EU-sponsored project AMI, the speech technology group decided to renew our efforts in automatic speaker segmentation and clustering, now in the domain of meeting recordings. This happens now in a broader context of speaker recognition, in which we have improved our own system a lot in recent NIST speaker recognition evaluations. Participating in NIST evaluations has proved to be of enormous benefit to us, not only in order to improve our own system and try and perform better each year within a better-performing group of peer systems, but also in order to better understand the essential problems of the task and evaluation metrics. We traditionally have had interest in the problem of evaluation itself, and specifically in drawing paralels between machine and human performance, both in absolute comparison and methods of analysis of results.

This paper describes our system as it was used to submit results to the NIST 2005 Rich Transcription spring evaluation [6]. Although we do not present new algorithms, in lieu of development time, we will try to document the implementation and experiences carefully, so that other researchers who may decide to start research in this field may benefit from them.

We will first describe our speech activity detection system, which has functioned as an input to the speaker segmentation and clustering system that will be described afterwards. Initially we will clarify the data we used for development testing.

2   Development Test Data

Because we initially didn't have access to the RT04s evaluation material (something which was corrected later), but had development test data of 10 AMI meetings, we worked with five AMI meetings as training material, and used the other for development testing, as shown in Table 1. For development of our SAD system, we had unfortunately decided to use the SAD reference file that was distributed with the AMI development test data. As was pointed out later by Xavier Anguera of ICSI, these contained a lot of errors, and we should have used the speaker diarization reference files instead. We did use the corrected SAD reference files of the training partition of AMI meetings for building silence and speech models for the SAD system. We also used the test split of AMI for parameter tuning of the speaker diarization system.

About a week before the evaluation deadline we received the RT04s evaluation data for development testing. We found that the SAD system trained on AMI data alone performed fairly well on these meetings. We used the RT04s material, exluding the CMU meetings, for checking that the AMI-tuned parameters of the speaker diarization system were working for these meetings as well.

In all experiments and submissions we used information from only one of all available microphones. We chose the lowest numbered microphone, so that

Table 1. The split of AMI development test meetings in training and development testing evaluation material

Training	Testing
ES2002a	ES2002c
ES2002d	ES2009b
ES2009c	ES2009d
IS1009a	IS1009b
IS1009c	IS1009d

our 'multiple distant microphone' submission can be considered 'single distant microphone' as well.

3   Speech Activity Detection System

Our first attempts in speaker diarization were based on a Broadcast News segmentation system that we have developed a number of years ago. One of the ways in which this domain differs from the meeting domain is that there are hardly any 'silences.' There are frequent interruptions in speech, but these are usually filled with music, jingles, tunes, or other acoustic events. The basic BIC segmentation method works not specifically for speech alone, and we have found that it performed satisfactorily to segment out short filled non-speech events. However, when applied to meeting data with significant amounts of silence, we found BIC did not do a good job of finding the silence segments and clustering them together. Moreover, since BIC works completely without acoustic training, BIC does not classify any silence clusters as non-speech. This is detrimental to speech diarization error rate (SDE), which for simple cases can be expressed as

$$\frac{\int C(\text{wrong speaker})\, dt}{\int C(\text{any speaker})\, dt} \tag{1}$$

where C denotes classification per time unit (e.g., frame). When in a meeting of duration T only T_s time was spoken by any of the speakers, and no speech activity detection is operational, this translates to false alarm time $T_{\text{fa}} = T - T_s$ and missed speech time $T_{\text{miss}} = 0$, which results in a minimum achievable SDE of

$$\frac{T - T_s}{T_s}. \tag{2}$$

For $T_s/T \approx 2/3$, which is a normal value in development test meetings, the minimum diarization error $\approx 50\,\%$, a number that can only grow if segmentation and clustering are not perfect. Thus the need for speech activity detection (SAD), as was also recognized by the community [7], caused the decision to include SAD as a separate task this year.

Our first attempts in SAD were based on the energy of the signal. Quite contrary to telephony data, such as is used in NIST speaker recognition evaluations, this tends not to work at all for distant microphones used in the meeting domain.

For instance, accepting all speech frames with an energy above a meeting-specific level which is 30 dB below the maximum energy lead to a SAD error of 52 %.

In a second attempt we used the Sonic speech recognition system [12] for segmenting into speech and non-speech fragments. We built two 'phone' Hidden Markov Models (HMMs) for 'speech' and 'non-speech.' Although training seemed to proceed normally we could not find decoder settings that would output anything, i.e., output files were empty. Because Sonic is designed to be used as large vocabulary speech recognition system it may be that the parameter setting range did not include the proper settings for a two-phone loop grammar.

In a last attempt we trained two Gaussian Mixture Models (GMMs) for 'speech' and 'non-speech.' We built a very straightforward 2-state Viterbi decoder to replace the more advanced Sonic decoder for this particular purpose. As speech features we used 12 PLP coefficients, augmented with log energy, and their deltas calculated over 7 consecutive frames of 16 ms. The GMM models consisted of 16 Gaussian mixtures, and we estimated them using 10 iterations of the EM algorithm. The average negative log likelihood per frame was much lower for the silence GMM (around 20) than the speech GMM (around 34), where we expect this error to be around 30 from experiences in text independent speaker Universal Background Models (UBMs) [13]. A reason might be that in the non-speech data there is less variability which is modeled more easily by the Gaussians than in the case of the speech data.

The decoder calculates in a single forward pass the sequence of states that maximized the likelihood to generate the observed data. Apart from the GMM parameters that determine the state likelihood we need to estimate transition probabilities a_{ij} that state i at time t is followed by state j at time $t + 1$. We used a fixed ratio of transition probabilities for $i \neq j$ w.r.t. $i = j$. We further introduced a prior probability p_i for observing a state i. Because there is a fixed number of states, the Viterbi procedure is actually fairly easy to implement in a matrix calculation program such as GNU Octave. In our implementation the main program loop spans 4 lines of code. After the maximum likelihood sequence of states has been determined, we smooth the sequence by first filtering it using a median filter of length M and subsequently convoluting it with a rectangular filter of R frames, favouring speech signals. Finally, speech segments with a duration less than $t_{\min}$ are discarded.

Due to late arrival of development test data for meeting locations other than AMI, we used only AMI meeting material for training the GMMs and tuning the decoding parameters, as shown in Table 1. The result of the manual parameter optimization is shown in Table 2. The resulting SAD error on the AMI development test evaluation split was 10.3 % error.

With the availability of the RT04s development test data we applied the SAD models and parameters as optimized for the AMI meeting rooms to this

Table 2. The optimum parameters for SAD

p_n/p_s	$a_{i\neq j}/a_{i=j}$	M	R	$t_{\min}$
0.01	1×10^{-5}	1	5	0.5 s

additional material, and found a SAD error of 2.3%. We were so pleased with this relatively low error rate that we decided not to change any of the parameters or models using the additional meeting material. In fact, ICSI had kindly offered to supply us with their SAD results, and had reported error rates of about 2%, so we concluded that our SAD system was performing reasonably well.

4 Speaker Segmentation and Clustering System

Chen and Gopalakrishnan have written an essential paper in the speaker segmentation and clustering technologies [4] that have later been refined by several others [3,15,5] and is used widely for speaker segmentation tasks in the NIST RT meeting tasks [8,2,11]. They introduced a method from general statistical modeling into the speech modeling technologies which can not only be applied to finding speaker segment and as clustering stop criterion, but also to find the number of Gaussian mixtures in a GMM or HMM speech model. Unfortunately, their formulas were not always flawless, and not all parameters as easy to interpret, a problem that has been largely resolved in [5].

The basic Bayesian Information Criterion (BIC) describes a balance between the goodness of fit of a given model M to given data $\boldsymbol{X} = \{\boldsymbol{x}_i\}$ and the number N_M of parameters in the model. Lacking a well defined symbol for the BIC it is defined as

$$\mathrm{BIC} = \log L(\boldsymbol{X}|M) - \frac{1}{2}\lambda N_M \log N_x, \tag{3}$$

where $L(\boldsymbol{X}|M)$ is the likelihood of the data given the model, N_x the number of data points in $\boldsymbol{X}$ and λ a 'penalty weight' parameter that should be 1. In the speaker segment problem the model is usually a d-dimensional Gaussian distribution with mean $\boldsymbol{\mu}$ and covariance matrix $\boldsymbol{\Sigma}$

$$N(\boldsymbol{x}_i, \boldsymbol{\mu}, \boldsymbol{\Sigma}) = \frac{\exp -\frac{1}{2}(\boldsymbol{x}_i - \boldsymbol{\mu})^T \boldsymbol{\Sigma}^{-1}(\boldsymbol{x}_i - \boldsymbol{\mu})}{(2\pi)^{d/2}\sqrt{|\boldsymbol{\Sigma}|}}. \tag{4}$$

Here d is the dimension of the features of $\boldsymbol{X}$ and $|\cdots|$ the determinant operator. In calculation of the log likelihood $L = \prod_i N(\boldsymbol{x}_i, \boldsymbol{\mu}, \boldsymbol{\Sigma})$ of the data $\boldsymbol{X}$ that is modeled by this Gaussian, the part in the exponential contributes $-N_x d/2$. Including the contribution from the normalizing constant we obtain

$$\log L(\boldsymbol{X}|N(\boldsymbol{\mu}, \boldsymbol{\Sigma})) = -\frac{N_x}{2}(\log|\boldsymbol{\Sigma}| + d\log 2\pi + d), \tag{5}$$

of which the last two terms are not dependent on the model parameters, and are therefore usually left out. Note that for this full covariance Gaussian model the number of parameters is $N_M = d + \frac{1}{2}d(d+1)$.

4.1 Segmentation with BIC

In the problem of speaker segmentation the BIC is applied as follows. A model for the total given speech signal $\boldsymbol{X} = \{\boldsymbol{x}_i\}$, $X : i = 1, \ldots, N_x$ is compared to two models for a hypothesized split $A: i = 1, \ldots, N_A$ and $B: i = N_A + 1, \ldots, N_A + N_B$ with $N_A + N_B = N_x$. When the difference $\Delta\mathrm{BIC} = \mathrm{BIC}_{A+B} - \mathrm{BIC}_x > 0$, it is assumed advantageous to assume two different speakers for the segments A and B. The difference in BIC is

$$\Delta\mathrm{BIC} = \frac{1}{2}\left(N_x \log|\boldsymbol{\Sigma}| - N_A \log|\boldsymbol{\Sigma}_A| - N_B \log|\boldsymbol{\Sigma}_B| - \lambda N_M \log N_x\right). \quad (6)$$

Note that the term with $\log N_x$ is the same for BIC_{A+B} and BIC_x, i.e., the same amount of data is observed in both models.

In practice we need an algorithm to find potential break points to evaluate $\Delta\mathrm{BIC}$. In our implementation we analyze a 'window' of audio of fixed duration, t_w, and look for potential speaker break points at times t_e, $t_e + t_c$, $t_e + 2t_c$, $\ldots$, $t_w - t_e$. We do not consider breakpoints at a time t_e from the 'edge,' because in determining the determinant of a d dimensional covariance matrix we need more than d data points (frames). We only evaluate 'candidate' breakpoints at t_c intervals because it reduces the computational load, and only a certain resolution of the speaker change point is required.

When positive $\Delta\mathrm{BIC}$ values are found, the maximum of those is chosen and accepted as a breakpoint provided that more than a user-specified N_p points have a positive $\Delta\mathrm{BIC}$ and the maximum is more than a standard deviation higher than the mean of these potential breakpoints. Once a segment boundary is chosen, the segment is split off and the remaining audio data is used for finding further breakpoints. If no breakpoint is found, the window is lengthened by new audio data of duration t_w, and a new series of values for $\Delta\mathrm{BIC}$ is considered. This implementation is similar to the ones described in the literature.

For computational efficiency, we calculate $|\boldsymbol{\Sigma}|$ from the sufficient statistics $s_t = \sum_{i=1}^{t} x_i$ and $c_t = \sum_{i=1}^{t} x_i x_i^T$, and bear in mind that the statistics for segment B are the difference between those for the total segment (which is constant for the fixed window) and for A. For each segment we record the beginning and ending times, as well as the sufficient statistics.

In Table 3 we summarize the values of the segmentation parameters we used.

Table 3. Values of the segmentation parameters. Durations are measured in seconds.

Frame t_f	Window t_w	Edge t_e	Candidate t_c	# positive N_p
0.016	5	1	0.096	5

4.2   Clustering with BIC

For speaker clustering the BIC is usually used as a stop criterion for agglomerative clustering. Once initial segments have been formed, the segments need to be clustered. As originally proposed in [4], we implemented an agglomerative clustering. Using some distance measure we can find the closest two clusters, and merge these. This process can be continued until the increase in BIC by merging two clusters is no longer positive. There are many ways of measuring a distance between two clusters c_i and c_j [5], and we chose the 'Gish distance' $G(c_i, c_j)$ [9] which is the log likelihood ratio between merged model Σ_m and separate models

$$G(c_i, c_j) = \frac{1}{2}\left((N_i + N_j) \log |\Sigma_m| - N_i \log |\Sigma_i| - N_j \log |\Sigma_j|\right). \tag{7}$$

The increase of BIC by merging these clusters should be positive

$$\frac{1}{2}\lambda_c N_M \log N_x - G(c_i, c_j) > 0. \tag{8}$$

Note that this difference in BIC differs from eq. 6 in some respects:

- it has an opposite sign, since we favour merging cluster rather than splitting segments
- the $\log N_x$ term is constant since in clustering we consider *all* available speech data, rather than only the speech segment that we consider to split in two parts, which has a duration of typically only a few times t_w. It is also possible to account only for the frames in the clusters being considered, this is known as a *local* BIC penalty [16].
- we have introduced a separate penalty weight λ_c for clustering.

In our implementation we continue with the sufficient statistics from the segmentation process. We calculate upper triangular distance matrix $D_{i<j} = G(c_i, c_j)$ and merge c_i and c_j by adding their sufficient statistics. After merging, we remove from the distance matrix row j and column j, and update row and column i in D_{ij}. Because we chose the Gish distance, the stop citerion (the increase in BIC) follows directly from the minimum distance by eq. 8. As noted by others [15], this agglomerative clustering is fairly computationally intensive, but it has the advantage that it does find the optimum clustering.

4.3   Parameter Tuning

Although the BIC method in principle does not need tunable parameters, development testing showed that the 'penalty parameters' λ and λ_c needed values different from unity in order to have a reasonable SDE. Specifically, we found the best SDE results for the AMI development test meetings when $\lambda = 1.5$ and $\lambda_c = 14$.

5   Results and Discussion

In Table 4 we tabulated the results for both development test (AMI and RT04s without CMU meetings) and RT05s evaluation.

Both SAD and speaker diarization results performed as could be expected from the development test results. The SDE is the highest of 3 site submissions, but only about 5%-point higher than the LIA system [10] which was the best performing system of RT04s. The SAD results, which were only computed as a

Table 4. SAD and speaker diarization results, in % error, for non-overlapping speaker segments. The last three columns show SDE results where the input to the clustering system is either our own SAD (primary evaluation system), ICSI's SAD and perfect SAD (post-evaluation).

| Test | SAD error | SDE SAD input from: | | |
		TNO	ICSI	perfect
AMI dev	10.3	35.7		45.9
RT04s – CMU	2.8	35.4		31.9
RT05s	5.0	35.1	37.1	32.3

necessary step for the speaker diarization, appear to be very competative. Only SRI-ICSI's more advance multiple microphone system [1] has slightly better performance.

Interesting to see is the shift in SDE from our own SAD as input to ICSI's SAD—even though ICSI SAD has better SAD performance, the SDE increases slightly from 35.1 % to 37.1 %. One reason might be that the parameter optimization had been carried out using our own SAD output. Using perfect SAD (as obtained from the reference transcription files after the evaluation) shows the SDE purely due to clustering errors, *i.e.*, the fraction of missed and false alarm speech is zero.

We did not attempt to use multiple microphone information, which, in the light of the results of other teams [1,10] turned out to be a wise decision, because they observed higher error rates when using multiple microphone data.

We found it most remarkable that we had to tune $\lambda_c = 14$ which is significantly greater than the theoretical value of 1. We have not seen such high values reported in the literature. Even though the high value tends to over-cluster, such that some speakers are missed completely, these speakers tend to be the ones that spoke very little. In the overall RT05s evaluation our system missed 13 speakers out of 53, but these amounted to only 0.4 % missed speaker time, and hence contributed to the SDE only a little bit. In the extreme case of lecture data, the skewedness is so great that this led the ICSI-SRI team to submit a 'system' that attributes all speech to the same speaker [1]. This effect has previously been noted by Jin *et al.* [11], and they introduced an interesting measure, the 'speaker speaking time entropy' which measures the skewedness of the speaking time distribution. They found that their per-meeting SDE increased with increasing speaker speaking time entropy. As an alternative to the standard SDE we might consider a measure that somehow incorporates the prior probability of a speaker speaking in the weighting of the speech segments. This would be an interesting subject for future research.

Acknowledgement

Part of this research was funded by the EC project AMI. We would like to thank ICSI, and in particular Xavier Anguera, for helping us by pointing out several inconsistencies in the data. We would like to thank Jon Fiscus for supplying information in a very responsive manner during the course of the evaluation.

References

1. Xavier Anguera, Chuck Wooters, Barbara Peskin, and Mateu Aguiló. Robust speaker segmentation for meetings: The ICSI-SRI spring 2005 diarization system. In *Proc. RT'05 Meeting Recognition Evaluation Workshop*, pages 26–38, Edinburgh, July 2005.
2. Steve Cassidy. The macquire speaker diarisation system for RT04s. http://www.nist.gov/speech/test_beds/mr_proj/documents/icassp/papers/P03.pdf, 2004.
3. Scott Shaobing Chen and P. S. Gopalakrishnan. Clustering via the Baysian Information Criterion with applications in speech recognition. In *Proc. ICASSP*, 1998.
4. Scott Shaobing Chen and P. S. Gopalakrishnan. Speaker, environment and channel change detection and clustering via the Bayesian Information Criterion. In *Proceedings of the Darpa Broadcast News Transcription and Understanding Workshop*, 1998.
5. P. Delacourt and C. J. Wellekens. Distbic: A speaker-based segmentation for audio indexing. *Speech Communication*, 32:111–126, 2000.
6. Jonathan Fiscus. The rich transcription 2005 spring meeting recognition evaluation. In *Proc. MLMI*, Lecture Notes in Computer Science. Springer, 2005.
7. Jonathan Fiscus. Spring 2005 (rt-05s) rich transcription meeting recognition evaluation plan. http://www.nist.gov/speech/tests/rt/rt2005/spring/rt05s-meeting-eval-plan-V1.pdf, 2005.
8. Corrine Fredouille, Daniel Moraru, Sylvain Meigner, Laurent Besacier, and Jean-François Bonastre. The NIST 2004 spring rich transcription evaluations: two axis merging strategy in the context of multiple distant microphones based meeting speaker segmentation. http://www.nist.gov/speech/test_beds/mr_proj/documents/icassp/papers/P02.pdf, 2004.
9. H. Gish and N. Schmidt. Text-independent speaker identication. *IEEE Signal Processing Magazine*, pages 18–21, 1994.
10. Dan Istrate, Corrine Fredouille, Sylvain Meigner, Laurent Besacier, and Jean François Bonastre. NIST RT'05S evaluation: Pre-processing techniques and speaker diarization on multiple microphones. In *Proc. RT'05 Meeting Recognition Evaluation Workshop*, pages 14–25, Edinburgh, July 2005.
11. Qin Jin, Kornel Laskowski, Tanja Schultz, and Alex Waibel. Speaker segmentation and clustering in meetings. http://www.nist.gov/speech/test_beds/mr_proj/documents/icassp/papers/P04a.pdf, 2004.
12. Bryan Pellom. Sonic: The university of colorado continuous speech recognizer. Technical Report TR-CSLR-2001-01, University of Colorado, Boulder, Colorado, March 2001.
13. D.A. Reynolds, T.F. Quatieri, and R.B. Dunn. Speaker verification using adapted gaussian mixture models. *Digital Signal Processing*, 10:19–41, 2000.
14. Tony Robinson, Mike Hochberg, and Steve Renals. *The use of recurrent networks in continuous speech recognition*, chapter 7, pages 233–258. Kluwer Academic Publishers, 1996.

15. Alain Tritschler and Ramesh Gopinath. Improved speaker segmentation and segments clustering using the Baysian Information Criterion. In *Proc. Eurospeech*, 1999.
16. Xuan Zhu, Claude Barras, Sylvain Meignier, and Jean-Luc Gauvain. Combining speaker identification and BIC for speaker diarization. In *Proc. Eurospeech*, pages 2441–2444, 2005.

The 2005 AMI System for the Transcription of Speech in Meetings

Thomas Hain[1], Lukas Burget[2], John Dines[3], Giulia Garau[4], Martin Karafiat[2],
Mike Lincoln[4], Iain McCowan[3], Darren Moore[3], Vincent Wan[1],
Roeland Ordelman[5], and Steve Renals[4]

[1] Department of Computer Science,
University of Sheffield, Sheffield S1 4DP, UK
[2] Faculty of Information Engineering,
Brno University of Technology, Brno, 612 66, Czech Republic
[3] IDIAP Research Institute, CH-1920 Martigny, Switzerland
[4] Centre for Speech Technology Research,
University of Edinburgh, Edinburgh EH8 9LW, UK
[5] Department of Electrical Engineering,
University of Twente, 7500AE Enschede, The Netherlands

Abstract. In this paper we describe the 2005 AMI system for the transcription of speech in meetings used in the 2005 NIST RT evaluations. The system was designed for participation in the speech to text part of the evaluations, in particular for transcription of speech recorded with multiple distant microphones and independent headset microphones. System performance was tested on both conference room and lecture style meetings. Although input sources are processed using different front-ends, the recognition process is based on a unified system architecture. The system operates in multiple passes and makes use of state of the art technologies such as discriminative training, vocal tract length normalisation, heteroscedastic linear discriminant analysis, speaker adaptation with maximum likelihood linear regression and minimum word error rate decoding. In this paper we describe the system performance on the official development and test sets for the NIST RT05s evaluations. The system was jointly developed in less than 10 months by a multi-site team and was shown to achieve competitive performance.

1 Introduction

Transcription of speech recorded in meetings has been the focus of attention for speech researchers for quite some time. However the complexity of the input puts considerable strain on the performance of such systems. Besides the acoustic complexity, the variety of input sources and the moving speaker problems, the transcription of spontaneous speech itself is complex and normally yields results above 15% word error rate (WER). Speech transcripts of meetings are not only of interest in their own right, but are an important input for higher-level processing. Projects like AMI (Augmented Multiparty Interaction) aim to investigate the use of machine based techniques to aid people in and outside of meetings to

S. Renals and S. Bengio (Eds.): MLMI 2005, LNCS 3869, pp. 450–462, 2006.

efficiently access meeting content. Meetings are an audio visual experience by nature, information is presented for example in the form of presentation slides, drawings on boards, and of course by verbal communication. The automatic transcription of speech in meetings is of crucial importance for meeting analysis, content analysis, summarisation, and analysis of dialogue structure.

As is often the case work on automatic recognition of speech in meetings is stimulated by yearly performance evaluations by the U.S. National Institute of Standards and Technology (NIST) [18]. Large scale work on conference room type meeting speech was initially facilitated by the collection of the ICSI meeting corpus [12] which was followed by trial NIST meeting transcription evaluations in Spring 2002. Further meeting resources were made available by NIST [8], Interactive System Labs (ISL) [2] and the Linguistic Data Consortium for the RT04s Meeting evaluations [18].

In this paper we describe the 2005 AMI system for the transcription of speech in meetings used for participation in the 2005 NIST RT evaluations (RT05s). The system was designed for participation in the speech-to-text part of the evaluations, in particular transcription of speech recorded with multiple distant microphones (MDM), the primary test condition, and individual headset microphones (IHM). Both input sources are processed using different front-ends, however the recognition process is based on a unified system architecture. The RT05s evaluations differ from those of previous years in that tests are conducted both on meetings in conference room style and lecture room style. The system presented here has been developed solely for the purpose of transcribing conference room style meetings, with the same system being used for the transcription of the lecture room meeting data[1]. Data from new sources have further enhanced the richness of the testing conditions in terms of input speech, recording conditions and content. The new data originates from data collection efforts as part of two European projects, AMI[2] and CHIL (Computers in the Human Interaction Loop[3]) as well as from collections at the Virginia Polytechnic and State University.

The rest of the paper is structured as follows: First we describe the data resources used followed by a description of our generic system architecture and the main system components, including an analysis of the performance of various components on the RT05s evaluation data sets. In following sections we give an overview of the complete system and its passes. This is contrasted with results using manual segmentation.

2   Meeting Resources

The ICSI Meeting corpus [12] is the largest meeting resource available consisting of 70 technical meetings at ICSI with a total of 73 hours of speech. The num-

---

[1] This excludes the use customised language models, see Section 4.4. For that reason we do not specifically report results on lecture room data unless required.

[2] See http://www.amiproject.org

[3] See http://chil.server.de.

ber of participants is variable and data is recorded with head-mounted and a total of four table-top microphones. We have not used any other microphones present in the room. Further meeting corpora were collected by NIST [8] and ISL [2], with 13 and 10 hours respectively. Both NIST and ISL meetings have unconstrained content (e.g. people playing games or discussing sales issues) and variable number of participants. In our development we made use of the official RT04s development and evaluation sets (rt04sdev and rt04seval). Both sets include 10 minute extracts from 8 meetings recorded at the 3 sites above and the Linguistic Data Consortium (LDC). As part of the AMI project a major collection and annotation effort of the AMI meeting corpus[3] is currently underway. Data is collected at three different instrumented meeting rooms in Europe (Edinburgh, IDIAP, TNO). The target size of the corpus is more than 100 hours of transcribed speech. The meeting language is English, but many participants are non-native speakers of the language. Each meeting normally has four participants and the corpus will be split into a scenario portion and an unconstrained meetings portion. Each scenario in the corpus consists of four meetings with the same participants working on a constrained task. For the benefit of the RT05s evaluations, AMI has released a preliminary development set (rt05samidev) and approximately 16 hours of scenario training data. In this work both resources were used.

For the purpose of development of systems for transcription of lecture room speech a development set (rt05slectdev) was provided by CHIL. However this was provided very late and due to time constraints could only be used for language model (LM) optimisation. In this paper we further report results on the RT05s evaluation sets from the conference room and lecture room data (rt05seval and rt05slecteval respectively). Both sets are based on 10 minute extracts from individual meetings. The IHM and MDM tests are conducted on the same 10 minute extract.

3   System Architecture

The system architecture overview presented in this section is generic to both the IHM and MDM systems. A more detailed description of system components is provided in the following section. The IHM and MDM systems differ only in the processing of the input audio and the use of input source specific acoustic models in the various processing stages. The system operates in a total of 6 passes. Figure 1 shows a schematic representation of the processes. In the first pass (P1) the input data is segmented and transformed into a stream of 39 dimensional MF-PLP feature vectors[22]. Speech segments have a start and an end time as well as a channel/speaker label. A first recognition pass is conducted with acoustic models trained using maximum likelihood estimation (MLE) and a trigram LM (see Section 4.4). The resegmented output of this pass is used only for estimation of the vocal tract length normalisation (VTLN) warp factors on a per input channel basis. In the second pass (P2) the VTLN warp factors are determined and the audio data is recoded with these warp factors.

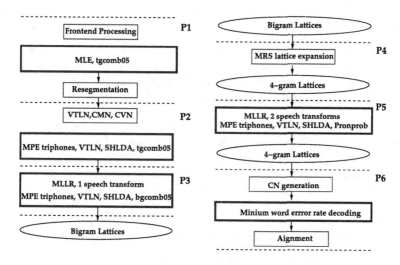

Fig. 1. Processing stages of the 2005 AMI meeting transcription system

Then a second decoding pass with acoustic models trained on VTLN data is performed. The P2 acoustic modelling includes a smoothed heteroscedastic linear discriminant analysis (SHLDA) input transform[15] and acoustic models are trained (in the IHM case) using the minimum phone error(MPE) criterion[20]. The output of P2 is used to adapt the acoustic model means and variances using maximum likelihood linear regression [7]. Two transforms, one for speech and one for silence are estimated. A third decoding pass (P3) uses MLLR adapted P2 models to generate bigram lattices. As all subsequent stages only process lattices to constrain the search space the use of a bigram in P3 avoids too harsh constraints.

In pass P4, the bigram lattices are first expanded using a trigram language model, followed by a second expansion using 4-gram LMs. For conference room data this expansion uses language models optimised for each meeting resource (MRS). The 4-gram lattices generated in P4 are used for rescoring in the following pass P5. Here models are adapted using up to two speech transforms using a regression class tree. Lattice rescoring further makes use of pronunciation probabilities estimated on the training data [11]. The output of this pass is a set of lattices which form the input to the final pass, P6. Here confusion networks [16] are formed and the most probable word from each confusion set is selected. The final output is then aligned using the P5 acoustic models.

4   System Components

In this section a more detailed discussion of the system components as outlined in Section 3 is presented. First a brief description of the front-end blocks, both for the IHM and MDM cases is given. This is followed by a description of acoustic and language model training.

4.1   Front-End Processing

A common system architecture was chosen for both IHM and MDM sub-systems. This was possible due to the enhancement based setup chosen for MDM processing. In both cases the descriptions below do not include the feature extraction process. For more details the reader is referred to [10].

Individual Headset Microphone Processing. The main task for the front-end processing of IHM data is speech activity detection (SAD). Figure 2 outlines the processes involved. First cross talk suppression is performed at the signal level using adaptive-LMS echo cancellation[17]. Additions to the basic system are: the use of multiple reference channels in cancellation; automatic estimation and correction of skew between channels; automatic cross-talk level estimation; and ignoring of channels which produce low levels of cross-talk. Updates are further made on a per sample basis to account for non-stationary 'echo' path.

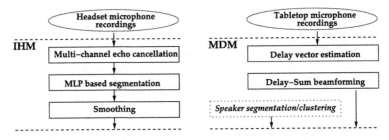

Fig. 2. Front-end processing of IHM and MDM data

The SAD system used here is a straight-forward statistical based approach with additional components to control cross-talk between channels. A 14 dimensional MF-PLP [22] feature vector is augmented with additional features: log energy, log energy normalised by the total energy on all channels, signal kurtosis, and a voicing strength measure based on the maximum amplitude in the speech cepstrum in the range of frequencies 50-300Hz [19,23]. A Multi-Layer-Perceptron (MLP) with a 31 frame input layer, a 5 unit hidden layer and an output layer of two classes is trained. Ten meetings from each meeting resource serve as training data totalling to around 20 hrs of data. A further five meetings from each corpus are used to determine early stopping of the parameter learning. The utterance segmentation uses Viterbi decoding with scaled likelihoods and a minimum segment duration of 0.5 seconds. In a final processing step the output of the segmenter is smoothed by padding segments with 0.1 seconds, merging overlapping segments in the process. Table 1 shows frame error rate results on the rt05seval before and after segmentation. Note that the relationship between false alarm and false reject rates differs substantially between meeting resources. The performance overall on the test data shows relatively high false reject rates. Smoothing the segment boundary estimates by padding allows to reduce the false reject rates significantly.

Table 1. Segmentation performance (in %) on rt05seval. FA denotes false acceptance, FR false reject, and speech the percentage of speech in the reference. TOT gives the overall performance whereas TOT(REL) are relative to the associated class.

	AMI	ISL	ICSI	NIST	VT	TOT	TOT(REL)
RAW							
FA	1.29	1.52	0.71	1.49	3.70	1.64	2.00
FR	4.49	3.03	3.36	2.81	1.12	2.94	16.23
speech	24.40	28.84	13.79	15.56	14.83	18.12	
SMOOTHED							
FA	1.90	2.55	1.21	2.05	4.34	2.22	2.71
FR	3.80	2.01	2.71	2.18	0.83	2.30	12.69
speech	24.40	28.84	13.79	15.56	14.83	18.12	

Multiple Distant Microphone Processing. The basic processing stages of MDM processing are outlined in Figure 2. Since the position of microphones in the meeting room is not fixed for this task an approach that does not require geometry information was used.

First gain calibration is performed by normalising the maximum amplitude level of each of the input files. Then a noise estimation and removal procedure is run. This in itself is a two pass process. On the first pass the noise spectrum $\Phi_{nn}(f)$ of each input channel is estimated as the noise power spectrum of the M lowest energy frames in the file ($M = 20$ was used. On the second pass a Wiener filter with transfer function $\frac{\Phi_{xx}(f) - \Phi_{nn}(f)}{\Phi_{xx}(f)}$ (where $\phi_{xx}(f)$ is the input signal spectrum) is applied to each channel to remove stationary noise. The noise coherence matrix Q, estimated over the M lowest energy frames, is computed. Finally delay vectors between each channel pair are calculated for every frame in the input sample. The delay between two channels is the time difference between the arrival of the dominant sound source and is calculated by finding the peak in the generalised cross correlation[13] between input frames across two channels.

The delay vector is given as the delays for all pairs with respect to a single reference channel - there are therefore N delays in each vector, with the delay for the reference channel equal to 0. Further a vector of relative scaling factors is calculated, corresponding to the ratio of frame energies between each channel and the reference channel. The start and end times in seconds, along with the delay and scaling factors are output for each frame. The delay and scaling vectors are then used to calculate beamforming filters for each frame using the standard superdirective technique [4,5]. Segments and speaker labels were provided by SRI/ICSI[21].

While this approach is robust to a variety of configurations, for a small number of sparsely located microphones (as for some rooms in the rt05seval set) delay estimation can be unreliable and significant spatial aliasing occurs.

4.2   Acoustic Models

Acoustic models are phonetic decision tree state clustered triphone models with standard left-to-right 3-state topology. Models are trained up to 16 mixture components using MLE with standard HTK[4] procedures and contain approximately 4000 states. For more details on the training process the reader is referred to [10]. In previous experiments [10] we found that maximum a posteriori (MAP)[9] adaptation from conversational telephone speech (CTS) models gave better performance than training solely on meeting data.

VTLN was applied both in training and testing, both on IHM and MDM. For training an iterative procedure was used alternating the estimation of warping factors and model parameter updates. For IHM initial warp factor estimates were obtained from CTS-adapted models. Experimental evidence shows improved WER performance with warp factor estimation at a reduced bandwidth of 3800Hz. Initial experiments using IHM models for warp factor estimation on MDM data yielded a performance degradation. Hence IHM VTLN models were adapted to the MDM VTLN data where a single training iteration was found to yield good results that could not be improved further.

Feature space transformation was applied in the form of smoothed heteroscedastic linear discriminant analysis (SHLDA) [15]. The transform was used to reduce a 52 dimensional feature vector (standard plus third derivatives) to 39 dimensions. HLDA estimation procedure[14] requires the estimation of full covariance matrices per Gaussian. SHLDA in addition uses smoothing of the covariance estimates by interpolating with standard LDA type within-class covariances. The adaptation of CTS models when using SHLDA is non-trival due to the reduced bandwidth of CTS data. To avoid further issues with discriminative training no CTS data was used in conjunction with SHLDA.

All further models were trained using the minimum phone error criterion [20]. The implementation of MPE used here is similar to that described in [20]. For this purpose numerator and denominator lattices were generated using the SHLDA models and a bigram LM interpolated with a unigram model that includes training set specific words. The phone times as obtained in recognition are used to improve speed in training. Only means and variances are modified and parameter update makes use of I-smoothing. Performance was found to stabilise after 10 training iterations[5].

Table 2 shows lattice rescoring results on rt05seval IHM for models of increasing complexity. Note the 0.3% performance degradation from the use of unadapted models which is compensated by 1.6% improvement from SHLDA. Another 2.8% absolute are gained by the use of MPE training. It can be observed that model improvement has little impact on the deletion rate.

4.3   Training Data Selection

Training data for IHM is given by the reference transcripts. In total 104 hours of speech were available from resources outlined in Section 2, albeit a significant proportion of the data is silence. The special processing setup for MDM data (see Section 4.1) however makes additional processing necessary as the system cannot

---

[4] The Hidden Markov Model Toolkit (HTK). http://htk.eng.cam.ac.uk.

[5] Both SHLDA and MPE are developed as part of the STK HMM toolkit: http://www.fit.vutbr.cz/speech/sw/stk.html.

Table 2. %WER on rt05seval IHM rescoring 4-gram lattices with pronunciation probabilities and various models. By default models are trained on meeting data only.

	TOT	Sub	Del	Ins	AMI	ISL	ICSI	NIST	VT
CTS adapted	39.1	20.0	13.4	5.7	39.9	35.1	36.0	46.9	37.6
CTS adapted, VTLN	36.9	18.5	13.0	5.5	37.0	33.1	34.4	45.2	34.8
VTLN	37.2	18.8	13.2	5.2	36.4	33.0	36.1	45.5	35.0
HLDA	35.7	17.8	13.4	4.6	36.0	31.0	33.9	43.3	34.6
SHLDA	35.6	17.7	13.3	4.5	35.6	30.3	34.5	42.8	34.7
SHLDA-MPE	32.9	15.8	13.3	3.8	32.8	27.8	32.3	39.8	31.9

Table 3. MDM Data selection. IHM denote IHM segments (inc. overlapped speech). sil-bound and word-bound denote methods for removing overlap (cut at silence or word boundaries), sn denotes silence normalisation.ASL denotes the average segment length.

	#Segments	Size (hours)	ASL (sec)	%Silence
IHM	136822	104.27	2.74	27.0
sil-bound	84044	62.33	2.67	21.0
word-bound	94940	65.78	2.49	21.1
word-bound + sn	96086	62.96	2.36	18.0

cope with overlapped speech. A straight forward exclusion of all segments with overlaps would have resulted in removal of more than 60% of the data and hence was not an option. Table 3 compares several data selection techniques based on alignments. *sil-bound* denotes cuts at the nearest boundary where silence occurs, *word-bound* the nearest word-boundary regardless of silence. With *sn* further silence beyond 0.2 seconds at segment boundaries and within segments was removed. The word-bound+sn configuration showed marginally better performance and was used for MDM model training.

4.4   Vocabulary, Language Models and Dictionaries

The recognition vocabulary is set to cover the 50000 most frequent words using a procedure outlined in[10]. The same vocabulary was used both for lecture and conference room style meetings. Pronunciation dictionaries are based on the UNISYN pronunciation lexicon [6] which was manually augmented[10]. Pronunciation probabilities are estimated from alignment of the training data[11].

As in previous work, LMs trained on a large number of corpora were used to derive meeting room specific and generic language models by optimisation of interpolation weights. The most important corpora are listed in Table 4. A full discussion of all source material would go beyond the scope of this paper. It is important to note that a collection of data from the web using tools and methods as provided by [1] was performed using both AMI and CHIL data as the basis. In both cases the proposed approach was altered to focus on previously unobserved contexts. This approach has in particular lead to a dramatic reduction in perplexity for lecture room data by more than 30%.

Table 4. Size of various text corpora in million words (MW)

Corpus	#words (MW)
Swbd/CHE	3.5
Fisher	10.5
Web (Swbd)	163
Web (fisher)	484
Web (fisher topics)	156
BBC - THISL	33
HUB4-LM96	152
SDR99-Newswire	39
ICSI/ISL/NIST/AMI	1.5
Web (ICSI)	128
Web (AMI)	100
Web (CHIL)	70

Table 5. Perplexities for 4-gram LMs on rt04dev and rt05samidev

Data source	Language models					
	ICSI	NIST	ISL	AMI	LDC	fgcomb05
ICSI	82.734	86.1662	87.3345	97.1024	109.86	84.1826
NIST	101.442	103.668	102.054	105.683	109.212	98.8722
ISL	110.124	110.99	106.66	119.327	114.483	108.588
AMI	92.9651	108.865	108.723	77.2817	101.714	84.1282
LDC	92.3824	92.761	87.6343	99.0105	84.2745	90.5354
AllDev	86.9236	93.2191	93.6604	92.0517	106.716	85.381

Table 5 shows perplexities for language models tuned to specific meeting resources as well as in combination. It is evident the meeting room specific models outperform the combined models. Hence the lattice expansion to 4-gram lattices (see Section 3) was performed using meeting resource specific models. This gave an additional 0.5% WER reduction on the rt04seval set.

4.5   Minimum Word Error Decoding

Minimum word error rate decoding[16] is a widely used technique to counter the fact that the standard speech recognition objective function is to minimise sentence instead of word error rate which is the measurement metric. Table 6 compares the performance both on IHM and MDM. In both case the gain from this technique was found to be moderate. The table also shows the effect of correcting the word times by alignment. Standard decoding adds between-word silence to the end of a word, thus artificially lengthening words. Secondly, confusion network decoding uses heuristic rules to define word times. Hence again re-alignment is needed to correct the times.

Table 6. %WERs on rt05seval showing the effect of CN decoding. Word times are corrected by alignment.

CN decoding	Word time correction	IHM	MDM
		32.1	44.2
	×	31.2	42.2
×		31.5	44.0
×	×	30.6	42.0

5   Overall System Performance

Table 7 shows WER results for the 2005 AMI meeting transcription system on a per pass basis. The result for P3 is higher than that for P2 due to the use of a bigram language model. The major reduction in WER at P6 can be explained by the use of alignment (see above). The high deletion rate is a main contributor to the error rate. Overall the WER reduction up to P6 is 10.5% absolute, however most of the gain is already obtained in P2.The associated results on rt05seval MDM are shown in Table 8. Note that a similar improvement is obtained to that observed on IHM data, again with relatively high deletion rates. Particularly poor performance on VT data has a considerable impact on performance (only 2 distant microphones!).

Table 7. %WER on rt05seval IHM

	TOT	Sub	Del	Ins	Fem	Male	AMI	ISL	ICSI	NIST	VT
P1	41.1	21.1	14.7	5.3	41.1	37.2	42.3	36.3	37.1	49.1	41.1
P2	33.1	15.9	13.4	3.9	33.1	28.2	33.4	27.2	32.8	39.5	32.8
P3	34.4	16.9	13.7	3.9	34.4	28.7	34.8	27.7	33.5	41.8	34.6
P4.tg	32.2	15.3	13.1	3.8	32.2	27.3	32.3	26.1	32.1	39.3	31.4
P4.fg	32.3	15.5	12.9	3.9	32.3	27.7	32.6	26.4	31.9	39.5	31.2
P5	32.1	15.3	12.8	4.0	32.1	27.4	32.7	26.3	31.8	39.1	30.5
P6	30.6	14.7	12.5	3.4	30.6	25.9	30.9	24.6	30.7	37.9	28.9

Table 8. %WER on rt05seval MDM

	TOT	Sub	Del	Ins	Fem	Male	AMI	ISL	ICSI	NIST	VT
P1	53.6	32.1	17.3	4.1	53.6	56.4	46.5	50.2	48.2	53.6	63.0
P2	50.8	31.3	14.8	4.7	50.8	51.4	44.7	46.7	43.6	51.6	60.4
P3	50.4	31.1	14.6	4.7	50.4	53.0	44.7	47.0	45.2	48.9	59.7
P4.tg	48.4	30.0	13.6	4.8	48.4	49.4	43.9	44.8	42.5	46.9	57.2
P4.fg	47.9	29.5	13.7	4.7	47.9	49.3	42.4	45.0	41.8	47.4	56.6
P5	44.2	26.0	14.0	4.1	44.2	42.6	38.6	38.9	39.2	43.8	53.2
P6	42.0	25.5	13.0	3.5	42.0	42.0	35.1	37.1	38.4	41.5	51.1

5.1 Manual Segmentation

In previous sections we have shown that automatic segmentation is still a main source of error. Table 9 compares results with reference and automatic segmentation. Both on MDM and IHM the automatic segmentation naturally increases deletion rates, however the effect is far stronger on IHM where the overall difference between automatic and manual segmentation is 6.4%. The gain from confusion network decoding is further decreased with automatic segmentation. The absolute gain from P1 to P6 is similar in absolute terms, with or without manual segmentation.

Table 9. %WER summary for rt05seval

	IHM				MDM			
	refseg		autoseg		refseg		autoseg	
	TOT	Del	TOT	Del	TOT	Del	TOT	Del
P1	34.9	7.1	41.1	14.7	50.6	11.8	53.6	17.3
P2	26.0	7.1	33.1	13.4	46.4	11.4	50.8	14.8
P3	27.4	7.4	34.4	13.7	47.8	12.5	50.4	14.6
P4	24.5	6.4	32.3	12.9	45.1	11.5	47.9	13.7
P5	24.5	6.3	32.1	12.8	42.0	12.2	44.2	14.0
P6	24.2	6.4	30.6	12.5	40.7	12.3	42.0	13.0

Table 10. %WER on rt05slecteval

	IHM				MDM			
	TOT	Sub	Del	Ins	TOT	Sub	Del	Ins
P1	44.4	26.4	5.0	12.9	65.0	47.6	9.9	7.5
P2	33.0	19.1	5.2	8.7	60.0	43.4	10.0	6.7
P3	33.7	19.7	5.3	8.6	59.9	43.0	11.0	5.9
P4	31.4	18.2	4.8	8.3	58.8	42.2	10.1	6.5
P5	31.1	18.2	4.6	8.3	54.8	38.7	11.2	5.0
P6	30.4	17.7	4.6	8.0	53.5	37.2	11.6	4.7

5.2 Lecture Room Meetings

Lecture room meetings as included in the RT05s evaluations originate only from one recording site. Presentation sessions are mixed with question/answer meetings where more than one speaker talks. In this work no development work was performed due to lack of time. The system for conference room meetings was used as described except for language models optimised on the associated development data with additionally collected web-data. For MDM transcription only the four microphones on the table were used. Table 10 shows WERs both on IHM and MDM recordings. It is interesting to note that the WERs are in the same range as on lecture room data, however the overall gain of the passes is larger. Deletion rates are considerably lower on IHM compared to the results on conference room data.

6   Conclusions

This is the first participation of the AMI-ASR team in NIST evaluation and the system presented here was developed from scratch in less than 10 months in a joint multi-site effort. The system was shown to yield very competitive performance for the transcription of meeting data in the NIST RT05s evaluation both on lecture and conference room data. We have also described and analysed a series of potential short-comings that will be addressed in the future. Particular emphasis will be placed on improving the IHM and MDM front-end processing.

Acknowledgements

This work was largely supported by the European Union 6th FWP IST Integrated Project AMI (Augmented Multi-party Interaction, FP6-506811). The authors thank the rest of the AMI-ASR team for their valuable contributions: Barbara Peskin, Jan Cernocky, Jithendra Vepa, and Chuck Wooters. We also would like to thank Andreas Stolcke and ICSI for providing the segments and speaker labels for MDM data, and the Cambridge University Engineering Department for providing the h5train03 CTS training set and for the right to use Gunnar Evermann's HDecode at the University of Sheffield.

References

1. I. Bulyko, M. Ostendorf, and A. Stolcke (2003). Getting More Mileage from Web Text Sources for Conversational Speech Language Modeling using Class-Dependent Mixtures. in Proc HLT'03.
2. S. Burger, V. MacLaren, H. Yu (2002). The ISL Meeting Corpus: The Impact of Meeting Type on Speech Style. In Proc. ICSLP'2002.
3. J. Carletta,S. Ashby, S. Bourban, M. Guillemot M. Kronenthal, G. Lathoud, M. Lincoln, I. McCowan, T. Hain, W. Kraaij, W. Post, J. Kadlec, P. Wellner, M. Flynn, and D. Reidsma (2005). The AMI Meeting Corpus. In Proc. MLMI'05, Edinburgh.
4. H. Cox, R. Zeskind, and I. Kooij (1986). Practical supergain. IEEE Trans. ASSP, Vol 34(3), pp 393–397.
5. H. Cox, R. Zeskind, and M. Owen (1987). Robust adaptive beamforming. IEEE Trans. ASSP, Vol. 35(10), pp. 1365–1376.
6. S. Fitt (2000). Documentation and user guide to UNISYN lexicon and post-lexical rules, Tech. Rep., Centre for Speech Technology Research, Edinburgh.
7. M.J.F. Gales and P.C. Woodland (1996). Mean and Variance Adaptation within the MLLR Framework. *Computer Speech & Language*, Vol. 10, pp. 249–264.
8. J.S. Garafolo, C.D. Laprun, M. Michel, V.M. Stanford, and E. Tabassi (2004). In Proc. 4th Intl. Conf. on Language Resources and Evaluation (LREC'04).
9. J.L. Gauvain and C. Lee (1994). MAP estimation for multivariate Gaussian mixture observation of Markov Chains, IEEE Tr. Speech& Audio Processing, Vol. 2, pp. 291–298.

10. T. Hain, L. Burget, J. Dines, I. McCowan, G. Garau, M. Karafiat, M. Lincoln, D. Moore, V. Wan, R. Ordelman and S. Renals (2005). The Development of the AMI System for the Transcription of Speech in Meetings, In Proc. MLMI'05, Edinburgh.

11. T. Hain (2005), Implicit modelling of pronunciation variation in automatic speech recognition. Speech Communication, Vol. 46(2), pp. 171–188.

12. A. Janin, D. Baron, J. Edwards, D. Ellis, D. Gelbart, N. Morgan, B. Peskin, T. Pfau, E. Shriberg, A. Stolcke and C. Wooters (2003). The ICSI Meeting Corpus. In Proc. ICASSP'03, Hong Kong.

13. C. H. Knapp and G. C. Carter (1976). The generalized correlation method for estimation of time delay/ IEEE Transactions on Acoustics, Speech and Signal Processing, Trans. ASSP, Vol 24, pp 320–327.

14. N. Kumar (1997), Investigation of Silicon-Auditory Models and Generalization of Linear Discriminant Analysis for Improved Speech Recognition.PhD thesis, John Hopkins University, Baltimore.

15. L. Burget (2004), Combination of Speech Features Using Smoothed Heteroscedastic Linear Discriminant Analysis. in Proc. ICSLP'04, p 4–7, Jeju Island, Korea.

16. L. Mangu, E. Brill and A. Stolcke (1999). Finding Consensus Among Words: Lattice-Based Word Error Minimization. In Proc. Eurospeech'99, pp. 495–498, Budapest.

17. D. Messerschmitt, D. Hedberg, C. Cole, A. Haoui and P. Winship (1989). Digital voice echo canceller with a TMS32020. Appl. Rep. SPRA129, Texas Instruments.

18. Spring 2004 (RT04S) Rich Transcription Meeting Recognition Evaluation Plan. NIST, US. Available at http://www.nist.gov/speech.

19. T. Pfau and D.P. W. Ellis (2001). Hidden Markov model based speech activity detection for the ICSI meeting project. Eurospeech'01.

20. D. Povey and P.C. Woodland (2002), Minimum Phone Error and I-Smoothing for Improved Discriminative Training, In Proc. ICASSP'02, Orlando.

21. A. Stolcke, C. Wooters, N. Mirghafori, T. Pirinen, I. Bulyko, D. Gelbart, M. Graciarena, S. Otterson, B. Peskin and M. Ostendorf (2004). Progress in Meeting Recognition: The ICSI-SRI-UW Spring 2004 Evaluation System. In Proc. NIST RT04S Workshop.

22. P.C. Woodland, M.J.F. Gales, D. Pye and S.J. Young (1997). Broadcast News Transcription using HTK. In Proc. ICASSP'97, pp. 719-722, Munich.

23. S. Wrigley, G. Brown, V. Wan and S. Renals (2005). Speech and crosstalk detection in multichannel audio. In IEEE Trans. Speech& Audio Proc., Vol 13(1), pp. 84–91.

Further Progress in Meeting Recognition: The ICSI-SRI Spring 2005 Speech-to-Text Evaluation System

Andreas Stolcke[1,2], Xavier Anguera[1,3], Kofi Boakye[1], Özgür Çetin[1],
František Grézl[1,4], Adam Janin[1], Arindam Mandal[5], Barbara Peskin[1],
Chuck Wooters[1], and Jing Zheng[2]

[1] International Computer Science Institute, Berkeley, CA, USA
[2] SRI International, Menlo Park, CA, USA
[3] Technical University of Catalonia, Barcelona, Spain
[4] Brno University of Technology, Czech Republic
[5] University of Washington, Seattle, WA, USA
stolcke@icsi.berkeley.edu

Abstract. We describe the development of our speech recognition system for the National Institute of Standards and Technology (NIST) Spring 2005 Meeting Rich Transcription (RT-05S) evaluation, highlighting improvements made since last year [1]. The system is based on the SRI-ICSI-UW RT-04F conversational telephone speech (CTS) recognition system, with meeting-adapted models and various audio preprocessing steps. This year's system features better delay-sum processing of distant microphone channels and energy-based crosstalk suppression for close-talking microphones. Acoustic modeling is improved by virtue of various enhancements to the background (CTS) models, including added training data, decision-tree based state tying, and the inclusion of discriminatively trained phone posterior features estimated by multilayer perceptrons. In particular, we make use of adaptation of both acoustic models and MLP features to the meeting domain. For distant microphone recognition we obtained considerable gains by combining and cross-adapting narrow-band (telephone) acoustic models with broadband (broadcast news) models. Language models (LMs) were improved with the inclusion of new meeting and web data. In spite of a lack of training data, we created effective LMs for the CHIL lecture domain. Results are reported on RT-04S and RT-05S meeting data. Measured on RT-04S conference data, we achieved an overall improvement of 17% relative in both MDM and IHM conditions compared to last year's evaluation system. Results on lecture data are comparable to the best reported results for that task.

1 Introduction

Meeting recognition continues to be a challenging task for speech technology for several reasons. Unrestricted speech, recognition from distant microphones, varying noise conditions, and multiple and overlapping speakers pose problems not found in other widely used benchmark tests. Furthermore, meetings pose the interesting problem of designing *portable* recognition systems, in two regards. First, because of the relative novelty of the task, and limited size of in-domain training corpora, it is advantageous to try to leverage methods and data that have been developed for other genres of speech,

S. Renals and S. Bengio (Eds.): MLMI 2005, LNCS 3869, pp. 463–475, 2006.

such as conversational telephone speech (CTS) and broadcast news (BN), for which one can draw on a longer development history and an order of magnitude more data. The second motivation for portability is that the meeting domain itself is varied, with different collection sites, acoustic conditions, and conversational styles and topics.

As for last year's meeting evaluation (RT-04S), our development strategy for RT-05S was to start with an existing CTS system[1] and adapt it to the meeting domain. This allowed us to leverage research between the corresponding CTS evaluations, from the Fall of 2003 (RT-03F) to the Fall of 2004 (RT-04F), and was crucial to developing a meeting system in the short period available. Acoustic models were adapted to the available conference room data (some of it new for this year), and language models were rebuilt for the conference and lecture room domains (no special acoustic models were created for the lecture domain). A new aspect in our acoustic modeling this year was the use of discriminatively trained Tandem/HATS features, and the fact that features were adapted to the new task, in addition to the more standard model adaptation. The acoustic preprocessing for meetings was also improved significantly, for both distant and individual microphone conditions.

The evaluation task and data are described in Section 2. Section 3 gives the system description, focusing on new developments relative to the 2004 system [1]. Results and discussion appear in Section 4, followed by conclusions and future work in Section 5.

2   Task and Data

2.1   Test Data

Evaluation data. The RT-05S conference room evaluation data (eval05) consisted of two meetings from each of the recording sites AMI (Augmented Multi-party Inter-action project), CMU (Carnegie Mellon University Interactive Systems Laboratory), ICSI, NIST, and VT (Virginia Tech). Systems were required to recognize a specific 12-minute segment from each meeting; however, data from the entire meeting was allowed for processing.[2] Separate evaluations were conducted in three conditions:

MDM Multiple distant microphones (primary)
IHM Individual headset microphones (required contrast)
SDM Single distant microphone (optional)

The lecture room data consisted of 120 minutes of seminars recorded by the Computers In the Human Interaction Loop (CHIL) consortium. In addition to the above conditions, lecture data provided the following recording conditions:

MSLA Multiple source-localization arrays (optional)
MM3A Multiple Mark III microphone arrays (optional). The MM3A condition has not yet been delivered for the evaluation set, and could be evaluated only on development data, using a single array.

---

[1] As explained later, we also made use of acoustic models developed for BN.
[2] We did not find significant gains from adapting on entire meetings, and, except in the acoustic preprocessing, used only the designated meeting excerpts.

It should be noted that microphones varied substantially by type and setup, even within each condition. For example, some of the AMI IHM data was recorded with head-mounted lapel microphones, and MDM recording devices ranged from low- and high-quality individual table-top microphones to AMI's circular microphone arrays. Meeting participants included both native and nonnative speakers of English (unlike in CTS evaluations).

Development data. The RT-04S evaluation data, consisting of eight 11-minute excerpts of meetings from CMU, ICSI, LDC (Linguistic Data Consortium), and NIST was designated as development data for RT-05S, and used by us as an unbiased test set (`eval04`). For most of the development we relied on the RT-04S development set, consisting of another 8 meetings from the same sources, and a newly provided set of 10 AMI meetings. Out of these we formed 10-meeting set that was balanced by meeting source (designated `dev04a`) and that served for optimization and system tuning. An additional 5 meetings (2 ICSI, 2 CMU, 1 LDC) were available from the RT-02 devtest set (used by us only for some LM tuning and speech/nonspeech model training). Note that the `eval05` "VT" meetings had no corresponding development data and thus served as a "blind" test. Excerpts from 5 CHIL lectures were available for development testing in the lecture room domain.

2.2 Training Data

Training data was available from AMI (35 meetings, 16 hours of speech after segmentation), CMU (17 meetings, 11 hours), ICSI (73 meetings, 74 hours), and NIST (15 meetings, 14 hours). The CMU data was of limited use in that only lapel and no distant microphone recordings were available.

Background training data for the (pre-adaptation) acoustic models consisted of the publicly available CTS and BN corpora. These included about 2300 hours of telephone speech from the Switchboard, CallHome English, and Fisher collections, and about 900 hours of BN data from the Hub-4 and TDT corpora.

3 System Description

3.1 Signal Processing and Segmentation

Distant microphone processing. All distant microphone channels (in both training and test) were first individually noise-filtered using a Wiener filter with typical engineering modifications, identically to last year [2,1].

Subsequently, for the MDM and MSLA conditions, a delay-and-sum beamforming technique was applied to combine all available distant microphone channels into a single enhanced signal, described in more detail in [3]. A time delay of arrival (TDOA) was computed between each input channel and a reference channel every 250 ms, using the GCC-PHAT algorithm [4] on 500 ms segments. The reference channel was chosen as the most centrally located microphone in the room, as specified by the SDM condition. For each step of 250 ms, a 500 ms segment was extracted for each channel and delayed according to the computed TDOA. Finally, the different channels were summed together, multiplied by a triangular window to avoid discontinuities between steps.

Speech regions were then identified using a speech/nonspeech two-class HMM decoder. Resulting segments were combined and padded with silence to satisfy certain duration constraints that had been empirically optimized for recognition accuracy. The algorithm and models were unchanged from last year [1], except that special speech/nonspeech models were trained exclusively from and for AMI meetings.

Finally, the segments were clustered into acoustically homogeneous partitions, which serve as pseudo-speaker units for normalization and adaptation. Last year we fixed the number of clusters at 4; this year the cluster number was chosen automatically, but such that each cluster contained at least 20 segments. We tried using the output of the ICSI-SRI diarization system [3] for segment clustering, so far without improvement in recognition accuracy. This could be because even within one speaker there is important acoustic variation (e.g., due to head movement) that is detected by the current clustering algorithm.

Close-talking microphone processing. The IHM input channels were segmented (without Wiener filtering) into speech and nonspeech regions using the same basic algorithm as for the distant microphone signals, using speech/nonspeech models trained on the close-talking training data (again, except for separate AMI processing, models are unchanged from 2004). No speaker clustering was performed, since it was assumed that each IHM channel corresponds to exactly one speaker. However, this year we added a crosstalk detector, with the goal of avoiding insertion of recognized speech from background speakers.[3]

The system generates start and end times for *foreground* speech segments by performing zero-level thresholding of a "crosstalk-compensated" energy-like signal derived from channel energy signals (but taking both positive and negative values). For each target channel $i = 1, 2, \ldots, N$ in the set of IHM channels, this crosstalk-compensated signal $E_{CC,i}$ is given by

$$E_{CC,i}(n) = E_{\text{offset},i}(n) - \frac{1}{N-1} \sum_{k \neq i} E_{\text{offset},k}(n) \quad . \tag{1}$$

Here $E_{\text{offset},k}$ is computed as $E_k(n) - \min_l E_k(l)$, that is, the signal energy minus the minimum signal energy over the channel. This minimum energy is used as an estimate of the noise floor.

The subtraction of the average of the nontarget energy signals is done with the expectation that regions in which crosstalk appears on the target channel (and most likely on other channels) will have values below the threshold in the resulting signal, as the crosstalk will appear as a region with significant energy in the averaged signal. The energy signals represent an average over a window of 25 ms with a step size of 10 ms. The presumed foreground segments thus detected are then intersected with the output of the speech/nonspeech decoder.

3.2 Acoustic Modeling and Adaptation

Decoding architecture. To motivate the choice of acoustic models, we first describe the SRI-ICSI-UW RT-04F CTS system, on which the meeting system is based (see

---

[3] We discarded the post-recognition crosstalk detector used last year that had proven ineffective.

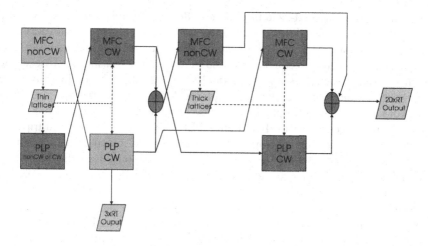

Fig. 1. SRI CTS recognition system. Rectangles represent decoding steps. Parallelograms represent decoding output (lattices or 1-best hypotheses). Solid arrows denote passing of hypotheses for adaptation or output. Dashed lines denote generation or use of word lattices for decoding. Crossed ovals denote confusion network system combination.

Figure 1). An "upper" (in the figure) tier of decoding steps is based on MFCC features; a parallel "lower" tier of decoding steps uses PLP features. The outputs from these two tiers are combined twice using word confusion networks (denoted by crossed ovals in the figure). Except for the initial decodings, the acoustic models are adapted to the output of a previous step from the respective other tier using MLLR (cross-adaptation). Lattices are generated initially to speed up subsequent decoding steps. The lattices are regenerated once later to improve their accuracy, after adapting to the outputs of the first combination step. The lattice generation steps use non-crossword (nonCW) triphone models, and decoding from lattices uses crossword (CW) models. Each decoding step generates either lattices or N-best lists, both of which are rescored with a 4-gram LM; N-best output is also rescored with duration models for words and pauses [5].

The final output is the result of a three-way system combination of MFCC-nonCW, MFCC-CW, and PLP-CW decoding branches. The entire system runs in under 20 times real time (20xRT).[4] For quick turnaround development it is useful to use a "fast" subset of the full system consisting of just two decoding steps (the light-shaded boxes in the figure); this fast system runs in 3xRT and exercises all the key elements of the full system except for confusion network combination.

Baseline models and test-time adaptation. The MFCC recognition models were derived from gender-dependent CTS models in the RT-04F system, which had been trained with the minimum phone error (MPE) criterion [6] on about 1400 hours of data. (All available native Fisher speakers were used, but to save training time, statistics were collected from only every other utterance). The MFCC models used 12 cepstral coef-

---

[4] Runtimes given assume operation with Gaussian shortlists. Since RT-05S did not impose a runtime limit we ran the system without shortlists, in about 25xRT.

ficients, energy, first-, second-, and third-order differences features, and 2×5 voicing features over a 5-frame window [7]. Cepstral features were computed with vocal tract length normalization (VTLN) and zero-mean and unit variance per speaker/cluster. The 62-component raw feature vector was reduced to 39 dimensions using heteroscedastic linear discriminant analysis (HLDA) [8]. After HLDA, a 25-dimensional Tandem/HATs feature vector estimated by multilayer perceptrons (MLPs) [9,10] was appended. Both within-word and cross-word triphone models were trained, for lattice generation and decoding from lattices, respectively. Baseline PLP CTS models (cross-word triphone only) were trained in analogous fashion, but did not include voicing or MLP features. All models this year were trained using decision-tree-based state tying, rather than SRI's traditional bottom-up genonic model clustering; this change had resulted in improved CTS performance.

In testing, all models underwent unsupervised adaptation to the test speaker or cluster, using maximum likelihood linear regression (MLLR) with multiple, phonetically defined regression classes. After the evaluation we experimented with regression classes that were generated in a data-driven manner by decision trees. The first MFCC and PLP adaptation passes used a phone-loop reference model; later passes adapted to prior recognition output. In addition, all but the first decoding used constrained MLLR in feature space, which was also employed in training (speaker adaptive training) [11].

Following work by the CMU-ISL team in RT-04S [12], we also experimented with PLP baseline models trained on BN data. Unlike the CTS versions, these models use the full signal bandwidth and are gender independent. Otherwise, the BN model used similar training, normalization, and adaptation techniques: VTLN, HLDA, feature-space CMLLR, and model-space MLLR.

Acoustic model task adaptation. All baseline models were adapted to the IHM and distant microphone conditions using the respective channels in the training data. Based on experiments with last year's system, we chose not to use the CMU data for model adaptation. Also, we found (in 2004) that there was no advantage to delay-summing the training data for MDM recognition, compared to pooling all the individual distant microphone signals into one training set. This meant that, conveniently, a single adapted model set could be used for all distant microphone test conditions. Last year we found only a very minor benefit from adapting acoustic models to individual meeting sources; this year the same pooled adaptation data was used for all meetings. The weight for adaptation data statistics was empirically optimized, and set at 20.

Last year's baseline models had been trained with maximum mutual information (MMI) estimation, and accordingly a version of MAP adaptation that adapted numerator and denominator statistics separately was employed [1]. This year's baseline models were created using MPE training [6], and we found it best to apply the MMI-MAP procedure in adaptation [13]. However, due to lack of time, we applied MMI-MAP only to the IHM models, and used the standard, less-involved ML-MAP procedure on the distant microphone models.

MLP feature adaptation. The MLPs estimating Tandem/HATS features had been trained on a large subset of the CTS training data [10] to perform frame-level phone discrimination. In addition to MAP-adapting the models based on these features, we explored adapting the features themselves to better match the meeting domain. This was accomplished by applying three additional backpropagation iterations to the CTS-trained MLPs, using the meeting data as training material. The KLT transform mapping the phone log posteriors was kept unchanged from the CTS system, so as to keep the features compatible with existing models. Because of time constraints and data availability, we were able to carry out this procedure only once, using CMU, ICSI, and NIST close-talking microphone data. However, as described in the next section, the adapted features gave improved results on all meeting sources, and for both IHM and distant microphone conditions; we therefore used the same adapted MLPs in all versions of our system.

3.3 Language Models

Three LMs were used in decoding: a multiword bigram for lattice generation, a multiword trigram for decoding from lattices, and a word 4-gram for lattice and N-best rescoring. The same set of language models is used for all conference meeting sources (we had found no advantage in tuning LMs to the meeting source). A second set of LMs is used for the lecture task.

For the conference room domain, the LMs were linearly interpolated mixtures of component LMs trained from the following sources: (a) Switchboard CTS transcripts, (b) Fisher CTS transcripts, (c) Hub-4 and TDT4 BN transcripts, (d) AMI, CMU, ICSI, and NIST meeting transcripts, and (e) world-wide-web data collected to match different topics and styles [14], namely RT-04S meeting sources, AMI meetings, and 525M words of Fisher-like conversational web data collected and published by UW for the RT-04F evaluation. We obtained best recognition results with mixture weights that had been tuned to minimize perplexity on heldout CMU, ICSI, LDC, and NIST (but not AMI) transcripts. The LM vocabulary consisted of 54,524 words, comprising all words in our CTS system (including all Hub-5 and all non-singleton Fisher words), all words in the ICSI, CMU, and NIST training transcripts, and all non-singleton words in the AMI training transcripts. The out-of-vocabulary rate was 0.40% on eval04 transcripts, and 0.19% on the 2005 AMI development transcripts.

For the lecture room domain, additional LM mixture components were built from (f) 0.1M words of TED oral transcripts and (g) 28M words of speech conference proceedings (suggested by [15]). Also, the Fisher-relevant web data was replaced by web data related to conference proceedings. The lecture LM mixture was then optimized on CHIL development transcripts (LM tuning and testing used a jackknifing scheme to avoid tuning on the data being tested on). No CHIL transcripts were used for N-gram training. The lecture LM vocabulary was an extension of the conference LM vocabulary, with 3791 additional frequent words found in the proceedings data. The out-of-vocabulary rate on the CHIL development data was 0.18%.

4 Results and Discussion

Here we present results measuring the effects of the system features and improvements described in the previous section. We will first present mostly conference meeting results, since those were the focus of our development. Lecture recognition results are summarized at the end.

4.1 MDM Delay-Sum Processing

For RT-04S, we applied the delay-sum beamforming *after* the segmentation step, with one TDOA estimate per waveform segment. This year, delay-summing was performed *before* segmentation, as described above. Table 1 compares SDM and MDM results with both methods. We observe that the new delay-sum method reduces word error rate (WER) for meetings with multiple distant microphones by 6.5% relative over the old method, and by 18.0% relative over the single-microphone condition. We also tested the new delay-sum algorithm, but retaining the old segmentation computed from SDM input, and found almost the same improvement as with segmentation based on the delay-summed signal (last row in Table 1. This shows that the improvement stems mostly from better recognition on the enhanced signal.

Table 1. Comparison of SDM and new and old MDM delay-sum methods, using RT-04S models and a fast decoding system. WERs on eval04 with and without CMU meetings (which had only one distant microphone channel) are given.

Method			eval04	
Input	Delay-sum	Segmentation on	w/CMU	w/o CMU
SDM	none	SDM	51.3	48.9
MDM	old	SDM	47.4	42.9
MDM	new	delay-summed	45.5	40.1
MDM	new	SDM	45.5	40.3

4.2 IHM Crosstalk Filtering

Table 2 shows IHM recognition results, without and with the new crosstalk suppression algorithm, as well as for an ideal segmentation derived from the NIST STM reference files. On both test sets, our crosstalk processing eliminates about one third of the word error difference between automatic and reference segmentation. However, broken down by meeting source the error patterns on the two test sets differ somewhat. On eval04 (as well as on our development data) the crosstalk filter never increased WER significantly.[5] On eval05, however, WER sometime increases, because of occasional deletions of foreground speech by the filter. This is especially a problem on the eval05 ICSI meetings, for reasons yet to be investigated. It should be noted that one of the eval05 NIST meetings is anomalous, in that a talker participates via a speakerphone, but without an associated IHM channel. Also, three channels do not contain any speech. Both these factors lead to very high insertion rates that our algorithm cannot yet effectively suppress.

4.3 Language Modeling

To evaluate the effectiveness of the various LM mixture components, we ran IHM recognition tests on eval04, AMI devtest data, and CHIL devtest data. Results are

---

[5] Here and elsewhere, we score on all eval04 personal microphone channels, including one ICSI lapel microphone channel that was removed from official scoring.

Table 2. IHM performance without and with crosstalk filtering, and with reference segmentation. Results on `eval04` obtained with RT-04S models, fast system; `eval05` with RT-05S models, full system. WERs are broken down by meeting source, and for `eval05` by error type (substitutions, deletions, insertions).

Crosstalk filter	eval04				eval05								
	All	CMU	ICSI	LDC	NIST	**All**	AMI	CMU	ICSI	NIST	VT	Sub	Del	Ins
No	**35.4**	39.7	27.4	44.7	27.1	**29.3**	22.1	23.3	20.5	45.8	35.8	11.0	10.3	8.0
Yes	**34.3**	39.3	25.2	43.0	27.3	**25.9**	23.3	23.3	24.5	34.5	23.6	11.0	11.5	3.4
Reference	**32.1**	36.9	23.9	40.3	24.3	**19.5**	19.2	19.9	16.8	21.4	20.6	11.2	6.7	1.6

Table 3. IHM WERs (in **bold**) and perplexities (in *italics*) with various LM mixtures on development data

Language model	eval04					2005 devtest	
	All	CMU	ICSI	LDC	NIST	AMI	CHIL
RT-04F (CTS)	**28.7** *95*	**32.1** *111*	**24.5** *78*	**34.1** *85*	**21.5** *109*	**39.8** *113*	**37.6** *320*
RT-04S	**28.7** *97*	**33.1** *117*	**22.0** *62*	**35.7** *97*	**21.1** *99*	**38.3** *107*	**31.5** *212*
RT-05S, no web	**28.9** *103*	**33.4** *121*	**22.0** *66*	**36.0** *101*	**21.5** *110*	**38.4** *100*	**27.6** *155*
RT-05S, w/web	**27.9** *92*	**32.5** *111*	**21.4** *59*	**34.9** *93*	**20.2** *90*	**37.3** *94*	**26.9** *148*

summarized in Table 3. More detailed results are reported in [16]. We note that the addition of AMI meeting transcripts, additional Fisher data, and new web data reduced WER by about 1.2% absolute on conference meetings relative to last year's meeting LM. Naturally, given the difference in topic and speaking styles, the adaptation to the lecture domain has a more dramatic effect, as the WER is reduced by 4.6%. Web data is quite important for conference meetings, lowering the WER by 1.3%-1.5%, but less so for lectures, where its effect is only a 0.7% absolute reduction. A possible explanation for this difference is that lecture-relevant material on the web is already available in the conference proceedings used in lecture LM training. Furthermore, we observe that the CTS LM mixture performs the best on the CMU and LDC meetings in terms of WER, and on the LDC meetings in terms of perplexity. This could be due to the sparseness of training data for these two sources, or to intra- and inter-source variability.

4.4   Acoustic Modeling

We tested a range of acoustic models to determine the contribution of baseline model improvements, Gaussian adaptation, MLP features (original and adapted), and CTS/BN model combination (for distant microphone recognition). Results are summarized in Table 4.[6] Below we point out the most important contrasts.

Lines (a) and (b) give results with CTS models underlying the RT-04S and RT-05S meeting models, respectively. We observe between 7% and 16% relative WER reduc-

---

[6] The original MDM submission had 30.0% WER, due to a VTLN bug that actually helped on `eval05`. Post-evaluation we found the BN model had not been adapted to female speakers; however, fixing this only reduced the WER to 30.1%.

Table 4. WERs using various sets of acoustic models and evaluation data for the conference test conditions. All results were obtained using the full recognition system and conference meeting LMs. Columns 2 and 3 indicate whether the Gaussian models and/or the MLP features were adapted to the meeting domain. "None" in column 3 indicates that MLP features were not used at all, whereas "no" means that CTS-trained MLPs were used. **Highlighted** results correspond to the final evaluation system.

Line	Baseline models	Gaussians adapted	MLP adapted	MDM eval04	MDM eval05	IHM eval04	IHM eval05
a	RT-03F CTS	no	no	48.3	40.2	33.2	30.8
b	RT-04F CTS	no	no	41.4	34.5	28.9	28.6
c	RT-04F CTS	no	yes	41.1	34.2	28.4	27.0
d	RT-04F CTS	ML-MAP	none	n/a	n/a	29.4	28.6
e	RT-04F CTS	ML-MAP	no	n/a	n/a	28.6	26.9
f	RT-04F CTS	ML-MAP	yes	40.3	32.2	28.3	26.2
g	RT-04F CTS+BN	ML-MAP	yes	**37.1**	**30.2**	28.0	26.3
h	RT-04F CTS	MMI-MAP	yes	n/a	n/a	**27.9**	**25.9**
i	RT-04F CTS+BN	ML-MAP+DT	yes	36.8	29.8	n/a	n/a
j	RT-04F CTS	MMI-MAP+DT	yes	n/a	n/a	28.1	25.6

tion as a result of added CTS data and improved modeling techniques.[7] Gaussian adaptation (e) and feature adaptation (c) each give about the same amount of improvement for IHM. Feature adaptation gives only a small gain for MDM because the MLPs were adapted on close-talking data only. Line (f) shows that Gaussian and feature adaptation are partly additive. The combined WER reduction is about 7-8% relative on `eval05` and 2-3% on `eval04`. MMI-MAP (h) gives an extra 1% relative IHM error reduction.

The combination of CTS-based MFCC models with BN-based PLP models (g) results in a large, 6-7% relative error reduction for MDM. Preliminary experiments had shown no gain for IHM, and the post-evaluation results given here show that there is no consistent gain over CTS-based PLP models. The reason might be that while CTS models are a better match to meeting speech in terms of speaking style, BN data contains more samples of distant microphones and noisy speech.

After the evaluation, we tested MLLR with decision-tree-generated regression classes (i, j), which resulted in another 1% relative improvement for most conditions, with the exception of `eval04` IHM data.

A comparison of adapted models without MLP features (d) and with adapted MLP features (f) shows an improvement of 8.4% relative on `eval05`. That is comparable to the 10% relative gain found in the CTS domain [10], and indicates good portability of the Tandem/HATS method.

Comparing the two evaluation sets, we notice that `eval05` is slightly easier (2% absolute) for IHM, and considerably easier (almost 10% absolute) for MDM. The absolute WER differences between line (a) and lines (g)/(h) are almost the same for the two test sets (about 10% for MDM and 5% for IHM). However, almost all the win on `eval04` seems to come from improvements in the baseline system, whereas for `eval05` the

---

[7] For comparison, the combined effect of all CTS model improvements was about 28% relative error reduction on in-domain (Fisher) data.

adaptation techniques contribute a larger gain. The reasons for this discrepancy still remain to be investigated.

4.5   Result Summary

Table 5 summarizes results on last year's and this year's evaluation sets, including on lecture room data. The lecture recognition system differed from the conference meeting system only in the LM (as described earlier), and in the configuration of the signal preprocessing. For MDM processing, we found that one of the CHIL tabletop microphones had much better signal-to-noise ratio than the others, and was best used alone, instead of in beamforming. Also, the speaker clustering for distant microphones proved detrimental and was omitted, no doubt because the lectures are dominated by a single speaker. For comparison with other lecture recognition work we include results on the development data, which corresponds to the CHIL January 2005 evaluation set.

Table 5. Evaluation system result summary

System	Conference Meetings						Lecture Meetings							
	eval04			eval05			CHIL devtest				eval05			
	MDM	SDM	IHM	MDM	SDM	IHM	MDM	MSLA	MM3A	IHM	MDM	MSLA	SDM	IHM
RT-04S	44.9	51.3	33.6											
RT-05S	37.1	43.0	27.9	30.2	40.9	25.9	51.6	51.0	49.7	26.9	52.0	44.8	51.9	28.0

Based on eval04 results, the overall reduction in word error compared to last year's system is 17.4% relative for MDM, and 16.9% for the IHM condition. Error rates are broadly comparable on eval04 and eval05, in spite of the latter containing different meeting sources, including one source that had not been seen in training or development (VT).

Word error rates on CHIL seminar lectures are comparable to conference meetings for the IHM condition. Distant microphone recognition shows 10% or more absolute higher WERs, which is not unexpected given the challenging acoustic conditions and the lack of in-domain training data. Results are in line with error rates reported by CHIL research sites [15].

5   Conclusions and Future Work

We have made considerable progress in the automatic transcription of conference meetings, as measured on NIST evaluation data. Substantial improvements came from meeting-specific preprocessing methods, as well as successful porting of CTS and BN models, MLP features, and decoding techniques, for an overall word error reduction of about 17% relative. We were also pleased that the system generalized well to previously unseen meeting sources and to the lecture domain, the latter with only minimal language model porting effort.

Major challenges remain, for example, in the recognition of distant speakers and overlapping speech. The single most important problem in IHM recognition remains the separation of foreground from background speech, especially when not all meeting participants are recorded individually. We also hope to benefit from tighter integration with our diarization system in the future.

Acknowledgments

This work was partly supported by the European Union 6th FWP IST Integrated Project AMI (Augmented Multi-party Interaction, FP6-506811), and by the Swiss National Science Foundation through NCCR's IM2 project. We thank Ivan Bulyko for assistance with LM preparation and web data collection; Lori Lamel for information concerning CHIL data and scripts for proceedings processing; Thomas Hain for information about AMI data; Barry Chen, Qifeng Zhu and Nelson Morgan for assistance and advice with MLP feature computation; and members of SRI's Speech Technology and Research Laboratory for assistance with the recognition system.

This paper contains corrections and additions to the version distributed at the NIST MLMI Meeting Recognition Workshop.

References

1. Stolcke, A., Wooters, C., Mirghafori, N., Pirinen, T., Bulyko, I., Gelbart, D., Graciarena, M., Otterson, S., Peskin, B., Ostendorf, M.: Progress in meeting recognition: The ICSI-SRI-UW Spring 2004 evaluation system. In: Proceedings NIST ICASSP 2004 Meeting Recognition Workshop, Montreal, National Institute of Standards and Technology (2004)
2. Adami, A., Burget, L., Dupont, S., Garudadri, H., Grezl, F., Hermansky, H., Jain, P., Kajarekar, S., Morgan, N., Sivadas, S.: Qualcomm-ICSI-OGI features for ASR. In Hansen, J.H.L., Pellom, B., eds.: Proc. ICSLP. Volume 1., Denver (2002) 4–7
3. Anguera, X., Wooters, C., Peskin, B., Aguiló, M.: Robust speaker segmentation for meetings: The ICSI-SRI Spring 2005 diarization system. In: Proceedings of the Rich Transcription 2005 Spring Meeting Recognition Evaluation, Edinburgh, National Institute of Standards and Technology (2005) 26–38
4. Flanagan, J.L., Johnston, J.D., Zahn, R., Elko, G.W.: Computer-steered microphone arrays for sound transduction in large rooms. J. Acoust. Soc. Am. **78** (1985) 1508–1518
5. Vergyri, D., Stolcke, A., Gadde, V.R.R., Ferrer, L., Shriberg, E.: Prosodic knowledge sources for automatic speech recognition. In: Proc. ICASSP. Volume 1., Hong Kong (2003) 208–211
6. Povey, D., Woodland, P.C.: Minimum phone error and I-smoothing for improved discriminative training. In: Proc. ICASSP. Volume 1., Orlando, FL (2002) 105–108
7. Graciarena, M., Franco, H., Zheng, J., Vergyri, D., Stolcke, A.: Voicing feature integration in SRI's Decipher LVCSR system. In: Proc. ICASSP. Volume 1., Montreal (2004) 921–924
8. Kumar, N.: Investigation of Silicon-Auditory Models and Generalization of Linear Discriminant Analysis for Improved Speech Recognition. PhD thesis, John Hopkins University, Baltimore (1997)
9. Morgan, N., Chen, B.Y., Zhu, Q., Stolcke, A.: TRAPping conversational speech: Extending TRAP/Tandem approaches to conversational telephone speech recognition. In: Proc. ICASSP. Volume 1., Montreal (2004) 536–539
10. Zhu, Q., Stolcke, A., Chen, B.Y., Morgan, N.: Using MLP features in SRI's conversational speech recognition system. In: Proc. Interspeech, Lisbon (2005) 2141–2144
11. Jin, H., Matsoukas, S., Schwartz, R., Kubala, F.: Fast robust inverse transform SAT and multistage adaptation. In: Proceedings DARPA Broadcast News Transcription and Understanding Workshop, Lansdowne, VA, Morgan Kaufmann (1998) 105–109

12. Metze, F., Fügen, C., Pan, Y., Waibel, A.: Automatically transcribing meetings using distant microphones. In: Proc. ICASSP. Volume 1., Philadelphia (2005) 989–902

13. Povey, D., Gales, M.J.F., Kim, D.Y., Woodland, P.C.: MMI-MAP and MPE-MAP for acoustic model adaptation. In: Proc. EUROSPEECH, Geneva (2003) 1981–1984

14. Bulyko, I., Ostendorf, M., Stolcke, A.: Getting more mileage from web text sources for conversational speech language modeling using class-dependent mixtures. In Hearst, M., Ostendorf, M., eds.: Proc. HLT-NAACL. Volume 2., Edmonton, Alberta, Canada, Association for Computational Linguistics (2003) 7–9

15. Lamel, L., Adda, G., Bilinski, E., Gauvain, J.L.: Transcribing lectures and seminars. In: Proc. Interspeech, Lisbon (2005)

16. Çetin, Ö., Stolcke, A.: Language modeling in the ICSI-SRI Spring 2005 meeting speech recognition evaluation system. Technical Report TR-05-06, International Computer Science Institute (2005)

Speaker Localization in CHIL Lectures: Evaluation Criteria and Results

Maurizio Omologo, Piergiorgio Svaizer, Alessio Brutti, and Luca Cristoforetti

ITC-irst, Povo, Trento, Italy
omologo@itc.it
http:shine.itc.it

Abstract. This work addresses the problem of automatic speaker localization and tracking in a real lecture scenario. Evaluation criteria recently adopted under CHIL and NIST benchmarking are outlined. Two speaker localization systems are described, which are based on the use of Generalized Cross Correlation Phase Transform analysis and Global Coherence Field. Benchmarking results, obtained on a set of 13 lectures, showed an average RMS error of about 30 cm in the speaker localization.

1 Introduction

Localization of active speakers is a challenging research area related to microphone arrays [1], with a large variety of foreseen possible applications, as videoconferencing, security, surveillance, smart home, etc. Many research activities and real implementations are described in the literature, mostly based on the solution of the Time Difference Of Arrival (TDOA) problem through the estimation of the phase tilt in the cross-power spectrum between two microphone signals. This phase information is derived by computing the Generalized Cross Correlation PHAse Transform (GCC-PHAT) introduced in [2] (as a possible alternative to a Maximum Likelihood estimator) and eventually adopted in [3] for speaker localization. To this regard, the geometry of the room and of the sensor set-up plays an important role in deriving an accurate speaker position from the resulting TDOA estimates.

Under CHIL [1] (Computer in the Human-Interaction Loop) European Project this research issue is tackled by different laboratories, working on a common experimental framework and, in particular, adopting similar distributed microphone networks. Evaluation criteria have been defined and then applied to compare performance of the given technologies. The most recent benchmarking was conducted under the NIST RT-Spring Evaluation 2005 (see "http://www.nist.gov/speech/tests/rt/rt2005/spring/"). The task refered primarily to locate, identify and track the lecturer while speaking in a seminar, which represents the first experimental context addressed under the CHIL project.

---

[1] This work was partially supported by the European Commission under the Integrated Project CHIL, contract number 506909.

S. Renals and S. Bengio (Eds.): MLMI 2005, LNCS 3869, pp. 476–487, 2006.

The remainder of this work will introduce the Speaker LOCalization (SLOC) problem, presenting the most commonly used techniques, addressing the evaluation criteria adopted under CHIL and NIST benchmarking, and finally reporting on results obtained by using two SLOC systems realized at ITC-irst.

2   Problem Definition

Let us consider a speaker, positioned in $\mathbf{p} = (x, y, z)$, that generates a speech signal $r(t)$, and a set of M sensors, with an arbitrary three-dimensional array geometry, placed in positions $\mathbf{p_0} = (x_0, y_0, z_0), ..., \mathbf{p_{M-1}} = (x_{M-1}, y_{M-1}, z_{M-1})$, and capturing the respective electrical signals $s_0(t), ..., s_{M-1}(t)$. Assuming that the acoustic waves associated with $r(t)$ propagate in a non reverberant noisy environment, the signal acquired by acoustic sensor i can be expressed as follows:

$$s_i(t) = \alpha_i r(t - \mathbf{t}_i) + v_i(t) \tag{1}$$

where α_i is an attenuation factor due to propagation effects, $v_i(t)$ includes additive noise components, and $\mathbf{t}_i$ denotes the propagation time of the wavefront from $\mathbf{p}$ to the i-th sensor. This propagation time can be expressed as $\mathbf{t}_i = \frac{d_i}{c}$ where c is the speed of sound and d_i is the distance between the source and the i-th microphone. The relative delay of the wavefront arrival between microphones i and k, can be expressed as $\delta_{ik} = \mathbf{t}_k - \mathbf{t}_i$.

In a real situation, the wave propagation is characterized by reflections on the surfaces and scattering by the objects inside the room. The speakers can be modeled as multiple directional acoustic emitters possibly moving in space and overlapping in time. Taking into account the reverberation effects, for one speaker the most suitable signal model in the discrete domain becomes:

$$s_i(n) = h_i * r(n) + v_i(n) \tag{2}$$

where * denotes convolution, $v_i(n)$ is an additive (background) noise signal at that sensor, and h_i is the channel impulse response between the speaker and the i-th sensor, which includes implicitly the propagation time $\mathbf{t}_i$. From the estimated propagation times (or, better, from the differences δ_{ik} in the arrival of the wavefront) at the sensors, one can derive the position of the speaker.

In particular, a single delay estimated between the signals of two microphones determines a surface (hyperboloid) of potential source position in the three-dimensional space. The surface can be reasonably approximated by a cone for distant sources (i.e., in case of far field assumption). When multiple delay estimates are derived from multiple microphone pairs, the "best intersection point" (according to a proper definition of a distance measure and a consequent minimization) is assumed as estimated candidate source position. A linear array allows source localization except for a rotation along the array axis. If the height of the source is assumed to be known, the linear array is sufficient for a two-dimensional localization. When a three-dimensional localization is requested, the array geometry should span all the three axes of a cartesian coordinate system.

In this case, microphone pairs at different heights and with different orientations inside the room are to be used.

All these aspects make the problem of speaker localization inside rooms a special case in the general topic of passive source localization by means of multiple sensors. Without lack of generality, in our case the active speaker corresponds to a wide-band, non-stationary acoustic emitter acting in closed space of small dimension in relation with the involved wavelengths. A lot of literature exists on the general topic, also reporting on methods that could not find direct application in the speaker localization scenario (correlation-based and autoregressive methods, eigenvalue-based analysis, MUSIC algorithm), in particular techniques either requiring a priori knowledge on the statistics of the emitters and the background noise, or requiring narrowband signals, or making assumption of far-field and low-reverberation (for more details see [4]). For speaker localization purposes, the most suitable methods are those based on the estimation of time delays δ_{ik}, as described in [1] and addressed in the following. Examples of real implementations are also described in the literature [5, 8].

3   Distributed Microphone Networks

In the CHIL project, Speaker Localization and Tracking in 3D is accomplished by adopting a distributed microphone network: this corresponds to have a set of arrays consisting of few microphones (e.g. T-shaped clusters of 4 microphones) spatially distributed in such a way that any time at least one cluster is in a favorable position to provide information about the direction of wavefront arrival.

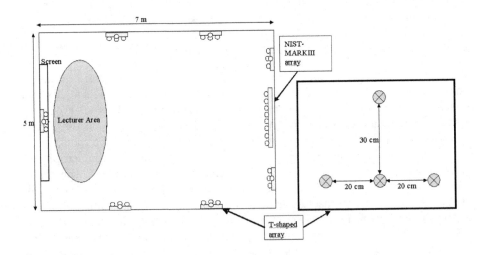

Fig. 1. Map of the CHIL room at ITC-irst: the room is equipped with one modified NIST MarkIII array and seven T-shaped arrays; the geometry of the latter ones is reported in the right part of the figure.

In practice, given the same number of sensors the main advantage of a distributed microphone network over a more traditional microphone array solution is in terms of better coverage in space, i.e. the potential for a better localization performance for every possible speaker position and head orientation. On the other hand, it is worth noting that spatial filtering (e.g. beamforming) can not, in general, be applied with such a distribution due to the limitation related to the spatial aliasing theorem [9]. Speech enhancement and acoustic feature extraction (for distant-talking speech recognition) based on a distributed microphone network represent challenging issues to investigate.

Figure 1 shows the map of the CHIL room at ITC-irst, where seven T-shaped arrays are placed at the same height (at about 2 meters). The Figure also shows the geometry of a T-shaped array, which consists of four omnidirectional microphones. This geometry allows to determine azimuth and elevation angles relative to each array; merging information from different arrays allows to localize the source in terms of (x,y,z) coordinates. Note that given a high number of microphones at the same height the evaluation of z coordinate may be biased.

4   Time Delay Estimation

Methods based on estimation of Time Difference Of Arrival (TDOA) at multiple microphones have been shown to be capable of accurate speaker localization even in relatively noisy and reverberant environments. The Phase Transform (PHAT) identifies a possible processor weighting in the GCC framework [2]. In the past, it was also defined as Cross-power Spectrum Phase (CSP), as discussed in [3] where it was applied for the first time to speaker localization, and ported into a first product for videoconferencing already based on a T-shaped array geometry (see "www.aethra.com"). Its computation is performed as follows. Denoting with l the time lag, and with $s_i(n)$ and $s_k(n)$ the discrete time sequences in the given interval, which were obtained by sampling signals acquired by microphones i and k, GCC-PHAT is defined as:

$$C_{ik}(t, l) = DFT^{-1} \left\{ \frac{DFT(s_i(n)) \cdot DFT^*(s_k(n))}{|DFT(s_i(n))| \cdot |DFT(s_k(n))|} \right\}. \tag{3}$$

In particular, as shown in [3, 4, 10], a GCC-PHAT based Coherence Measure (CM) function $C_{ik}(t_0, \tau)$, computed for an interval centered at time instant t_0, has a prominent peak at delay $\tau = \delta_{ik}$ corresponding to the direction of arrival.

Due to the theoretical independence of GCC-PHAT based CM from spectral characteristics of the input signals, maximizing it in the range of possible lags leads to an effective TDOA estimation even in presence of noise and reverberation. More details on the influence of acoustics and environmental conditions on speaker localization accuracy can be found in [11]. Starting from this basic method, many other similar solutions to speaker localization have been proposed in the literature during the last decade [1].

Alternative techniques have also been proposed as for instance that described in [12]: in this case, time delays derive from the analysis of the multichannel spatial correlation matrix, which takes advantage of the redundancy among multiple microphones to reduce the effects of noise and reverberation. However, preliminary experiments conducted under CHIL did not show a remarkable improvement in using that technique rather than GCC-PHAT [13].

Among the most recent proposals, a technique described in [14] deserves to be mentioned for next investigation, which derives time delay estimates by applying a blind source separation to the given input channels.

5   Global Coherence Field

A Global Coherence Field (GCF) is a function, defined over the space of possible sound source locations, which represents the plausibility that a sound source is active at a given point. It was introduced in [4], related to the Coherence Measure, and it is conceptually similar to Power Field (PF) introduced in [15]. More recently, in Chapter 8 of [1], Steered Response Power(SRP)-PHAT was introduced, which is equivalent to GCF.

Power Field (PF) represents the power of the signal obtained at the output of a beamformer, as a function of the point of space at which the array is steered. In other words, if the location space is subdivided by a grid Σ of potential source locations $\mathbf{p_l} = (x_l, y_l, z_l)$ and the corresponding sets η of steering delays are used to "scan" the space by means of the array, the power of the output signal, when the array is steered at a given location, can be used to derive a degree of plausibility that the source is located at that point. Now, let us consider a set Ω of Q microphone pairs and denote with $\delta_{ik}(x, y, z)$ the theoretical delay for the microphone pair (i, k) if the source is at position (x, y, z). Once the Coherence Measure $C_{ik}(t, \delta_{ik}(x, y, z))$ has been computed at instant t, for each microphone pair (i, k) belonging to Ω, GCF is expressed as:

$$GCF_\Omega(t, x, y, z) = \frac{1}{Q} \sum_{(i,k) \in \Omega} C_{ik}(t, \delta_{ik}(x, y, z)). \qquad (4)$$

Note that GCF is more informative than PF for SLOC purposes, especially for a distributed microphone network where beamforming should not be applied due to spatial aliasing. In fact, GCF is defined by considering the average coherence between signals realigned by the beamformer, instead of the power of its output. Figure 2 shows an example of GCF restricted to a plane (x, y).

6   ITC-irst SLOC Systems

The following of this work will address the evaluation of two SLOC systems realized at ITC-irst. The first one is based on a two-step procedure:

– In the first step, two horizontal microphone pairs (one per T-shaped array, with a distance of 40 cm between the microphones) are used to derive two delay estimates by using GCC-PHAT; from the two resulting directions a (x,y) position is computed.

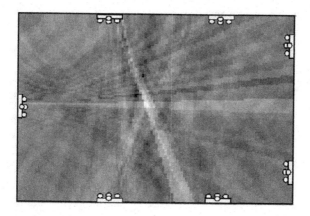

Fig. 2. GCC-PHAT based two-dimensional GCF computed using the 5 leftmost microphone clusters. GCF magnitude is represented by the brightness of the plotted points. The brightest spot in the center of the room corresponds to the active speaker.

– In the second step, two vertical microphone pairs are used to compute two GCC-PHAT functions. From the delay corresponding to the maximum in the two functions, the z-coordinate estimate is derived.

The second system works in a straightforward manner; in fact, it is based on maximizing GCF over all the possible positions in the room (on a grid of 10 cm x 10 cm).

Both systems can produce a set of coordinates every frame (i.e. about 90 ms); however, a postprocessing based on the maxima of the GCC-PHAT functions and on a related thresholding and smoothing leads to the decision about eventually classifying a given frame as speech. In other words, the latter step plays the role of a speech activity detector. Tuning of the systems was conducted on the basis of performance obtained on a development data set.

7   SLOC Evaluation

Most of the literature addressing speaker localization is based on simulations and often reports on performance expressed in terms of accuracy (e.g. bias and standard deviation) of delay estimates. On the other hand, in this work we directly address the problem of evaluating a SLOC technology in terms of localization accuracy in a real scenario. The accuracy of a speaker localization system is affected by many factors: the number of exploited microphones, their sensitivity, their spatial and spectral response, their relative geometric position, their distance from the speaker. In the CHIL project, a very similar set-up was adopted at the partners' sites in order to minimize fluctuations in performance due to the above mentioned factors; this way, sharing development and test data across the partners can lead to a reliable and fair evaluation of the different technologies.

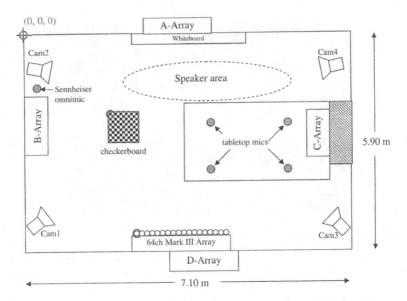

Fig. 3. Map of the CHIL room at Karlsruhe University (reported with the kind permission of Karlsruhe University). The 2-step procedure used a horizontal and a vertical microphone pair for each of the two arrays B and D. In the GCF-based procedure, GCF was computed from one horizontal microphone pair for each of arrays B, C, and D.

Estimating SLOC accuracy in a real scenario implies the need of a reference consisting in a labeled real database. For the first CHIL/NIST benchmarking, a database of 13 lectures was used, which were recorded between November 2004 and February 2005 in the CHIL room available at Karlsruhe University (see "http://chil.server.de" for further information). Figure 3 shows the map of the room, characterized by a reverberation time of about 450 ms. The location of the centroid of the speaker's head in the images from the four calibrated video cameras was manually marked every 667 milliseconds. Starting from these hand-marked labels, the true position of the speaker's head in three dimensions was calculated using the technique described in [16]. The resulting ground truth positions are accurate to within approximately 10 cm.

7.1   Type of Errors

In the given scenario two types of localization tasks are defined: *Accurate*, corresponding to a situation for which an extremely reliable coordinate reference is available; *Rough* used to face with situations in which a reliable reference is not available (this happens when the lecturer is interrupted by the audience, and inspecting videorecordings does not allow to recognize where was the speaker).

Basically, SLOC performance is evaluated by means of the Euclidean distance (or RMS) applied to the coordinates provided by the localization system (p_l) and to the corresponding reference coordinates checked by the manual transcriber

(p_r). The localization errors are classified in two classes [12, 17]: anomalies or *gross errors*; non-anomalies or *fine errors*. Given a distance function $d(p\_l, p\_r)$ between the two set of coordinates, and a threshold E_r in the related error, which represents a circle (or a sphere, in the 3-dimensional version) around the true source position p_r, a localization error is classified as anomalous or *gross error* if $d(p\_l, p\_r) > E\_r$; otherwise, it is classified as a non-anomalous or *fine error*. Thresholds for the discrimination between fine and gross errors will be different from *Accurate* localization tasks to *Rough* localization tasks: for instance, in a lecture scenario the threshold can be 50 cm for the *Accurate* localization task and 1 meter for the *Rough* localization task. For what concerns the classification between gross and fine errors, one can also compute the localization rate P_{cor}, as suggested in [18], which is defined as the number of fine errors (NFE) over the total number of frames (NT) for which the system has produced a localization result, i.e. $P_{cor} = NFE/NT$.

7.2   Speech Activity Detection Constraints

In principle, a speaker localization system may produce a set of coordinates at a high rate, for instance equal to the TDOA analysis rate. However, in a realistic application one needs to have a system able to track smoothly the position of the speaker. Hence, an overproduction of speaker positions have to be postprocessed anyway in order to derive one position for a longer temporal segment. The adoption of an updating rate in the range of 1-10 Hz seems to be reasonable. This choice is also consistent with typical rates adopted for vision technologies, and so with a potential integration between audio and image processing systems for person localization and tracking purposes.

So, in order to evaluate different SLOC technologies a common evaluation rate is here adopted; the example given in Figure 4 (see also the Appendix) refers to the assumption of an evaluation temporal segment equal to 100 ms. If a speaker localization system provides coordinates with a faster rate, the evaluation tool averages the coordinates, on a 100 ms window centered around the given time instant. If the speaker localization system produces data with a slower rate, or is not able to produce a set of coordinates for some frames labelled as "one speaker" by the human labelers, the evaluation tool will classify those missing data as deletion errors. Figure 4 provides one example for each of the following situations: an averaging, a localization at the given evaluation frame rate, a deletion, and a false alarm. Actually, introducing here deletion and false alarm rates is due to the fact that a speaker localization system includes an implicit acoustic event detection process. In a real application we can assume that one is interested in a good localization accuracy as well as in a low, and balanced, rate of deletions and false alarms, as discussed in the following.

7.3   SLOC Evaluation Tool

Based on the above mentioned approach and concepts, ITC-irst developed a SLOC evaluation software under the CHIL project. The same software was then

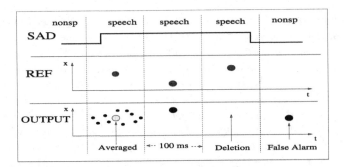

Fig. 4. Examples of outputs of the localization system for the x coordinate: SAD is the bilevel information of speech/non-speech activity, REF is the reference transcription of the x coordinate, OUTPUT shows the results of the localization system in the case of output at higher frame rate than 10 Hz, in the case of output at 10 Hz and in cases of deletion and false alarm, respectively.

adopted by NIST for RT-Spring Eval 2005 benchmarking [2]. A dummy example of how this software works is reported in Appendix. In particular, one can find: the content of the reference (manual labeling) file for a sequence of 1.3 seconds; a second list of data representing the output of a SLOC system; a third list reporting the output of the evaluation software for every frame (i.e. every 100 ms); finally, a list of indicators of performance, which let one be able to interpret a SLOC system potential from different perspectives.

7.4 NIST/CHIL Evaluation

The NIST RT-Spring Eval 2005 activity was conducted on excerpts of 13 lectures, as previously mentioned. The test recordings had an overall duration of about 66 minutes. A reference file (similar to that reported in the Appendix) was available for every lecture, with a labeling time step of 667 ms. The total number of reference frames was 5788. For 4241 of them, a set of coordinates corresponding to the active speaker location was available. It is worth noting that the recordings were selected among sequences in which most of the time there was no interruption by the audience.

The two ITC-irst systems above described were evaluated on the given test data. Although 16 microphone channels were available, for both SLOC systems a subset of microphones was used. In more detail, two T-shaped arrays (namely B and D) of the UKA room were used for the first system (based on GCC-PHAT). For the second system (based on GCC-PHAT and GCF) the T-shaped arrays B,C,D were used, since the array A (positioned close to the lecturer) was less informative. In fact, in most of the recordings the lecturer was oriented towards the audience; preliminary experiments on a development set had shown that by including array A slightly decreased performance.

---

[2] See also "http://www.nist.gov/speech/tests/rt/rt2005/spring/", where the source code and the document "SpeakerLocEval-V5.0-2005-01-18.pdf" can be downloaded.

Table 1 reports on the results, which show (see the first two rows) that both systems produced on the average two localizations per second (in fact, Average Frame Rate is 1.94 and 2.25). In both cases, the RMS of fine errors is close to 20 cm and the RMS of fine and gross errors together is a little higher than 30 cm. The good performance of the system is also confirmed by the localization rates, equal to 0.95 and 0.92, which shows that most of the errors are under the threshold of 50 cm. The bias is neglectable in all the three coordinates, even considering both fine and gross errors; this also shows that the video calibration process was consistent enough. Finally, the False Alarm Rate and the Deletion Rate are in both cases between 0.39 and 0.48, which corresponds to a satisfactory balanced situation. On the other hand, by setting the GCF-threshold of the voice activity detector in different ways, system behaviour changes substantially. Given a threshold equal to 0, deletion and false alarm rates are almost equal to 0 and 1, respectively, while the average frame rate is more than 6. Finally, the last row (with GCF-threshold=0.75) shows a case in which the error rate is improved but deletion rate becomes unacceptable (i.e. the evaluation is done on 175 frames).

Table 1. Results obtained applying the two SLOC systems developed at ITC-irst to the NIST-RT Spring Eval2005 test set.The last two lines refer to different settings of the GCF threshold for speech activity detection.

Technique	Average Frame Rate[s]	Number of Loc. frames	False Alarm Rate	Deletion Rate	Locali- zation Rate	RMSE fine [mm]	RMSE fine+ gross [mm]	Bias fine+ gross [mm]
2step	2.25	2539	0.42	0.41	0.95	203	309	(59,-78,-41)
GCF(0.38)	1.94	2273	0.39	0.48	0.92	198	327	(40,-47,-51)
GCF(0)	6.21	3962	0.81	0.07	0.87	226	479	(43,-64,-77)
GCF(0.75)	0.07	175	0.03	0.96	0.91	159	238	(80,-22,-57)

8   Conclusions and Future Work

In this work, the evaluation of a speaker localization system in a real lecture scenario has been addressed. Although good performance has been obtained, the given task can be considered of medium difficulty due to the limited movements of the lecturer in a rather small area and to a preliminary selection of test sequences in which there was almost no interference from the audience.

Next activities include the study of speaker localization in more complex scenarios as meetings and interactive seminars, in which different speakers can be active, even at the same time. To this regard, the entire distributed microphone network can be exploited to improve system performance; GCF and its extension to the Oriented GCF (OGCF) [19] represent good techniques along this direction. Finally, the integration of audio and video processing is envisaged to obtain a multi-modal person tracking in a more complex but probably more effective framework than using a single modality. To this regard, evaluation criteria and related tools are expected to be updated.

Acknowledgements

The authors would like to thank the anonymous reviewers for valuable suggestions. Thanks also to University of Karlsruhe, to all the CHIL partners who
contributed to the activities on SLOC (in particular to data collection and labeling), and to Jon Fiscus (NIST) for the effort in managing in a short time
(with all related technical problems) SLOC evaluation for RT-Spring Eval 2005.

References

1. M. Brandstein, D. Ward, "Microphone Arrays", *Springer Verlag*, 2001.
2. C.H. Knapp, C. Carter, "The Generalized Correlation Method for Estimation of
   Time Delay", *IEEE Trans. on ASSP*, vol. 24, pp. 320–327, 1976.
3. M. Omologo, P. Svaizer, "Acoustic Event Localization using a Crosspower-
   Spectrum Phase based Techniques", *Proc. IEEE ICASSP*, Adelaide 1994, vol. 2,
   pp. 273–276.
4. R. De Mori, "Spoken Dialogues with Computers", Ch. 2, *Academic Press*, 1998.
5. D.V. Rabinkin, R.J. Ranomeron, J.C. French, and J.L. Flanagan,""A DSP Implementation of Source Location using Microphone Arrays", Proc. of SPIE 2846,1996.
6. H. Wang, P. Chu, " Voice Source Localization for Automatic Camera Pointing
   System in Videoconferencing", Proc. of ICASSP, 1997.
7. Y.A. Huang, J. Benesty, G.W. Elko, "Microphone Arrays for Video Camera Steering" in "Acoustic Signal Processing for Telecommunication", S.L. Gay and J. Benesty Editors, *Kluwer Academic Publishers*, 2000.
8. H.F. Silverman et al.,"Performance of Real-Time Source Location Estimators for
   a Large-Aperture Microphone Array", *IEEE Trans. on SAP*, vol. 13,n. 4, 2005.
9. H.L. Van Trees, "Optimum Array Processing-Part IV", *John Wiley&Sons*, 2002.
10. M. Omologo, P. Svaizer, "Use of the Crosspower-Spectrum Phase in Acoustic Event
    Location", *IEEE Trans. on SAP*, vol. 5, n. 3, pp. 288–292, May 1997.
11. M. Omologo, P. Svaizer, "Acoustic Source Localization in Noisy and Reverberant
    Environment using CSP Analysis", *Proc. IEEE ICASSP*, 1996.
12. J. Chen, J. Benesty, Y. Huang "Robust Time Delay Estimation exploiting Redun-
    dancy among Multiple Microphones", *IEEE Trans. on SAP*, vol. 11, n. 6, 2003.
13. D. Macho et al., "Automatic Speech Activity Detection, Source Localization, and
    Speech Recognition on the CHIL Seminar Corpus", *Proceedings of ICME*, 2005.
14. H. Buchner et al., "Simultaneous Localization of Multiple Sound Sources using
    Blind Adaptive MIMO Filtering", Proc. of ICASSP. 2005.
15. V. Alvarado, "Talker Localization and Optimal Placement of Microphones for a
    Linear Microphone Array using Stochastic Region Contraction", PhD Thesis, *Tech-
    nical Report LEMS-69*, Brown University, 1990.
16. D. Focken and R. Stiefelhagen, "Towards Vision-based 3-d People Tracking in a
    Smart Room", in IEEE Int. Conf. Multimodal Interfaces, 2002.
17. B. Champagne, S. Bedard, A. Stephenne "Performance of Time Delay Estimation
    in the Presence of Room Reverberation", *IEEE Trans. on SAP*, vol. 4, 1996.
18. T .Nishiura, T. Yamada, S. Nakamura, and K. Shikano,"Localization of Multiple
    Sound Source based on a CSP analysis with a Microphone Array", ICASSP 2000.
19. A. Brutti, M. Omologo, P. Svaizer,"Oriented Global Coherence Field for the Es-
    timation of the Head Orientation in Smart Rooms equipped with Distributed Mi-
    crophone Arrays", Proc. of Interspeech, 2005.

Appendix: Evaluation Input-Output

Reference

Ti-me[s]	Spea-kers	Noi-se so-urces	Spea-ker ID	x [cm]	y [cm]	z [cm]	Ti-me[s]	Spea-kers	Noi-se so-urces	Spea-ker ID	x [cm]	y [cm]	z [cm]
0	1	0	lect	400	200	180	0.7	1	0	aud	120	150	110
0.1	0	1	-	-	-	-	0.8	2	0	-	ND	ND	ND
0.2	1	0	lect	395	250	180	0.9	1	0	aud	120	150	115
0.3	2	1	-	ND	ND	ND	1.0	1	0	lect	398	238	180
0.4	1	0	aud	120	150	120	1.1	0	1	-	-	-	-
0.5	1	0	lect	410	225	170	1.2	1	0	aud	120	150	100
0.6	0	2	-	-	-	-	1.3	2	1	-	ND	ND	ND

Output of the localization system

Time [s]	x [cm]	y [cm]	z [cm]	Time [s]	x [cm]	y [cm]	z [cm]
0	396	198	180	0.6	300	310	115
0.2	405	239	185	0.7	125	170	118
0.4	110	181	110	0.9	200	220	94
0.5	430	280	177	1.0	410	224	186

Output of the evaluation software

Time [s]	Err [cm]	Classification	Time [s]	Err [cm]	Classification
0	4.5	Fine Error(Lect.)	0.7	22.1	Fine Error(Aud.)
0.1	ND	No Speaker	0.8	ND	Ignored
0.2	15.7	Fine Error(Lect.)	0.9	108.4	Gross Error(Aud.)
0.3	ND	Ignored	1.0	19.4	Fine Error Lecturer
0.4	34.1	Fine Error(Aud.)	1.1	ND	No Speaker
0.5	58.9	Gross Error(Lect.)	1.2	ND	Deletion(Aud.)
0.6	ND	False Alarm	1.3	ND	Ignored

Evaluation Summary	Lecturer	Audience	Overall
Pcor	0.75(=3/4)	0.67(=2/3)	0.71(=5/7)
Bias fine (x,y,z)[cm]	(6.0, -9.0, 3.7)	(-2.5, 25.5, -1.0)	(2.6, 4.8, 1.8)
Bias fine+gross (x,y,z)[cm]	(9.5, 7.0, 4.5)	(25.0, 40.3, -7.7)	(16.1, 21.3, -0.7)
RMSE fine [cm]	14.6	28.7	21.4
RMSE fine+gross [cm]	32.1	66.8	50.0
Deletion Rate	0(=0/4)	0.25(=1/4)	0.12(=1/8)

False Alarm Rate=0.33(=1/3)

Author Index

Lecture Notes in Computer Science

For information about Vols. 1–3779

please contact your bookseller or Springer